The Psychology of Being Human

The Psychology of Being Human

Elton B. McNeil
University of Michigan, *Ann Arbor*

Canfield Press 𝚽 San Francisco
A Department of Harper & Row, Publishers, Inc.
New York   Evanston   London

Art	Pamela Vesterby
Cartoons	Tony Hall
Copyediting	Linda Jean Harris
Cover Design	Bonnie Russell
Design	Joseph Fay
Photographic Research	Kay Y. James

The Psychology of Being Human

Harper & Row, Publishers, Inc.
10 East 53rd Street
New York, N.Y. 10022

Library of Congress Cataloging in Publication Data

McNeil, Elton Burbank, 1924–1974
    The psychology of being human.

    1. Psychology. I. Title. DNLM: 1. Psychology.
BF121 M169p 1974
BF121.M296   150   73-23125
ISBN 0-06-385442-2

    76   10 9 8 7 6

Preface

Every teacher is, in a sense, a frustrated actor-performer. The longer he works at his craft the more convinced he becomes that he has uncovered a successful formula to convey to students something of the excitement and fascination of the particular intellectual pursuits that have occupied his own educational life. In this sense, every textbook is a kind of well-intentioned ego-trip by a professor who honestly believes he can come closer to target-center than did those who wrote before him. Thus, if I am to be honest with you, it is necessary to confess that this book was written for many of these same reasons.

This book is about psychology in the manner that I would say to you, "I'd like you to meet a very good friend of mine. I think you will like one another, and this may well be the beginning of a beautiful and permanent friendship." If your thoughts run in the same direction as mine, this ought to be a book that holds your interest, that answers a great many questions that have rattled around in the back of your mind for some time now—a book that makes psychology come alive for you and become a meaningful part of your daily life.

Why? Because, in addition to the topics that have traditionally been thought necessary to a basic understanding of psychology, a lot of information not usually found in introductory textbooks is also included without making the reading burdensome. A brief look at the content and the organization of the book will help to explain how this has been accomplished.

The text proper (printed in black ink throughout to set it off from other material) has been written in a narrative fashion that attempts to communicate the flavor of psychology while minimizing its jargon. This text is designed to be read by any interested person, with or without previous knowledge of the field. It is intended for the student who might stop at one course in psychology, as well as for the student who will need a solid background for more advanced courses. Thus, the now-classic experiments that helped to establish psychology as a science are presented, as are the physiological correlates of psychological behavior, but the rigorous experimental and biological aspects of psychology have been down-played. As the title suggests, this text has been written for human beings who are interested in and capable of achieving their full potential of being human. For this reason, I have devoted whole chapters to subjects treated only in passing in other texts—for example, "Aging and Death," "Sex," "Styles of Living," "Consciousness," and "The

World of Work." I hope that the reader will come away from this book not only with a broad perspective of the many and oftentimes divergent viewpoints of psychology, its basic vocabulary, and the research methods of the discipline, but also with an ability to understand, predict, and control his behavior and that of the people who surround him.

Interspersed throughout the chapters are *boxes* (printed in maroon ink) which take specific topics and expand them beyond their treatment in the text itself. The boxes have been set off so the text can maintain its flow and continuity. Also, they serve as convenient stopping points where the reader can pause for reflection, contemplate an application or example, or be exposed to a different perspective. Their subject matter varies from chapter to chapter. Some examples: studies being conducted today, the results of which are still inconclusive ("How We Feel Pain"—in relation to acupuncture); new approaches to long-time fields of study, including new methods made possible by advanced technology ("Unlocking the Brain"); physiological aspects of material discussed in text ("The Glandular System"); consideration of questions the student might have when reading the text ("What Are Psychologists Really Like?"); information on a phenomenon that is of high-interest but that neither medicine nor psychology has yet been able to explain ("Phantom Limbs").

In the margin column of the text (also printed in maroon ink) are what I prefer to call *teasers,* because they entice the student to think about a particular psychological concept in a new way. For the most part, these are comprised of anecdotal information that professors (myself included) often use to "spice up" their lectures, and I wanted a way to share in a textbook some of the material that my students have found fascinating over the years. More importantly, I feel, is that these marginal notes indicate that psychology is not an isolated discipline, but one that must interact with all fields of endeavor if we are truly to understand what being human is all about.

Psychological issues follow each chapter and are printed on tinted pages. Although I have tried throughout the book to integrate psychological theory with its practical applications, I have used the psychological issues as the springboard for showing how the principles of psychology apply, and are of concern, to all of us. The information that has been compiled on behavior control, parascience, hypnosis, the generation gap, encounter groups, overeating, the poor, suicide, and many other such topics has met with conflicting responses from psychologists. There is no universal agreement about these things, and that is why they are "issues." These areas demand more attention, primarily because students want to know what the discipline has to say about our world and how psychological methods and theories can help us find new approaches to age-old human problems.

The organization of the text is such that it will fit in with a wide variety of lecture plans. The chapters are modular in that they need not be read in any particular sequence. I have followed a somewhat traditional outline of topics with the knowledge that those instructors who wish to start their students on the less rigorous, more applied areas of psychology presented in later chapters may do so with no loss of continuity. Also, the text itself is relatively brief, despite the overall number of pages, for much space has been devoted to artistic and photographic illustrations of the concepts under discussion. Depending on an instructor's needs, certain chapters or issues could be assigned or omitted to make this text appropriate in either one- or two-semester courses.

As mentioned earlier, this text incorporates a wide range of theoretical viewpoints and tries to introduce the student to the work of all schools of psychology—behavioral, developmental, clinical, comparative, physiological, humanist, and so on. This might sound ambitious, but I feel that the beginning student must achieve an overview of what psychology is all about and understand that there are continuing disagreements about the research methods and the orientations of its practitioners.

To aid the student, summaries for each chapter and issue have been prepared by a most talented writer, Ellen Weber. Even though I have tried to work around the jargon of psychology, some terminology cannot—and should not—be avoided in an introductory text. Thus, in addition to the "in-context" definitions of such words, I refer the reader to the glossary, compiled by Frances P. Bowles. Along with the student guide written to accompany the book by Robert McNally, these materials should allow the reader to study and review the text in a fairly straightforward manner.

This book was fashioned directly by the day-to-day classroom experience. It was critiqued, edited, polished, and shaped to its final form by a team of dedicated specialists in publication. In particular, Gracia A. Alkema must be singled out for praise. Without her work in coordinating the editing, art, design, and production of the project, this book would be no more than a hopeless jumble of exceedingly sloppy notes that would never have seen the light of day.

I am also indebted to the consulting reviewers for their appraisal of the manuscript and for their suggestions in improving it: Suzanne Adams, Merritt College; James D. Andrews, City College of San Francisco; Robert Buckhout, Brooklyn College; Lucy Freund, Loop College; Richard Graf, California State University, San Diego; Michael Hughmanick, West Valley College; Thomas McCloud, Wayne County Community College; Edward Poindexter, San Jose City College; Robert Smith, Orange Coast College. Thanks go to all of them not only for their reviews but also for their work in compiling the instructor's manual and test bank that accompany this text.

In addition, I wish to acknowledge all of the other individuals who helped to make this book come alive, and whose names are listed on the copyright page. Further, the whole staff of Canfield Press should be thanked for their contributions at various stages of the project—from acting as couriers to proofreading the index. This really has been a massive effort, and without the cooperation of all these dedicated people the end product would be considerably different.

Finally, to all readers of this text, may I say that I hope the study of psychology will provide as much pleasure for you as it has for me.

Elton B. McNeil

Contents

PART ONE

THE SCIENCE OF PSYCHOLOGY

CHAPTER ONE   **The Methods of Science**

No MATTER WHERE YOU LOOK, things seem to be going downhill. As bad as the evening news sounds on Monday, it gets worse on Tuesday. The newspapers are filled with stories of wrongdoing, and occasionally good news slips in under the guise of human interest. Sometimes, only the comics bring a smile to our faces—and often a cynical one at that. Of course life isn't all bad, and maybe its really true that good news is no news. But if you asked the man on the street what he thought about the quality of our present lives, he would probably say it is pretty poor.

I would guess that most of you would say so too, even if you refuse to watch the news or have canceled your morning paper. You—like all of us—are continually affected by society's affairs. And, like the rest of us, you contribute to society's affairs. For that is the nature of being human.

Society's attitudes, for example, have probably determined how you were raised, what you learned in school and out of it, who your friends are, and maybe even whether you are poor or rich. Of course, you had something to say about this too. Out of an unlimited number of choices, you chose only certain people as your friends. You chose certain activities to spend your money on, and you decided what you would study in school. Eventually your decisions began going beyond yourself. You started to vote; you littered; you bought a host of products because you wanted to be beautiful. How did you make all these decisions? Were they merely a reflection of society's teachings, or did something more come from somewhere inside you? How much do you contribute to society's problems, and how much of your contribution does not result from how society shaped you? How much does the world contribute to your problems and to your well-being? How much are they your own doing? In other words, how do you interact with your environment?

The science of psychology has been defined in a number of different ways. We should look at psychology, not just as a science, but also as a method of exploration, intent on discovering answers to these questions about being human. The work of psychologists encompasses a variety of fields—from how we see to why we rob banks. Psychology is a rather new science, compared with fields such as physics, and that is why much of its work is still in the stage of theory rather than fact. That is also why psychology can be more exciting than other fields. It gives even the novices a chance to do some exploration on their own.

Not all of psychology is theory, however, and we have already begun to apply many of the ideas psychologists have come up with. Some applications have failed. Many have succeeded, however, and with each new idea the science of psychology comes closer to solving some of the puzzles about what's gone wrong with the world. By the time you have finished reading this book, you will probably have many more answers than you have now, and you may have even gained some ideas that you can put together into your own theories. But if you are going to examine psychology's findings, it is important for you to know how psychology began and how psychologists have gone about investigating the highly complex nature of being human.

3

The Methods of Science

The world of poetry, mythology, and religion represent the world as a man would like to have it, while science represents the world as he gradually comes to discover it.—Joseph Wood Krutch

Psychology Today

The word *psychology* is derived from two Greek terms: *psyche* meaning soul or life principle, and *logos* meaning discourse. Early psychology was mental philosophy that included topics broader than the study of the mind. Then, about 400 years ago, mental philosophers began to translate the word psyche as "mind," and psychology was defined as "the study of the mind." In this century psychology was redefined as "the science of behavior," and this change fundamentally altered the direction of psychology and the kinds of questions it asked.

      Contemporary psychology covers such a diversity of activities and interests that, as Erasmus Hoch (1962) said: "His subject matter being the kind it is, the psychologist finds himself pulled in many directions at once. The stuff of human problems is everywhere. To define the boundaries of the science today is to have to shift them tomorrow. Where behavior or thought or attitude or motivation is, there psychology is" (pp. 11–12).

      It is almost impossible to describe what modern psychologists are really like since they do so many different things and identify themselves in so many different ways. We can, however, briefly touch on the main points of each of the different kinds of psychology.

Experimental Psychology.   Experimental psychology is the oldest specialty within psychology. It began with the introspective study of sensory processes and has expanded over the years to encompass research on perception, cogni-

5

PSYCHOLOGISTS AT WORK
In 1970, membership in the American Psychological Association was about 30,000. Not everyone is a joiner, of course, and one estimate of those who don't belong sets the figure at 10,000. Thus, as a rough estimate there are probably 40,000 psychologists in America. Sixty percent of them are applied psychologists who work at clinical or counseling psychology. Slightly less than 40 percent of us work in academic settings, and the others work in industry, hospitals, government agencies, or private practice.

tion, emotion, thinking, and learning. Experimental psychologists can be found conducting research in almost every field of psychology.

Industrial Psychology.　Psychologists in this field may work with special tests for selecting and classifying personnel, dealing with morale problems among workers, developing training programs, investigating man-machine relationships, or doing research on any industrial problem involving human factors. One specialized branch of industrial psychology is *human engineering*. The human-factors scientist may combine his knowledge with that of industrial, electrical, or aeronautical engineers in designing equipment and work settings that allow maximum efficiency and comfort.

Social Psychology.　Social psychology involves the study of the impact of groups on individual behavior. The study of propaganda, attitude change, prejudice, and intergroup relations are included in this field, but social psychology is so broadly defined that it encompasses many other topics of interest. Like other psychologists, the social psychologist studies individual behavior, reactions, and perceptions and how these are influenced by man's membership in human groups.

Education and School Psychology.　Educational psychology focuses on the study of psychological problems relating to education. The educational psychologist may use measures of achievement, study ways to improve teaching techniques, or work with children who have special educational problems. The school psychologist has many similar professional interests but is employed by the school system to work with disturbed children and their parents, to develop the testing and evaluation program, and to diagnose special problems, such as retardation or giftedness in pupils.

Developmental Psychology.　This field is devoted to the study of behavioral development from birth to old age. Developmental psychologists may study physical maturation, the acquisition of learned behaviors, the development of perceptual and intellectual processes, or the development of personality. In a way, developmental psychology is the study of all psychological processes from the viewpoint of how they change over the years.

Personality Psychology.　This is the study of the whole person in light of the underlying processes that cause him to act as he does. Personality consists of a number of distinctive traits, and the psychologist attempts to understand how these traits are organized, where they come from, and how they influence a person's relations with others.

Clinical Psychology.　Clinical psychologists are concerned with identifying and understanding psychological problems and with finding ways to help people who have difficulty adjusting to daily life. They work in schools, hospitals, private practice, and community centers, where they diagnose abnormal behavior, search for its causes, and provide therapy for those who need it.

Counseling Psychology.   Psychologists trained in counseling offer advice and direction to people who have personal problems (such as difficulties in marriage, education, or jobs) but do not seem to be affected by mental disorder. Often counseling and clinical psychology overlap, as do many of the psychological fields of study.

And Many Others.   The list of kinds of psychologists would stretch almost endlessly, of course. In my own university, there are colleagues who identify themselves as mathematical psychologists, psycholinguists, survey researchers, community psychologists, and, to top it off, general psychologists. There are more, but by now the point is clear that there are no absolute or sharp dividing lines between the various specialties. My own identity as a psychologist might serve as an example. I began as a general, experimental psychologist, was then trained to be a clinical psychologist, worked as an educational consultant to school systems and as a school psychologist, directed a training center for persons planning to work with emotionally disturbed and delinquent boys, worked on the psychological aspects of disarmament proposals, and was a field selection officer for the Peace Corps. The best way to identify the psychol-

---

What Are Psychologists Really Like?

There is no answer to the question: "What are psychologists really like?" except to say that there are probably 40,000 of them in the country; and, like the members of every other profession, they are as much different as they are alike.

Anne Roe (1961) is one of the few psychologists to take a close look at what scientists are really like. She points out that most accounts of scientists emphasize the objectivity of their work and describe them as cold, detached, and impassive observers of phenomena. But Roe's research suggests that nothing could be further from the truth. She is convinced that the creative scientist is always very deeply involved emotionally and personally in his work.

She feels that the fundamentals of the creative process are probably the same in all fields. In those fields where an advance in knowledge is sought, however, there is an additional requirement—the need for a large store of knowledge and experience. The broader the scientist's experience and the more extensive his stock of knowl-

edge, the greater the possibility of a real breakthrough.

She notes that, while intelligence and creativity are not identical, intelligence does play a role in scientific forms of creativity—the minimum intelligence required for creative production in science is higher than average.

The personality of the scientist is also an important contributor to his or her success. Truly creative scientists, according to Roe, are more observant than others and value this quality. They are more independent and dominant. They tend to be radical, resist group standards and controls, and are highly egocentric. They have strong egos and have no feelings of guilt about their independence of thought and action. Their interpersonal relations are generally limited, and they are not very social or talkative. (This does not apply to social scientists.) This is true partly because they show a much greater preoccupation with things and ideas than with people.

Scientists, it appears, are a strange breed. Some laboratory psychologists fit the description exactly, whereas psychologists who work with people usually don't fit it.

ogist is not by his early training but by the research and practice that currently interest him or her.

Modern psychologists are not exact likenesses of the historical figures who shaped the early days of our professional discipline. But everyone interested in the field should get an idea of the unique flavor of psychology by quickly looking at its early origins.

The Difference between Psychologists and Psychiatrists

Psychology and psychiatry differ primarily in their training and professional activities. Psychiatry is a medical specialty primarily involved with the diagnosis and treatment of mental illness. Psychiatrists take the same basic course work in medicine as other physicians, but afterward they spend additional years studying psychiatry.

While the psychiatrist is being trained in medicine, the clinical psychologist (following his Bachelor's Degree) enters graduate school to study psychology and research methodology. After a minimum of three years of study and a full year of internship, the clinical psychologist earns a Ph.D. degree. Actually, it takes the average clinical psychologist closer to five or more years to complete training.

The work of psychiatrists and clinical psychologists is similar in some respects and different in others. Both professions diagnose abnormal behavior, for example, but the clinical psychologist more often uses psychological tests while the psychiatrist uses other methods. Both may administer therapy for emotional disturbances but when the therapy involves drugs, surgery, or other medical treatments, of course, only the psychiatrist is qualified.

PSYCHOLOGICAL PUBLIC OPINION
Because of psychology's overlap with psychiatry, the distinction between these two fields has been difficult for the layman to grasp. In an opinion survey taken in St. Louis, the general public overestimated the annual income of both psychiatrists and psychologists and underestimated how long it takes either of them to finish their training and education. When the respondents were asked what profession they preferred their own son to follow (the choice offered was surgeon, engineer, lawyer, dentist, or psychologist), the psychologists finished last (Thumin and Zebelmen, 1967).

Psychology's Roots

Psychology traces its roots back to the early Greek and Roman philosophers and their speculations about the nature of things. Even today the highest graduate degree offered in the sciences and humanities is the doctorate in philosophy, the Ph.D. And, it is only within the past 75 or 80 years that university courses in psychology have been taught in departments of psychology. Earlier, psychology was the province of philosophy departments.

Despite their enormous contributions to Western thought, some of the ancient Greek philosophers confused the growth of psychological knowledge with incorrect ideas. Aristotle, for example, made the mistake of locating the mental functions in the heart. Centuries passed before this view was corrected, and mental functions assigned to the brain. References to the problems of human behavior appeared again in the writings of philosophers of the seventeenth and eighteenth centuries. Before the nineteenth century, however, psychology did not exist as a distinctive discipline.

Two directions of development, one in philosophy and the other in the physical and biological sciences, had much to do with the early nature of psychology. The first development was the concern in British philosophy of the nineteenth century with the nature of ideas and how ideas are associated in the mind. The British philosopher, John Locke (1632–1704), for example, attempted to answer questions about how we can obtain valid information about the physical world. Locke concluded that all knowledge comes from sensory experience and that man's intellect is at first a *tabula rasa*—a blank tablet on which sensory experience makes its marks. All knowledge, Locke believed, no matter how complex or abstract, derives from sensory encounters with the physical world.

The second development was in the biological and physical sciences of nineteenth-century Germany. In 1879 Wilhelm Wundt, a German physiologist and philosopher, opened a psychological laboratory at the University of Leipzig. A few years earlier William James had established a laboratory at Harvard University, but James's laboratory was used solely for purposes of instruction and demonstration. For this reason, most psychologists consider Wundt to be "the father of scientific psychology." In this early period of scientific psychology "schools" or "systems" of psychology were established, and each school revolved around a particular subject matter and the methods used to investigate it. As psychology matured, the schools or systems of its early development tended to disappear.

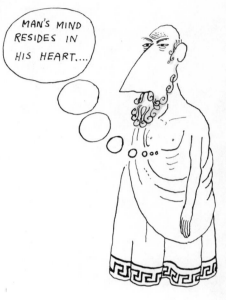

Structuralism. The system of psychology founded by Wundt was known as *structuralism* because the focus was on discovering the "structure" or anatomy of conscious processes. The subject matter of structuralism was consciousness, and the major method employed by the structuralists was called *introspection*. To introspect, a subject was supposed to look at his own conscious experience as objectively as possible while perceiving and judging various stimuli under controlled laboratory conditions. Sensations, images, and feelings were studied since structuralists felt that these elements combined in different ways in most conscious activities. These elements were not merely added together but combined to produce something quite different from the separate parts. The process was viewed as a kind of "mental chemistry."

Functionalism. Wundt's psychology was thought by the German psychologists to be a "pure science" because there was no practical application of findings. It was Wundt's students from America—James, Dewey, Cattell, and others—who became interested in finding some practical application of the study of conscious processes. American psychology became a functional and applied psychology that developed into the fields of child psychology, educational psychology, and mental testing, among others.

Behaviorism. The development of behaviorism can be traced to the influence of a former functionalist, John B. Watson. Becoming dissatisfied with functionalism early in his career, he asserted that the only proper subject matter for psychology was behavior. This assertion coupled with the development of objective experimental methods brought the study of conscious processes to a virtual end.

Watson shifted the subject matter of psychology to an emphasis on

PSYCHOLOGY TODAY
"Our responsibility is less to assume the role of experts and try to apply psychology ourselves than to give it away to the people who really need it—and that includes everyone. The practice of valid psychology by nonpsychologists will inevitably change people's conception of themselves and what they can do. When we have accomplished that, we will really have caused a psychological revolution." [Miller, 1969, p. 16]

learned behavior, believing that the environment is all-important and that virtually all human behavior is learned. Watson doubted there was any such thing as a human mind. He was aware that human beings had thoughts, but he believed that these were simply a form of talking to oneself by making tiny movements of the vocal cords. He also knew people had feelings, but he believed these were only a form of conditioned glandular response to a stimulus in the environment.

Gestalt Psychology.   The gestalt psychologists argued that the study of consciousness would never progress by analyzing it into elements. They insisted that, in the very process of breaking the mind into its pieces, scientists were destroying the essence of the human mind. To their way of thinking, it was like trying to study how fish live by taking them out of water. The word *Gestalt* is a German word most often translated to mean "form" or "organization." Gestalt psychology emphasizes the whole, the form, or what is called the configuration of mental activities in general and perception in particular. The gestalt school was formed in Germany, but its leaders moved to America in the 1930s with the rise of Hitler.

Individual and Dynamic Psychology.   Individual and dynamic psychology is primarily concerned with motivation and the dynamics (functioning) of personality. Sigmund Freud, the founder of the psychoanalytic movement, is best known for developing a complicated theory of personality to explain the causes of mental disorders. But psychoanalysis is also a theory of behavior and a set of techniques useful in the treatment of mental disorders. While psychoanalysis was evolving, World War I exploded and changed American psychology significantly. During that war, psychological testing was used for the selection and classification of soldiers for various army duties. For efficiency, group tests of intellectual ability (the Army Alpha and the Army Beta) were developed and administered to more than two million men. Then, during the period between World War I and World War II, individual psychology grew the fastest. It had come of age in the sense that psychology was seen as being useful for all human beings and not just for those who were emotionally disturbed.

Even though their fields of interest may vary, psychologists of all kinds pursue the same aims of scientific endeavor. We are scientists first and psychologists second. Thus, to understand psychology and psychologists, it is necessary to take a closer look at the purpose of science and the scientific method.

The Purpose of Science

Psychology is a science that seeks to measure, explain, and change behavior. And, compared with mathematics, physics, biology, or chemistry, it is a young science. Since early times man has been interested in learning about himself and has wondered about the forces that affect him. Yet, only recently has man developed a science of psychology designed to get accurate answers. Psychologists follow a sequence of steps known as the *scientific method* because it is characteristic of virtually every scientific endeavor. This method includes five steps: selecting a problem, stating the hypothesis, forming and conducting an experiment, organizing the data, and drawing conclusions from the facts that are revealed.

Psychology deals with the description, causation, prediction, and control of phenomena. Careful descriptions of behavioral events, collection of data, and interpretations of the factors underlying such data are the goals of the research psychologist. At times, these data may be applied to practical problems of predicting and controlling behavior. Psychologists add to scientific knowledge when systematic, objective, controlled procedures are used to study behavior.

When a psychologist wishes to study the relationship between variables, he uses the experimental method whereby he manipulates one set of variables to see if it affects the other set of variables. The basic principle of the experimental method is the control of relevant variables that affect the experiment. Thus, the experimenter identifies variables of interest to him and then invents ways to manipulate these variables and control other factors that may influence his results.

Conducting an experiment typically involves three steps: first, formulating a hypothesis about a relationship between events; second, collecting data while using proper controls and measuring techniques; and, third, interpreting the results, usually by means of statistical procedures. Using these steps, psychologists seek to explain, predict, and control the forces that influence human behavior.

There is a broad, general agreement among scientists that certain features are essential if findings are to be declared scientific (Fincher, 1964). Science tends to conform to the following characteristics. It is:

- Rational—it uses reason and logic.
- Empirical—it is based on observations.
- Self-corrective—facts and observations modify previous conclusions.
- Systematic—the search for facts is systematic and organized.
- Objective—findings must be repeatable.
- Quantitative—science measures as well as describes events.

We have described the nature of science, but science is a human enterprise. We must now look to the nature of the psychologist-scientist.

The Social Scientific Method

Now we are ready to describe what psychologists do when they do research. Donald Marquis (1948) described the application of the scientific method

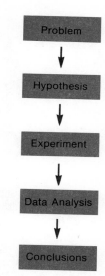

The five major steps of the scientific method.

to human affairs as a progressive sequence of events involving the following steps:

1. *Formulating the problem.*

   The social scientist's way of asking a question differs from that of the lay person. A scientific question must be formulated in precise, researchable terms. No scientific investigation can begin if the question posed is too general or can't be defined precisely.

2. *Reviewing existing knowledge.*

   The researcher must know of the scientific labors that have gone before his own. It is seldom that his topic has not been touched

Subjects
(13-Months-Old Boys)

Independent Variable
(Fence Between
Boys and Their Mothers)

Dependent Variable
(Boys' Behavior Measured)

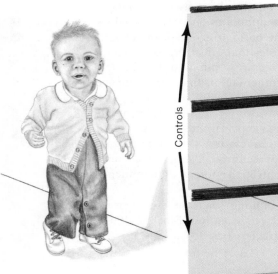
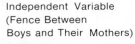
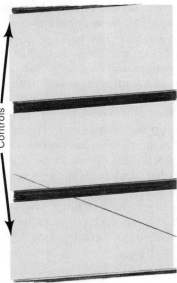

Controls

Example of a social scientific experiment. The hypothesis for the above is that a child will become frustrated when he is deprived of maternal contact. To test the hypothesis, the experimenter selected his subjects, and then devised the independent variable—separating boys from their mothers via a fence. He controlled the other factors in the environment. Next, he placed the boy's mother on one side of the fence, and the little boy on the other. The child's behavior (the dependent variable) was observed and recorded as he coped with this unexpected barrier. After many repetitions of this experiment, the experimenter will have enough raw data from which he can draw conclusions about the accuracy of his hypothesis.

on by some other scientist. From the study of previous efforts, he may decide to ask a different question or modify the one he originally asked.

3. *Making preliminary observations.*

   Every scientist is a hoarder of facts, observations, and insights. With this collection of facts already known, the scientist begins to probe about, organize his observations, and start to give meaning to what he has observed. The scientist may use a *pilot study* in which he uses crude methods to test a small population of subjects to determine whether further investigation is justified. The pilot study often indicates the ideas are much more difficult to test than was originally expected. The scientist then modifies his methods and techniques.

4. *Constructing a hypothesis.*

   After completing the first three steps, the researcher is ready to make an educated, scientific guess about the relationship of one thing to another. This hypothesis must be checked out through experimentation.

5. *Verifying the hypothesis.*

   The test must be run with techniques approved by other social scientists. The scientist cannot rely on magic or on logic alone. He must conduct controlled experiments whereby the question asked will be answered in a trustworthy and repeatable fashion. The selection of research techniques depends on the nature of the investigation being conducted, on the population of subjects available, and on the kind of answer being sought. The choice of a technique is never easy since a number of instruments may be appropriate.

As Lowe (1959) notes, the psychologist is increasingly called upon to leave his laboratory and move out into the real world. When he leaves the laboratory to deal with human problems, he finds himself concerned less with what *is* than with what *should* be. It is this encounter with real life that poses ethical issues for the psychologist. The industrial, educational, or clinical psychologist works for others and is tempted to compromise some of his values. Or, his own values may influence those of other people. For example, every choice of a therapist involves an implicit acceptance of some set of values (Williamson, 1958). Further, patients who improve through therapy seem to revise their values to resemble those of the therapist (Rosenthal, 1955). The psychologist's task is not an easy one in a society that has a multiplicity of competing values and attitudes.

The Tools of the Method

Thought and the mind of man are the cardinal tools of the scientific and the experimental method. One of the first steps is *inductive thinking*—the

THE SOCIAL SCIENTIST
" 'A social scientist is a man who, if he has two little boys, sends one to Sunday School every Sunday and keeps the other one home as an experimental control group.' . . . The scientific method is a way of trying to make sense out of the booming, buzzing confusion of the universe. It is an intellectual stance toward information. The scientific method is a set of assumptions about when a fact is a fact . . . this century has seen a larger and larger proportion of scholars using the scientific method as a means to the end of learning more about human social behavior. Every year, more students are exposed to science as a frame of reference. The mass media report and comment upon information gathered by observation, interviews, and questionnaires. Political leaders, educators, businessmen, church administrators make policy decisions based upon data gathered by social scientists. . . ." [Mack, 1964, pp. 24–25]

The Scientific Method at Work

The French scientist Louis Pasteur took bottles of sterile nutritional jelly to high altitudes and exposed them to the mountain air. Then he exposed similarly sterile bottles of jelly to the ordinary atmosphere of his home town. Repeating the experiment a great many times, he observed that molds and tiny organisms always grew in the jelly that was in contact with air at low altitudes. Yet they never appeared in jelly exposed to rarefied mountain air. Pasteur concluded that organisms flourished in the air of dusty, dirty cities. He discovered that the air is alive with forms of life that grow and multiply in our food, which

must then be treated before it is safe to eat. Today we *pasteurize* our milk, refrigerate other foods, and add chemicals to slow down bacterial growth. We also pasteurize beer with heat in order to kill the organisms that thrive in it.

The point of the story is not how to make a better draft beer, but rather, to underscore the role of meticulously conducted experimentation in scientific discovery. A scientist is human and is unhappy when experiments prove his ideas wrong. But he learns to lose as gracefully as he wins.

process of starting with observed facts and constructing a theory that is consistent with those facts. The scientist begins with particular instances and evolves from them a general rule that accounts for the known facts. After constructing a theory that is consistent with the facts, a logical deduction is made about predictable consequences of the theory. If the theory is true the scientist bets his professional reputation that he can predict certain events will take place under specified conditions. If he makes the bet, he must construct an experiment that will prove whether he is right or wrong. He must verify his theory experimentally by collecting new facts and observations that support or refute his predictions.

As he begins to design an experiment, he thinks of events he can manipulate. What the psychologist manipulates is called the *independent variable*. The result that he observes is called the *dependent variable*. In psychological research, the independent variable is almost always a stimulus, and the dependent variable is almost always a response. Thus, the experimental method may be defined by three components: (1) manipulation of one or more independent variables, (2) control of related variables, and (3) observation of one or more dependent variables. There are four basic approaches to the study of human behavior. They involve: (1) collecting and analyzing existing documents, (2) asking people questions, (3) watching people, and (4) experimenting. These approaches can be combined to take advantage of the strengths of each.

Whatever variables the scientist uses or invents as tools in his experiment, he must define them operationally. An *operational definition* is one which tells what he is going to do or what procedure he plans to use. It defines terms by describing what operations are used to understand them. For example, the scientist might operationally define those who have charisma by saying that "charismatic" subjects are persons who always get a standing ovation when they enter a room.

In the comic-strip version of the psychologist, the researcher is usually found ecstatically at work in a laboratory filled with rats, computers, or mysterious brain-exchanging contraptions. Psychologists do work in laboratories a great deal, but they also employ a number of other common techniques in their search for data to confirm their hypotheses or teach them something new about human nature. Each research method has its own advantages and, as you will see throughout this book, its own drawbacks. So psychologists must choose the methods carefully, according to the information they seek. We can briefly review some of these methods here.

Observation. The researcher may produce his own psychological version of "Candid Camera," observing and systematically recording events or phenomena as they occur naturally. He may use cameras, tape recorders, or his own eyes to look for characteristics of the situation which seem to be related to the question he has posed. This technique is employed where any manipulations on the part of the experimenter would destroy the phenomenon he is trying to study.

Psychological Tests.   Psychological tests have been devised to enable researchers to determine how an individual measures up to the rest of the population in regard to particular personality traits, aptitudes, vocational preferences, general intelligence, or other characteristics or behaviors.

Case History.   A case history is the study of one individual in depth in order to find out as much as possible about the causes and characteristics of a particular behavior he displays. Personality tests, intelligence tests, biographies, interviews, and observations may all be used to get a complete picture of an individual. Case histories are employed most frequently in the study of abnormal behavior or psychopathology. It permits psychologists to examine a number of different variables which may all have contributed to the behavior.

CAMPUS PSYCHOLOGY CENTERS
A questionnaire administered to 376 college students on three campuses found consistent differences in the reactions students had to hearing the names "Counseling Center" and "Psychological Center." The name "Counseling Center" was associated with the treatment of minor problems. "Psychological Center" was associated with the treatment of more serious problems. The "Psychological Center" was seen as more medical, expensive, professional, embarrassing to go to, and competent than the "Counseling Center" (Sieveking and Chappell, 1970).

Surveys.   When psychologists want to know how members of a population feel about a certain issue, they conduct surveys. Surveys permit psychologists to gather a large amount of data in a short time. The psychologists may survey an entire population, or they may select a smaller group which they believe is representative of the larger population. Those surveyed are asked to answer specific questions which relate to the attitudes or emotions that psychologists are trying to study.

Correlational Studies.   Much of psychological theory is a result of studies in which psychologists have demonstrated a relationship (or correlation) between two or more characteristics of individuals they have studied. Often the data used have been collected through the methods we have just discussed, or the data may have come from records kept by institutions such as schools, hospitals, or the Bureau of the Census. For example, suppose the psychologist wanted to know if intelligence had anything to do with a person's income. He would select a large number of individuals, and for each one he would determine their annual income and their scores on an intelligence test. If he does this for enough people, he may begin to see that every person of low income ranks low in intelligence, or that every person with high income ranks low in intelligence, or that there is no consistent relationship either way.

The major drawback to correlational studies, case histories, surveys, personality tests, and simple observation is that, even when a relationship between variables has been established, there is no way to tell which variable is the cause, and which the effect. That is, did the low income lead to low intelligence, or did the low intelligence lead to low income? Did an individual's early history lead to his abnormal behavior, or did his abnormal behavior cause him to be treated poorly when he was young? Or did some other factor cause them both?

The primary advantage of conducting studies in a laboratory setting is that the experimenter can control the entire experimental situation. He can manipulate the variables one at a time and thereby determine cause and effect relationships. He can be more certain about what is happening to each individual. He can randomly assign subjects to different experimental groups, and he can eliminate or minimize factors that might give him false results.

The problem with laboratory experiments is that they tend to rely on subjects that are not necessarily representative of the general human population. The laboratory rat and the male college sophomore have long been the most popular subjects for psychological research—mostly because they are easily available to researchers. Studies have also been carried out on almost every other species of animal besides man: houseflies, elephants, worms, racoons, kangaroos, and most of the monkey family.

Psychologists use animal subjects for a number of reasons. They are less complex than human beings, and their behavior is, therefore, more easily observed. The experimenter can control hereditary and environmental influences and—because most species have shorter life spans than man—the psy-

chologist can investigate the transmission of various effects over several generations. He can also use experimental techniques that would be considered immoral if applied to humans.

Despite these advantages, psychologists have always debated whether anything learned from a laboratory rat can be applied to the human race. More recently, psychologists have begun to wonder whether anything learned from a human laboratory subject has much bearing on the rest of the human race. For one thing, the laboratory setting is far from naturalistic. It is hard to see how the contrived nature of the experimental situation can really duplicate that of real life. Also, subjects in a laboratory know that they are being studied. In such a situation, it is not likely that the individual will act naturally or spontaneously. He may try to please or displease the experimenter or act in a way he thinks is proper, rather than as he would in real life. To some extent, psychologists—particularly social psychologists—have tried to compensate for these drawbacks by running experiments in natural settings, where subjects are unaware of being watched. Of course, what is gained in reality is lost in control. The experimenter cannot be sure that the subjects are responding only to his manipulations and not to the forces of everyday life. As Ralph Rosnow (1970) says about the human subject: "The Good Subject for behavioral research, like the proverbial Boy Scout, makes a habit of being useful to others. . . . The Good Subject tries to comply with what he sees as the experimenter's scientific desires" (p. 26).

The bulk of psychological findings on human subjects reported in journals in the 1960s was derived from male college students (Schultz, 1969; Smart 1966). This bright, young, affluent group cannot possibly reflect the average person in our country nor tell us much about poor people, racial minorities, women, or old people. As Schultz (1969) says: "The situation is cause for serious and constructive alarm within psychology. . . . If our source of data is open to question then surely one can legitimately question the validity of that data. We cannot continue to base some 80 percent of our human subject data on college students and still call our work a science of human behavior" (p. 224).

There is no easy answer to the problem of selecting human subjects for psychological research. A student of psychology must be aware of this difficulty, however, and ask with each study he reads: "Who were the subjects? Are their responses typical of what my own would be? Do their findings apply to me?"

Keeping It Honest

From long experience with research, psychologists have learned that the subjects in any study are quite susceptible to influence by the experimenter, even when this influence is subtle and indirect. The experimenter's tone of

SOCIAL SCIENCE SEX BIAS
Holmes and Jorgensen (1971) asked whether personality and social psychologists study men more than women. To answer the question, they examined issues of three relevant journals published in 1966 and all the issues of a single journal in 1946 and 1956, recording the sex and source of subjects. Males appeared as subjects twice as often as females—a ratio even greater than that favoring college student subjects over noncollege student subjects. Bias in favor of studying males is as great or greater with noncollege subjects as with college student subjects.

voice can convey a great deal of information. If his preferences are implied, there is a tendency for subjects to do what the experimenter seems to want. Experimenters make special efforts, of course, to be as neutral and consistent as possible, but they know subtle cues can be picked up and influence the subject's behavior. To avoid these effects, psychologists devised solutions to the problem of bias.

The easiest solution is to keep the experimenter ignorant about parts of the experiment. This is usually referred to as keeping the experimenter "blind" to information that would let him influence others. Thus, if he does not know which experimental condition he is dealing with, there is no way he can unconsciously change his behavior. It is a lot like watching a ball game and not knowing who to root for since you don't know which team you bet on. If there are slight differences in the experimenter's behavior from one experimental session to another, the differences won't be systematic and corrupt the findings.

In some experiments, of course, it is not possible to keep the experimenter totally blind about which subjects are in which experimental condition. A limited degree of blindness can be introduced into an experiment if two experimenters are used. One of them is made responsible for the experimental manipulation, and the other is concerned only with the dependent measure. It is important, of course, that neither knows what the other is doing to whom. If this complicated stratagem is not possible, most experimenters hide experimental knowledge from themselves as much as possible. For example, the subjects may be assigned code numbers; instructions may be standardized on tapes or typed sheets; and so forth. It is often impossible to eliminate experimental bias completely, even though psychologists try. In these cases (and often we don't know which ones they are), we can depend on replication to serve as a double check. If other psychologists repeat your experiment using your methods and instruments and don't get the same kind of results, then your original findings are called into question. The system is not perfect, but psychologists try harder than most.

Scientists Disagree

There is little fundamental disagreement about the usefulness of the scientific and experimental methods when applied to problems in the natural sciences. In part this is true because working scientists understand that the method is no more than a question-answering tool. As the scientist Claude Bernard said in 1865: "The idea is a seed; the method is the earth furnishing the conditions in which it may develop, flourish, and give the best fruit according to its nature. But as only what has been sown in the ground will ever grow in it, so nothing will be developed by the experimental method except the ideas submitted to it. The method itself gives birth to nothing."

THE N-RAYS

In 1902 the French physicist M. Blondot reported the discovery of the N-ray. This mysterious ray was observed in action as it made luminous paint glow more brightly when Blondot lowered the lights in the experimental room. Within two years nearly 80 scientific articles were devoted to discussion of the N-ray. It soon became apparent that the N-ray must be an exclusively French phenomenon since American, German, and Italian scientists couldn't make it work in their laboratories. After a series of tests, it was evident that the action of the N-rays was mostly in the eye of the beholder. As it happened, Blondot tried to judge the changes in paint luminosity using only his naked eye illuminated by a flickering gas light.

By 1909 the short history of the N-ray came to an end, and the moral was clear—human beings are imperfect measuring and calibrating instruments. Today's computers, oscilloscopes, tachistoscopes, and the like provide a degree of reliability unknown to the early experimenters.

The Scientific Method Isn't Perfect

Several psychologists have come to believe that the use of the strict scientific method is the very thing that will keep psychology from being an authentic science of man. In a speech before the American Psychological Association in 1972, Carl Rogers, clinical psychologist and one of the founders of the encounter group movement, challenged psychologists with this idea. Rogers explained that psychology has always been an insecure science, holding fast to the ideal of the scientific method to prove that it is as worthy of being considered a science as is physics. But Rogers points out that physics threw out the old conception of science long ago. Physicists today readily admit to the use of procedures—particularly inner processes—that do not follow the scientific method as we have outlined in this chapter. Rogers believes that psychologists cannot continue to base their theories only on observed behaviors but must also deal with less quantifiable data, such as introspection. Such data have at least as much meaning as contrived experiments for the study of man.

The insecurity of psychologists is what makes them reject parascientific phenomena as worthy of study, Rogers says. They are afraid that psychology will lose its significance as a science if it admits to the possibility of other realities. Yet, says Rogers, incidents of clairvoyance or precognition continue to occur. Some have even been tested experimentally, and much of the evidence is difficult to deny. Because of the mounting evidence, Rogers says: "We will have a harder and harder time closing our eyes to the possibility of another reality (or realities), operating on rules quite different from our well-known common-sense empirical reality, the only one known to most psychologists" (p. 385).

"Perhaps," says Rogers, "in the coming generation of younger psychologists, hopefully unencumbered by university prohibitions and resistances, there may be a few who will dare to investigate the possibility that there is a lawful reality which is not open to our five senses; a reality in which present, past, and future are intermingled, in which space is not a barrier, and time has disappeared; a reality which can be perceived and known only when we are passively receptive, rather than actively bent on knowing. It is one of the most exciting challenges posed to psychology" (p. 386).

Source: Carl Rogers. "Some New Challenges." *American Psychologist,* May 1973, pp. 379–86.

The issue in recent years has more to do with applying the scientific method to human beings. The comments of two critic psychologists can make this point clear.

> *Psychology, which once sought to free itself from its philosophic-religious tradition, now has an opportunity to free itself from its reliance on the natural-science model. . . . A major obstacle to the development of an authentic psychology is man's intrinsic* psychophobia—*man's fear of acknowledging the truth about his own mind* . . . the major function of social science, including psychology, should be to make man aware of the forces that operate on him. [Bakan, 1972, pp. 87–88]

Rosenberg (1971) puts it in another way: "I suggest that rigorous science as it is presently applied is not the road to understanding human behavior. To study the typewriter that a novelist used is not the way to understand his novel" (p. 68).

The argument began years ago and continues to this day. It is for the psychologists of the future to decide whether psychology will continue to pursue the aims of science or declare itself an art form or a philosophy of man.

Summary

1. The word *psychology* comes from the Greek terms *psyche* and *logos,* meaning study of the mind. Psychological inquiry began in the time of the Greek and Roman philosophers, but the interest in psychology as a science was a result of the philosophies of John Locke and the work of Wilhelm Wundt. Both of these men believed in the importance of man's sensory experience for understanding the physical world.

2. The earliest school of thought in psychology was *structuralism.* It focused on the study of the element's of one's own consciousness: sensations, images, and feelings. The *functionalism* school of thought was founded in an effort to find useful applications for the study of conscious processes.

3. The theories of the behaviorist John B. Watson soon brought the study of conscious processes to an end. He asserted that the only proper topic for psychological study was behavior and that all behavior was learned. The influence of the behaviorists contributed to the new definition of psychology as the science of behavior.

4. The gestalt theorists objected to the psychological tendency to break down human processes into their elements. They believed that the only way to understand man would be to study the configuration of his mental activities.

5. The early twentieth century saw the beginnings of the *dynamic* and *individual* schools of psychology. From both groups, new ideas were generated about the nature of abnormal behavior. But the two schools were also responsible for the idea that psychology was useful even for normal individuals.

6. Today psychology is concerned with a wide variety of subjects, and no psychologist deals with them all. Most psychologists change research interests frequently throughout their careers.

7. Contrary to the popular stereotype, scientists appear to be creative individuals who are nonconformists. They are independent, have few interpersonal relationships, and are not particularly sociable. Most psychologists do not fit this picture of the scientist, however, perhaps because of the nature of the subject matter they are dealing with.

8. Psychologists and psychiatrists differ both in training and in the methods they use for the treatment of emotional disturbance. In addition, only psychiatrists are permitted to prescribe drugs, surgery, or other medical treatments for psychological problems.

9. The purpose of psychological research is to describe, understand, predict, and thus be able to control, behavior. Psychologists have

adopted the scientific method from the older sciences to pursue these aims. The scientific method is a systematic way to select problems, collect information, and interpret one's findings.

10. The social scientific method consists of five steps: (1) formulating the problem, (2) reviewing the research that has already been done in the area, (3) making preliminary observations, (4) forming a hypothesis about how your problem will be resolved, and (5) conducting a study to verify or reject the hypothesis.

11. In conducting an experiment, the psychologist manipulates those variables he thinks affect the phenomenon he is trying to understand. He arranges certain events to occur *(independent variables)* and watches the results *(dependent variables)*. At the same time, he controls for other variables which might influence the outcome. The experimental method may be carried out in the laboratory or in real life.

12. Despite the advantages, controlled experiments may not give true results if: (1) the artificial manipulations do not replicate normal behavior, (2) subjects know they are being studied, (3) subjects are not representative of the general population, and (4) the experimenter's bias interferes with subject behavior.

13. In attempts to eliminate experimenter bias, experimenters may tape instructions, keep themselves ignorant of experimental conditions, or disguise the identity of the subjects they are testing.

14. Psychologists do not always collect their information through controlled laboratory experiments. Other methods include observation, surveys, psychological tests, and case histories. Usually these data are then analyzed in correlational studies.

15. Many psychological theories stem from correlational studies in which the psychologist tries to determine if two or more variables in his data are related to each other. Despite their wide use, correlational methods only establish whether or not there is a relationship between the variables and how strong that relationship is. They do not say anything about which variable causes the other or if they are both effects of a third, unknown factor.

16. Some psychologists object to the use of the scientific method, saying that it is not appropriate for understanding the nature of man's mind. Some suggest that man must return to introspection about his own experiences.

PSYCHOLOGICAL ISSUE

Parascience

The world of mysticism and the occult begins with a set of premises that differ sharply from those of the "scientific" world. It is for this reason that scientific-parascientific communication has so often been a "dialogue of the deaf" in which both speak persuasively, but neither listens (Metzner, 1971). The term *parascience* (*para* meaning "beside, apart from, or accessory to") is a fairer choice of terms than the traditional, derogatory label, *pseudoscience* (*pseudo* meaning "false"). As Kaufmann (1968) observed: "Some aspects of science itself developed out of magic, and whatever the dissimilarities, it shares with magic the urge to know the . . . world, and the belief that Man can be more than a passive, uncomprehending thing in it" (p. 7).

Ideas Whose Time Has Come.   There seem to be times in human history when the conditions are right for certain ideas to be born. What Germans call the *Zeitgeist* (the spirit of the times) seems to prevail, and scientists working independently of one another make the same discovery at almost the same moment in time. There are numerous examples of scientific ideas that are born only to waste away from neglect until, years later, the scientific world is ready to assimilate them, connect them to other bodies of fact or theory, and apply them to problems previously unsolvable.

Recent times have seen the rise of astrology, numerology, witchcraft, satanism, Ouija boards, Tarot cards, and a multitude of other approaches to the mystery of man. Ninety percent of American newspapers carry daily astrological forecasts, and as many as two million Ouija boards are purchased each year in this scientifically sophisticated society.

In 1865, Claude Bernard insisted that if the *facts* used for the basis of reasoning are ill-established or erroneous, everything will crumble. Indeed, errors in scientific theories often originate in errors of fact. But it is this disagreement about what is or is not "fact" that triggers most of the hostile dialogue between parascientists and scientists.

Scientists must seem *un*reasonable to parascientists but, as Gardner (1952) pointed out, this very stubbornness "forces the scientist with a novel view to mass considerable evidence before his theory can be seriously entertained. If this situation did not exist, science would be reduced to shambles by having to examine every new-fangled notion that came along. Clearly, working scientists have more important tasks" (p. 11).

The Psychologist and Personal Bias

The realm of parascience is a particularly difficult one to treat in an objective, impartial manner. This is so for me, not only because it is an area of study usually defined as *outside* science, but also because of the personal convictions I have accumulated over a period of many years. I label these convictions scholarly conclusions. Those who disagree with me would call them personal biases.

Do I have an open or closed mind about parascientific phenomena? Questions like this are at the center of much scientific controversy. In the scientific method, objectivity and impersonal concern with "the facts and only the facts" has long been a professional watchword. There are areas of experimental endeavor, however, in which "the facts" are hard to come by and the argument over trustworthy fact is fueled more by emotion than by incontrovertible evidence.

What I have labeled "parascience" is only one of many such areas of marked disagreement among dedicated researchers. In other scientific areas, personal bias is harder to detect, and often a psychologist is unaware that his view of "the facts" may appear distorted or blurred to others. If you one day join the ranks of social scientists, you will be confronted with the same challenge to your objectivity. As a social scientist you will be forced to decide when, or if, you will personally declare certain directions of exploration to be unscientific. You can begin this decision-making process now by examining your current convictions to see which can easily be changed if adequate proof is presented, which would require a remarkable level of unarguable evidence, and which convictions would be nearly impossible to abandon even in the face of startling "facts" to the contrary.

Since we are all human, this is what the pursuit of science is all about—the making of imperfect man into a more perfect instrument of factual discovery. My own bias with regard to parascientific phenomena is apparent. More psychologists share my position than disagree with it, but each of you must decide these issues for yourself. History tells us with great certainty that the "facts" of the year 2000 will most assuredly not correspond with the "facts" of the mid-1970s.

So, read what I have written, subtract what you take to be my personal bias, and "keep your options open" so that tomorrow can be significantly better than today. You are well-advised to retain your skepticism about what you read and to consider the possibility that those of us who have gone before you have figured it out all wrong.

The Varieties of Parascience

The parasciences are too many in number to describe in detail, but a brief outline of a few of them can serve as an illustration of the ways man has sought to unlock the secrets of nature and the universe. Phrenology is the one endeavor that is closest to modern psychology.

Phrenology   Phrenology began with the following series of assumptions: (1) the brain is the physical organ of the mind, (2) the shape and size of the various parts of the growing brain represent the over- or underdevelopment of personality traits, and (3) the bumps and hollows of the skull reflect the shape of the brain it contains. It followed logically that the phrenologist need only measure head bumps to determine the shape of the brain and diagnose the personality of his patient.

Phrenology began with Franz Joseph Gall's (1758–1828) curiosity about a possible relationship between the physical characteristics and psychological qualities of man. Gall concluded that the mind was composed of 37 powers or propensities (firmness, reverence, acquisitiveness, and combativeness, for example). He theoretically located these powers in specific parts of the brain. The physician Johann Kaspar Spurzheim (1776–1832) modified some of Gall's theories and made a number of further observations.

By 1840 phrenology had become a popular craze offering a quick, "scientific," inexpensive way to get vocational guidance and assure happiness. There were phrenology parlors scattered across the country, and traveling phrenologists crisscrossed the nation on lecture tours. Phrenology had a reasonable ring to it in that day and age, even though today's scientists reject the notion that the brain is like a muscle that becomes weak or strong depending on how much it is exercised.

Graphology   The practitioners of graphology—the analysis of handwriting—have made astonishing claims about its uses. One modern advocate maintained: "I am convinced that in the hands of a skilled practitioner, graphology can assist corporations in the selection of productive and reliable employees, can aid therapists in evaluating their patients, and can help youths choose their careers by pinpointing talents and personality traits. I believe that graphology could aid in difficult medical diagnoses" (Anthony, 1967, p. 30).

Graphology and Psychology.   The classic work by psychologists in this area was that of Allport and Vernon in 1933. In their investigations of human behavior they included handwriting on the assumption that (1) personality is consistent, (2) movement is expressive of personality, and (3) the gestures and other expressive movements of an individual are consistent with one another. They had no intention of confirming or disconfirming the claims of graphology, but their studies are often cited by graphologists as evidence that there is reliability and consistency in human expressive activity of all sorts—including handwriting.

Anthony insists that graphology is a legitimate subdiscipline of psychology, but few psychologists would agree with him. And, few psychologists study handwriting analysis enough to do effective research on its claims. What little psychological research has been accomplished has not been encouraging to the graphologists. In one appraisal of a series of handwriting studies, McNeil and Blum (1952) revealed a number of weaknesses. Some of these were: "failure to consider consistency of an individual's handwriting and reliability of raters' judgments; lack of specificity of criteria used to evaluate handwriting; inadequacies of the global matching method; and dubious character of some of the personality variables" (p. 483).

Psychological research in graphology continues to languish today, but popular fascination has not diminished accordingly. "The 'easy art' of handwriting analysis has answered the needs of the drawing room psychologizers who seek a dramatic new path to personal popularity" (Anthony, 1963, p. 76).

The Occult Parasciences

For centuries, people have planned their life events with one eye on reality and the other on the signs of the zodiac. And now, the ancient art of astrology has entered the computer age. Computer-cast horoscopes are available, the cost of which can be charged to another technological breakthrough, the credit card.

Astrology   Astrology has long captivated the interest of persons of all ages in our society. It "seeks to blend in varied proportions the fundamental methods of ancient and medieval astrology with the broad psychological knowledge which has been spread throughout the United States" (Rudhyar, 1968, p. 7). The information astrologers offer to believers is often related to mysterious and ancient wisdom amassed over the centuries. What precisely this wisdom was and what exactly the ancients achieved with their knowledge somehow never gets discussed. The facts are probably not really relevant if man believes that the patterns he observes in the sky give order to the apparent chaos and confusion of daily life.

Astrology is one way to convince ourselves that we are not alone and unnoticed in this life. The belief in astrology (or any parascientific phenomenon) is an *emotional* rather than a rational event. What *feels* right

Counterscience. The study of the stars as a guide to behavior and personality is receiving its most serious appraisal since the scientific revolution swept it off the shelf of intellectually respectable learning some years ago. The resurgence of interest in astrology has variously been attributed to:
- The collapse of religious faith,
- A loss of confidence in pure reason as a guide to action, and
- The spreading interest, particularly among the young, in Oriental mysticism.

The notion that heavenly bodies influence human behavior is among mankind's oldest beliefs.

and true to an individual *is* truth to him, and no massive accumulation of so-called scientific data can shake the foundation on which such belief is based. The belief itself is comforting and probably harmless, if it does not become the sole focus of existence.

The Ouija Board The name *ouija* is a combination of the French *oui* and the German *ja,* and literally means "yes-yes." The Ouija board has the letters of the alphabet, the words *yes* and *no,* and the numbers 1 through 10 printed on its surface. The tiny Ouija table (a small surface with three short legs) moves

Songs I Never Heard Before. When Rosemary Brown was seven, the great composer Franz Liszt appeared to her and told her he would visit her again after she had grown up. He did. And he began to pass on to her his musical compositions—totally new and unheard by the living world. Mrs. Brown, a London housewife, has been visited not only by Liszt but by Beethoven, Debussy, Chopin, Schubert, Bach, and other musical geniuses who have given her over 400 new compositions. "Leading authorities" have said that no one could have composed that much music, written in a dozen different styles, without being a musical genius. Yet Rosemary Brown had limited musical training, knew very little musical notation, and almost no musical theory. Her communication with long-dead composers was not limited to musical information. In two instances, Franz Liszt told her to enter the football pools (a form of lottery in England), and she won both times. [Brown, 1971]

The Spiritualists. Spiritualists are often categorized merely as mediums who contact the "other side" by holding séances to call up some departed spirit. But this is only one of their functions. Spiritualists often spend as much or more time healing and counseling as they do holding séances. Their information, in true spiritualist tradition, comes from "spirit guides"—friendly sources on the "spirit side" who offer secret information to those on the "earth plane."

about the larger board spelling out words, answering yes or no, or adding up numbers, in response to the pressure of the fingertips of the participants. Believers are convinced that answers to their questions are furnished by a supernatural force that guides their fingers to the truth. Nonbelieving psychologists are convinced that this phenomenon is less ghostly and more an instance of the simple physical expression of an unconscious wish for evidence of a guiding force in the universe. It is a harmless pastime as long as you don't begin to take it too seriously and guide your life and your decisions according to "messages" received from the spirit world.

Satanism and Other Mysteries Recently a major airline offered a "Psychic Tour" of Great Britain which included a visit to a psychic healing center, a séance, and a day at Stonehenge with the chief of Britain's Most Ancient Order of Druids. Each tourist received his own astro-numerology chart, and flight dates were astrologically plotted to be favorable. The current popularity of such psychic attractions attests to the nature of our times. In an age when everyone except computer cards gets duly stapled, folded, and mutilated, one boon is the feeling of being the manipulator instead of the one who is eternally manipulated. Much of the occult is man's attempt to become godlike, to master the world around him. It is, in short, magic—the earliest of man's religious responses.

How fares magic in this modern world? As reported in *Time* magazine:

In Oakland, California, when the moon is full, a group of college-educated people gather in a house in a mid-

dle-class *neighborhood, remove their clothes, and whirl through the double spiral of a witches' dance. In southern New Jersey, a 30-year-old receptionist winds thread around a voodoo doll and sticks steel pins into it in a determined effort to harass a rival at the office into resigning. In Chicago, from 75 to 100 otherwise ordinary people . . . take instruction in ancient witchcraft and ceremonial magic from a high priest and priestess.* [June 19, 1972]

These new "occultniks" have been accused of being either intellectual frauds, financial swindlers, or dis-

Satanism. "Blessed are the strong, for they shall possess the earth. If a man smite you on one cheek, SMASH him on the other!" This inverted gospel—from Anton Szandor La Vey's *The Satanic Bible*—sets the tone for today's leading brand of Satanism, the San Francisco-based Church of Satan. Founded in 1966 by La Vey, a former circus animal trainer, the Church of Satan offers a mirror image of most of the beliefs and ethics of traditional Christianity. La Vey's sinister balderdash reaches hundreds of thousands through the black gospel of *The Satanic Bible* and his second book, *The Compleat Witch.* [*Time,* June 19, 1972]

Witchcraft.   White witches historically derived their presumed power from beneficent forces of nature and used it to heal, resolve disputes, and achieve good for others. Such benevolent magic may also include defensive spells against the maledictions of black witches. The black witches invoke power from the darker forces of nature—or Satan—and generally employ their magic for themselves, either in an attempt to acquire something or to cast a malicious spell on an enemy.

During an initiation ceremony at a "white" witch coven in Louisville, Kentucky, the high priestess faces an altar with paraphernalia to be used during the ritual. At left is a close-up of the Book of Magick, handwritten in occult code. The symbols date to ancient times.

turbed individuals who frequently mistake psychoses for psychic phenomena.

The flying saucer phenomena of the 1950s provide additional insight into the emotional and social aspects of belief in the occult. According to Buckner's (1966) analysis of flying saucers, excitement about Unidentified Flying Objects (UFOs) began in 1947 producing a period of public sensitization to the notion that there were mysterious things flying around our planet. From April through July 1952, *Life* magazine carried articles about flying saucers, which increased the number of UFO sightings about tenfold. Before long, the flying saucer craze entered a new phase Buckner calls "occult colonization"—people began to report UFOs landing and making contact with humans. By the mid-1950s,

The Ghostly Writer.   Harlow (1961) tells of a St. Louis housewife named Mrs. Curran who wrote down poetry and novels that were supposedly dictated by a woman who lived 300 years ago. Mrs. Curran received her initial message through an Ouija board one evening in 1913. The Ouija pointer identified the woman as Patience Worth who had lived in seventeenth-century England. In the writings Patience dictated, she spoke of birds, flowers, and trees that are native only to England. She had an intimate knowledge of archaic forms of the English language and often spoke of customs long since abandoned in England but common during the Elizabethan period.

In 1928 Patience told the housewife that her earthly work had been accomplished and that she was leaving. The novels of Patience Worth have not stood the test of time, however. Her "absolute genius" is now forgotten.

a large body of publications had appeared suggesting the possibility that we were being watched by aliens from outer space. Flying saucer clubs were formed. National UFO conventions were held, and a lecture circuit was established. As Buckner observed:

The social world of the occult "seeker" is a very unusual one. The seeker moves in a world populated by astral spirits, cosmic truths, astrologers, lost continents, magic healing, human "auras," "second comings," telepathy, and vibrations. A typical occult seeker will probably have been . . . a member of four or five smaller specific cults. The pattern of membership is one of continuous movement from one idea to another. Seekers stay with a cult until they are satisfied that they can learn no more from it, or that it has nothing to offer, and then they move on. [p. 11]

Much of the parascience that some young people are "into" today is an open rather than closed cult. That is, the believer need not adhere to a fixed dogma or doctrine but only respect the mystic beliefs of others and share the common mood of mystery.

Flying Saucers.   The Air Force went out of the Unidentified Flying Object (UFO) business after a blue-ribbon study by University of Colorado scientists concluded the UFO reports were mostly hokum. There have been 25,000 UFO reports in the last 25 years. With the accepted range of 10 to 20 percent unexplained sightings, 100 to 200 out of an average of 1,000 reports each year simply cannot be brushed off as hoaxes, conventional aircraft, meteors, reflections on clouds, or other natural phenomena. That is a big enough margin to keep the believers hoping and a small enough margin for the nonbelievers to dismiss flying saucers as a figment of someone's overactive imagination.

This is, perhaps, as concise a statement as we can make of the psychological view of the resurgence of the occult and its handmaidens in modern times. The prosperity of parascience today may be a direct consequence of the terror of these times.

Summary

1.   Like psychology, parascience is an attempt to make sense out of the world and to control one's environment. The recent upsurge in parascientific interest seems to be related to the dissolution of many of the traditional institutions to which man has always looked for support.

2.   Although most parascientific phenomena have yet to be substantiated scientifically, believers usually resist scientific assaults to their beliefs.

3.   Parascientific phenomena are difficult to study with the scientific method. In addition, some psychologists would prefer not to deal with these areas because they believe they are not worthy of scientific investigation. Other psychologists, however, such as Carl Rogers, feel it is important that psychologists admit to the possibility of other realities and attempt to deal with them as part of their science.

HUMAN BEHAVIOR

IN THE FOLLOWING THREE CHAPTERS, you will begin to see how the methods of science can be applied to the study of man. We will explore the human brain and nervous system, the processes of learning and remembering, and theories of personality. Most of us take the brain and nervous system for granted, hardly considering the miraculously complex design contained in our body. We become suddenly concerned about this biological "computer" encased in our skull only when it stops functioning—either in ourselves or in others. Then, we may become alarmed or interested enough to want to learn more about it. Many people may not know, for example, that the brain is actually composed of two interlocking organs. And most of us are only dimly aware of the advances that have been made in controlling certain operations of the brain by the implantation of electrodes.

We tend to be more concerned with the issues of learning and remembering since these processes are more conscious aspects of our daily existence. We are aware that we can learn and then forget, but only in recent years has scientific research made clear progress in detailing the nature of these critical events. With each scientific advance, we move one step closer to the possibility of controlling human behavior and society. One other target of research has been that illusive quality called *personality*. Each person has his own unique set of traits, and for centuries thinkers have tried to account for the incredible diversity in human nature. Psychologists have devised tests of all kinds to assess our differences, and they have fashioned numerous theories to explain our quirks or to help us change our directions. For most of us, it is a big enough job to get to know ourselves and to understand more about why we are the way we are.

The Brain and the Nervous System

*A sound mind in a sound body, is a
short but full description of a happy
state in this world.*—John Locke

One striking fact about the nerves and the brain is the length of time it
took to discover them. Most of our knowledge of these bodily systems is
very recent in historical time. But this knowledge is still largely irrelevant
to most of us, since we seldom think of any part of our body until it starts
to malfunction. A headache makes us acutely aware of the housing that holds
our brain. It is vitally important to know something of what happens inside
the body and in our nervous system if we are to be able to understand human
behavior.

The human nervous system is a miracle of complexity when compared
to forms of life much lower on the evolutionary scale. Animals such as the
one-celled amoeba, for example, don't have a nervous system, and the entire
cell body itself is responsive to stimulation. The nervous system got its primitive
beginning when specialized cells, called *neurons,* spread evenly through the
outer layers of the body in different species as evolution proceeded. When
any part of this nerve net is stimulated, impulses spread out along the net
from that point and produce muscle responses in the areas where the neurons
are activated. There is nothing very complex in such a nervous system.

A further stage in the evolution of the nervous system appears in some
flatworms (planaria). In these animals, the nerves form a system much more
like that of man with the neurons arranged in a bundle called a nerve cord.
This is a kind of primitive spinal cord with the cell bodies of the neurons
concentrated in the head to form something similar to a brain.

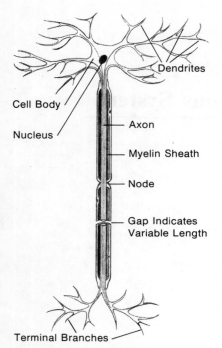

Cell Body

Nucleus

Dendrites

Axon

Myelin Sheath

Node

Gap Indicates
Variable Length

Terminal Branches

The neuron is the basic unit of the nervous system.

The Nervous System

The specialized cells called neurons are the basic building blocks of the nervous system. Each neuron is a living cell with a nucleus of the kind common to all cells. It consists of three principal parts: the *cell body,* which contains the nucleus; the *dendrites,* or many short fibers that project from the cell body and receive activity from nearby cells; and the *axon,* a long fiber that extends away from one side of the cell body and transmits activity to other neurons or to muscles and glands. Nerve impulses normally move in one direction—from the dendrites, through the cell body, and along the axon to the dendrites or cell body of the next neuron, or to a muscle or gland. While all neurons have these general features, they differ greatly in their dimensions. A neuron in the spinal cord may have an axon two or three feet in length, whereas neurons in the brain may cover only a few thousandths of an inch.

The neurons that collect messages from inside and outside the body and transmit them *to* the spinal cord or to the brain are called *afferent,* or sensory, neurons. Messages carried *from* the spinal cord or the brain to the muscles and glands go via *efferent,* or motor, neurons. Some neurons (usually in the brain or spinal cord) make the connection between incoming and outgoing messages. These are *association* neurons.

The Message Travels

Information we get from stimuli is transmitted through the nervous system in two ways. There is *axonal* transmission—the movement of nerve impulses *with* a neuron. And there is also *synaptic* transmission—the transfer of impulses *between* neurons. A nerve impulse in the human body may travel anywhere from 2 to 200 miles an hour, depending upon the diameter of the axon and a number of other factors.

In axonal transmission, solutions of two different chemicals (sodium and potassium) are found on both sides of the axon membrane, and this membrane is selectively permeable or porous. As a result of this selective permeability, the concentration of sodium ions is much higher on the outer side, and the concentration of potassium ions is much higher inside the axon. This means that the external and internal solutions have different electrical voltages. Most of the time, the inside of the axon is electrically negative compared to the outside. In this condition the axon is said to be *polarized,* and the inside-outside voltage difference is called the membrane potential. The transmission of a nerve impulse ("firing") changes this polarity—some of the potassium ions move outward through the membrane and some of the sodium ions move inward, and this sets up the charge necessary for the firing.

For a few milliseconds after the axon has "fired" and the membrane

The Glandular System

The body is equipped with another communications network besides the nervous system, known as the *endocrine glands.* These glands serve two main functions. The first is to maintain a steady metabolic state within the body. For example, if the level of sugar in the bloodstream increases beyond a certain amount, the pancreas, one of the endocrine glands, releases *insulin,* which moves the sugar out of the bloodstream into cells, thus restoring the blood to its normal chemical composition. The other function of the endocrines is to coordinate periodic physical changes, both permanent changes like sexual maturation and temporary ones like fear and flight.

All endocrine glands have a common characteristic: they possess no ducts as do the salivary glands or the tear glands of the eye. Rather, they discharge their substances directly into the bloodstream, which then carries the hormones to all parts of the body. For this reason, the endocrines are sometimes called the *ductless glands.* The substances produced by the endocrine glands and poured into the blood stream are called *hormones.* The *pituitary* is the master gland, which secretes a number of different hormones that have a profound effect upon the body. As you grow up, the pituitary secretes a growth hormone that regulates the development of the body. If the pituitary produces too little of this growth hormone, development is arrested and you may become a dwarf. With too much of the hormone, you may grow into a giant. At the time of puberty, the pituitary begins to secrete another hormone to activate the sex glands.

The *adrenal glands* rest on top of the kidneys. Each of them has two parts with quite different functions. The inner part (*adrenal medulla*) secretes *adrenalin* and *noradrenalin,* which affect the rate of heartbeat, raise the blood pressure, and cause the liver to release increased quantities of sugar into the blood to provide additional energy. They also tend to relax the smooth muscles of the digestive system, tense the striped muscles used for movement, shift the flow of blood from the digestive organs to the muscles, and make blood coagulate more quickly in cases of injury.

In times of fear or anger, the endocrine system works

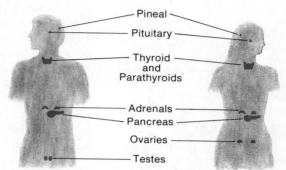

Location of the endocrine glands in the male and the female.

at top speed to produce extraordinary levels of physical activity. When in danger, you can perform feats of strength and endurance that would ordinarily be beyond your capacity. When you are angry you can fight harder than you realized was possible. And, if injured, your body will minimize the damage by having your blood clot faster than under ordinary circumstances.

The *adrenal cortex* (outer layer) produces a number of hormones called *corticoids.* An undersupply of these hormones will cause death. They maintain a salt balance in the body and turn the body's proteins into sugar.

The *thyroid gland* is a tissue lodged on either side of the windpipe. People with goiter, in which the thyroid gland becomes unusually large, have overactive thyroids that cause them to lose weight and have muscle tremors. The heart beats faster than normal, and behavior becomes markedly excitable and nervous. People with an underactive thyroid tend to be placid, tire easily, and are often sleepy. They are inactive and gain excessive weight.

The hormonal system works in conjunction with the nervous system, and each system depends on the other. The rates of secretion of the pituitary and the adrenal medulla are directly controlled by the neurons that innervate them (supply them with nervous energy). Other endocrines are controlled chemically—several of them by secretions of the anterior pituitary gland. The anterior pituitary is in turn controlled by the secretions of the endocrine glands it influences.

---

potential is more negative than it is normally, the membrane is temporarily unexcitable and cannot be fired again. This interval is known as the absolute refractory period. As the membrane returns to normal, there is a short period during which a stronger-than-normal stimulus is required to fire an impulse. This is called the relative refractory period.

THE NERVOUS SYSTEM DESIGN

"Starting from the periphery of the body, fibers from neighboring individual neurons are first grouped together as a nerve. In man . . . the fibers of the nerves are sorted out on arriving at the backbone, entering the spinal column at various levels, where they join with many thousands of fibers from other levels, forming together the main cable between the input/output devices and the brain. . . . This main cable of the spinal cord reaches the brain with an accumulation of several million separate conducting nerve fibers. About half of these fibers are busy bringing information to the brain while the other half are busy transmitting to the muscles and glands the instructions that constitute the results of the brain's data-processing and computing activities." [Wooldridge, 1963]

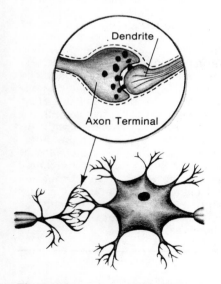

The synapse. A nerve impulse crosses the synapse in one direction only—from axon to dendrite. The enlargement shows the tiny sacs are filled with transmitter substances.

Each axon requires a certain level or threshold of stimulus intensity before a nerve impulse can be produced in it. If the strength of the stimulus is below this threshold, there is no firing of a nerve impulse. However, if the stimulus strength is anywhere above the threshold—just barely or very far above—the axon fires. Thus the axon fires either completely or not at all, which is known as the all-or-none principle. The size of the nerve impulse is always the same for any particular axon, regardless of the size of the stimulus. But the stimulus must be at or above the threshold. In some ways, it is like firing a gun. You must pull the trigger hard enough to fire the gun, but pulling harder on the trigger will not cause the bullet to travel any faster or any further.

Some nerve fibers are insulated by a myelin sheath. The sheath of these myelinated fibers is interrupted about every two millimeters by little pinched-off places called nodes, where the myelin sheath is very thin or totally absent. The transmission of nerve messages jumps along the fiber from node to node and thus is much more rapid in myelinated fibers than in non-myelinated nerve fibers. The myelin sheath of many of the nerve fibers in the brain is partial or incomplete at birth. This suggests that the maturation of some of the infant's sensory and motor apparatus may be related to the gradual process of myelination as he grows older.

The Synapse

Toward the end of the axon, a great many small fibers branch out, each ending in a tiny knob called an *axon terminal.* A microscopic gap separates the end of each of these terminals from the dendrites or cell body of other neurons. This tiny space is a *synapse,* and if the neural impulse is to travel on to the next neuron it must travel across this gap. It can bridge this gap because some axon terminals contain many tiny oval sacs called *synaptic vesicles.* When the nerve impulse reaches the end of the axon, it causes some of these vesicles to burst and release a chemical transmitter substance that travels across the gap and may cause the second neuron to fire, if a sufficient number of vesicles burst.

At this point you must wonder why these neural communication lines do not get hopelessly jammed. This doesn't happen because each type of receptor cell communicates to higher nerve centers through its own particular set of neural pathways. These separate routes, much like telephone lines, keep the messages separate and distinct.

The Nervous System Divisions

The nervous system consists of the brain, the spinal cord, and the nerves that connect these to *receptors* (cells in the sense organs) and *effectors* (muscles and glands). The brain and spinal cord make up the central nervous system, whereas other nerves make up the peripheral nervous system. The peripheral

Central Nervous System

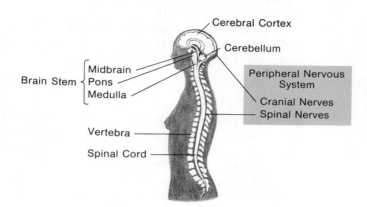

Structural diagram of the human nervous system. Functionally, the sensory and motor nerves are located in both the cranium and the spine.

nervous system, in turn, contains the two kinds of nerves mentioned before—sensory nerves, which carry messages from the sense organs to the central nervous system; and motor nerves, which carry messages from the central nervous system out to the muscles and glands.

It sounds a little complicated at first, but the peripheral nervous system is divided further according to which parts of the body it serves. Involuntary muscles and glands are controlled by the *autonomic nervous system,* and body movements are controlled by the *somatic nervous system.* The autonomic nervous system has two branches—the *sympathetic* and *parasympathetic* divisions. Both these divisions are directly involved in controlling and integrating the actions of the glands and blood vessels within the body, but they do so by waging a constant tug-of-war. The nerve fibers of the sympathetic division are busiest when the body is responding to stress, as when you are frightened or angry. They carry messages that tell the body to prepare for an emergency, to get ready to act quickly and decisively. In response to messages from the sympathetic division, your heart pounds, you breathe faster, your pupils enlarge, digestion stops, and blood is redistributed in your body. When you react to sudden stress, it involves almost all of your body.

The nerve fibers of the parasympathetic division connect to all the same organs as the sympathetic nerve fibers, but the messages they carry often tell the organs to do just the opposite of what the sympathetic division directs. The parasympathetic division most often sends messages that reduce the emergency reaction, but it is involved in more than just returning the body to normal after stress. It also handles all restorative and ruminative functions. Following a stressful situation, the parasympathetic division signals the heart to beat at its normal rate. It relays messages for the stomach muscles to relax, digestion to begin, breathing to slow down, and the pupils of the

Sympathetic		Parasympathetic
	Eye	
Dilates Pupil of Eye		Constricts Pupil of Eye
	Lungs	
Dilates Bronchi of Lungs		Constricts Bronchi of Lungs
	Heart	
Stimulates Beat		Inhibits Beat
	Adrenal Gland	
Inhibits Digestive Process		Stimulates Digestive Process
	Stomach, Spleen, Pancreas	
Stimulates		No Action

Different effects of the sympathetic and parasympathetic divisions on some parts of the body.

eyes to contract once more. Usually these two systems work together. The sympathetic division arouses the body. The parasympathetic division allows it to relax following a crisis.

The nervous system is far from complete at this point. We have yet to describe the brain and spinal cord, without which we would not be able to sense and respond to our environment.

The Brain

In the early days of brain study, the brain was removed after death and sliced into sections for examination, but very little valuable information was discovered through this method. Today a variety of approaches to research on the brain are being employed.

The development of microelectrodes as small as one thousandth of a millimeter, for example, has allowed scientists to record the activity in a single neuron. This procedure allows researchers to track stimulation and make discoveries about brain function never possible before. With such refined

FINDING THE BRAIN

It took man most of his history to pinpoint mental functioning in the brain. Aristotle believed that man's mind (or soul) resided in his heart, for if his heart were pierced, he almost always died. The brain was often considered to be little more than a radiator where hot blood was pumped to be cooled off. Another view, sometimes attributed to the early Egyptians, was that a "little man" or homunculus lived in the skull and pulled the strings that operated the muscles of our bodies. The problem couldn't be solved scientifically until we found out enough about electricity and chemistry to understand how the brain actually functions. It took until the late 1700s before the seat of consciousness was fixed within the confines of the skull.

Unlocking the Brain

The brain is a difficult organ to study. It is locked up inside a bony skull and protected by several layers of membrane and cushioning fluid. Our knowledge of the brain—what it does, what it is capable of, and which areas are responsible for each function—increases only as quickly as researchers can figure out new methods for studying this mysterious part of ourselves. In the last few decades, however, scientists have developed and perfected a number of methods that are beginning to unlock some of the secrets of our brains.

Electrical stimulation of the brain (ESB). Because the transmission of impulses through the nervous system is electric in nature, researchers can use electricity to stimulate the functioning of particular areas of the brain. They place electrodes in the area of the brain they wish to study and pass an electric current through the electrode. The current stimulates that area of the brain in the same way an impulse from another neuron would. The researchers can stimulate brain regions and observer how the behavior of their subjects changes.

Electrical recording. Just as researchers can stimulate the brain with electric current to map out its functions, they can record the electrical activity produced by different areas of the brain. The electric potentials of neuronal activity are amplified and converted by a machine into written records which appear as lines on a graph. The researchers may, for example, present a visual stimulus to a subject hooked up to a machine and record

how part of his brain reacts while processing this new information. Brain researchers have developed such precise recording methods that they can record the activity of one neuron. With larger electrodes implanted in the brain, they can record the summed activity of many neurons to pinpoint the functions of specific areas in the brain. They can also study patterns of brain activity produced in several regions of the brain by placing electrodes on the surface of the skull and recording them on the electroencephalograph (EEG).

Chemical stimulation and inhibition. Sometimes researchers inject chemicals into certain parts of the brain. The chemicals may be activators or inhibitors. As with ESB, the experimenters apply the chemicals and then observe the behavior of the organism to determine the precise function of the area in question.

Lesions. Because of accidents or surgery, certain areas of the brain are destroyed, inactivated, or removed. Psychologists study individuals with brain lesions to observe the behavioral changes that result from the loss of functioning of a particular brain region.

Split-brain surgery. One type of surgery that has yielded a great deal of information about the brain is the severing of the corpus callosum, the nervous tissue which connects the left and right hemispheres of the brain. Individuals who have split brains appear quite normal but share a few peculiarities which demonstrate the specialized functions of each hemisphere of the brain.

equipment, the electrical effects of nervous activity can be measured, and the path of a nervous impulse from its origin to the brain can be mapped. The continuing electrical rhythm and tide of the nervous system can be recorded over time. The linking together of instruments like the electroencephalograph (EEG) and the computer allows brain explorers to "read" brains at a level not even imagined years ago.

The discovery of the effects of electrical stimulation of the brain was another breakthrough. Work with patients having brain surgery and on experimental animals with permanently implanted brain electrodes has made it possible to "map" sensory and motor activity of the brain. Recent experiments with electrode implantation in human subjects, coupled with radio-signal stimulation from a distance, have furnished completely new information.

The traditional methods of studying brain function are still in use and still contribute added insight about the mystery of the mind. For example, researchers have traditionally studied cases in which accidental brain damage

EEG Tracings

Excited

Eyes Closed

Eyes Open

Deep Sleep

Dreaming

Patterns of brain activity recorded by the electroencephalograph under various circumstances.

has caused nerve degeneration. When such nerve death or degeneration happens, the pathways of nerve fibers can be traced microscopically through the incredible maze of the brain in a way not otherwise possible. Whenever disease or injury occurs in specific, circumscribed areas of the brain, it is possible to learn more about the function of that area by observing the symptoms produced by such injury. In the same fashion, the necessary surgical removal of parts of the brain can make a valuable contribution to treatment of future patients as well as add to our general store of knowledge about the brain.

The Spinal Cord

Through the hollow center of the connected vertebrae of the backbone runs the major nerve of the body, the *spinal cord*. It provides certain basic connections between motor and sensory neurons and serves as the pathway for nervous

Biofeedback

The technique of biofeedback uses electronic instruments to amplify changes in the brain, which reflect bodily fluctuations occurring in blood pressure, heart rate, muscle contractions, and so on. The changes in the brain are indicated by signals in the instruments (such as a sound or a light) which can allow a person to identify internal changes and, hopefully, learn to control them. Just as you learn to ride a bicycle by feeling your body move and correcting your movements to keep balance, you can learn to relax and alter your brain waves by getting feedback from an electroencephalograph (Luce and Peper, 1971). Using the kind of conscious concentration practiced by meditators along with the electroencephalograph to guide them, biofeedback experimenters are trying to learn to manipulate the brain from states of high alertness to states of rest.

Thus, you can learn to sit with your eyes closed and "will" certain brain wave patterns to occur. The brain-wave patterns are named according to letters in the Greek alphabet—alpha, beta, delta, and theta. The alpha rhythm in particular has stirred a great deal of interest since subjects report they are relaxed or feel like they are floating on air when it appears. Subjects have commented that it is as if a force is flowing through them or they have "a lonely, serene feeling of being in harmony with the universe" (Hoover, 1972). When alpha brain waves appear, other subjects report a state of "alert tranquillity and calm," closely resembling that described by the masters of Zen and Yoga meditation. In fact, experts in Zen and Yoga learn control of their alpha waves far more

rapidly than the average person. People who have practiced meditation for six months to a year all show the same EEG characteristics: high alpha while meditating, low alpha when they were not (Kamiya, 1968).

Conscious control of the alpha waves of the brain is not really of any practical use at the moment. But, it has been suggested that conscious production of alpha waves may one day increase our creativity and lead us to ways to control our internal states of mind. Some of the more enthusiastic advocates of biofeedback think it is a greater invention than fire or the wheel—an invention that may open the door to the secrets of inner space or be the next step in human evolution (Rorvik, 1970).

impulses traveling from the outlying portions of the body to the brain. A cross section of the spinal cord shows that it comprises two different regions. The dark tissue forming the "H" at the center of the cord is known as *gray matter.* It consists of cell bodies and nerve fibers without myelin sheaths. The nearly instantaneous, reflex connections of sensory and motor nerves are found in the gray matter. The *white matter,* which derives its color and its name from the myelin sheathing of its nerve fibers, surrounds the gray matter and carries messages to and from the brain.

The Basic Structure of the Brain

Compared to his animal neighbors, man is a creature of modest physical endowment. He has a poor sense of smell, just average hearing, only passable vision, thin skin, weak jaws and teeth, unimpressive muscular strength, middling running speed, and so-so stamina. His one saving grace, the one that distinguishes man from the rest of the animals and allows him to master his environment, is his brain.

At first glance, the brain seems an unlikely candidate for such distinction. The organ has the consistency of soft cheese, and with its many convolutions and ridges, it looks and feels something like a giant, mushy walnut. But in cellular terms the brain is impressive. It contains about 110 billion cells, 10 billion neurons and 100 billion *glia,* which provide nourishment and support for the neurons. In terms of relative size, man's brain is the largest of all brains. For the sake of comparison, a dog, a gorilla, and a man of the same body size would have brains of one-half, one, and three pounds respectively.

The simplest brains, found in certain primitive animals, are nothing more than bulbous swellings at the end of the spinal cord, and this description essentially fits the human brain. The brain is composed of three basic structures. The enlarged and knobby protrusion of the spinal cord is the *brainstem.* Behind the brainstem sits the ball-like mass of the *cerebellum.* Enveloping the whole of the brainstem and most of the cerebellum is the *cerebral cortex.* The wrinkles and folds of the surface layer of the cerebral cortex give the brain its characteristic appearance.

The brainstem comprises several connected structures, each with its own distinct functions. The *medulla,* at the very base of the brainstem, controls such basic physical rhythms as heartbeat and breathing, and it contains the reflex centers for vomiting, sneezing, coughing, and swallowing. Above the medulla is the *pons,* which houses ascending and descending nerve tracts and a cross-connection between the brainstem and the cerebellum. The *midbrain* acts as a relay center in complex reflexes involving hearing and vision and in the reception of pain. The exact role of the *thalamus* is not well understood, but it seems to sort incoming sensory messages and route them to the appropriate region of the cerebral cortex. The *hypothalamus,* to the front and

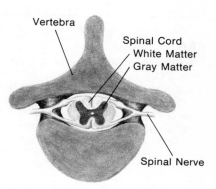

Vertebra

Spinal Cord
White Matter
Gray Matter

Spinal Nerve

The spinal nerve emerging from the spinal cord.

THE REFLEX
When you react to sudden pain or drop a hot potato, you do so without stopping to think about it. The action is accomplished in the spinal cord without involving the higher brain centers. The impulse moves along the sensory nerve to the spinal cord and out the spinal cord via the motor nerve of the hand. Any action more complex than the reflexive withdrawal of the hand would involve the higher brain centers. The nerve impulse would travel all the way to the cerebral cortex where orders would then be given for appropriate action. Thus, if the frying-pan handle is fairly hot but not enough to produce reflex action, your brain may tell you to pass it from hand to hand until you can safely set it down somewhere.

EEG

The presence of electrical current in the brain was discovered by an English physician, Richard Caton, in 1875. But it wasn't until 1924 that Hans Berger, a German neurologist, used his ordinary radio equipment to amplify the brain's electrical activity so that he could record it on graph paper. The fluctuations of current in the brain appeared on this first electroencephalograph (EEG) as a bunch of squiggly lines. On closer observation, however, Berger noticed that the fluctuations were regular. They changed in a consistent manner with the state of mind of the individual. We now call these rhythmic fluctuations of brain impulses *brain waves.*

A brain wave can be described by its frequency and amplitude. *Frequency* is the rate at which the wave travels. It is usually spoken of as the number of times the rhythmic fluctuation repeats itself in one second. This can be seen on the EEG as the number of cycles of the wave which appear within a designated space on the graph.

Amplitude is the intensity of the brain wave. On the EEG, amplitude is judged according to the height that the wave reaches at its peak.

The various regions of the brain do not emit the same brain wave simultaneously. If you placed an electrode on the scalp of an individual, the EEG would pick up, not one simple brain wave, but many waves of differing amplitudes and frequencies. This has presented a great deal of difficulty to researchers trying to interpret the large amount of data they receive from even one EEG recording. Through advanced techniques and the use of computers, however, researchers have been able to distinguish four basic brain waves, each with its own characteristic frequency. These are *alpha, beta, theta,* and *delta* waves. Although none of these waves is ever emitted exclusively by the brain at any one time, the state of mind of the individual may make one wave more pronounced than the others.

In addition to distinguishing between these four brain waves, the EEG has been put to a variety of uses. In medicine, for example, the EEG has been employed to diagnose brain tumors since areas adjacent to tumors emit distorted brain waves. The different forms of epileptic seizures also have their own characteristic brain waves. The EEG can be used to monitor attacks that might otherwise go unnoticed and to interpret the effects of treatment. The EEG has further been used by researchers in their attempts to understand sleep and dreaming.

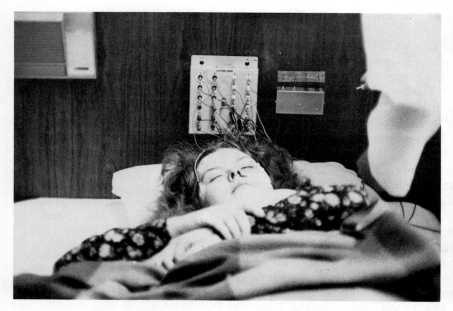

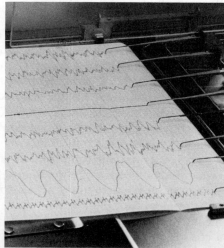

Recording the activity of brain waves during sleep at the Stanford University Sleep Disorders Clinic in Palo Alto, California.

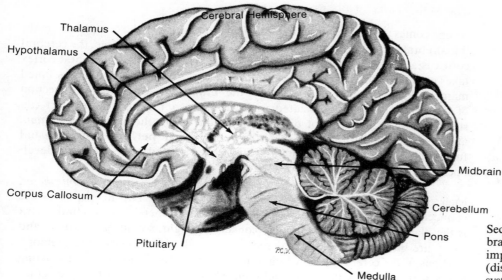

Thalamus

Hypothalamus

Cerebral Hemisphere

Corpus Callosum

Pituitary

Midbrain

Cerebellum

Pons

Medulla

Sectional view of the right half of the brain shown from the midline. It is important to note that the pituitary (discussed in the box on the glandular system) is under control of the hypothalamus, and that this connection coordinates the nervous and endocrine systems.

underside of the thalamus, is the most important automatic control point in the brain. It monitors particular activities such as eating, drinking, sex, sleeping, and temperature regulation, and it plays a direct role in the patterns of emotional behavior we call rage, terror, and pleasure.

Messages coming into the brain pass through nerve fiber tracts along the backside of the brainstem, while outgoing information follows neural pathways on the front side. Between these two regions lies a core of nerve tissue known as the *reticular activating system,* which runs the entire length of the brainstem. The reticular activating system is connected to the sensory nerves, and it performs an information-filtering process called *sensory gating.* The reticular system monitors incoming information, decides what is important, alerts higher brain centers that significant information is on its way, and discards insignificant messages to keep them from jamming neural pathways. Thus the reticular activating system is responsible for deciding how the brain will use its time to deal with the environment.

The cerebellum is positioned behind the brainstem and is largely occupied with automatic controls of body position and motion. It monitors the tension of arm muscles, for example, and keeps track of where the arm is in relation to the rest of the body and the surroundings. When you make a conscious wish to move your arm, the cerebellum acts as a kind of intermediary between command and execution, translating the order into a series of specific motor impulses that results in a coordinated and controlled movement.

The Many Tasks of the Cerebral Cortex

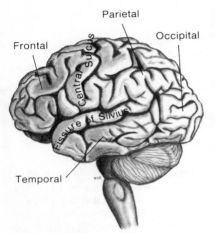

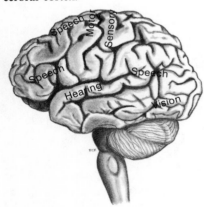

Above, the lobes of the cerebral cortex located in relation to the two main fissures. Below, some of the sensory and motor projection areas of the cerbral cortex.

As one comes up the evolutionary scale from the simple to the complex animals, the cerebral cortex grows markedly in size. In a shark, for example, the cerebral cortex is a very small portion of the brain. By contrast, man's cerebral cortex takes up 80 percent of his brain. As the cortex has grown larger, it has assumed many tasks performed originally by the brainstem. Cut away the section of the cerebral cortex associated with vision in a rat, and the subject can still see, although it cannot distinguish patterns. Do the same to a human, and he will be blind. The midbrain of the rat performs basic visual functions, but in man these functions have been passed on to the more developed cerebral cortex.

The cerebral cortex is composed of two separate halves, or *hemispheres,* each of which operates independently of the other. The hemispheres are connected by the *corpus callosum,* a body of nerve fibers. The cerebral cortex is the place where sensory impulses concerning sight, sound, taste, smell, and touch are interpreted, and it is the site of thought, intelligence, and memory. Portions of the cerebral cortex integrate the sensory and motor systems, acting like a sort of final switchboard between what comes in and what goes out.

Two prominent grooves, or *fissures,* run through the cerebral cortex; the central sulcus passes through the top of the cortex, and the fissure of Silvius runs from the bottom toward the top at an oblique angle. Using these fissures as reference points, the cerebral cortex is divided into regions, or *lobes.* The front portion of the cortex is the *frontal lobe.* Behind the central sulcus lie the *parietal* and *occipital lobes,* and the *temporal lobe* is found beneath the fissure of Silvius and the frontal lobes.

Fortunately for brain researchers, the cerebral cortex lies just under the skull, making it accessible to mapping by systematic probing with electrodes. A narrow band of cortex at the rear of the frontal lobe controls the motor responses of the whole body. Just across the central sulcus into the parietal lobe is another strip of cortex, which controls the sensory responses of the whole body. By no means are the amount of sensory and motor tissue devoted to a particular part of the body a function of the size of that particular portion of the anatomy. For example, the hands and mouth make up only a small percentage of the volume of the body, but they merit almost half of the motor cortex. The hearing area of the cortex is located within the fissure of Silvius on the temporal lobe. The occipital lobe is the site of the visual cortex. Cortical regions associated with speech are found in the frontal, parietal, and temporal lobes.

A curious feature of the human cortex are the portions which demonstrate no specific response when stimulated electrically. These so-called silent areas are known as the *associational cortex.* Since man's associational cortex is relatively far larger than that found in other animals, it's reasonable to assume that it plays a major role in making us human. However, its precise functions are not yet fully known.

The frontal lobes are mostly associational cortex. Not so long ago, many mental patients were "treated" by removing their frontal lobes, an operation known as lobectomy, or by severing the connections between the frontal lobes and the remainder of the brain (lobotomy). Most people subjected to this treatment showed marked personality change, but the particular change varied from one case to another, thus making it hard to say what the normal role of the frontal lobes is. At the present state of the science, most researchers agree that the frontal lobe is crucial to intention and will. We know more about the associational areas of the occipital lobe. Experiments show that this region is involved in discriminating among various kinds of stimuli, a mental function basic to learning and orderly thinking. It is thought, but by no means proven, that we will eventually find that learning and memory are located in the occipital lobe.

The Split Brain

Corpus callosum nerve fibers run from one hemisphere of the brain to the other. These fibers form an important communication network referred to as the transfer area because it transfers information received by one half of the brain to the other half.

PHINEAS P. GAGE
In 1868, the foreman of a road gang, Phineas P. Gage, was in a dynamite accident which rammed a four-feet long, one-inch thick crowbar through his jaw, up through the frontal lobe of his brain, and out the top of his head. Mr. Gage survived this accident, but there was a marked change in his personality. He became like a child. He had fits of temper when he didn't get his way, made elaborate plans and then changed his mind suddenly, and swore a blue streak at any time or place. Mr. Gage's experience illustrates that to a large extent the frontal lobes are responsible for what we call social control and personality.

Phantom Limbs

The messages coming into the brain sometimes contain seriously false information. Sometimes the brain is told what is happening at the body's extremities but simply cannot "learn" that the body no longer is the same as it once was. Phantom limbs are an illustrative case in point.

When it is necessary to amputate a limb, the amputee usually reports feeling a phantom limb almost immediately after surgery. The limb has a definite shape, and it moves the way a normal limb would. At first the phantom limb feels normal in size and shape, and the new amputee may reach out for objects with a nonexistent hand, try to step onto the floor with a phantom leg, or clench missing fists.

As time passes, however, the limb begins to change shape. The leg or arm becomes shorter, and may even fade away altogether, so that the phantom foot or hand seems to be hanging in mid-air. Sometimes the limb slowly telescopes into the stump until only a hand or foot remains at the stump. Over the years the phantom may become less distinct and disappear. If the patient wears an artificial limb, however, the phantom usually remains vivid and may correlate perfectly with the movement and shape of the artificial limb. [Melzack, 1970, p. 63]

In addition, about 30 percent of amputees report pain in phantom limbs. This pain tends to decrease and eventually disappears, but for about 5 to 10 percent of the amputees the pain is severe and may become worse over the years. The pain usually starts just after the surgery, but sometimes it does not appear for weeks, months, or years.

No acceptable theory explains this pain in phantom limbs, and surgeons have tried every known technique to relieve it but without much success. When medical methods fail, psychological reasons for the pain are suspected. Even though the pain goes away in some instances with psychotherapy or hypnosis, these usually don't work either. Emotional problems can contribute to pain, but this is not the major cause of pain in phantom limbs. We simply don't know why this happens in amputees, but the suspicion is that it will one day be traced to some as yet unknown aspect of our brain function.

NEUROPSYCHOLOGY
"By pinpointing the brain lesions responsible for specific behavioral disorders we hope to develop a means of early diagnosis and precise location of brain injuries (including those from tumors or from hemorrhage) so that they can be treated by surgery as soon as possible. Second, neuropsychological investigation should . . . lead to better understanding of the components of complex psychological functions for which the operations of the different parts of the brain are responsible." [Luria, 1970, p. 17]

In most persons the left half of the brain is dominant, controlling speech and the activity of a more skilled right hand. The right half of the brain, however, is specialized for form perception and perception of spatial relations. These differences are not absolute: the right hemisphere has some speech comprehension, and the left hemisphere does not completely lack space and form perception. But large injury to the left temporal lobe in most persons produces a severe aphasia, with disturbance of comprehension as well as of the production of speech, and injury to the right temporal lobe disturbs visual pattern perception and other nonverbal abilities. [Hebb, 1972, p. 53]

According to Ornstein (1973), the left hemisphere is also involved with analytic thinking, especially language and logic. This hemisphere seems to process information sequentially, which is necessary for logical thought for it depends on sequence and order.

The right hemisphere, by contrast, appears to be primarily responsible for orientation in space, artistic talents, body awareness, and recognition of faces. It processes information more diffusely than does the left hemisphere. The activities of the right and left hemispheres are not exclusive of each other. Rather, each "half-brain" is a specialist in its functions.

Thus, the brain of the higher animals and man is a double organ, consisting of right and left hemispheres connected by a bridge of nerve tissue (the corpus callosum). When the connection between the two halves of the cerebrum is cut, each hemisphere functions independently, as if it were a complete brain in itself. This odd feature of the brain structure has stimulated a great deal of research that has revealed some startling facts.

Disconnecting the Hemispheres

The first findings from hemisphere disconnection in animals revealed that cats and monkeys with split brains can't be distinguished from normal animals in most of their activities. They show no obvious disturbance of coordination and easily maintain their internal functions. They are alert and active, respond to situations in the usual manner, and perform about as well as normal animals when tested with standard measures of learning ability. Their individual traits of personality and temperament seem to remain the same. When specially designed tests were used, however, it became apparent that the split brain is not, after all, entirely normal in its functions. The split-brain animal behaves as if it had two entirely separate brains (Sperry, 1964).

When experimenters severed the hemispheres in chimpanzees with one eye connected to one half of the brain and the other eye connected to the other half, a strange situation developed. A' chimp's eyes were alternately blindfolded after this surgery, and the animal was then trained to do task X with one eye and task Y with the other eye. The chimp learned two different tasks as if he had two brains. The eye that learned task X couldn't recognize task Y, and vice versa. Of course, when the corpus callosum is left intact, the information learned in one hemisphere is transferred to the other, even if one eye is blindfolded.

It was predictable that experimentation with human beings was soon to follow. A number of human patients have undergone the brain-splitting operation as a part of standard medical procedures. Surgeons have performed this operation on people afflicted with uncontrollable epilepsy, in hopes of confining seizures to one hemisphere. The operation has proved to be remarkably successful, producing an almost total elimination of all attacks and no serious impairment of mental faculties.

In the studies of Gazzaniga (1967) dating back to 1961, the first split-brain patient was a 48-year-old war veteran. The operation produced no noticeable change in the patient's temperament, personality, or general intelligence. All the evidence indicated that separation of the hemispheres created two independent spheres of consciousness. Gazzaniga has even speculated that, if a human brain were divided in a very young person, it is possible both hemispheres could separately and independently develop mental functions at the level attained only in the left hemisphere of normal individuals.

Sperry (1968) reports similar results for a patient who had suffered epileptic seizures for more than ten years and had grown worse despite treatment. At the time of the operation, the patient was averaging two serious attacks a week and had begun to have severe seizures that could have been fatal. In the five and a half years since surgery, the man has not had a single major convulsion.

The Two Visual Worlds

Each brain hemisphere has its own set of visual images and memories. The separate existence of these visual inner worlds is most apparent in tests that require speech or writing, since the brain center for speech and writing is located in the dominant brain hemisphere (the *left* hemisphere in right-handed people). When the brain is surgically split and a picture presented to the right half of the visual field, it will be transmitted to the left hemisphere. If you were the patient, you would be able to describe what you saw in speech or writing. When the same picture is shown to your left eye only (and hence transmitted to the right hemisphere), you will insist you saw nothing at all or only a flash of light. In fact, you will act as if you were blind in the left half of your visual field. Now, if you were asked to point with your left hand to a picture or object that matches the one you were shown, you could do it with no trouble. In short, the halves of the brain cannot respond in the same ways.

An interesting question arises about what happens if two different pictures are flashed at the same time to the left and right eyes. Say an *X* is shown to the left eye, and an *O* to the right. If the patient is blindfolded and asked to draw what he saw with his left hand, he can reproduce the

IT'S A RIGHT-HANDED WORLD

Try playing the violin, cutting with scissors, playing golf, or opening most refrigerator doors with your left hand, and you will learn just how right-handed our culture is. A southpaw learns that eating dinner with a right-hander requires extra caution to avoid bruised elbows. Pilots find most of the aircraft controls are on the right. And, in the very old days, the teacher would crack a ruler across your knuckles if she caught you writing left-handed. Try and buy a TV with all the color controls on the left side of the set. Somehow, during evolution the two halves of the human brain began to specialize, and the left side of it became dominant for the almost 94 percent of us who are right handed. About 15 to 20 percent of us are ambidextrous and can use either hand equally well. A very few are so good at it they are highly paid "switch-hitters" in baseball (Barsley, 1968).

figure on the left—that is, the *X*. But if you ask him what he has drawn, he will tell you he drew a circle! The left hemisphere does not seem to know what the right hemisphere saw and drew.

Another demonstration of the differing mental awareness in the two hemispheres can be done by asking the split-brain person to identify objects using only the sense of touch. He can easily describe and name orally or in writing objects that are put into his right hand, but if the same objects are put into his left hand, he can only make wild guesses. He may even seem unaware that anything at all is in his left hand. He does know something is there, of course, and he can demonstrate this if he is asked to find a matching object with his left hand rather than tell you what he is feeling. Even when he finds the proper matching object, he is liable to tell you that he just guessed and didn't know exactly what he was doing.

Interestingly, the approximately 5 percent of the population who are left handed (most of the split-brain studies were naturally done on right-handers) show a mixed set of results. Some are no different from right-handers. Some show completely reversed brain function, and in others both hemispheres have verbal ability. Although we have known about the crude functions of the separate hemispheres for many years, it has only been in the last five years or so that sophisticated research efforts have promised to unlock some of the eternal mysteries of the brain.

Summary

1. The basic unit of the nervous system is the *neuron*, a cell specialized for the transmission of impulses through the body. Nerve impulses in the neuron move from the dendrites, through the cell body, and along the axon to another neuron, muscle, or gland.

2. Neurons are distinguished according to function. *Afferent* or *sensory* neurons collect messages and transmit them to the central nervous system. *Efferent* or *motor* neurons carry messages to muscles and glands. *Association* neurons, found in the brain and spinal cord, connect incoming and outgoing messages.

3. The cell membrane of each neuron forms a barrier between a negatively charged solution inside and a positive solution outside. When the neuron picks up an impulse, the cell membrane allows the positive solution to pass through, temporarily depolarizing the cell. In this way the impulse is transmitted along the length of the axon to the axonal terminals.

4. The all-or-none principle refers to the fact that neurons will fire only if the impulse they pick up is of a certain minimum intensity. The neuron will fire at its maximum intensity as long as this minimum threshold is reached.

5. Transmission of impulses across the *synapse* (the space between neurons) is accomplished through the release of a chemical substance from the small sacs at the end of the axon terminals.

6. The peripheral nervous system consists of two subsystems: the *autonomic,* which controls involuntary muscles and glands, and the *somatic,* which controls voluntary body movements. The autonomic nervous system is further divided into the *sympathetic* nervous system, which controls and integrates the body's reaction to emergencies, and the *parasympathetic* nervous system, which allows the body to return to its normal operating level and which takes care of restorative and ruminative functions.

7. Advanced electrical recording methods have enabled scientists to measure the activity of a single neuron, or larger areas, in the brain. Scientists have also implanted electrodes in the brain to stimulate brain activity and map the behavior that each brain area controls.

8. The electroencephalograph is a machine that amplifies and records patterns of electrical activity in the brain known as *brain waves.* These waves have a characteristic *amplitude* (intensity) and *frequency* (speed). Researchers have identified four basic frequencies of brain waves which appear to be related to different states of mind.

9. In neuropsychology, researchers study the behavior of persons with brain lesions to determine the functions of the damaged areas. For instance, studies done with people who have had the corpus callosum of their brains severed yield important information about the separate functions of the hemispheres of the brain.

10. *Biofeedback* is the process by which electric instruments are used to amplify and report changes in the body. It is hoped that individuals can use this "feedback" to control their internal states. Of particular interest is control over the production of alpha brain waves, which are associated with relaxed states and increased creativity.

11. The *central nervous system* consists of the spinal cord and the brain. The spinal cord is made up of bundles of long nerve fibers. The white matter, on the outside of the cord, conducts messages to the brain. The grey matter, on the inside, is responsible for reflex action.

12. The brain is essentially a bulbous swelling at the end of the spinal cord. It is made up of three basic structures: The *brainstem,* the *cerebellum,* and the *cerebral cortex.*

13. The *medulla* controls breathing, heartbeat, and similar activities which occur involuntarily. The *pons* serves as a connection between

the brainstem and the cerebellum. The *midbrain* relays messages involved in hearing and vision and in the reception of pain. The *thalamus* is believed to process and route sensory messages to the appropriate area of the cerebral cortex.

14. The importance of the *hypothalamus* is demonstrated by the activities it controls and by the fact that it is largely involved in patterns of emotional behavior.

15. The *cerebral cortex,* which surrounds all of the brain, receives information from all the sensory systems and is also responsible for skilled, finer movements.

16. The *cerebellum,* located behind the brainstem, takes care of balance and coordination.

17. The *reticular activating system* in the brain alerts the higher centers when important messages are about to be received. In *sensory gating,* powerful messages from one sense are attended to, while messages from the other senses are momentarily ignored.

18. The two hemispheres of the cerebral cortex operate separately, and they are connected by the *corpus callosum.*

19. The two major fissures of the cerebral cortex help us describe the location of the four main lobes—the frontal, parietal, occipital, and temporal. In turn, these lobes serve as reference points when researchers *map* the brain through electrical probing.

20. Areas of the cerebral cortex which show no specific response when stimulated electrically are known as *associational cortex,* the precise functions of which are not yet known. We know the most about the associational areas of the occipital lobe, and we might eventually find that learning and memory are located here.

21. In right-handed individuals, the left hemisphere of the brain is dominant, controlling speech and the activity of the skilled right hand. The right hemisphere is more concerned with space and form perception. Each hemisphere of the brain receives sensory information from the opposite side of the body.

22. Persons with split brains have two visual worlds, because information coming to one hemisphere cannot be transferred to the other. Because of their special functions, the halves of the brain cannot respond to stimuli in the same way.

23. The endocrine system is made up of organs called *glands,* which secrete substances called *hormones* directly into the bloodstream. Some of the glands are controlled by the nervous system, whereas others respond to chemical changes within the body itself. The endocrine glands control chemical reactions all over the body, helping to maintain it within certain bounds.

PSYCHOLOGICAL ISSUE

Electrical Stimulation of the Brain

Would you stand in a ring without cape or sword if this bull were charging at you? You might if you were José Delgado, and if you had a radio transmitter (like he did) to send messages to electrodes implanted in the bull's brain. More information on Delgado's work can be found by turning the page.

In 1954 James Olds, in collaboration with Peter Milner, implanted electrodes in rats to study the reticular formation of the brain. One electrode landed in an area Olds had not intended to hit, and the rat kept returning to the place on the table where that part of its brain had been stimulated. Olds demonstrated that the rat would learn to run mazes to get the electrical current—to get its brain reward. In other words, stimulation of some brain pathways was found to be a reward for the rat, whereas stimulation of other sites was aversive or punishing. This discovery of centers for pleasure and pain was soon extended to human beings via electrical stimulation of the brain (ESB).

ESB and Humans

Stimulation of the human brain with electrically activated wires has a long history. As early as 1870 Fritsch and Hitzig had the novel idea of stimulating the brain in this way. They found that when a certain area of the exposed brain was touched—the motor area, for instance—an involuntary motor response (a response of the arms, legs, or trunk) occurred as a function of the particular area stimulated. This discovery was an impetus to research that has taught us much of what is now known about the brain. At least the general nature of the brain was known a fair time ago: it is electrochemical; it contains nerves; it is the principal controller of complex behavior; and it is divided into sections responsible for specific behaviors.

In an operation nearly 100 years later, a neurosurgeon discovered that, by touching an electrode to a specific portion of the brain, the patient relived, as if in a movie or dream, a part of his past life—a childhood birthday party, an exciting trip, or other incident. As long as the electrode was held in place, the patient continued to relive the incident, as if it were stored on video tape inside the brain. When the electrode was removed, the "movie" stopped. If the neurosurgeon was able to penetrate the exact same spot again with the electrode, the movie continued from where it left off (Penfield, 1959).

The Stimoceiver

José Delgado is both a brain researcher and an "impassioned" prophet of a new "psychocivilized" society whose members influence and alter their own mental functions to create a "happier, less destructive, and better behaved man" (Scarf, 1970, p. 46). Delgado suggests that, if the brain can be made capable of reshaping its own structure and functions, it can take a new step in the course of human evolution. Perhaps, the first step is Delgado's experiment with two-way, direct radio communication between a computer and the brain of a chimpanzee.

Delgado's methods of electrical brain stimulation involve drilling a small hole in the skull of the subject, introducing fine insulated electrode wires into precise, preplanned locations in the brain, and connecting the wires to a socket anchored to the skull. Then, the experimental subject is simply plugged in like any other home appliance. Some of the chimps first used in surgery have had up to 100 electrode contacts implanted for more than four years. When Delgado turns on the switches, a chimp can be made to open or shut its eyes, turn its head, hop, yawn, sneeze, stick out its tongue, or flex its limbs.

Not all ESB reactions are as simple as these. One of Delgado's monkeys, when stimulated, would stop what she was doing, change expression, turn her head to the right, stand up on two feet and circle to the right, climb a pole and descend, and growl and attack another monkey. Through the course of 20,000 stimulations, this behavior was repeated in the same order each time.

Delgado developed the "stimoceiver"—a one-ounce transmitter-receiver able to stimulate the brain by remote radio command and record the electrical activity of the brain. He has done several experiments with the stimoceiver, the most dramatic being when Delgado halted the charge of an enraged bull. In another experiment, one monkey in a colony learned to activate the radio stimulator to inhibit the aggressiveness of the mean-tempered boss-monkey of the group.

Epilepsy and the Computer. Delgado's experiments with stimoceivers suggests that unwanted patterns of brain activity—those associated with epilepsy, for example—might be recognized by a computer-at-a-distance and inhibited or dampened before they reach the critical phase that produces an epileptic seizure. The epileptic could have a cerebral pacemaker installed that would work something like a brain-wave thermostat. When brain activity of a preseizure sort begins to appear, the signals could be flashed to a preprogrammed computer that would react instantly, by radio, to stimulate those areas of the brain that would counteract and forestall the seizure. Epilepsy as well as other disorders triggered by brain activity might then be brought under control without drugs or conscious awareness on the part of the patient.

Since the brain contains areas that can be crudely designated as positive or negative, it would seem possible to alter life-long patterns of anxiety, fear, or violent behavior simply by exact stimulation of selected parts of the brain. ESB is an efficient and easy procedure for assuring socially acceptable behavior, but human beings still react negatively to physical control of their minds. For most of us, the idea of walking through life with electrodes implanted in our brains is pretty repulsive to contemplate.

ESB and Pain

Although we spend half a billion dollars each year on aspirin and other pain relievers, we actually know very little about pain. The variety of conditions under which pain is felt and the failure to discover a specific pain center in the brain has led theorists to conclude that pain is a general property of brain functioning.

Human beings display great individual differences in reports of feeling pain. When morphine is used for pain following surgery, about a third of the patients get relief; another third get as much relief from a placebo; and a final third are relieved by neither placebo nor morphine (Beecher, 1959). Some people are insensitive, or indifferent, to pain and, rarely, this abnormality may be present from birth.

In animals, pain can be a learned response. Dogs reared in very restricted physical and social environments, for example, turn out to be intellectually and socially "retarded" and, surprisingly, grossly insensitive to pain (Melzack and Scott, 1957). The reaction to pain can be "unlearned" in dogs. The Russian physiologist Ivan Pavlov paired food with a painful stimulus for dogs, and after many such pairings the dog would salivate when the painful stimulus was presented. The dog would also give no evidence of pain or even mild discomfort.

Pain in human beings can be similarly manipulated using the new electronic advances such as the stimoceiver. Persons who have suffered incurable and almost constant pain from some affliction are now walking around with tiny pain-killing radio receivers implanted in their chests. When the patient switches on the radio, it feeds a signal into the patient's spinal cord. In most cases, this relieves the pain for as long as the radio remains on. The theory is that the radio signals raise the pain threshold by canceling out pain impulses in the spinal cord before they reach the brain. This system has been used chiefly on patients who suffer low-grade, constant pain from back injuries and disc-surgery failures. About a quarter of the patients suffer pain from cancer. The pain-blocking effect is not great enough to prevent the person from feeling any pain, but it blocks the dull pain that may linger for hours. Most patients run the transmitter about 8 hours a day, and the relief continues after it is off. Some, however, must run it 24 hours daily in order to be free of pain.

Electrical stimulation of the brain and other parts of the nervous system is a part of behavioral science that has just blossomed. It holds an enormous promise for the future since many of the psychological theories about human action and reaction have been constructed with too little knowledge about the structure

ESB for the Criminally Insane. A confessed murderer-rapist, confined 18 years ago to a hospital for the criminally insane, was a prospect for experimental brain surgery to eliminate his uncontrollable rages. But, the surgery could also change his personality in other, unpredictable ways. The patient was scheduled for an operation to implant electrodes deep in his brain. This would allow doctors to send electrical impulses into his brain to see whether they could trigger his rages and so pinpoint defective portions of his brain. If the offending areas were not extensive, they would then be destroyed by surgery. It was hoped this would free the patient from the rages and resulting violent acts which have plagued him since childhood. Ultimately, the state-financed project was to include 24 similar mental patients, half to undergo surgery and half to receive drugs. The project was canceled following public protest. The patient was released from custody when it was discovered he had been confined under a law that had since been declared unconstitutional.

and operation of the brain. As we will later see, a great many of the mysteries of human behavior may become understandable as we learn more about how the brain and consciousness work together.

Summary

1. Research in electrical stimulation of the brain (ESB) has demonstrated that animals can be made to perform various activities merely by stimulating certain areas of their brains with electricity. José Delgado, a leading researcher, has used ESB to inhibit an attack by a bull and aggression in a monkey.

2. These findings, plus the discovery that stimulation of areas in the brain can cause pain or pleasure, have generated a controversy over the proper use of ESB. It has so far been used productively to relieve pain by inhibiting pain centers in the brain.

Learning and Remembering

The mind is slow in unlearning what it has been long in learning.—Seneca

How can experience or practice produce relatively permanent changes in our responses? Without learning we would be little different from the helpless infants we were at birth. It is difficult to explain learning, however, since no one ever saw learning take place. So, when we speak of learning, we are referring to a construct, an idea about something that happens inside you. If you walk into a bar sober and come out singing and staggering hours later, we infer that your condition changed because you were drinking. In a way, that's how we theorize about learning.

Learning

All learning theories are organized, complex sets of guesses about how experience changes us. The earliest guesses about learning used the notion of *instinct* as an explanation.

Instinct

In relation to human beings, we often use the term *instinct* and we often use it inaccurately. We may talk about a maternal instinct in a new mother, or a killer instinct in a mass murderer, but by doing so we are confusing automatic or impulsive behavior with behavior that is inherited and unlearned. Psychologists tend to avoid the word entirely. Instead, they refer to *instinctive behavior,* or an *inherited pattern of behavior.* Three conditions are necessary for a pattern to be classified as instinctive behavior: (1) It must be a general characteristic of the species. (2) There must be evidence that it is not learned—i.e., that it appears at the appropriate moment without previous training. (3) It must be obviously different from reflexive behavior (which is an automatic response to a stimulus). Thus, it may be touched off by a stimulus, but it must not be controlled by it. Further, instinctive behaviors need not be present at birth, for growth and maturation may need to take place before the organism is able to perform certain behaviors.

Patterns of instinctive behavior are found in many species, particularly in birds, insects, and fishes. Mother birds, for example, build nests, lay eggs, secure food, and return to the nest to feed the young without having learned to do so. A cat bearing her first litter will instinctively eat the placenta (the afterbirth membrane), kill any kittens that have been born deformed, and then nurse the healthy young. Behaviors such as these are instinctive because they conform with the conditions described above: All members of the species exhibit them, they are not learned, and they are not reflexive but complex.

Since an inherited pattern of response is not a learned response, it seems likely that few, if any, human behaviors are instinctive. Almost everything man does to help himself adapt to the world around him is learned, and in turn, he teaches his offspring how to adapt. The role of heredity should not be ignored or even down-played, however. We are certain that our lives are shaped to some extent by the particular physical, glandular, and nervous equipment we inherit. But when it comes to how and why we behave as we do, what we are born with seems less important than what we learn.

Although human behavior does not appear to be instinctive, there may still be *critical periods* for learning the behaviors we exhibit. A critical period is when an organism is ready to learn certain things, and the timing seems to be determined by the stage of maturation. Research has not yet established if such periods exist in humans, but experiments with animals provide evidence that there are critical times for learning in certain species.

A Critical Learning Period

Scott (1969) raised a newborn female lamb on a bottle and kept it in the house for ten days. The lamb quickly became closely attached to members of the family and followed them everywhere, much like Mary's Little Lamb of storybook fame. When the lamb was introduced to other sheep, it paid them no attention and three years later was still wandering around the field by itself while the rest of the flock stayed together as normal sheep usually do.

This phenomenon is described as a *critical-period effect,* referring to a special period of time during which a relatively small amount of learning produces a major and lasting effect. Such critical periods are not the same for all animals.

Scott and his co-workers conducted a fascinating "wild-dog" experiment

Seven little ducklings all in a row follow Konrad Lorenz as a result of being *imprinted* shortly after hatching. Imprinting occurred at a critical period when the ducklings were ready to make the social response of following and saw Lorenz as the object to be followed. They continued to make the same response whenever they saw him—and Lorenz was stuck with his adoptive family.

in which they placed a tame, pregnant bitch in a one-acre field surrounded by a high board fence. When the puppies were born, they were fed through a hole in the fence so that they had no human contact beyond quick glimpses through narrow cracks between the boards. Then, at different ages, individual puppies were taken out of the field and given contact with human beings for a week before returning to their enclosure.

The researchers discovered that puppies removed during the first five weeks of life behaved much like normal puppies. At seven weeks puppies began to be shy, and at fourteen weeks they had become wild animals who were so fearful of humans that they could be tamed only by confinement, forced contact, and hand feeding. This experiment demonstrated that dogs have a critical period for the formation of social attachments.

There are many examples of critical periods in learning, but the now classic example of what is now called *imprinting* was provided by Konrad Lorenz. In 1952, Lorenz found that, shortly after hatching from their eggs, ducklings would follow him as if he were their mother (if he quacked like a mother mallard and walked in a squatting position). Later experimenters used a tape recording of the duck call during imprinting (Hess, 1959) and learned that ducks are imprintable only at a certain time. There is a critical age, in hours, at which the duckling is most responsive to a mother figure.

We suggested above the humans *might* have critical learning periods. If so, it seems most likely that they would exist in relation to our learning of language. And there might also be optimum times for humans to learn certain other skills. But since we do not yet have definitive answers to questions

Ivan Petrovitch Pavlov.

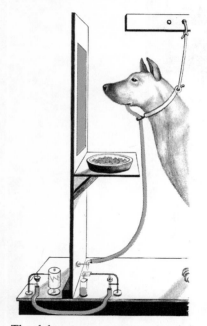

The laboratory apparatus used by Pavlov. The tube, attached to the salivary gland, collects any saliva secreted, and the number of drops is recorded on a revolving drum outside the chamber. An attendant can watch through a one-way mirror and deliver food by remote control. Thus, there is nothing to distract the dog except food and any other signals the attendant wishes to introduce.

about critical learning periods in humans, we must consider other ideas about how we learn. We can begin with a consideration of the conditioned response—a basic fact of learning.

Learning and Conditioning

The story of the conditioned response begins with the work of the Russian physiologist Ivan Pavlov (1849–1936). He was a man so dedicated that he reportedly lost his temper once at an assistant who was late because of having to walk through the streets during the Russian revolution in order to get there. Pavlov was experimenting on the salivary and digestive glands to measure the effect of gastric juices and to understand how digestion works, when he made a discovery. He noticed that if food was put directly into the stomach it did not produce enough digestive juices to allow normal digestion. He also noted that, even when no food was placed in the mouth, digestive juices would begin to flow when the animal merely *saw* the food. His most surprising discovery was that laboratory animals would begin to salivate just by seeing the experimenter who had previously fed them. The same thing happens if you pick up your dog's feeding dish; he starts to respond as if it were time to eat. If you could measure the flow of his saliva, you would see that his body is indeed getting ready to eat. Pavlov called this reaction a *conditional response*—a response that depends on certain conditions. Sometimes called *Pavlovian* or *classical* conditioning (because of Pavlov's now-classical experiments), the term preferred by many today is *respondent conditioning*.

Trying to understand this odd event—which he at first called "psychic secretions"—Pavlov connected tubes directly to the salivary glands and constructed measuring devices that would record the salivary flow. He knew dogs would salivate when they tasted food. Since no special conditions were needed to evoke this response, he labeled this the unconditioned response. He reasoned dogs can learn to start salivating at the mere *sight* of food, and he called *this* a conditioned response. Pavlov then proceeded to teach dogs to salivate to a whole series of other signals. To accomplish this, a stimulus (a light, for example) was presented for a brief period of time when food dropped into the dog's feeding tray. As the pairing of light and food recur time after time, the light itself begins to produce salivation. Every so often the light is presented without food, and salivation still occurs. The light, thus, becomes a *conditional stimulus,* which was once neutral but which now produces a response.

In respondent conditioning, then, two stimuli are paired; one is conditioned (elicits no response at first), the other is unconditioned (consistently elicits a response). After the two stimuli are presented to the subject together numerous times, one of them—the unconditioned one—may be omitted, and the response to the conditioned stimulus by itself will be similar to (but not identical with) the response to the unconditioned one. The subject learns to

Lucky Shoes, Lucky Hairpin

Old-time Dodger pitcher Alan Foster forgot his baseball shoes on a road trip and borrowed a pair from a teammate. That night he pitched a no-hitter and later, needless to say, bought the shoes from his friend. They became his most prized possession.

Rube Waddel, a Philadelphia Athletic pitching great of long ago, had a hairpin fetish. However, the hairpin he possessed was only powerful as long as he won. If he lost a game, he would look for another hairpin (which had to be found on the street), and he would not pitch until he found another (Gmelch, 1971).

Most people who act superstitiously defend their actions by saying that they don't really believe that an object causes good or bad luck, but they're just not taking any chances. So there are a great many unsuperstitious people who carry lucky charms, knock on wood, avoid black cats, don't walk under ladders, wear a lucky shirt to a tough interview, and get a little nervous when they break a mirror. How is it that so many seemingly trivial acts continue to hold so much importance for so many individuals? It's simply a matter of operant conditioning, say the learning theorists.

In 1957, Morse and Skinner demonstrated how superstitious behavior can be produced in animals. They put hungry pigeons in small cages and fed them every so often. The animals were fed regardless of what they did in the cage. Yet most birds (but not all) developed patterns of "superstitious" behavior. They began to repeat certain behaviors in order to get more food, even though feeding was not at all contingent on the behavior. One bird learned to make two or three counterclockwise turns about the cage trying to cause the food hopper to drop more food. Another bird learned to jerk its head repeatedly, and still another learned to make pecking or brushing movements toward the floor. Whatever the pigeon happened to be doing when the food was delivered became a reinforced response and thus was likely to occur more often subsequently.

Skinner (1953) argues that humans resemble pigeons in forming superstitions. If you say, wear, or do something just before a good experience or outcome (reinforcement), there is a chance that you will associate the reward with your actions. In the reverse case, if you *expect* bad luck to follow the appearance of a black cat, you will be especially sensitive to any event that can be interpreted as unfortunate. If such an event takes place, it will confirm your belief about bad luck and black cats.

All of this is based on the principles of learning. When the reward is meant to follow your actions, your subsequent repetition of the reinforced response makes a good deal of sense. But accidents will happen, and, even when the reward is only coincidental, you may still respond to it as if someone were trying to reinforce your behavior.

---

respond to a stimulus in a way he had not responded before, and this is called the conditioned response. Or, we can say the subject has been respondently conditioned. Although it is a very simple form of learning, respondent conditioning reveals a series of facets of learning that have some more direct and important applications to human beings.

Generalization

We have all observed that a young child will confuse similar stimuli more frequently than will an older child. A three-year-old may think all four-legged animals are dogs, but an older child becomes capable of better discrimination. Pavlov's experiments with stimulus *generalization* showed that a dog who was conditioned to respond to the tone of a tuning fork would also respond to the sound of a buzzer, the click of a metronome, or the ringing of a bell once the original conditioning had taken place. In generalization, the greater the similarity between stimuli, the greater the similarity in response. For

CONDITIONING
BEFORE BIRTH
Spelt (1948) discovered it was possible to condition a fetus in the mother's uterus during the last two months of pregnancy. A very loud noise was used as the unconditioned stimulus and vibration of the mother's abdomen as the conditioned stimulus. After pairing the noise and vibration about 15 or 20 times, the fetus would move in response to the vibration alone. Spelt also found that he could extinguish this conditioned response, that spontaneous recovery occurred, and that the conditioned response could be retained over a three-week period.

humans, too, there is generalization among the various stimuli we are exposed to in daily life.

Responses can also generalize in the sense that a subject will make a substitute response when unable to make the specific conditioned response. Thus, a dog that has learned to give a conditioned response with its front left paw will respond with its front right paw, if for some reason the use of the left paw is impossible. The conditioning is still there even if the usual response mechanism is no longer available. In much the same way, human beings transfer old responses to new situations.

Discrimination

Imagine the kind of mess life would be in if we were unable to *discriminate* between one stimulus and another. As it is, we learn to tell the difference between two stimuli even when they are very similar to one another. The undiscriminating child who calls all men "daddy" learns that he is rewarded with attention and approval only when he is referring to his own father. In much the same way, we learn to tell the difference between many similar objects and events in life. We learn to spot our own automobile in a crowded parking lot and recognize friends in the crush of a crowd.

Extinction

THE EXTINCTION OF LEARNING
The techniques of unlearning involve reinforcement. A rat, for example, may have learned to press a bar to get food. When it finds that pressing the bar no longer produces food, it will push the bar less and less frequently. Frustration leads to a brief increase in activity, but as the frustration builds the behavior gets extinguished.

A conditioned response is not necessarily permanent since it is possible to eliminate it. This process is called *extinction*. If a conditioned fear exists, it can be extinguished by presenting the feared object without the unconditioned stimulus (pain or injury from what we fear). In a classic example of extinction, a child named Peter was afraid of rabbits. To extinguish this fear, a rabbit was brought into the room while the child was eating. At first it was quite distant from the child, but each day the rabbit was moved a little closer until Peter would tolerate its presence. The repeated contacts with the rabbit in the presence of food (and in the absence of fear) allowed the fear response to be eliminated. Conditioned responses do not disappear simply through the passage of time, but rather some new conditioning (counterconditioning) is required.

It should be noted that the conditioned or learned response is the one that becomes extinguished and not the unconditioned one. Conditioned behavior can later reappear without additional conditioning, even though extinction had appeared to be successful. This is known as *spontaneous recovery*. If a rest interval follows the extinction of a conditioned response, it will reappear spontaneously but in a somewhat weaker form. If conditioning is done again using the same stimuli, the original response will quickly be strengthened. In fact, reconditioning is a faster learning process than original conditioning. As Pavlov argued, the conditioned response is never completely extinguished.

It is only blocked from being actively produced by new conditioning.

It is wise to extinguish a fear soon after it is acquired. If you are in a car accident, you are encouraged to resume driving as soon as it is reasonably possible. A man thrown from a horse is advised to get right back in the saddle to extinguish the fear that even one incident may condition in the individual.

Operant Conditioning

We make random responses from the moment of birth. When one of these responses is closely followed by a reward that gratifies a need or achieves some goal, this movement is likely to be repeated more often than other random behaviors. If the reward or reinforcement is unpleasant or painful,

---

How To Be An Operant Operator

If you want to try operant conditioning on others, the first thing you must figure out is how to get the individual to make the first correct response so you can reinforce it. There are many ways this can be done, and each of the ways has some advantages and some disadvantages.

Motivate your subject. Increase your experimental subject's motivation to make a lot of responses so you can get the one you want to reinforce. If the subject is a rat, you can electrify the floor of its cage to keep the rat moving. If you have a human subject you can promise him future reward or threaten him with punishment or deprivation.

Eliminate old reinforcers. If motivation alone doesn't work, you may decide to search for something that is inhibiting the response you are looking for and try to eliminate the inhibitor. If, for example, your subject doesn't want to dance, he may perhaps be easily embarrassed in public. In a private place he may be able to dance up a storm. Finding out what reinforcers are maintaining the inhibitions and removing those factors helps produce the response you are looking for.

Act as a model. If you are getting nowhere, you might try telling your subject exactly what you want him to do—either by verbal instructions or, sometimes more successful, by acting as a model. We all do this when we try to teach others a complicated task. When I learned to fly the instructor (often in despair) would execute the maneuver and have me follow him through by doing what he did rather than what he tried to explain.

Limit your subject's responses. Sometimes you have to structure the environment if you want to encourage a particular type of responding. If you want an animal to learn to pull a lever, you can make it more likely to happen if the animal is in a Skinner Box where a bar is the only thing available.

Shaping. Don't be discouraged if your pigeon isn't about to walk over to the bar and press it. You can work with available behaviors. Try to shape the behavior, so that any response that is even roughly close to what you want can be reinforced. Then, one step at a time, reward responses that are progressively more like the desired response. In time these partial behaviors will be shaped into a sequence that will produce the action you want.

Force the response. If shaping isn't fast enough, you can force the response. When you teach your dog tricks, you often do so by saying "shake hands" and then lifting up his paw until he learns what the words mean. In a way, then, you can not only lead your horse to water, but you can also make him drink, if you need to.

Much of our behavior has been influenced by the shaping, modeling, motivating, and coercing of the people around us—particularly our parents. Once they got us to perform the desired response, the rest was easy. They simply reinforced us with praise each time we said "thank you" or ate everything on our plates. It may seem a little frightening how easy it is to operant condition someone. Most of us, however, including parents, have neither the time nor patience it takes to purposefully condition the more significant and complex behaviors of thought and emotions.

Operant conditioning at work. Morgan, a pilot whale, is trained to make deep ocean recoveries of such objects as experimental torpedos. On the top left he is preparing to fasten a grabber claw to a torpedo. On the bottom left he has fastened the device, which allows a balloon to inflate and float the torpedo to the surface. Above, Morgan gets his reward—a fish snack.

the behavior is less likely to occur in the future. This is the basis of *operant conditioning,* a sequence well known by animal trainers who make an animal obey by selectively rewarding and punishing it. Whereas respondent conditioning is most often associated with involuntary responses, operant conditioning is focused on voluntary responses.

Operant conditioning works on the principle that, if a behavior or a response has been instrumental in producing reinforcement, that behavior or response will become stronger. The more often the response is reinforced, the stronger it will become. Thus an operant response "operates" on the environment by producing some reward. This fact has led to an expanding field of applying learning theory to a host of animal and human experiences.

Operant conditioning began with E. L. Thorndike's (1911) *Law of Effect,* which states that responses may be altered depending on the effects they produce in the environment. He observed that responses leading to satisfying effects are strengthened, whereas responses leading to annoying effects are weakened. In the beginning of most operant-conditioning situations, there is a period during which the subject is free to be active and randomly explore his environment. After becoming habituated or accustomed to the situation, the subject (if an animal) will begin to explore at random until it finds whatever lever or switch is to be used in the experiment. At first pulling the lever or pushing the switch will not be associated with the appearance of food, but the connection is made in very short order and further training can begin.

Bars and food pellets are not necessary reinforcement for people, of course. As Greenspoon (1955) demonstrated, the use of certain words (like *I, me,* or plural nouns) can be reinforced simply by having the experimenter say "mm-hmm" when the words are used. In Greenspoon's experiment, subjects later indicated that they were unaware of the relationship between their responses and the reinforcement. They learned to make specific responses without an awareness of what it was they learned.

The classic story of experimental operant conditioning is about the student who attends class faithfully and sits in the front of the class. As the first month of the class rolls by, he or she regularly makes visible movements (head shaking or other expressions) of disagreement with the professor. As the semester wears on, the gesturing slowly alters to nodding agreement with the brilliant lecture of the professor. This "playing-out" of the role of an educational convert who is persuaded by the intellect and logic of the professor is, in theory, guaranteed to assure an A in the class. I don't know if the theory has ever been tested (you might try it as a scientific research project), but the idea behind it is clear—the professor was being "operant conditioned" by the daily sight of a student skeptic who, slowly and painfully, was converted to a "believer" by the sheer weight of professorial brilliance.

Reinforcement

The concepts of reinforcement and reward in learning theory need to be explained since they are important to both respondent conditioning and to the idea of operant conditioning. Positive reinforcement refers to stimuli which strengthen responses. Negative reinforcement designates stimuli "which strengthen responses by their removal." In negative reinforcement something is taken away (an aversive stimulus such as a bright light or a shock) to strengthen the response. In positive reinforcement something is added, and the response is strengthened. Positive and negative reinforcers play a vital part in our daily lives. We labor to achieve goals. We adjust the environment when it irritates us. We study to get educated, or we go to church to get right with God. In each instance we seek reward or reinforcement in our behavior. What reinforces each of us may be different, but clearly we all abandon behaviors that go unrewarded.

For humans, positive and negative reinforcers may be of equal importance, and the number and variety of reinforcers is far greater than in animals. People differ in what reinforces them, and we all have our own unique set of interests or events that are reinforcing. The special preferences that reinforce us contribute to the differences in our personalities.

White (1959) suggests that the master reinforcer that keeps most of us motivated over long periods of time is the need to confirm our sense of

OPERANT BODY CONTROL

It is possible to train animals to change their heart rate, blood pressure, and intestinal contractions by operant conditioning techniques (Miller, 1969). Miller and Banuazizi (1968), for example, trained rats to modify heart rate and intestinal contraction. One group of rats was rewarded for an increase in heart rate and another for a decrease by using a procedure (shaping) such that any increase or decrease at all was rewarded at first and then reward was given only for marked increases or decreases. They were able to slow a rat's heart rate from 350 beats per minute to 230 in a short period of time and to increase or decrease intestinal contractions to roughly the same degree.

Attempts are being made to translate these experiments into usable human terms. If they are successful, we will have achieved an exceptional level of control over autonomic responses once thought beyond conscious control.

HUMOROUS REINFORCEMENT

One group of psychology students decided to turn the tables and demonstrate the effects of reinforcement on their instructor (Sanford, 1965). On alternate days, they either laughed at anything even remotely funny in the instructor's lecture or did not crack a smile throughout the entire period. They reported a great day-to-day variation in the amount of humor or attempted humor in the lectures. On days when humor was reinforced, there were many attempts to produce it. On the days when the best jokes produced only grim silence, lectures soon became dedicatedly serious.

THE BEHAVIOR
CHAIN
Learning a series of related behaviors is called chaining. *A behavior chain is a sequence of acts in which each act serves as a stimulus for the next act to be performed. The best example of a behavior chain is driving. In sequence, you take out your keys, unlock the car, open the door, sit down in the driver's seat, fasten your seatbelt, put it in neutral, turn on the ignition, shift into gear, check the traffic, and press down on the accelerator. These acts become an automatic sequence or series of learned acts that occur in a well-established order.*

BARNABUS PERFORMS
Pierrel and Sherman (1963) taught their rat Barnabus to climb a spiral staircase, cross a narrow drawbridge, go up a ladder, pull a toy car over by a chain, get into the car and pedal it to a second ladder, climb this ladder, crawl through a tube, board an elevator, pull a chain to raise a flat, and lower himself back to the starting platform where he would press a lever to get a food pellet. After the pellet was eaten, the remarkable sequence of behaviors began all over again.

personal competence. Being able to master our external or internal environment is rewarding whether it is learning to ride a bike, being the best student in class, or keeping cool when everyone else panics. It is rewarding and positively reinforcing to feel that we are capable human beings. To the contrary, it is punishing and negatively reinforcing to see ourselves as helpless, ineffective people.

Schedules of Reinforcement

The rate at which reinforcements for behavior occur may follow different patterns that experimenters call *schedules of reinforcement.* Since no one gets rewarded or reinforced all the time for everything he or she does, experimental work in learning has focused on partial reinforcement. Partial reinforcement schedules can be set up experimentally by using time, the number of responses, or the rate of response between reinforcements as schedule rewards. Examples of schedules of reinforcement would include the following.

Fixed-ratio Schedules. These schedules involve reinforcement after a fixed number of responses. Here, the word *ratios* refers to the proportion of the unreinforced trials to reinforced responses. If every fifth response is reinforced, the fixed-ratio schedule would be 5:1. Five responses must be made for one reward, and the faster you respond, the more reward you get. If you have a job that pays for the number of pieces of work you turn out in a day or an hour, you are working on a fixed-ratio schedule.

Variable-ratio Schedule. In a variable-ratio schedule, the subject is rewarded after a variable number of responses. He might be rewarded after he has made three responses, or thirteen. The experimenter sets up a ratio for the subject and this is the basis for determining the average number of responses. The subject doesn't know which response will make the reward appear, but he is learning that the payoff will be made after *some* response. If we liken a nickel to a response, it is similar to playing a slot machine. You never know which nickel will get rewarded, but you keep putting money in the machine since you know that some nickel will trigger a jackpot.

Fixed-interval Schedules. These schedules require a certain amount of time and the subject learns to respond after a specific time period has passed. Animals such as rats do not learn time, of course, but they learn a certain pattern of motor responses. The rate of making these responses begins to increase as the time for reinforcement gets near. Humans *do* learn time, and students respond to the fixed intervals at which college examinations take place. They cram just before the exam, lay off right afterwards, and start to study again as the next exam approaches.

Variable-interval Schedule.   If the interval of time is allowed to vary from when a reinforcement is given. This is the similar to doing your course work every day because the instructor gives you surprise quizzes.

Punishment

People often confuse negative reinforcement with punishment, but the two are not the same. Reinforcement, whether it is positive or negative, is meant to *increase* the probability that a certain response will be made. Again, when you positively reinforce a behavior, you are rewarding the subject for exhibiting that behavior. Thus the subject will learn to exhibit it more often. With negative reinforcement you remove a behavior reinforcer that is unpleasant when the subject exhibits the behavior you are trying to encourage (in other words, you allow the subject to avoid a negative experience). Punishment, on the other hand, attempts to *decrease* the probability that a certain response will occur—or, another way of saying it is that it attempts to eliminate undesirable behavior. Punishment can take the form of applying an unpleasant stimulus, or withholding a pleasant stimulus, whenever the subject exhibits undesirable behavior. An animal's bar-pressing behavior is reinforced when he presses a lever and either receives food (positive reinforcement) or avoids an aversive stimulus such as shock (negative reinforcement). In either case, the bar pressing will increase. But bar pressing will decrease when, after the animal presses the bar, food supply is cut off or an electrical current is turned on. The outcome of the bar-pressing behavior is punishing and the animal will cease to exhibit it.

Social Operant Conditioning

The whole purpose behind operant conditioning is, of course, to get other people to make or stop making a certain response. Every time you have an argument with someone who doesn't share your opinion or belief, you try to "operant condition" them by what you say and by the feelings you express toward what *they* say. By being "amazed at how wrong they are," you suggest that every sensible person would believe as you do. The unspoken message, of course, is that, if the other person continues to hold his incorrect beliefs, then he can no longer be your friend and will be dismissed from regard as a stupid person. This kind of operant conditioning works if the operator is sufficiently skilled in knowing how not to go too far and cause resentment in the other person over being considered stupid. As we all know, some people get "stubborn" about their opinions, just because they resent the way we go about persuading them of their error.

In much the same way as eliminating a classical conditioned response, all of us will stop an operant behavior such as putting quarters in a slot machine that stops paying off. We will stop shopping at a store that begins

OPERANT CULTURAL ENGINEERING
In Walden Two, *Skinner (1948) employs operant conditioning techniques, which he called "cultural engineering." To develop frustration tolerance in children, for example, intermittent reinforcement was used from an early age. As Skinner describes it: "Our engineering job was to* preserve *them by fortifying the child against discouragement. We introduce discouragement as carefully as we introduce any other emotional situation, beginning at about six months. Some of the toys in our air-conditioned cubicles are designed to build perseverance. A bit of a tune from a music-box, or a pattern of flashing lights, is arranged to follow an appropriate response —say, pulling on a ring.*
Later the ring must be pulled twice, later still three or five or ten times. It's possible to build up fantastically perseverative behavior without encountering frustration or rage."
[p. 101]

to give bad service and ignore people who have "put us on" so often that we no longer trust or believe them. Interestingly, there is a kind of "spontaneous recovery" in operant conditioning just as there is in classical conditioning. After a period of freedom from negative reinforcement, you may again come back to the nonpaying slot machine, the shop that did not treat you well, or the con artist who always tries to talk you into a bad deal.

Generalization and discrimination of stimuli also occur in operant conditioning. *Stimulus generalization* is when you react to a new stimulus in a way very similar to the way you have learned to react to another stimulus. Thus, if your operantly conditioned response is to trust your parents and friends (since they have always been predictably trustworthy), you may approach each new acquaintance with the same trust, sometimes to be sadly disappointed. Generalizing previous experience to present situations may be misleading. *Response generalization* is when you respond differently to the same stimulus. Say, for example, you have learned one behavior (smoking cigarettes) connected to a certain stimulus, but for some reason (perhaps no cigarettes) you can no longer exhibit the original behavior. What you would probably do would be to substitute another behavior (smoking a pipe, if one were available) that is similar to the originally learned behavior.

As an exercise in understanding the concept of operant conditioning and its related features of extinction, spontaneous recovery, and stimulus and response generalization, pose an experimental problem for yourself. Pick out someone who holds a point of view that differs from your own but that is reasonably subject to influence. Possible topics might be car models, popular records, current movies, or even baseball teams. (A topic such as religion might not be good since its roots in belief reach deep and cannot be unemotionally reexamined.) Now, try operant conditioning as a means of bringing that person to your point of view. Ask yourself what reinforcement you plan to use, what schedule of reinforcement will be applied, how you will extinguish the old response, how you will furnish a basis for new discriminations and for eliminating old generalizations, and how you will judge the effectiveness and permanence of your operant conditioning. As the old saying goes, if at first you don't succeed, try, try again.

Remembering

Asimov (1967) reports estimates that the brain, in a lifetime, absorbs as many as one quadrillion—1,000,000,000,000,000—separate bits of information. From an avalanche of sensory stimulation, we select certain material and register it in our consciousness. We then manage to retain it and make it available for retrieval at some later date. When we fail to remember, we are never sure whether the failure was in registration, retention, or retrieval. An intriguing facet of the study of memory is the unanswered question of what kinds of changes in the nervous system account for our capacity to remember.

SAVINGS
In relearning by the savings method, something previously learned is later learned again. When this is done, the subject usually learns faster than he did the first time. The number of trials required to master the relearned material can be compared with the number of trials it took to master it originally, and the difference between the first and second learnings is the savings in trials or time. In general, relearning shows the greatest amount of retention over the longest period of time. Simply reorganizing material shows the highest immediate retention following the original learning. And recall shows the smallest amount of retention.

Improving Remembering:
Or, Studying Made Easier

When you want to remember something important, what do you do? Tie a string around your finger? Write it down? Say it to yourself over and over? Ask a friend to remind you later? We all have our own ways of insuring that we remember certain things, but some of our methods are more successful than others. Thus, when people say they have a bad memory, it is more likely that they are just bad at remembering. All memories can be improved to some extent simply by applying some of the principles psychologists have learned in their study of remembering and forgetting.

1. *Have a system.* Organizing your information into a system is one way to improve your memory because it cuts down the number of individual items you have to remember. It links them together so that one piece of information naturally leads to another. Here are some of the systems you can try:

Visual imagery is one system. The brain seems to have two different memory systems—one for visual memory and one for linguistic material (Haber, 1970). The reach of visual memory is apparently enormous. Thus, if you wanted to learn a list of objects, one way to do it would be to visualize each one in combination with the next.

In the pocket system, small objects are remembered by picturing them placed in different pockets of a suit.

A third system is to use a code. You are no doubt aware of how easy it is to remember lyrics to entire songs or commercials, even though the simplest historical fact continually slips your mind. This is proof that it pays to organize verbal information so that one fact links itself to another. There is probably not a single American who has gone beyond the second grade and doesn't know the year Columbus sailed for America. How come? Because "in fourteen hundred ninety-two, Columbus sailed the ocean blue."

Codes work by organizing individual bits of information so they make sense when put together. Thus, department stores may conceal the prices of items by using code letters.

Some of these systems may seem impractical for everyday remembering, but the principle can be applied to something you are doing right now—studying. When you are reviewing a text, try to learn the material in a unit, so it makes some sense. Try to recall chapter headings and subheadings. Attempt to recite details under each heading. Keep track of what you missed, and link those items in some way to the items you always get right.

In addition to ways of organizing the material you want to remember, psychologists have discovered a number of other techniques that will help you remember material for a final exam, the names of guests at your party, a list of French verbs, or your lines for the next little theater production.

2. *Overlearning.* If you must learn a list of items, you are better off if you do more than learn until that point when you can recall the complete list once without error. If you continue to practice after this point, it will affect how much of the material you will be able to remember later.

3. *Recitation.* Recitation is repeating to yourself what you have just learned. Active recitation while you are reading leads to better retention because it focuses attention on the subject at hand. It ensures that you will be able to retrieve (not merely recognize) the material when it is needed. Thus, when subjects in one study spent nearly 80 percent of their reading time stopping and reciting what they were learning, they recalled what they had learned better than did a control group that read without taking frequent breaks for recitation (Gates, 1958).

4. *Review.* The principle of savings states that it will take you fewer trials to learn old material—even when it has apparently been forgotten—than it takes to learn new. Therefore, if you know you will be tested on material learned early in the term, it pays to review the material every so often to refresh your memory about the parts you know and to learn those parts you had trouble with the first time. The more you review during the term, the less time you will have to spend going over old material for the final.

5. *Spaced practice.* Studies indicate that spacing study periods is more efficient than learning material all at once, at least with some types of information. This is because your attention tends to wander over long periods of time and because what you have learned has a chance to consolidate if you take a break. Thus, four 15-minute intervals of study will probably enable better recall of the material than a one-hour study session.

6. *Sleep.* What we have learned about retroactive inhibition suggests that you are most apt to retain material if you go to sleep immediately after learning it. There are no intervening activities to interfere with consolidation and, therefore, retention.

7. *Feedback.* It helps too if you are informed of your progress, either by being told how well or poorly you are doing or by seeing the results so you can correct your errors.

Forgetting

One ancient explanation says that forgetting occurs when memories are not used. The problem with this explanation is that some learning is retained for a lifetime (even though it may not be used for decades), whereas other information is forgotten instantly.

Underwood (1957) had his subjects learn nine different lists of nonsense syllables. He believed that the last lists would be remembered best, but the results showed just the opposite. His subjects remembered 71 percent of the first list learned but remembered only 27 percent of the last list. Underwood concluded that the previously learned material *interfered* with new material. He also observed that the more you know, the more you are able to forget.

Two particular factors affect the amount of material remembered: the time interval that elapses before retention is measured and the strength of the original learning. The length of the forgetting interval affects memory in a predictable fashion: the longer the interval, the less the retention. The greatest memory loss happens soon after learning, and the rate of loss declines as time passes. Thus, memory losses are slower after the initial forgetting, but they still occur.

The strength of original learning is, of course, directly related to retention. The greater the degree of original learning, the greater the retention. Retention of well-learned material is the same, despite differences in the learning ability of subjects or differences in the difficulty of the material. Slow learners and fast learners both forget at the same rate, and easily learned material is probably not retained any longer than is difficult material.

Interference

Forgetting can be caused by activities that interfere with what has been learned, and this can happen either before or after the learning takes place. If the interference occurs *before* the learned activity, then the forgetting is due to *proactive inhibition* where material learned earlier causes forgetting and confusion of both sets of material. For example, if I give you a series of telephone numbers to remember and then add others to the list, the first numbers learned can interfere with learning the additional ones. If I add another set of numbers after you learn the first list, it may produce *retroactive inhibition*. You learn the second list easily, but it forces part of the first list out of your mind.

Another interpretation of interference theory says that we forget because new material interferes with the *processing* of what is being learned. Thus, some types of new material can cause processing problems for material already learned and being stored (Massaro, 1970).

It is also possible that interference occurs because the new material is so similar to the old and produces conflict between the new learning and the old. Thus, when you have been driving a standard-shift car and then

THE
SERIAL-POSITION
EFFECT
It has been observed that, if you are learning a list of digits, the first and last numbers seem easier to remember than the middle ones. This serial-position effect seems to happen since first and last numbers are particularly noticeable, marking the beginning and end of the list. This effect can be demonstrated by presenting items or numbers in a circular list where there is no beginning or end. Then, the serial-position effect is markedly reduced.

Sleep Learning

We "waste" one-third of our life sleeping, and it would be nice if we could devote that time to learning and still get our rest. Early studies of sleep learning found that it worked, but there was a catch. It seemed that no one was sure the "sleep learners" were really asleep. To correct for this experimental flaw, Emmons and Simon (1956) played a recording of ten one-syllable words only when electroencephalograms showed that the subjects were really asleep. When the subject began to wake up (as indicated by the EEG), the experimenter would turn the record off, turning it on again only when the EEG sleep returned.

To test learning, the sleeping subjects were asked to choose, from a list of 50 words, those words that had been played during sleep. They didn't do any better than control subjects. The conclusion drawn from this and a number of other tests of sleep learning is that subjects do not learn while asleep. They learn only if they are awake.

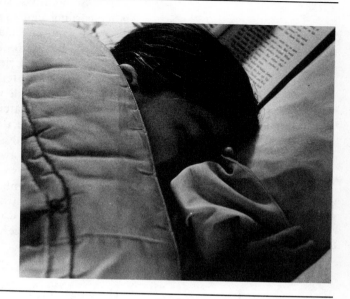

drive one with an automatic transmission, you may keep moving your foot to a nonexistent clutch. This mistake is not forgetting; it is interference with new learning, which causes you to have difficulty (Ceraso, 1967).

Consolidation Theory

Evidence shows that once new information enters memory, a period of time is required for it to consolidate and become permanent. Consolidation theory proposes that changes in the nervous system produced by learning must undergo a consolidation phase during which, if the memory trace is in any way disrupted, memory loss occurs. If disruption doesn't happen then the trace consolidates into long-term memory. Thus, persons who suffer brain injury usually have amnesia for events that occurred just before the accident. This loss may cover a period from several minutes to more than an hour before the accident (Russell and Nathan, 1964). Similarly, if you get a head injury in an automobile accident, you may have no recollection of the events that caused the accident.

Memory loss of this sort can be produced in the laboratory by using electroconvulsive shock. If a laboratory animal is taught a task and then given an electric shock that produces temporary unconsciousness, it will forget what it learned, depending on the time period between learning and being shocked. Immediately after learning, electroconvulsive shock produces much more forgetting than shock given after a delay.

Some drugs (strychnine, nicotine, caffeine, or amphetamine) given just after learning seem to speed up consolidation. Animals so stimulated need fewer learning trials and make fewer errors. It has been suggested that these drugs accelerate the neurological processes in memory consolidation, although how they do this is not clear (McGaugh, 1970).

In practical terms, consolidation theory suggests that, if you study first and then rest for a while, it will give the memory storage system time to consolidate the material. Some years ago Newman (1939) experimented to determine the effect of sleep following learning. Each member of a group of subjects read the same stories. Then, half the group went to sleep, while the others stayed awake and went about their daily activities. After eight hours, both groups were tested to see how much of the stories they remembered. Both groups remembered the parts essential to the story, but the trivial parts were remembered twice as well by the sleepers. Newman suggests we do not forget because we do not use material but because it is interfered with before it has had a chance to consolidate.

Memory—Short-Term and Long-Term

The longer we have had a memory, the stronger will be its trace in our brain, and the more difficult it is to lose it. Short-term memories, for example, can be temporarily erased by blows on the head or powerful electric shocks. Memories acquired just before an accident can sometimes be permanently erased. New memories are short term until they have been transferred to storage, or long-term memory. We need to consider both varieties of memory in our discussion here.

Short-Term Memory

Short-term memory capacity is assumed to be small and rather limited in scope. Once its limits are reached, previously learned information must be pushed out for new information to be absorbed. Short-term memory operates on a continuous cycle in which a few short-term memories are transferred to long-term storage but most are discarded and lost to us.

One theory suggests that short-term memory is stored in the nervous system as a memory trace, a theoretical nerve pathway (a kind of "sensory memory") on which information is carried. If the information is not used at once or shifted to storage along with long-term information, this trace fades and is lost.

Short-term memories involve the storage and retrieval of information that is remembered for a very short period of time, sometimes for only seconds. Sometimes, they don't even last as long as we need them. Thus, you may look up an unfamiliar telephone number but get distracted before you dial and forget the number when you return to dialing. Or, when you are introduced

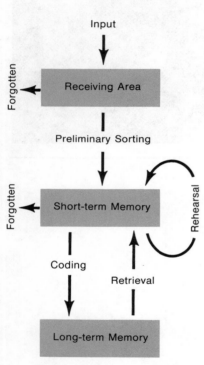

One way to diagram the flow of information in human memory. The *receiving area* registers everything that hits our senses and then discards most of it. Information sorted from this stage makes up *short-term memory.* In turn, if something is to be stored in *long-term memory,* it must be rehearsed often before it can be coded and passed along. What is not rehearsed is forgotten and lost beyond recall—only the information stored in long-term memory can be retrieved.

Molecules and Memory

Some researchers believe that memory is stored in ribonucleic acid (RNA). RNA is involved in protein production in the body's cells, and in the development and configuration of transmitter substances. RNA molecules can hold an enormous amount of chemical information, which theorists suggest can be translated into what we call memory.

There is some evidence to support the theory that RNA plays a vital role in memory. After rats learned how to get to food at the end of a maze, protein inhibitors were injected into the animals, and, a day or so later, the learning seemed to have been forgotten (Flexner and Flexner, 1968). The possibility of molecular memory mechanisms seemed all the more fascinating In light of the experiments conducted by James McConnell and his fellow researchers.

McConnell (1962) devised a classical conditioning experiment in which he subjected planaria (flatworms), about an inch and a half long, to a flash of light and then to an electric shock. Their bodies contracted at the shock and, eventually, began to contract as soon as the light was turned on even when the shock did not follow. They had become conditioned. That is, they "learned" that the light meant a coming shock. McConnell hypothesized that the worms formed new RNA molecules to register that bit of learning and memory, and this is how he tried to prove it.

The conditioned planaria were chopped up and fed to untrained planaria which were then put through the same learning process. McConnell reported that these planaria learned to react to the light faster than did ordinary planaria. They had, McConnell suggested, incorporated the RNA molecules from their food to acquire the "memory" it contained.

Allan L. Jacobson, who had worked with McConnell, took the experiments one step further. He extracted RNA from conditioned planaria and injected it into unconditioned ones. That worked too. The conditioning was apparently injected along with the RNA. Jacobson also conditioned rats and hamsters to respond to the sound of a click or the flash of a light by going to a feeding box. Once conditioned, the animals were killed, and RNA from their brains was injected into animals that hadn't been conditioned. Jacobson found that the animals getting these injections were easier to train. The injections even worked across species. In other words, a rat could benefit by injections of RNA from a hamster.

Excitement over the possible role of RNA has been enhanced by experiments indicating that RNA injected from trained rats can actually reproduce a learned response in untrained rats (Golub et al., 1970). But the role of RNA in learning and memory is not yet an established fact, particularly because many scientists have reported difficulty in replicating the transfer experiments. But if it can ever be satisfactorily demonstrated that learning is indeed coded on the RNA molecule and is capable of transfer from one organism to another, the learning possibilities seem endless. You could speculate that students of the future may be able to learn physics or math just by receiving an injection of RNA extracted from their instructor—a costly but effective process. But, then, what would be the point of final exams?

to a lot of people, their names are forgotten at almost the same rate that new names are mentioned. In the end, only the last name is remembered.

Short-term memory can retain items fairly well for the first few seconds. After about 12 seconds, however, recall is very poor, and after 20 seconds it disappears entirely. Some items do not disappear this quickly but are coded and processed and passed along to long-term memory.

Long-Term Memory

Long-term memories last for days, years, or sometimes a lifetime, and they are thought to reflect permanent changes in the brain. They resist interference from other learned material. The long-term memory has a vast capacity since the information is organized by being rehearsed, coded, and constantly revised as new material comes in. It is a dynamic, continually shifting network of memory in which recollections from all of the senses can be stored.

One attempt to explain the differences between short-term and long-term memory was made by Donald O. Hebb. He suggested that the nervous system records sensory input by means of a pattern of neural activity involving a reverberating circuit established in randomly connected neurons. Hebb posited that the nerve impulse must circulate a number of times in a closed, self-exciting circuit until some type of permanent anatomical change occurs in the synaptic connections between the neurons. At some later time, the same group of cells will fire when stimulated again by the same type of sensory input. Thus there is a reverberating circuit for short-term memory, and some form of permanent change in the synaptic connections for long-term memory.

Summary

1. When we talk about learning, we are talking about the way an individual is changed by his experience. Since we can't actually see learning take place, a change in behavior is used as evidence that learning has occurred.

2. Animals have certain innate patterns of behavior that occur naturally, no matter what the animal's experience. Such inborn patterns of behavior are called *instincts.* Since an instinct is something that is not learned, it appears that humans have few, if any, instinctive patterns of behavior.

3. Many animals have a critical period soon after birth, at which time they can be permanently conditioned with a relatively small amount of learning. Humans *might* have a critical learning period for language, but research has not yet established this as fact.

4. Respondent (classical) conditioning is the process in which the capacity to elicit a response is transferred from one stimulus to another. If a neutral stimulus is presented with a stimulus that normally evokes a response, the neutral event by itself eventually comes to elicit the response.

5. Once a response is conditioned to a particular stimulus, it can often be elicited by similar, but not identical, stimuli. This is called *stimulus generalization. Response generalization* is said to occur if a particular stimulus can elicit similar but not identical responses without any additional learning.

6. *Discrimination* is the opposite of generalization. It is the ability to tell the difference between two similar stimuli and respond to them differently.

7. *Extinction* is the method by which conditioning is eliminated. If you repeatedly present the conditioned stimulus without the unconditioned stimulus, you will eventually extinguish the condi-

tioned response. The ability of a conditioned response to automatically reappear after extinction is known as *spontaneous recovery.*

8. A behavior chain is a sequence of learned responses that occur in a well-established order. In a behavior chain, each act serves as a stimulus for the next response.

9. In *operant conditioning,* the subject is taught to make a particular response in order to receive something he wants. Operant conditioning usually focuses on voluntary responses, whereas respondent conditioning deals mainly with reflex or involuntary acts. In addition, with respondent conditioning the stimulus occurs *before* the response in order to produce it. In operant conditioning, the reinforcing stimulus occurs *after* the response has been given.

10. One task of operant conditioning is to get the subject to initially perform the response so that you can reinforce it. This may be accomplished by modeling the desired behavior, forcing it, or shaping existing responses into the desired activity.

11. Reinforcement is any event that strengthens the response. *Positive reinforcement* is the application of a favorable event after the response. *Negative reinforcement* is the withdrawal of an aversive event. With both positive and negative reinforcement, however, the stimulus following the response increases the probability that it will occur.

12. Skinner has suggested that superstitious behavior occurs when a reinforcement is accidentally paired with a particular response. Since learning principles work whether they are purposeful or not, the subject will view the desired event as being contingent on his performing the "reinforced" behavior.

13. When reinforcement is delivered only after a fixed number of responses has occurred, the reinforcement is on a *fixed-ratio schedule. Fixed-interval schedules* are those in which reinforcements for the response are given only after a certain amount of time has passed. With *variable-ratio schedules,* the subject is rewarded after he has made a number of responses, but he never knows how many responses it will take to get the reward. *Variable-interval schedules* are when the intervals of time between reinforcements change from trial to trial.

14. Punishment is any event which reduces the probability that a response will occur. Punishment may be in the form of removing a pleasant stimulus or applying an unpleasant stimulus.

15. The principles of generalization, discrimination, extinction and spontaneous recovery apply to operant as well as respondent conditioning. Extinction occurs in operant conditioning when a previously reinforced response is no longer rewarded.

16. If you learn something once, forget it, and then learn it again, it will take you fewer trials to learn the material the second time.

17. Most memory loss occurs soon after learning, and the rate of loss declines as time passes. However, the longer the time interval or period of forgetting, the less the retention.

18. Some researchers believe that memory storage takes place in ribonucleic acid (RNA). Experiments with planaria and rats indicate that transferring the RNA from conditioned animals to naive ones also transfers the conditioning.

19. Forgetting can be caused by interference from other activities. If material learned earlier interferes with new material, *proactive inhibition* is taking place. *Retroactive inhibition* is said to occur when new material interferes with remembering the old.

20. Some psychologists believe that inhibition occurs because acquiring one set of information interferes with the processing of the other. Others believe that interference occurs because the new material is similar to the old.

21. Short-term memory holds information for only a few seconds. Because it has a limited capacity, most short-term memories are pushed out and lost when new material is acquired. Some short-term memories, however, are transferred to long-term memory.

22. Long-term memory lasts for days, years, or a lifetime, and has a vast capacity for information storage and retrieval. Long-term memory is thought to involve a permanent change in the brain. Because of this, a period of time after learning is probably necessary for the information to consolidate and become permanent.

23. Donald O. Hebb suggested that nerve impulses reverberate in a circuit when they are introduced into short-term memory. For a memory to become long term, the impulses must circulate a number of times until there is an anatomical change in the synapses between the neurons.

24. We remember best when we go to sleep right after learning or review. This happens because there are no intervening activities to interfere with consolidation. The principles of interference and consolidation also suggest that spaced study periods, with rests in between, enable better recall.

Learning and Behavior Control

"Today's behavioral psychologists are the architects and engineers of the Brave New World." The behavioral psychologist McConnell said it, I didn't. What people seem to be worried about is that he may be right. Scientific behavior control could present serious threats to our individual liberties. Those who are alarmed feel that behavioral scientists are implying the individual is incapable of managing his own affairs or of even knowing what is best for him.

Behavioral scientists began to move out of the campus psychology laboratory some 20 years ago. They are now likely to be found in mental hospitals, rehabilitation wards, prisons, nursing homes, day-care centers, factories, movie theaters, national parks, or community mental-health centers (Goodall, 1972). Their work has changed over the years, but its roots still lead back to the basic principles formulated by B. F. Skinner and his associates observing pigeons and rats in their Skinner boxes. Today, the real question is not whether man should be controlled, but *how* he should be controlled. Will he be controlled by the erratic forces of nature or by man himself (Andrews and Karlins, 1971, p. 39)?

The issue of controlling human behavior has ignited widespread argument among professionals and lay persons alike. Two kinds of application of this theory have aroused particular public comment—punishment and token reward systems.

Punishment

In recent years some behavior therapists have used punishment as a therapeutic tool. Psychologists have found punishment to be one of the fastest, most effective techniques for ridding people of troublesome behaviors. The public response was predictable.

Had the findings been a vaccine against some disease, there would have been headlines and congratulations. But the treatment is not called "vaccination," it is called "punishment." The word brings with it images of anger, whips, screams. So instead of celebrating a new scientific

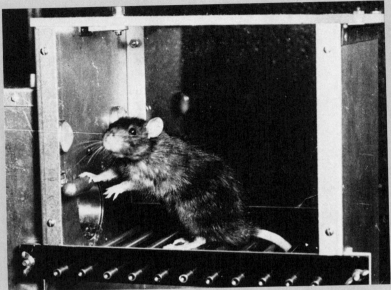

In developing techniques of operant conditioning, B. F. Skinner would put rats and pigeons into Skinner boxes and allow them to explore. Eventually, the animals would display accidentally the behavior Skinner wanted to reinforce. The pigeon would peck at the wall; the rat would press a bar. When these behaviors occurred, Skinner rewarded his subjects with food pellets and the animals quickly learned that repeating the behavior would produce more food.

advance, we feel apprehensive; we look for a hint of sadism . . . somehow, pain inflicted by a human being seems different—barbaric and repellent. [Baer, 1971, p. 33]

Baer argues that public resistance to the use of punishment is based on moral, not scientific, grounds. But the moral position that pain is bad and should always be avoided becomes *immoral* if it prevents us from correcting the learned behavior that puts some persons in even greater pain. And, Baer points out, punishment works. "Anyone with a hand to swing is equipped with a punishing device. Mail-order catalogs list a number of inexpensive and reliable cattle prods that deliver punishing but undamaging electric shocks" (p. 37).

In most human situations, punishment rarely needs to be very harsh to teach avoidance of one response in favor of another. Most people respond to mild punishment as a signal to begin new response patterns. Further, mild punishment such as criticism, frowning, or shaking one's head can designate undesirable behavior very clearly. If an alternative of correct behavior exists, mild punishments can be effective.

Behaviorists argue that some combination of reward and punishment is used from the beginning of human learning. This first occurs in the satisfaction or deprivation of physiological needs for food and pain avoidance. When the child develops, this is followed by approval or disapproval from other persons. In turn, these events fashion the self-rewarding or self-punishing action of the child's superego, or conscience. Life, to the behaviorist, is an unending series of rewards and punishments. If we wish to control human behavior, it is necessary only to systematize and regularize the forces of learning. One way in which this can be done is through a token economy.

Token Economies

The notion of a token economy, like most techniques used by the behavior controllers, had its origins in animal experiments. Chimpanzees started it all in 1930 when they demonstrated they could associate poker chips and grapes (Wolfe, 1936). The chimps learned to put a poker chip in a slot machine to obtain grapes. They would also press a bar to obtain more chips and save up a number of chips to exchange for grapes at a later time. The chimpanzees also learned an unrelated task—weightlifting—to obtain chips. This meant that poker chips had become symbols of reward that were valued in themselves. Since these early discoveries, token economies of a more complicated sort have been established for human beings. Token systems have been designed for adolescent boys with behavior problems such as juvenile delinquency or failure in school.

The Token Community. Miller (1969) described a token-economy program conducted with low-income mothers. The idea was to train mothers in self-help. The mothers' self-help activities were reinforced by "freedom credits." They were taught to begin controlling their own environment by earning tokens for attending meetings and doing jobs that helped themselves and others. In a food project, items such as meat, canned goods, and produce could be exchanged for freedom credits. The program has expanded with tokens being used to influence and shape new self-help activities.

Ayllon and Azrin (1965) reported a series of six experiments with a token economy and demonstrated that the behavior changed as a function of the token reinforcement. In one experiment with work assignments on the ward of a hospital, patients selected the job they preferred most and received tokens for their labors. After ten days they were told that they could continue working on this job but would get no tokens for their work. Of the eight patients observed, seven switched jobs immediately, and the eighth patient switched a few days later. In the third phase of the experiment, the jobs that the patients had originally preferred were once again awarded tokens. All eight patients switched back to their original jobs. Ayllon and Azrin's experiment demonstrated that tokens were effective in producing desired behavior.

The success of experimental token economies cannot be denied. The problem is the ethical and social questions raised by the rapid refinement of technical know-how in controlling human behavior.

The Controlled Society?

What are the ethics of manipulating the behavior of others? Social scientists of all theoretical persuasions have vigorously joined the debate about the propriety of managing the lives of others. Those opposed to planned behavior control feel it is immoral to deliberately control another person's behavior, principally because it dehumanizes the person subject to such control. Whenever an individual is deprived of his right to make choices, he becomes a thing or a number—not a person. Human beings, the critics argue, should not be forced to comply with the wishes of others, nor should they be seduced into agreeing for their own good.

This ethical debate began some time ago. In 1956 the humanist Carl Rogers and the behaviorist B. F. Skinner outlined different directions that psychological knowledge might pursue. Skinner (1972) has stated:

What is needed is a new conception of human behavior which is compatible with the implications of a scientific analysis. All men control and are controlled. The question of government in the broadest possible sense is not how freedom is to be preserved but what kinds of control are to be used and to what ends. [p. 247]

In rebuttal, Rogers insisted:

If this line of reasoning is correct, it appears that some form of Walden Two *or of* 1984 *(and at a deep philosophic level they are indistinguishable) is coming. The fact that it would surely arrive piecemeal, rather than all at once, does not greatly change the fundamental issues. In any event, as Skinner had indicated in his writings, we would then look back upon the concepts of human freedom, the capacity for choice, the responsibility for choice, and the worth of the human individual as historical curiosities which once existed by cultural accident as values in a prescientific civilization.* [1972, p. 255]

The urgency of the issue has become increasingly apparent as psychological scientific know-how has brought us closer to the moment when man can actually control his fellow man. The choices available to us were outlined in part by Carl Rogers.

We can choose to use our growing knowledge to enslave people in ways never dreamed of before, depersonalizing them, controlling them by means so carefully selected that they will perhaps never be aware of their loss of personhood. . . . Or, at the other end of the spectrum of choice, we can choose to use the behavioral sciences in ways which will free, not control; . . . which will facilitate each person in his self-directed process of becoming; which will aid individuals [and] groups . . . in freshly adaptive ways of meeting life and its problems. [1972, pp. 258–59]

Skinner (1971) doesn't share this view in his book *Beyond Freedom and Dignity.* He argues that man must finally surrender the individual rights he has always held precious and redesign his culture for survival by instituting a system of behavioral controls designed to reinforce socially acceptable behavior and eliminate undesirable and selfish behavior. In Skinner's world, man will stop polluting, overpopulating, rioting, and making war—not because he has learned that the results are disastrous—but because he has been *conditioned* to want whatever serves the best interests of the group.

The question for Skinner is whether we will rely on accidents to bring about cultural evolution or whether we will design and construct an environment suitable for the human beings of tomorrow. His position is that our behavior is already being managed today in ways we cannot control. Skinner observes that we immunize ourselves against disease and must now immunize ourselves against accidentally applied external control.

The question for most of us is whether we will master learning theory or whether learning theory will master us. We are aware of the unending barrage of attempts to control, influence, and limit us. Further, we are aware that living in a community with others is bound to restrict and restrain our personal freedom. Given these conditions, we each need to decide how much of our learning needs to be spontaneous and free for our own sake and how much needs to be controlled for the sake of us all.

B. F. Skinner (1904–   ).

Summary

1.   Psychologists have begun to apply the principles of learning to a number of natural settings, mainly as a therapeutic tool. Many people object to the use of behavioral engineering because of the control it exerts over people without their realization. Others object because a great deal of behavior control for therapeutic purposes involves punishment.

2.   A leading spokesman for institutionalized behavior control is psychologist B. F. Skinner. He argues that such controls are necessary to man's survival because they are the only things that will eliminate man's polluting, overpopulating, war-like behaviors.

Theories of Personality

My clothes keep my various selves buttoned up together, and enable all these otherwise irreconcilable aggregates of psychological phenomena to pass themselves off as one person. —Logan Pearsall Smith

Personality can be described as the pattern of characteristic ways of behaving and thinking that make up the individual's style of adjusting to his environment. The word *personality* is usually applied to characteristics that play a major part in the individual's adjustment to his environment, and personality theories attempt to organize human behavior around general principles that will help us understand why people are different. Theories examine the patterns of relationship among characteristics and how these patterns get established. All of us are personality theorists who try to read other people as well as ourselves.

The apparently accurate readings of human personality by fortune-tellers and palm readers depend on the fact that almost every known psychological trait can be observed to some degree in everyone. Personality traits are often viewed as being distributed along a continuum ranging from a lot to a little. The approach that "character readers" use is to make interpretations in such general terms that they could apply to almost anyone. In addition, if statements of personality analysis tend to be flattering, they will find even greater favor with the eager listener.

This technique of using generalized personality interpretations has been demonstrated by psychologists (Ulrich, Stachnik, and Stainton, 1963) using a quite simple experimental procedure. In this procedure, research subjects take a "personality test" and then are given an interpretation of what the test revealed about them. The catch is that all subjects receive identical interpretations worded in a manner designed to fit most persons. Such a broad

NICE GUYS CALLED
PRONE TO CANCER

"Some behavioral scientists believe there is a 'cancer-prone personality' that has a significantly greater-than-average probability of coming down with malignant disease. . . . This person fits the pattern of an establishment square who lives by the rules and expects others to do the same, who rarely exhibits anger or hostility, and who in general tries to get along with his fellow man.

"One study suggests that the cancer-prone person is less able to roll with the punch of stress than the average man or woman.

"This may make him or her more susceptible to the factors that cause cancer, among which—it is now believed—viruses may be predominant or at least extremely important. . . ." [Detroit Free Press, April 8, 1971]

When studying personality, psychologists often use drawings as projective tests—to determine, for example, how children view men and women. These three drawings were all done by ten-year-olds. The top one was drawn by a girl, and the other two were done by identical twin boys.

personality analysis might read something like this: You are not a stubborn person, but once you have examined the relevant facts you make up your own mind and stick to your guns. You pride yourself on being an independent thinker and are not likely to accept others' opinions without satisfactory proof. You need to have other people like and admire you, but you won't go to excessive lengths to win their approval. Whereas you have some personal shortcomings, you are usually able to compensate for them, and you have a great deal of unused capacity which you have not yet turned to your advantage. At times you are extroverted, affable, and sociable, but at other times you are more reserved and wary. Some of your aspirations tend to be unrealistic, and you are not always certain you have made the right decision or done the right thing. You have a need for a certain amount of change and variety and become frustrated when hemmed in by too many restrictions and limitations.

An incredibly high percentage of people respond to such a meaningless conglomeration of personality statements as if the "interpretation" were a precise, insightful view of themselves. Psychologists, however, have no investment in the need to please people by telling them only what they want to hear about themselves. To the contrary, psychologists work incessantly to rid their personality descriptions of unreliable, unmeasurable, meaningless terms that seem to fit everyone but actually fit no one accurately. This task has proved to be a particularly difficult one. As we will see, a variety of theories have been devised in the effort to understand human personality.

Before a psychologist can begin the study of personality, he must decide whether his goal is to understand and predict characteristics of single individuals or to find generalized human characteristics that apply to all or most people. That is, he must decide between an *idiographic* or *nomothetic* approach to personality.

If he decides to formulate general statements about behavior (the nomothetic approach, from the Greek word *nomo* meaning law), he will seek to discover laws of behavior that, within reason, apply to all individuals. If the psychologist chooses to understand particular individuals and their unique characteristics (the idiographic approach), he will explore the special organization of traits and behavior patterns in that person (as clinical psychologists do). The idiographic psychologist would be aware that two individuals may get the same score on a personality inventory of aggressiveness; yet one of them may be submissive when he is with members of his family and hostile with outsiders, whereas the other may be angry and demanding when with his family but inhibited in business life. The two are alike, yet different.

A leading exponent of the idiographic view was Gordon Allport (1962), who suggested that psychologists should study the individual personality through personal documents—autobiographies, oral reports, letters written by the individual, and the like. These, Allport feels, are valuable tools in personality research.

Type Theory

The earliest attempt to classify human personalities probably involved *type theory* whereby the varieties of human beings were sorted into types (the happy-go-lucky person, the pessimist, the worry wart, and so on). With the type theory, people were described and reacted to in terms of their central or cardinal characteristics. To date, a satisfactory type theory has not been devised. Past and present type theories have not gained widespread support (Vernon, 1964) partly because the individual is expected to possess all the characteristics of that type. A single term or name cannot sum up all of an individual's personality, and such stereotypes tend to ignore individual differences. Type theories in particular tend to neglect the influence of culture.

Trait Theory

In contrast to type theories that use a limited number of characteristics to describe personality, trait theories use a great many dimensions that are thought to be common to all men. For example, Allport (1961a) distinguishes between what he calls "common" and "individual" traits in the structure of personality. Common traits appear in different amounts in all men. Individual traits (or "personal dispositions" as Allport prefers to call them) are characteristics that are not found in all persons and may not even exist in more than one specific individual. Personality for Allport consists of such traits, some of which are unique and some of which are found in differing degrees in all men. To understand personality, Allport feels we must assess, not only the similarities and differences among individuals, but also the unique characteristics in one individual personality.

One problem, however, is that when behavior is described in terms of traits, we still don't know how the traits fit together in a particular individual. A trait of stinginess, for example, may appear in various ways in different individuals. Many psychologists believe that a more workable way to approach personality is to understand how we develop our personal styles of life.

Psychodynamic Theories

Theories stressing the notion that personality is not a static thing are referred to as *psychodynamic theories.* According to the psychodynamic approach, personality reflects the act of living and an interplay of forces, feelings, and events. An analogy might be the difference between a parked car and a car in motion. The important concept is *dynamic.* Psychodynamic theory is often discussed together with *developmental* theory (even though the two are different) because both emphasize the importance of an individual's life history. These theories stress that personality is always determined by the types of

 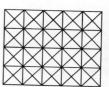

Another way in which psychologists try to identify personality traits is the embedded figures test, which is made up of items similar to the one above. The idea is to find the simple figure in the more complex one.

experience the individual has had while growing up. Today, psychodynamic theories have a wider acceptance than trait or type theories, and psychoanalytic or Freudian theory is the most prominent among them.

Jakob Freud's family, a fairly large one, was photographed in 1876 with six of seven children. Twenty-year-old Sigmund is standing behind his mother, and the baby of the family, Alexander, sits on the floor. The lieutenant is Amalie Freud's younger brother.

THE PATH TO CIVILIZATION

*Freud suggested that the development of civilization became possible when the energy of man was freed from basic survival needs. Converting primitive impulses to civilized ends is not always completely satisfying, however, and the tensions of "being civilized" periodically produce explosive behavior such as war. Imperfect as it may be, the ability to "sublimate" makes possible the ideas, values, attitudes, and activity that characterize the civilized adult human being (*Civilization and Its Discontents*, 1930).*

Freud

Freud devised the best known and most widely studied of all the personality theories and was the first theorist to stress the developmental aspects of personality. He also was the first to note the decisive role of infancy and childhood in establishing an individual's basic character structure. Freud thought the personality was almost formed by the time the child entered school and that personality development after this time consisted of elaborating and refining the basic structure.

Freud was convinced that there are conflicting emotional forces within each individual and that these forces affect each individual's personality and behavior. He concluded that most emotional problems stem from a conflict between the patient's conscious self and his unconscious needs, desires, and wishes. *Psychoanalysis* thus is a theory of personality that deals with the *structure* and *development* of the unique individual.

Freud was concerned with the motivational forces that exist in all human

A Biography of Freud

Born in Moravia (now Czechoslovakia) in 1856, Sigmund Freud was the son of middle-class Jewish parents. When he was three, Freud's family emigrated to Vienna, Austria, where he spent most of his life. Although the Freuds were quite poor during Sigmund's childhood, he managed to obtain financial assistance from a Jewish philanthropic society in order to enter the medical facility at the University of Vienna in 1873.

Although Freud delayed his medical degree for two years to pursue his research, he eventually entered Vienna General Hospital as a resident assistant physician, where his interests quickly focused on psychiatry. After obtaining his medical degree, Freud traveled to Paris to study under the famous neurologist Marc Charcot. At the time, Charcot was studying an emotional disorder known as hysteria. There is little doubt that Charcot's interests greatly influenced Freud's later pursuits. When he returned to Vienna, Freud opened a practice as a neurologist and was soon a well-respected physician. But Freud's interests centered on the psychological rather than physical aspects of the brain.

In the course of his practice, Freud saw many hysterical patients. At first he treated them with hypnosis but soon began to employ the cathartic method developed by Josef Breuer. In this method, patients lose their symptoms by delving into painful memories while under hypnosis. Freud noted that many of his patients revealed unacceptable wishes in their forgotten memories, and this discovery led the physician to his theory of repression.

Between the years 1895 and 1900, Freud published several of his most important and famous works, describing his theories of the unconscious and defense mechanisms, and touching on the idea of infantile sexuality and hostility toward one's parents. *The Interpretation of Dreams,* which was published during this period, presented many of these revolutionary ideas, yet the book was largely ignored by scientists in Europe, as was most of Freud's work until 1905. In this year, Freud published a much more explicit account of his theories on infantile sexuality and their relation to adult neurosis. *Three Essays on the Theory of Sexuality* shocked the intellectuals of nineteenth-century Vienna, and Freud quickly became the most unpopular scientist of the day.

Despite the severe criticism he received, Freud continued to publish his theories and evidence in their support. Much of his later work was devoted to expansion and modification of his original formulations and applications of his psychodynamic views to other fields. Most of his books were criticized severely by experts in the

Sigmund poses with his fiancée Martha Bernays, whom he married in 1886.

fields, primarily because Freud's speculations attacked many heretofore unquestioned beliefs. Toward the end of his life, however, Freud began to receive the recognition he deserved for his courageous exploration of the human mind. He was initiated into several scientific societies, received the Goethe Award for his writing, and was made a corresponding member of the prestigious Royal Society on his eightieth birthday.

During this period of recognition, the Nazi persecutions had caused many of Freud's supporters to flee Germany, and Freud's books were confiscated and burned in Berlin. Freud's publishing company, which he had founded in 1919, suffered tremendously from the loss of sales in Germany, but Freud insisted upon remaining in Vienna and continuing the firm's operations. When the Nazis invaded Austria in 1938, Freud was persuaded to emigrate to England. One year later, a recurring cancer of the mouth from which Freud had suffered since 1923 terminated his life.

SIGMUND FREUD
(1856–1939)

Volumes have been written about Freud, but no written word can capture the full meaning of his solitary search for keys to the mind. His theories were scoffed at by his peers and declared taboo by the "wiser" men of his day. Perhaps only Socrates, Galileo, and a few other pioneers have shared the feelings which accompanied his lonely exploration of the truth behind man's nature.

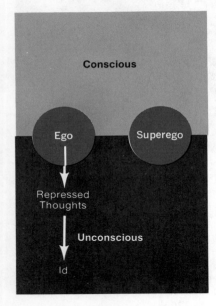

In Freud's conception of personality, both the ego and the superego are situated partly in the conscious and partly in the unconscious. The id, however, is completely in the unconscious and has contact with the outside world only through the ego. The ego, in turn, represses thoughts arising from the id which the superego determines are socially or morally unacceptable (after a drawing in Freud, 1966).

beings and the conflicts that arise because all human behavior is dominated by biological urges that must be controlled and regulated if man is to become civilized. These instinctual, biological urges make up the *libido* and furnish the basic psychic energy that motivates every aspect of a person's behavior. Thus, to Freud, man begins as a biological organism but becomes a human personality by taming his biology.

For Freud, the structure of the personality contained elements or functions which he labeled the *id*, the *ego*, and the *superego*—three distinct and separate (but interrelated and interlacing) systems of psychic function. The *id*, according to Freud, is the reservoir of basic biological urges that motivate the individual. The id is hunger, thirst, sexual impulses, and other needs that assure survival or bring pleasure or relief from pain and discomfort. It remains an unchanging, powerful, active force throughout life, but its insistent demands are tempered and controlled by the ego.

The *ego* directs and controls the id by requiring it to seek gratification within socially acceptable bounds. If the id wants to destroy another human being who is frustrating the id's quest for gratification, the ego decides whether this can or cannot easily and safely be done. Unlike the id, most of the ego's actions are conscious. The ego thus acts like an executive who sees to it that the gratification of impulses will not be painful, dangerous, or destructive to the organism. In other words, the id powers the human vehicle; the ego

OH NO! — IT'S SUPEREGO!

EGO

steers it on a safe course; and, as we will see, the *superego* insists that the ego obey the traffic laws even when there is no expectation that the violation will be caught or punished.

The *superego* is that force within the self which acquires the values and ideals of parents and society. The superego is the moral part of the self. It looks to the ideal rather than the real, what ought to be rather than what is. Further, the superego limits the sexual or aggressive impulses of the id. It pressures the ego to respond to socially approved moral goals rather than impulse gratifying ones. Thus, the ego is trapped between the impulses of the id and the controls of the superego. The conflict of id, ego, and superego causes anxiety, which, in turn, creates defense mechanisms. You are anxious because your impulses (if freely expressed at the wrong time and place) can get you into trouble socially or can make you have an attack of conscience that tells you what a rotten person you are.

Psychopathy

According to psychodynamic theory, human psychopathy is the outcome of early thwarting experiences and frustrations which warp the growing child. The particular kind of emotional disorder that will appear depends on when such traumatic events occur and what positive events take place to compensate for the trauma. Thus, the psychologically crippled adult must try to cope with the stress of daily life while still grappling with the personal inadequacies left over from a painful childhood. A harassed husband, for example, may respond to an angry wife not as an adult male but rather as a child who fears his mother doesn't love him and will abandon him.

During each of the several stages of development Freud described, a unique set of anxieties may emerge as a result of conflict or frustration. If these childhood anxieties and the defenses used against them continue unmodified into adulthood, pathological personality traits may result. The anxious child, fearful of losing parental love and support if he violates parental wishes, may become the cautious adult unable to free himself from the fear that other people won't approve of him.

Freud's concepts of the peculiar anxieties and conflicts that arise while growing up must be viewed in terms of the three developmental stages. Freud designated these as the oral, anal, and phallic stages.

The Oral Stage. According to Freud, an infant can become fixated in the oral (sucking) stage if he finds being fed too pleasurable (excessive gratification) or if nursing is painfully frustrating. Overgratification at the sucking stage, according to Freud, can lead to an unreasonably self-assured adult, whereas a painful sucking period can produce excessive dependency in the adult. Frustration during the oral stage might also lead to aggressive oral habits such as sarcasm or verbal hostility in later life.

Psychopathic Personality: The Mask of Sanity

One of the most interesting of the so-called "personality disorders" is the psychopathic personality. It is often hard to recognize the psychopath at first because he wears, as Cleckley once said, "the mask of sanity." But if you follow his exploits for just a little while, it becomes more apparent that his emotions, motivations, and actions are very different from the ones most of us share.

The psychopath carries into adult life the characteristics we usually attribute to a spoiled child. He is impulsive, undisciplined, and will take immediate gratification rather than wait for later gratification of a superior sort. He does what pleases him now and lets the future care for itself. His escapades are often excused because of his intelligence, charm, and promises to reform, and because he is more interesting than most people. But it soon becomes apparent that the psychopath feels no remorse for his wrongdoing and has no intention of changing his ways. He is an emotionally blunted human being, indifferent to the feelings of others, and without the capability of feeling things like anxiety, guilt, love, or loyalty. However, the psychopath has learned to imitate the emotions others are expressing so that he can "use" people for his own purposes.

Based on the observations of a number of theorists and clinical workers, Coleman (1964) assembled the following characteristics of psychopathic personalities:

- Inadequate development of a conscience.
- Low frustration tolerance, poor judgment, egocentricity, impulsivity, and irresponsibility.
- The search for immediate gratification and an absence of long-range goals.
- An absence of sufficient anxiety or guilt for self-control.
- An inability to learn from previous impulsive actions.
- Charm and a sense of humor used to exploit others.
- Social relationships without love, depth, or loyalty.
- Hostility toward, and rejection of, authority.
- Lack of insight into his behavior.

The particular antisocial behavior the psychopath chooses may vary considerably, but the quality of his dealings with other people remains the same. Thus a psychopathic personality may become an unprincipled businessman, a dishonest lawyer, a crooked politician, a quack doctor, a prostitute, or an imposter of some other sort. Quite notorious people, such as the Nazi Field Marshal Goering, are known to have been psychopaths.

The peculiar set of characteristics that makes up the psychopath has generated a number of theories about how an individual gets to be that way. Some investigators have suggested that the behavior is related to abnormalities in the brain, but EEG studies fail to bear this out. Hans Eysenck suggested that the physiological problem is that the psychopath has a slower rate of conditioning than the ordinary individual. He fails to learn the associations between wrongdoing and punishment and does not acquire the conditioned responses necessary for socialization.

The childhood environment of the psychopath has often been citied as a major force in the development of antisocial personalities. In 1945, Greenacre wrote the classic description of the ingredients that might lead to the psychopathic pattern: a successful father who, although a community leader, is distant and frightening to the son, and a pleasure-loving, self-centered mother who indulges her child. Parent-child relationships in such a family might amount to "buying-off" the child rather than expressing true affection or concern. These parents are worried about how things appear, and they may teach the child to pretend, protect the family reputation, and appear to be meeting the expectations of others. Charm is an acceptable substitute for achievement, and failure is dismissed as unimportant or blamed on others.

Another developmental theory was formulated by Lykken (1957) and suggests that the psychopath's inability to learn social lessons might be due to an absence of anxiety in childhood. Comparing psychopaths with non-psychopathic controls, Lykken concluded that psychopaths were less anxious than others. The findings of many other researchers have confirmed these observations. Without anxiety we do not learn. With a limited amount of anxiety we learn a little. With adequate anxiety we learn what is necessary to survive the emotional give-and-take of society.

The psychopath is an extreme example of one kind of possible personality development. Yet like all other forms of personality, its various characteristics may be partially present in all of us. At certain times, places, and social situations, any one of us may behave in psychopathic ways. The difference is that what most of us do rarely and usually feel guilty about afterwards is a way of life for the psychopath.

The Anal Stage.   The period of toilet training (the anal stage) can similarly lead to unique patterns in the adult personality. When a child is toilet trained, he has for the first time acquired the power to successfully resist his parents' demands; he can now choose to satisfy or frustrate their desires. During the toilet-training battle, the child may adopt attitudes toward parental authority which will continue throughout life. If too much anxiety is present at toilet training, the child may grow up to be compulsively clean and orderly and become intolerant of those who fail to be the same. To ensure that everything is tidy in his life, he may dictate to others and enforce severe and arbitrary rules much like those his parents imposed upon him. Severe toilet-training procedures may also lead to a personality marked by anger. This person tries to frighten others into pleasing him. If the parents lose in the toilet-training contest, and the child learns he can always get his way, he may develop a lifelong pattern of self-assertion, negativism, personal untidiness, and dominance over others.

The Phallic Stage.   In the phallic stage of development, Freud believed a psychological struggle took place between the child and the parent of the same sex for the affection of the parent of the opposite sex. Freud labeled this psychological conflict the *Oedipus complex.* Freud considered success or failure in this conflict to be at the core of either normal psychological development or neurotic disorder. For boys, failure to resolve the Oedipal conflict meant growing up with an intense fear that a powerful and jealous father might punish him for his feelings toward the mother. If the Oedipal conflict is adequately managed, the boy learns to control his envy and hostility toward the father. He identifies with his father's power and masculinity and converts these into motivation for accomplishment in life. Girls eventually renounce their attraction to the father, and, if the Oedipal conflict is resolved, they will find a male to take the place of the father. Many women in America today, of course, are convinced there are other alternatives in living beyond simply searching for a male to replace the romanticized image of their fathers. Thus, resolving the Oedipal conflict need not be judged by the standard of "finding" a man.

In addition to the life problems that can be sustained during the developmental stages, Freud described various kinds of anxiety that the adult personality must somehow contend with.

Anxiety

Anxiety is that vague, unpleasant feeling that suggests something bad is about to happen. It is so closely related to the emotion of fear that there is no sharp dividing line between the two. In general, fear is a reaction to a specific stimulus, whereas anxiety remains vague and has no immediately apparent cause. You can fear a car that has careened wildly into your lane on a freeway, but you suffer from anxiety if you are generally apprehensive about driving in traffic. Anxiety, thus, is an exceptionally uncomfortable experience that is hard to cope with because it has no easily identifiable source.

Aside from anxiety caused by environmental threats (*reality anxiety* about polluted air, for example), Freud described neurotic anxiety and moral anxiety (feelings of guilt). *Neurotic anxiety* is fear that the instincts will cause the person to do something he will be punished for. *Moral anxiety* is having a guilty conscience (doing something or thinking of doing something that violates the moral code learned from the parents).

Man is able to remember the past, know the present, and anticipate the future, and this knowing makes us vulnerable to the threat of what is yet to happen. We become tense about possible injury or harm, and that tension is experienced as painful, distressing anxiety. Most of us deal with anxiety by solving the problem posed by the threat. Learning to swim, for example, can eliminate anxiety about going near the water. But when anxiety mounts too high, the ego is forced to defend itself—to deny, distort, or falsify reality to protect psychological well-being.

Anxiety and Defense

Anxiety warns you of impending danger so that you may do something to avoid it. When the pressure of anxiety is excessive and cannot be relieved by practical, problem-solving methods, the ego must use "impractical" methods called *defense mechanisms.* Defense mechanisms have two primary characteristics. For one, they deny, falsify, or distort reality. Second, they operate unconsciously so that the person is never aware of them.

Complicated psychological maneuverings begin in the early years of childhood as the human psychological apparatus deals with the multitude of threats, conflicts, and frustrations that are a part of growing up. The outcome of the way we handle hundreds and thousands of little contests with anxiety and frustration sets the pattern of adult behavior we call personality. It will help us understand Freud's developmental theory if we look briefly at how some of the various defense mechanisms work.

Displacement and Sublimation.   When the object that will gratify an instinctual urge is not accessible, displacement to a new object takes place. The development of personality consists of an extended series of such displacements. Since we cannot always have what we want when we want it, we learn to accept substitutes. Substitute objects are rarely as satisfying as the original objects, and the search for more perfect objects continues as a motivating force in our behavior.

Miller and Bugelski (1948), for example, studied displacement of aggressive impulses to demonstrate this. A group of boys at a summer camp were asked to fill out questionnaires regarding their attitudes toward two minority groups—Mexicans and Japanese. They were told (while filling out the questionnaires) that they were going to miss a social event they really enjoyed. A comparison was then made between the answers filled in before and after the frustrating announcement. Miller and Bugelski found a substantial increase in negative attitudes following the frustration. This increase in negativity was interpreted as a displacement of the hostility aroused by the announcement. The experimenters believed that hostility felt toward the adults who told them the bad news was displaced to the minority groups.

When displacements fit cultural aims, they are called *sublimations*. But since sublimation does not produce complete satisfaction, the result is usually tension or nervousness—the price we pay for civilization.

Rationalization.   Rationalization is the most common of defense mechanisms. It is an attempt to find logical reasons for disappointments, or it can be described as the attempt to substitute "good" reasons for our "real" reasons. We use rationalization to conceal from ourselves the fact that we have acted from motives that conflict with our standards. Thus, a student cheats on an examination, but he rationalizes by saying that everybody cheats. The man who mistreats his wife may rationalize his behavior by claiming that she needs a strong, dominant male as a mate. Or, if we fail to do what we set out to do, we may insist that we didn't really want to do it in the first place.

Intellectualization.   This mechanism may resemble rationalization, but in intellectualization we are concerned with emotions—particularly anxiety. The discussions in college dormitories and coffee shops over questions of religion, sex, and morality may be examples of such intellectualization. The anxiety related to these questions is dismissed by analyzing them intellectually and converting them to theory rather than action. By intellectualizing, problems are detached from the self and removed from unpleasant emotional consequences.

Projection.   If you think that nobody can be trusted, you may be right. Or, you may be projecting your own unconscious impulse to be dishonest with others. Thus, the censor who thinks modern movies are filthy may be concealing his or her own strong interest in such sexual activity—an interest that would produce anxiety if allowed into consciousness.

In a now classic study of projection, college men who knew one another well were asked to rate their fraternity brothers on a scale of four traits: Stinginess, obstinacy, disorderliness, and bashfulness. The experimenters found that some members of the fraternity were indeed quite stingy, obstinate, disorderly, or bashful. Yet when the subjects rated themselves on these traits, some of them would not admit that they possessed these traits. The significant finding was that the students who were in fact stingy or obstinate (but were unaware of it or unwilling to admit it) were most inclined to attribute these

MULTIPLE
PERSONALITY
The case of Eve White and her alternate personalities known as Eve Black and Jane (Thigpen and Cleckley, 1954, 1957; Lancaster, 1958) tells us something about the nature of personality organization.

Eve White was a dedicated young mother who went to a therapist complaining of severe headaches. During one of her interviews, she reported that she had been hearing "voices," and then she suddenly underwent a striking personality change and became a gay, flirtatious personality who called herself Eve Black. The personality Eve Black was aware of the thoughts and behavior of Eve White, but Eve White did not suspect Eve Black's existence. Later a third, more mature personality emerged who called herself Jane. The personalities of Eve White and Eve Black had apparently both existed since an exceptionally unhappy early childhood. As a measure of defense, distinct urges of the self became isolated from one another and formed separate personalities.

traits to others. Thus, the student who was regarded by his fraternity brothers as being stingy described *himself* as generous but was likely to rate his friends as stingy. The researchers assumed the accuser was getting rid of his anxiety by projecting his stinginess onto others.

This brief view of Freud's theories implies that developing a "normal" personality is a treacherous process resulting in a near miracle. In a sense this is an accurate conclusion. Psychoanalytic theory suggests that the cost of becoming civilized must be paid by each of us by becoming less than our potential would otherwise allow. Perhaps no one passes the test of personality formation with a perfect score.

The Psychoanalytic Dissenters

There is more than a little disagreement about the important parts of the human puzzle. There is even greater disagreement over what the completed picture should look like. The history of theoretical dissent among some of Freud's followers is a fascinating chronicle of the relations between a master and his disciples. Freud's theories of infantile sexuality shocked the educated citizens of Vienna in the late 1800s, and he was rejected by the intellectuals of his time. His years of "splendid isolation" were ended, however, by the establishment of an inner circle of followers interested in establishing the discipline of psychoanalysis. In 1902, Alfred Adler and a few Viennese physicians gathered on Wednesday nights at Freud's home to establish the first Psychoanalytic Society. In 1907, Carl Jung, a psychiatrist in Zurich, Switzerland, joined the exclusive group. Before long, a series of theoretical conflicts occurred, and Adler and Jung (each for different reasons) left the group to go their own theoretical ways.

Carl Jung

Jung was from his earliest days deeply involved in mysticism, spiritualism, and the occult. He applied the psychological insights gained from Freud to the material that had fascinated him when he was young—myths, fables, and ancient legends. These interests then flavored his interpretation of man's nature. Once considered Freud's "Crown Prince," Jung became a dissident renegade whose views struck a more responsive chord "among speculative philosophers, poets, and religionists than in medical psychiatry" (Alexander and Selesnick, 1966, p. 244).

Jung's analytical psychology is not a complete and systematic outline of human personality development. Further, his ideas are expressed in terms unfamiliar to most of us, since he sometimes adopted Freudian terms but gave them different meanings. Personality, for Jung, is fashioned according to the nature of the balance achieved between conscious and unconscious forces. Jung's conception of the unconscious, however, differs from that of

Carl Jung, 1875–1961.

Freud. Jung distinguished two levels of the unconscious: (1) the *personal unconscious*—which encompasses the most common conception of the unconscious (repressed or forgotten material); and (2) the *collective unconscious*—a part of the human psyche which is filled with "primordial images" or "archetypes." According to Jung, these archetypes consist of primitive, tribal, ancestral experiences garnered over the millions of years of human existence. The collective unconscious is common to all humans, having survived throughout our evolution as a race. These archetypes are not easy to describe, however, since they refer to universal human experiences such as mothers, the earth, caves, and so on.

Jung observed that each of us must master a varied series of obstacles as our personality forms from infancy to adulthood. Personality disorder can result from our failure to master any of the many challenges of life. We may be badly adjusted to social and cultural demands if we have failed to achieve personal *individuation* (developing all parts of our personality in a balanced form), or if we cannot rise to the stage of *transcendent function* (uniting the parts of personality into a fully realized self).

In addition, Jung believed unconscious forces (properly used) are necessary for healthy, integrated personalities. The collective unconscious with its archetypal predispositions to primitive patterns of thinking is an integral part of man—a part that produces disorder if it is ignored and forced to seek expression in twisted forms such as delusions or hallucinations.

Alfred Adler

Adler deviated from both Freud and Jung by believing that we must look to the social urges of man if we are to understand what motivates him. Adler developed an ego-psychology that focused on real or imagined feelings of inferiority. Adler had overcome a series of handicaps early in his own life. Because of rickets he did not walk until four years of age; he then developed pneumonia, which was followed by a series of accidents. These experiences suggested to him that mankind relied heavily on his brain as a means of compensating for felt inferiority.

Striving thus became a key word in the Adlerian system of human psychology. Security is accomplished by denying one's feelings of inferiority through the accomplishment of some master goal in life. Once this goal is firmly fixed in mind (it is usually a conscious goal), heredity, experience, and environment are blended together in a life style designed to lead to later success. Life goals and life styles are established early and become vital contributors to the ultimate shape of the personality. Since much of human achievement is accomplished through our social interactions, Adler gives the social community a key position in healthy psychic life. For Adler, man is a social being rather than a sexual creature—driven mercilessly throughout life to achieve a goal that will allow him to escape a feeling of inferiority.

INDIVIDUAL PSYCHOLOGY

In our quest for security, all of us overcompensate for our felt individual inferiority complex. Our striving and our overcompensation make unique individuals of each of us, which is the reason why Adler's philosophy is called "Individual Psychology."

The Neo-Freudians

Theorists such as Harry Stack Sullivan, Karen Horney, Erich Fromm, and Erik H. Erikson published major statements on psychoanalytic theory during a period from the late 1930s through the early 1950s. Each, in his or her own distinct way, suggested basic revisions in Freudian theory. The neo-Freudians reexamined the facts of human development from birth to maturity and interpreted them differently. Deemphasizing Freud's reliance on notions of instinctual energy and libido (the id), the neo-Freudians (or culturalists) argued that human motivations were much more complicated. They were frequently determined by the demands of the culture and pivoted on the kinds of human relations that exist between child and parent. For one neo-Freudian, Erik Erikson, Freudian theory is just a beginning. To understand personality development, one must place more emphasis on the influences of society.

Karen Horney, 1885–1952.

Erikson and Personality.   Erikson developed a theory of personality involving the psycho*social* stages that confront the growing individual. He accepts Freud's concept of ego but does not use the concepts of id and superego. He contends that personality development happens throughout an individual's life. In Erikson's general scheme, the ego forms the individual's adjustment, decisions, beliefs, and attitudes, much as in Freud's description.

Erikson's theory also posits that human beings pass through eight stages of development and, at each stage, face a *psychosocial crisis* of adjustment to the social and cultural environment. The eight stages are not fixed or rigid, and the individual may fail to solve any one or more of the psychosocial conflicts at one time yet clear up that conflict later. Erikson's eight stages are as follows.

1. *Trust versus mistrust.* In his first year of life the infant depends on others to feed him, carry him about, and dress him. The mother and father cuddle him, talk to him, and play with him, and these interactions determine his attitude later in life. If well cared for and if physical needs are met, he learns to trust his environment. If not, he will become fearful and mistrust himself and the people and objects around him.

2. *Autonomy versus doubt.* In the second and third years, the child will learn to walk, talk, and do things for himself. If his parents are inconsistent in their disciplinary techniques, are overprotective, or show disapproval when he exercises his initiative, the child will become doubtful and ashamed of himself. If parents encourage him to use initiative, are consistent in discipline, and allow him

independence, he is likely to be able to cope with situations requiring choice, control, and autonomy.

3. *Initiative versus guilt.* By four and five years of age, motor skills have developed, and he comes more and more into contact with friends, neighbors, and relatives. If his activities are encouraged by his parents, he will find it easier to go out on his own. If the child's activity and inquisitiveness are inhibited by his parents, he will develop feelings of guilt whenever he tries to be independent.

4. *Industry versus inferiority.* From about age six to eleven, the child learns to manipulate objects and events by himself. If encouraged, he will develop a sense of industry, will enjoy being curious, and seek intellectual stimulation. If not, he will develop a sense of inferiority and have to be bribed or cajoled to complete a task.

5. *Identity versus role confusion.* Between the ages of 12 and 18 sexuality emerges, and the adolescent faces a social crisis in finding himself. He must integrate all that he has previously experienced in order to develop a sense of ego identity. He must decide what he wants out of life, what he believes in, and who he is. He must form his own identity. Erikson believes that this is the single most significant conflict he will face.

6. *Intimacy versus isolation.* If he has achieved a sense of identity, then he can form close relationships and share with others. If not, he will be unable to relate intimately to others and may develop a sense of isolation, feeling there is no one but himself he can depend on in the world.

7. *Generativity versus self-absorption.* By middle age the individual must have decided about the outside world, the future, and his readiness to contribute to it. By *generativity* Erikson means the individual's ability to look outside himself and be concerned with other people. If he cannot do this, he will be self-centered rather than productive and happy.

8. *Integrity versus despair.* Old age is a time for reflection. By then most of life's work is complete, and the individual must retire from his active pursuits. If life has been a pleasure and a sense of unity has been achieved within himself and with others, it will be a happy time. If he feels that life was full of disappointments and failures, and he cannot face life at this age, he will develop a sense of despair.

Neo-Freudians like Erikson have drifted away from the original direction and emphasis of psychoanalysis. Their theoretical revisions of Freudian theory have, in recent years, been extended by humanists and behaviorists whose theories we shall examine shortly.

Learning Theory

Many learning theorists have focused their attention on trying to find consistent relationships between stimulus conditions and behavior. They have felt that a theory of personality is necessary at this stage in our knowledge of personality.

According to learning theory, secondary drives develop from primary drives. Thus, hunger and thirst are satisfied by the mother, and, gradually, the infant learns to desire the mother's presence. Thus, the drives for affiliation, approval, and dependency are learned through association with the satisfaction of primary drives. According to Dollard and Miller (1950), the social motives in the personality of an adult are learned derivatives of primary drives.

The values of reinforcers are also learned. The reinforcing value of a formerly neutral object is acquired through association with primary reinforcement gained by the satisfaction of physiological needs such as hunger or need for sleep. Objects that acquire such reinforcing properties are labeled *secondary reinforcers.* They become significant for the individual and direct behavior as well as shape personality. Learning theorists stress the importance of the child's early years, but these early experiences and their impact on personality development are described in terms of learning processes rather than mysterious, unconscious, dynamic forces.

Learning theory is also the basis of behavioral theory, which, as we will see, presents a conception of man that is quite distinct from that of the psychodynamic theorists.

Behavioral Theory

Behavior theories view the source of disorder in terms of reinforcement and try to explore the nature of the environmental reinforcements that shape the behavior of the individual. The neurotic's responses are judged inadequate because most people do not behave as he does. However, this statement merely says that the neurotic responds to a different set of stimuli and is reinforced by an inappropriate set of rewards.

Learning theory regards neurotic symptoms as habits which are learned like any other habits. For Eysenck (1959), there is no neurosis underlying the symptom but merely the symptom itself. His motto is: "Get rid of the symptom, and you have eliminated the neurosis." Eysenck makes it clear though that *all* symptoms must be removed, not just the visible symptoms. *Behavior therapy,* a term coined by Eysenck, involves extinguishing *all* the conditioned responses which the patient complains about and all patterns of response that are meaningfully related to the symptoms. Behaviorists insist that, when the social-learning history of maladaptive behavior is fully known, the principles of learning can provide a complete explanation of psychopathological phenomena. Meanwhile, behavior therapy is a way of systematically applying learning-theory principles to the problem of changing behavior.

Behavior therapy reports a generally high rate of success. Not only is undesirable behavior eliminated, but new ways of behaving are also established.

Behavior therapists note that the ultimate goal of therapy is to have the patient abandon external reinforcers and substitute internal ones which will become self-perpetuating. Once a patient has experienced mastery and success, he will hopefully continue to repeat these experiences because they provide inner satisfaction.

Behavior modification involves a series of small steps (successive approximations) toward the final desired outcome. For instance, if a behavior

Physique and Personality

Among the most ancient ideas about personality is the notion that physique and personality are somehow connected. Many early personality theories were rooted in observations of the relationship between physical types and psychological traits. Scientists of this persuasion postulate that, since heredity contributes in large measure to constitutional variations among individuals, it may also be a key to understanding personality and behavior. Of course common sense also suggests that one's personality may contribute to or be affected by one's weight, height, or strength.

Early in this century Ernest Kretschmer suggested that tendencies toward certain forms of serious emotional disorder were associated with particular body types. Schizophrenics, according to Kretschmer, tend to be somewhat smaller and thinner than the average person. Manic-depressive disorders were associated with round, stocky, heavy physiques, and other varieties of schizophrenia were associated with persons having strong, muscular builds.

Sheldon (1940, 1954) classified human body types on a seven-point scale with three basic dimensions: ectomorph, mesomorph, and endomorph. In his system of rating body build, the *ectomorph* is thin, long-boned, poorly muscled, and delicate. The *mesomorph* is well muscled and athletically built. The *endomorph* is heavy and fat. Body typing is accomplished by assigning each subject a "somatotype" that reflects the contribution of each of these dimensions to an overall description of his physical structure.

Some studies have negated the significance of somatotypes in determining personality. For example, a study of semistarvation revealed that somatotypes vary with nutrition. All the subjects in the starvation experiment eventually approached or reached the ectomorphic physique. The investigators concluded that "the technique

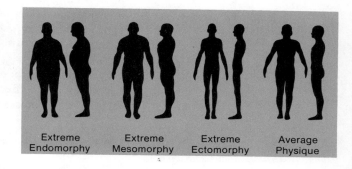

Extreme   Extreme   Extreme   Average
Endomorphy   Mesomorphy   Ectomorphy   Physique

of somatotyping would appear to be more useful for determining the state of nutrition than for determining the inherent constitution" (Keys et al., 1950, p. 153).

Whether or not there really is a significant relationship between physique and personality, most of us act as if there were. In an attempt to demonstrate how most of us react to stereotypes about body build, Lerner and Korn (1972), for example, studied three age groups of males (5–6 years, 14–15 years, and 19–20 years). The subjects were asked what body build they preferred and why they wanted to have the preferred physique. The results indicated that at all age levels males held a predominantly favorable view of the mesomorph, a markedly unfavorable view of the endomorph, and a somewhat less negative but still unfavorable view of the ectomorph.

Common sense observations over the centuries have yet to be translated into a scientifically trustworthy system of personality. The problem remains unsolved—we can type physique with a high degree of accuracy, but the elusive concept of personality is not nearly as well tamed. When we eventually understand as much about personality as we do about judging human physique, perhaps this direction of research will be more productive.

therapist treated a chronic nail-biter, he would find those rare moments when the patient was not biting his nails and reward those moments in an effort to gradually extend them. It is a positive rather than a negative approach and ensures the patient some degree of success early in treatment. Behavior therapists agree that it is not necessary for the patient to gain insight into the original cause of his problems.

Some theorists insist that the behavior model of personality differs from the psychoanalytic model only in the terminology used and that, in fact, the two models are very similar. It is clear there are certain similarities. The motivating role of anxiety in the Freudian system is similar to the drive-producing conditioned responses of learning theory. This fact, behavior therapists would insist, may account for the observation that persons admitted to a psychiatric hospital with highly deviant and disorganized behavior often appear normal in a short period without any active therapeutic intervention. Removal from a stressful or otherwise unfavorable environment may trigger such changes.

Another group of theorists who have extended Freudian thought and taken it in quite different directions is that of the humanists, whose personality theories we shall examine next.

Humanistic Theories

Every person born into this world represents "something new, something that never existed before, something original and unique" (Gale, 1969). For humanists, it is the uniqueness of each human being—his value, dignity, and worth as an individual—that is important.

The terms *humanist, self-actualizing theorist, phenomenologist,* or *existentialist* are only rough indications of the actual theoretical positions of these psychologists. Certainly, all of them would be offended by being imprisoned by such restrictive labels. Phenomenologists or humanists have been tagged "self-theorists" or "self-actualization" theorists since they state that life is only understandable in terms of the meaning of the experiences of each individual. To understand each man, we must comprehend the particular dilemmas he faces and study the state of his consciousness as he experiences various events in his life.

Carl Rogers

Carl Rogers's theory centers on the phenomenal self—the image each person has of himself. This image may or may not correspond to reality as others might judge it. As infants, each of us learns to need love, and each behaves as he does in order to ensure that he will get love. Thus, we learn to behave in ways that will please others. Before long, these learned patterns of behavior please us as well.

HUMANISM
*Humanists assume that behavior is meaningful and is caused by a great number of complex physical, psychological, and sociocultural factors. People are dynamic individual organisms involved in the process of "becoming."
Self-development produces a conglomeration of selves: the motivated self, the attitudinal self, the physical self, the intellectual self, the psychosexual self, the learning self, and the personalized self.*

Becoming a well-adjusted, well-integrated adult is most easily done if we are not beaten down by other people's rejection of us, by low self-regard, by anxiety, or by conflict. If the self develops in an open, flexible, expansive manner, the individual will continue on the road to self-actualization. If too great a gap develops between the self and the ideal we want to become, progress in actualization comes to a halt, and future experiences become threatening rather than growth inducing.

One source of disorder in Rogerian self-theory is the child's attempt to become what *others* want him to be rather than what *he* really wants to be. Beginning early in life, the child is exposed to a series of experiences and feelings which he must assemble into an image of himself. In the course of his personality development, the child is bound to encounter conflicts between the ideal of self and the true nature that seems to contradict it. He is expected, for example, to be generous but feels possessive.

When breakdown takes place, the self-structure comes apart, and behavior and emotion become unpredictable. Put simply, it can be said that self-actualization is a life-long process similar to struggling in quicksand: one only sinks deeper when the thrashing about becomes disorganized and purposeless.

Abraham Maslow

Maslow, like Rogers, begins with the theoretical assumption that human beings are innately good. In other words, humans would be able to actualize their true natures were it not for a succession of frustrating stumbling blocks. Man begins with a "given" inner nature containing instinct-like needs, capacities, and talents that seek to become a reality (actualized). The struggle to satisfy urgent basic needs must be won before men can strive for full self-actualization. This given inner nature, however, is easily distorted by learned attitudes, social pressures, accidents, habits, and so forth.

Maslow believed that the child beginning his journey toward full expression must have a benign, accepting, supportive environment. If this is absent, the child may grow into an adult who is anxious about gratifying physiological and safety needs and who may be incapable of handling the issues of belongingness, love, esteem, or self-actualization. If uncrippled by fear, the mature, healthy person moves steadily, if slowly, toward self-actualization. He seeks delight in new experiences and moves, without compulsion, toward the higher and more complex forms of realizing his capacities.

Maslow is less concerned with disorder than are most personality theorists because he feels that historically too much work has been devoted to the neurotic parts of personality, and not enough attention focused on achieving a fully developed being. He is aware, however, that many of us reach physical adulthood without having gone very far beyond the young child's anxious concern about physiological needs and safety. Personality disorder is a reflection of the crippling effects of a poisonous childhood environment. If the child is forced, prodded, or threatened, he may ultimately allow himself to be shaped by others rather than grow from within. The innate nature of the child dies when he is forced to choose between his own nature and his needs for safety, food, love, and the approval of others. In this contest, the child is hopelessly outmatched.

Summary

1. Personality is the pattern of characteristic behaviors and thoughts we use to deal with the environment. How each of us develops his own unique characteristics, how these individual behaviors fit into a meaningful pattern, and how we can differentiate among the patterns are the concerns of personality theories.

2. There are two approaches to personality theory. In the *idiographic approach,* psychologists attempt to discover the unique characteristics of a particular person. The *nomothetic approach* attempts to discover laws of personality and behavior that apply to all individuals.

3. To some extent, every known personality trait can be found in everyone in differing degrees. One reason we seem to share personality traits is that we are all raised in the same culture and therefore share many of the values about proper behavior.

4. Type theory was an early attempt at classifying personalities. Individuals were categorized and labeled according to the central characteristic they displayed. The problem with such a method was that psychologists expected that the labeled individual would possess all the accompanying characteristics of that type. In reality, however, many people who share a central trait are otherwise not alike.

5. Trait theory attempted to describe individuals by noting a great number of personality characteristics. The problem here was that, even with a list of traits for each person, you had no idea how they all fitted together or which traits were dominant.

6. Psychologists have spent a good deal of energy trying to prove or disprove the idea that physique and personality are somehow related. Whether or not they are really connected, many of us judge people's personalities according to their physical types.

7. Psychodynamic theories of personality attempt to describe personality in terms of forces that are continually motivating the individual's behaviors. Many psychodynamic theories are also developmental theories, in that they stress the importance of experiences an individual has while growing up.

8. The psychoanalytic theory of man, formulated by Sigmund Freud, views personality formation as the direct result of the need to satisfy instinctual, biological urges.

9. In the psychoanalytic view, personality consists of three parts: (1) the *id,* whose aim is to seek gratification of instinctual needs; (2) the *ego,* whose role is to schedule this gratification; and (3) the *superego,* whose goal is to uphold the standards and ideals of parents and society.

10. According to psychoanalytic theory, pathology is a result of adult life stresses following a frustrating childhood whose conflicts have not been resolved. The particular form of pathology depends on the stage of development in which the particular crisis occurred.

11. Anxiety is a vague unpleasant feeling that suggests something bad is about to happen. According to Freud, an attack of anxiety is caused by internal conflict between the id, ego, and superego. Anxiety serves as a warning that forbidden wishes or thoughts are attempting to make themselves known to the conscious mind.

12. Freud noted that there are really three types of anxiety: (1) *reality anxiety,* caused by real environmental threats; (2) *moral anxiety,* or a guilty conscience; and (3) *neurotic anxiety,* the fear that forbidden instincts will emerge and cause the person to do something he will be punished for.

13. Freud postulated that individuals use *defense mechanisms* to cope with anxiety. We deny or distort the reality that is causing the anxiety attack. Defense mechanisms are successful only if we remain unaware that they are at work.

14. Carl Jung agreed with Freud that personality was the outcome of the balance between conscious and unconscious forces. However, Jung thought the unconscious consisted of two parts: the personal and the collective. Poor adjustment, Jung said, resulted from the failure to achieve a balance among the various parts of the personality or to fit the pieces of personality into an integrated whole.

15. Alfred Adler believed that personality development was a result of an individual's need to overcome inferiority by striving to master a major goal in life.

16. Neo-Freudians like Karen Horney, Harry Stack Sullivan, Erich Fromm, and Erik Erikson modified Freud's theories because they believed that human motivations were more complicated than Freud originally suggested.

17. Erik H. Erikson, for example, postulated that individuals must pass through eight psychosocial stages of development to achieve healthy personalities. At each stage, there is a crisis that must

be resolved, but the most significant of these, Erikson said, is the *identity crisis,* which occurs between the ages of 12 and 18.

18. The behavioral theory of personality states that all personality development can be explained in terms of learning principles. Thus social motivation and objects that have reinforcing properties acquire their importance through association in the early years with the satisfaction of primary drives like hunger and thirst.

19. In the behavioral view, pathological behavior is a result of faulty learning and can be traced to the reinforcement pattern to which individuals have been exposed.

20. Unlike psychodynamic therapists, behavior therapists believe that the pathological behavior is the neurosis—not a symptom of it. The object of behavior therapy is to remove the behavior or add new ones by using conditioning techniques. They feel there is no need to delve into possible unconscious causes of the problem.

21. Humanistic theories of personality development stress the importance of each individual's fully realizing his own unique way of experiencing life.

22. According to Carl Rogers, the self will develop fully if it experiences an accepting environment in which love and attention are not contingent on becoming the person *others* want us to be. If a person grows up doing things in order not to be rejected, he will continue to encounter conflicts between what he thinks he should be and his true self.

23. Abraham Maslow suggested that, if a person grows up but is still anxious about gratifying basic physiological needs, he will never proceed to satisfy higher needs like belonging, love, or self-actualization.

24. The psychopathic personality is one example of the way in which personality can be distorted. His lack of concern about rules and the feelings of others has been attributed to a number of causes, such as poor models set by his parents, the inability to associate wrongdoing with punishment, or the lack of anxiety while he was growing up.

PSYCHOLOGICAL ISSUE

Self-Esteem

Human babies usually appear to recognize themselves in mirrors when they are about 10 months old. Some retarded persons, however, may never reach this stage of self-recognition. When most animals see themselves in a mirror, they react as if the reflection were another animal. If, for example, a baby chicken is put alone in a box it will begin chirping high-pitched distress calls and attempt to escape. If another chick, or a mirror, is put in the box the distress calls dwindle to almost zero. Aside from some of our fellow primates, the ability to recognize oneself in a mirror seems to be limited to man.

Awareness of self and self-esteem are particularly relevant variables in human personality. Coopersmith (1968) has noted the relationship between self-esteem and psychological health and asserted it is important that we devote more attention to building up the *constructive* aspects of human personality. For Coopersmith, the most important factor for effective behavior is self-esteem.

Coopersmith on Self-Esteem

In their research Coopersmith (1968) and his co-workers found that youngsters with a high degree of self-esteem are active, expressive individuals who tend to be successful both academically and socially. They lead rather than merely listen in discussions. They are eager to express opinions, do not avoid disagreement, and are not particularly sensitive to criticism. In addition, they are highly interested in public affairs, show little destructiveness in early childhood, and are little troubled by feelings of anxiety. They appear to trust their own perceptions and reactions and have confidence that their efforts will be successful. They approach other persons with the expectation that they will be well received. Their general optimism stems not from fantasies but rather from a well-founded assessment of their abilities, social skills, and personal qualities. They are not self-conscious or preoccupied with personal difficulties. They are much less frequently afflicted with psychosomatic troubles such as insomnia, fatigue, headaches, or intestinal upset than are persons of low self-esteem.

Boys with low self-esteem present a picture of discouragement and depression. They feel isolated, unlovable, incapable of expressing or defending themselves, and too weak to confront or overcome their deficiencies. They are fearful of angering others and shrink from exposing themselves to notice in any way. In the presence of a social group, they remain in the shadows, listening rather than participating. They are sensitive to criticism, self-conscious, and preoccupied with inner

problems. This dwelling on their own difficulties not only intensifies their feelings of defeat but also isolates them from opportunities for friendly, supporting relationships. In the words of Epstein and Komorita (1971): "It is likely that the low-self-esteem person will 'externalize' responsibility for his actions and attribute the consequences of his behavior to factors beyond his control. On the other hand, the high-self-esteem individual presumably views himself as determining the outcome of his behavior" (p. 2). Thus, one's confidence that life can be gratifying may rest squarely on the self-concept, which may decide whether one succeeds or fails in life.

When Coopersmith looked into the backgrounds of boys who possessed high self-esteem, he found that close relationships existed between the boys and their parents. The mothers and fathers showed interest in the boys' welfare, were available for discussion of problems, and encouraged mutual activities. They clearly indicated that they regarded the boy as a significant person worthy of their deep interest. The boys came to regard themselves in a similar, favorable light.

The parents of the high-self-esteem children also proved to be less permissive than the parents of children with low self-esteem. Though the less permissive parents demanded high standards of behavior and were strict and consistent in enforcing rules, their discipline was not harsh or punitive. By comparison, the parents of the low-self-esteem boys tended to be exceptionally permissive, yet used harsh punishment when their children gave them trouble.

Buss on Self-Esteem

In the words of Buss (1973):

There are two kinds of self-judgments, one temporary and other enduring. Temporary self-evaluation refers to specific behaviors [in] particular situations: "That was stupid of me," "I played very well today," or "I really out-maneuvered them this time." These transient reactions, limited in time and place, are of less interest to the student of personality than are the more generalized and enduring evaluations each person makes of himself. The latter evaluations are more central to the self and represent the residuals of some of the most fundamental life experiences: affection from others and one's own achievements. [p. 495]

Buss has designed a *model of self-esteem* to account for the ups-and-downs we all experience in our feelings about ourselves.

The core of self-esteem is formed by the unconditional love of the parents. They love the child simply because he is theirs. They make no demands and place no conditions on their affection. Thus, the infant learns that the most important figures in his life think he is valuable merely because he exists. Love without limits or conditions forms a major part of the core of self-esteem. It creates a permanent feeling of self-love and the expectation that others will offer affection. There is also a peripheral self-esteem that consists of (1) the continued affection of the parents (now with conditions laid down—more love when the child is good, less when he is bad) and (2) the affection of other members of the family and a wider circle of friends. This second part of peripheral self-esteem depends on accomplishments. At first the child performs to please his parents, but gradually his goals are based more and more on group norms.

According to Buss, by middle childhood the core of self-esteem has been established. If the core is sufficient, the person will always be able to fall back on a reserve of self-love. If the core is insufficient, the person will always be driven to seek affection or to demand respect for achievement. "The person who seems *driven* to appeal for love or *driven* to accomplish requires inordinate esteem from others to compensate for his lack of self-esteem. Without a sufficient core of self-esteem, he needs continual assurance of his own worth" (Buss, 1973, p. 497).

Together, the work of Coopersmith and the theorizing of Buss underscore the importance of self-esteem as a core facet of the personality. We may each have personalities composed of differing traits in differing degrees, but these combinations are not very significant, compared to the degree to which we are able to esteem ourselves and behave accordingly.

Summary

1.   Recent research on self-esteem indicates that the way one feels about oneself will make a great difference in behavior. People with low self-esteem isolated themselves from others, were sensitive to criticism, and were preoccupied with their own problems. These people tended to attribute their problems to circumstances beyond their control.

2.   High self-esteem appears to be related to a background in which parents express interest in their children's welfare, are available for discussion and activities, and are less permissive than parents of low-self-esteem children.

3.   Buss notes that self-esteem comes from a childhood environment in which love is given without conditions but given more when the child is good. If the core of self-esteem has not developed by middle childhood, says Buss, the person will spend his life being driven by the need to gain approval from others.

PART THREE

THE SPAN OF LIFE

FROM BIRTH TO DEATH, life is a psychological problem. This simple fact is why we need to bring the span of life into the scope of our study. We must know about the beginnings of life, the conflicts involved in growing up, and the special problems that come with aging and death. Every age group is interesting, of course, but infants and children are particularly fascinating for psychologists who follow the developmental view of human nature. According to this viewpoint, a continuity is maintained from the past to the present, and thus the present can best be understood in terms of its past history. This is why many psychologists have seen children as excellent subjects for the discovery of the general principles and lawful relationships that are part of everyone's being.

As children grow up, they learn desirable values and behaviors. This process of *socialization* (the shaping of a person into what the society considers an acceptable form) is crucial to our understanding of ourselves and our society. Socialization pervades every area of human experience, determining how we perceive, understand, react, and behave. But then, of course, change is ever-present, and the child who grows into a man or woman must also face new stresses and challenges presented by the eventuality of old age and impending death. The demands and psychological problems of life may be different at every stage, but it is certain that they never disappear. To the end of understanding them more fully, then, let's begin at the beginning.

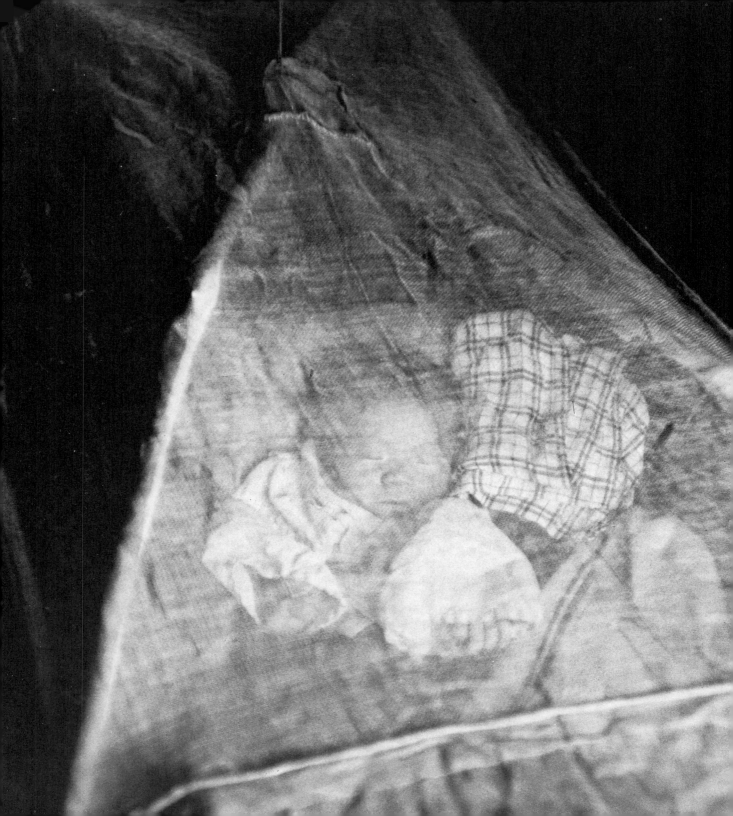

The Beginnings of Life

Being born, we die; our end is the consequence of our beginning.—Manilius

For all the evolutionary distance we have traveled, mankind is, in the view of one modern writer, little more than a bright, sexy primate. "There are one hundred and ninety-three living species of monkeys and apes. One hundred and ninety-two of them are covered with hair. The exception is a naked ape self-named *Homo sapiens*. This unusual and highly successful species spends a great deal of time examining his higher motives and an equal amount of time studiously ignoring his fundamental ones" (Morris, 1967, p. 9). Psychologically, at least, we are sexy primates and a great deal more.

Evolution

Darwin

The work of the biologist Charles Darwin (1809–1882) affected the development of child psychology and imparted to it some of its present flavor. It was Darwin more than anyone else who directed psychologists toward the study of animal behavior through the impact of his theory of evolution. To explain evolution, Darwin formulated a theory called *natural selection*. He carefully noted that although all members of a given species share basic characteristics, they also vary markedly in many ways. As an example, look at the people around you next time you are in a crowded place; notice how different they are in terms of height, weight, skin and hair color, and intelligence. Darwin also noted that each species produces many offspring that do not reach adulthood. Only the best adapted offspring, those most able to survive, live to maturity and reproduce. This is the meaning of *survival of the fittest.* The fittest live to pass their adaptive characteristics on to their offspring, while those that are less fit die and do not reproduce. Thus, a species gradually changes over time to meet the demands of its environment. Over the billions of years of the earth's existence, the original one-celled organisms have given rise to life forms as diverse as bread molds, oak trees, fish, hummingbirds, and humans.

Darwin's major contribution was in pointing out how the development of humankind had probably come about. He carefully collected and interpreted evidence on evolution as a general phenomenon for 17 years. But not until the last pages of *The Origin of the Species* did he write one sentence that very gently hinted that natural selection might be a key factor in explaining man. The intimation was that man might not be a special creation of God with an exclusive soul but rather an animal on the same scale as his dogs and his cows. Few ideas in the course of history have had such overwhelming ramifications.

Evolution and Psychology

The effect of Darwin's studies on psychology, and especially child psychology, is best illustrated in the early work of G. Stanley Hall (1846–1924) who studied the contents of children's minds. He was convinced that much of human behavior could be explained by understanding man's evolutionary history. Hall introduced objective methods to study of children during the process of development. Some of Hall's ideas may seem misguided to us today, but they were not considered especially strange by his contemporaries. A German biologist and philosopher, Ernst Haeckel (1834–1919), had proposed that each individual recapitulates the physical evolution of his species. In other words, the development of the embryo shows vestiges of all evolutionary stages, such as human gill slits indicating that land species evolved from a watery background—i.e., fish. Hall's work took him in a different direction from Haeckel's studies, but some similarities are apparent.

Hall thought of adolescence as the individual equivalent in development to the sociocultural dawn of civilization for all mankind. In other words, he believed each of us—from birth to maturity—relives the history of mankind's evolution. Thus, the years before adolescence are like a reliving of the evolution of mankind before we had recorded history. Some of the conclusions Hall drew from his parallels between individual and societal development led to a few uncommon theoretical ideas.

Hall, for example, believed in the virtue of returning to the simple truths of "nature." In his work *The Contents of Children's Minds* (1883), he described city life as an unnatural setting that defrauded children. He said, in fact, that a few days in the country could raise a child's IQ more than one or two semesters of school training could. Hall looked wistfully to the advantages of primitive life, but he also looked ahead to life in a future in which man could become superman. It takes an enthusiastic man to look backward and forward simultaneously and see value in both.

One current enthusiast of the evolutionary point of view is Arnold Buss (1973), who stated that "social and developmental psychologists are looking more closely at man's heritage for clues to a better understanding of human behavior; and behavioral genetics (the study of the effect of heredity on behavior) has become important enough to be included as a chapter in many introductory psychology texts" (p. 2). For Buss, evolution places man in his true perspective—an animal sharing features with lower animals, yet a unique species with features no other animal has.

Genetics

The basic mechanisms of heredity are contained in the structures called *chromosomes,* which, in turn, contain thousands of smaller units called genes. All mature, normal body cells (with the exception of red blood cells which do not have nuclei) contain chromosomes, but only the chromosomes in the nucleus of the sex cells affect human heredity. At conception we receive 23 chromosomes from each of our parents. These 46 chromosomes with their thousands of genes represent our hereditary potentials.

Genes always act in pairs. One gene of each pair is located on a chromosome coming from the mother, and the other gene is located at the same place on a corresponding chromosome coming from the father. If the two genes of a pair are identical, then the resulting hereditary trait is referred to as a *homozygous* trait. If the two genes are different, then the resulting trait is said to be a *heterozygous* trait. In the case where the two genes are different (heterozygous), one member of the pair—the *dominant* gene— suppresses the effects of the other member—the *recessive* gene. Thus, a recessive gene determines a hereditary characteristic *only* if it is paired with another recessive gene. A dominant gene has its effect regardless of the dominance or recessiveness of the other gene. Thus, when a dominant gene is present, it will be *visible* in the physical makeup of the person.

Looking somewhat like an entangled piece of yarn, within the cell nucleus, the chromosome is the basic carrier of genetic information.

Dominant and Recessive Characteristics

Dominant Characteristics	Recessive Characteristics
Curly Hair	Straight Hair
Dark Hair	Light Hair
Brown Eyes	Blue Eyes
Normal Sight	Night Blindness
Normal Hair	Baldness
Normal Color Vision	Color Blindness
Normal Blood	Hemophilia
Normal Hearing	Deaf-mutism

If genes for blond and brown hair make up the gene pair, the individual will always have brown hair because brown is the dominant gene. Similarly, if a child inherits genes for blue and brown eyes and for straight and curly hair, he will have brown eyes and wavy hair—brown and wavy being the two dominant genes. If a person has a dominant gene for brown eyes and a recessive gene for blue, his *phenotype* (appearance) will be brown eyes, but his *genotype* (genetic makeup) will be one brown-eye gene and one blue-eye gene. And when an individual inherits two genes that are the same (both dominant or both recessive), his phenotype and genotype are also the same for that characteristic.

How this complicated series of genetic events occurs was illuminated two decades ago by the three scientsts, J. D. Watson, F. H. C. Crick, and M. H. F. Wilkins. They deduced the molecular structure of the chemical substance that makes up all genetic material, and for this achievement, they won the 1962 Nobel Prize in Medicine and Physiology.

Watson and Crick came up with a model of *DNA* (deoxyribonucleic acid) that indicated how this molecule could act as the storer of genetic information and as the carrier (responsible for its transfer from cell to cell in the development of an individual organism). DNA, the genetic material, resembles a twisted ladder. When a cell divides, the two sides of the DNA molecule come apart or "unzip" down the middle. Each side then replicates itself. This means that when a DNA chain splits through the middle bonds, it picks up a new complementary half. Thus, each of the two new cells contains a complete DNA molecule identical to the one in the "parent" cell. The "rungs" of the DNA ladder are composed of chemical substances, which can be paired in specific ways to allow for the storing or "coding" of the genetic material.

The DNA code carries information to direct the cell's manufacture of proteins. After a DNA ladder unzips, a molecule known as *messenger RNA* forms along it. RNA is similar to DNA. The information on the DNA is transcribed onto complementary bases on the RNA. The RNA carries the information to one of the protein factories of the cell. There a molecule known as *transfer RNA* brings the components of the protein and assembles them according to the chemical instructions coded onto the messenger RNA. Thus DNA directs the synthesis of proteins in the cell and ultimately the beginnings of life in a new human being.

Eugenics

Eugenics is the science of the improvement of the hereditary qualities of a race or breed—in this case the human race. There are two basic ways in which human eugenics can be accomplished—selection and transformation.

Selectionist Eugenics.   These are the familiar techniques used to domesticate animals and plants. Specimens with characteristics we like are chosen. Those

SEXLESS REPRODUCTION
The Nobel Prize-winning geneticist Joshua Lederberg predicts we will soon be able to duplicate human beings from the cells of a single person (bypassing the traditional egg and sperm process). Without sex, we may be producing more people and enjoying it less. Steel wombs, embryo transplants, egg banks, and artificial insemination have little human warmth and love, but Robert Francoeur (1970) feels the day will soon arrive when procreation will be totally separated from sexual intercourse. As this reality moves closer to us, it will be necessary to develop a new ethic suited to the times—an ethic that treats man as his own maker and truly in his own image.

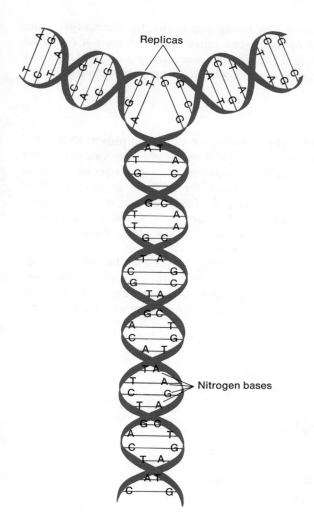

Replicas

Nitrogen bases

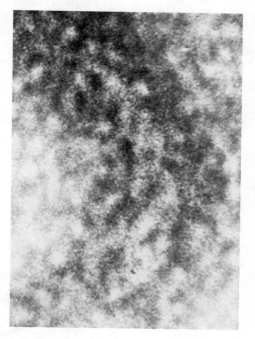

The line drawing at the left shows a replicating DNA molecule; the four nitrogen bases which construct the rungs are adenine (A), thymine (T), guanine (G), and cytosine (C). The photograph below is a greatly magnified shot of the double helix, as the twisted ladder of the DNA molecule is called.

we don't like are removed, and from this selection process we get thoroughbred dogs and horses, plump chickens, fancy-tailed fighting fish, and lean-meat pigs. It is a fairly slow and inefficient system, however.

Artificial insemination is another means of managing heredity. It works for animals, but with human beings it is harder to decide what kinds of persons are the ideal ones to populate the future.

Transformationist Eugenics. Another approach aimed at the improvement of the human race is based on the idea that undesirable genes could be eliminated from the population's genetic pool by keeping persons with "bad seed" away from "breedable" companions of the other sex. Also, we are able

TEST-TUBE BABIES

Dr. Robert G. Edwards of England's Cambridge University recently announced he had successfully created the early stages of a human embryo in a test tube by mixing male sperm with an egg surgically removed from a woman's ovary. He theorized that the embryo could develop into a normal baby, when implanted in a woman's womb. Using female volunteers who are unable to conceive, Dr. Edwards removes an egg surgically, combines it with sperm from the husband, and implants the fertilized egg in the donor at the proper time.

to alter genetic structure today by operating chemically, by microsurgery, and by radiation. Although most of these gene transformations are not beneficial as of now, they point the way to increasing the speed, magnitude, and economy by which the occupants of future times will be chosen—if such a course is what we want.

Biological Engineering

There is another way in which the human race can be improved that is not properly termed *eugenics*. Through *biological engineering,* we can chemically and surgically change a number of individual biological characteristics *without* altering the genetic structure. In recent years, for example, great strides have been made with prenatal surgery by which the fetus may one day be routinely removed from the mother, repaired, and returned to the womb to grow to full term and a healthy birth. Continued advances along these lines will continue to startle us in the decades ahead.

At the moment, biological engineering is not capable of producing significant changes in the quality of the population, but the possibility exists. The potential of such engineering raises serious moral questions. One area of concern is the creation of what are called *clones*—or exact copies—of a

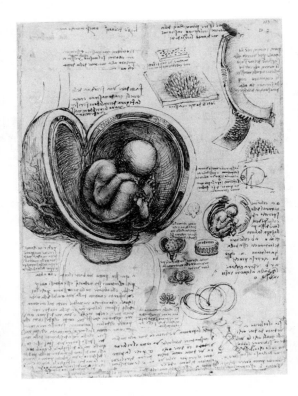

Leonardo da Vinci, the creator of scientific illustration, combined the insight of the artist and the diagrammatical clarity of the scientist in this drawing of *Embryo in the Womb,* c. 1510.

human being who already exists. All cells (except, as we mentioned before, red blood cells) contain the proper number of chromosomes to start a new individual. If these cells could be induced to divide the way the fertilized egg does, they would divide, subdivide, and multiply until they developed into a new human being. In theory, as Rivers (1972) points out: "A body cell could be taken from a donor—scraped from his arm, perhaps—and be chemically induced to start dividing. The cell could be implanted in an artificial womb or in the uterus of a woman, where, presumably, it would develop like a normal fetus. The baby would be genetically identical to the donor of the cell—his twin, a generation removed. It would have only one true parent. . . . Clones have already been produced from carrots and frogs" (p. 24).

Genetic Defects

About 250,000 of the four million American babies born each year have birth defects. About 20 percent of these are attributed to heredity, and another 20 percent attributed to environmental factors during pregnancy. The remaining 60 percent are thought to result from chromosomal abnormalities (Stock, 1969).

Birth defects that affect metabolism can have serious consequences for development, but some of these defects can be detected by tests performed on newborn infants. An example is the disease called PKU (phenylketonuria). PKU prevents the body's full utilization of food proteins and causes a buildup in the blood of a chemical called phenylalanine. Too much phenylalanine disturbs brain and nervous system functioning by causing the destruction of brain cells. Children with PKU show severe mental retardation, hyperactivity, and epileptic-type seizures.

PKU is a recessive genetic trait, and when both parents contribute a recessive PKU gene, the child will be afflicted by the defect. PKU can be controlled by careful management of the diet if the babies are identified early. Even some older children who show PKU damage have been aided by diet control, but nothing much can be done to reverse damage already done.

There are other defects that involve chromosome deviations. One type of mental retardation called *Mongolism* or *Down's syndrome* is caused by extra pieces of chromosomal material. An interesting relationship has been discovered between this defect and the mother's age. Half of the cases of Mongolism are born to mothers who are 38 years of age or older.

Sex-related defects can also be caused by chromosomal abnormalities. The factor for sex type is carried by one of the chromosomes coming from each parent. Some sperm cells carry an X factor for sex (female), whereas other sperm cells carry a Y factor for sex (male). All egg cells carry only the X factor for sex. If a Y-carrying sperm cell fertilizes an egg cell, then the pattern XY is formed—the male. If a sperm cell carrying an X factor fertilizes the egg cell, then the pattern XX occurs—the female.

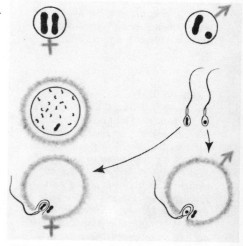

The sex of a child is determined by the sperm of the father. When a sperm with the larger X chromosome fertilizes the egg, a female is produced. When fertilization takes place by a sperm with the smaller Y chromosome, a male will result.

AN END TO BIRTH DEFECTS?

All told, more than 1,000 different types of birth defects are known. In the future, a great number of these might be eliminated. We may see the use of a hollow needle not only to "tap" the uterus but also to give the ailing fetus a blood transfusion to replace as much as 90 percent of its thin, watery blood with a load of healthy, enriched red corpuscles. Such transfusions have already been given as early as the twenty-second week of pregnancy, enabling the fetus to survive either until term or at least until sufficiently developed (at 32 weeks) to survive a premature delivery. People at work on the frontiers of obstetrics foresee not just an end to birth defects but also the enhancement of intelligence and improvement of the bodily organs by "genetic engineering." Now there is a device allowing doctors to peer at a baby inside the mother's womb. The instrument, called a fetoscope, helps physicians monitor the infant's development, spot physical defects, and take blood samples from the fetus.

FROZEN EMBRYOS

Mice embryos frozen and preserved at temperatures as low as 452 degrees below zero Fahrenheit survived and developed normally after being implanted in the wombs of other mice. More than 2,500 embryos, each consisting of only a few cells, were slowly frozen with liquid nitrogen, stored for up to eight days, and then slowly thawed out. The slowness in freezing and thawing was a key to success.

Between 50 and 70 percent of them developed in test tubes, and more than 40 percent of the embryos in the pregnant mice gave rise to apparently normal full-term fetuses or newborn mice.

Deviations do occur, and an individual could have an XXY or XYY genetic makeup, with a total of 47 chromosomes in all. With the XXY makeup, the chromosomal abnormalities cause a problem known as *Klinefelter's syndrome*. With this defect, the male genitals fail to develop normally. Investigations of the XYY makeup, on the other hand, suggest that such males are often very tall, unusually aggressive, and below normal in intelligence.

Life Before Birth

If a baby went on growing as rapidly *after* birth as he did during his last month *before* birth, he would weigh something like 160 pounds on his first birthday. Yet, the last month is the *slowest* of all his nine months of prenatal development. In the first month alone, the newly formed organism increases to nearly 10,000 times its initial size. In the first three months it progresses from a simple roundish dot to an infinitely complicated human form—unfinished, but recognizably a baby-to-be.

The new life grows in the *placenta*—a network of blood vessels and membranes attached to the wall of the uterus on one of its sides and to the *umbilical* cord on the other side. Materials from the mother's blood system, to provide nourishment and respiration for the developing child, pass through the placenta to the blood vessels of the umbilical cord and to the blood system of the child. Waste materials from the child are carried by the blood vessels of the umbilical cord through the placenta to be eliminated by the blood system of the mother.

The *amniotic sac* is filled with a clear liquid (98 percent water) in which the embyro floats and is free to grow without restraint or interference. The temperature of the amniotic fluid seldom varies as much as one degree.

The first few days after conception are called the period of the *zygote* (fertilized egg). When the zygote implants itself in the uterine wall (on about the fourth day), it is called an *embryo*. The period of the embryo continues from this time until eleven weeks, and during this period, all the essential elements of the anatomy of the child will begin. The brain, heart, and liver are the first organs formed. The heart begins to beat during this period, the liver begins to manufacture its own red blood cells, and the limbs appear in budlike form.

In nearly every respect the embryo is formed by the end of the third month, although it is only three inches long and weighs about one ounce. It is now called a *fetus,* and it has the general form and structure of a human baby. During this period, bone tissue will replace cartilage in the skeleton, and most of the anatomical details will be finished. The developing child will make his first movements, and there will be a rapid increase in size and weight.

Superstitions and myths once existed which said that, during the period between three months and birth, a pregnant woman can affect her unborn

Human Ovum (Egg)

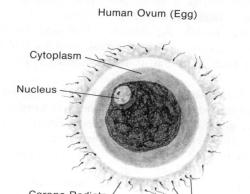

Cytoplasm

Nucleus

Corona Radiata

Sperm

Human Sperm Cell

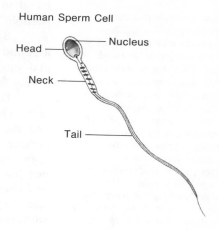

Nucleus

Head

Neck

Tail

The Formation of Life

Human conception occurs as a result of sexual intercourse when the sex cell of the male (sperm) unites with the sex cell of the female (egg). These sex cells are produced in the testes of the male or the ovaries of the female. The sperm of the male has a flat, oval-shaped cell body and a long, thread-like tail. In all, the cell body of the sperm is about 1/5,000 of an inch in size. It contains one-half (23) of the chromosomes needed to form life. The millions of sperm are carried in a fluid called semen, and, when deposited in the female, the cells live from two to five days. Sperm move by a whiplash action of the tail at a rate of about three to six inches per hour. Only one sperm is needed to fertilize an egg cell. Yet, despite the millions of sperm in each ejaculation, none may survive to reach the egg cell.

The egg cell is much larger than the sperm (about 1/180 of an inch) and consists mostly of nutritive material. It too has a cell nucleus with 23 chromosomes. The egg cell doesn't live long either, usually for only a few hours and at most for two days. Normally, the two ovaries of the female take turns in producing one egg cell a month.

The egg cell is discharged from the ovary into the tube (oviduct) that goes to the uterus. The sperm cells deposited in the vagina of the female during sexual intercourse move upward through the uterus, and the sex cells usually meet somewhere in the oviduct. When they get together, the sperm cell penetrates the egg, thus assembling the full number of the chromosomes—46—needed for reproduction. Conception has occurred. When this happens, the membrane around the newly fertilized cell changes to form a barrier to keep other sperm from entering. The fertilized egg now continues moving to the uterus, and there it attaches itself to the uterine wall. The fertilized egg in the uterus sets up a special hormone action that will stop the menstrual cycle and build up the uterine tissues to sustain life for the next 270 days.

child by the things she sees, thinks, or hears. These tales made no anatomical sense, of course, because the umbilical cord is the only connection between mother and fetus, and the umbilical cord contains no nerves. The nervous systems of mother and child are entirely separate, and nothing the mother thinks or perceives can directly affect her offspring. "Like its nervous system, the fetus's circulatory system is completely independent from its mother's. The fetus manufactures all its own blood. Molecules of material pass from one blood stream to the other—the traffic goes both ways, from mother to

THE ULTRASONIC BEAM

Doctors now know that some low-weight babies are actually full-term infants who for various reasons have not grown as much as they should. This weight difference is crucial because the kind of care that is appropriate for a premature baby may actually be dangerous to a full-term, but underweight baby. A new device that beams ultrasonic waves into the uterus can now provide a three-dimensional "map" of the unborn child that doctors can compare with other maps to determine precisely if the fetus is the right size for his age. Some hospitals now have charts that detail the age at which various muscular reflexes develop. By comparing a newborn's reflexes with these charts, doctors can tell whether the infant is an underweight nine-month-old or a premature seven-month-old and plan treatment accordingly.

The human fetus at two stages of development. At the left, magnified twelve times, the fetus is about three weeks old. At the right, magnified one-and-one-half times, it is approximately six weeks old.

fetus and vice versa—but the bloods never mix. The mother does not supply blood to the fetus, and nothing like a transfusion from mother to fetus is possible" (Thoms and Bliven, 1958, pp. 119–20).

By the end of the sixth month, the fetus is a foot long, weighs about a pound and a half, and can hiccup, move its facial muscles, feel pressure, and sneeze. If the fetus is born as much as three months before its time, it may survive.

During the prenatal period the child is affected by the external environment. The fetus is capable of responding to external stimuli (vibrations, X-rays, and the mother's diet and general health), and these stimuli can make a difference in its later life. The percentage of abnormal births induced by X-ray radiation was extremely high as early as 1929. Inadequate maternal diet has been known to produce stillborn, immature, or premature infants, and drugs taken by the mother also can affect the health of the fetus. In some cases, the newborn infant has had to undergo a period of "physiological withdrawal," if the mother were addicted to drugs prior to the birth of the child.

The circulatory system of the mother and the developing organism are separate, but research has shown that some maternal infections may be transmitted across the placental barrier and affect the developmental process. Maternal German measles (rubella), for example, can cause fetal abnormalities such as blindness, deafness, brain damage, and heart disease. Other viruses and some bacteria (such as smallpox, chicken pox, mumps, malaria, and syphilis) may infect the fetus so that the disease is present in the newborn.

Other environmental events may have effects on the growing organism. Smoking by the mother has been shown to lower the birth weight of the baby, and the mother's use of alcohol, hallucinogenic drugs, and some medications may also affect the child.

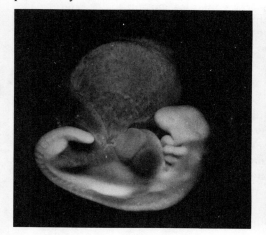

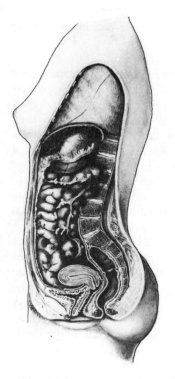
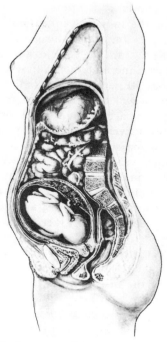
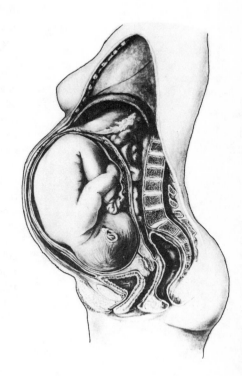

These cutaway views show that by the end of pregnancy, the upper point of the uterus has pushed up almost to the breastbone of the mother. In these later months, the fetus folds upon itself to conform to the shape of the uterine cavity.

Birth

Labor and childbirth seem such natural biological processes that it is difficult to assess the role psychology plays in bringing the young into the world. Newton (1970) suggests the duration and pain of the birth process may be culturally determined. He uses the examples of birth practices among the Curra Indians of Central America and the Siriono Indians of Bolivia to make his point.

Curra Indian girls are not supposed to learn the truth about sex and childbirth until the marriage ceremony. To their dismay, they then learn that pregnancy and birth are fearful female events. Midwives will attend them at the time of birth, and all men and children will be shunted away from the labor area. The process of labor will be extreme and prolonged.

Childbirth among the Siriono is quite different. Birth is an open, public event which all interested parties may attend. The mother labors in a hammock in the hut while her visitors gossip, compare notes, and pass the time of

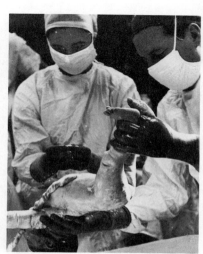

day. Compared with the Curra culture, birth among the Siriono is casual and relaxed, and labor is brief.

To test the influence of environment and culture on labor, Newton, Foshee, and Newton (1966) turned to experimental studies of mice. They found that if pregnant mice are disturbed while giving birth there is a statistically significant increase in the time they are in labor. Disturbance slowed labor by about 70 percent. In a similar fashion, in other experiments, they found that birth will more easily occur in familiar, convenient places. When moved from their accustomed sights, smells, and sounds the mice delivered less easily and delivered more dead pups in the litter.

It might be speculatively concluded that in mice and humans there is a degree of psychological control over the process of childbirth—a degree of control that makes it a newsworthy event in those rare instances when women deliver children in taxi cabs or on hospital lawns.

On a purely chance basis, an equal number of children of both sexes should be conceived, but, in fact, there are between 120 and 160 males conceived for every 100 females. During the prenatal period, for reasons we do not yet understand, 50 percent more male fetuses die than female. By the time of birth, then, there are approximately 105 to 106 male babies for every 100 female. In the first month after birth, 40 percent more male babies than female babies die, and among the prematurely born 50 percent more males than females die. This ratio continues for the period between five and nine years of age. It gets worse between ten and fourteen years (70 percent more boys than girls), and worse yet between fifteen and nineteen years (145 percent more boys than girls). By the time a male child reaches adulthood, he is in the "minority sex."

THE NEWBORN

The Newborn. *Breathing and heartbeat rapid and irregular. Moves arms, legs, fingers, head and neck randomly, without control. A talented and busy mouth: sucks, swallows, coughs, sneezes, tastes sweet and sour, spits, burps, vomits, cries. Startle response to cold or hot food or bath. Urination 18 times, defecation 4 to 7 times daily. Sleeps 20 hours a day.*

2 Weeks. Eyes begin to focus on objects.

4 Weeks. Can lift head; eyes focus a little better but not well. Awakens early, screaming for food. Sometimes stops crying after feeding, rocking, changing diapers, or bubbling.

8 Weeks. Follows an object with eyes. Smiles. [Haimowitz and Haimowitz, 1960, p. 122]

The Newborn Child

The newborn child is a remarkably capable organism from the moment he begins to breathe. He can see, hear, and smell, and is sensitive to pain, touch, and change in position. The only one of the five senses that may not be functioning immediately at birth is taste. . . . The newborn's behavioral equipment is also remarkably well developed. When only two hours old, he will follow a rapidly moving light with his eyes; his pupils will dilate in darkness and constrict in light; he will suck a finger or nipple inserted into his mouth; he will turn in the direction in which his cheek or the corner of his mouth is touched. He can cry, cough, turn away, vomit, lift his chin from a prone position, and grasp an object placed in his palm. His body will react to a loud sound. He can flex and extend his limbs, smack his lips, and chew his fingers. [Kagan, 1968, p. 451]

The human infant is nearly helpless but the one thing it can best do from birth is suck. Sucking begins as a *reflex* action, and the infant uses

Multiple Births

When more than one egg cell is produced and fertilized, multiple conceptions occur, and multiple births may result. Two egg cells fertilized by two sperm cells produce individuals called *fraternal twins*. Fraternal twins need not be very much alike since each is the result of the union of different sex cells. The hereditary potentials each receives can be quite different. Similarly more egg cells may be produced and fertilized by separate sperm cells resulting in fraternal triplets, quadruplets, and quintuplets. In the past few years the use of fertility drugs has produced a number of instances in which more than one egg cell is produced by the female reproductive system at a time.

Sometimes, a single egg cell that has been fertilized by a single sperm cell divides soon after fertilization and produces two individuals called *identical twins*. Because identical twins come from a single fertilization, the genetic material each possesses is the same.

When a single, fertilized egg does not complete the cleavage it started, *Siamese twins* are produced. Siamese twins may be joined on the body surface, or they may share one set of internal organs. The possibility of surgically separating them depends on how they are joined.

it in several ways—to obtain nutrition, to reduce discomfort, and to explore the world. Even on the first day of life, the child has some control over his sucking and can adapt it to changes in the environment. Almost as soon as he is born, he can look, but he cannot look and suck at the same time. The newborn infant sucks with his eyes shut tight. If he begins to look at something, he stops sucking. By two or three months of age, when a burst-and-pause sucking pattern has become established, the baby will suck in bursts and look during the intervening pauses. All infants show differences in temperament and activity levels, however, which are biologically determined from the moment of conception.

Development and Maturation

The development of an infant is an orderly process, even though its rate is not constant in individuals. Different parts of the body develop in independent patterns and sequences at first. During the first month after birth, a baby will develop some control over his neck and head. By four to six months, the child can hold his head upright while lying on his stomach. Behaviors such as crawling and walking appear anywhere from ten months to eighteen months after birth, although some babies do start crawling earlier than this.

The *rate* of behavior development in an individual is not constant since the rate of maturation of physical processes does not proceed in a continuous, smooth fashion. The rate of maturation of the early years is not matched by similar growth in later childhood. Though parents become concerned over a less-than-average rate of physical development and are proud when their child achieves something ahead of the average, this relative progress is not related to the extent of the child's later development.

Observations on the effects of restriction of movement on development have been made with human infants. In some cultures, it is a custom to

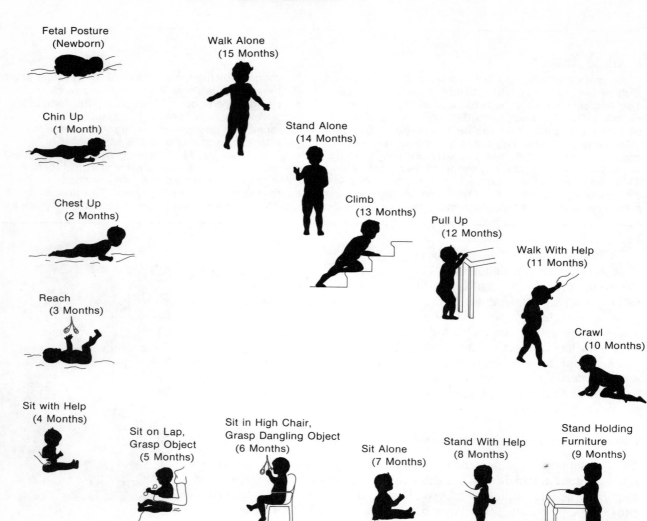

Fetal Posture
(Newborn)

Chin Up
(1 Month)

Chest Up
(2 Months)

Reach
(3 Months)

Sit with Help
(4 Months)

Sit on Lap,
Grasp Object
(5 Months)

Sit in High Chair,
Grasp Dangling Object
(6 Months)

Sit Alone
(7 Months)

Stand With Help
(8 Months)

Stand Holding
Furniture
(9 Months)

Walk Alone
(15 Months)

Stand Alone
(14 Months)

Climb
(13 Months)

Pull Up
(12 Months)

Walk With Help
(11 Months)

Crawl
(10 Months)

Although there are individual differences, children usually develop their motor skills in this sequence (after Shirley, 1933). From birth to first step, the child goes through stages of gradually increasing his ability to control bodily movements. The average times at which these stages occur are indicated above.

swaddle an infant—to wrap him in long, narrow bands of cloth to restrict his movements. When researchers compared the development of a group of infants who had been swaddled until one year of age with the development of infants who had not been restricted, they found that, although the swaddled children displayed poor muscular coordination when first released, they caught up with the unswaddled chldren after only a short period of practice and with no permanent impairment (Orlansky, 1949). This suggests that motor development is largely a matter of *maturation* rather than learning.

Ages, stages, and phases of growth are arbitrary divisions of the human experience that we use to make sense of the process of development. Stages and phases are statistical statements of events that, on the average, will happen to most children in our culture. But human beings seldom follow the blueprints drawn for them. Their "stages" do not always occur on time or in the proper sequence. Nonetheless, these descriptive phases of development reflect a mixture of maturational and learning effects on behavior.

Maturation and Learning

The infant grows and learns. By *growth* is meant physical or physiological change with the passage of time. *Learning,* as we have already discussed in Chapter 3, refers to the modification of behavior that occurs as a consequence of experience. When we speak of *maturation,* we mean the process by which the potential of the human organism unfolds. It is the ripening of the physical equipment combined with a change in the capacity to perform. A distinction is usually made between those changes that take place as a consequence of learning and those produced by growth and maturation.

Maturation may be a ripening of capacity in the individual or the growth of some neurological or anatomical structure which makes new performances possible. In psychological terms, maturation is development that takes place in the absence of specific experience or practice. The usual assumption is that maturation is a genetic process which triggers a child's capacity to learn. Maturation is most often judged by the chronological age of the child, but this measure often fails to be meaningful since tempo and rate of growth can vary widely within the individual.

Most behavior is a consequence of both maturation and learning. But learning is most effective when the organism is physically ready for it. In general, attempts to train children before maturational readiness bring temporary results at best. Try teaching a three-year-old to ride a two-wheeled bike, for example.

In some cases, the course of normal maturation and learning get distorted by unusual life circumstances. We refer to these cases as "deprived children"—deprived of the usual learning and training which capitalize on the child's maturational readiness.

The most obvious instances of deprived children are those who have reportedly been raised among animals. This photograph taken in Lucknow, India, shows a "wolf boy" named Ramu eating raw meat. The examining British specialist said he had no doubts the child was reared among animals. Note the scars on the boy's head.

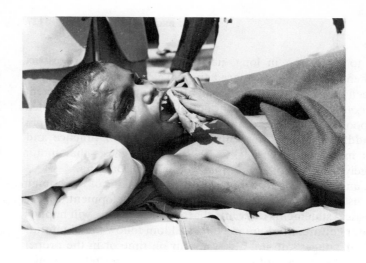

Deprived Children

Many observers have reported profound effects on the behavior and well-being of the infant when it is separated from its mother for a prolonged period of time. Ribble (1944) applied the term *marasmus* to the physical and psychological "wasting away" that she observed in infants deprived of their mothers. A few years later, Spitz described the physical and behavioral characteristics of institutional children who had received less maternal attention than most children.

The immediate reaction reported in infants under two years of age is highly regular. The sequence usually is violent crying followed by a steady and progressive withdrawal from people and surroundings. Moreover, physical as well as psychological damage occurs. The children in one series of studies (Spitz, 1945; 1946) were grossly underweight, small for their age, quite subject to infection, and generally retarded in the acquisition of the expected developmental skills. The physical damage is progressive, and, after five months of separation, the progression cannot be reversed. However, children who are separated from mothers with whom they had had a poor relationship in the first place show much less disturbance, as do infants who are rapidly provided with a good substitute mother.

Depriving the infant of his mother or the parent figure who provides him with a warm, basic relationship also seems to be disastrous for socialization. However, it is difficult to generalize about the specific characteristics of the deprived infant, since there are so many different kinds of deprivation.

Summary

1. Charles Darwin's theory of evolution stated that all present-day animals had a common ancestry. Darwin's ideas made it likely that the study of animal behavior could tell us something about our own.

2. According to Darwin's theory of natural selection, evolution occurred when deviates of a species were born with characteristics that were better suited to the environment than those of the normals. They would be more likely to survive and, therefore, reproduce. These special characteristics would be passed on to future generations through heredity.

3. Darwin's theories suggested to some psychologists that, if we knew more about evolution, we might know more about human behavior and its causes. G. Stanley Hall, for example, believed that man in his development from conception to adolescence repeated or relived the stages of mankind's evolution.

4. Genes are units of heredity found on structures called *chromosomes*. We receive 23 chromosomes from each parent when we are conceived. For every gene we receive from one parent, we receive a corresponding gene for the same trait from the other parent.

5. *Phenotype* is the appearance of the individual, and *genotype* is his genetic makeup. They are not necessarily the same. If the genes for a particular trait are identical, then the hereditary trait is *homozygous*. If they are different, the trait is *heterozygous*. When the genes are different, the dominant gene determines the resulting phenotype.

6. One of the 23 chromosomes carried by each parent contains a sex factor. All eggs carry an X factor, whereas sperm may carry either an X or Y. If a sperm with an X fertilizes the egg, the result is an XX pattern—a female. If a sperm carrying the Y factor fertilizes the egg, an XY pattern results, and a male is born.

7. *Fraternal twins* occur when two eggs are fertilized at the same time by two different sperm. Thus fraternal twins may share no more of their biological makeup than normal siblings. *Identical twins* occur when one egg is fertilized but splits before it begins to divide into a multicellular organism. Identical twins have identical genetic makeup.

8. *DNA* is a molecule, found in the nucleus of a cell, that contains the hereditary information. When a cell divides, the DNA replicates itself so that each new cell contains the same hereditary store.

9. DNA controls the production of proteins by the cell by manufacturing RNA. *Messenger RNA* carries the genetic messages to tell the cell what protein it is to produce. *Transfer RNA* picks up the necessary components and brings them to the place in the cell body where the protein is made. The interaction of DNA and RNA determines whether the cell becomes blood, tissue, or bone.

10. *Eugenics* is the science by which hereditary qualities in a race are improved. The improvement can be accomplished by (1) selectively breeding those members of a species whose characteristics we like; and (2) preventing individuals with genetic abnormalities from breeding, and then altering the genes of those who are allowed to breed.

11. *Biological engineering* is the method by which an individual's biological characteristics are altered without touching the hereditary material.

12. Because all cells, not just sex cells, contain the number of chromosomes (46) necessary to start a new individual, genetic engineers are experimenting with *cloning*. This is a process by which an ordinary cell is induced to divide and multiply to form an exact copy of the animal or plant the cell originally came from.

13. Birth defects may result from heredity, environmental factors during pregnancy, or accidental coding errors in the DNA molecules.

14. The developing embryo lives in its mother's womb, receiving nourishment and oxygen, and discharging wastes through the umbilical cord. The nervous system and blood supply of the two are completely separate although maternal infections and addictions can be transmitted to the developing child.

15. At age three months in the womb, the new life begins to take the form and structure of a human baby. At this point it is called a *fetus*. By the sixth month, the fetus is a foot long. It can move its facial muscles and sneeze.

16. The length of labor and degree of pain involved appear to differ among cultures, according to whether childbirth is perceived as a joy or as something to be feared.

17. The newborn child is capable of many reflexive actions immediately after birth. From this point, it develops better physical equipment and a capacity to perform through maturation.

18. *Maturation* is the process by which heredity continues to unfold the child's genetic potential after birth. Development caused by maturation and not learning will occur even without practice. Much of learning, in fact, cannot take place until maturation brings the developing child to a stage of readiness.

19. Children who have been separated from their mothers often experience intense psychological and physical impairment, including loss of weight, loss of resistance to infection, and a general retardation in the acquisition of motor and mental skills.

PSYCHOLOGICAL ISSUE

Birth Order

Being the firstborn child in your family is important if you want to increase your odds of becoming an astronaut or president. If you are not quite as ambitious as all that, it is still important to get here before all your other brothers and sisters. Everything you will ever be does not, of course, depend simply on the order of your birth. But it does seem to make a difference in the kind of person you will eventually become.

So You Want to Be President?   Psychologist Louis Stewart analyzed presidential elections in periods of social crisis (during or just before wars) and discovered that eight of the nine men elected during these times were firstborn or only sons. In less stressful times, of 21 presidents elected only 8 were firstborn or only sons. Apparently we're willing to give the kid brother a chance when things are going smoothly, but if there is trouble we tend to lean on the older brother (Goodall, 1972). If you want to be president but weren't the firstborn, the next best is to be third in line. Thirty-two percent of all presidents were third sons. Only one has been a fourthborn, and none has been born later even though families used to be quite large.

Scientific psychology has been interested for some decades in the effects of birth order or ordinal position in the family on intellectual achievement and social adjustment. Data suggest that a great proportion of you taking psychology classes are firstborn children—more than would be expected by chance. Schachter's (1963) findings are that more graduate students in psychology and education are firstborn, more medical students are firstborn, and that the firstborn have a higher high-school grade-point average than laterborn children. The firstborn female is a more successful interpersonal strategist compared with a laterborn female. Her form of strategy, however, is said to involve using her good looks to "work on" the instructor. Thus, for example, the firstborn female tends to sit in front of the class, to see the instructor after class, and to visit the instructor during his office hours significantly more than do laterborn females. Research evidence suggests that the second male and the first female are similar in their skillful, manipulative, interpersonal abilities. The first male and second female have been found to be equally unskilled in manipulation (Singer, 1964).

Times Don't Change Much.   The relation of order of birth to achievement has been investigated for a hundred years. The first known data appear in Sir Francis Galton's *English Men of Science,* published in 1874. Galton selected eminent scientists of that time and found a more-than-chance number of only sons and firstborn sons among them. [Altus, 1966]

Thirty years later, Havelock Ellis (1926) published *A Study of British Genius,* based on the biographies of 975 eminent men and 55 eminent women. The probability of appearance in the *Dictionary of National Biography* was much greater for a firstborn than for a middle child. The youngest was similarly favored over the intermediate child.

Why Should Birth Order Make a Difference?

There are several possible reasons and many theories why birth order affects the child. The firstborn usually has the smallest birth weight in the family. Yet within a couple of years this child will be heavier and taller than laterborn children at the same stage and age of growing up. By adulthood, no significant differences will remain in height or weight between eldest and laterborn siblings (Clausen, 1966).

Usually, no other children will get the amount of attention, energy, and concern that the firstborn receives before a brother or sister comes along. The firstborn is also more likely to be a planned child and more likely to be breast-fed for a longer period of time (Sears, Maccoby, and Levin, 1957). But, he must also suffer inexperienced parents who may be unsure of themselves and therefore less consistent in taking care of him. The parents will spend more time with him, talk to him more, and spank him more often than they will the children who come later.

Parents regularly report they are much more relaxed with laterborn children than with their firstborn (McArthur, 1956; Sears, 1950). They also display greater permissiveness about the behavior of their laterborn children, whereas they tend to be overconcerned with the details of upbringing with their first child. This concern and anxiety is eventually reflected in the child's image of himself and produces the need to win approval, which is never fully satisfied.

One of the most consistent findings relating to birth order is that firstborn children achieve eminence in higher proportion than do their siblings. Many factors account for this success. One of the most important is that achievement in academic pursuits must start very early, and firstborns perform better in the classroom from the beginning. They are not smarter, but they try harder to achieve in the school setting. This striving seems to reflect the aspirations and pressures of the parents (after all, it is their first entry in the race of life). With this background under their belts, firstborns tend to go on to become serious, conscientious adults.

The Need to Affiliate

Our modern concern with birth order was triggered by a study done in 1959 by Stanley Schachter. By accident, really, he found that college-age female students who were firstborn or only children regularly chose to wait with other people when they expected to receive a painful electric shock in an experiment. Interestingly those who were laterborns didn't care as much whether they awaited alone or with others. Schachter thought this difference between "firsts and onlies" and "laterborns" was due to motivation. He argued that firstborns must have a stronger need to affiliate than do laterborns, and that this motivational difference is particularly apparent under conditions of stress.

Schachter's research turned up some interesting findings in a study on the effectiveness of fighter pilots as a function of birth order. Firstborns are inferior to laterborns in this role presumably because of increased anxiety about being on their own during periods of stress. Being with others seems to be comforting to firstborns (Wrightsman, 1960), but laboratory experiments may be too artificial to tell us how firstborns handle their affiliative needs when anxious. Irving Sarnoff and Philip Zimbardo (1961), in fact, maintain that this reaction depends on what emotion the firstborn is feeling. Indeed, the evidence on the association between birth order and affiliative behavior has been confusing (Warren, 1966).

No Cheers for the First Born.   Some researchers have suggested that firstborns find physical pain or the prospect of being hurt more frightening than do laterborn individuals. Thus, when told they were to be given severe electric shock, firstborn females reported more fear than did laterborn females, and they asked the experimenter to stop actual electric shock sooner than did laterborn females.

Nisbett (1968) figured that, if this were true, you would expect firstborns to stay away from activities where the risk of physical injury was high. He checked their participation in dangerous sports and found that they are less likely to play sports involving high risk than are laterborn persons.

Sibling Position

Walter Toman (1970) has a fascinating theory that, although parents are important in deciding what kind of person you will become, the order of your birth and the number of brothers and sisters you have is even more important. As families expand, Toman thinks children turn to each other for the psychological support they cannot get from the parents. Thus, brothers and sisters (siblings) have a vital impact on the way you learn to relate to others. The kind of person you choose for a spouse, friend, or working partner may be determined by the kinds of siblings you lived with while growing up. Adult relationships may duplicate the ones you have had with brothers and sisters. According to Toman, the more exact the duplication, the greater the chance that your adult relationships will last and be happy. A boy raised with sisters, for example, gets used to interacting with girls, and females lose the "different" or "strange" quality to him. But, a boy raised with brothers may feel uncomfortable around women and prefer the company of men. Sibling position is particularly important in Toman's theory. He believes oldest children will learn to be leaders, just as younger children will get used to being followers. Thus, firstborns will grow up looking for relationships they can dominate, whereas the opposite will be true if you are a younger child in the family.

Toman uses his theory to predict how marriages will work:

Suppose that the older brother of a sister *marries the* younger sister of a brother. *They are getting in marriage precisely the peer relation that they had at home. He is used to a girl his junior, and she to a boy her senior. Hence there should be no conflict over their dominance rights. And both of them are used to the other sex, so they should have no great sex conflicts either. If this fellow had married an oldest sister of sisters, however, he could have expected some problems. Both partners would expect to have seniority rights and each one would try to rule the other. In addition, the wife would have had little experience in getting along with men.* [Toman, 1970, p. 45]

If you are an only child, however, you have a serious disadvantage as far as marriage goes. The only child has only parents to learn from and may have a hard time getting along with peers. You may be looking for a father or mother rather than a peer when you marry, and you may not want to have children of your own since you want to remain a child yourself. You can be an only child even if you have brothers and sisters, if you differ more than six years in age from them. The age gap lets you grow up like an only child,

The Only Child. Despite statistics that show only children very often grow up to be outstanding, there has been a longstanding prejudice against the one-child family. The usual notion is that an only child will be "spoiled"—that he's overindulged, maladjusted, egocentric, and never learns the give and take of life (Kramer, 1972). Some parents, in fact, feel they must have a second child just to salvage the first. Most only children actually enjoy striking advantages both as children and adults. A disproportionately high number of only children appear as National Merit Scholars, science prize winners, astronauts, doctors, and persons listed in *Who's Who in America*.

and you may react accordingly. If you have children, you should keep in mind, Toman says, that parents tend to treat their children according to how they themselves were treated as siblings. You may simply repeat the family pattern you knew as a child.

You can analyze yourself and your relationship to your brothers and sisters using Toman's system (1970). Here are some examples:

Oldest Brother of Brother(s) (OBB). He is a man's man: aggressive, assertive, in control at most times. He is the leader of men, whether he takes over by force or cunning. He gets along well with other males, especially when they are not older. The OBB is a perfectionist in most areas of his life.

Youngest Brother of Brother(s) (YBB). The YBB can be daring and imaginative but also annoying and irritating. He is an irregular worker, sometimes excellent and other times unproductive. He is at his best in artistic or scientific endeavors. He is not a true leader. He will squander his own and other people's money equally freely, and he enjoys making fabulous gifts on the spur of the moment. The YBB flocks to prophets, advisers, and psychotherapy. He loves whatever attention he gets.

Oldest Brother of Sister(s) (OBS). This is the true ladies' man. The OBS adores women—as friends, colleagues, lovers, wife. Love is the most important thing in life, and he is not one of the boys or a man's man.

Youngest Brother of Sister(s) (YBS). Girls absolutely adore him, love him, and clean up after him. No matter where he is or what he is doing, there is usually a female around to take care of his needs. Not surprisingly, he does not make a terribly good father.

Oldest Sister of Sister(s) (OSS). She is dominant, assertive, and bossy. When she cannot take charge of others and tell them what to do, she will be unhappy, angry, or sullen. She is a good worker, in a position of leadership. She is competent, responsible, and she gets things done efficiently. Her best marriage choice would be a youngest brother of sisters.

Youngest Sister of Sister(s) (YSS). She wants an adventurous and colorful life, likes entertainment and change, and may seek them haphazardly and spontaneously. Her bouncy enthusiasm helps her retain her youthfulness far into old age. She is quick and charming, willful, and somewhat pretentious, gullible, and emotional—and a brat. She may have trouble in marriage, since she has not accustomed to living with a male, so it will take a dominant and indulgent man to handle her—an oldest brother of sisters, perhaps.

Oldest Sister of Brother(s) (OSB). Like all firstborns, she is independent, strong, practical, and concrete. She relates easily to men. They are important to her, and they tend to like her. The OSB will want children, and they will come to her with troubles and complaints rather than to their father. She will enjoy taking care not only of her husband but also of any number of children.

Youngest Sister of Brother(s) (YSB). The YSB is everything a traditional man wants a girl to be: feminine, friendly, kind, tactful, and submissive but not subservient—a good companion and good sport. She gets along well with male co-workers, but women do not always like her.

Toman's is an interesting approach to the problem of birth order, but it is difficult to tell how accurate these broad descriptions are. Like all theories that put people into neat categories, it fits everyone a little, some a lot, and others not at all. Since most of us

Birth Order and the Nursery School. McGurk and Lewis (1972) studied the social behavior of 14 firstborn, 10 secondborn, and 28 third- and later-born children averaging just less than four years of age in small nursery school groups. Their analysis indicated that secondborn children sought more adult help and more adult approval than first- or laterborns. They also spent more time in individual activity, were generally more talkative, and expressed more negative emotions than the others. These findings suggest that the effect of birth order is well established early in life—earlier than most theorists would have guessed.

are subject to a thousand and one influences in our lives, sibling position is just one of many ways we learn about people. It depends on the particulars of your own family structure whether this one influence becomes significant. It is apparent we have not yet properly assessed the meaning and impact of birth order in human life.

Summary

1. Most of the research done on birth order indicates that more firstborn than laterborn children achieve eminence. One reason this may be so is that firstborns do better in school. This performance is in turn based on the fact that firstborns try harder to achieve because of the aspirations and pressures of their parents.

2. Because parents tend to handle their firstborns with great anxiety and a lack of confidence, many firstborn children probably grow up feeling a need to win approval to bolster their belief in themselves.

3. Walter Toman has suggested that the number of brothers and sisters you grew up with is more important than birth order. Brothers and sisters influence the way you learn to relate to others more than do parents. Further, you will tend to replicate your family situation through your choice of spouse and in the way you treat your children.

Growing Up

Children have neither past nor future; they enjoy the present, which very few of us do. —La Bruyère

As the popular song goes: "God bless the child who's got his own." But, in that very quest of self and pursuit of "one's own," every child also goes through a period of learning the essentials of social living. He acquires certain desirable behaviors and values and inhibits undesirable ones. To teach children the essential lessons of social living, adults take advantage of mechanisms already present in the child. These are, according to Janis, Mahl, Kagan, and Holt (1969): (1) the desire for recognition, acceptance, and affection; (2) the urge to avoid punishment and rejection; (3) identification; and (4) imitation of loved ones. Using the mechanisms of *imitation* and *identification,* the child attempts to achieve a reasonable balance between dependence and independence in relationships with others. We can look first at how this balance between dependence and independence is achieved.

Psychological Development

Independence and Dependence

The child is, at first, dependent on others for his well-being. But, as he becomes independent (able to rely on his own resources, capacities, and skills), he learns to be his own person. If an anxious mother is frightened by life, she will, unfortunately, unduly protect her child by intervening before the child can call on his own resources.

If the child is regularly rewarded and seldom punished for dependent

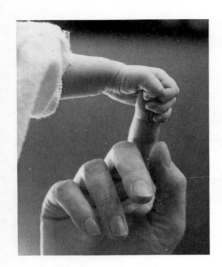

behavior, he or she will learn to react in dependent ways. In most families, the growing child gets a mixed and inconsistent set of messages about dependence and independence. He is urged to be independent in some situations and encouraged to be dependent in others. From these mixed communications, every child must sort out a message meaningful to himself. This is not an easy task, and children fluctuate unpredictably between dependent and independent behaviors as they grow up. The parental problem is no easier. Parents, too, vacillate between telling the child "You are old enough to do it yourself" and "You are too young to be allowed to do that."

Dependency and passivity, once formed, remain stable over the years. As Kagan and Moss (1960) have indicated, this may occur because our culture encourages and reinforces dependent behavior in females but discourages and punishes it in males.

Growing children work out the problem of dependence and independence by using the mechanisms of imitation or identification.

Imitation

Children consciously and unconsciously imitate people whom they admire and feel close to. Boys will often imitate males, whereas girls will most often imitate females. Copying and matched-dependent behavior are two forms of imitation. When a child copies behavior he deliberately tries to precisely duplicate a way of responding, even though he may not understand it. With matched-dependent behavior, the child may only approximate the behavior of the model, perhaps modifying it to fit his own personal style.

Theorists make a distinction between identification and imitation by describing imitation as superficial and identification as a process that alters the self in permanent ways. However, behavioral theorists such as Bandura and Walters (1963) suggest that this is a semantic and artificial distinction. When children imitate others, parents usually exercise control by punishing certain behaviors and rewarding others. However, if the parent does not supervise the child closely or treats these imitations lightly, the behavioral lesson may be imprinted indelibly and become nearly impossible to eradicate. Imitation can be controlled and guided only if the parents understand its importance and intervene when unacceptable patterns are chosen.

Identification

Identification describes how a child assembles a self-picture by "becoming like" his parents and a variety of other persons he encounters. Apparently, the child may become "like" others without consciously imitating their mannerisms or values.

Thus, the kind of person the child begins to become may reflect not only the direct parental teachings but also a multitude of characteristics possessed by others. Often parents cannot understand the child who turns out distinctly different from the conscious lessons he was taught. But the child can make negative as well as positive evaluations in the process of identification. Psychodynamic theorists suggest there is a variety of kinds of identification. *Defensive identification,* for example, occurs when the child patterns himself after others in order to achieve the power and status they possess. *Identification with the aggressor* is when the child becomes "like" the hostile, angry, punishing parent or peer. *Developmental identification* refers to the affectionate bond between mother and child early in life.

The various kinds of identification can blend in the developing personality. Thus, the boy identifies with his father, not *only* because the father is warm and nurturant, but because the father can be the prime source of reward and punishment.

For psychoanalytic theorists, the process of identification is the primary way children internalize a code of values. Our conscience can be traced to the emotional ties we formed with our parents and other important persons in our early life.

Learning Sexual Roles

The child must learn a great many social roles. For males, society has defined the vocational role as primary and the father and husband role as secondary. The reverse is true for women. Boys are taught to achieve, and girls are raised to conform. Most societies foster achievement and self-reliance in boys while teaching obedience, nurturance, and responsibility as desired characteristics

THE MALE CHAUVINISTS OF OLD

The Greek philosophers viewed woman as an evil influence or deficient object. Pythagoras wrote: "There is a good principle which has created order, light, and man; and a bad principle which has created chaos, darkness, and woman." Plato thanked the gods he was free (neither slave nor woman), and Aristotle suggested we regard the female nature as afflicted with a kind of natural defectiveness.

Similar examples can be drawn from early Semitic tradition. "One group of Bedouins says that women were created from the sins of the satans, another that she was manufactured from the tail of a monkey. From the South Slavs we get other details. In this case God absentmindedly laid aside Adam's rib when He was performing the operation recorded in the Bible. A dog came along, snatched up the rib and ran off with it. God chased the thief but only succeeded in snatching off its tail. The best that could be done was to make a woman out of it." [Hays, 1964, p. 12]

Protest and Identity

The cry of "power to the people" first echoed in the 1800s in Russia when the children of nobility were arrested for protesting against the status quo. In the United States, the Oberlin Peace Society was formed by students in 1843. Protest marches were held at Princeton in 1859, and the strike against war by the National Student League was held in 1934. Modern student movements combine old elements into new protests.

The Student Search for Identity. From about 1960 to 1968 the war babies came of age, and the 18- to 24-year-old age group increased by 43 percent (Douglas, 1970). With five and a half million students in college, it takes only 2 percent of them, or about 100,000 young citizens, to give any revolutionary effort a sense of power.

The source of student unrest could be traced to the exceptional prolongation of adolescence in industrialized cultures (Berger, 1969). Adolescence is no longer a brief transitional stage between child and man. It is a segment of life that may last, psychologically, for as long as 15 years. In this artificial interim, it is not surprising that the young develop their own cultural style replete with goals, values, traditions, sources of motivation, and satisfactions, designed to compensate for this delayed maturity. For some students, the university has become a home territory that comfortably fills a decade of their life.

Kenneth Keniston (1967) noted that student dissenters fell along a continuum stretching between activists at one end and culturally alienated students at the other. The activists were in the middle of demonstrations protesting the injustice being done to others less fortunate than themselves. The activists worked within the American system to improve it as they felt it should be improved. The culturally alienated were strictly opposed to the "Establishment" or the "System" but were so pessimistic that they did not become directly involved. Dropping out, for them, was the only sensible option.

A psychoanalytic view of the relations between generations argues that the sons are attacking the authority of their fathers. Feuer (1969), for example, argues that, in their irrational rebellion, the sons exist apart and alienated from their fathers and all they stand for. Feuer contends that guilt over their rebellion leads the sons into self-defeating actions which drive them into self-destructive failure. In his view student protests are oriented symbolically to the destruction of the father and elimination of his authority.

Other theorists interpret the student protest movement in terms of children living out the *ideals* of their fathers (Flacks, 1967; Keniston, 1967). The sons are *like* their

fathers, only more so. If the fathers are liberal politically (but tend to preach more than they practice), the sons have become liberal or radical both as preachers and practitioners. This is hardly generational conflict. Young people, in this view, cannot be explained and understood simply as a generation in revolt. For most of them, this is not an effort to break free of the constricting, tradition-oriented, or obsolete values of parents. Keniston states:

Whereas the protesting student is likely to accept the basic political and social values of his parents, the alienated student almost always rejects his parents' values. In particular, he is likely to see his father as a man who has "sold out" to the pressures for success and status in American society; he is determined to avoid the fate that overtook his father. [1967, p. 113]

Watts, Lynch, and Whittaker (1969) differentiate between the family relationships of the activists and the alienated. Activists were raised by educated, upper-middle-class parents who were interested in national politics. Alienated youths showed a marked degree of estrangement from their families as compared to the activists. The data suggest that a basic determinant of whether youth will actively confront social ills or passively retreat into an alienated subculture is whether they perceive that they have a supportive parental background (Whittaker and Watts, 1971). Solomon and Fishman (1964) found with their sample of Washington peace demonstrators that 50 percent of the protestors said their parents approved of their activity. Similar family support was discovered by Miller's (1969) study of demonstrators arrested at the 1968 Democratic National Convention: 48 percent of the demonstrators indicated that both parents approved of their behavior, and 59 percent reported that at least one parent approved.

for girls. As Hartley (1959) so aptly put it, in our society boys come to understand that, "they should know what girls don't know—how to climb, how to make a fire, how to carry things; they should have more ability than girls; they need to know how to stay out of trouble; they need to know arithmetic and spelling more than girls do" (p. 460).

Learning to Be Male

Each child must achieve a set of beliefs about the match between his biological and psychological characteristics. The education in sex-role identity begins early in life as children are taught to masculinize and feminize their environment. Lions are seen as masculine, whereas housecats are treated as feminine.

To be male is to inhibit dependency and passivity and become suitably assertive, aggressive, and strong. Almost every culture on this planet promotes these values in the male (Kagan, 1969). Courage, inner direction, autonomy, technological skill, a considerable amount of toughness in mind and body are expected in males (Sexton, 1969, p. 15). Boys are disciplined to repress tender feelings. They may not cry, and they must not do anything that will label them "sissy." They must fight when they would rather run away or compete destructively when they might prefer to cooperate. A study of kindergarten children (Hartley, 1959) also showed that more distinctive sex-role behavior is demanded from boys than from girls at this same age. The problem of male identification is made even harder when the father is seldom around or is seen as a remote and punitive person.

THE RISKY MALE

A prevalent belief in our culture is that men should, and do, take greater risks than women. For the child, a man's role is defined to a considerable extent in terms of courage.

"A number of children (735 boys and 312 girls) between the ages of 6 and 16 participated in a decision-making game designed to assess their willingness to take risks. The results indicated a sex difference in risk-taking propensity which emerged between the ninth and eleventh year of age. The difference was in the direction of our cultural stereotype: boys were bolder than girls." [Slovic, 1966, p. 169]

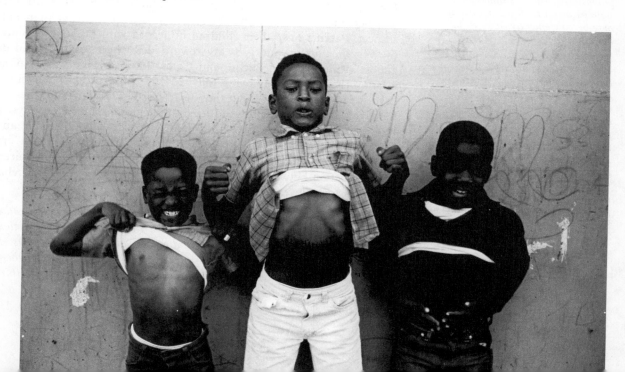

For Kagan (1969) there are two important six-year periods of sex-identity development—one before puberty when peers teach the boy what the important sex-role characteristics ought to be and one in adolescence when his sex-role identity either passes or fails the critical test of heterosexual adjustment. The heterosexual role dictated for the male by society is not an easy one to master as he grows older. Helen Hacker (1957) has listed the role prescription as (1) being patient, gentle, understanding—yet sturdy as an oak; (2) being a person whom a wife can rely on to make decisions but who leaves her free to make her own; (3) having a compulsion to succeed in gainful employment; and (4) being capable of evoking orgasm in his mate. This prescription may be filled effortlessly when we are young, but it becomes more difficult as the male grows older.

In this technological time in history, the male has the added burden of learning new skills, attitudes, and values or being declared outmoded and obsolete (Frankel, 1958). Today's male may feel that, whereas society allows his wife, as the mother of grown children, to rest in knowledge of labor completed, his own work can never be quite finished. "All through American society, the male's behavior shows that he actually is experiencing a change which affects his traditional roles as father, lover, and provider. This change may be summed up in a single word: *emasculation*" (Ruitenbeek, 1967).

Learning to Be Female

Like the male, the female child must learn acceptable sexual attitudes, beliefs, and behaviors. This training for femaleness begins earlier than most people suspect. Parents raise their children in accord with popular stereotypes from the very beginning, and girls are rewarded for being passive and dependent almost at once (Barry, Bacon, and Child, 1957). In one study, six-month-old infant girls were already being touched and spoken to by their mothers more than were infant boys. When they were thirteen months old, these girls were more reluctant than the boys to leave their mothers. When a physical barrier was placed between mother and child, the girls tended to cry and motion for help, whereas the boys made more active attempts to get around the barrier (Goldberg and Lewis, 1969). There is no way to measure precisely the connection between these sex differences and the mothers' behavior, but it is hard to believe that the two are not linked.

As children grow older, more explicit sex-role training is introduced. Boys are encouraged to take more of an interest in mathematics and science. Boys, not girls, are given chemistry sets and microscopes for Christmas. Moreover, all children quickly learn that mommy is proud to be a moron when it comes to mathematics and science, whereas daddy knows all about those things. When a young boy returns from school all excited over a biology class, he is almost certain to be encouraged to think of becoming a physician. A girl with similar

LIKE BROTHER, LIKE SISTER

"Several investigators . . . maintain that children in the same family tend to acquire each other's characteristics. They propose that a male will acquire feminine response tendencies from a sister and masculine response tendencies from a brother. Consequently, males with a sister are expected to display a more feminine behavior pattern than males with a brother. This proposition, which assumes that siblings adopt each other's behavior, may be conveniently labeled the imitation hypothesis.

"For example, Brim . . . concluded that boys with sisters are more feminine and less masculine than boys with brothers, particularly among the secondborns. Rosenberg and Sutton-Smith . . . studied game preferences of children of ages 9–12 and found that among boys with one sibling, boys with sisters displayed more feminine preferences than boys with brothers. . . . At all age levels, males with sisters seem more feminine than males with brothers."
[Leventhal, 1970, p. 452]

enthusiasm is told that she might want to consider nurse's training later so she can have "an interesting job to fall back upon in case." [Bern, 1970, p. 91]

Through the socialization process, we train females to model themselves after the ideal feminine image and to meet the expectations held for women as a group. According to Freeman (1970), this process leads to a female self-image that is characteristically "uncertain, anxious, nervous, hasty, careless, fearful, dull, childish, helpless, sorry, timid, clumsy, stupid, silly, and domestic." Freeman continues to state:

On the more positive side women felt they were understanding, tender, sympathetic, pure, generous, affectionate, loving, moral, kind, grateful and patient. This is not a very favorable self-image, but it does correspond fairly well to the myths about what women are like. The image has some "nice" qualities, but they are not the ones normally required for the kinds of achievement to which society gives its highest rewards. [p. 37]

To counteract the inevitable sex-role stereotyping, some modern-day parents are undertaking what is called nonsexist child rearing. The attempt is to treat each child as a total human being, without regard for the old stereotypes of what a boy or girl should be or do. Considering the massive reinforcement that children receive daily through school and the media, it is not surprising that the nonsexist experiments have so far produced traditionally masculine boys and feminine girls.

The Disorders of Childhood

The President's Joint Commission on the Mental Health of Children published a report entitled *Crisis in Mental Health: Challenge for the 1970s*. The report described the emotionally disturbed child in terms of arrested personality development that deprives him of accurate perception of the world about him, adequate impulse control, and appropriate interpersonal relationships. The Joint Commission calculated that approximately 6 percent of our children are psychotic. About 2 or 3 percent are severely disturbed, and an additional 8 to 10 percent of our young have emotional problems serious enough to be designated as neurosis. Many of the problems in this last category are manifested in one particular behavioral problem the child displays. These special symptoms are difficult to diagnose because the reaction may be short-lived.

Feeding Disturbances.   Feeding disorders first become clinical problems during the ages of two to three years old. Food and its consumption can become a battleground for the parent and child, and the scars of the conflict may last a lifetime.

Overeating. The obese child is effectively isolated from full participation in the activities of his peers. Rejected and ridiculed by others, he eases his distress by eating ravenously. He only gains more weight and further widens the interpersonal breech with his age mates. The happy, well-adjusted fat person can only be a myth in a society so obsessed with slenderness. The truth is that in study after study researchers have described overweight children as immature, dependent, maladjusted, fundamentally unhappy, timid, inhibited, fearful, and tense. These negative characteristics are often carefully hidden behind a placid, cheerful facade.

Because there is almost no evidence that serious weight difficulties result from constitutional predisposition (glandular difficulties), we must look to psychological interpretations of the problem. Psychogenic explanations of obesity run the gamut of human emotional complications. They include the overprotective mother who compensates for feeling unloved by lavishing attention on the child and the hostile parent who denies feelings of hostility by becoming oversolicitous. Behavioral theorists stress simply that the child may imitate the eating habits and life style of the parents or be selectively reinforced for hearty eating behavior.

Undereating. The single predictable outcome of failing to meet parental standards of food intake is an onslaught of parental bribing, threatening, and coaxing. The "starving" child can command an incredible amount of parental

time and energy, and, if the child wants to engage in a contest of wills, not eating is one of the very best ways to go about it.

Serious undereating (clinically labeled *anorexia nervosa* or nervous loss of appetite) may be an emotional variant of the loss of appetite every one of us experiences when unhappy, hurt, or frightened. But when semistarvation looms on the horizon, poor appetite becomes a serious problem. This most often appears during adolescence or early adulthood. In some cases, minimal food intake may be made more complicated by vomiting, vitamin deficiency, diarrhea, or anemia. Women seem more prone to this disorder than men.

Strange Appetites. When a child eats substances usually considered inedible (clay, plaster, charcoal, dirt, paint, and the like), the term *pica* is applied. Many strange objects find their way to the mouths of the very young, but when this kind of consumption becomes marked and seemingly intentional, it constitutes a physical and emotional problem. This problem is greater for boys than for girls, more frequent for prematurely born children, and more apparent among members of lower socioeconomic groups. Pica has most often been viewed as a response to poor nutritional conditions. But, it is difficult to disentangle cause and effect since inadequate diets are so often embedded in a context of disorganized family life.

Toilet-Training Disturbances. If toilet training has been ineffective by age three, *enuresis* (lack of bladder control) and *encopresis* (lack of bowel control) become clinical problems. Nocturnal or nighttime problems with elimination normally are greatest at about nine years of age and, shortly thereafter, show a significant decline. The rate of such disorders is remarkably high among children saddled with other emotional disorders.

Enuresis. This is a far more frequent problem for boys than girls, and seriously enuretic children may have a number of other infantile habits such as thumb sucking, teeth grinding, head banging, and rocking. The inability to control one's own bladder may have a psychological effect by convincing the child that his genital apparatus is broken or imperfectly formed. Dynamic causes suggested for enuresis may include regression following stress produced by separation from a parent or birth of a sibling. In some cases the child may be capitalizing on parental annoyance and wetting the bed as a means of expressing his resentment and irritation at their demands.

Treatment of enuresis along behavioral or conditioning lines began in the late 1930s when Mowrer had an enuretic child sleep on a special pad containing two pieces of bronze screening between the heavy cotton fabrics. If the child urinated during the night, the fluid penetrated to the metal conductor causing a door bell to ring, waking the child and reminding him to go to the bathroom. After several experiences with this conditioning procedure, the child learned to waken in response to less pressing degrees of bladder tension and go to the bathroom. Such devices are still in use and seem to be effective in as many as 70 percent of the cases.

Encopresis. Lack of bowel control and fecal soiling is, like enuresis, a problem primarily for male children. This problem is thought to be indicative of more serious emotional disturbance than enuresis since soiling usually occurs during the waking hours rather than in sleep. Some soilers alternate between defecating and prolonged withholding of feces—in some cases withholding can last

for weeks at a time. If the child learns that defecating is a disgusting, repulsive act, he may avoid defecating as long as he can, and when he inadvertently does lose control he may hide the evidence.

Toilet training is a perfect time and means for any child to display a growing thrust for independence. The child quickly learns that he and only he can truly control the time and place of his bowel movements, and this new found knowledge gives him the power to resist his parents.

Disorders of Sleep. For most children, resistance to bedtime is a now-and-then problem that never becomes very severe. When sleeping is regularly disturbed (excessive wakefulness, restless sleep, nightmares), it is indicative of disorder in the child's psychological adjustment. For analytically oriented theorists, problems of sleeping can be traced to a variety of circumstances. Sleep may represent an anxiety-provoking separation from parents or a time of aloneness in which guilt or fear may surface. Many children need a favorite toy, a pacifier, or a security blanket for sleep to be untroubled.

Behavioral theorists believe that sleeping is less a matter of psychic tranquillity than an issue in habit training. If a regular bedtime schedule is established and consistently enforced, they say, such problems need not arise in the first place.

Tics and Motor Habits. Among the first signs of developmental disturbances are distressing motor habits such as rhythmic head banging, repetitive rocking motions, hair pulling, or muscular twitches and tics. These symptoms may occur in as many as 15 percent of the total population of children. They most often appear just before going to sleep. With rhythmic movements the child seems to be soothing himself in the absence of other stimulation. We are not certain, however, that this pattern of behavior is truly predictive of disorder. More distressing are involuntary movements of small groups of muscles, which are called tics. Children who display tics are generally tense, anxious, and sensitive to criticism, but they rarely carry such responses to adult life.

The Joint Commission on the Mental Health of Children noted in their report that while more than ten million of those under age 25 could benefit from therapeutic help or guidance, fewer than 500,000 are being served by available mental health facilities. For years Americans have been criticized for responding with too little alarm to the serious mental health needs of its children. As a nation we do not seem to be able to respond to mental illness with the outpouring of empathy we accord to other handicaps and problems.

Adolescence

Prolonged adolescence is a luxury affordable only by advanced civilizations. In many parts of the world, adult responsibility comes exceptionally early. In Mexico, boys may be expected to assume an adult's burden by the age of 12 or 14, and in South Vietnam it has been common for boys in their earliest teens to fight alongside men.

Physical Adolescence

Today's children grow faster, reach puberty earlier, and attain their adult height earlier. Adolescents also grow taller than they did 60 or 70 years ago. A normal male in the United States will be as much as one inch taller and ten pounds heavier than his father, whereas the normal girl will be almost one inch taller, two pounds heavier, and begin menstrual periods about ten months earlier than her mother.

Maturing—Early and Late

In our society, the ideal for males is large physical size and strength. If these are achieved early in life, both peers and adults respond with increased respect and acceptance. The adolescent who appears physically immature, however, has a handicap. The resultant feelings of inadequacy, defensiveness, and insecurity produce what has been labeled "small-boy behavior."

The early or late onset of pubescence has a substantial impact on personal and social adjustment. Late maturers are viewed by adults as being less physically attractive, less moderate in their behavior, and more affected and tense. Similarly, peers view late maturers as much more restless, less reserved, and less grown-up. In social activities, late-maturing adolescents are not selected as leaders. In later life, these late maturers tend to continue to have less self-control, be less responsible, and be more inclined to turn to others for help (Jones, 1957).

Time of maturation does not have quite the same effect on girls. Late physical maturation is an asset for girls, whereas early maturation appears to be a liability (Jones, 1949). The reason is again cultural. The early-maturing girl may tend to acquire a stocky, muscular physique, whereas the late maturer may be slim and therefore more in keeping with the feminine ideal of our society. Moreover, the early-maturing girl is not only out of step with other girls of her age but also substantially different in physical status from the males of her age. In general, boys lag about two years behind girls in puberty. With later adolescence, these physical differences become less marked and so interfere less with social development.

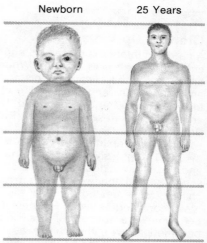

Newborn   25 Years

Proportions of the body change markedly from birth to maturity (adapted from Jackson, 1929).

Finding Jesus

In recent times, we have witnessed the phenomenon of a mind-boggling variety of religious forms among the young, including spiritualism, Zen Buddhism, pentecostalism, and drug-induced religious experiences (Cooper, 1971; Greeley, 1971; Walsh, 1971). The "Jesus People" are among the newly converted.

The tenets of belief among the Jesus People are quite direct. The Bible is taken as being literally true, and miracles can really happen (*Time*, 1971). Jesus is a martyr to the cause of peace and brotherhood, a fellow rebel, and a living God with whom they can and must establish an intense personal relationship. Moreover, the Ten Commandments are strictly adhered to.

For better or worse, Jesus has become a heavy trip for some of the young, white, middle-class, suburbanites. Yet the Jesus bag is only one more evidence, to parents, of the faddishness of the young. The public concern about the "Children of God" (one of the Jesus groups) caused some to ask whether young people were being "hypnotized," "brainwashed," or "robotized" by their peers or religious leaders (Ward, 1971). And for some parents, this is the only explanation that makes sense. However, Adams and Fox (1972) feel the Jesus trip is tailor-made for adolescents who are struggling with achieving their own identities. The commitment to Jesus preserves childhood morality "with its absolutistic definitions of right and wrong," and provides an ideology that, because it is based on personal experience "is unchallengeable and thereby not available for analysis." The Jesus trip also provides adolescents with approval and affirmation by peers. Adams and Fox conclude that the Jesus trip is a step backward from maturity. Like drugs, it is used as a way of avoiding the anxieties that are a natural part of the identity crisis. With a display of religious fervor, young converts try to substitute a packaged, prearranged identity as a shortcut to the hard labor of evolving one distinctly their own.

As Adams and Fox (1972) indicate:

In normal development the new dimensions of identity are added to the previously established identity, modifying it to some degree; some parts of one's previous identity will be discarded, submerged or eradicated by new behavior. Instead of progressing toward adult ethics, the Jesus person clutches tenaciously to childhood morality, with its simplistic black-and-white, right-and-wrong judgments. Rather than developing behavior oriented towards reality, he flies into ideational, ideological abstractions to numb his awareness of his newly arisen needs. [p. 53]

Growing Up Violent

A newborn infant expresses his aggressive feelings in an entirely uncontrolled manner. Whenever he is the least bit frustrated, he cries, flails his arms, and strikes out at anything within range. When the child gets old enough to venture into the outside world, he will learn a pattern and style of aggressive behavior. Patterson, Littman, and Bricker (1967) made continuous observations of four-year-old children at nursery school. They recorded a total of 2,583 aggressive acts and the consequences. The findings showed that the more structured the nursery-school setting, the fewer the aggressive responses. When children were treated permissively, they were apt to behave more aggressively. Further, if a child's aggressive behavior were successful (his victim gave up a toy or became passive), the child was likely to increase his aggressiveness. If the behavior were unsuccessful or met counteraggression, the child was less likely to behave aggressively in the future. Aggression must pay since the child who was highly aggressive and assertive at the beginning of the nursery school sessions continued to be aggressive over a period of several months.

The world of the nursery school, like most settings, contains some very active, aggressive people and some relatively inactive people who initiate little aggression and do not encounter much aggression from others. The problem in socialization is not to teach a child never to aggress but to teach him when aggression is appropriate or inappropriate. The first mechanism by which this learning occurs is reinforcement. When a particular behavior is rewarded, an individual is more likely to repeat that behavior in the future. When it is punished, he is less likely to repeat it. The child is punished when he punches his brother, throws stones at the girl next door, or bites his mother, and he learns not to do these things. He is rewarded when he restrains himself despite frustrations, and he learns this also. The complication is that not all learning about aggression is controlled by human reinforcement. Children watch television, and television contains a great deal of aggression and violence that no doubt has an impact on their behavior.

The Psychological Tasks of Adolescence

Developmental tasks are the challenges that individuals face at different periods in their lives. The small child must master the complexities of learning to walk and talk. Later, the child learns important skills such as playing games and reading. Ten tasks are particularly significant for the adolescent. These are: (1) achieving more mature relations with age mates of both sexes; (2) achieving a masculine or feminine social role; (3) accepting one's physique and using one's body effectively; (4) achieving emotional independence from parents and other adults; (5) achieving assurance of economic independence; (6) selecting and preparing for an occupation; (7) preparing for marriage and family life; (8) developing intellectual skills and concepts necessary for civic competence; (9) achieving socially responsible behavior; and (10) acquiring a set of values as a guide to behavior (Havighurst, 1953).

Scattered through the days of youth are episodes of deep unhappiness and discouragement. Few adolescents have not thought at one time or another that life was simply too difficult to bear much longer. Meissner (1966), for example, reported that adolescent boys indicated on a questionnaire that they experienced a marked increase in depression, sadness, dissatisfaction with life. They had feelings of being misunderstood and feelings of loneliness as they grew older. More than 50 percent were worried about their studies. In general, boys are more severely distressed by the demands of maturity than are girls because of the social concept of maleness.

As every adolescent learns, becoming an adult does not involve a sudden and highly visible change in status. For most people, the change to adulthood is so gradual that it is usually apparent only after it has taken place. Entrance into adulthood does not signal the end of change, however, since there is no period in life that is free of developmental tasks.

Styles of Child Rearing

The styles of child rearing that once worked well are no longer prevalent. As one observer wrote:

> *To begin with, families used to be bigger—not in terms of more children so much as more adults—grandparents, uncles, aunts, cousins. Those relatives who didn't live with you lived nearby. You often went to their houses. They came as often to yours, and stayed for dinner. You knew them all—the old folks, the middle-aged, the older cousins. And they knew you. This had its good side and its bad side . . . they all minded your business throughout the years. They wanted to know where you had been, where you were going, and why. If they didn't like your answers, they said so (particularly if you had told them the truth). Not just your relatives minded your business. Everybody in the neighborhood did. Your parents would know what you had done before you got back home. People on the street would tell you to button your jacket, and ask why you weren't in church last Sunday.* [Bronfenbrenner, 1967]

Modern suburbia has reduced the extended family to a nuclear one with only two adults. The functioning neighborhood—where it has not decayed into an urban or rural slum—has withered to a small circle of friends, most of them accessible only by car or telephone. As we have become a different kind of society, our methods of child rearing have also changed. We can look at a few of them here.

Permissive Child Rearing

The permissive parent tries to react in a nonpunitive, affirmative manner toward the child's impulses, desires, and actions. The parent may consult with the child about policy decisions, give explanations for family rules, and make few demands for household responsibility. The parent is presented as a resource for the child to use as he wishes, not as an ideal for the child to imitate or as someone responsible for shaping behavior. The child is allowed to regulate his own activities as much as possible and exercise self-control in response to reason and not overt power.

HOW TO BE A
SUCCESSFUL
MOTHER
If you are looking for formulas for the upbringing of an achievement-oriented son, try mixing together one fairly bright little boy, a father who is totally respected, and a mother who is devoted, intelligent, and sensitive. According to Robert Frager (1972), this is how both Japanese and Jewish families instill high levels of ambition in young boys of average intelligence. Mothers are devoted, loving, and nurturing. They cajole rather than criticize and nag constantly but good naturedly. Their children are welcomed into the adult scene, but they are accepted as children. Fathers are looked up to by everyone in the family, but they leave the job of child rearing to their competent, strong wives.

Both Japanese and Jewish mothers make their children aware of the great debt they owe to their parents. The children, particularly the boys, feel guilty if they make their mothers suffer by misbehavior or by failing to live up to expectations of success.

THE MEDIEVAL
CHILD
*"The medieval child usually learned
his letters with the local priest or a
monk from a nearby monastery, but
the age at which he started his
primary education would be dictated
by his personal circumstances. Often,
a boy would not start to learn Latin,
without which all but the most basic
learning was impossible, until he
was in his teens, sometimes even 20
or older, simply because his
economic situation prevented it. Old
men, young men, adolescents, and
children could all be found sitting in
the same classroom, learning the
same lessons. . . . In the early
sixteenth century, groups of students
ranging in age from the early
twenties to a mere ten would wander
in search of learning from France to
Germany and back again. They lived
like hippies and wandered like
gypsies, begging, stealing, fighting,
yet they were always hungry for
books."* [Plumb, 1972, p. 83]

THE CHANGING
WORLD OF
CHILDHOOD
*"By 1600 a new attitude was
growing, based on the concepts that
childhood was innocent and that it
was the duty of adults to preserve
this innocence. . . . Increasingly, the
child became a special creature with
a different nature and different
needs, which required separation and
protection from the adult world. By
1700 . . . the child possessed his own
literature, books carefully pruned of
adult sophistication or broad humor,
but also especially written for the
young mind. The period between
seven and adolescence was becoming
a world of its own."* [Plumb, 1972,
p. 83]

Authoritarian Child Rearing

The authoritarian parent deliberately attempts to shape, control, and evaluate the behavior and attitudes of the child according to an absolute standard of conduct. These parents value obedience as a virtue and use punitive measures to curb rebellion in the child. The child is kept in his place and taught respect for work. Order and traditional structure are valued, and there is little verbal give and take. "Do it because I told you to" is sufficient reason for obedience.

Democratic Child Rearing

The democratic parent tries to lead the child in a rational manner, encouraging verbal give and take. The reasoning behind policies is shared with the child, and his objections are discussed when he refuses to conform. Firm control may be exercised at points of parent-child divergence, but the child is not imprisoned in such restrictions. The child's individual interests and special ways are recognized, but standards are still set for conduct.

Parenthood

The fate of the child depends upon the psychological environment into which he is born. The emotional involvement he has with his parents, whether he receives affection and acceptance, is a crucial factor. Each infant also needs to feel his world is safe and satisfying if he is to develop what Erikson calls *basic trust.* Without this basic trust, the infant begins to defend himself against a threatening, depriving world where he may never feel comfortable. Obviously, the nature of the child's environment depends on what kind of parents he has, whether he is part of a one-parent or two-parent family, and which social class he is born into.

Along with a great many other critics of the modern scene, Robert Hawkins (1972) notes that the number of children with behavior problems has become so large that only a required parent-training program in our public schools can hope to reverse the trend. He is convinced that the home has failed to prepare the child for school. According to Hawkins, the child "then gets caught in vicious circles that lead to underachievement, disruptiveness, truancy, destructive acts, social isolation, inability to be pleased with his own work, anxiety, excessive fantasy, allegiance with other outcasts, and innumerable other problems" (p. 30).

Hawkins recommends a compulsory parent-training course that would reach virtually all potential parents in the schools. In his proposal students would be given practical child-rearing experience in a day-care center affiliated with his high school. This nursery school would serve as a laboratory in which every student would work with young children. The students would learn

HUMANISTIC CHILD
REARING
*Allan De Witt Button (1969), in his
book* The Authentic Child, *makes a
statement about love and freedom
for children: "Existentialism
proclaims freedom, unfettered, often
frightening freedom, and it is only in
freedom that we can attain full
humanity" (p. 10). When freedom to
develop is provided children, they
grow into healthy, secure adults.
There is no humanistic prescription
for child rearing since existentialism
is a state of mind. Raising an
authentic child, rather, is a way of
life that determines what happens in
every exchange between mother
and child.*

*The humanistic approach to
children begins with the assumption
that all human beings are born
authentic and become corrupt or
inauthentic in the give and take of
parent-child relationships. If parents
love the child, listen to him, respect
his human dignity, commiserate with
him, and guide him, he will be free
to be himself—free to choose rather
than simply react to threat and
pressure.*

to identify behavior accurately, and they might be required to develop a
personal relationship with a child. Students might also learn the use of punishment, discrimination training, prompting, and shaping (Hawkins, 1972).

Mothering in Monkeys

Experimental work with motherhood in monkeys has exposed some important
dimensions of mothering. Harry and Margaret Harlow (Harlow, 1958; Harlow,
1959; Harlow and Harlow, 1961; Harlow and Harlow, 1962; Harlow and
Harlow, 1965) have helped us to put the mother-child relationship into a
new perspective. Although scientists have long suspected that pathological
patterns of behavior in infancy might be traced to the nature of the mother-
child relationship, ethical and humane considerations made it impossible to
perform human experiments to shed light on the problem. The Harlows did
the next best thing. They raised rhesus monkeys in various environments.
Some were provided with inadequate mothers, and some were completely

deprived of mothers. Some monkeys were kept with siblings according to experimental design, and some had surrogate mothers made of terrycloth and wire.

The original terrycloth mother surrogate used by Harlow was a relatively complicated apparatus that had a number of drawbacks. The worst problem was that the infant monkeys soiled the cloth bodies so badly that a considerable laundry bill mounted up. This problem was solved by constructing simplified surrogates (heated or unheated), which consisted of a rod pushed through a cloth-covered cylinder. The infant monkeys clearly preferred the warm "mother," but this preference changed as they grew older. Harlow then devised a hollowed-out board covered by a cotton athletic sock. This "mother" managed to provide security for young monkeys.

The Harlows conducted a series of experiments which furnished guidelines to the study of human infants. When male and female rhesus monkeys were raised in total isolation for the first two years of life, they developed very slowly, were unable to interact effectively with other monkeys, could not defend themselves, and displayed little interest in sex in later years. *The greater the deprivation by isolation, the greater the ultimate social damage.* When monkeys were raised in cages where they could see, hear, and smell—but not touch—others of their species, they too developed abnormal patterns of behavior (self-injury, inability to mate, fixed staring into space, and rocking motions).

The mother surrogates used in these experiments were nearly perfect monkey mothers. That is, they were warm, soft, always supplied milk, never hurt or scolded the infant, and were on call day and night. Yet, these inanimate parents could not respond to their young, and this seemed to be the crucial difference in producing pathology or normality. When the children of these wire-and-cloth mothers had children of their own, they proved to be terrible mothers. They ignored, rejected, or beat their children.

It has been noted again and again that six or more months of total social isolation following birth produces profound and apparently permanent social deficits in rhesus monkeys. These monkeys fail to develop appropriate play, aggressive, sexual, and maternal behaviors. Instead, they display abnormalities such as self-clasping, huddling, and rocking behaviors. In the past, attempts to rehabilitate these isolated subjects were not successful. But, successful rehabilitation could be done. After being removed from isolation, the abnormal monkeys were permitted to interact with socially normal monkeys three months younger than themselves. Within a few weeks disturbance behaviors decreased substantially and were replaced by primitive, socially directed activity. After six months of such exposure, the isolate subjects could not easily be distinguished from the other monkeys.

In discussing human motherhood, of course we must remember that human infants are not nearly as independent or capable of fending for themselves as are young monkeys.

Human Motherhood

Although the institution of motherhood is under no serious threat right now, not every observer is entranced by the scene. Jeanne Binstock (1972), for example, looks at motherhood in the following terms:

> Mothers have traditionally been the world's largest occupational group. Half the population was assigned to a single task—producing people, with all the resulting obligations of child care. The huge allocation of human resources was absolutely necessary to maintain an adequate adult population in the face of war and disease, and it was a logical assignment of roles. After all, what else could any group of people do if they were almost always pregnant, . . . in danger of dying every 18 months, or needed to be constantly available for feeding children. The job title was Mother, and, just as in other occupational groups, the job was invested with an occupational mystique, a jargon, a particular life style, and some specialized technical skills. [p. 99]

Binstock is convinced that 20 years from now the act of giving birth will be no more than an occupational specialty. This vision is shared by Peck (1972) who argues that women have been coerced into the mother role, which should be only one of several options for women. Peck is convinced our society sets "baby traps" for women.

> Within our culture, from earliest baby-girlhood, you learn that you should want children. And you learn from many teachers. . . . That cuddly doll is the first bait in the baby trap. . . . There are the ads: one glorious Clairol mother, many gleaming children; mother in mink cavorting through snow with children; mother skillfully applying band-aid to her six-year-old's knee; mother and daughter doing laundry together with Ivory Snow. . . . It's the trap of the glossy situation TV series, where the doll-like mother manages home and family with freedom and expertise. It's the trap of the magazines, with their incessant articles on the "motherhood" theme. [pp. 19–20]

Even though women are increasingly free to choose alternatives to motherhood, childbearing is still socially defined as the "normal," if not the primary, function of women. And, there are a great many reasons presented to the female to encourage her to have children. A childless woman may wish to be like her friends or relatives who already have children, or she may feel isolated from friends who have become mothers. She may desire a child in order to be able to participate in activities and conversations with other mothers. Having a child may confirm her feminine identity and demonstrate her adequacy as a woman (Flapan, 1969).

A woman who feels that her mother was inadequate and unfulfilled in motherhood may look forward to childrearing as a means of demonstrating her own ability to be a good mother. She may be determined to create a more satisfying family life than the one she experienced as a child.

We also need to mention the positive reasons for being a mother—love,

MOTHERHOOD, WHO NEEDS IT?
Betty Rollin (1970) quotes the psychiatrist Dr. Richard Rabkin who says: "Women don't need to be mothers any more than they need spaghetti. But if you're in a world where everyone is eating spaghetti, thinking they need it and want it, you will think so too.

"And, over the centuries the myth of 'maternal instinct' was buttressed by laws which made her a chattel and denied her education.

"So if the music is lousy, how come everyone's dancing? Because the motherhood minuet is taught free from birth, and whether or not she has rhythm or likes the music, every woman is expected to do it." [p. 17]

affection, tenderness, the need to nurture others, the chance to guide and teach another human being, or simply the creative achievement of having a child. No evidence suggests that motherhood is an "instinctive" or necessary role for all women, and, of course, many people do have children for the wrong reasons and consequently rear them badly.

The Father

In some societies it is normal for a father to be absent or rarely present, and this may be a norm in some of the . . . suburbs of modern cities. Nevertheless, Western cultures usually treat father-absent families as abnormal—a product of social disorganization, implying that they are less than ideal environments for maturing children. [Biller, 1970, p. 407]

You would never guess the father was a vital force in child development if you judged by the psychological literature. In years past the father was, as a matter of course, a guide and model for his son and an ideal image for the daughter. As Ruitenbeek (1967) asks: "Whatever happened to father's chair? The father's chair was a majestic symbol of his position as head of the family. And, knowing who and what he was gave the other members of the family circle a more stable sense of their own identity."

The Missing Father

More than one-tenth of the children in the United States live in households where no father is present, and the incidence of fatherless families is especially high among the lower class (Miller, 1958). The sociologist Talcott Parsons (1947) suggested that, in our culture, the delinquent and antisocial behavior of some boys later in life may be related to the difficulty the boy has had in establishing his identity as a man. The male child surrounded only by feminine influences may protest this state of mother domination by becoming a tough caricature of the male—a sexually experienced, drug-taking fighter. This and other forms of social protest may be an unconscious reaction to a fatherless home and a school system dominated by women.

The father need not be physically absent from the family setting to be an ineffective model for his children. The passive, easily-dominated, timid, unsuccessful, and uninterested father can be invisible in the home, if not actually absent from it. Father absence during the early years may take its toll in a variety of unsuspected ways. Sears, Pintler, and Sears (1946) found that boys from father-absent homes were indistinguishable from girls in aggressiveness and in how they played with dolls. In other words, sex-typing seemed delayed. In such family settings, the mother is forced to assume both the father and the mother role, and the lessons the children will learn from her are not tempered by any masculine influence.

THE ABSENT FATHER AND THE PEACE CORPS
Peace Corps volunteers who completed the full two-year tour of duty were compared with those who left their assignments early. The comparison dimension was "father absence" for at least five years before the volunteers' fifteenth birthday. The results were startling—those who failed as volunteers and came home early were significantly more often reared in "father-absent" homes. What do these findings reflect? Less flexibility in unusual situations? Less ability to tolerate stress? Greater dependence on others? We have yet to find the answer.

FATHER ABSENCE
AND CONSCIENCE
DEVELOPMENT
*"A father-absent and a
father-present group—controlled for
sex, IQ, and social class—were
compared concerning seven moral
attributes and overt aggression. All
subjects were seventh-grade white
children. . . . Father-absent boys
obtained lower scores for all the
moral indexes—significantly lower
for internal moral judgment,
maximum guilt following
transgressions, acceptance of blame,
moral values, and rule conformity.
They were also rated by teachers as
significantly more aggressive than
father-present boys. . . . Evidence is
presented that . . . some but not all
of the effects of father absence are
attributable to the lack of a parental
model. Evidence is also presented
which suggests that the effects of
father absence on boys may be
partly mediated by the resulting
changes in the mother's child-rearing
practices."* [Hoffman, 1971, p. 400]

A wealth of evidence points to the importance of the father-son relationship in masculine development. Stolz et al. (1954) reported that four-
to eight-year-old boys, who had been separated from their fathers for the
first two years of their lives, were generally regarded by their fathers as "sissies."
The study also revealed that these boys were less aggressive and independent
in their peer relations than boys who had not been separated from their fathers.
In a study done in Norway, Lynn and Sawrey (1959) studied eight- and
nine-year-old children whose fathers were sailors and therefore absent at least
nine months a year. Interviews with mothers indicated that the father-absent
boys (compared with father-present boys) showed more compensatory masculinity. In other words, these boys behaved in an exaggeratedly masculine
manner.

There have also been several investigations which reveal that the father-absent child often suffers from intellectual deficits (Bronfenbrenner, 1967;
Deutsch and Brown, 1964). In addition, a number of studies suggest that
father-absent boys have more difficulty forming peer relationships than do
father-present boys (Mitchell and Wilson, 1967).

DAGWOOD THE
AMERICAN FATHER?
Blondie *was one of the most
popular, if not the most popular,
American comic strip until the rise
of* Peanuts *in recent years. Dagwood
Bumstead, as many commentators
have pointed out, is an infantile,
weak, greedy, and incompetent
figure.*
*"Dagwood is kind, dutiful,
diligent, well-meaning within his
limits; but he has so completely
given up any claim to authority that
the family would constantly risk
disintegration and disaster, if it were
not for Blondie. . . . Food . . . (the
Dagwood Sandwich) . . . seems to be
his only real source of gratification,
which suggests that he is a case of
arrested development. . . . Dagwood
. . . is browbeaten by a domineering
and assertive wife, is abused by his
boss, and is generally a failure in
everything he tries, although his
intentions are often generous and he
means well."* [Berger, 1973]

Father and Daughter

Many theorists believe the father plays an important part in the development of his daughter's sex role. Though young fatherless girls do not show masculine behavior, it is in part through experiences with her father that the daughter acquires the social skills and confidence necessary to interact appropriately with members of the opposite sex. "If the absence of a father is related specifically to lack of the opportunity to develop emotional security and skills in interacting with males, the deficiency probably would not become apparent in girls until the age of puberty, when there is increased interaction between the sexes" (Hetherington, 1973, p. 49).

A series of studies done by Hetherington (1972; 1973) suggest that the effects of father absence on daughters appear during adolescence and are manifested mainly as an inability to interact appropriately with males. Several groups of girls were tested in one study. The first group came from intact families with both parents living in the home. The second group came from families where the father was absent due to divorce. The third group came from families where the father was absent due to death. None of the father-absent families had any males living in the home after the separation from the father occurred. Hetherington found that adolescent girls who had grown up without fathers repeatedly displayed inappropriate patterns of behavior in relating to males. "Girls whose fathers had died exhibited severe sexual anxiety, shyness, and discomfort around males. Girls whose fathers were absent because of divorce exhibited tension and inappropriately assertive, seductive, or sometimes promiscuous behavior with male peers and adults. Yet neither group had difficulty relating to female peers" (1973, p. 49).

Interestingly, both groups of father-absent girls felt insecure and apprehensive around male peers and adults, but they showed their insecurity in different ways. Girls whose parents were divorced reported more heterosexual activity than any other group. They dated earlier and more frequently than other girls and were more likely to have had sexual intercourse. In contrast, girls whose fathers had died reported late starts on dating and seemed to be sexually inhibited (Hetherington, 1973).

We can see that death, divorce, or one-parent absence are critical features of the family structure of many of our citizens. Often, children who least need these additional burdens are the very ones who are saddled with them. Over six million children today are growing up in fatherless homes. We must be careful to note that temporary father absence cannot be equated with continuing father absence, nor can planned and socially approved absence be equated with socially disapproved absence. Studies consistently report differences between children whose fathers are dead and children whose parents are divorced or separated. The adverse effects of the father's absence are more marked in children whose fathers are dead. Few studies, however, have compared the effects of tense, conflict-ridden two-parent homes with harmonious, well-organized one-parent homes. A careful reading of the literature on fatherless homes leaves many questions unanswered. Few studies have been replicated by other researchers, and this fact alone should make us suspicious of statements about the role of the father in producing serious pathology in children.

Summary

1. The socialization of children—the technique by which we teach young people to accept society's values and roles—is accomplished by (1) reinforcing or punishing the child; (2) the child's *imitation* of others; and (3) the child's *identification* with others.

2. Consciously and unconsciously, children imitate people whom they admire. Imitation may take the form of *copying behavior* or *matched-dependent behavior*—that is, adapting general behaviors of the model to his own particular style.

3. Identification is the process of becoming like someone else. It may involve direct imitation of that person's mannerisms, or it may be a more general alteration of character. Imitation involves superficial behaviors, whereas identification leads to deeper changes in the person.

4. Identification may occur for a number of reasons: (1) to give the child a feeling of power (*defensive identification*); (2) to allow the child to be like a hostile or punishing parent (*aggressor identification*); or (3) as a result of an affectionate bond between parent and child (*developmental identification*).

5. According to psychoanalytic theories, identification with one's parents, and consequently with the parental values, is the primary way children internalize society's standards, making the standards part of the conscience.

6. When children learn the psychological characteristics associated with their physical sex, they are said to have acquired their *sex-role identity*. In most societies, the sex role of males includes achievement in a vocation, self-reliance, and aggressiveness. For females the role is one of obedience, dependence, and motherhood.

7. In families where the father is absent a great deal of the time, it is difficult for boys to find a model for masculine behaviors. In addition, the growing demands on men in their vocations and significant changes in the traditional home structures make it increasingly difficult for men to maintain their sex-role identity.

8. In addition to modeling effects, sex roles are learned when children are reinforced for behavior appropriate to their sex and reprimanded for acting like the opposite sex. As children grow older,

sex-role training becomes even more explicit, particularly in terms of what subjects and careers it is appropriate for each sex to pursue.

9. Some parents have tried nonsexist child rearing, where children are neither rewarded for appropriate behavior nor punished for inappropriate behavior. Nonsexist child rearing is often thwarted by the larger society, which prefers to socialize its children into roles already designed for them.

10. If a child's physical development is delayed, he may come to have feelings of inadequacy, defensiveness, and insecurity. These self-impressions, coupled with the way peers and adults react to late maturers, may cause these individuals to be less responsible, less dominant, and more dependent on others later in life.

11. There are several styles of child rearing, each based on a different philosophy. The permissive parent allows the child a great deal of latitude in regulating his own activities, rarely punishes the child, and makes few demands on him for proper behavior. The parent is viewed more as a friend rather than someone responsible for shaping the child's behavior.

12. By contrast, authoritarian parents deliberately shape the child's behavior, make obedience a virtue in itself, and punish the child when he misbehaves. The democratic parent deals with the child in a rational manner but exercises control if necessary to shape the child's conduct.

13. According to humanists, it is important to treat the child as a person—which means loving him, listening to him, respecting his dignity, and guiding him.

14. The child's relationship with his parents can make a great difference in his identity and in how he views the world as he grows up. According to Erik Erikson, the child must develop *basic trust* from his home life, or he will always view the world as a threat.

15. Many pathological patterns of behavior in infancy have been attributed to difficulties in the parent-child relationship. Symptomatic problems such as obesity, undereating, toilet-training problems, and nervous tics are often explained as the result of unconsciously hostile parents, overprotective mothers, the child's need to show independence or gain security, or poor habit-training by the parents.

16. Harlow's experiments with monkeys demonstrated that, if infants are reared without mothers for over six months, they develop slowly and have difficulty interacting with peers. They also become very poor mothers themselves.

17. Although human motherhood is still defined as the norm, there is no instinct for motherhood in women. Many women, in fact, have children for the wrong reasons, and this is often reflected in the child's development.

18. Boys who grow up without fathers may have difficulty achieving a masculine identity. The resulting behaviors may be less aggressive and independent, or the boys may compensate by becoming tough guys, out to prove that maternal domination had no effect on their masculinity.

19. For the daughter, the father's absence may lead to difficulties in acquiring the social skills and confidence necessary for interacting with the opposite sex. Such girls may become inappropriately assertive or extremely shy toward men.

20. The child begins life by displaying his aggression any way he wants, but he soon learns that there are acceptable patterns for aggressive behavior. Through proper reinforcement, the child can be taught when aggression is appropriate and when it is not.

21. Student dissent may be generated by the fact that today's youth have a prolonged adolescence before they enter the adult world. In this period, they try to develop a cultural style that gives them a sense of identity distinctly different from either childhood or adulthood.

22. Research on student protestors indicates that activists are generally not people rebelling against their families but actually share many political beliefs with their parents and believe in working through the system to achieve them. Those who do not actively protest but merely drop out when disaffected with society are the ones most in conflict with parental values.

PSYCHOLOGICAL ISSUE

Morality

What constitutes personal or political morality? As a result of the confrontations and destruction of property that attended the student demonstrations of the 1960s, many administrators, politicians, and parents claim that the younger generation is morally bankrupt. Protestors have countered by saying that it is their elders who lack a sense of moral justice. Is it just a matter of opinion, or can we scientifically investigate what morality really is?

Parents try their best to get their children to take over some reasonable facsimile of parental standards of conduct so the children will act according to social rules even when they are not being watched by the parents. If this attempt succeeds, it is called *morality*. Still, few of us can agree exactly what morality is or what it ought to be—even though we have been preoccupied with this problem since the beginnings of recorded history.

Moral Trust

In recent times, there has apparently been a loss of faith in how moral or trustworthy other people are. But as Hochreich and Rotter (1970) observe: "It has become a cliché to say that college students today are less trustful of the establishment, their elders, our social institutions, etc., than at any time in the past. It is also a cliché among the educated to point out that complaints of this type have been made since Socrates' time and to imply that protest and distrust may take different forms but are nevertheless constant characteristics of youth" (p. 299).

Cliché or not, there seems to be clear support for the notion that our society's efforts at moral training have produced disenchantment among the young adults who will one day determine the future direction of our culture. Wrightsman and Baker (1969) tested incoming freshman college students on items such as trust. Defining trust as "the extent to which people are seen as moral, honest or reliable," they found a decrease in trust in two general categories: (1) items having to do with the establishment (national and international politics, the judiciary, the mass media), and (2) items dealing with our society (the hypocrisy, self-seeking, and competitive character of people in general).

To understand how this could happen, we need to look at how children learn morality and learn to become "moral" adults. Psychological studies of morality may reasonably be said to have begun with, or been

Changing Concepts of Morality.   An analysis by Zube (1972) of selected issues of the *Ladies Home Journal* from 1948 to 1969 reveals shifts in value orientations—most notably from future to present and from doing to being. She noted several trends: (1) morality as a rather permanent inflexible set of standards becomes a more fluid concept which each defines for himself; (2) psychological explanation for understanding behaviors becomes used increasingly to justify behaviors; and (3) the importance of mental health for the good of family and society gives way to concern with psychological adjustments to meet the needs of the individual.

stimulated by, Piaget's notions of stages in moral development.

Piaget   Piaget (1948) proposed the presence of two stages: moral realism and autonomous morality. In the stage of *moral realism,* the child accepts rules as given from authority. In the stage of *autonomous morality* (moral independence), the individual modifies rules to fit the needs of the situation. Piaget observed, for example, that when young children (aged three years) play marbles together, they do so with no rules for cooperative play. They don't really play "together." From ages three to five each child is *egocentric* and considers his own point of view the only possible one. He is unable to put himself in someone else's place because he is not fully aware the other person has a point of view. By the age of seven or eight, *incipient cooperation* emerges, and there is some concern about rules although they are still rather vague. Then, around age eleven or twelve, there is a period of *codification of rules.* Every detail of the game is fixed and agreed upon in advance.

To the three-year-old, rules are received almost without thought. During the next few years, rules are held sacred and untouchable. Four- and five-year-olds see rules as coming from adults and lasting forever. During the ages from ten to eleven years old, a rule is a law based on mutual consent. At this age, rules are modifiable.

Between the stage of moral realism and the stage of moral independence, feelings about the seriousness of crime also change. Take clumsiness and lying, for example. The young of any species are unusually clumsy, and the child attaches meaning to adults' reactions to his constant breaking and spilling. Children are concerned about accidentally destroying the world around them (and the anger it produces in adults), and, when very young, they learn that intentions make very little difference in the seriousness of the crime committed. It is the amount of damage that counts. The worse the mess, the more guilty you should feel. When they get older, they discover that an intentional act of destruction is much more serious (even if smaller) than an accidental big catastrophe.

The same is true for telling a lie. Among the very young, the intention to deceive another person is less important than how big the lie is. Older children learn it is not how far-fetched their story is but the motives and intentions involved that count. On this progression from moral realism to moral independence, we learn a great deal about the kinds of punishment that fit each crime.

Kohlberg   Stimulated by Piaget's work, Kohlberg (1963; 1968) has defined the following stages of moral reasoning and levels of moral development.

Level I.   Premoral
  Stage 1.   Punishment and obedience orientation
  Stage 2.   Naive instrumental hedonism
Level II.   Morality of conventional role conformity
  Stage 3.   "Good-boy" morality of maintaining good relations, approval of others
  Stage 4.   Authority-maintaining morality
Level III.   Morality of self-accepted moral principles
  Stage 5.   Morality of contract, of individual rights, and of democratically accepted law
  Stage 6.   Morality of individual principles of conscience

To test the relationship between age and progress through the different levels, Kohlberg uses a series

Male and Female Morality. Teachers tend to regard girls as being more moral than boys. But Krebs (1968) has found that, when moral behavior is assessed by comparing boys and girls on moral judgment and the ability to resist temptations to cheat, girls are *not* more moral than boys. Krebs suggests, simply, that girls may just be sneakier than boys!

of stories that contain classic moral dilemmas. For example:

In Europe, a woman was near death from a special kind of cancer. There was one drug that the doctors thought might save her. It was a form of radium that a druggist in the same town had recently discovered. The drug was expensive to make, but the druggist was charging ten times what the drug cost him to make. He paid $200 for the radium and charged $2,000 for a small dose of the drug. The sick woman's husband, Heinz, went to everyone he knew to borrow the money, but he could only get together about $1,000, which is half of what it cost. He told the druggist that his wife was dying and asked him to sell it cheaper or let him pay later. But the druggist said, "No, I discovered the drug and I'm going to make money from it." So Heinz got desperate and broke into the man's store to steal the drug for his wife.

The subject is presented with this dilemma and then asked questions about the incident: "Should Heinz have done it?" "Was it wrong or right?" "Would a good husband do that?" "Did the druggist have the right to charge that much?" "Heinz was caught; should the judge send him to jail for stealing or should he be let go?" "Why?" Subjects are presented with ten such moral dilemmas and interviewed about each incident.

If the stages in moral development are universal, they should reach across different societies, and it should be possible to find the same stages in a variety of cultural settings. Studies undertaken in Taiwan, Mexico, and Turkey do find results comparable to those of studies in the United States (Kohlberg, 1968; 1969). Although the rate of development by age varies from culture to culture, the existence of the stages has been supported by Kohlberg's data. In our own society, it was found that level I covered persons up to 7. By age 13, people are at level II. By 16, level II is still detected, but level III also appears.

Haan, Smith, and Block (1968) examined the level of moral development of students who had been actively involved in the Free Speech Movement at Berkeley. Their data suggest that politically active students (as compared with inactives) defined moral values as going beyond the values of their institution. Their allegiance was to general human values and social justice rather than to the form of justice they experienced in their university.

Kohlberg believes that if a person is to achieve the highest stage of moral development he must pass through the other five stages. In doing so, the individual reorganizes his experience and moves toward a more mature level of moral judgment.

Not Quite Moral

Heilman, Hodgson, and Hornstein (1972) conducted a "memory experiment" in which 68 college-student volunteers were given the chance to cause accidental damage to a graduate student and get away with it. Each had been directed to a room where a box of slides was precariously balanced on a shelf under a booby-trapped, drop-leaf table. When the subject leaned forward on the table to take the memory tests, the table leaf collapsed, an ashtray fell on the shelf, and the slide box catapulted onto the floor. In some cases, a note had been attached that read: "These slides have taken hours to put in order for use in final defense of my Ph.D. dissertation tonight at 8 P.M. Will return at 7:45 to collect." For other subjects, the note stated that the box contained only vacation slides for a party. In some cases, the note said that any damage would be "unrectifiable" because "the master sheet is gone," whereas in other cases the written comment said: "It would be a drag to redo them."

When many subjects were run under these various conditions, it became apparent that some people simply are not concerned by the more minor troubles they cause. Fifty-seven percent of the subjects who thought they had inflicted great harm left a note or notified a nearby secretary, but only 17 percent of the students who were convinced they had accidentally caused a minor mishap did anything about it. When the harm seemed to be great, 73 percent admitted the accident—*if* the note indicated that the damage could be corrected.

The most interesting subjects were those (equally distributed across the various conditions) who were so "uninvolved" that they did not even seem to take note of what they had done. They consistently failed to read the note on the box, failed to report their accident, and, as it happened, tended to cheat on the recall tasks they had been recruited to perform. The fact that more than 15 percent of the total sample did this suggests it is time psychologists begin to devote more time to the study of morality and social responsibility.

Summary

1.   Piaget suggested that the child goes through two different stages of moral development. In the first stage, *moral realism,* the child accepts rules as given. In the second stage, *autonomous morality,* the child understands that rules can be modified to fit a particular situation.

2.   From the ages of three to about eleven, the child remains in the stage of moral realism. After eleven, however, he realizes that rules are based on mutual consent and can be modified.

3.   Kohlberg suggested a more complicated series of moral levels that individuals must pass through before achieveing the highest level—that of developing one's own moral principles. Individuals in most cultures seem to go through these stages, but the rate at which each individual achieves each stage varies with the culture.

Aging and Death

*There are people who, like houses,
are beautiful in dilapidation.*
—Logan Pearsall Smith

Neanderthal man, if he were lucky and a fast runner, could expect to live to the ripe old age of 30 years. The ancient Greeks didn't live much longer—35 years on an average. "In a prosperous modern society, a man of seventy is about three times as likely to die during his next year as a man of thirty, and about fifty times as likely as a boy of ten" (Comfort, 1966, pp. 151–52). We may live longer than Neanderthal man, but we cannot escape the process of aging and death.

Aging

We all harbor the secret hope that researchers will make it possible for us to live longer, and a few biologists insist they are close to discovering how to prolong life. One idea being researched is that each person inherits a given amount of vitality at birth and that this gets used up by stress, accidents, and illnesses. In other words, each of us can experience only so much illness and stress before the wear and tear of sickness exhausts the amount of bodily energy issued at birth. A different theory assumes that every human being has a built-in "time clock" destined to run down at a rate determined by the environment and way of life the person is exposed to. According to this theory, people who take care of themselves can last longer than those who have a rough life. Experimentation with rats, for example, has demonstrated that if the rat's food supply is sharply reduced to a subsistence level, the rat's life span gets dramatically lengthened and in some cases doubled. There is also a biochemical theory of aging. This theory suggests that fatal cell

WOMEN WITHOUT
MEN
*There are 4.5 million more women
in the total population than men,
according to Department of Labor
statistics for November 1972. The
number increases as ages go up,
with 2.6 million more women in the
70-and-over age group. The majority
of women 55 and over are single,
widowed, or divorced. The majority
of men in that age group are
married. Labor statistics for March
1971 show that in the 55 to 64 age
group there are three times more
women than men without spouses.
There are three and one-half times
more spouseless women in the 65 to
69 age group, and five times more in
the 70-and-over group.*

165

THE RECIPE

John Jefferson, who just turned 106, has a simple prescription for long life: "Drink a fifth of whisky twice a month—the first and the fifteenth." Jefferson, who was born in Oklahoma when it was still Indian territory, added that for good measure he smokes about ten cigars a month as well as a pipe. He also says he participates in a Bible study once a week with a minister who visits his home. He has 9 children surviving from a total of 14, 39 grandchildren, 66 great-grandchildren, and 17 great-great-grandchildren.

Whisky is a secret source of longevity that hasn't hurt two other extremely old citizens. Charlie Smith, probably the oldest man in the United States at 130 or thereabouts, told a Los Angeles adult school class that his secret is a concoction of rye whisky, fruit, and cola, followed by a couple of aspirins. Alvin Wetmore, who recently celebrated his 102nd birthday, doesn't give it direct credit, but still enjoys three glasses of whisky a day (the doctor's limit) along with a pack of cigarettes.

degeneration occurs when harmful chemicals build up in the body. For natural or man-made, accidental reasons, chemical elements may produce an unstable chemical balance that is finally fatal to the individual.

Living and dying depend on the billions of bodily cells that form the cornerstone of human existence. The "error" theory of death suggests that cell reproduction is much like photographing a photograph, printing a negative, and, then photographing the new photograph. Thus, in cellular life what may be happening to all of us is the reproduction of successive copies of lower and lower quality till death finally happens. This notion is also labeled the "copy of a copy of a copy" theory—a process whereby human bodies gradually weaken and wither away.

A recent and urgent concern is the possibility that our cells die for ecological reasons. That is, the air we breathe, the water we drink, and the food we eat may poison us over a long period of time. Poisons accumulate, age us, and kill us. "The assumption is that there are poisons which slow down the function of cells and ultimately kill many of them. When enough cells reach some critical stage of poisoning, the organism collapses" (Still, 1958, pp. 301–302). There is also a "loss of control" theory which suggests that aging slows down all our nervous and chemical reactions. This "rigidity" deprives us of the ability to bounce back when sick, ward off infection, heal when damaged, or summon the necessary energy to meet a crisis.

We can't determine which of these theories of aging and death is true. Perhaps, aging and death are complicated events involving a multitude of processes going on at the same time. Perhaps the truly important thing is *how* we live our lives rather than how *long* it lasts. It is very possible to be one age physiologically but psychologically quite another age. Perhaps all of us should reckon our real age as Montagu (1962) proposed—age based on flexibility, personality, and maturity rather than on the years that have passed.

Personality and Aging

Bernice Neugarten (1972) has long been deeply concerned about the effects of the aging process on personality. She notes, for instance, that in her interviews 40-year-olds saw the environment as one that rewards boldness and risk taking, and they saw themselves as having the energy to take advantage of the opportunities presented in the outer world. By contrast 60-year-olds saw the environment as being complex, dangerous, and something to be dealt with in conforming and accommodating ways. Older people seem to move toward more eccentric, self-preoccupied positions and to attend increasingly to the control and satisfaction of personal needs. The evidence was clear that, over a long time span, there was shrinkage in social-life space.

Neugarten concludes that personality organization or personality type is the pivotal factor in predicting which individuals will age successfully. Within

Shangri-La?

Drink four cups of rum and smoke up to 60 cigarettes a day and still live 100 years, or even longer. That is a surprisingly common experience in the Valley of Vilcabamba, a strange sort of Shangri-La in Ecuador. When death finally does overtake the people of Vilcabamba, it is usually said to be the result of "an accident, or of catching influenza from the few outsiders who visit the place." Observers suggest, as clues to the people's longevity, the utter tranquillity of the valley, its ideal climate, and the low-calorie diet that has little meat but a lot of garden-fresh fruit and vegetables.

The two oldest people in the valley are José David, 142, and Miguel Carpio, 123. They are not exceptional. Statistics indicate that more than 7 percent of the valley residents live past age 80, compared with well under 1 percent for Ecuador as a whole. While the people drink two to four cups of rum a day and smoke 40 to 60 cigarettes, the rum is unrefined and the tobacco is grown in their gardens and then wrapped either in leaves or toilet paper to make cigarettes.

broad limits, patterns of aging can be predicted from the character of the individual in middle age.

It has become increasingly evident that each person interprets his present situation in terms of what his expectations have been. Man is a thinking and planning animal, he looks around, compares himself with others, anticipates; then compares reality with his anticipations, . . . The statement, "I am 50 years old" has little significance; but, rather, "I am 50 years old and farther ahead than I expected to be," or "farther behind than other men in the same line of work." In such everyday phrases, the individual gives content and meaning to the passage of time. [Neugarten, 1972, p. 13]

For some people, the failure to meet challenges and change in old age can be disastrous.

The Involutional Reactions

When people become "old folks," there are a great many physical and psychological obstacles to be overcome. Parents or grandparents who are undergoing the psychological disorders that can come with old age may have heated encounters with young people. Such disorders appear in middle and late-middle life. Because they occur when there are metabolic and endocrinal changes in human physiology, it has long been assumed that the disorder is biologically caused. This human involutional ("turning in") period occurs roughly from 40 to 55 years of age in women and from 50 to 65 years in men. As Cameron (1963) noted, the "involutional" age is also the age at which depressive reactions are most common.

The psychological response of women to the primary sign of involution—*menopause*—is considered crucial to the appearance of disturbed reactions. Menopause signals an end to the woman's reproductive functions, and the idea of "being less than a whole, productive woman" can find its reflection in the psychological state of the female. It can produce extreme changes in mood, irritability, depression, and other disturbances. If the woman is convinced she is now useless and if she becomes envious of younger females, menopause will be a traumatic change of life for her (White, 1964).

The male equivalent of the female's menopause is called the *andropause* or male *climacteric*. This is only roughly similar to menopause since there is little evidence that the same physiological events are occurring. The aging male does undergo some change in neurological and endocrinological balance at this time of life, but this event is easily managed by most men and may not even come clearly to their attention.

The problem for both men and women is to distinguish between the purely *physical* symptoms of aging and the patient's *psychological* reactions to these events. In a culture so attached to youth, the involutional period

can pose an excruciating threat of impotence, helplessness, and uselessness. In its classic form, the involutional period has been described as producing *involutional melancholia*—a delusional, anxious, agitated depression. This reaction often has visible precursors in the form of mild, transient neurosis-like symptoms. Attempted suicide is not uncommon at this time since a profound depression may develop, centered on a conviction of total worthlessness and uselessness to society. The fact that this happens to old people in our society is due, in part, to the social role assigned older persons in our culture.

The reported "normality" of the patient just before the appearance of these symptoms is difficult to comprehend. The disorder strikes seemingly ordinary and untroubled people, but if we look deeper we see that this state is the end result of a life without preparation for the critical test of aging. Middle and old age is inevitably the time for balancing accounts and measuring the discrepancy between what one aspired to and what one achieved. As the time of death looms nearer, it can provoke serious distress and a deep sense of longing for the chance to do it all over again. But, it is too late and everyone knows it.

Growing Old When Young

Recent comment on increasing longevity is not very encouraging. On the psychological side, we are exhorted to maintain a useful, satisfying role in society and keep a positive view of life (Palmore, 1969). But certainly this is a vague guide to longevity. On the physical side, many of us have sweated hard and long to resemble athletes, but good physical condition while young is no guarantee for prolonged life. In Polednak and Damon's (1970) study of Harvard athletes, major athletes tended to have the shortest lives. Minor athletes had the longest lives, and nonathletes met death somewhere between the two. Actually, Tarzan would have about the same life expectancy as the rest of us.

Kastenbaum (1971) asked what would happen if a young person were placed in an accelerated environment so that he performed as slowly as the aged person in a normal environment. He and his co-workers timed subjects in practice runs where they were instructed to work quickly but accurately. Then Kastenbaum required subjects to make their decisions faster and faster—at up to twice their original rate. They concluded that some of the psychological changes that eventually appear in the aged actually begin years before when a person is considered young and flexible.

Kastenbaum also investigated what happens when a person is placed in an environment that makes him feel disregarded and ineffective—another circumstance the aged sometimes experience. Participants played a game in which they acted as advisers to a city government. As the game goes on, conditions in the city change. Officials are replaced, and the adviser finds himself treated as an "old-timer." As Kastenbaum reported:

THE BEST IS YET
TO COME
"Casanova wrote his memoirs between his 63rd and 73rd years. Galileo summarized his life's work at 68. Tolstoy, at 67, completed a definitive treatise on art. Shaw wrote some of his greatest plays in his late 70s.... Had Freud died before his 40th birthday, we would hardly know of him. He published The Interpretation of Dreams *when he was 44 and* The Ego and The Id *when he was 67."* [Butler, 1971, p. 51]

His advice is still requested routinely, but it becomes clear that nobody is paying attention. His role is empty, yet he must continue to go through the motions. Those we have tested in this situation show impotent rage, and preoccupation with bodily discomfort, and tend to go off on tangents about the "old times" when they were powerful and effective. [p. 54]

Lessons such as these make it evident that it is not easy to be old in our society. Even though we don't consciously or deliberately make old people obsolete, the demoralizing effect is the same.

Age and Civilization

In our society, cities are developed primarily for the benefit of the mobile, employed, consuming, young citizens. Modern cities tend to be efficient (shopping centers, medical centers, massive department stores) only if you are young and mobile. These "developments" may be nightmares for the aged (Birren, 1970).

Compared with other civilizations, we effectively deny our older citizens a role in maintaining control over younger persons. In preindustrial cultures, the aged were in an enviable position. They owned or controlled property and resources, and their years of experience were vital to the continuation of the culture. They were living links to the past, had rapport with the gods, and dominated the extended family. As Rosow (1965) reports, the position of old persons is better if the economy is close to the edge of starvation. The greater the struggle to survive, the relatively better off old people are, since every pair of helping hands becomes important. In our culture, by contrast, we have retirement villages in California, Florida, and Arizona.

The cultural, economic, and social conditions of today have produced what Rosenfelt (1965) calls "the elderly mystique." Despite a determined effort to think young, time takes its inevitable toll, and the aging person begins to believe all the social myths about old people. When the aging male takes stock of himself, he resigns himself to being a cultural discard.

As a worker, he has become a liability. His rigidity, his out-of-date training, his proneness to disabling illness, not to mention his irritability, lowered efficiency, and arrogant manner, all militate against the likelihood of his being hired or promoted. Fussduddiness is his special quality. Besides, he is more than the pension plan ever bargained for. Moreover, there are younger people available for the vacant positions, and they are thought to need them more. [Rosenfelt, 1965, p. 39]

The *facts* of aging are less important than the *mystique* that elderly people come to accept as being true. These beliefs encourage the old-timer to withdraw from meaningful participation in the culture. In this way, the aged contribute to their own cultural downfall.

THE GRAY PANTHERS

The Gray Panthers are out to change a society that "wants to keep the elderly out of the way, playing bingo and shuffleboard." By adopting a new life style of independence, the Gray Panthers stress action, in contrast to most older adults' service-oriented organizations. They focus on transportation, health maintenance, banking, tax reform, and putting old people in charge of their nursing homes. Working with the Gray Panthers are a number of young people—the Panther Cubs. The two groups discovered that "age-ism" goes both ways—hurting both the young and old and depriving both groups of the right to control their own lives.

Because of the inordinate emphasis placed on youthful appearance in recent years, many people approaching middle age panic and try to stop the aging process—often at great cost and with few results. The best recommendation for those who wish to look and feel young (or who simply wish to stay healthy) is a moderate program of regular exercise.

YOUNG AGAIN, SURGICALLY

Robert M. Goldwyn (1972) of the Harvard Medical School reports that the typical patient seeking a youthful appearance through surgery is a white, middle- or upper-class married female about 48 years old. She is energetic, active socially and professionally, and is usually trying to match her youthful outlook with a similarly youthful appearance. A smaller number of women wish to appear younger for professional reasons or to please younger mates or lovers. Goldwyn reports a high degree of emotional instability among seekers of antiaging surgery. He discourages patients who will be happy with nothing less than anatomical perfection or those who expect cosmetic surgery to erase career or marital difficulties.

The Youth Drugs

The eternal quest for youth takes some people thousands of miles seeking doctors who offer a cure-all for aging. Some experts call the treatments undiluted quackery. One magic potion is called Gerovital H-3. The liquid is injected into the buttock, creating some soreness in the limbs, but according to the advertisements, it can turn gray hair black. It has been claimed that Gerovital cures heart and brain disorders, rheumatism, arteriosclerosis, depression, and skin problems among other problems of aging.

Scientists say the powers of Gerovital are unproven. But the American Medical Association, during its 1968 conference on quackery, concluded that, if Americans cannot find the quacks they want in the United States, they will go halfway around the world for them. For almost 40 years, since the discovery of Gerovital by Dr. Ana Aslan, a Romanian cardiologist, believers have sought out the drug both in Romania and from "underground" sources elsewhere. Gerovital is prohibited by the U.S. Food and Drug Administration, but reportedly it is illegally available in New York at outrageous prices.

At a spa called Renaissance in the Bahamas, therapy for aging includes swallowing chicken embryos. Patients have paid $1,500 apiece, plus hotel bill, for a ten-day treatment since Dr. Ivan Popov, a Yugoslavian youth doctor, opened the "reconditioning center." The chicken embryo, about an inch in diameter and seven to nine days old, is swallowed whole—and live. Patients swallow the embryo daily for two or three weeks. Later they show "a marked restoration of vitality, a tremendous amount of energy, zest, ambition and improvement in their ability to perform all the body functions."

Popov and his associates turn to the sea for another part of their treatment. Sea water which may have bits of plankton and grains of sand mixed up in it is used for massaging and taking baths and showers. Using atomizers, patients also inhale it. But no matter how many bizarre or unusual efforts are made to prolong youth, death is unrelenting. No one yet knows how it may be waylaid.

Death

If you worry about dying you are not alone. Your doctor may be even more worried than you are—not about *your* death but about his own. Perhaps he even decided to study medicine to find an answer to the riddle of life and death (Kasper, 1959). Knowing as much as they do, doctors may feel even more helpless than most of us do about the chances of staying alive. You have to think about it sooner or later, and in a number of colleges courses death has finally joined the curriculum.

School for Death

The idea of schooling for death is not as new as you might think. In Aldous Huxley's book *Brave New World,* every child regularly spent two mornings a week in the wards of a hospital for the dying. At these times, they were offered delightful toys to play with and special treats to eat. When it came time for these same people to die (as old adults), they would enter the same hospital and find themselves in a familiar environment made lively with music. No hospital staff member would try to delay death, but they would provide happy, gracious care until death occurred.

Learning about death is less fictional at the University of Cincinnati. Students there visit cemeteries, morgues, and funeral homes. At the University of Minnesota, they are trying on coffins for size and planning their own funerals. At the Wayne State University Center for Psychological Studies of Dying, they are using a facsimile of the death certificate to explore attitudes toward mortality. Subjects fill in the certificate estimating when, where, and how they expect to die, the length of time they will spend on their deathbeds, and how they expect their corpses will be disposed of. Students are also listening to taped interviews with dying persons to learn more about the reality of dying and to change their picture of death.

The systematic study of death can help make your own eventual death more real. Studying death can also help students be realistic about what will kill them. Cancer kills about 16 percent of us, yet only 4.2 percent of us expect to die of it. We think heart attacks will get us instead.

The subject of death has long fascinated artists, even as it has fascinated all of us at some point in our lives. Kathe Kollwitz's lithograph, *Death Seizing a Woman,* focuses attention on the terrified expression on a mother's face as Death envelopes her from behind.

DEATH IS A GROWTH INDUSTRY

Death has become a growth industry in the United States. After remaining fairly static for nearly 40 years, the mortality trend has turned sharply upward. The Social Security Administration has projected 2.297 million deaths annually by 1980—a number that is more than 20 percent higher than the recorded deaths during 1970. Those grim statistics represent a growing market for the $2-billion funeral-service business. Burials conducted at public expense average between $300 and $600, but others run as high as $25,000. The average funeral cost in the United States runs from $1,200 to $1,500.

Psychosocial Death

You can walk out of the doctor's office after a thorough physical examination and drop dead of a heart attack before you get to your car. How can it happen? Perhaps, because your physician was looking for the wrong warning signals. He might have been too busy peering at the body's machinery and not looking at the psychological condition of its owner. Victims of unannounced heart attacks are reported to have been "running sad" for some time before it happened. Wives and friends reveal the victim had been depressed and that this psychological state was complicated by sudden, unpleasant developments in personal or work life. Heart attack and death followed quickly.

The idea that you can die a *psychosocial* death—die psychologically before your body actually fails you—suggests that you ought to be able to prolong your life if you have good reason to hang on. Avery Weisman (1972) claims it happens all the time—that you can even postpone death in order not to miss your birthday. He reports one study that examined death dates for 348 famous Americans. The researchers reasoned that famous persons would look forward to their birthdays and the public celebrations and gifts that went with them. If there were significantly fewer deaths just before birthdays compared to just after them, we might conclude that death can be made to wait until after the party is over. The researchers checked to see how many could have been *expected* to die in any given month and compared the figure with the average number of public figures who actually *did* die in the month before their birthdays. Statistically, at least, too few died. About 12 or so persons each month postponed their deaths until after their birthdays were celebrated. In the four-month period following the birthdays of one group of famous people, the mathematical expectation was for 116 deaths. In fact, there were 140. When this group of famous people was subdivided into categories of most, average, and least famous, the postponement of death was even more apparent. The more famous you are, the better you can hang on to life—until after your birthday.

Other evidence suggests that people can postpone dying so they can witness special occasions. In New York City, for example, there are fewer deaths than expected before the Jewish Day of Atonement. There is also a drop in deaths just before presidential elections. Thus, we at least have a clue that emotional factors do have something to do with the time of our death.

Voodoo Death.   All this may be news to you, but it is old stuff to the people of Haiti. They don't separate illness into mental and physical categories as we do, nor do they assume that illness is always due to natural causes rather than supernatural ones. Illness, disease, and early death are commonplace in less developed societies where man must depend on nature for his fortune. This strengthens the belief that man is always at the mercy of a mixture of natural and supernatural forces.

HAPPY ANNIVERSARY!
Hilgard and Newman (1959) describe what has been labeled the "anniversary reaction." On the anniversary of the death of a loved one, the surviving mate or friend may develop symptoms similar to those that caused the death of the deceased. Or, the survivor may experience intense anxiety about the possibility of his own death. This often is a delayed emotional reaction that happens to those who never properly grieved for the loved one at the time of his or her death. In part, it is fear about suffering the same fate, and in part it is a way of expressing guilt—a way of saying "I should have felt more deeply when you died, I should have missed you more, and I should not have adjusted so well after you were gone."

Voodoo is a mixture of primitive religion and superstition. It centers around a faith in spirits (Loa), which can be either good or evil. A witch doctor can cast a Loa spell that will cause death, and this spell cannot be removed except by calling on a "greater" witch doctor or having the original one remove it (Bach, 1961). When people become ill and seem to waste away without any evidence of a physical disease, they are thought to be "hexed," and only the removal of the curse can restore health.

Sudden Death.   On a human level, researchers explored the causes of sudden and unexpected death among American soldiers who were not in combat at the time of their death (Moritz and Zambeck, 1946). Studying a sample of 1,000 sudden deaths between 1942 and 1946, they chose men who were young and healthy, who had died within 24 hours after their symptoms appeared, and who were not engaged in heavy physical activity at the time of death. In most of these cases, no physical cause of death could be determined. We still don't know why sudden death happens, but we have to seriously consider the possibility that—like voodoo—people can be hexed by problems in their life and just give up. When this happens, the body responds to the psychological signals being sent to it and functions in a way that proves to be fatal.

YOU AND DEATH
A poll revealed that students had the following thoughts about death.
* • You are both awed by death and attracted to the thought of it.*
* • You believe psychological factors can influence or even cause death.*
* • Forty-three percent of you believe people consciously or unconsciously participate in their own deaths.*
* • Half of you have wanted to die at one time or another in your life but most of the wishers have been women.*
* • You are against traditional funeral rites, services, and the cost of funerals.*
* • One-third of you say you would donate your bodies to medical schools or science.*
* • Most of you (82 percent) would donate your heart for transplant to friends or relatives (Shneidman, 1971).*

If these attitudes and beliefs don't change as you get older, you will revolutionize the death industry by the year 2000.

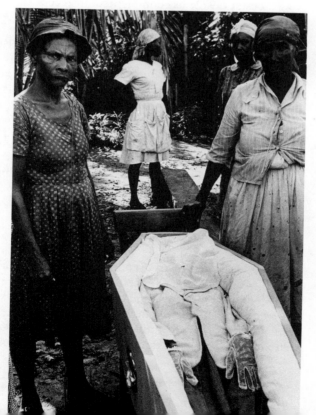

A Living Will

The Euthanasia Educational Council in New York has prepared a will to be used by any interested person. Although the will is not legally binding, there has been an extraordinary number of requests for copies (they may be obtained by writing the Council at 250 West 57 St., New York 10019). Many people seem to feel, at least while they are in good health, that they want a "dignified" death unmarred by artificial means to prolong life. What are the implications of such a document—medically, religiously, legally, socially, and morally?

To My Family, My Physician, My Clergyman, My Lawyer:

If the time comes when I can no longer take part in decisions for my own future, let this statement stand as the testament of my wishes:

If there is no reasonable expectation of my recovery from physical or mental disability, I, _____ request that I be allowed to die and not be kept alive by artificial means or heroic measures. Death is as much a reality as birth, growth, maturity, and old age—it is the one certainty. I do not fear death as much as I fear the indignity of deterioration, dependence, and hopeless pain. I ask that medication be mercifully administered to me for terminal suffering even if it hastens the moment of death.

This request is made after careful consideration. Although this document is not legally binding, you who care for me will, I hope, feel morally bound to follow its mandate. I recognize that it places a heavy burden of responsibility on you, and it is with the intention of sharing that responsibility and of mitigating any feelings of guilt that this statement is made.

Signed_____

Date_____

Witnesses _____

ANGELS OF MERCY

You are most likely to die in a hospital. During your last hours, most of your contact will be with nurses, who will play a role in the fact of your death.

"So long as hope is real, and nurses feel they are working to save a life, they are apt to become intensely involved. High involvement is also likely when it seems especially tragic that the patient should die—he is young, has great promise, has an important job, has a devoted family dependent upon him. A gifted or beautiful patient has great appeal and the threat of death distresses nurses and drives them harder" [Glaser & Strauss, 1965, p. 28]. *On the other hand, when death is certain, nurses (without deliberately intending to) may begin to delay responding to the patient who signals for care* [Bowers et al., 1964].

Lester (1972) has commented on recent cases of persons who suddenly dropped dead and were then subjected to extensive postmortem probings.

> *If we come to believe there is no solution either because of forces beyond our control (helplessness) or because of our own worthlessness and inability to cope (hopelessness), we may be driven not only to give up, but ultimately into the deadly "giving up-given up" complex, in which "for the helpless patient there is no present and for the hopeless there is no future." This mental state does not cause disease . . . nor is it necessary or sufficient for disease to develop. But it does reduce the body's ability to deal with potentially pathogenic processes.* [p. 52]

Helplessness and hopelessness it may be, but we are still a long way from explaining how such attitudes or beliefs work physiologically to produce death.

Death and the Hospital

Glaser and Strauss (1965) report a favorite story about death and hospitals: "Once upon a time a patient died and went to heaven, but was not certain where he was. Puzzled, he asked a nurse who was standing nearby: 'Nurse, am I dead?' The answer she gave him was: 'Have you asked your doctor?' " Even when death is certain and the patient acknowledges the fact, a little charade is played with him because he is frequently ignorant about other aspects of his death. A patient who knows that he is dying may be convinced that death is still some months away. Staff members may conceal their own knowledge of the expected time of death or hide their expectation that the patient is going to deteriorate badly before dying. Although it contradicts the usual priorities in patient care, a patient dying in a medically "interesting" way or suffering from an "interesting" condition may receive special attention as a "teaching case."

Perhaps, as David Dempsey (1971) suggested, we will eventually take death seriously, stop treating it as a taboo, and learn to confront its approach. However, despite evidence that the overwhelming majority of hospital patients want to know the nature and severity of their illnesses, hospital procedures together with professional attitudes prevent this from happening. The average

Death and Choice

Nowadays it is likely that when you get old and are troubled by a variety of physical and psychological problems, you will be sent to a nursing home. And when that happens, it may kill you before your time. In one study of 40 people who applied to a nursing home in Cleveland, Ohio, 23 died within a month after mailing the application. As it turned out, most of those who died were applicants whose families had decided they should be put away. Those who did not die were persons who had made applications on their own (Ferrare, 1962).

Applicants to the home were interviewed and classified according to whether or not they felt they had a choice in going to the home. It was learned that, within ten weeks of being admitted to the home, all but one woman in the no-choice group had died. In contrast, all but one of those who felt they did have a choice were still living. Apparently old people have more than a little choice about when they will die.

If you are financially well off, you go to a nursing home. If you are not, you are likely to be sent to a mental institution to die (Markson, 1971). And die you will. An examination was made of the medical records of 174 elderly patients admitted to a state mental hospital in New York City during an eight-month period in 1967. It showed that elderly people with a multiplicity of serious physical illnesses were being sent to the mental hospital. Out of 174 patients, 44 died within 30 days of admission. Interestingly, men whose families had pressed for their admission were more likely to die within a month than men referred by other agencies.

Those who work with the dying insist that subtle psy-

chological changes signal when the end is near. Lieberman (1968), for example, reported that the chief nurse in one home for the aged was able to predict who would die months before any clear-cut physical changes were evident to others. She couldn't tell exactly how she knew; it was just that these patients "seemed to act differently." Lieberman became convinced this made sense. His studies reveal that the psychological changes preceding death reflect a lessened ability to cope with environmental demands. The patient loses his ability to organize and integrate what is happening around him. These are psychological symptoms of impending death that may actually represent a last desperate attempt by the victim to pull his world together when he feels the end is coming.

American who is fatally ill will probably die without the dignity or tranquillity that might make the passage more bearable. He is likely to die in a drug-induced stupor that destroys consciousness of his last moments. Dempsey noted that it is even "harder" to die today since the electroencephalograph sometimes records brain-wave patterns even after the physical signs of life, such as heartbeat and respiration, can no longer be measured.

After Death

When you finally do depart from this life, one of several new possibilities is available to you. It may be that your generation will be buried in a different style. Recently, a company began constructing a high-rise mausoleum in Nashville, and at least two more similar facilities are planned in Tennessee. The first floor of the 20-story facility will open with 2,183 crypts. Eventually, the Nashville Mausoleum will have space for 100,000 crypts.

If you find you are not quite ready when your time comes, you might try freezing out the Grim Reaper. You have to die first, but this may only be temporary if you are frozen in liquid nitrogen. In theory, at least, all you have to do is wait for a few hundred years until doctors can cure whatever killed you. When they have thawed you out and repaired the necessary parts, you can pick up life just where you left off—or almost. These ideas are clearly theoretical since, so far, no one has figured out how the "defrosting" process can be made to work.

If the new science of *cryonics* catches on there may be millions of "immortals" patiently waiting to be reborn in some future century. But there will be problems (Ettinger, 1964). If freezing and unfreezing is ever perfected, it may turn out that living forever is boring. The citizens of the future also may not be so enthusiastic about a population explosion caused by people left over from ancient times. If you did come back, your great-great-grandchildren would be older than you. You might be drafted in World War XII, and if inflation continues for another 500 years, the million dollars you

This Is Going to Hurt *You* More Than It Hurts *Me*

The friendly, smiling doctor in whose tender hands you have placed your life may someday kill you. "Few doctors today subscribe to the principle of mercy killing, but there are equally few who do not practice it. Sometimes treatment is simply discontinued. Less frequently, a patient will be allowed to make the decision himself, if he is conscious, with a bottle of sleeping pills left by the bedside. Apparently the most common solution is to turn off the life-support system. All of these are forms of 'passive euthanasia.' Nobody knows just how many hopeless patients die this way because nobody wants to talk about it, but it is the rare physician who at some time has not 'pulled the plug.' Or, more likely, who has not instructed the nurse to do it, for one of the moral dilemmas of 'heroic' medicine is just who shall become the executioner when the time comes." [Dempsey, 1971, p. 64]

saved might only be worth $3.63. Death isn't much, but it may be better than a frozen future.

PLEASE DO NOT USE ICE FOR COLD DRINKS, COCKTAILS, ETC.

Summary

1. There are a number of theories concerning the time when death will occur. Some theorists suggest that we are born with a given amount of vitality. This vitality will be used up quickly or slowly, depending on how much stress we are exposed to.

2. Other theorists suggest that death occurs when too many harmful chemicals build up in the body, causing fatal cell degeneration. Connected with this idea is the possibility that chemicals found in polluted air and water are the cause of most cell degeneration.

3. The "loss of control" theory postulates that, as aging occurs, our nervous and chemical reactions slow down so that at some point we are unable to resist infection and crisis.

4. Along with these physiological theories of death is the possibility that death may occur without any real physical problem. Psychosocial death occurs when one dies psychologically. Only afterwards does the body stop operating.

HOW NOT TO BE DECLARED "DEAD ON ARRIVAL"

If something serious happens to you and you are transported to the emergency room of your local hospital, you will be a lot better off if you are young, white, sober, well-dressed, and "respectable looking." What's wrong with you doesn't seem to count as much. The older you are (beyond a certain age), the less likely it is you will get a thorough examination, the more likely you will be declared dead, and the fewer staff efforts there will be to help you live.

"A young child was brought into the emergency room with no registering heartbeat, respiration, or pulse—the standard 'signs of death'—and was, through a rather dramatic stimulation procedure involving the coordinated work of a large team of doctors and nurses, revived for a period of eleven hours. On the same evening, shortly after the child's arrival, an elderly person who presented the same physical signs, with—as one physician later stated in conversation—no discernible differences from the child in skin color, warmth, etc., arrived in the emergency room and was almost immediately pronounced dead, with no attempts at stimulation instituted." [Sudnow, 1967, p. 37]

5. It has been suggested that those who react the worst to the process of aging are people who find they have not met the expectations they had when younger. Difficulty with aging can usually be predicted according to the individual's perception of his situation during middle age.

6. The *involutional period* is marked by a depression that includes feelings of worthlessness and uselessness. Although behavior is generally quite normal until the involutional symptoms appear, most people who react in this way have not really prepared themselves for the confrontation between their ambitions and achievements.

7. In women, the involutional period occurs between the ages of 40 and 55 and usually accompanies the *menopause,* which signals the end of reproductive functioning. For many women, the inability to produce children causes feelings of incompleteness and uselessness.

8. For men the involutional period (*andropause* or *climacteric*) occurs between the ages of 50 to 60. The physiological changes occurring in the male are present but hardly noticed.

9. The difficulties experienced with aging can largely be attributed to living in a civilization that prizes youth and casts its aged aside. In many other societies, the elderly are accorded a great deal of respect because of their knowledge and experience.

10. The mystique surrounding old age is that the elderly are poor workers, irritable people, slow, inflexible, and inefficient. Whether or not this is true for each individual, most old people come to believe it is true and therefore believe that they should drop out of any useful social role.

11. The mystique regarding age is so great that many aged people desperately attempt to regain their youth through expensive surgery and drugs. Surgery may help people look younger, but drugs have not been proven successful in restoring youth.

12. *Sudden death* is the term for an inexplicable phenomenon in which individuals, faced with severe life problems, suddenly drop dead. Doctors are unable to determine any physiological cause for such deaths.

13. It has been suggested that sudden death occurs when we come to believe that our problems have no solution. This may happen because we can't do anything to control our lives (helplessness) or because we feel worthless and unable to cope any longer (hopelessness). This phenomenon very much resembles what happens to voodoo believers who, knowing that they have been cursed, may just give up and die.

14. Evidence of the psychological nature of death has been found in studies of nursing homes. Individuals who are sent away to nursing homes or mental hospitals by relatives die quickly. Individuals who *choose* to go to the homes go on living in their new environments. This suggests that the ability to direct one's own life may be an important factor in successful aging and longevity.

15. Nurses suggest that they can tell the difference between patients who will soon die and those who won't just from their psychological state. One explanation for this is that patients who are giving up have a decreased ability to cope with the demands of their environment.

16. The topic of death is largely taboo in our society, and this may be another reason why so many of us have difficulty accepting aging and death. Most hospitals refuse to tell dying patients the truth, even though most patients say they prefer to know the truth so they can live out their last moments in dignity.

17. Some hospitals go to extremes to keep patients alive, but a newer attitude is to let the terminal patient decide for himself when he wants to die. Euthanasia, or mercy killing, is rarely practiced. But for patients whose agony is prolonged, some doctors may turn off the system that has been keeping them alive.

18. *Cryonics* is the science of freezing individuals who are dead before their bodies degenerate. When doctors find the cure for whatever killed them, they can be thawed, repaired, and sent back to the world to continue living. The idea may be comforting to dying individuals, but the problems of future population explosions may cancel the advantages.

The Generation Gap

The Old Testament saying, "And there is no new thing under the sun," might well be applied to hair length. Although it has been a major issue in recent young-old confrontations, the length of one's locks has shortened and lengthened throughout history. Here, friends of J. C. Fremont, the general who conquered California in the Mexican-American War, gather in 1848.

The generation gap is an ancient phenomenon. Hieroglyphics in Egyptian tombs complain of the younger generation's unwillingness to respect the wisdom of their elders and honor the established laws of the society. Perhaps, it is the fate of the young always to push for change while their elders defend the status quo.

The Adult View   Margaret Mead (1970) believes there is a generation gap today that has nothing to do with parents and children. The gap, rather, is between all the people born and brought up after World War II and all those who were born before it. Some of those on the adult side of the gap have risen to the defense of the new generation and tried to accept their new beliefs as an improvement over the values of past times. Zoellner (1968), for example, is one enthusiast who felt that only the supremely healthy person among those pushing 50 could have as many honest moments as persons now under 30. To him, today's young are the first American generation that is free to form its own morality rather than accept a hand-me-down from elders. Charles Wyzanski (1968) says it is quite right that the young should talk about us as hypocrites, since

The Changing Gap.   Modern-day conflict between the young and their elders is different from that of the past. In previous eras, the young were impatient to enter the system and to have the privileges their seniors did. The only questions were who should be in the driver's seat and when the generational change of drivers should take place. In recent years, some of the young "feel as if they were locked in the back of a vehicle that has been built to corrupt specifications, was unsafe at any speed, and was being driven by a middle-aged drunk. They don't want to drive; they don't even want to go where the car is going, and they sometimes distrust the examiners too much even to be willing to apply for a license. What they want is to get out while they are still alive; if they succeed in that, they will try to camp where they happen to be, hoping to make it if they can stay together and leave ambition and the Great Society to us." [Friedenberg, 1969, pp. 22–23]

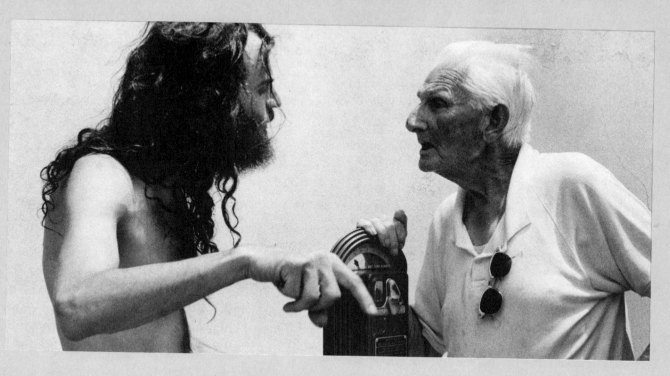

we are. The young may accurately diagnose the hypocrisy and shallowness of many adult interpersonal relationships, but they have yet to devise a better formula.

Many adults are unhappy with the rebellious image of the adolescent, even though they acknowledge that young people have more knowledge, cultural advantages, and sophistication than previous generations. Many adults simply are not convinced that the "new species" is an improvement over themselves at a young age. Elizabeth Hurlock (1966) is one of these disenchanted adults. She describes the new species of American young people in these unflattering terms:

• The young are driven by a compulsion to follow the herd and fear to be original or different—they are frighteningly conformist.

• The young are preoccupied with status symbols that will indicate they are an accepted member of a worthwhile peer group.

• The young are irresponsible about anything that requires effort or interferes with their search for pleasure.

• They are anti-intellectual despite the fact that more and more of them attend college.

• They are, understandably, not understood by the older generation. Their new values are hedonistic and self-seeking.

• They are disrespectful of age and experience and disregard age-old rules and laws. They have become the first affluent generation of juvenile delinquents.

• They have an unrealistic level of aspiration for cultural change and improvement.

After this lengthy damnation of the young, Hurlock concludes that this generation is not likely to produce superior adults. As she notes, the young are not happy now, and there is little reason to anticipate that they will be happier later in life.

Is There a Gap?

According to Joseph Adelson (1970), the idea of a generation gap is no more than "pop" sociology—a false idea whose time has come in the course of man's affairs. Like every false idea, it bears just enough truth to make it believable. Adelson insists that it is not the fact of greater sexual freedom, the difference in generational politics, widespread alienation, nor the marijuana culture that makes the difference. It is, rather, that the young and old share a belief that there is a significant difference between them. Adelson insists that, if scientific evidence rather than the popular media is examined, no extensive degree of alienation can be demonstrated between parents and their children. In a study of youngsters from 12 to 18 years old in all regions and social classes in America, Adelson and Douvan concluded that few signs exist of serious conflicts between parents and the young. According to their study, there is much less arbitrary parental authority and much less open rebellion than is popularly supposed.

Adelson observes that to identify the young with liberal or radical tendencies only makes sense if one's focus of vision is narrowly concentrated on the occupants of the elite university campus. The whole of American youth has a quite different complexion. The young who went to the factory rather than college are evidently appalled at what appears to be the collapse of patriotism and respect for law.

Despite radical inroads into our society, about 80 percent of the young tend to be traditionalists in their values, and there is as great a gap among the different groups of the young as there is between young rebels and their elders. The facts are that no one really knows how deeply the generational division runs, how rapidly change is taking place, or in which segments of the population the change is truly significant. We don't truly know how much is fact and how much is popular rhetoric. The revolution may exist only in the minds of those who wish it to be true. What generational revolution there is, according to Adelson, may amount

The Ancient Gap. The generation gap has always existed in America. "To the stuffy, inhibited, puritanical parents of the 1920s, the gin-swizzling, rowdy, belligerent, sexually promiscuous adolescent was a shameful enigma. That was indeed a 'Lost Generation' which could be found in illegal speakeasys or in the indelible pages of F. Scott Fitzgerald. Nor was the serious-minded, socially conscious adolescent of the 30s any less of a mystery to his adult contemporaries. The fact that he denounced capitalistic society from corner soapboxes, crusaded on picket lines and wrote inflammatory poetry was a bitter thorn in the side of his depression-plagued, morally repressed and rigidly conformist parent. In the 40s, the alumni of the firebrand, rebellious 'Lost Generation'—now paunchy and middle-aged—despairingly found that they had spewn forth a generation of spineless, 'adjust' jellyfish who worshipped security above ambition; silence above protest." [Gustin, 1961, p. 78]

to no more than an attempt by the young to claim credit for a movement begun years before their birth and only now peaking.

Parents at the Gap

Today's 35- to 55-year-old parents never had the luxury of being able to relax in child rearing as did the parents at the turn of the century who could dismiss their failed children as the "black sheep of the family." In the early 1900s parents unquestioningly accepted the prevailing belief that heredity was a prime determinant of behavior. Millions of ordinary people were convinced that bad children were a result of bad seed or weak stock, that crime was hereditary, and that spanking a child every day should be enough to put him on the straight and narrow path to righteousness.

By the late 1930s a new and powerful image of the child gained ascendancy when Freudian concepts revolutionized child-rearing practices. Suddenly, mothers began to talk about "the rights of infants," the need for "oral gratification," and the importance of freedom from repression and inhibition. Permissiveness was the only way out for parents now confused about which way to turn.

This growing faith in the trustworthiness of science had its greatest impact on the middle-class parents of today. They became thoroughly imbued with the notion that, unless they were obtuse, evil, or stupid, they should be able to rear a near-perfect child. This belief evoked painful feelings of guilt if they failed to measure up to "scientific" expectations. An historically unparalleled degree of absorption with the young was begun by a parent generation deprived of its own adolescence. Today's adult parents are certain they understand the years between puberty and adulthood simply because they lived through them. But any comparison between the years of the Great Depression and those of the most recent decade only demonstrates what a dramatic difference there is between adolescent behavior of the past and of the present.

Margaret Mead (1970) observes that our elders could once say, "I have been young and *you* never have been old." But today's young people can reply: "You have never been young in the world I am young in, and you never can be." This is the common experience of pioneers and their children. In this sense, all of us who were born and reared before the 1940s are immigrants. Like first-generation pioneers, we were reared to have skills and values that are only partly appropriate in this new time. Nevertheless, we are the elders who still control government and power. And like the immigrants from colonizing countries, we cling to the belief that our children will turn out to be like us.

Perhaps the feeling of the generational gap is best conveyed in the plaintive wail of the father who states: "I survived the Great Depression, World War II, three economic recessions, and a heart attack. Now my 18-year-old kid sneers and tells me I don't know what life is all about!" For Kalish (1969) the generation gap is neither new nor limited to a division between youth and the middle-aged establishment. Lack of understanding and communication between genera-

"Spontaneous" Relationships.   Some of the young believe the only meaningful contacts with others are spontaneous ones, but this dogma of spontaneity can often be used as an excuse for irresponsibility. It's a drag if relationships have to be worked at. If you are "spontaneous" and "open," demands for responsibility by a partner can be dismissed as neurotic possessiveness. Doing your own thing can be a rationalization for ignoring the needs of the partner. "Another syndrome characterizing the way youth avoid intimacy is shared love, or what we call *spreading it thin.* The best example is the girl, commonly a member of hip communities or a commune, who takes on the role of Earth Mother. She loves and cares for everyone; and because she does not refuse anyone, she is responsible to no one in particular." [Salisbury and Salisbury, 1971, p. 179]

tions is just as likely to occur between a 70-year-old man and his 42-year-old son. "If their conflict is not as widely publicized as that between the latter and his 20-year-old son, it is probably because the conflict is less dramatic and less intense, rather than because of fewer differences in basic values" (p. 83).

It is instructive to consider some of the details of the gap Kalish describes between a 42-year-old man and his 70-year-old father. The father would have been born at the turn of the century. He grew up in a world without telephones, TV, movies, automobiles, running water, electricity, social security, or income taxes. When he was about 30 years old, the Great Depression left him penniless and unemployed with a family to feed. Surviving at a near subsistence level for a number of years, it was a considerable sacrifice for the father to send his son to the university to get the education that would keep him from undergoing the same experience. The aged father cannot at all comprehend the disruption and discontent in what was once a stable, predictable society. "Progress" is too rapid and bewildering to him. He has retreated and severed contact with much of the world.

His 42-year-old son remembers being poor for a long time when he was young and recalls being taught the value of getting an education and working hard to succeed. He followed this dictum scrupulously, moved steadily up the economic ladder, and has been able to give his children all the "advantages" he never had. As Kalish points out, the son's children will now have grown up in times distinctly different from that of their father as well as their grandfather. They may or may not hold similar views about hard work. The 42-year-old son may or may not have children in college, but the news of riots, sexual freedom in male-female dormitories, marijuana smoking, and student strikes is simply beyond his comprehension and violates his principles. What is clear is that the faster our society changes, the greater will be the psychological gap between generations. It would be interesting to speculate about the gap that will develop between today's 18- to 25-year-olds and their children in the year 2000.

Summary

1.   During the past few years there has been much discussion of the generation gap. Yet sociologists differ as to whether or not there really is a gap—and, if so, whom does it separate?

2.   Margaret Mead suggests that the generation gap is not just between today's counterculture youth and their parents. On one side of the gap are all those born before World War II, whereas all those born after the war are on the other side.

3.   Adelson suggests that the gap has been created—not by any *real* differences between two generations—but by each group's belief that it is significantly different from the other. Actually, says Adelson, in most families there is really very little parent-child conflict. Most American youths follow the traditional values of their parents.

4.   Kalish suggests that an equally important conflict exists between a middle-aged parent and his old-aged father. The two grew up in strikingly different societies.

5.   Most of these ideas point up the fact that the generation gap is a result of growing up in different worlds. The faster the society changes in the future, the greater each generation gap will be.

MOTIVATION AND EMOTION

ALTHOUGH THE MAGNIFICENT COMPLEXITY of the human brain has been compared to the wonders of modern computers, man—unlike the computer—is a *motivated* being who feels *emotions*. These two features of our existence bring us to the awareness that the experience of being human is, indeed, unique. Motivation and emotion bring us our greatest satisfactions and cause us the greatest pain. In recent times, for example, we have all witnessed the sad spectacle of men in the political arena who were impelled by psychological motives powerful enough to allow them to disregard the conventional ethics and morality of our society. The Watergate affair was a dramatic demonstration of how the needs for power and achievement can destroy us as well as carry us to great heights. The waves of emotional responses that followed the Watergate exposures covered the gamut of human reaction—anger, rage, resentment, pity, amazement, fear, and even boredom.

For most of us, events that take place on a national scale are much less urgent than the motives and emotions that are part of our immediate, day-by-day existence. Perhaps, some of you have learned how the basic motives of hunger and thirst can change your usual patterns of behavior. Or consider for a moment why you select certain people as your friends or why you are leading your life as you are. Hopefully, the chapters in this unit will better prepare you to understand our uniquely human motivations and emotions.

Motivation

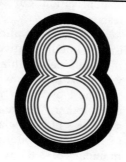

*We would often be ashamed
of our finest actions if the world
understood all the motives that
produced them.* —La Rochefoucauld

Most of us think we know why we do what we do—even if we don't always
tell ourselves the truth in every instance. And, most of us try to guess why
other people do what *they* do. These interests are what the study of motivation
is all about. Since no one has ever seen a motive with the naked eye, what
we call *motivation* is obviously an idea psychologists have used in answering
their questions about *why* people act the way they do. This question *why*
is so crucial to the study of human beings that almost all psychologists have
it constantly on their minds.

    If you think about it for a minute, you will discover you already know
a great deal about human motivation. If you didn't, your daily life would
be pretty miserable. You would freeze wearing your sandals, shorts, and T-shirt
on a winter's day. You would feel a gnawing sensation in your stomach and
a parched sensation in your mouth and throat and not know you are hungry
and thirsty. And you might feel painfully uncomfortable without understanding
you are overdue in eliminating waste products from your body. Before very
long you would invent the ideas of *deprivation* and *need* and attach them
to these sensations. Then, as you noticed how restless these sensations made
you, you would come up with the idea that you are *driven* (compelled, urged,
or pressured) to restore the painless condition you remember experiencing.
You would invent the ideas of *drive* and *homeostasis* (returning your bodily
condition to a balanced state). If your thirst sensations were the most painful
and your eyes lighted up when you saw a water fountain, you would have
learned that motivated behavior is goal-directed behavior.

Stages of Motivation

Stimulus

Motive

Behavior

Goal Attainment

As your inventions multiplied you would soon learn that motivation may be *overt* (visible) and/or *covert* (hidden). You would further learn that it is not always possible to guess a person's motivation from his overt behavior since the person himself may be unaware of the motivation behind the behavior. Thus, the analysis of motivation by psychologists has depended on the concepts of *need* and *drive*. We all experience needs such as the need for food and the need for social contact. We become aware of our needs when we are in a *state of deprivation* and our needs are unfulfilled. During a state of deprivation, our system suffers from an imbalance, and this causes us to respond.

The observation was made more than a century ago that living organisms maintain relatively constant internal states. Thus your body temperature is maintained within a fairly constant range despite extreme temperature variations in the environment. In fact, each of us experiences the fluctuation of a host of bodily needs and deprivations that rise and fall in relation to one another. We are almost always adjusting and trying to maintain a steady, satisfying physiological state. The human body is, in other words, a system of fluctuating conditions that produces physiological motivational states. In moments of total relaxation, you can become aware of how much of your activity is a kind of housekeeping or caretaking of your body—you feed it, water it, rest it, tend to its temperature, and clean it a great part of every day. Imagine for a moment how your life would be changed if you were blessed with an automatic homeostasis for all your needs and had no physiologically caused motivation.

The tendency to maintain a balanced physiological state called *homeostasis* applies to body temperature; regulation of sugar, salt, fat, and proteins in the blood; water intake; and an adequate oxygen supply.

The sequence of events in physiologically motivated states can be summarized like this. A condition of *need* comes to exist (either through deprivation or some harmful stimulation). This need is then reflected in active behavior *(drive)* that is characterized by tension and energy. This leads to *preparatory activity* (for example, looking for places where food or water can be found). This *goal-directed activity* leads to an object that can reduce the drive. Food, for example, is an incentive that satisfies the hunger drive through *consummatory behavior* (the act of eating). The motivated behavior sequence ends with a return to physiological balance.

All of these ideas of need, drive, goals, and homeostasis work pretty well if we only talk about how to keep our body happy. But, as we will see, in the realm of psychological motives, we need more complicated concepts to make sense of human behavior. Whereas it is easy to understand that we all get hungry and look for a place to eat, it is harder to explain why some of us are pizza freaks, some like to dress up and eat by candlelight, some dislike eating alone, and still others won't touch anything but "health" foods and vitamins. We obviously need some theoretical system to put together our physiological and psychological motivations. We need to know, for example, why there is so much variability in human behavior even around a common physiological need like hunger. We also need to know why it is so difficult to guess the motives of other persons, to understand why they are not motivated by the same needs we are, and why they satisfy their needs in ways we find unattractive.

Theories of Motivation

The various approaches to motivation can be roughly classified as *hedonistic, instinctual, cognitive,* and *drive theories.*

The *hedonistic theory* of motivation is an ancient idea that suggests man's primary motivation is to seek pleasure and avoid pain. The early eighteenth and nineteenth century versions of this theory assumed that man's decisions are fully conscious calculations of how to maintain a simple balance of pleasure and pain. The unconscious parts of man's motives were not considered. Theorists insisted that those who seem to seek pain or avoid pleasure (masochists, suicides, Puritans) are really "pleasured by their pain" and thus do not violate the basic principle of this theory.

Monetary rewards are, for some people, a prime source of motivation.

The human organism is born with some fixed, instinctual reactions to food, water, sexual stimulation, and pain. These stimuli seem to produce immediate and intense responses that do not have to be learned. *Instinct theory* assumes that man is motivated as much by what he inherited physiologically as by what he learns as he grows up. This concept has recently become more important due to the discovery of *imprinting* during critical periods in the early life of most animals. Instinct theorists argue that perhaps our inheritance acts to fix our response to certain parts of our environment during particular phases of our lives. Man's motivation, then, would be partly fixed before the learning that he experiences in subsequent years. At one time in the past it was thought there might even be *social instincts,* a set of innate responses passed genetically through the species. However, when the list of social instincts became too long and complicated, the idea was abandoned. Also there was evidence that actions which seem instinctual for a human in one culture are totally irrelevant and not practiced in other cultures.

Cognitive theories of motivation avoid notions of simple hedonism or fixed instincts and attribute to man a rational capacity to make choices. Cognitive theories favor the concepts of *willing* and *desiring,* which give purpose to human behavior. This notion of *free will* is highly suspect among psychologists, even though the issue has reared its head ever since man began thinking about his behavior. The issue of free will concerns cognitive theorists because they begin with the assumptions that man is a rational being and that man is aware of his needs and desires. The cognitive theorists care less about what starts behavior than they do about how man decides between alternative ideas and values.

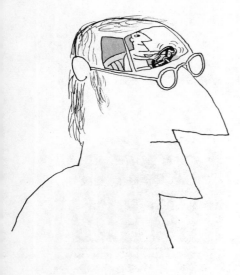

Drive theories occupy a prominent place in modern theory. Drive theorists believe that the more powerful the drive, the more fixed and persistent will be the habits of behavior associated with it. Thus, why man acts as he does and becomes the kind of person he does is thought to be traceable to the pattern of learned reactions accumulated in the process of satisfying needs and drives.

Birch and Veroff (1966) have suggested another way to phrase the issue of motivation. They stress that the aim of studying motivation is to be able to predict "when an organism will shift from one activity to another, what activity the organism will shift to, and also the intensity with which the organism will engage in the activity" (p. 2). To Birch and Veroff, the action you will take depends on the varying strengths of competing tendencies with the strongest one determining the action. Thus, the study of motivation involves assessing the strength of motive tendencies by means of understanding *incentives to action*. Birch and Veroff (1966) describe motivation in terms of seven incentive systems: sensory, curiosity, affiliative, aggressive, achievement, power, and independence. These systems propel the individual to interact with the environment. As Birch and Veroff suggest:

Organisms typically confront developmental problems of regulating their bodily (sensory) experience; reacting to new stimuli (curiosity); depending on contact with others (affiliation); reacting to frustration by others (aggression); evaluating their own performance (achievement); withstanding influence by others (power); and operating on their own (independence). [p. 42]

Another way to look at the basis for motivation is Altman's (1966) classification of biological drives. According to Altman, there are: (1) *vegetative* drives that push us to seek the chemicals we need to maintain our existence; (2) *emergency* drives that motivate us to act when threatened; (3) *reproductive* drives that involve us in sexual activity; and (4) *"educational"* drives that involve curiosity and exploration. Among these needs, first things must come first. We can reproduce and "educate" ourselves only if we face no severe emergency or threat and only if we have achieved a stable vegetative balance that lets us turn our attention to other matters.

In several respects, Altman's approach slices the motivational pie in a fashion similar to the earlier ideas of Maslow. Maslow (1962) views the person as having an inner nature that is constantly unfolding and growing, even if this growth is not easily visible to others. The human capacity to develop, for Maslow, is like that of a tiny seed that contains a tremendous potential for growth. Even in adverse circumstances, it will grow despite the odds against it. Seeds differ in their ability to survive and so do humans. Maslow (1943) felt there are certain basic needs humans must meet before they can be concerned with satisfying other needs. Maslow designed a theoretical pyramid of human needs, which included (from the bottom going up): The basic physiological needs of food, air, and the like; safety and security

Maslow's pyramid of human needs.

(pyramid labels, top to bottom: Self-actualization; Self-esteem Needs; Love and Belonging Needs; Safety and Security Needs; Stimulation Needs (Sex, Activity, Exploration); Basic Physiological Needs (Food, Air, Temperature))

needs; love and belonging needs; self-esteem needs; and the need of self-actualization.

Maslow says we must first satisfy one set of needs before we can become involved with satisfying the next set. Maslow feels some of us may live our entire lives stuck on just one set of needs. It is obvious that there are millions of people who will live out their lives at the bottom of the pyramid, barely able to keep themselves and their families alive. Some few of us move beyond safety and security needs only to fashion a life style that is devoted entirely to the search for love from others. These people never have enough time or energy left to actualize the potentials they were born with.

Maslow (1962) maintained that self-actualizing people have certain qualities, which include efficient perception of reality; spontaneity and unconventionality of thought; acceptance of themselves, others, and nature; independence from their environment; concern for basic philosophical and ethical issues; and a new appreciation for ordinary events. Maslow's theory

---

A Sampler of Murray's List of Social Motives

Abasement. To submit passively to external force and to accept injury, blame, criticism, or punishment. To become resigned to fate and admit inferiority, error, or defeat. To blame or belittle the self and to seek and enjoy pain, punishment, illness, and misfortune.

Autonomy. To be free of restraint, break out of confinement, resist coercion and restriction. To be independent and free to act according to impulse.

Deference. To admire and support a superior. To praise, honor, or yield to the influence of another. To conform to custom and follow rules.

Exhibition. To make an impression, to be visible, to excite, amaze, fascinate, entertain, shock, or amuse others.

Nurturance. To give sympathy and gratify the needs of a helpless object: an infant or any object that is weak, disabled, tired, inexperienced, infirm, defeated, humiliated, lonely, dejected, sick, mentally confused. To assist an object in danger. To feed, help, support, console, protect, comfort, nurse, heal.

Play. To have "fun" without any other purpose. To laugh, make jokes, seek relaxation from stress, or to participate in games, sports, and the like.

Succorance. To have one's needs gratified. To be nursed, supported, sustained, protected, loved, guided, and indulged.

Source: Hall and Lindzey, 1970.

MOTIVES AND FAITH

Two fundamentalist preachers died after refusing medical attention for strychnine they drank at a religious service to test their faith. Members of the rescue squad went to the church, but persons who attended the service refused to permit the preachers to be taken to a hospital. One person at the service said copperhead snakes and rattlesnakes were handled by some members of the congregation. The Holiness sect bases its belief in snake handling on verse 18 of the 18th chapter of Mark, reading: "They will pick up serpents, and if they drink any deadly thing, it will not hurt them." Both preachers had been bitten by snakes at previous services.

of motivation called attention to a number of unclear dimensions of psychological motives that other personality theorists neglected.

We must keep in mind that the list of human needs on a psychological level is endless. Some classifications include the need for achievement, deference, autonomy, exhibition, affiliation, dominance, aggression, or change.

Ernest Hilgard (1962) attempted to negotiate a compromise among motivation theorists by suggesting that motives can be categorized into three types: Survival motives, social motives, and ego-integrative motives. *Survival motives* would encompass those that are usually considered physiological in nature and would also include related motives of activity and rest, escape from bodily injury and pain, and curiosity. The *social motives* would involve other human beings. Interpersonal relations, although vital to survival, may not have the same urgency as the raw physiological motives. As Hilgard indicates, sex is physiological and necessary for survival of the species, yet is not needed for the survival of the individual organism. Dominance, submission, and aggression would also fall into the category of social motives. The *ego-integrative motives* resemble the self-actualization motives of Maslow. These motives have to do with mastery and self-respect. Mastery, for example, suggests the urge to construct, invent, grow things, or exert power. Ego-integrative motives are intimately related to the ideas we have of a self—a self that has values and beliefs, makes choices, has preferences, subscribes to a philosophy of life, and pursues goals and aims.

Looking at the need systems of Altman, Maslow, or Hilgard, we may be discouraged about the possibility of ever finding an adequate means of encompassing all man's complex motivations under a single theoretical system. The fundamental nature of motivation remains a mystery to theoreticians, even though they are aware of the importance of such a concept for our understanding of the driving forces that activate the organism. We can, however, look more closely at what is known about our various levels of needs.

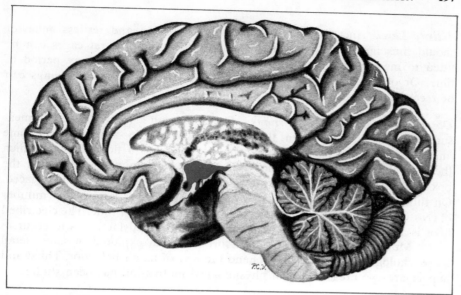

The hypothalamus, shown here in color, is a small region at the base of the brain, right above the back part of the mouth. It functions in emotion, thirst, hunger, sleep, and sex—in other words, in all physiological motivation.

Physiological Motives

Unless our physiological needs are satisfied we cannot continue to exist. Without food, water, and oxygen, we perish. These instinctive, biological needs are insistent and unreasoning since our survival depends on them.

The food-deprived state may be described as a state of *need*. This need is physiological, but a state of physiological need has psychological consequences. These psychological consequences of needs are called *drives*. A drive does not always get stronger as the need gets stronger.

Measuring Drives

There are four popular means of measuring the level of drive in a motivated organism. These involve performance, choice, activity level, and obstacle reactions.

Performance Role. If an animal has learned to press a bar in order to get food pellets, it will press the bar more rapidly when hungry. The rate of bar-pressing may be used as a measure of drive. Time can be another drive measure. How quickly an animal starts to run down an alley to a food box, or the running speed itself, can be used to assess drive.

Choice. If more than one drive exists at a time, the relative strength of each drive can be measured by letting the animal choose one incentive or reward. The animal may be presented with water in one arm of the maze and food in the other, so a choice must be made.

Activity Level. Increased drive leads to restlessness, and restless behavior should thus increase as the drive increases. To test this, rat cages can be fitted to measure the amount and kind of activity through any period of time. Or observations of movement and restlessness in human beings can be recorded and coded to assess drive.

Obstacle and Obstruction Reactions. Drive strength can be assessed by measuring how much punishment the organism will take to satisfy a drive. Some animal experiments use an *obstruction* box that has a floor through which the animal may be given a shock. The motivated animal is placed in the box and allowed to run across the uncharged floor to where food is placed. On future runs the shock is turned on, and a record is kept of the number of crossings that the animal will make in a given period of time. The electrified floor is an obstacle that must be overcome if need satisfaction is to occur.

Motivation of a physiological sort has been explored in some detail by psychologists trying to comprehend the *why* of man's behavior. Thirst and hunger are two areas in which physiological motivation has been studied.

Thirst

We can go without food substantially longer than we can go without water. This simplifies some aspects of the relationship between need and drive states. It is obvious when we are thirsty. A dry throat and mouth tells us we need water, but easing this dryness is only one factor in alleviating the thirst drive. Dogs subjected to different degrees of water deficit will drink amounts of water directly proportional to the known deficits (Adolph,, 1941), and this accurate estimation of the need for water cannot be explained in terms of dryness in the mouth and throat alone. The brain seems to exert major control over the amount of drinking in various species (Andersson, 1953).

Man can live for weeks without food but can survive only a few days without water. Men who have been deprived of both food and water for long periods of time report that the sensations of thirst soon become maddening, but the pangs of hunger tend to disappear after a few days. Experiments with rats reveal that thirsty animals will learn to find a reward of water more quickly than hungry ones learn to find food.

The thirst drive is controlled by delicate biochemical balances within the body and has been linked to the level of salt in the bloodstream. Salt causes water to leave the body's cells, and a high level of salt in the blood will cause the cells to become dehydrated. When the level of salt in the blood reaches a certain point, a *thirst center* in the hypothalamus is stimulated and activates the thirst drive. Drinking returns the system to normal.

Hunger

Hunger comes from the body's need for food used in growth, bodily repair, maintenance of health, manufacture of energy, and so on. We know we are hungry because of *hunger pangs* caused by contractions of the stomach muscles. In a classic experiment, a subject swallows a deflated balloon with a long, thin tube attached to it. Once in the stomach, the balloon is inflated until it reaches the stomach walls and is affected by stomach contractions. When the muscles contract, the balloon contracts, and air is forced up the tube. When there are no contractions, no air is forced up the tube. The subject is told to press a key whenever he feels a hunger pang, and the tube and the key are attached to a recorder. In general, whenever the subject indicated hunger, his stomach muscles were contracting.

This does not mean that the hunger drive is caused by stomach contractions. Human beings whose stomachs have been removed surgically still feel hunger pangs, and rats whose stomachs are removed still behave like hungry rats. Hunger pangs are just one indication of hunger. A relationship also exists between blood sugar level and hunger. When blood from a starved dog was injected into a normal dog, the stomach of the injected animal soon produced the kind of contractions found in hunger. Injection of blood from a well-fed animal would then stop the contractions.

Normally animals will regulate the amount of food they eat. They know when they are full. The satiation of the hunger drive is regulated in two ways: taste in the mouth and signals from the bloodstream. These are then translated into a feeling of fullness in the stomach. When animals chew and swallow food that does not reach the stomach (because an opening is cut into the passageway to the stomach and the food extracted), the animals behave as though they were well fed, and they stop eating. In much the same way, rats stop eating when signals from the bloodstream are received by the stomach.

A Need for Electrical Stimulation?

For a long time we had assumed that naturally occurring needs—for food, water, and sex, for example—were probably more powerful than any other motivating forces. But studies by J. Olds indicate that even nature may be overruled. Olds (1958) demonstrated that rats that normally press a bar only 25 times an hour for food will press it more than 200 times an hour when pressing the bar is immediately followed by electrical stimulation to certain areas of the brain. The increased performance of rats for brain stimulation was one indication that this was a stronger drive than hunger. Olds also tried the obstacle technique. He placed a rat in a box and let it press the lever three times to get stimulation. Then this lever stopped working and the rat had to cross an electrically charged floor to get to another one. Olds found that the rat would not only cross the electrified grid to receive stimulation but that it would endure twice as much pain as would be endured by a rat that was trying to obtain food after going hungry for 24 hours. Now if they could only package it and sell it to dieters.

The Balanced Diet.   Food preferences may arise from specific bodily needs, and a diet that is deficient in some essential food may cause specific drives that can be satisfied only by the appropriate foods. When rats are put on a fat-free diet and then offered a choice among fat, sugar, and wheat, they show a marked preference for fat. Rats deprived of sugar will prefer sugar. Rats can also have specific hungers for protein, thiamine, riboflavin, salt, phosphorus, sodium, and calcium. We are not certain how specific hungers are regulated in the body, but it is assumed that the needed foods must taste better to the animal than unneeded foods. When the taste nerves of rats are cut, the animals will not select a balanced diet (Richter, 1943).

The physiologically motivated organism is in a state of physiological imbalance. Activity and behavior are designed simply to restore the balance. In contrast, as we now explore the great variety of human psychological motives, it will become apparent that the concepts of needs, drives, goals, and homeostasis become enormously more complicated and difficult to explain.

Psychological Motives

Man's needs obviously reach beyond satisfying bodily deprivation. Along with some other primates, man has drives toward stimulation. We need to interact with our environment and seek stimulating experiences. These drives are not essential for survival, but they somehow contribute to our psychological health and our feeling of contentment. Our psychological motives, of course, come in all varieties, and we will discuss some of them here.

Curiosity and Exploration

The first reaction of an animal placed in an unfamiliar environment is *habituation*. This means that it will first carefully explore its surroundings to overcome its fear of the new setting. But experimenters noticed that animal subjects

will also engage in exploration and manipulation of objects without being stimulated by any obvious motivation. Monkeys, for example, will explore their surroundings and manipulate objects apparently just for the fun of it.

In a series of studies designed to explore the curiosity drive, Butler (1954) gave monkeys mechanical puzzles involving a pin, a hook and eye, and a clasp. To solve this puzzle the monkeys had to manipulate its parts in an exact order. The monkeys soon learned how to do it, and if the experimenter presented the puzzle again, the monkey would rework it hour after hour with no reward except the joy of working the puzzle. Everyone knows what it means to "monkey around" with an object, and that is, evidently, where the saying comes from.

Welker (1961) and Dember (1961) report that a great many studies reveal that rats will also work for the opportunity to explore a new environment. Even when deprived of food and water for several days, they will prefer to explore a new environment rather than stop to eat or drink.

Hill (1956) limited the activity of rats to see whether the opportunity to be active would be an incentive. He found that animals would indeed learn tasks in order to be rewarded by the opportunity to be active. They appeared to enjoy activity just for its own sake.

These may be what Berlyne (1966) calls investigatory responses—responses that make an unfamiliar object a familiar one by picking it up, tearing it apart, or examining it. Such responses also seem to be a natural part of human life. They can be observed in the first few months of life when the human infant learns to manipulate objects for entertainment. Between five and seven months the infant will remove a cloth covering his face and play the peekaboo game. At eight to ten months he will begin to look behind or beneath other things. By eleven months he will experiment with things in various ways (Piaget, 1952).

Affection and Contact

Harlow (1970) demonstrated a number of features of the drive for contact or affection in his experiments with monkeys. Using surrogate mothers, Harlow found that young monkeys preferred a cloth mother to a wire mother, a vinyl mother to a sandpaper mother, a mother with breasts and milk to one with neither, a stationary mother to a rocking mother, a warm mother to a cold mother, and a mother with no face to a mother who at first has no face and is then given one.

In one experiment, Harlow had a group of monkeys fed by a cloth mother and another group fed by a wire mother. He thought that, if affection in monkeys was caused by the satisfaction of some basic drive such as hunger, the monkeys would show affection for the mother that fed it. But this did not happen. In fact, all the monkeys preferred to cuddle up to a cloth mother. The monkeys fed by a wire mother would return to the cloth mother, and the monkeys fed by a cloth mother rarely approached the nonfeeding wire mother.

Man needs security, needs to interact with others with love, needs to seek new experiences, and needs to be accepted and approved by others for healthy development. But since all behavior must be physiologically processed, it is hard to draw a clear line between physiological and psychological motivation. In addition, the people in our social environment greatly influence our motives and our behavior. Years ago psychologists assembled lists of social drives. These lists were interesting, but no one could agree what "psychological" or "social" drives should be included. We assume that man has a need for achievement, for example. But is it also true that we have (as Freud suggested) an inborn need or drive for aggression? Do we have needs for dependency or for independence? Are human beings approval-seeking creatures, and does our approval-seeking behavior qualify as a need or as a drive? I am afraid there is no easy answer to these questions as far as psychologists are concerned. What we do know is that certain behaviors get reinforced. This reinforcement proves to be satisfying, and our needs get reduced.

When Motives Appear

Motives are not always expressed and they do not always result in behavior. Knowing how to do something does not necessarily mean you *will* do it, any more than wanting to do something means you *can* do it. The appearance of motivated behavior is determined by several factors.

It depends, for example, on the *availability of the response.* You can't fly by flapping your arms however much you might be motivated to do so. This fact introduces the idea of *expectancy*—the probability of attaining the desired goal. If you have tried to fly and failed, your motivation would not take the form of action. *Anxiety* is another factor in the appearance of motivated behavior. If you are anxious about displaying the behavior (you might expect negative consequences will follow), you will *inhibit* behavior that is directed toward the goal of flying.

A similar kind of inhibition might come from a different source. You may decide that arm flapping is not rational behavior and is therefore inconsistent with your self-definition as a sane person. Finally, you would consider the *context* of your behavior before you put your motivation into action. There is a right time and place for behavior, and trying to fly in the middle of a church service might not be the wisest move.

Functional Autonomy of Motives

A man who has become accustomed to going to work every day, even if he does not like his job, may find upon retirement that he still has the urge to continue going in to work. The motive to work remains with him although there is no longer any need for him to work. His motive has become *functionally autonomous*. It continues in strength long after the original set of circumstances has ceased to exist.

Gordon W. Allport used the concept of functional autonomy to explain motives such as the retired sailor's desire to return to the sea, the successful city businessman's longing for the farm life of his youth, and the miser's urge to hoard. Allport suggests that in the beginning each of these motives served a definite purpose and did not exist for itself alone. The sailor may have been forced to go to sea as the only job available. At first he may even have hated it. But, it provided him with a living, and he learned to like it.

There is evidence this also happens in animals. Rats that have never run a maze for a food reward will, after a few trials, learn the shortest path to the food and learn to avoid blind alleys. When the maze has been learned and the rats are put into another maze, it is not necessary to make the rats hungry or to have food at the end of the maze. The rats will run the new maze and learn to avoid blind alleys just because they have acquired the habit of maze running. This is called *externalization* of drive in which the motive of maze running has become functionally autonomous.

Motives in Conflict

A single motive seldom operates in isolation, and often our motives interfere with one another. Motives can conflict in several ways. Some of these are called *approach-avoidance, approach-approach,* and *avoidance-avoidance* conflicts.

Approach-Avoidance Conflict.   In conflicts of this kind, there is one goal but two motives. One motive leads us to approach the goal-object, and the other tells us to avoid it. An example of such conflict is the hungry dieter who

Approach-Avoidance

Approach-Approach

Avoidance-Avoidance

wants to eat and also wants to leave food alone. This conflict may be visible as the person alternately approaches and avoids the refrigerator, unable to decide which impulse to follow. It is the same with every attractive temptation. When we are tempted to do or think of the act, we feel guilty. This deters us but also leaves us in conflict.

Approach-Approach Conflict. This type of conflict may take the form of two goals competing with each other. An example may be when two good movies are showing in town and you can't see both and can't stand to wait till they reach TV.

Avoidance-Avoidance Conflict. In this case there are two goals, neither of which is desirable but one of which must be chosen. This is the kind of conflict faced by war protestors when, for reasons of conscience, they had to choose between the draft and going to prison. Neither is attractive, but no other real choices may be possible.

Every day may bring a variety of conflict situations, which we usually resolve quickly. On occasion we may even be in a multiple conflict which combines all three of the preceding types. Usually even this situation is soon resolved, and we forget that it occurred. In contrast, the neurotic person is in continual conflict and may never resolve it without outside help. When such help is needed, it is unwise to seek it from the amateur psychologists among our friends. We may, however, seek the guidance of a competent counselor.

Unconscious Motives

Whether we are conscious of our motives or not has little to do with their importance. All of us are conscious, of course, of many of our motives. We know some of the goals we seek and why we seek them. Often, however, we are not even aware of our goals, and, consequently, we are unable to explain why we seek them.

Certainly all of us realize that many processes go on within our bodies without our conscious awareness. We seldom know just what our internal organs are doing at a given moment. It does not worry us that most of the time the beating of our hearts and the digestion of our food go on without our conscious knowledge. By the same token, we should be neither surprised nor worried that some of our motives direct our behavior without our being aware of the process.

Sometimes we remain unaware of very strong motives because of a process called *repression.* Through repression unpleasant memories may be kept from consciousness. Yet these memories may continue to motivate us strongly. The clinical psychologist and the psychiatrist discover such repressed unconscious motivations in many of their patients.

When Motives Are Suspect

Recently psychologists have taken a closer look at personal and social motives involved with influencing and manipulating other people. The interest is new, but the inspiration can be traced to the sixteenth century.

The city of Florence in the 1500s is best remembered for one of its citizens, Niccolo Machiavelli. Machiavelli's views of man and how men should and could be manipulated has survived the centuries, and today's psychologists are tempted to believe there may be modern-day Machiavellis among us. Christie (1970), for example, became curious about the nature of individuals who are effective in manipulating others, and had some hunches about what the perfect manipulator would be like. The modern Machiavelli, he felt, is not basically concerned with morality in the conventional sense. He is cool and detached with other people since becoming emotionally involved with another person makes it difficult to treat that person as an object. Today's Machiavelli, like the one of ancient times, is more concerned with means than ends, more interested in the act of manipulating others than in what he is manipulating them for. Christie is not describing a pathologically disturbed, neurotic, or psychotic person. The Machiavellian manipulator may function quite successfully in the real world.

To test these observations, a scale of Machiavellianism (Mach scale) was constructed containing items drawn from Machiavelli's writings. For example, Machiavelli wrote that, "The best way to handle people is to tell them what they want to hear." New statements with a similar orientation were also included on the Mach scale. "Barnum was probably right when he said there's a sucker born every minute." Agreement with such statements indicates agreement with Machiavellian views. A person is Machiavellian to the extent that his answer to items on the Mach scale agree with the answers Machiavelli might have given.

With his co-worker Frances Geis, Christie conducted an experiment to test the results of the Mach scale, and reported:

Geis and I have the impression that the High Machiavellian is an effective manipulator not because he reads the other person and takes advantage of his weakness, but because his insensitivity to the other person permits him to bull his way through in pursuit of coolly rational goals. The Low Mach's empathic ability prevents him from being detached enough to take advantage of the other. [1970, p. 86]

Testing subjects with a revised version corrected for biases in the original Mach scale, Christie and Geis further pursued the question of Machiavellian motives and behavior. They found that males are generally more Machiavellian than females and that high Machs do not do better than low Machs on measures of intelligence or ability. Interestingly, high Machs were more likely to be professionals who control and manipulate people in everyday life.

NICCOLO MACHIAVELLI
"Niccolo Machiavelli lived in Italy 400 years ago, but his influence has survived to this day. Not only is his name used to describe the person who manipulates others through guile, deceit, and opportunism. . . , but Machiavelli's ideas have also been adopted—either outwardly or tacitly—by countless politicians, military officers, [and] business executives." [Wrightsman, 1973, p. 87]

Lawyers, psychiatrists, and behavioral scientists, for example, are more Machiavellian than accountants, surgeons, or natural scientists. Surprisingly, young adults proved to have higher Mach scores than older adults. Perhaps, the Brave New World will not be as loving a place as it has been portrayed.

The Cheaters

"Highly Machiavellian and un-Machiavellian college students participated in an experimental task involving two persons (Exline, Thibaut, Hickey, and Gumpert, 1970). While the experimenter was absent from the room, the other participant (a confederate of the experimenter) induced the subject to cheat on the task. (On the first attempts, highly Machiavellian subjects resisted cheating more strongly than un-Machiavellian subjects.) Later, during the post-experimental interview (ostensibly done to document the subjects' approaches to the task), the experimenter became suspicious and accused each participant of cheating. Highly Machiavellian cheaters looked the interrogator in the eye and denied cheating longer than less Machiavellian felons. Moreover, highly Machiavellian subjects confessed less often and lied more plausibly after the accusation than un-Machiavellian subjects." *Source:* Christie, 1970, p. 88.

Summary

1. The study of motivation is the study of *why* we do the things we do. Psychologists want to know where our motivations come from and how they affect the behaviors we pursue. Motivated behavior is behavior directed toward a goal. The behavior is initiated by a physiological need or psychological drive.

2. There are a number of ways psychologists have approached the questions of where our physiological and psychological motivations come from and why we choose certain ones over others. Most of the views can be classified as either *hedonistic, instinctual, cognitive,* or *drive theories.*

3. The *hedonistic* viewpoint says that man is motivated to seek pleasure and avoid pain. All of man's behavior stems from these complementary motivations.

4. *Instinctual* theorists have suggested that man's motivations are inherited or at least fixed during a critical period in early life. The theory of social instincts has been modified a great deal because of evidence demonstrating how much human behavior differs among cultures.

5. *Cognitive* theorists stress that man consciously directs behavior according to his needs. Thus the cognitive theorist is more interested in how man selects the goal-directed activity than in how the motivated activity got there.

6. *Drive* theorists suggest that man learns behaviors when they are responsible for the reduction of a drive because drive reduction is reinforcing. If motivation is strong, then the habits of behavior associated with achieving the goal will also be very strong.

7. Some psychologists have tried to determine what types of drives there are and which ones will dominate over others. Several alternative systems have been suggested, but as yet no one system has been agreed upon.

8. Abraham Maslow suggested that man has a pyramid of needs and that each set of needs has to be satisfied before the next set can be attempted. At the bottom of the hierarchy are the basic physiological needs. At the top is self-actualization.

9. Physiological motivations are related to *homeostasis,* which is the tendency for the body to remain in or return to a balanced state. Physiological motivation occurs when a physiological imbalance— such as deprivation or unpleasant stimulation—occurs. A bodily need arises from this state, and this need in turn triggers a motive, or drive, to fill the need. The drive causes us to engage in goal-directed activity—that is behavior which leads to satisfying the need. When the need is filled, bodily balance is restored, and motivation ceases.

10. The strength of a drive can be measured according to what the motivated organism will do to satisfy its needs. One can judge the intensity of a drive, therefore, by noting: (1) how often the organism performs the goal-directed behavior; (2) which of two goals it will work for; (3) how much punishment it will endure to achieve its goal; and (4) its overall level of activity.

11. Thirst appears to be a stronger drive than hunger. The thirst drive is activated by the hypothalamus when the level of salt in the bloodstream reaches a certain point.

12. Although hunger pangs—contractions of the stomach muscles— coincide with feelings of hunger, the hunger drive is not caused by stomach contractions. The level of sugar in the blood initiates or stops the hunger drive.

13. Exploration and curiosity appear to be inborn motives, directed to the goal of simply finding out. Animals will often work just for the opportunity to explore a new environment. Manipulating responses also seems to be inherently motivated, as even the youngest infants engage in manipulative play merely for entertainment.

14. Harlow's experiments with monkeys indicate that certain aspects of the drive for affiliation and affection may be inborn. It is not certain how much of man's need for affiliation is inborn. Psychologists are reasonably sure that many social behaviors acquire their motivating value and become needs because they are reinforced.

15. Some activities that were originated to satisfy one particular need may eventually acquire *functional autonomy*—that is, the individual is motivated to perform the activity even though the original need no longer exists.

16. Whether motivated behavior will actually occur depends on one's expectancy about obtaining the goal, one's anxiety about displaying the behavior, and one's ability to make the motivated response.

17. *Approach-avoidance conflict* occurs when two motives are connected to the same goal. One of these motives is to obtain the goal, whereas the other is to avoid it.

18. The *approach-approach conflict* occurs when you desire two goals but can only pursue one. The *avoidance-avoidance conflict* occurs when you are forced to choose between two equally undesirable alternatives.

19. Sometimes we are unaware of the particular motivations directing our behavior. This is because we repress certain memories and impulses, but they affect our behavior anyway.

20. Machiavellian motivation is the desire to manipulate others regardless of what one will achieve by such manipulation. Persons who score high on the Mach scale seem to be so insensitive to others that they can take advantage of them without qualms.

PSYCHOLOGICAL ISSUE

The Need for Achievement

We can begin by assuming you wouldn't be reading these words if you didn't have a need for achievement. The achievement motive can be characterized as the striving to increase or to maintain one's competence in activities where a standard of excellence is thought to apply. One can either succeed or fail in the execution of such activities. "Standards of excellence, therefore, are the mark of the achievement motive insofar as the individual perceives such standards as personally binding, compelling, or 'obligating' " (Heckhausen, 1968, p. 108).

If we can agree you have a need to achieve then we know something about you. We know, for example, that high achievers volunteer more for experiments, take a more active role in college, try harder to obtain knowledge of results, and consider themselves more responsible for outcomes (Atkinson, 1964). This suggests that high achievers believe that they will win and that they can influence the course of events. Researchers have also found out that college students with a high need for achievement perceive their parents as distant rather than as close, whereas students with a low need for achievement describe their parents as friendly and helpful. Students with a high achievement need also see themselves as more independent of authority than do students with a low need for achievement (McClelland, Atkinson, Clark, and Lowell, 1953).

These facts have been learned by showing pictures to people and then asking them to write stories about the pictures. The four pictures originally used by McClelland (McClelland et al., 1953) depicted a work situation (a man at a machine), an academic situation (a boy at a desk), a father-and-son picture, and a boy who appears to be daydreaming. Subjects are shown these pictures and asked to tell what is happening at the moment, what led up to the situation, what is being thought, and what the outcome will be. Then the subjects' responses are scored for the number of achievement-related ideas or themes that their stories contain. It is interesting that when the subjects are given a questionnaire about their desire for achievement their answers do not agree very closely with the themes that emerge in the stories they make up.

There also seems to be a correlation between the learning of the achievement motive and the nature of childhood training. Adults who are high in achievement motive were apparently subjected as children to relatively rigorous training in independence. The mothers of eight- to ten-year-old boys who were high in need for achievement reported that their children were expected to have mastered at an early age such independent behaviors as obeying traffic lights, entertaining themselves, earning their own spending money, and choosing their own clothes. In contrast, the mothers of boys low in need for achievement reported that they expected the same level of independence at a significantly later age (Winterbottom, 1953).

The sources of achievement motivation have also been described by Heckhausen (1967). As the child masters tasks, he is pleased with solving the problem and pleased with *himself* for having done so. The child develops self-attitudes through his successes and failures. Gradually, the successful child begins to seek challenges to test himself, and his achievement motivation increases. The unsuccessful child avoids the risks of competition. His achievement motivation drops, and he learns to fear failure.

Risk taking and confidence about one's ability has a great deal to do with what battlefields you will enter in life and how high you will aspire.

Level of Aspiration

When undertaking a task, we usually set goals for ourselves. The goals we hope to achieve on a particular trial are called our *levels of aspiration,* and they are influenced by the groups with whom we compare ourselves. If we know the performance of some particular group and are then asked how well we hope to do, we will set our goals in relation to the performance of the group. If it is a group we think would be better at the task, we set our goals below their expected performance. If we expect them to be less skilled, we set our goals at about their performance level. If we

have tried the task before, we will usually set our goal just a little above our usual performance. What we then experience as success or failure will depend—not on an absolute measure of performance—but on how our performance compares with our level of aspiration.

Individuals who are high in achievement motive tend to be realistic about taking risks. They avoid tasks in which they are almost sure to succeed but receive very low rewards. They also avoid tasks in which they are almost sure to fail but could gain very high rewards. This is particularly true of individuals who are high in achievement motive and low in anxiety. People with a high degree of achievement motive and a low level of anxiety tend to prefer jobs where they have a fair chance of success and can obtain reasonable rewards. People who are low in achievement motive and high in anxiety are inclined either to settle for an easier but lower-paying job or aim for a high-paying job that is probably beyond their abilities.

In a study in which college students reported on incidents in their own lives (Child and Whiting, 1949), each student wrote a description of three well-remembered incidents: one involving frustration which prevented him from reaching a goal, one involving achievement of a goal following frustration, and one involving attainment of a goal without noticeable frustration. After the frustrating incidents had been reported, the students were asked to describe the effect of the incident upon their level of aspiration. It was clear that total frustration led students to lower their level of aspiration, but success in goal attainment led a large proportion to raise their level of aspiration. Past successes and failures as well as personality factors influence goal setting.

Working-class children, in contrast to their middle-class peers, may not become strongly concerned about achievement unless concrete rewards are available. Investigations have found such social class differences. Boys from the middle and upper social classes score higher on achievement motivation than working-class boys.

One group of researchers (Hoffman, Mitsos, and

Protz, 1958) had their subjects (middle-class and working-class students) perform a task either for a cash reward or for no material prize. In comparison to the working-class youngsters, the middle-class subjects showed less variation in performance from the reward to the no-reward situation. They were more apt to work just as hard when there was no specific prize as when there was a definite reward to be gained, apparently because many of them had internalized the desire to do well. The working-class students were more likely to exhibit good performance only when a concrete reward was available.

Cultural Influences on Achievement Motivation

If ideas on high and low need for achievement are correct, nations seeking rapid economic and technological progress should try to produce a high level of achievement motivation in their populations. A variety of conditions affect achievement motivation, and some of them can be controlled by governmental, educational, and parental policies. However, it would require an exceptionally totalitarian society to control all the important forces leading to achievement. For reasons that are not fully clear, societies high in achievement motivation at one period of history do not necessarily turn out to be achievement-oriented years later. Bradburn and Berlew (reported in McClelland, 1961, pp. 132–49) examined samples of English literary writings from about 1500 to 1830 for signs of achievement motivation. They related these motivation scores to actual economic developments reflected in the increase in coal imports to London above that to be expected from the general trend. They found that the average achievement motivation levels in the samples of English literature predicted the rate of gain in coal imports 50 years later.

McClelland (1958) studied the relationship between the achievement motivation of the ancient Greeks and the economic activity of their society. He measured achievement motivation by counting the number of achievement themes occurring in samples of literature from three periods of Greek history: a period of growth (from 900 B.C. to 475 B.C.), a period of high development (from 475 B.C. to 362 B.C.), and a period of decline (from 362 B.C. to 100 B.C.). The extent of the Greek area of trade was used as an index of economic activity. It was discovered that achievement themes were significantly more frequent in the period of growth than in either of the other two periods. By 450 B.C., achievement themes in Greek literature had fallen off greatly, and from 450 B.C. onward there was a decline both in the trade area and in the frequency of achievement themes in Greek literature.

McClelland (1965) uncovered the fact that the amount of achievement imagery in children's textbooks of 30 countries in the 1920s was related to the economic development in those countries 20 years later. The more the achievement imagery, the greater the economic development. Studying only American textbooks between 1810 and 1950 and using a different measure, De Charms and Moeller (1962) found that their measure of achievement imagery rose until about 1890 and then declined. During that period, themes involving moral teaching declined, whereas themes involving affiliation increased. Perhaps history is written in the achievement themes of our children's school books.

Pursuing the idea that people can learn to be more successful by being taught achievement motives, McClelland (1965, 1969) developed a ten-day training program for businessmen in this country and in India. Both groups' scores of need for achievement increased following the program.

The Female Achiever

The woman motivated to achieve finds herself trapped in a male-dominated society. For her, success may mean failure.

Thus consciously or unconsciously the girl equates intellectual achievement with loss of femininity. A bright woman is caught in a double bind. In testing and other achievement-oriented situations she worries not only about failure, but also about success. If she fails, she is not living up to her own standards of performance; if she succeeds she is not living up to societal expectations about the female role. . . . For women, then, the desire to achieve is often contaminated by what I call the motive to avoid success. [Horner, 1969, pp. 37–38]

The problem of prejudice against intellectual achievement in women is prevalent among females as well as males, as Philip Goldberg (1968) demonstrated. He asked female college students to rate a number of professional articles from each of six different fields. The articles were assembled in two sets of booklets, one set attributed to a male author (John T. McKay) and an identical set attributed to a female author (Joan T. McKay). After reading the articles, each student rated them for value, competence, persuasiveness, writing style, and the like.

When testing female subjects, Goldberg found that the same article was given significantly lower ratings when it was presumed to have been written by a female author than when the subjects thought it was written by a male author. The female students not only downgraded articles in the traditionally male-dominated professional fields such as law and city planning, but they also gave low ratings to articles by female authors in the fields of dietetics and elementary education. The women readers seemingly rated male authors as better at everything.

If a woman is convinced she can successfully combine marriage, a family, and a career she may, according to Bloustein (1968), be in for a rude shock since society promises what it is not willing to deliver. As a married woman with children, she will be told to take second best in her career since she is expected to go where her husband's work dictates.

Bem (1970) notes that society insists that self-fulfillment for women is possible if they are motivated enough to go and get it. ("She is free to choose; no one's standing in her way.") This belief ignores the fact that a life time of socialization gives a woman far less than an equal chance to make such a decision. Even though there are no significant biological deterrents to such accomplishments, there are a great many social obstacles. (In contrast to our society, women in the Soviet Union make up 75 percent of the physicians and about 35 percent of the engineers.) As Bem comments, when a "newborn child is a girl, we can usually predict with confidence how she will be spending her time 25 years later. Her individuality doesn't have to be considered because it will be irrelevant" (1970, p. 95).

Summary

1. An achievement motive is the desire to achieve or maintain a high degree of competence in an activity that has a standard of excellence. Persons with high achievement motivation set for themselves standards of excellence that are not only desirable but also obligatory.

2. The achievement motive seems to be related to earlier childhood training in independence. The achievement motive forms when the child accomplishes a task, discovers he is pleased with himself, and proceeds to develop his self-attitudes according to his successes and failures.

3. How high a goal one sets for oneself in a particular task is called the *level of aspiration.* We all tend to choose our levels of aspiration according to the amount of frustration or success we have experienced in the past. High-achievement motivated individuals appear to set more realistic goals—and therefore encounter less frustration—than low-achievement motivated persons.

4. Unlike middle-class children, lower-class children become more concerned about achievement when there are material rewards involved. Thus middle-class children generally score higher on achievement motivation than lower-class children.

5. Women who have high-achievement motives may experience an approach-avoidance conflict when it comes to the goal of success. A woman desires achievement to live up to her own standards, but she also realizes that success in roles other than motherhood is frowned upon as a failure in fulfilling feminine roles and responsibilities.

Overeating

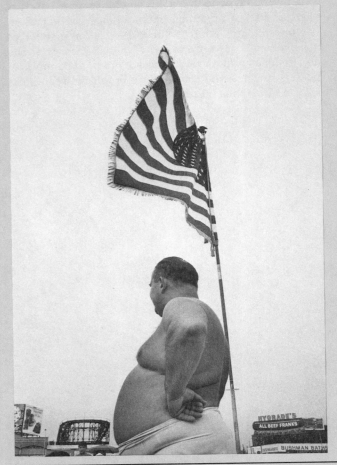

Dieticians estimate that from 10 to 25 percent of the American public is overweight, and medical experts report that only 12 out of 100 patients who seek a physician's help actually lose weight. Worse yet, 10 of these 12 gain back their excess pounds within a year or two.

Much of our overweight problem stems from the eating habits we have acquired as a result of living in an affluent culture. As nutrition expert Jean Mayer (1970) says:

Never in history, nowhere else in the world, have such huge numbers of human beings eaten so much, burned away so little of the food by activity and accumulated so much of the surplus in their bodies as fat. . . . The evidence is disturbing. In studies I did in 1953, 15 percent of the kids who were graduating from high schools in the Boston area were obese. By the same criteria, it is now 20 percent. I would call that a sharp rise—up one-third in 16 years. . . . These figures understate the national problem, of course, because they deal only with teen-agers. You get fatter as you get older even if you don't get heavier. [p. 43]

Infants, of course, can't tell they are affluent. But parents can, and they feed their young accordingly. Mayer found that with normal-weight parents, 7 percent of the children are obese. If one parent is obese, then 40 percent of their children are obese. If both parents are obese, 80 percent of the kids are seriously overweight. Early nutritional patterns may be the beginning, but the lack of exercise and activity is probably the end point in accumulating fat. A weight lifter can consume 7,000 calories a day and still be all muscle. Most of us can eat far less than half that amount and end up swimming in our own lard.

For various reasons, too many of us are overweight. Some of us eat too frequently. Some of us don't know when to stop after we start eating, and some load up on rich, fattening foods. Others may eat properly but simply don't burn up enough energy by exercise or physical activity.

Supposedly, if you learn why you eat too much, you ought to be able to stop, without spending the

---

Programmed for Fat. A University of Michigan psychologist suggests that being overweight is a normal, even ideal, condition for some people. His theory is that overweight people are "biologically programmed" to be pudgy because their bodies contain more than the average number of fat cells. For them, obesity is the natural shape of things, and dieting themselves below their "physiologically dictated normal weight" could be dangerous. If everyone has a given number of fat cells that can neither be increased through overeating nor decreased by dieting, then eating habits can only temporarily alter the size of each cell and cannot change their total number. Thus, a naturally fat person who diets may be literally starving himself into a permanent energy deficiency. The villains that establish a person's fat level are heredity and the early eating experiences of infancy. Since a fat person can't do anything about either of these factors later in life, it is unfair to attribute his eating habits to a lack of will power [Nisbett, 1968].

---

rest of your life dieting. But before you get your hopes up, I should note that so far our studies on eating motivations have not yet found a single theory or simple answer for obesity. However, research by psychologists has furnished a number of interesting facts that may aid our understanding of some of the motivations for overeating.

Fat Eaters and Thin Eaters

Let's start with the stomach and work our way to the psyche. Stunkard and Koch (1964) had their research subjects skip breakfast and come to the laboratory at 9:00 A.M. and swallow a balloon. For the next four hours they had their stomach contractions recorded. Every 15 minutes during this experiment they were asked: "Do you feel hungry?" Then a record of stomach contractions was compared with reports of hunger. For normal-weight subjects, stomach contractions and reports of hunger coincided closely. When the stomach contracted, hunger was reported. The subject was likely to say that he did not feel hungry when there was no stomach contraction. For obese people, however, this wasn't true. When the obese subject said he was

hungry, it had surprisingly little to do with the state of his belly.

Pursuing this lead, Schacter, Goldman, and Gordon (1968) designed an experiment that would vary the physiological sensations of food deprivation. In other words, some subjects had empty stomachs, and others had full stomachs just before an eating experiment. When a subject arrived at the lab he was either fed roast beef sandwiches or fed nothing. Then he was told that his job was to taste crackers and judge whether each cracker was salty, cheesy, garlicky, and so forth. He could taste as many crackers or as few as he wished to make up his mind on each trial. As the subjects tasted and rated crackers for 15 minutes, the researchers simply counted the number of crackers they ate. There were, of course, two types of subjects: obese subjects (from 14 to 75 percent overweight) and normal subjects (from 8 percent underweight to 9 percent overweight).

The results of this experiment probably won't surprise you. Normal subjects ate fewer crackers when their stomachs were full of roast beef sandwiches than when their stomachs were empty. The obese subjects ate as much or slightly more when their stomachs were full. In other words, if you are obese, the condition of your stomach has nothing to do with your eating behavior. Rather, eating is determined by outside cues such as the sight, smell, and taste of food. The normals

---

Overeaters Anonymous. Patterned very closely after Alcoholics Anonymous, Overeaters Anonymous was founded in 1960 by two California women and has since spread throughout the country. Members meet weekly to talk about their problems. Food is often not mentioned at all, because the focus is on the problems that cause overeating. The organization has no official diet, doesn't require members to "weigh in," and doesn't even care if they're not fat. A compulsive overeater is self-defined.

The underlying theories parallel those of Alcoholics Anonymous. Overeating is a disease one can never consider entirely cured, only arrested. People fighting the compulsion should fight it "one day at a time." Victory requires the help of God.

---

respond to the same stimuli, of course, and these external factors will affect what, where, and how much they eat. The difference is that their eating responses are regulated by their physiological state of hunger.

Goldman, Jaffa, and Schacter (1968) summed up the results of a series of eating studies in the following way:

The eating behavior of the obese is under external rather than internal, control. In effect, the obese seem stimulus-bound. When a food-relevant cue is present, the obese are more likely to eat and to eat a great deal than are normals. When such a cue is absent, the obese are less likely to try to eat or to complain about hunger. . . . There is evidence that, in the absence of food-relevant cues, the obese have a far easier time fasting than do normals, while in the presence of such cues, they have a harder time fasting. [p. 137]

One fascinating food cue is the passage of time. Four to six hours after eating one meal, we have the urge to eat another. Thus, if time is manipulated, the habitual eating behavior of subjects may be affected. Schacter (1971) decided to gimmick two clocks so that one ran at half normal speed and the other at twice normal speed. Subjects were led to a windowless room containing one of the rigged clocks and left alone with nothing to do for half an hour.

Later, the experimenter would enter the room carrying a box of crackers while nibbling on one. Putting the box down, he would invite the subject to help himself and then give the subject a "personality inventory" to fill out. In all, the subject was left alone with the box of crackers for exactly ten minutes. Schacter found that the obese subjects ate almost twice as much when they thought the time was 6:05 as when they believed it was 5:20. This phony elapse of time stimulated eating among the obese, but it had the opposite effect on normal subjects.

In a related study, Schacter examined the eating schedules imposed on pilots by time-zone changes. The Air France flights from Paris to New York and from Paris to Montreal were chosen. Members of these flight crews leave Paris at noon, fly for eight hours, and land in America between 2:00 and 3:00 P.M. Eastern time. Flight-crew members eat lunch shortly after takeoff and do not eat another meal until they land in North America at a time too late for lunch and too early for dinner. Schacter's theory was that the fatter fliers (since they were sensitive to external rather than internal cues about eating) would quickly adapt to local eating schedules and not notice the difference between American mealtimes and the messages from their bellies. This proved to be the case. The fatter fliers waited until dinner time in the new time zone to eat, even though they hadn't eaten for eight hours. The normal-weight fliers ate right after landing, regardless of the hour.

To Fast or Not To Fast. On Yom Kippur, the Jewish Day of Atonement, the devout Jew must go without food or water for 24 hours. Reasoning that tempting foods and food cues would be particularly scarce on this occasion, Schacter (1968) expected fat Jews would be more likely to fast than would normal Jews. The study revealed that 83.3 percent of fat Jews fasted, as compared with 68.8 percent of normal-weight Jews. Fat people eat when something to eat is readily available and go without if they are not exposed to such temptation.

Taking It Off

The seriousness of the American problem of obesity is underscored by the startling fact that books about dieting outsell books on sex. If you are determined to shed weight, it will help if you know in advance a few details about hunger. For example, the stomach contractions that signal hunger stop shortly after your usual lunch hour whether you eat or not. Your hunger pangs will start again as supper time approaches, but these too will pass. If you stop eating entirely, you will be exceptionally hungry for three to five days as the centers in your brain and the muscles in your stomach keep expecting meals to appear. By the end of five days of total starvation, however, your body will have started to learn that food simply isn't going to be coming. The stomach contractions will eventually cease almost entirely, and hunger won't bother you as much. Thus, one way to break the hunger "habit" is to put yourself on a very irregular eating schedule that trains your body not to be hungry.

But before you start doing tricks to fool your body, you should examine some of the nonphysiological motives that make you either eat too much, too often, or the wrong foods. You may not be aware of it, but there is a good chance that somehow you are receiving reinforcement for your poor eating habits. The reinforcement may just come from the satisfaction of your own needs, but it may also come from others. For this reason, behavioral psychologists suggest that you pay attention to the social dimension of eating. That is, become aware of who is around when you eat and what their response is to your eating habits. There may be someone in your life who wants you to stay fat. The work of behaviorist Richard B. Stuart demonstrates how this might come about.

Stuart (1972) studied men who had fat wives. He had 14 married couples make tape recordings of their dinner-time conversations and found that the men were seven times more likely to talk about food than were their wives (all of whom were on diets). The husbands were four times more likely to offer food to their dieting wives (compared with wives offering food to husbands), and the husbands were twelve times as likely to criticize their wives' eating behavior as they were to praise it. When Stuart interviewed 55 husbands of dieting women, he concluded that many husbands take strange pleasure in coaxing or goading their wives to become fat. Once the wife becomes overweight, the husband then throws it up to her in family arguments. Interestingly, Stuart suggests that husbands who are no longer fond of their wives could blame their lost interest on the fact that their wives had become fat. For some of the men, a fat wife was a safe wife—one who would not be attractive enough to other men to be unfaithful.

Behavioral theorists suggest that it is necessary for

Starvation. In an experiment conducted at the University of Minnesota during World War II, psychologists observed systematic starvation among volunteers over a six-month period. As the starvation period continued, the subjects became increasingly silent and apathetic. Their movements slowed down, and most of the time they remained immobile since any activity was extremely fatiguing. Their favorite topic of conversation was food. At night they dreamed of food, and they read cookbooks as if they were sexy novels. They complained they felt "old" much of the time. Interest in girls declined and finally vanished.

you to understand what reinforces your fatness if you want to change the way you are. The reinforcers may be found in your own needs and motives, or they may exist in the needs and motives of others.

Summary

1. Studies indicate that people who are obese are motivated to eat by external cues, whereas normal people eat according to internal physiological cues about hunger.

2. Overeating may also be caused by inadvertent reinforcement of poor eating habits. The reinforcement may come from others who prefer you to be obese. Or it may come from the satisfaction of your own physiological or psychological needs.

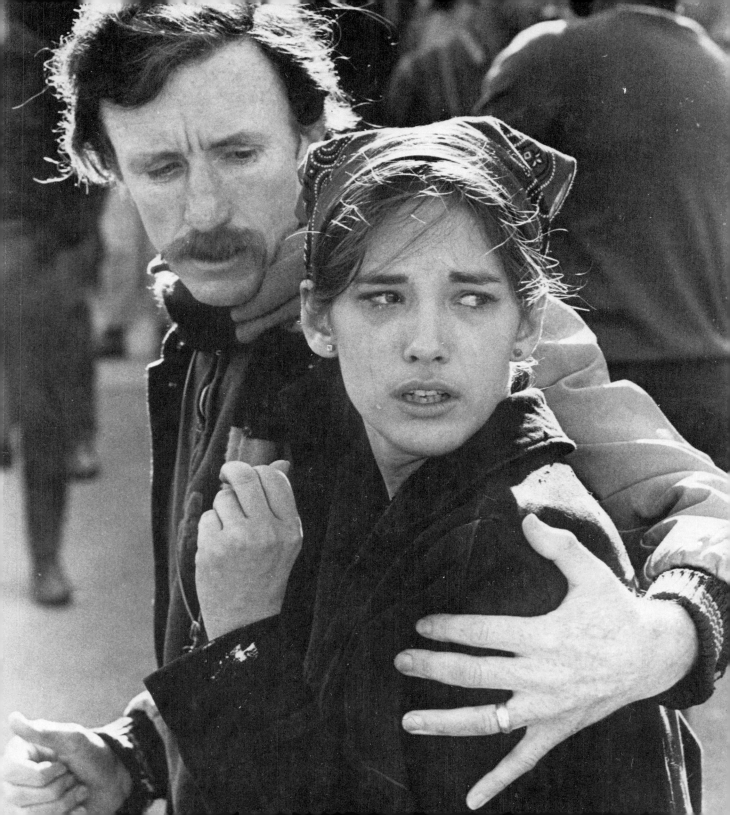

Emotion

Suppose, when man finally explores the distant places of the universe, he stumbles on a planet populated by beings much like himself but incapable of experiencing what we call emotion. Suppose these beings existed without any of our feelings of triumph or failure, joy or sorrow, pleasure and displeasure. To us, it would be like living with all the juices wrung out of it—a colorless, monotonous, one-dimensional existence. It would be difficult to relate to those beings since it would be much like making friends with a computer or a television set. They could think, react, and respond but would have no feelings. Imagine for a moment that the person closest to you had absolutely *no* reaction to you one way or another. Suppose your friend gave only a logical response to "the facts" and no more. Before long, you would begin to have an emotional reaction to the *lack* of emotion in your friend. Of course, our fictional other-planetary "beings" would be hard pressed to comprehend the strange and unpredictable reactions of their human visitors suffering from some strange affliction called emotion.

In a sense, this chapter can be considered an attempt to explain human emotion. The most obvious expressions of emotion that we see in our fellow humans are the intense ones of joy, pain, fear, grief, anger. It would be misleading, however, to suggest that all of the emotions to which we give labels are experienced by everyone. We have devised such labels to help us talk about different emotional states, but what *I* mean by "joy" may not be the same as what *you* mean. Furthermore, you may have devised a relative scale of joy for yourself. For example, when you say you feel "joyous," you might mean that you feel "sort of happy" or "extremely happy," according

219

to your personal scale. No wonder we have trouble at times attaching a proper name to the emotions we are experiencing! And no wonder we are often helpless to explain them to other people!

In fact, we even have trouble coming up with a *definition* of emotion. Since laymen seem to understand intuitively what is meant by the word, some psychologists do not attempt to formulate a technical definition at all. Others characterize emotion as the reflection of *physiological changes* in our bodies, or as the force that *motivates* us, or as the subjective *feelings* we experience. It is probably most accurate to say that emotion is a combination of all of these. That physiological changes do take place is not questioned. Whether they trigger the emotional state or whether it is the other way around, however, is not clear. And we know that emotions and motives are closely interwoven; but again, how and to what extent they are intertwined cannot be stated precisely. Further, the subjective aspect of emotion is, obviously, something that cannot be measured accurately. Still, research has revealed some tendencies that seem to hold true for many different people. For instance, the same physiological changes in two different people (or in the same person at different times) can elicit different descriptions of the emotional state being experienced. At one time, the state could be described as fear; at another time, anger. Also, different bodily changes can occur at different times, even though we say we feel the *same* emotion. Thus, a further definition of emotion could be that we *organize* and *interpret* the sensations within our bodies by way of a mental process which labels these sensations in accordance with the particular environmental context. The factors include the actual physiological change, our organization of the sensations produced from that change, and our interpretation of the information to decide, for example, whether we are "blue" or "up." A complication is that after we decide how we feel, further physiological changes may take place to keep our body state in tune with our mental conclusion. Have you ever told yourself you were going to enjoy an evening with your boring relatives no matter what, and then be a bit surprised later on when you realize you actually are enjoying yourself?

Before we go any further, consider the words *feel* and *feelings* as used in the previous paragraphs. In our day-to-day life, we commonly use *emotions* and *feelings* synonymously. But the two are not exactly the same. If someone asks you, "How are you feeling?" he probably wants to know about the overall state of your being. You might answer with a description of your physical ills, but that would only be a partial answer. You not only feel objects (as with the sense of touch), but on another level you feel sensations—pain, cold, warmth, and so on. And on still another level you feel love, affection, hate, anger, amazement, sorrow, astonishment, joy, puzzlement, disappointment, hope—the nouns we have created to describe the emotions we experience are practically limitless. Only with this last kind of "feeling" are you called upon to *evaluate* consciously what's going on inside of you and to decide what you are going to label it.

By now it should be obvious that emotions are not something we can touch, or observe, or categorize into nice little compartments. So how do we determine the emotional state of those we come in contact with? "Through facial expression, gestures, and body postures, for starters," you might answer. But there are problems with these cues of nonverbal behavior—one of the most obvious being that different cultures have different modes of emotional expression. Whereas we consider sticking out one's tongue a sign of defiance, the Chinese view it as an expression of surprise. And even in our own culture, our emotions are often misread—even by those closest to us. Why? Because unless the stimulus situation is known to others, we can mask our emotion in facial expression to conceal how we feel. In particular, it is difficult to gauge another's emotions by facial expression. We can tell whether someone is feeling happy or sad, but it becomes increasingly difficult to distinguish between emotions when they are not intense. Further, some people's threshold for experiencing emotions is so high that they may appear to be unemotional to others. For many reasons, then, we often misjudge. In our discussion of emotions, let us first see how they develop and are learned.

Where Do Emotions Come From?

Several theories have been proposed to explain where emotions, and the behavior that results, come from. Like the proverbial chicken and the egg, the theories center around the question of whether the physiological arousal or the perception of emotion comes first. As yet no one is certain which theory is true.

The James-Lange Theory. Most of us believe that our feelings occur first and this is what stimulates our bodies to react. But William James and Carl Lange proposed that an emotional experience actually occurs in the opposite way. That is, the body reacts first, and, by noting our bodily responses, we determine which emotion we are experiencing. James claimed that if we ran into a wild animal in the forest, we would tremble and then run away. The trembling and running would make us recognize the emotion of fear. Our conscious feelings, in other words, would result from our body's experiences.

The Cannon-Bard Theory. The Cannon-Bard theory is another way of approaching the James-Lange theory. Cannon and Bard concluded that the thalamic-hypothalamic region of the brain is the center of emotion and that the emotional experience and the bodily responses occur simultaneously because of the integrated functioning of the thalamus and hypothalamus. According to them, nerve impulses travel to the cerebral cortex in the usual way except that emotional impulses pass through the thalamic region of the brain. The emotional impulse then splits, with part of the impulse continuing to the cortex and part passing through to the hypothalamus. Thus, impulses are sent from the hypothalamus to the cortex (where the emotion is perceived) and to the muscles and internal organs where an emotional reaction occurs. The thalamus and hypothalamus are responsible for producing both the cognitive and bodily reactions to emotional stimuli.

Cognitive theory. Cognitive theory is similar to the James-Lange theory in suggesting that we derive our perception of emotion from our bodily experiences. However, the cognitive theorists go one step further. They suggest that we will select an emotion to go along with the physiological arousal according to the situation we are in. If we experience arousal while with a member of the opposite sex, we may interpret the emotion as love. If we experience the same arousal while confronted with a lion, we will experience fear. The same form of physiological arousal, therefore, might lead to two different emotions, depending on surrounding circumstances.

To demonstrate the validity of this theory, Schacter and Singer (1962) had a physician inject subjects with the chemical epinephrine, which causes increased arousal in the form of shaking hands, flushed face, and a pounding heart. Some subjects were told what the real effects of the injection would be, whereas others were only told that it might make their feet numb. It was hypothesized that subjects who were incorrectly informed about the effects of epinephrine would attribute their physiological arousal to an emotion relevant to the social situation of the experiment. Those who knew that the epinephrine was the reason for their arousal would not experience any strong emotion.

Then, two different social situations were created to which the physiological arousal could be ascribed. In one situation, the subject would have reason to expect to feel excited and enthusiastic. In the other situation, he might feel angry. In the first situation, the subject watched a confederate acting in a wild and silly way, playing with a hula hoop and shooting wads of paper at a wastebasket. In the anger situation, the confederate was told to object strenuously to a questionnaire which he and the real subject were filling out. The confederate escalated his protest until he finally tore up the questionnaire and left the room. Schacter and Singer expected that when the subject was misinformed about the effects of the epinephrine, he would report feeling the same as the confederate—happy or angry depending on how the confederate behaved.

In general the results supported the hypothesis. The subjects in the different experimental treatments attributed their physiological arousal to happiness or anger depending on the social context they were in. Once they had interpreted the stimulus of their physiological state as an emotion, they then behaved in a way appropriate to that particular emotion.

These experiments suggest that emotion is what we label it and that it has a great deal to do with the meaning we give to the world around us. Perhaps this explains why something that thrills you only produces a mild interest in me. And what thrills you today is not likely to stimulate you later in your life. Many young people complain about the inability of the older generation to respond to the wonders of being alive. But, if the meaning we give to our cognitions has some effect on the emotions we experience, then it is no wonder that, as the meaning of things changes, so will our emotions.

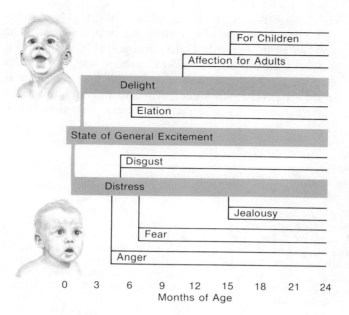

One way to depict the development of emotion in human infants. The first expression of emotion is one of general excitement, and from this the two main branches of distress and delight develop. Within a few short months, these categories branch even further and become more and more complex (adapted from Bridges, 1932).

The Development of Emotions

According to the evolutionary theorist Charles Darwin, emotions evolved and persisted in human beings because they were important for our survival as individuals and as a species. In a book written in 1873, *The Expression of Emotions in Man and Animals,* Darwin suggested that many of our ways of expressing emotions are left over from a time when such expressions were an important part of our survival. (When angry, we sometimes make a face that bares our teeth, even though we don't bite our enemies much anymore.)

In relation to humans, such theories remain hypothetical, though we do know that there may be differences in the inherited degree of excitability or emotionality in animals of different species or breed. Studies with the laboratory white rat and the wild gray rat have substantiated that there is a definite connection between heredity and savageness in this animal. The white rat is tamed easily; the gray rat is not. Crossbreeding produces some offspring that show the tame disposition of the white parent and some that exhibit the savageness of the gray parent (Stone, 1932).

Some evidence indicates that there is a hereditary basis for human emotionality as well. Although we do not know that any particular emotion can be inherited, it is believed that the *ability* to be emotional is. When identical twins were compared with pairs of siblings and with pairs of unrelated children, the highest correlation in the bodily states associated with emotion was found with the identical twins than with the siblings, and a higher correlation with the siblings than with the unrelated children (Jost and Sontag, 1944).

It may be useful to distinguish between *emotion* and emotional *expression*. At birth, the only clearly recognizable display of emotional expression is one of unfocused excitement. Babies wriggle, jerk, and thrash about—not as a specific response to specific stimuli but as a general reaction to changes in the external environment. Also, all babies smile and cry, well before they have the capability of learning these expressions from others. Moreover, these

---

The Emotion Detector

Emotion detectors are popularly called lie detectors. Actually, machines can't tell the difference between a human truth and a human lie. They can only register differences in mechanical and electrical stimulation they receive from people who are either telling the truth or lying. People have the emotions; machines record the physiological aspects of emotion; and the operator of the machine decides whether a lie has been told. Even before such machines were invented, lie detection rested on the observation that physiological arousal is a part of our emotions.

The Bedouins of Arabia once required conflicting witnesses to lick a hot iron; the one whose tongue was burned was considered to be lying. The ancient Chinese, it is said, made someone who was being questioned chew rice powder and spit it out; if the powder was dry, the suspect was guilty. In ancient Britain a suspect who could not swallow a "trial slice" of bread and cheese was also found guilty. All these tests were based on the early observation of a physiological change that often accompanies emotional tension: the flow of saliva decreases and the mouth becomes dry. [Smith, 1967]

The first attempt to record the physiological aspects of lying was made in 1895 by Cesare Lombroso, an Italian criminologist who measured changes of pulse rate and blood pressure in suspected criminals as they were being questioned. He reported some success in identifying guilty individuals. But in 1921 John A. Larson, a policeman, constructed the basic model of the present "lie detector"—a machine to record blood pressure, pulse rate, and respiration. Leonard Keeler, an associate of Larson's, refined this device and added another measurement—the *galvanic skin response* (GSR). The galvanic skin response is a measure of the resistance of the skin to the conduction of electricity. It is detected by placing two electrodes on the fingers or other parts of the hand and passing a small electric current through the skin via the electrodes.

The rate of flow of the current will vary according to the resistance of the skin. In highly emotional states, the GSR shows a decrease in resistance of the skin. This is probably caused by the sweating of the palms that comes with tension. The decreased skin resistance is registered on the polygraph as a change in the rate of flow of the electric current. This is an indication that the individual has been aroused by the question and may be lying.

The design and use of the *polygraph,* or lie detector, is based on the belief that the liar knows he is telling a lie, that he lies deliberately, and that his deception is accompanied by one or more emotional response such as guilt, anxiety, and fear. These emotions produce involuntary physiological responses that are under the control of the autonomic nervous sytem.

What complicates lie detection is that the physiological responses associated with lying are to some extent under voluntary control. A good liar may never show his colors on the polygraph. Moreover, not everyone reacts to lying in the same way. Some people are emotionally sensitive even to neutral stimuli, while others are unresponsive even to normally arousing stimuli. Also since the assumption is that the liar knows he is lying, a problem is caused by the individual who genuinely believes he is telling the truth, even when he isn't. Finally, the examiner's manner, attitude, and tone of voice can influence the kind of physiological response produced.

Because all of these pitfalls can lead to false conclusions about a suspect, polygraph evidence has not been admissible in a court of law, although the device can be used freely in investigations on a voluntary basis. Polygraphers claim anywhere from 95 to 100 percent accuracy, and in a recent laboratory experiment the polygraph demonstrated 92 percent accuracy in locating the guilty person (Davidson, 1968). But we must remember that even this margin of error may be responsible for convicting an innocent man.

behaviors (or, more accurately, *reflexive behaviors*) appear spontaneously in both blind and deaf children. Unfortunately, we do not know whether smiling and crying are indications of emotion or whether children smile and cry without emotion. Most likely, crying is an inborn response to internal physical needs or discomfort. But as a child grows and develops, and experiences more of the world about him, he starts to differentiate among emotional states. There are emotions (envy, greed, jealousy) that we recognize in children and adults that we do not distinguish in infants. Thus, it seems clear that some emotions at least must be fashioned during intellectual and perceptual development and through enlarged experience. According to Bridges (1932), emotions develop in a treelike pattern, and from the state of general excitement, the infant begins to exhibit specific emotional states. By the time the infant is three months old, he appears to have feelings of distress and delight. Signs of increasingly complex emotions emerge in the child as development and maturation proceed. Note that we say that the child *appears* to have these feelings, for obviously the young child cannot communicate verbally to tell us what he's experiencing.

It is believed that all of us are born with the capacity for emotion. Beyond that, we learn most of the emotions we experience, and the more we experience, the more our emotions are modified. We learn, for example, which stimuli should provoke, or are appropriate to, which emotions. A young child, for instance, may scream as much when he stubs his toe as when his favorite toy is taken from him. There is no gradation in emotional response. Later, he begins to evaluate between minor and major annoyances, and his responses become proportional to the stimulus or event. A child may be curious about everything and afraid of nothing when very young, but when he starts to attach meaning and positive or negative feelings to particular events, he does develop fears and apprehensions. Later, his growing intellectual ability enables him to analyze his responses; whereas when he was younger, he forgot his anger or fear as soon as the cause was removed.

Before we explore both the physiological and psychological dimensions of emotional man in greater detail, recall what we mentioned previously about emotions assuming the status of motives. Anger, for example, may motivate you to seek revenge at any cost. Fear may limit your freedom to explore, and envy or jealousy may impel you to act in ways that you are secretly ashamed of. The search for pleasurable feelings and the need to avoid unpleasant feeling-states may be a central force in how you organize the details of your life.

The fact that we are emotion-experiencing beings has certain drawbacks that need to be considered. Though our emotions may motivate us or drive us on to significant accomplishments, they may also destroy us. Our feelings get linked to our physiological functioning during the process of growing up. What we "feel" psychologically produces concomitant "feelings" in our body, and these may be costly to our well-being.

When Emotions Destroy

One way emotion can be destructive is by producing ulcers. Grayson (1972) reports, for example, that at least one-third of the air traffic controllers in America suffer from peptic ulcers. In March 1970, 111 air traffic controllers of the Federal Aviation Administration walked off the job and staged a "sick-out." Sixty-six of them were diagnosed with some sort of pathological gastrointestinal disorder. Thirty-six were found to have peptic ulcers. Air traffic controllers suffer a much higher incidence of peptic ulcers than any other profession or group—including physicians, alcoholics, coronary patients, clerks, airline stewards, rural workers, and lawyers. According to the National Health Survey of the National Center of Health Statistics, peptic ulcers are presently one of the leading chronic conditions causing disability.

The tensions in the air traffic controller's job have been related to the occurrence of the disease. The primary source of stress is the fear of midair collisions. If the controller is involved in a near collision, he cannot exercise the "fight or flight" response which often acts as a tension release in other situations. Rather, he must suppress any such reaction while trapped at a radarscope, forced to continue issuing cool, concise commands into a microphone.

Emotions and ulcers go together for other animals as well. Brady's (1958) studies of ulcers in monkeys at the Walter Reed Army Institute of Research is illustrative. In some of his experiments, monkeys were kept in restraining chairs where they could move their heads and limbs but not their bodies. The monkeys were conditioned in various ways while sitting in these chairs. These experimental procedures seemed to impose considerable emotional stress on the animals and brought about dramatic alterations in the hormone content of their blood. In fact, some animals died. Brady reported:

> *At first we considered this merely a stroke of bad luck, but the post-mortem findings showed that more than bad luck was involved. Many of the dead monkeys had developed ulcers as well as other extensive gastrointestinal damage. Such pathological conditions are normally rare in laboratory animals, and previous experiments with monkeys kept in restraining chairs up to six months convinced us that restraint alone did not produce the ulcers. Evidently the conditioning procedures were to blame.* [p. 235]

Brady and his co-workers investigated and found that one of the procedures which showed a high correlation with ulcers involved training the monkey to avoid an electric shock by pressing a lever. The animal received a brief shock on the feet at regular intervals (about every 20 seconds), but it could avoid the shock if it learned to press the lever at least once in every 20-second interval. Before long, the monkeys learned to press the lever far more often than once every 20 seconds.

A controlled experiment was set up using two monkeys in "yoked chairs." Both monkeys received shocks, but only one monkey could prevent them. The experimental or what they called the "executive" monkey could prevent shocks to himself and his partner by pressing the lever. The control

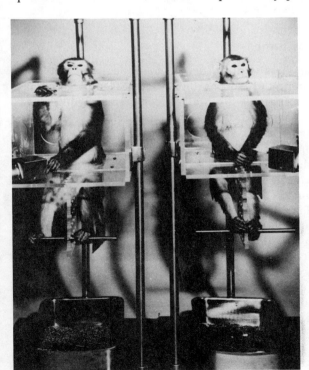

The "executive" monkey experiment conducted by Brady (1958). Although both monkeys were equipped with control levers, only the one on the left could prevent his partner and himself from being shocked.

monkey's lever was a dummy. Thus, both animals were subjected to the same number of shocks at the same time, but only the executive monkey faced the stress of having to press the lever. The monkeys were placed on a continuous schedule of alternate periods of shock avoidance and rest at an interval of six hours for each period.

After 23 days of the schedule, the executive monkey died. It pressed the lever steadily through the first two hours of its last session. The "executive" and the control monkey were examined, and Brady concluded that the crucial factor was not the degree or even the frequency of stress but the relationship between the length of the stress periods and the rest periods. The six-hours-on, six-hours-off schedule had produced ulcers. No other schedule they tried produced ulcers at all. "Emotional stress, it appears must be intermittent—turning the animal's system on and off, so to speak—if it is to cause ulcers" (Brady, 1958, p. 238).

Very similar findings were reported by Weiss (1972) using rats. He reported that, when rats were able to predict when shocks would occur, they showed relatively little ulceration. When rats received the shocks unpredictably, they showed a considerable amount of ulceration. His results clearly demonstrated that the psychological variable of predictability, rather than the shock itself, was the main determinant of ulcer severity.

Clearly, emotions can be destructive enough to kill us. But they can also bring us joy and satisfaction and protect us in threatening situations. We can now take a closer look at emotion acting in situations that involve sexual arousal and in situations where we experience fear.

Sexual Behavior and Hormones

HORMONES AND AGGRESSION

Animal studies have noted there is a link between the male hormone testosterone and aggression. In the mouse, for example, fighting among males commences with the onset of puberty, when hormone levels are rising abruptly. Female mice fight only rarely, as do males that have been castrated. When male castrates are given testosterone injections, however, they display normal male adult fighting behavior within a matter of hours. Also, a high correlation exists between the levels of testosterone and the position each animal holds in the dominance hierarchy. With monkeys, for example, dominance and aggression tend to increase in proportion to the amount of male hormone the animal has.

Sexual behavior in lower animals is often tied to a particular part of the year. Most migrating birds mate only during the spring season. As the days grow longer and longer, some part of the brain becomes more active than usual and the hormones that begin the sexual cycle are released. However, it usually takes the sight of the bird's mate to trigger the instinctive sexual response patterns. For example, the brilliant tail feathers of the peacock serve not only to attract the peahen, but also to set off an increased production of the hormone estrogen in her. The peahen's response to the male's display activates those parts of the male's brain concerned with mating behavior and as the neural circuits controlling the male's behavior are triggered, they stimulate an increased production of androgens in his sex glands. When these male hormones are released into the bloodstream, they stimulate sexual activity by causing appropriate neurons in the brain to fire. They also cause the glands to secrete even more hormones until the male's drive level is high enough for the sexual-reproductive cycle to be completed.

The relation of hormones and sexual behavior in humans is, of course, less direct than in animals. For one thing, the sex drive in humans is not

THE MATERNAL MOTIVE

The maternal motive is produced by a combination of hormones secreted during pregnancy and shortly afterward. One of the most important is a product of the pituitary gland, prolactin. Prolactin is stimulated by the presence of a fetus in the uterus. In turn, prolactin stimulates the mammary glands to produce milk for nursing the young. When prolactin is injected into a virgin female rat that has been given the young of another rat, for example, the injected rat will accept the young and care for them in much the same way that the natural mother would.

as closely tied to the female reproductive cycle. The human female's receptivity to the male is determined more by psychological factors than it is by the type of hormones her body is producing at any moment. In other words, how we feel has more to do with our cognitions and values than with blood chemistry. Sexual behavior in humans is mostly under the control of the brain, but hormone levels do have an effect. In most instances, they form a backdrop for human emotion that can enhance or inhibit feelings and their expression in behavior. But physical changes do take place in our bodies, and our emotional reactions to our arousal helps to determine our sexual behavior.

Both sexes produce both sex hormones, and in females as well as males testosterone appears to be the hormone which most strongly influences levels of sexual urge. Most of the male hormones produced by females are secreted by the adrenals. Women who have had their adrenals removed suffer a dramatic loss in sexual desire. In contrast, women who have had their ovaries removed rarely respond with loss of sex drive. In addition, women receiving testosterone injections report experiencing a marked surge in sexual desire.

Psychological events can *cause* physical events as well as *be* caused by them. A psychological state thus can influence hormone production, just as the hormones influence psychological states. The same holds true for the emotion we call fear and the severe fears we call phobia.

HORMONES AND SEXUAL CHOICE

Women who have undergone menopause and experience a decrease in sexual desire come to life again sexually if they receive androgen, the male sex hormone. Similarly, men whose desires are waning can be stirred to action again by the administration of additional androgen.

About thirty years ago experimentalists sought to determine if intake of the male hormone by homosexuals would reverse their patterns of behavior and make them more interested in women. The experiment was a failure.

Testosterone influences sexual impulses in both sexes, but has nothing to do with determining the sex of the individual toward whom heightened sexual interest will be directed.

Fear and Anger

Animals such as lions, which survive by fighting and killing their prey, have large quantities of a chemical called *noradrenalin* in their systems. Rabbits, which survive by running away, have large quantities of the chemical *adrenalin*. Thus, it would appear that the physiological effects of noradrenalin and the emotion of anger (with the attendant behavior of "fight") are closely connected. On the other hand, the emotion of fear (and the attendant behavior of "flight") seems to be associated with adrenalin.

In many emotional states the rate of heartbeat can jump from the normal of 72 beats per minute to as high as 180 beats. The composition of the blood changes so that the number of red corpuscles (which carry oxygen) increases markedly. And the hormones secreted by the endocrine glands produce changes in the sugar level, acidity, and amounts of adrenalin and noradrenalin in the bloodstream.

With anger, there is a tendency for the heart rate to go down. Blood pressure goes up; muscular tension increases; and, most of all, the number of galvanic skin reflexes (based on increased sweat-gland activity) rises sharply. With fear, there is a tendency toward faster breathing, peaks of muscular tension, and increased electrical conductivity of the skin. As we studied in Chapter 2, it is the sympathetic division of the autonomic nervous system that tells the body to prepare for an emergency.

The movements of the stomach and intestines, associated with the digestion and absorption of food, usually stop during anger and rage. The body's metabolic rate tends to go up, and food in the bloodstream and the body tissues is burned off at a faster rate. The breathing pattern changes in rate and depth, and the angry person may gasp or pant. The salivary glands stop working and cause the feeling of dryness in the mouth that so often occurs with fear and anger. In contrast, the sweat glands may be overactive and produce a dripping forehead or the "cold sweat" that sometimes accompanies fear. In addition, the pupils of the eyes may enlarge, giving the wide-eyed look that is characteristic of rage, excitement, and pain.

Ax (1953) performed a series of experiments to determine whether or not fear and anger produce different physiological patterns of response. The laboratory assistants produced anger by making derogatory remarks to the subjects during the course of the experiment. They provoked fear by acting uncertain about how to operate some dangerous-looking electronic equipment. Ax then recorded pulse rate, heartbeat, galvanic skin responses, respiration, hand- and face-skin temperature, and eyelid movement.

Fear produced changes in three response areas: respiration increased; palmar-skin resistance decreased (when you have sweaty palms, there is decreased resistance to a low voltage electrical current); and there were outbursts of high muscular tension. A different pattern was recorded for anger: heart rate decreased; the number of galvanic skin responses increased; overall muscular tension increased; and blood pressure increased. Ax found that the

FEAR AND ANXIETY
Fear is usually described as a reaction to immediate and evident danger. Anxiety is described as an apprehensive response to future possible dangers. What a child fears and what makes him anxious change as he grows older. Releasing a harmless snake in the presence of an infant or a child younger than two years of age usually produces only curiosity as a response. By age three or four, children are at least cautious about the strange wriggling object. By four, they display visible fear responses.

pattern of fear resembled the pattern produced by the injection of the hormone adrenalin. The pattern of anger resembled the action produced by the injection of noradrenalin.

Our physiological response to fear or anger is a critical event in our lives, but we must not neglect the psychological consequences of strong emotions. Extreme emotions can interfere with our adjustment to life. Extraordinary fear, called *phobia*, is an illustration of how emotions can alter our existence.

Phobia

The fears of infancy and early childhood are usually quite concrete. As the child grows older, however, fears become abstract and often include nonexistent threats. Everyone is frightened by what they only partly comprehend. These fears range from an intense dread of immediately present dangers (such as fire) to uneasiness about painful events that are possible, if not probable. As Kessler (1966) points out, a school-age child may express a dislike for dogs and be uneasy around them. This may be quite normal. But, when the child becomes preoccupied with the possibility of encountering a dog and lives in a constant state of anticipatory anxiety, his feeling goes beyond simple fear and borders on phobia.

Jersild, Markey, and Jersild (1960) interviewed 398 children from five to twelve years of age and found the following order of fears (from most to least frightening): supernatural agents (ghosts, witches, corpses, mysterious events); being alone, in the dark, in a strange place, or being lost; attack by animals; and bodily injury, falling, illness, traffic accidents, operations, hurts, and pains. Angelino, Dollins, and Mech (1956) discovered a positive relationship between socioeconomic background and the number and kinds of fears that children have. Lower-class boys feared switchblades, whippings,

THE TWO PHOBIAS
Dixon (1957) and his co-workers made statistical groupings of phobic responses reported by patients and concluded such symptoms could be grouped into two categories: fear of separation and fear of harm. Persons phobic about being left alone, being in the dark, or taking journeys are anxious, primarily, about interpersonal relations. Those whose fears are focused on harm (surgery, hospitals, or pain) share the common fears of most of us, but the intensity of their reaction refers most directly to developmental experiences that have been inadequate to provide the maturity needed to face the harsh realities of life.

Counterphobia

One way to deal with phobic feelings is to take defensive (counterphobic) measures rather than avoid the feared object. The phobic person can consciously and deliberately seek mastery of what he fears in order to deny to himself (and others) the truth of the anxiety that nibbles at his consciousness. Thus, some adults indulge vigorously in precisely those behaviors they dread most, even though they may be unaware of the source of their fascination with such actions. Cameron (1963) describes this as a form of "reactive courage." Those who fear heights may climb mountains. Those who fear speed may drive racing cars. And those who suffer from claustrophobia may devote their lives to "spelunking"—the exploration of confining caves and narrow passage ways in the bowels of the earth.

This is not to suggest that the heroes and daredevils of our culture are all emotionally disturbed, obsessively counterphobic human beings. It is merely a way of noting that, for some, dangerous acts are a means of demonstrating to themselves and to others that they have mastered the most common fears—that they are free of anxiety.

OUTER SPACE
PHOBIA
*Phobias reflect the degree of
technical sophistication of the
society. Kerry (1960), for example,
reported four patients who had
intense phobias centering on outer
space. They were anxious about
residing on a planet that, like a
gigantic space ship, hurtled through
space at an incredible speed.*

THE NUMBER 13
*"The case illustrates particularly
well the expansion of a phobia. The
patient began by staying in bed on
the thirteenth day of the month so
that he would not come in contact
with calendars and newspaper dates.
Soon he discovered that
"twenty-seventh" contained thirteen
letters, and he was condemned to
bed two days each month. He next
began going to work by a
roundabout route to avoid the
thirteen-letter sign, "Peter
Robinson," that hung prominently
on the direct route. Presently he
experienced uneasiness when people
said, "Oh, good morning," or when
they said, "Good afternoon" without
the "Oh" that would have given the
greeting a safe fifteen letters. He
began hopping over the thirteenth
step in a flight of stairs, counting
his own footsteps, counting the
streets he passed, until finally he
had time for nothing but avoiding
the number thirteen."* [White,
1964, pp. 257–58]

robbers, killers, and guns. Upper-class boys feared car accidents, getting killed, juvenile delinquents, and disaster.

The persistent, irrational, morbid fear called phobia is so common in the early years that it has been designated the "normal neurosis" of childhood.

The Psychoanalytic View

According to classic psychoanalytic theory, phobias are symptoms issuing from unacceptable basic urges that have been repressed from consciousness. When repression is effective, phobia symptoms need not exist. But, when repression fails, the anxiety properly belonging somewhere else is displaced to a related but undeserving object, person, or situation. In this way, harmless objects (water, cats, snakes, and the like) become objects of enormous fear and are anxiously avoided. When avoidance is not possible, intense anxiety may produce gross psychological disorganization in the phobic person. Thus, a phobia may effectively protect the individual from recognizing the true nature of his emotional problem. It may protect him from the conscious awareness of an intolerable impulse as, for example, the desire to kill a parent.

The classic example of phobia was the case reported by Sigmund Freud—of little Hans, a five-year-old boy who lived in terror of horses. Hans's phobia, according to Freud, was not so much fear of horses as fear of his own frightening impulses. First Hans repressed his frightening wish to attack his father. Then, fearing the father might somehow learn of this wish and punish him horribly, Hans "solved" the problem by fearing horses instead of the father. Since Hans both loved and hated his father, he also resolved his mixed feelings. He now could hate horses while loving his father.

One phobia unique to childhood is school phobia. School may become a source of terror or acute discomfort for the child. These phobias can occur at any age, but most appear in younger children. Psychoanalytic theorists have considered fear of separation from the mother as a cause for the child's reluctance to attend school. They regard mother-and-child as a single interacting unit. Neurotic, overprotective, and fearful mothers may see to it that the child acquires crippling phobias. It is rare, however, for a school-phobic child to have this as his only symptom of emotional disturbance. Usually, school phobia is merely one of a series of related difficulties. Among the psychic conflicts theorized to exist in school phobia, the roles of ambivalence and aggression are seen as most important. In other words, the child is unwilling to separate from the mother but may also have unrecognized resentment toward her. The child's feelings of love and hate may be expressed in the anguish he causes his mother each morning when he invents another excuse to stay home from school.

Phobias can be acquired in several ways. They can be learned from parents or from traumatic experiences with the feared object. Or they can be a resolution to psychic conflict.

Skydiving and Fear

"For a novice sports parachutist, a parachute jump represents an acute approach-avoidance conflict. On the one hand, there is the excitement and thrill of a new adventure, and on the other, the fear of injury and death. Many jumpers say that their first few jumps were the most terrifying experiences of their lives. . . . Experienced jumpers, understandably, present an entirely different picture. If they are afraid, they don't show it. . . . In a study we ran in 1965, we had novice and experienced sports parachutists rate the degree of fear they felt at different times before, at, and after a jump . . . the peak of anxiety for both groups occurred *before* rather than *at* the time of the jump. . . . Novices showed increasing anxiety up to the moment of the jump, when they also felt most afraid. Experienced jumpers, by contrast, rated themselves most afraid on the morning of the jump, though their level of physiological arousal did not peak until after they were airborne; by the moment of the jump their arousal had declined to normal levels. It seems that the early rise of subjective fear and the later rise of physiological arousal in the experienced parachutists served as early warning signals that prevented the fear and arousal from becoming excessive."

Source: Fenz and Epstein, 1967, pp. 233–45.

The Behavioral View

In contrast to psychoanalytic theorists, behaviorists contend that some human phobias are generated by the attachment of intense fear responses to otherwise neutral objects or situations. Yates (1970), for example, notes that, even in Freud's case of Little Hans, it was true that the child also experienced a series of traumatic exposures to horses during the time his phobia developed.

In the last ten years, school phobias have attracted the attention of behavioral therapists who suggest that labeling school avoidance as phobia is oversimplifying the issue. They point out that truants are even more successfully and regularly absent from school, yet they are not called phobic.

Behavioral methods of treatment have been quite successful in returning children to school. In some studies a comparison between these methods and the traditional psychoanalytic approach is possible, but it is important to remember that the theories behind these different methods are not similar. Gelder and Marks (1968) reported that, on the average, phobic patients exposed to desensitization procedures improved more in four months than they did in two previous years of exposure to group psychotherapy. Patients treated with behavioral methods, once free of phobic symptoms, do not seem to substitute a new set of symptoms for the ones they had.

The behaviorists' version of "Little Hans" is Watson and Rayner's (1920) "Little Albert." Albert, an 11-month-old child, had a white rat put into his room. As he reached for it, the experimenter struck a steel bar, making a very loud noise. The sequence was repeated until Albert developed a genuine phobia about white rats. As the experiment continued, Albert developed a fear of all furry things, fur coats, wool, and even cotton. Wolpe and Rachman (1960) have used the following model in discussing the cause of Albert's phobia: (1) phobias are learned responses; (2) phobic stimuli, simple or complex,

HOW TO CURE FEAR
OF SNAKES
A great many people are afraid of snakes. Psychologists have used this fact to test out certain kinds of fear-removal techniques. The experimental design is simple. Sort out college students who are afraid of snakes, and expose them to different approaches to removing the fears. Then find out which approach is best by measuring the number of "cured" people. Psychologists soon learned that there are a great many effective ways to eliminate fear of snakes. Cooper, Furst, and Bridges (1969) gave harmless snakes to fearful students and told them, simply, that, if they held and handled the snakes again and again and acted as though they were unafraid, they would get over their fears. It worked.

Before Little Albert "learned" to be afraid of white rats, he played with all sorts of white fuzzy things. Afterward, even a cuddly rabbit caused him great distress.

develop when they are associated in time and space with fear-producing situations; (3) neutral stimuli directly connected with the fear-producing situation are more likely to trigger phobia than are irrelevant stimuli present at the same time; (4) repetition of this association between fear situations and phobic objects will strengthen the phobia; and (5) generalization from the original phobic stimulus to stimuli of a similar nature can easily occur.

This conception of the source of phobic problems may not be as different from the psychoanalytic view as it first appears. In their studies of phobia, Gelder and Marks (1966) found that when they used a matched sample of persons who did *not* get treatment, seven out of ten of them improved symptomatically in both the experimental and control groups. In a later work, Gelder, Marks, Wolff, and Clark (1967) concluded that both desensitization and psychotherapy can contribute in different ways to the treatment of phobic persons; neither approach can be relied on for every person.

How do you decide whether the psychoanalytic or behavioral approach to the treatment of phobia is correct? Perhaps no decision is necessary. Either may be appropriate for different people. For many cases of childhood phobia, it may be that the traditional psychoanalytic treatment is best. For other kinds of phobias, behavioral therapy may be most effective. Behavioral therapists have been very successful with fairly well delineated, circumscribed disorders, and they have treated some fears and phobias without bothering to explore the source of the patient's anxiety. Their therapeutic methods are basically a-historical, dealing exclusively with the present. Variants of their primary techniques are being employed by a mushrooming number of practitioners. Of course, the techniques of classical or respondent conditioning which we discussed in Chapter 3 can also be used to extinguish a phobia. In this case, the phobia is first respondently conditioned, then deconditioned.

If different phobias can come about for different reasons and in different life circumstances, then different methods of treatment are called for. In dealing with emotional difficulties, it is apparent that a proper diagnosis must precede any therapeutic plan.

Summary

1. According to the theories of evolutionist Charles Darwin, the capacity to feel and express emotions developed in both animals and man to aid their survival. Although man appears to inherit a *capacity* for emotion, not everyone experiences the same emotions or to the same degree.

2. In addition to learning the emotion itself, we learn which stimuli specific emotions are attached to. Sometimes we are conditioned to react positively or negatively to certain stimuli before we understand their meaning.

3. Because we often seek pleasant feelings and avoid unpleasant ones, our emotions sometimes act as motivators. In addition, specific emotions may motivate you to perform certain behaviors.

4. The subjective feelings of emotion are always accompanied by a state of physiological arousal. Because of this, our emotions may sometimes lead to bodily damage.

5. The *James-Lange theory* suggests that we experience the subjective feeling of emotion after we become aware of our physiological state of arousal. The *Cannon-Bard theory* states that physiological arousal and subjective emotion occur at the same time. *Cognitive theorists* suggest that the emotions we attribute to a state of physiological arousal will vary not with the type of arousal but with the situation we are in.

6. Studies involving the executive-monkey setup demonstrated that stress itself does not necessarily cause physical damage. Rather, the predictability of the negative stimulus determines when stress will be destructive.

7. Lie detectors, also called *polygraphs,* are machines that record changes in physiological arousal occurring when individuals feel guilty, anxious, or fearful about telling lies. Polygraphs measure blood pressure, respiration, heart rate, and the galvanic skin response (GSR).

8. The galvanic skin response (GSR) is a measurement of the change in resistance of the skin to electrical current. When we are emotionally aroused, the GSR shows a decrease in skin resistance, probably due to increased sweating of the palms.

9. The production of hormones can cause certain psychological events in humans. But emotions can also influence the production of hormones.

10. In man the sexual response is only partly controlled by hormones, and psychological factors play a more important role.

11. The state of physiological arousal associated with anger and the fighting response are similar to those caused by *noradrenalin.* This hormone is found in the blood of individuals and animals who express anger in fear-provoking situations.

12. The emotions of fear and flight are associated with a physiological pattern similar to that produced by the hormone *adrenalin.* The blood of animals who run rather than fight when exposed to fearful situations contains adrenalin.

13. A *phobia* is an intense, irrational fear that often causes an individual to go to extremes to avoid the fearful situation. The psychoanalytic view is that phobias occur when an unacceptable impulse

is displaced to a related, but dissimilar, object, which then can be avoided.

14. According to the behaviorists, phobias occur when a neutral stimulus becomes associated with a fearful situation. The neutral stimulus is more likely to acquire phobic properties if it is somehow relevant to the fearful event, even when it is not the cause. Stimuli similar to the particular phobia acquire phobic properties through the principle of generalization.

15. According to the behavioral view, phobias can be eliminated through desensitization. This is a step-by-step procedure in which progressively more fearful stimuli are presented to the phobic individual in the absence of any real danger. Psychoanalytic theorists, on the other hand, treat phobias by examining the individual's past history to uncover the unacceptable impulse that the phobia represents.

16. Some people deal with their phobias by *counterphobic* behavior. They place themselves in situations they fear most in order to prove to themselves and others that they are really not afraid.

PSYCHOLOGICAL ISSUE

Stress

When we talk about the "stress and strain" of modern life, we mean simply the pressures caused by competition in school and in the working world, social demands, worries about economic security, and so on. No time in human history has been free of such stresses and strains, but severe and prolonged psychological stresses can cause actual physical diseases.

The term *stress* is usually applied to any human condition that leads to the mobilization of bodily resources and the expenditure of more energy than usual. Stressful conditions have a physical cause (bodily injury, lack of sleep, inadequate or improper food) or result from psychological states (insecurity and loss of love). The body reacts to these stressors with three stages of adjustment, which Hans Selye (1956) refers to as the *general-adaptation syndrome.*

The first stage of the general-adaptation syndrome is the *alarm reaction.* The activity of the autonomic nervous system increases to produce an emergency physiological pattern. The second stage is the *stage of resistance* in which the organism attempts to resist stress by increased secretions of various glands. If the original stressor does not disappear, or if new stressors are added, the glandular system cannot continue to function at this high rate. Then, the last stage, or *stage of exhaustion,* occurs as the organism fails to withstand the stressors. If stress continues, death may result.

As Lazarus (1966) indicates, stress is "a universal human . . . phenomenon [that] results in intense and distressing experience and appears to be a tremendous influence in behavior" (p. 2). Stress is the outcome of a perceived threat to one's life or well-being. A vital aspect of stress is that the individual *continually* anticipates a threatening confrontation with some harmful condition. In measuring and appraising the relationship between stress and psychological adjustment, researchers need access to the psychological experiences of the person to determine what has been viewed as threatening and stressful throughout life.

Initially it seemed that the concept of stress would

tie together a great many loose ends from physiology and psychology. It might bind together notions about various states such as anxiety, conflict, emotional distress, extreme environmental conditions, ego-threat, frustration, threat to security, tension, and arousal (Appley and Trumbull, 1967).

The problem is that not all potentially stressful stimuli always induce stress. In addition, neither of us will react in identical or predictable ways under stress. You may get sharper, more accurate, and efficient under stress, whereas I may come apart at the seams and be unable to perform adequately. One critical feature of stress is that we cannot judge it either by measuring the environmental stimulus or by assessing the behavioral response the organism makes to it. As Arnold (1967) said: "We cannot really speak of psychological stress without considering . . . [the

person's] . . . subjective evaluation, for what is stress for one may be a welcome challenge to another" (p. 126).

Lazarus (1966) proposed that any analysis of stress must deal with the problem of threat—the anticipation of harm. Lazarus underscores the coping features of a person's responses to threat. How any one threat is appraised may produce quite different reactions, ranging from an angry attack to withdrawal or paralyzing anxiety. However we react, each instance of threat and stress affects our psychological well-being.

Stress and Mental Health

Our environment obviously affects our mental health, but the possibility that the social environment can trigger emotional disturbance is a more complicated

notion. The push-pull of stressful social pressures and consequent personal reactions produces some deformity in the psychological state of the individual. People, like molecules, react to stress by slowly and subtly altering their characteristic ways of adapting to new environmental demands. When humans adapt to stress, we are concerned with how much distortion there will be in personality organization. There may be changes in a person's resilience, ego-strength, ability, or inner resources. In reference to these dimensions, Langner and Michael (1963) suggested:

If these terms seem almost mystical, it is because we know so little about what makes for a mentally healthy person. If we knew more about the origins of mental health we wouldn't have to ask ourselves how two people faced with the same apparent stress—such as military service, a concentration camp, or a death of a loved one—can react so differently, one with extreme strain, the other with relatively little. [p. 7]

People have an unhealthy tendency to produce unexpected reactions. They may destroy themselves by reacting to the anticipation of stress, or they may live through it and then cripple themselves with their memories. Once you are burned you will probably be twice as fearful since new stress is added to the weight of all the painful stresses of the past. Memory of a significant or painful stress can haunt a person as long as he lives, and every new trauma may evoke the disturbing memory.

Stress is a relative rather than absolute condition, which can become as circular as a merry-go-round. Social stress evokes strain, and strained reactions produce new social stress to be dealt with. Most riders on this merry-go-round make no forward progress, even though the full fare of mental debilitation must still be paid.

Langner and Michael (1963) studied the mental health of citizens living in midtown Manhattan, focusing on the emotional impact of economics on the human psyche. They questioned a sample of adults who were children in the Great Depression and discovered that 42 percent of those whose fathers had oc-

cupied a high socioeconomic status before the crash recalled that their parents experienced financial problems during the depression. In many cases these "problems" involved adjusting to not having enough money to maintain a previous life style or to attain the life style to which they aspired. Such financial problems could hardly be classed as true economic deprivation, but they did produce a *subjective* feeling of deprivation relative to the financial aspirations of the family.

The crucial conclusion of the study was that the children of parents who "often" had a hard time "making ends meet" during the depression suffered substantially greater mental-health risk than persons whose parents endured less financial and social hardship during the 1930s. The children of parents who only "sometimes" or "rarely" experienced difficulty or "never" had a hard time in the depression years survived with even fewer mental-health scars.

These findings confirmed a continuing suspicion among mental health theorists that the mental health of an adult may be traceable to distressed child-parent relationships resulting from "hard times." Many mothers were compelled to go to work to keep the family economically intact. The daily absence of the mother was not in itself enough to produce emotional disturbance, but the angry, resentful, depressed mother who worked under duress may have been. The proportion of working mothers increased markedly for persons who now recall exceptionally hard times during the depression. In families which "never" had hard times, only 19.4 percent of the mothers worked, but 44.8 percent of the mothers worked in families which "often" had hard times. Keep in mind that most of these working mothers had school-age children, and 25 percent of the mothers with preschool children worked at least part time during the year. The depression thus left an indelible imprint on the mental life of its children. Social scientists who gamble will quote you odds of three to two that, if you experienced economic deprivation in childhood, you will show greater emotional difficulty as an adult than if all had gone well in your family during those bleak years.

Poor is a relative term, of course, and many of the present-day American poor would be envied by a large portion of people in most countries of the world. When we compare the descriptions of poverty in the nineteenth century with those of today, the difference is astonishing. The important point to establish is that in every society the poor person assesses his position in life by *comparing* it to the position of others.

Being poor is one kind of possible stress. Many other forces cause stress and produce the subjective feelings of strain. Man is an emotional animal. His positive emotions reach heights no lesser species can even begin to comprehend, and his negative emotions produce a level and kind of despair the other species are spared in their time on this planet.

Summary

1.   *Stress* is any physiological or psychological condition that causes the body to mobilize its resources and expend more energy than usual. Stress occurs whenever one perceives a threat to his well-being.

2.   It is difficult to judge which environmental conditions will cause stress, since each individual may perceive threat differently. For this reason some people perform well under pressure, whereas others buckle or become ill under the stress.

3.   The body's reaction to stress occurs in three stages, known as the *general-adaptation syndrome.* First, the activity of the autonomic nervous system increases to cope with the emergency. Then, the body attempts to resist stress through increased glandular secretions. Finally, if the stress does not disappear, the body is forced to give up in exhaustion.

4.   Studies of children of the Great Depression indicate that memories of past traumas will increase the severity of the adult's reactions to stress. The greater mental-health risk found in people who have been through hard times may be related to poor parent-child relationships that occurred during those difficult times.

THOUGHT AND INTELLIGENCE

LIKE MOTIVATION AND EMOTION, man's capacity to think is unique to the experience of being human. If man has an undisputed claim to superiority over his animal cousins, it lies in the human ability to form concepts, to reason and solve complex problems, and to master language. Man has accomplished miraculous feats because he can apply his intelligence by means of abstract thought. He can manipulate symbols and ideas, record what he thinks, and communicate it to others. Even the highest primates lack this vital ability to communicate about the past and future.

Man's intelligence also allows him to be creative. The astonishing extremes in human creativity, such as the spectrum of musical geniuses, are still mysteries in man's creative history. Of course, intelligence is only one part of being human, even though our society in particular has put a disproportionate emphasis on it. On the constructive side, we have attempted to design an educational system that fosters the growth of a student's aptitude and intelligence. But as we shall see in later chapters, man's role as the thinking species on this planet has not always produced beneficial effects—on himself or on his environment. Intelligence, the capacity to solve problems, and language are powerful weapons. They can be the basis of our destruction or our salvation.

Thought and Language

I think I think; therefore, I think I am.—Ambrose Bierce

Human thought and language are the capacities that separate man from other animals. Through thought and language, we fashion decisions in completely new situations by recalling the past and thinking ahead to the consequences of various alternative actions. *Thinking* can be defined as the acquisition and manipulation of symbols and ideas through the unique process called *language*.

Concepts and Thought

The most common kind of thinking involves the formation of *concepts* which let you classify your experiences. Thus, if you look at a collection of items, such as a gallon of milk, a bottle of beer, and a quart of orange juice, you know these objects go together because they are all liquids in containers. When you add nonliquid, edible objects to the items, you must form a new concept for grouping them together. They may now be described as groceries.

Concepts are considered mediators that link a single response to a number of different stimuli. A *verbal mediator* or label allows us to react appropriately to new stimuli the first time we encounter it. One aspect of the mediating process is called the *reversal shift* (Kendler and Kendler, 1967). A subject can be presented with two squares at a time, which he must learn to choose between. The squares differ in size (large and small) as well as color (black and white). In experiments, the subject is reinforced or rewarded for choosing a square either on the basis of color or size. For example, the subject might be rewarded every time he chooses the large square regardless

245

FEEDBACK

More often than not problem solving is an activity that involves at least one other person. The degree to which feedback from another person is important becomes evident when it is restricted. Bavelas (1957) gave one subject a diagram for the arrangement of dominoes while, on the other end of a telephone, his partner had the dominoes and tried to follow directions. The communication was only one-way so there could be no feedback. The partner receiving instructions, but unable to communicate, soon found himself bewildered. No pair of problem solvers managed to get the problem solved. When the second man could react with a push-button for "Yes" or "No," the problem was solved, and the subjects no longer felt they had been stuck with a stupid co-worker!

of its color. Then he must learn to *reverse* his responses (the reversal shift). In other words, he must now learn to choose the small square in order to get a reward. There is also a *nonreversal shift* where the subject must learn to choose by color. This brings in a dimension that was previously irrelevant.

The fact that people can successfully reverse their thinking and concepts may depend on the ability to use verbal mediators. They are able to tell themselves that size is the critical variable, and they can then switch from large to small if large stops being rewarded. Since very young children or animals can't use verbal mediators, they have more difficulty with reversal shifts but less difficulty with nonreversal shifts.

The abilities to fashion abstractions, form concepts, and hold in mind the past, present, and future allow man to solve the problems that confront him. This problem-solving aspect of thought is what we want to consider in greater detail.

Problem Solving

Thinking and reasoning in problem solving may be deductive or inductive. In *deductive* reasoning, we go from the general to the particular. In other words, we have some previous general knowledge and then we draw conclusions from this available data. Sherlock Holmes has been described as a master of deduction.

In *inductive* reasoning, the thinker starts from what is known and leaps intuitively to a new thought or hypothesis about the matter. Inductive reasoning can lead in several directions and creatively produce an entirely new approach to problem solving. Albert Einstein was an inductive thinker who reached conclusions that violated all known laws of physics.

There are a great many elements in the problem-solving process that we need to keep in mind as we consider how our problems are managed.

Trial and Error

All of us have some experiences with *trial and error*. This approach involves trying all possible solutions one by one until the correct solution appears. The method can be useful in solving simple problems such as finding the right key to open a door, but it is an impossible method (in terms of time) for finding the proper numbers on a combination lock.

Thorndike experimented with trial and error by putting cats in a puzzle box and watching them use random approaches before they managed to escape. For Thorndike's cats, problem solving had more to do with learning than thinking.

The animals could not solve the problem of escape from pure thought about the problem. The mechanism to release the doors was not visible, so the cats couldn't have figured out how the doors worked even if they had been smart enough to do so.

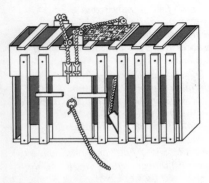

Thorndike's puzzle box.

Solving Problems in Groups

Is it true that "two heads are better than one" or do "too many cooks spoil the stew"? There are arguments on both sides of the issue. It took thousands of scientists and technicians working harmoniously to conquer outer space, but Albert Einstein worked alone and announced the theory of relativity at age 26. Since the decision to work alone or with others has great practical implications, we can consider some of the factors that make group performance superior or that hamper group solutions.

The major advantage of working in groups is that you can pool your unique resources with those of others, and the different contributions of each group member can be combined into a new whole. The members of a group differ not only in intelligence but also in motivation. Some are more willing than others to do hard work, and some problems require time-consuming, painstaking chores. Working alone you may or may not be motivated to put forth the necessary effort. But with a group, the drudgery can be divided equally among the members. As the saying goes, "many hands make light work."

It is also easier for us to see other people's mistakes than to be aware of our own. Annoying as it may be, having our errors corrected by others is frequently helpful. Not only can the group filter out errors, but it may also stimulate ideas which would not have occurred to individuals working alone.

The most obvious disadvantage to group effort is the familiar impulse to let somebody else take the responsibility and slack off in our own effort. In addition, individuals come to the group bringing a variety of motives and these may interfere with the group enterprise. Some may want, consciously or unconsciously, to sabotage the group effort. Others may have self-oriented needs such as defeating rivals, impressing another group member, expressing pent-up feelings, or winning group approval. Members of a group may all want to solve the problem, yet have quite different ideas about how to go about it. If people are unwilling to compromise these different ideas can clash.

In addition, your status in a group also makes a difference in whether your ideas are incorporated in the group solution. Communication is important in group thinking, but it may be hampered by status differences. A group member may not want to criticize the ideas of high-ranking individuals, and low-ranking individuals may not want to speak out at all.

Many of these problems are negligible when groups use *brainstorming* to tackle their problems. The technique of brainstorming started with the assumption that creative

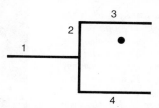

Can a group solve this puzzle faster than an individual? Set up a mini-test by giving the puzzle to several of your friends together, and then try to solve it on your own. The rules: Arrange four matchsticks as shown above and place a piece of "dirt" in the "shovel." By moving only two matchsticks, get the dirt out of the shovel. No, you can't move the dirt! Solution appears on page 261.

ideas will be greatest when everyone feels free to communicate suggestions about a problem at hand. When a group is assembled to solve a problem, it is asked to follow some specific ground rules. During the initial phase of brainstorming (*green-light stage*), group members can put forth any idea they wish—no matter how impractical or ridiculous it may at first appear. No one is allowed to criticize anyone else's ideas. In this stage "killer thoughts" are forbidden: "We tried that before and it didn't work"; "You will never get people to cooperate"; "It's too expensive." All of the ideas are recorded until the flow of ideas dries up. Then in the next phase (*red-light stage*), all the suggestions are examined, evaluated, and criticized until a solution agreeable to the group is found. In many situations, brainstorming seems to work well. In others, it appears to be less effective than allowing individuals to work alone.

In an early study on brainstorming by Taylor, Berry, and Block (1958), subjects were assigned at random to work alone or in five-man groups. In both conditions five problems were posed, and 12 minutes were allowed to work on each one. The comparisons of individuals and groups in terms of the quantity and the originality of ideas produced showed that individuals working alone scored higher than the groups. (Individuals had an average of 68.1 ideas compared to 37.5 for groups.) Individuals also produced more creative ideas.

The fact remains that history records a preponderance of individual accomplishments and seldom reports spectacular group endeavors that have changed the course of mankind. Yet we know that groups have been incredibly successful. Perhaps the answer to whether groups or individuals are better problem solvers is: It depends—on the kind of problem undertaken and, of course, on the group.

THE THINKING CHESS PLAYER

Most of us would think of the chess master who can play 12 boards of "blindfold" chess simultaneously as a model of intense thought and concentration. The psychologist and master chess-player Fine (1965) has commented on the skills and thought processes of such men. He observes that, as a result of long experience with the game, both the board and the pieces acquire so many associations for the player that it becomes impossible for him to think of the board separately from the pieces or of the pieces with no relationship to the board. The master player also thinks in terms of symbols, and it is impossible for him to think of the moves without the symbolic language which chess players use to describe their plays.

THE TWO-STRING REASONING PROBLEM

Imagine this situation: You're in a room with two strings hanging from the ceiling, a chair, and a table on which are a six-inch piece of wire, a cup, a pair of pliers, and some paper. You are told that you must tie the two pieces of string together, but no matter how much you stretch, you can't reach the second string while you're holding onto the first. Your arms need to be two feet longer, or you need to figure out a different way to solve the problem. Think about it for a bit before looking at the answer.

Answer: If you can set the second string in motion, it will swing toward you while you are grasping the first. Only one object on the table, however, is heavy enough to do this—the pliers.

Insight

When a problem seems impossible to solve, sometimes the answer unexpectedly appears all at once in the form of an awareness known as *insight*. It has been suggested that, during the period of time when there seems to be no progress, the thinker is actually reshuffling his similar past experiences and searching for a solution. When this subconscious search uncovers the right combination of elements to solve the problem, the solution pops full blown into mind.

Kohler conducted a famous series of experiments with apes to demonstrate this phenomenon in the process of problem solving. The experimental task was for the apes to get food which had been placed out of reach in a basket suspended from the roof of the cage. The basket would swing back and forth when a string was pulled, and near it was a scaffolding which the ape could use to reach the basket as it swung by. Kohler's apes appeared to solve the problem suddenly rather than to stumble onto the solution while making random, trial-and-error responses. Once they had the solution, they used it successfully every time thereafter.

Insight need not always be a completely sudden event, of course. Sometimes it appears only after a number of trial-and-error experiments have failed. Birch (1945) placed food out of the reach of chimpanzees so they could get it only by using a hoe to rake it toward them. The chimps that had previously played with sticks and learned to use them for digging could solve the problem easily. Animals that did not have this earlier experience never solved the problem.

Functional Fixedness

When facing a problem we sometimes get a mental set which fixes or limits the way the problem is tackled. Experiments have shown that we find it difficult to solve a problem if we are required to use a *familiar* object in a *novel* way. Psychologists call this *functional fixedness.* If you think of an object in terms of its normal use, you remain "fixed" to that expectation and have trouble thinking of it in a different way. Thus, the more you use an object, the harder it is to think of novel uses for it. This fixation may be less powerful when the object is not used for a while. If, for example, a hammer is not used for some time, you might be more likely to use it to prop something up than if you had just used it to bang a nail into the wall (Adamson and Taylor, 1954).

Rigidity in thinking may result from a certain mental set just before you approach the problem, or it can be caused by existing, habitual ways of thinking or behaving. This may explain why you can labor over a problem for hours and get nowhere, whereas someone who is new to the problem can walk in and see the solution at once. A classic story illustrates this case. It was reported that a semitrailer was too tall for a bridge that it tried to go under. Its top crashed into the bottom of the bridge, and it became hopelessly stuck. As the story goes, a great many solutions were tried to get the truck out, but none of them worked until a little boy came along and asked the people why they didn't just let the air out of the truck's tires. They did and it worked. Their functional fixedness in problem solving had made them blind to the possibilities of the tires.

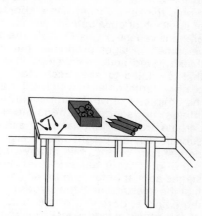

A test of functional fixedness. Subjects are shown items like those on the table above and are asked to mount one candle vertically on the wall. If you can't figure out how to do it, the solution appears on page 261.

Language

We use language in our thinking even when we are not speaking aloud. We think in a kind of shorthand that may skip a number of logical steps. When a decision or conclusion is reached, we must then translate the thought into language if we wish to communicate with others.

If you estimate the number of words you speak in a day, a month, or a year you would find that even if you are not a particularly talkative person you will speak a billion words in a lifetime. The number of words that you hear during the same lifetime is tremendous.

A student attending classes and holding frequent conversations with fellow students might hear 100,000 words in a day. If he has a modest reading speed of, say, 300 words per minute and spends five hours a day reading, he would cover 90,000 words a day. Such a student, then, could easily be exposed to three-quarters of a billion words a year. . . . Not all these words would be different, of course; indeed, it is likely that about one in ten is the word the. *. . . Even though an individual may not use certain words more than once in a very long time, if he is highly educated he may have a vocabulary of well*

Giant in the Nursery: Jean Piaget

In the course of . . . many years of research into children's thinking, Piaget has elaborated a general theory of intellectual development which, in its scope and comprehensiveness, rivals Freud's theory of personality development. Piaget proposes that intelligence—adaptive thinking and action—develops in a sequence of stages that is related to age. Each stage sees the elaboration of new mental abilities which set the limits and determine the character of what can be learned during that period. (Piaget finds incomprehensible Harvard psychologist Jerome Bruner's famous hypothesis to the effect that "any subject can be taught effectively in some intellectually honest form to any child at any stage of development.") Although Piaget believes that the order in which the stages appear holds true for all children, he also believes that the ages at which the stages evolve will depend upon the native endowment of the child and upon the quality of the physical and social environment in which he is reared. In a very real sense, then, Piaget's is both a nature *and* a nurture theory.

The first stage in the development of intelligence (usually 0–2 years) Piaget calls the sensory-motor period and it is concerned with the evolution of those abilities necessary to construct and reconstruct objects. To illustrate, Piaget observed that when he held a cigarette case in front of his daughter Jacqueline (who was 8 months old at the time) and then dropped it, she did not follow the trajectory of the case but continued looking at his hand. Even at 8 months (Lucienne and Laurent succeeded in following the object at about 5 months but had been exposed to more experiments than Jacqueline), she was not able to reconstruct the path of the object which she had seen dropped in front of her.

Toward the end of this period, however, Jacqueline was even able to reconstruct the position of objects which had undergone hidden displacement. When she was 19 months old, Piaget placed a coin in his hand and then placed his hand under a coverlet where he dropped the coin before removing his hand. Jacqueline first looked in his hand and then immediately lifted the coverlet and found the coin. This reconstruction was accomplished with the aid of an elementary form of reasoning. The coin was in the hand, the hand was under the coverlet, the coin was not in the hand so the coin is under the coverlet. Such reasoning, it must be said, is accomplished without the aid of language and by means of mental images.

The second stage (usually 2–7 years), which Piaget calls the preoperational stage, bears witness to the elaboration of the symbolic function, those abilities which have to do with representing things. The presence of these new abilities is shown by the gradual acquisition of language, the first indications of dreams and night terrors, the advent of symbolic play (two sticks at right angles are an airplane) and the first attempts at drawing and graphic representation.

At the beginning of this stage the child tends to identify words and symbols with the objects they are intended to represent. He is upset if someone tramps on a stone which he has designated as a turtle. And he believes that names are as much a part of objects as their color and form. (The child at this point is like the old gentleman who, when asked why noodles are called noodles, replied that "they are white like noodles, soft like noodles and taste like noodles so we call them noodles.")

By the end of this period the child can clearly distinguish between words and symbols and what they represent. He now recognizes that names are arbitrary designations. The child's discovery of the arbitrariness of names is often manifested in the "name calling" so prevalent during the early school years.

At the next stage (usually 7–11 years) the child acquires what Piaget calls concrete operations, internalized actions that permit the child to do "in his head" what before he would have had to accomplish through real actions. Concrete operations enable the child to think about things. To illustrate, in one study Piaget presented 5-, 6- and 7-year-old children with six sticks in a row and asked them to take the same number of sticks from a pile on the table. The young children solved the problem by placing their sticks beneath the sample and matching the sticks one by one. The older children, merely picked up the six sticks and held them in their hands. The older children had counted the sticks mentally and hence felt no need to actually match them with the sticks in the row. It should be said that even the youngest children were able to count to six, so that this was not a factor in their performance.

Concrete operations also enable children to deal with the relations among classes of things. In another study Piaget presented 5-, 6- and 7-year-old children with a box containing 20 white and seven brown wooden beads. Each child was first asked if there were more white or more brown beads and all were able to say that there were more white than brown beads. Then Piaget asked, "Are there more white or more wooden beads?" The young children could not fathom the question and replied that "there are more white than brown beads." For such children classes are not regarded as abstractions but are thought of as concrete places. (I once asked a pre-operational child if he could be a Protestant and an American at the same time, to which he replied, "No," and then as an afterthought, "only if you move.")

When a child thought of a bead in the white "place" he could not think of it as being in the wooden "place" since objects cannot be in two places at once. He could only compare the white with the brown "places." The older children, who had attained concrete operations, encountered no difficulty with the task and readily replied that "there are more wooden than white beads because all of the beads are wooden and only some are white." By the end of the concrete operational period, children are remarkably adept at doing thought problems and at combining and dividing class concepts.

During the last stage (usually 12–15 years) there gradually emerge what Piaget calls formal operations and which, in effect, permit adolescents to think about their thoughts, to construct ideals and to reason realistically about the future. Formal operations also enable young people to reason about contrary-to-fact propositions. If, for example, a child is asked to assume that coal is white he is likely to reply, "But coal is black," whereas the adolescent can accept the contrary-to-fact assumption and reason from it.

Formal operational thought also makes possible the understanding of metaphor. It is for this reason that political and other satirical cartoons are not understood until adolescence. The child's inability to understand metaphor helps to explain why books such as "Alice in Wonderland" and "Gulliver's Travels" are enjoyed at different levels during childhood, . . . adolescence, and adulthood, when their social significance can be understood.

No new mental systems emerge after the formal operations, which are the common coin of adult thought. After adolescence, mental growth takes the form—it is hoped—of a gradual increase in wisdom.

This capsule summary of Piaget's theory of intellectual development would not be complete without some words about Piaget's position with respect to language and thought. Piaget regards thought and language as different but closely related systems. Language, to a much greater extent than thought, is determined by particular forms of environmental stimulation. Inner-city Negro children, who tend to be retarded in language development, are much less retarded with respect to the ages at which they attain concrete operations. Indeed, not only inner-city children but children in bush Africa, Hong Kong and Appalachia all attain concrete operations at about the same age as middle-class children in Geneva and Boston.

Source: "Giant in the Nursery: Jean Piaget," by David Elkind. © 1968 by the New York Times Company. Reprinted by permission.

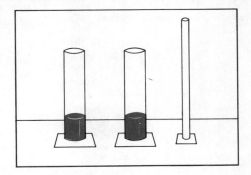

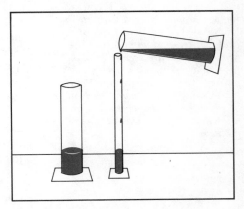

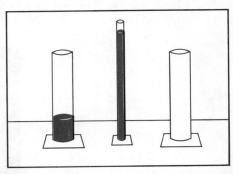

A problem used to study the development of thinking in children (after Piaget and Inhelder, 1962). Children of different ages agree that the amount of water in the two identical beakers is the same. Then, when the water in one beaker is poured into a taller beaker, the children are asked if there is still the same amount of water in the two beakers. Children under seven years of age say the taller beaker now has more water, but older children say the amounts are equal.

In 1950 I became acquainted with Vicki, the chimpanzee raised by Keith and Cathy Hayes, when she visited the University of Michigan Psychological Clinic. At that time the possibility was being considered that Vicki was unable to learn to speak English in part because she simply was not intelligent enough. Just for the fun of it we tried administering simple intelligence tests suited for a child that might be Vicki's mental age. The testing room was soon a shambles as Vicki romped around, played with all the "toys," swiped my wallet out of my back pocket, and climbed out the window to the fire escape to make faces and screeching noises at passing Ann Arbor citizens. From the test items Vicki completed (none of which involved speech), it was clear that stupidity was not her problem.

over 100,000 different words, particularly if one includes all the proper names of people and places that he knows. [Carroll, 1964, p. 2]

Of course, compared to other animals, man is a big talker. His ability to communicate about the past and future is apparently lacking in even the highest primate forms (Hockett, 1960). Animals don't speak or communicate as humans do, but that is not because psychologists haven't tried to teach them.

If I Could Talk Like the Humans

In the past 40 years a number of efforts have been made to teach human language to chimpanzees. In the 1930s, Winthrop and Luella Kellogg raised a female chimpanzee named Gua along with their infant son Donald. By the age of 16 months, Gua could understand about 100 words, but she never tried to speak to the Kelloggs. In the late 1940s, Keith and Cathy Hayes (1951) raised a chimpanzee named Vicki in their home. She learned a large number of words and with some difficulty could mouth the words *mama, papa,* and *cup.*

Since 1966 Ann and David Premack (1972) have been teaching the chimpanzee Sarah to read and write using various shapes and colors of plastic to represent words. Sarah now has a "vocabulary" of about 130 terms. The first step for the Premacks was to exploit knowledge that was already present.

In teaching Sarah we first mapped the simple social transaction of giving, which is something the chimpanzee does both in nature and in the laboratory. Considered in terms of cognitive and perceptual elements, the verb "give" involves a relation between two individuals and one object, that is, between the donor,

Reproduced Figures	Word List One	Stimulus Figure	Word List Two	Reproduced Figures
	Curtains in a Window		Diamond in a Rectangle	
	Bottle		Stirrup	
	Crescent Moon		Letter "C"	
	Beehive		Hat	
	Eyeglasses		Dumbbells	
	Seven		Four	
	Ship's Wheel		Sun	
	Hourglass		Table	
	Kidney Bean		Canoe	
	Pine Tree		Trowel	
	Gun		Broom	
	Two		Eight	

In a study designed to show the influence of language on our perceptions, two groups of subjects were shown stimulus figures similar to the ones in the middle column of this illustration. Each group was given a different set of words as the figures were presented, and later the subjects were asked to redraw the figures from memory. Consistently the redrawn items looked more like the words associated with them than like the original figures themselves (after Carmichael, Hogan, and Walter, 1932).

the recipient and the object being transferred. . . . Once she wrote "Give apple Gussie," and the trainer promptly gave the apple to another chimpanzee named Gussie. Sarah never repeated the sentence. At every stage she was required to observe the proper word sequence. "Give apple" was accepted but "Apple give" was not. When donors were to be named, Sarah had to identify all the members of the social transaction: "Mary give apple Sarah." [1972, p. 95]

Over the years Sarah has managed to learn a simple language that includes some of the characteristic features of natural language. The Premack's objective was to reduce complex notions to a series of simple and highly learnable steps. The program used to teach Sarah to communicate has been successfully applied to people who have language difficulties caused by brain damage.

Language Theories

Learning theorists (Mowrer, 1958; Skinner, 1957) feel that language follows the same learning principles as any other behavior. The infant acquires lan-

POW WOW
Nonverbal communication can convey some kinds of information that would take a great many words to describe. And, perhaps, part of the meaning would still be lost in translation. Most of us can comprehend a great number of gestures and nonverbal signs even if they are made by persons speaking a different language. In one study several hundred high-school and college students were asked to guess the meanings of some gestures used by American Indians. Both groups showed a better than chance understanding. More intelligent students were able to decode the gestures better than others. In general, deaf students performed better than students with normal hearing (Rowe et al., 1960).

SIGN TALK

There is more than one kind of hand language. Fingerspelling has a symbol for each letter of the alphabet, and words are spelled in the air. The language that most of the deaf people in this country use is called American Sign Language (ASL). Some aspects of the roots of language can be discovered by studying how a deaf person uses sign language. Bellugi and Klima made a careful study of people born unable to hear and therefore unable to speak. They researched how deaf children of deaf parents learn sign language and compared the form and structure of spoken and sign languages. "The deaf cannot communicate unless they can see each other; they analyze language by sight whereas we analyze language by sound. As a result, sign language is not simply parallel to or derivative of spoken English. In its deepest and most interesting respects, sign seems to be a language in its own right, with properties that are different from spoken languages in general and from English in particular." [Bellugi and Klima, 1972, p. 61]

guage skills largely by reinforced imitation of models. Short language units are combined into larger units, which are also reinforced if they are correct.

According to learning theory, some of the child's babblings will be reinforced and others will not, since reinforcement most often follows sounds that are similar to adult speech. Persons in the child's environment reward or reinforce the sounds used in their own language, and before long the child produces only those sounds that earn reinforcement. Reinforcement may be given for imitating sounds as well as for certain spontaneously produced sounds. The mother's voice (and its association with food and comfort) acts as a secondary reinforcer. The theory holds that imitated sounds are repeated because they provide a pleasurable experience for the child, and good imitations will be reinforced by adults who provide more attention.

There is some evidence to support the idea that vocalizations in three-month-old infants can be increased by reinforcements (Rheingold, Gewirtz, and Ross, 1959). But simple reinforcement theories may still not be a sufficient explanation. Lenneberg (1969) recorded the environmental sounds and the vocalizations of two groups of infants. Six infants were born of deaf parents, and six were born with hearing parents. The children who had two deaf parents experienced little in the way of normal speech sounds from their mothers and fathers, and other sounds in their homes (from TV, radio, and voices) were significantly less than the sounds heard in the homes of the other children. However, these dramatic environmental differences made no difference between the vocalizations of the babies in the two groups. In both groups of babies there was crying, cooing, and fussing. Lenneberg concluded: "Thus the earliest development of human sounds appears to be relatively independent of the amount, nature, or timing of the sounds made by parents" (1969, p. 637).

Additional questions were raised by Wahler (1969) who found that mothers in a natural situation did not reinforce vocalizations selectively. In other words, they did not reinforce only the sounds that resembled adult speech. They reinforced any sound about as much as any other, and the children still learned to make the appropriate sounds.

Speech Disturbances

When we consider the complexity of learning to speak clearly and coherently in a smooth, uninterrupted flow, the wonder is that so many of us master the task and so few of us end up stuttering or stammering. Stuttering is an exceptionally complex event that is difficult to differentiate (except in extreme cases) from the speech patterns of nonstutterers. It is actually a question of the degree of fluency of speech. Everyone stutters a little, but some people stutter almost every time they speak.

Stuttering usually begins early in life (at three to four years of age), but it is most often diagnosed in school settings at age seven or eight. Boys stutter more than girls, and rough estimates suggest that it occurs in 1 to 3 percent of the children in our school population. Only rarely is an organic or structural basis found for this disorder. Attempts to demonstrate clear personality differences between stutterers and nonstutterers have failed more often than they have succeeded.

Psychodynamic explanations of stuttering stress the presence of a mixture of sexual and aggressive motives for these mild disorders of speech. Stuttering is thought to reflect tension and conflict on the part of the speaker. For example, if you wish to harm the person to whom you are speaking, your stutter could be an attempt to hold such impulses in check by halting or hesitating when you communicate. A less complicated explanation suggests that, when a child is tense and anxious for any number of reasons, his speech may be disrupted as an expression of his feelings. A pattern of stuttering can, of course, be self-perpetuating once it is firmly established. The experience of failing to communicate can sensitize the child to anticipate more failure later on.

Behavioral theorists view speech problems—how they begin and how they continue—as imperfectly learned behavior. The speech behavior may have suffered interference because of perceptual defects that scramble the feedback control we use to think, speak, hear ourselves, and then speak some more.

An equally popular theory states that "stuttering arises when circumstances make a young child anxious about his speech; that is, fearful that he will not be able to speak properly. It is claimed that the very existence of the concept of stuttering channels the behavior of parents and teachers into unwittingly fostering the development of stuttering out of the normal speech errors that nearly every child makes" (Carroll, 1964, p. 72). If such a theory were true, then all stutterers should be anxious about their speech and a reduction in anxiety should diminish stuttering. Although it has been clearly demonstrated that stutterers do have great speech anxiety, there is little systematic evidence that stuttering is reduced with a reduction in anxiety.

Systematic desensitization has had some success as a therapeutic technique that can be applied to situations such as fear of public speaking. But despite a long history of theorizing and attempts to solve the problem, there is remarkably little trustworthy experimentation that conclusively favors one theoretical or therapeutic view over another. With speech as with every other aspect of expressive human behavior, it is undoubtedly time to recognize that we are dealing with a disorder that can have more than one sort of cause.

LANGUAGE IN APHASIA

Aphasia *(lack of speech) is a condition in which a person who has already acquired language suddenly loses some or all of it because of brain damage. The ability to conceptualize and to manipulate concepts by language symbols is lost, and, consequently, there is a loss of ability to use abstractions and to generalize. All aphasia cases are different. "Cases differ not only in severity but also in kinds of loss. In some cases the loss seems to lie predominantly in speech 'reception' (recognition and understanding), whereas in others, the defect is manifested chiefly in a reduced ability to express thoughts. Among the latter, some are chiefly handicapped by an inability to find particular words for concepts (anomia), and others by incapacity to form coherent sentences (syntactical aphasia)."* [Carroll, 1964, p. 70]

Lenneberg has stressed the importance of biology as the basic mechanism for language development. He feels that the ability to develop a real language is unique in man, and there is no known case of a group of human beings without language. This suggests that our linguistic ability is probably innate. Our ability to speak and understand a language can be attributed more to our genetic makeup than to reinforcements by parents. As Lenneberg (1969) points out, children speak neither sooner nor later than the time at which they reach the necessary stage of physical maturation.

Noam Chomsky is a psycholinguist who also believes that man has an *innate* capacity for dealing with the linguistic characteristics of all languages (Chomsky and Halle, 1968; Chomsky, 1969). In his view, language is learned according to rules that let a speaker generate a variety of novel sentences just as a listener can understand the new sentences he hears. Chomsky states that a precondition for language development is the existence of given principles "intrinsic to the mind." These principles are also basic to perceiving, learning, and thinking. Thus, when a child learns language, he is engaging in a kind of theory construction. Chomsky notes that all children could not develop the same basic theory if the innate properties of mental organization did not exist.

Other theorists state that to learn language the child must be able to make cognitive judgments about the world around him. He must be able to tell one speech sound from another, to reproduce these sounds, and to comprehend their meaning. Environmental influences are important in the development of language, and the kind of adult speech young children hear affects the speed of language acquisition and mastery of grammatical structure. An experiment conducted by Cazden (Ervin-Tripp, 1966) compared experimental and control groups of black children aged 28 to 38 months. These children were exposed to two and one-half hours of treatment each week in which adults responded to them in full and grammatically correct sentences. This rich verbal stimulation produced the predicted improvement in the experimental groups. Thus, training at home lets some children enter the world of language sooner and better equipped than others.

The Development of Language

Human speech is made possible by the coordinated use of the diaphragm, lungs, chest muscles, vocal cords, mouth, lips, and tongue. Of these body parts, the vocal cords (two membranes stretched across the inside of the larynx) are critical since we could not speak above a whisper without them. The lungs are used like a bellows which, when squeezed by the chest muscles, forces air up the windpipe and past the vocal cords making them vibrate. But vibration alone is not enough. To produce high and low tones (and all the tones in between), we must be able to raise or lower the larynx (voice box). You can understand how this works by feeling your Adam's apple rise when you make a high tone and lower when you make a low tone. After the tone is sounded, you must then shape it with the muscles of the mouth, lips, and tongue. Once these mechanics of speech are mastered, all of the complications of language learning still lie ahead.

A ruler of Egypt in the seventh century B.C. wanted to know what the original, universal language of mankind was. To find out, he conducted the first controlled psychological experiment in recorded history—an experiment in developmental psycholinguistics reported by Herodotus. The ruler took two infants and gave them to a shepherd to be brought up with his flocks under strict orders that no one should utter a word in their presence. The king wanted to learn whether isolated children would speak Egyptian words first and thereby prove that Egyptians were the original race of mankind. We don't know for sure how the experiment turned out, but we have since learned that children all over the world learn their native language first.

The first sound issuing from the speech apparatus is the "birth cry." It is identical in all humans, announcing the entry of an infant into the world. From this first noise, the incredible variety of sounds that make up adult language will be constructed. The first words a child learns contain a front-of-the-mouth consonant (*p, m, b,* or *t*) and a back-of-the-mouth vowel (*e* or *a*). This may be the reason why the words for mama and papa are quite similar in many languages.

The development of speech follows a fairly stable sequence. Most children begin to babble at about six months. They say their first word at about one year and begin to combine words by from eighteen to twenty-four months. Around the age of four and a half, the basic grammar of adult speech is in use.

Vocalization is very limited during the first months of life, but by about six months infants are producing a great variety of sounds and putting them together in various combinations. During this babbling phase, infants can produce all the sounds that form the basis of any language. At this stage you can't tell the babbling of an American baby from that of any infant the world over (Atkinson, MacWhinney, and Stoel, 1970). At around nine months, the range of babbled sounds starts to narrow. The child has seemingly completed his experiments with sounds and begun practicing syllables that will make up his first words. As Slobin (1972, pp. 73–74) indicates:

In all cultures the child's first word generally is a noun or proper name, identifying some object, animal, or person he sees every day. At about two years—give or take a few months—a child begins to put two words together to form rudimentary sentences. The two-word stage seems to be universal. . . . To get his meaning across, a child at the two-word stage relies heavily on gesture, tone, and context. . . . By the time he reaches the end of the two-word stage, the child has much of the basic grammatical machinery he needs to acquire any particular native language. . . . These rules occur, in varying degrees, in all languages, so that all languages are about equally easy for children to learn.

PHONEMES

Language is based on a number of basic sounds called phonemes. *The English language has about 45 phonemes, which reflect the different ways we pronounce the vowels and consonants of our alphabet. Some languages have as few as 15 phonemes, and others have as many as 85. A* morpheme *is another structure of language. Morphemes can be root words, prefixes, or suffixes and may contain from two to six phonemes.*

When phonemes are correctly combined, they give language a form and structure. The correct combination of phonemes makes nonsense words easier to remember. Brown and Hildum (1956) reported that it is easier to remember nonsense words that have correct phoneme combinations (stroop, skile) than nonsense words that do not have correct combinations (zbax, xrop, gtbil).

THINKING WITHOUT LANGUAGE

It is possible to think without using language. Einstein reported that some of his thoughts came to him in visual terms. Some composers claim they "hear" the music before they write it down or play it on an instrument. You can mentally visualize physical activities without really using language, but most of your thinking is dependent on language.

REPEATED LANGUAGE

Statistical counts of word usage indicate that we repeat ourselves on the average of 1 word every 10 to 15 words. There are 50 commonly used words that make up about 60 percent of all the words we speak and 45 percent of all the words we write. We repeat a very few words and arrange and rearrange them in a great number of ways and thus express an almost infinite number of ideas.

COLORFUL LANGUAGE

Bassa (a Liberian language), Shona (a language of Rhodesia), and the English language all designate the color spectrum in related ways (Gleason, 1961). In English we identify six color ranges. Four exist in Shona, and just two in Bassa. For example, red and purple are designated by the same term in Shona. In both Bassa and Shona, the full color spectrum is described by only two or four categories.

It is a common observation that every child's ability to express ideas grows faster than his ability to fashion the ideas in complete sentences.

As the child grows older, he will learn about sports and games, animals, getting hurt, the good guys and the bad guys, and things like witches and ghosts. In order to talk about all these things—or even understand them—the child needs language. And when he learns it, he learns a system of responses both for communicating with others (*inter*individual communication) and for facilitating his own thought and action (*intra*individual communication) (Carroll, 1964).

With speech, the child can actively interact with adults (Luria, 1961). The child can develop a verbal self, whereby he discovers and denotes himself with descriptive words. An important part of his later self-image will be furnished by the verbal feedback that he receives from those who approve or disapprove of his actions, thoughts, and feelings. Language will let him feel the psychological pain of criticism. Language becomes both the means by which parents socialize the child and the means by which the child responds in the dialogues to come.

Age and increased language capacity signal the start of new and greater demands for socialized behavior on the part of the child. As Watson (1965) reports, there is probably a cause and effect relationship between these two developments. The change from egocentric to sociocentric speech partly stems from rewards for socially oriented speech while egocentric speech is being discouraged. In turn, this shift in speech patterns aids the socialization process. "When the child can understand instructions, when he can ask and answer questions, when he can defend a course of action, when he can tell what he is doing, then he is in a position to profit . . . from the socialization efforts of those around him. Every parent knows how much more facility there is in controlling a child's behavior when his understanding of spoken language improves" (Watson, 1965, p. 326).

Black English

If I asked you to tell me the rules of putting words together into a proper sentence, you might have difficulty doing so. Yet you can easily tell if there is something wrong with a sentence. Thus if I say, "The soldiers the street down marched," you know it is wrong because the words do not follow the usual adjective-noun-verb-adverb sequence of English sentences.

Cultural complications due to social class or ethnic group follow hard on the heels of "correct" or "incorrect" usage of the same language. Sigelman (1972) notes that there are at least three reasons why children from different segments of society differ in language development. According to the hypothesis of *developmental lag,* a lower-class child will say something like, "They mine," because his language development is retarded. Given time, he will learn to supply the missing verb that has not been provided in language stimulation at home. The middle-class parent typically names objects and encourages conversation, and this accelerates the child's learning of language.

The hypothesis of *cumulative deficit* suggests that the lower-class child has failed to define the possessive relationship properly. His speech therefore reflects deficient learning of important relationships between words. As time goes on he will not catch up but will grow increasingly unable to use language for expressing complex and abstract thoughts. His language leads to a way of experiencing and thinking that does not transfer to the classroom. Thus, deficiencies in the child's speech may underline deficiencies in his cognitive ability. Both deficits are cumulative and grow deeper with age. The deficit theorist naturally recommends active, extensive, and early intervention to teach the language skills necessary for success at school.

Finally, the hypothesis of *difference* maintains that the lower-class child simply uses the dialect he has been taught—a dialect that omits the verb *to be* in certain sentences. If the child is measured by middle-class standards of English, he may seem to have problems. But by the norms of his own community, he is making the same language progress as his middle-class counterpart. Lower-class children learn dialects that are simply different from those of the middle class. Difference theorists naturally argue that the only reason for teaching the child a second dialect is that it is rewarded by the society at large.

Black English differs from standard English not only in its sounds but also in its structure. The way words are put together does not always fit English grammar books, and the method of expressing time or tense differs in significant ways.

The so-called "problem" of black English was clearly pointed out by Susan Houston (1973) when she observed that some researchers believe that black English is a "primitive" language. They claim that the oddities in a black child's speech are due to the limiting and concrete nature of this primitive language and to the basically nonverbal attitude of blacks. Believing this, the researchers Carl Bereiter and Siegfried Engelmann (1966) suggested that black English cannot express abstract concepts and consequently produces intellectual deficiencies in black children. They even suggested that black English lacks words and uses instead continuous blends of meaning they call "giant words" or word sentences. As evidence, they noted that black children often are unable to repeat standard English sentences correctly, saying "Da-re-truh" when they have heard "That is a red truck." They might answer most questions in an interview with "Uh-know" (I don't know).

Labov and Cohen (1967) concluded that ghetto children, listening to standard English, recode what they hear, retaining the meaning of the sentence but converting it from standard to nonstandard form. When asked to repeat sentences containing the negative "nobody ever," over half of the boys interviewed regularly replaced it with "nobody never."

Baratz (1969) found that, when the tables were turned, black, lower-class children were better at reproducing *non*standard sentences than were white, middle-class children. Both groups changed the original sentence to make it resemble the speech they know and regularly use. Further, the difficulties that lower-class blacks have in repeating standard English are shared by lower-class white children (Garvey and McFarlane, 1970).

Stewart (1964) proposed that nonstandard English spoken by uneducated blacks throughout the country was not derived from white colonial English. He suggests that the African slaves developed a simplified communication system (pidgin English), which became the language of their children. Thus, the Gullah dialect around Charleston, South Carolina, represents a

BLACK ENGLISH IN SCHOOL

"Teachers sometimes make the situation worse with their attitudes toward black English. Typically, they view the children's speech as 'bad English' characterized by 'lazy pronunciation,' 'poor grammar,' and 'short, jagged words.' One result of this attitude is poor mental health on the part of the pupils. A child is quick to grasp the feeling that while school speech is 'good,' his own speech is 'bad,' and that by extension he himself is somehow inadequate and without value. . . . One difference that is startling to middle-class speakers is the fact that black English words appear to leave off some consonant sounds at the end of words. Like Italian, Japanese and West African words, they are more likely to end in vowel sounds. Standard English boot is pronounced boo in black English. What is wha. Sure is sho. Your is yo. This kind of difference can make for confusion in the classroom." [Seymour, 1972, pp. 78–79]

blending of African and European language systems. After years of alteration of the English language black dialects may still carry remnants of West African languages.

McDavid (1966) and others insist that it is unnecessary to refer to African languages to understand why nonstandard English differs from other American dialects. They argue that white prejudices have segregated blacks and caused the formation of a distinct dialect just as isolated white groups in the Appalachian Mountain region have formed their own dialect.

A part of the difficulty in answering these questions about language stems from the methods used to uncover the basic data. Labov (1970), for example, believes that every language-testing situation is a social situation. In one interview, a boy's language performance was particularly poor even though the interviewer was a friendly black from Harlem. Labov then arranged a second interview, which included the boy's best friend, a bag of potato chips, and the interviewer sitting on the floor. The second speech sample was clearly superior and a better representative of the child's command of language. The important observation is that most lower-class subjects don't get such second chances. When researchers compare test performance with spontaneous speech outside the testing situation, there is frequently a difference between a child's competence (his knowledge of language) and his performance (what he actually says in a certain situation) (Sigel and Perry, 1968).

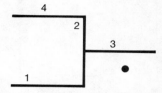

To solve the matchstick problem, *slide* match 2 up so that the end of it touches the end of match 1. Then, move match 4 so that it is above and parallel to match 1. Match 3 thus becomes the handle and the dirt is out of the shovel.

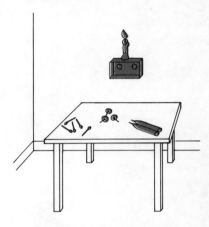

Solution to the functional fixedness problem. When the tacks are shown in the box, many people tend to think of the box simply as a container and not as a possible candleholder.

Summary

1. The process we call *thinking* is the mental manipulation of symbols and ideas. The abilities to deal with abstraction and to hold in mind the past, present, and future allow us to reason and to solve problems.

2. *Concepts* are categories by which we group a variety of objects or ideas according to their similar characteristics. Concepts are also mediators in that they allow us to react to a variety of new stimuli because they resemble stimuli with which we are familiar.

3. In order to solve our problems, we may use *deductive* or *inductive* reasoning. In deductive reasoning, we combine bits of knowledge and draw conclusions from the available data. In inductive reasoning, we start with present knowledge and think up various hypotheses leading from that. Of the two, inductive reasoning is more closely associated with creative thinking.

4. We may also solve a problem through trial and error—that is, by trying all the possibilities until one works.

5. When a problem is difficult we may leave it for a while, and then the answer suddenly comes to us. This burst of awareness is called *insight*. During the period we seem to have forgotten

the problem, the pieces of the puzzle are supposedly being shifted around unconsciously. When the combination is right, the solution pops into consciousness.

6. Sometimes our mental set limits the way we go about solving a problem. This is called *functional fixedness,* because it usually occurs when we are required to use familiar objects or ideas in a novel way.

7. Piaget suggested that the development of thought occurs in stages, and each stage is necessary before the next. According to Piaget, the age at which these stages evolve depends both on the child's natural endowment and his environment.

8. The child begins the *sensory-motor stage* believing that objects totally disappear when they disappear from view. By the end of this stage, however, objects out of sight are no longer out of mind, and the child has learned the permanence of objects and people.

9. During the *preoperational stage,* the child learns that objects can be represented by symbols or names. Since language is the symbolic representation of objects and actions, the child has thus acquired a basis for language at this point.

10. In the *concrete operations stage,* the child learns how to do things in his head, whereas before he had to actually manipulate objects to decide how certain actions would affect them. At this point, the child also learns the meaning and use of concepts.

11. In the last stage, *formal operations,* the child becomes capable of thinking about his thoughts, reasoning, and constructing ideas.

12. Numerous experiments have been conducted to teach chimpanzees how to talk. Although getting the animal to speak has been totally unsuccessful, some researchers have found that animals can acquire a large vocabulary if they use objects or sign language to represent words.

13. Behavioral theorists suggest that we learn language largely by being reinforced for imitating adult models or making sounds similar to adult speech. Studies of the children of deaf parents, and of normal mothers and their children, reveal that babies can develop speech regardless of the amount of sound the parents make, or how consistently they reinforce the child's speech.

14. Other theories of language state that the ability to speak is a result of genetic makeup, rather than reinforcement. Speech will not occur, then, until the child reaches a particular stage of maturation.

15. Connected to this idea is Chomsky's view that there are certain linguistic characteristics common to all languages. Chomsky be-

lieves that all children inherit an understanding of these linguistic principles and thus have a capacity to learn any language when they are born.

16. Whether or not heredity is responsible for the development of speech, the speed at which language is acquired and the grammatical structure the child will use are affected by his environment.

17. Speech occurs when the lungs force air up through the windpipe and past the vocal cords to make them vibrate. To make sounds that are high or low, the voice box (larynx) moves up or down. The tone is shaped into speech by the muscles of the mouth and lips.

18. Stuttering is an interference in speech, the cause of which is as yet uncertain. Psychodynamic theorists suggest that stuttering is an attempt to hold back harmful impulses. Learning theorists suggest that it is a result of faulty learning of speech. A widely accepted theory is that stuttering is due to a high level of anxiety on the part of the speaker who is fearful about making mistakes when he speaks.

19. Throughout the world, speech appears to develop the same way. It begins with a birth cry and develops into a variety of sounds from which adult language will be constructed. Babbling begins at six months, and by nine months the child begins practicing the syllables that will make up his first words. The first words are made up of the sounds children make most easily.

20. Every language consists of a number of *phonemes*—the basic sounds used to pronounce each vowel and consonant in the alphabet. The arrangement of phonemes makes it possible to recognize when words are really a part of the language and when they are nonsensical.

21. When the child has acquired language, he can be better socialized because he understands adults and because he can be rewarded for sociocentric—rather than egocentric—speech.

22. Black English has been attributed to three possible causes: (1) a result of retarded language development that can be improved with time; (2) a failure to learn important relationships between words, which gets worse as time goes on; and (3) the simple and correct learning of a dialect.

23. Those who believe in reeducating persons who use black English suggest that this dialect cannot be used to express abstract concepts and thus produces intellectual deficiencies in black children. However, it may be that the child understands proper English speech but just doesn't use it.

PSYCHOLOGICAL ISSUE

Creativity

These drawings are similar to those given in the Welsh Figure Preference Test, which uses the cognitive variable of *complexity* as a characteristic of the creative person. Subjects who have been identified as creative (based on the results of other tests) prefer the drawings on the right, whereas subjects chosen at random prefer the simpler drawings on the left.

We are often astonished by past examples of extremes in human creativity. The list of musical prodigies, for example, is long. Handel played the clavichord "when but an infant" and was composing by the age of 11. Haydn played and composed at the age of 6. Mozart played the harpsichord at 3, was composing at 4, and was on a tour at age 6. Chopin played in public at the age of 8; Liszt, at 9; Verdi, at 10; Schubert, at 12; and Rossini, at 14. Mendelssohn was playing and composing by the age of 9, Debussy at 11, Dvorak at 12, and Berlioz at 14. Wagner conducted one of his own compositions in public when he was 17.

As if this information were not oppressive enough, let me remind you that John Stuart Mill began the study of Greek at age 3, and by the age of 8 he had read Xenophon, Herodotus, and Plato and had begun to study geometry and algebra. At 12 he began logic, reading Aristotle in the original Greek. The next year he began the study of political economy, and at 16 he was publishing controversial articles in that field (Pressey, 1955). In more modern times the mathematician Norbert Wiener entered college at 11 and completed his doctorate at Harvard by age 18. Those of us who are more average sometimes feel comforted by the notion that creative people are strange, deviant, and perhaps a little crazy. But, unfortunately, the evidence suggests otherwise.

Creativity and Madness

Artist Van Gogh cut off his ear and later took his life. Edgar Allan Poe frequently wrote under the influence of narcotics. Indeed, some creative works have come from the "mentally disturbed," but only a few truly creative people are seriously disturbed even if many seem quite eccentric. For one thing, creative people do not always conform to society, and this may account for studies showing that highly creative people lean toward the abnormal on personality tests. The appearance of abnormality may go along with the

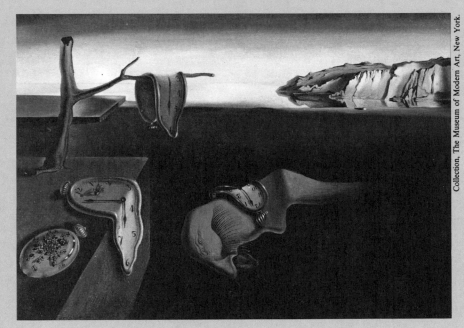

Collection, The Museum of Modern Art, New York.

Have you ever complained, when looking at the work of a contemporary artist, that you "just don't understand?" The creativity of such a person as Salvador Dali might not be appreciated by all of us, but he certainly views things in an unusual way—as evidenced in this 1931 painting, *The Persistence of Memory*.

tendency to be different from others, but this is not necessarily a sign of mental disturbance. Creative people seem to be able to enjoy the bizarre while still maintaining a grasp on reality.

Frank Barron (1972) clarified this issue in his comparison of a group of young creative artists with a group of hospitalized mental patients diagnosed as schizophrenic. He found the following distinguishing characteristics:

1.   Clinical schizophrenia, in contrast to artistic unconventionality or oddness, is marked by apathy, despair, dread, and a sort of spiritual death.

2.   In schizophrenia there is confusion, bizarre ideation, delusion of control by others, and loss of stable self-regulation of mood.

3.   The artist, by contrast, finds joy in life, is not self-pitying, is reasonably worried about practical matters, and functions well physically. [p. 44]

There were similarities, of course. About an equal number of artists and schizophrenic patients reported odd sensations such as ringing in their ears, peculiar odors, unaccountable numbness in parts of their body at times. Both groups preferred solitude to the company of other persons, and they shared a feeling of lack of love from parents and a rejection of home and many common social values. Both groups also expressed high levels of tension, restlessness, strain, and impulsive outbursts.

Barron concluded that his findings suggest an unusual state of psychic affairs in creative artists. They seem to be able to incorporate emotionally disturbing experiences and then combine them with rationality, very high conceptual intelligence, and honesty. Artists, Barron says, are capable of "dreaming awake," and this makes the difference in their personal adjustment.

The fact that creative people are often individualistic and independent is not surprising. Truly creative work is characterized by its distinctiveness and originality. The scientist or writer who was unduly sensitive to the opinions of others would find it difficult to innovate anything.

The Creative Process

The several stages in the creative process have been described as: (1) preparation, (2) incubation, (3) illumination, and (4) verification or revision. Preparing for creative thinking may involve making a great many false starts for short or long periods of time. Preparation is a process of "sorting out" and organizing that may amount to no more than arriving at a clear statement of what the problem is.

A next possible step is an unexpected one—some scientists stop working on the problem or stop consciously thinking about it. Some creative thinkers deliberately put the problem out of mind and simply let the issue incubate for a while as they relax, play, read, or go to sleep. While their attention is thus diverted, some part of their mental apparatus is proba-

bly still turning over and examining the problem. Dreams may reflect this process.

Inventor James Watt had been working on lead shot for shotguns. The standard process, a costly one, involved cutting or chopping metal. About this time Watt had a recurring dream. He seemed to be walking through a heavy storm; instead of rain, he was showered with tiny lead pellets. The next morning, he interpreted his dream to mean that molten lead, falling through the air, would harden into small spheres. Watt melted several pounds of lead and flung it from the bell tower of a church that had a water-filled moat at its base. Hastening down the stairs, he scooped tiny lead pellets from the moat and revolutionized the lead-shot industry. [Krippner and Hughes, 1970, p. 42]

The sudden appearance of an idea after the period of incubation is the "illumination" regularly reported by creative thinkers. This illumination triggers the intensive work necessary to check out the idea or invention. The evaluation and testing process may then stimulate new ideas which allow the basic invention to be modified or improved.

The Creative Classroom. How can we educate the exceptional child if we do not understand him? This vital question can be emphasized with a bizarre example. Imagine a teacher who has to design the curriculum for the following group of gifted children: Bach, J.; Curie, M.; DaVinci, L.; Darwin, C.; Einstein, A.; Freud, S.; Hitler, A.; Kant, I.; Lincoln, A.; Marx, K.; Newton, I.; Shakespeare, W.; and Whitman, W. The sense of helplessness we would feel in such a situation is mute evidence of the mismatch of methods and goals that probably would occur. Undoubtedly, we should resort to a solution that characterizes current plans for special education. We would "enrich" and "accelerate" with the unspoken hope that creativity would somehow emerge.

Lehman (1953) contends that creative contributions in the sciences are most regularly produced by men between the ages of 30 and 40. In most fields the gifted contributor not only produces his best work at a relatively early age but is most productive (counting the total number of works produced) during these same early years.

This timing of creativity may be related to the high energy level of younger people. Of course, regardless of age, the more productive the creative individual is, the more likely he is to create a work of outstanding significance. In nearly all fields of intellectual endeavor, eminent workers tend to produce more works than their less distinguished colleagues.

Fostering Creativity. To foster creativity, every plan of intellectual growth must demand the following characteristics from its students:
- an insatiable urge to inquire into the nature of the world;
- a willingness to be skeptical of man's most cherished beliefs;
- a capacity to pursue this inquiry in the face of opposition.

Henry (1963) suggests that if we truly want to induce completely creative thinking, we should teach children to question the Ten Commandments, patriotism, the two-party system, monogamy, and the laws against incest.

Intelligence and Creativity

Wallach and Kogan (1967) did an extensive study of 151 fifth-grade, middle-class children. They used measures of creativity that would allow a creative child to be of either low intelligence or high intelligence. By their measures, a child who was relatively low in creativity could also be of either high or low intelligence. Their descriptive accounts of children with various combinations of intelligence and creativity make fascinating reading.

High Creativity–High Intelligence. In the classroom, these children tend to be particularly high in their degree of attention span and concentration on academic work. They also are the most socially "healthy" of the four groups. They have the strongest inclination to be friends with others, and others also have the strongest inclination to be friends with them.

Low Creativity–High Intelligence. These children were least likely of all four groups to engage in disruptive activities in the classroom. They tended to hesitate about expressing opinions and seemed rather unwilling to take chances. They were characterized by a coolness or reserve in relations with their peers. The possibility of making an error seems particularly painful to these children.

High Creativity–Low Intelligence. Such young people tend to exhibit disruptive behavior in the classroom. They are the least able to concentrate and pay attention in class, the lowest in self-confidence, and the most likely to express the conviction that they are no good. They seem convinced that their case is a hopeless one. They are relatively isolated socially. Not only do they avoid contact with other children, but they also are shunned by their peers more than any other group.

Low Creativity–Low Intelligence. Despite this combination of apparent handicaps, these children seem to make up for it to some degree in the social sphere. They are more extroverted socially, less hesitant, and more self-confident than the children of low intelligence but high creativity.

The Creative Samples. Smith (1968) made an analysis of 105 investigations appearing in the psychological journals between 1956 and 1965 and revealed that the study of creativity has some odd characteristics. For example, 60 percent of the studies used university students. Approximately 80 percent of the studies used subjects who were intellectually superior or highly talented. Of 39 reports, 38 investigations used subjects from urban settings.

The lack of a unified, widely accepted theory of creativity has produced difficulties in establishing a useful, operational definition. Further, the criteria for the validity of creativity tests are often subjective.

Farson (1967) insists that if we seek creativity, education must not be limited solely to activities which seem to involve thinking. We must develop the other dimensions of humanness—the senses, feelings and emotions, taste and judgment, and an understanding of how humans relate to one another. We seem to want creativity in the young—but only if it follows all the rules, isn't too noisy, pleases the adults, and doesn't rock the social boat—conditions certain to kill all creativity in our offspring.

The relationship between intelligence and creativity was explored in adolescents by Getzels and Jackson (1961). These researchers selected subjects on the basis of an IQ test, several measures of creativity, and a word-association test. Two experimental groups were formed on the basis of an intelligence quotient and an overall creativity score. One group was made up of high-creativity subjects who were in the top 20 percent of the creativity measures but *below* the top 20 percent in intelligence. The other group included high-intelligence subjects who were in the top 20 percent for intelligence but *below* the top 20 percent on the creativity measures. Comparing the two groups in school achievement, the researchers found them to be about equal. (Both were superior to other pupils in their school.) Teachers rated the high-IQ subjects as more desirable to have in class than the high-creativity pupils.

Ingenuity. Flanagan (1963) tried to measure ingenuity in response to stories such as the following:

A very rare wind storm destroyed the transmission tower of a television station in a small town. The station was located in a town in a flat prairie with no tall buildings. Its former 300-foot tower enabled it to serve a large farming community, and the management wanted to restore service while a new tower was being erected. The problem was temporarily solved by using a _____ .

Along similar lines, Getzels and Jackson (1962) had subjects write endings for fables such as "The Mischievous Dog."

A rascally dog used to run quietly to the heels of every passerby and bite them without warning. So his master was obliged to tie a bell around the cur's neck that he might give notice wherever he went. This the dog thought very fine indeed, and he went about tinkling it in pride all over town. But an old hound said _____ .

Testing Creativity with Words. Guilford (1954) asked his subjects to name as many uses as they could for common objects such as a brick, toothpick, or paper clip.

Mednick (1962) tested creativity by asking for a fourth word which is associated with each of sets of three words such as: *rat-blue-cottage; surprise-line-birthday; out-dog-cat; wheel-electric-high.*

Getzels and Jackson (1962) asked children to write as many meanings as they could for words such as: *duck, sack, pitch, fair.*

Summary

1.   Creative people may have an unusual state of psychic affairs. But unlike the mentally ill, they can use their mental oddities with reason and for a purpose. In addition, creative people must be somewhat insensitive to criticism in order to produce anything unusual or new. Thus, it is quite likely that creative people would seem eccentric and be mindless of society's rules.

2.   The creative process seems to involve four stages: preparation, incubation, illumination, and verification of the idea.

3.   A number of studies have been done to identify creative children and determine whether or not high intelligence is also involved. Because there is no accepted theory of creativity, it is difficult to be certain that tests purporting to measure creative ability really do so. Above a certain IQ level, intelligence is probably not important.

4.   Many psychologists have tried to determine how they might induce creativity in school children. The answer seems to be that we would have to change many traditional ideas about education and allow the children to question everything in which our society believes.

Intelligence

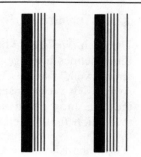

Curiosity is one of the most permanent and certain characteristics of a vigorous intellect.—Samuel Johnson

So much has been written and said about intelligence that it is necessary to put this concept into a suitable perspective before getting immersed in its details. Intelligence is only one aspect of being human, even though our society seems obsessed with it and apparently cannot respond to intelligence differences in a realistic way. David McClelland (1973) outlined one aspect of the problem when he appraised the role that intelligence and aptitude tests are thought to play in our culture. McClelland selected eight top students (all with straight A's) from a class in the late 1940s at Wesleyan University. In the early 1960s, he contrasted what these top students were doing with what eight really poor students were doing. To his surprise, McClelland could not distinguish the two lists of men 15 to 18 years after college. There were lawyers, doctors, research scientists, and college and high-school teachers in both groups. The only difference was that the people with better grades got into better law schools or medical schools. But even this supposed advantage did not produce notably more successful careers.

Findings such as these have been documented by a great many researchers. Berg (1970) summarized a series of studies showing that neither the amount of education nor grades in school are related to vocational success as a factory worker, bank teller, or air traffic controller. Holland and Richards (1965) and Elton and Shevel (1969) have shown that no consistent relationships exist between scholastic aptitude scores of college students and their actual accomplishments in social leadership, the arts, science, music, writing, or speech and drama.

THE HEAVY HEAD

There is a correlation between the brain size of various animal species and the ability of those species to solve problems. The correlation is not perfect, and there are a number of crude exceptions such as elephant brains that weigh 13 pounds and whale brains at 19 pounds. The principle of brain weight and ability holds true, however, if brain weight is figured as a proportion of body weight. Thus, an elephant's brain, compared to his size, is 1/1,000 of its weight. The ratio for the whale is 1/10,000. The ratio for man is 1/60 (Asimov, 1965).

271

EDUCATIONAL IQ
Cronbach (1960) reviewed studies on the relationship between intelligence and educational attainment; he found that people with Ph.D. degrees had IQs averaging about 130. The average IQ for all college graduates was 120, and for high-school graduates it was 110. These IQ scores are for groups and tell us little about any individual case. Educational attainment depends on more than intelligence alone, but these test scores do reflect relevant intellectual abilities in academic work.

GROUP TESTS
The massive beginning of widespread intelligence testing took place during World War I when nearly two million men were tested for intelligence and assigned to various army jobs accordingly. During World War I, Otis and other psychologists constructed two group intelligence tests—one for literates (the Army Alpha) and the other for illiterates (the Army Beta). These tests have evolved into the Army General Classification Test and the Armed Forces Qualification Test. Group intelligence tests are widely used in schools, industry, and in branches of government. Some of the most widely used are the California Test of Mental Maturity, the Otis Quick-Scoring Mental Ability Tests, the Cooperative School and College Ability Tests, and the Scholastic Aptitude Tests.

Yet, over the years the use of intelligence tests has not diminished much. The arguments against intelligence tests have involved criticisms of the secrecy surrounding test data, invasion of privacy, rigidity in using test scores, types of talent selected by tests, and the question of fairness to minority groups (Black, 1963; Gross, 1962; Hoffman, 1962). The arguments and counterarguments will undoubtedly continue for years to come. It is worthwhile now to look at human intelligence to understand the part it plays in our lives.

The Measure of Intelligence

The term *intelligence* has as many definitions as there are tests for the ability. Binet defines intelligence as "the ability to judge well, understand well, and reason well," whereas Terman defines it as the "capacity for abstract thinking." Arriving at a consensus on the definition is probably impossible. In a sense, the tests most often used to assess intelligence also define it, if we accept the notion that "intelligence is whatever intelligence tests measure."

The Binet-Simon Test

In the early 1900s the Minister of Public Instruction in Paris, France, needed to know which students required special instruction and which should go to a regular school. Since guessing someone's intelligence was hardly an accurate way to make such an important decision, he sought more objective methods. In 1904, a commission was established to determine ways to distinguish between bright and dull children. It was led by Dr. Alfred Binet and his co-worker Dr. Theodore Simon. They began using four factors as a rough guide: direction (the ability to set up a goal and work toward it); adaptation (the ability to adapt oneself to the problem and use appropriate means to solve it); comprehension (the ability to understand the problem); and self-evaluation (the ability to evaluate one's performance and determine if the problem is being approached properly).

Binet assumed that the nature of intelligence changes with age, and thus the items selected must be graded by both age and difficulty. He assigned to each test item a certain number of months' "credit" of mental age. Thus, in every six test items applied to an age group, each test item would count as two months' credit of mental age. The six items would total to one year of mental age, if all were answered correctly by the child.

Binet thus introduced the concept of *mental* age (MA). If a child can pass the items on which the average six-year-old child is successful, that child is said to have a mental age of six years. And, if a six-year-old can come up with the correct answers to the tests passed by the average nine-year-old, that child is considered accelerated in his mental development. But, if a ten-year-old can pass only the items passed by a nine-year-old, he is considered retarded (compared to a bright child).

Using both a child's mental age and chronological age, we are able to compute an *Intelligence Quotient* (IQ) using the formula:

$$IQ = \frac{MA \text{ mental age}}{CA \text{ chrono age}} \times 100$$

When mental age is more than chronological age, you will have an IQ greater than 100. If chronological age is more than mental age, then the IQ is less than 100. You should note that the number 100 is completely artificial. Had it been done differently, the average IQ could have been 50 (or any other number for that matter) depending on what we multiply the $\frac{MA}{CA}$ by. An IQ of 100 simply says that someone's mental age and chronological age are the same.

Perhaps a few samples of these calculations will make the idea of an IQ clearer. Suppose you are ten years old and pass only enough tests to get a mental age of eight. Then, $\left(\frac{MA\ 8}{CA\ 10}\right) \times 100 = 80$. Suppose you are ten years old and have a mental age of twelve. Then $\left(\frac{MA\ 12}{CA\ 10}\right) \times 100 = 120$.

Percentage Distribution of IQs and Classifications		
IQ	Classification	Approximate Percent in Standardization Sample
140 and above	Very Superior	1
120–139	Superior	10
110–119	High Average	18
90–109	Average	47
80–89	Low Average	15
70–79	Borderline	6
69 and below	Mental defective	3

SOURCE: From Terman and Merrill, 1960.

The Stanford-Binet

L. M. Terman of Stanford University tested almost 3,000 children with Binet's tests and arranged the tests by mental-age levels. In 1916, he published the Stanford Revision of the Binet. Since Binet built the test on the assumption of a single "general-intelligence" factor, this affected the choice of individual items used for questions. In turn, Terman limited his choice to items from the school curriculum that school authorities thought important: reading, writing, arithmetic. Thus Stanford IQ tests score "scholastic-performance intelligence"—not "general intelligence." In standardizing the test, only the children of white, English-speaking parents were used. The *Stanford-Binet* became an Anglo IQ test, according to Garcia (1972).

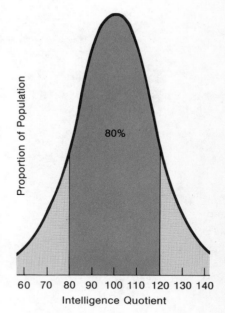

When we plot the distribution of IQs listed in the table, we come up with a curve like the one above. Note that 80 percent of the population falls within the range described as "average."

In addition to the intelligence tests discussed in this chapter are all sorts of tests that have been devised to measure aptitude. One of the items in the MacQuarrie Test for Mechanical Ability is similar to the one above. The idea is to trace each numbered line with your eye and enter the number of that line in the appropriate square on the right.

Spearman

In about the same years that Binet was developing his intelligence test, Charles Spearman, a British psychologist and statistician, proposed that only a single general-intelligence factor (called g) was needed to account for the regular correlations among different measures of mental ability.

He described g as a kind of well or spring of mental energy that flows into everything the individual does. The person who is "well-endowed" is able to understand things quickly, make wise decisions, and behaves intelligently in a variety of situations. He realized that performance on a particular task was not entirely a function of g but also involved an additional factor specific to each task. These specific factors he labeled s factors. Performance on a reasoning test thus might involve a specific as well as general talent.

Thurstone

L. L. Thurstone thought Spearman's concept of general intelligence needed some elaboration, and he devised a list of seven primary mental abilities (Thurstone, 1938) he designated as:

S—Spatial ability
P—Perceptual speed
N—Numerical ability
V—Verbal meaning
M—Memory
W—Word fluency
R—Reasoning

Still another way of viewing intelligence is illustrated by this three-dimensional cube, in which each cell represents one unique intellectual ability. J. P. Guilford (1967) disagreed with Spearman's and Thurston's ideas and suggested that there was not just one, or a few, but as many as 120 intellectual abilities. These abilities vary according to the *contents,* the psychological *operations* or processes, and the type of *products* required.

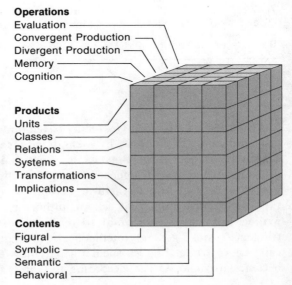

Operations
Evaluation
Convergent Production
Divergent Production
Memory
Cognition

Products
Units
Classes
Relations
Systems
Transformations
Implications

Contents
Figural
Symbolic
Semantic
Behavioral

The Neural Efficiency Analyzer—A Bias-Free Test or Just a "Neat Gadget"?

The quest for a culture-free measure of intelligence has thus far eluded designers of paper-and-pencil tests. Now, a renegade psychologist from north of the border is marketing an electronic device which he claims measures the brain's physical ability to learn and is not subject to environmental, emotional, or cultural influences. Recent popular magazine articles have billed Dr. John Ertl's neural efficiency analyzer as the successor to the IQ test. Ertl, director of the University of Ottawa's Center for Cybernetic Studies, doesn't go quite that far. But he insists that his device measures one component of intelligence: speed of information transmission within the brain.

Wearing a modified football helmet lined with electrodes, the subject relaxes in front of a strobe light. A compact unit containing a computer and an EEG measures the time it takes flashes of light to register as changes in the subject's brain-wave patterns. These changes are called "cortical evoked potentials."

After a minute, and more than 100 flashes, the device reads out an average score in milliseconds. The shorter the intervals (called latency scores), the greater the efficiency of information processing, Ertl claims. He says the process is entirely involuntary and can be performed on newborn infants (Asher, 1973).

These abilities were thought to be independent of one another. For example, if you are high on spatial ability, you might be low on reasoning. Thurstone devised tests for each of these factors, and they are known as the *Thurstone Primary Mental Abilities* tests (PMA). As it turned out these primary mental abilities were not independent at all, and each tended to correlate positively with the others.

The Wechsler Intelligence Scales

David Wechsler devised an intelligence scale for adults and adolescents in 1939 and revised the test called the *Wechsler Adult Intelligence Scale* (WAIS) in 1955. He defines intelligence as the "aggregate or global capacity of the individual to act purposefully, to think rationally, and to deal effectively with his environment" (1944).

The original tests were named Wechsler-Bellevue I and Wechsler-Bellevue II and were designed for use with adults. Later forms are the Wechsler Intelligence Scale for Children (WISC), the Wechsler-Adult Intelligence Scale (WAIS), and the Wechsler Preschool and Primary Scale of Intelligence (WPPSI, for children of ages four through six and a half years).

In contrast to the Stanford-Binet, the WAIS is organized into ten subtests each containing items arranged in order of difficulty. Because of this arrangement, the examiner usually continues until a certain number of questions have been missed. On some subtests, the score is the number of correct responses. On other subtests, the score is determined by how much time is taken to solve the problems or complete the task. The raw scores of these subtests are then converted into a weighted score, and the total number of weighted scores is added to get the IQ. This weighting of scores allows each part of the test to contribute an equal amount to the total score.

HEREDITY AND IQ
Evidence for the role of heredity in intelligence comes from studies of the IQ scores of parents and their children. On the average, the correlation between the IQs of parents and their natural children is about 0.50, but between parents and their adopted children, it is about 0.25. The IQs of fraternal twins correlate about 0.55, while the IQs of identical twins correlate about 0.90. Even if reared apart in different environments, the IQs of identical twins correlate 0.75.

AGE AND INTELLIGENCE

Different age groups of people have been measured at a single point in time. From such tests, it is evident that intelligence reaches its peak at about 30 and then begins to decline with increasing rapidity as we approach old age.

Honzik, Macfarlane, and Allen (1948) made a study over the years of more than 200 children and found that between six and eighteen years of age, 85 percent of the group varied ten or more IQ points, and nearly 10 percent of them fluctuated at least thirty points. The less bright you are, the more stable your IQ seems to be when you are older as well as when you are younger. It is also true that the older you are when you take an intelligence test, the more stable the IQ figure will be. Scores obtained after age six or seven usually correlate more highly with adult intelligence than do scores during the preschool years. Thus, an IQ score at age two may barely reflect the IQ you will score at age five. By the time you are seven years old, however, the correlation with a later IQ score rises remarkably.

The Dimensions of Intelligence

The psychologist H. M. Skeels announced in the 1930s that he had been able to increase the IQ of apparently mentally retarded children by putting them in a different environment. Skeels was working at an orphanage in Iowa where there were too many orphans and not enough facilities. The children lived in a bleak, unstimulating environment. Their cribs had white sheets draped over the sides which prevented them from seeing other children,

Test Motivation

Everyone taking an intelligence test does not bring to the testing situation the same type or degree of motivation. For example, a number of reports (Mussen, 1953; Rosen and D'Andrade, 1959; Merbaum, 1960) indicate lower-class southern black children show less concern for achievement and excellence of performance than do lower-class southern white children. Irvin Katz (1964) proposed that black behavior in a testing situation may be a function of "(a) social threat; i.e., Negroes were fearful of instigating white hostility through greater assertiveness, (b) low task motivation in confrontation with white achievement standards, . . . or (c) failure threat"

(p. 391). In addition, a great many studies (Katz, Epps, and Axelson, 1964; Katz and Greenbaum, 1963; Katz, Henchy, and Allen, 1968; I. Katz, 1967) report that the performance of black college students in both testing and laboratory situations is influenced by the race of the experimenter, the presence of other subjects of the same or another race, the nature of the task, the nature of the instructions, and the personality characteristics of the subjects. Using northern black boys from ages seven to ten, Katz, Henchy, and Allen (1968), for example, report significantly better performances on a verbal-learning task when a black rather than a white experimenter was present.

and there were no toys to play with. During the infant years, human contacts were limited to overworked nurses, and at two years of age the child joined 30 to 35 other children in cramped quarters where they ate, slept, and played according to a rigid schedule.

Skeels noticed two baby girls who were "pitiful little creatures." They were undersized, sad, inactive, and spent most of their days whining and rocking back and forth in their beds. Some time later he observed "two outstanding little girls. They were alert, smiling, running about, responding to the playful attention of adults, and generally behaving and looking like any other toddlers." He was surprised to learn that these were the same two babies he had seen before. He tested them and found they had almost normal IQs. He waited a year and again tested them. They now had a measured intelligence that was in the range of normal children their age.

Exploring what had happened to these girls, Skeels found that they had each been "adopted" by an older retarded woman at the institution who devoted many hours every day to caring for the children. The employees of the institution also spent time with them doing a number of activities not available to the other children.

Skeels then decided to try an experiment with ten more orphans who

Test Standardization

The standardization of intelligence tests such as the Stanford-Binet or the Wechsler consists of administering the test to large, representative samples of children and adults of various ages and calculating their scores. The construction of intelligence tests is done so that the distribution of scores obtained by a large group of people is usually "normal" in shape. If the distribution of IQs is "normal," then the odds of having a given IQ score may be determined. IQ scores may be classified into approximate ranges, and those falling within a given range are categorized by descriptive names. Thus, for example, a descriptive classification of the Wechsler test would be as follows:

IQ	Description	Percent in that Range
130 and above	Very superior	2.2
120–129	Superior	6.7
110–119	Bright normal	16.1
90–109	Average	50.0
80–89	Dull normal	16.1
70–79	Borderline	6.7
69 and below	Mental defective	2.2

The idea of average intelligence is a statistical notion since the average score on most IQ tests is around 100,

If the IQ is	It will be equaled or excelled by this number of persons out of 10,000
160	1
152	8
140	70
130	300
120	1,100
110	2,700
100	5,000
90	7,300
80	8,900
70	9,700
60	9,900

[Pintner, Dragositz, and Kushner, 1944]

and about 50 percent of a large sample of persons will fall within 10 points of the average. Thus the average, or normal, IQ range is artificially set at 90 to 109 (the range within which 50 percent of the population will score).

had been rated as retarded. Again, each child was lodged with older retardates who could give him love, attention, and stimulation. The children were tested regularly for several years afterwards. In every case, the children improved in health, happiness, maturity, and intelligence. The children in the experimental group showed an increase in intelligence, ranging from 7 to 58 IQ points, with an average increase of 28 IQ points. All but one of the children who stayed in the orphanage showed a loss in tested intelligence, ranging from 8 to 45 IQ points, with the average loss close to 30 points.

Skeels returned to study the children in both groups 30 years later and found the groups were even more different than before. The average length of stay in state institutions for children in the experimental group had been about 5 years, whereas the average length of stay for members of the control group was 22 years.

The Jensen Controversy

The media have recently given much attention to the views of Arthur Jensen, a psychologist who believes that heredity accounts for about 80 percent of the IQ differences among individuals and that innate differences may exist between blacks and whites.

Jensen's (1969) denial that IQ differences result from environmental differences and test biases naturally started a storm of protest among social scientists. Jensen's concept of "heritability" of intelligence implied that genetic factors were more crucial to IQ than the environment in which one is forced to grow up. In addition, Jensen felt that the massive educational programs established for the deprived young in recent years were bound to fail to change the condition of society.

The Jensen controversy stems from the observation by many psychologists that on the average the tested IQ of blacks is 5 to 20 points lower than that of whites, depending on the test administered. At the highest end of the IQ scale both blacks and whites are present, but there are more whites at this end than blacks.

Jensen does not dispute that environmental factors play a part in the obtained differences. As he stated: "No one, to my knowledge, questions the role of environmental factors, including influences from past history, in determining at least some of the variance between racial groups in standard measures of intelligence, school performance, and occupational status" (Jensen, 1969b, pp. 79–80). But Jensen also feels that genetic factors in racial behavioral differences have been greatly ignored because of a social taboo against even discussing such possibilities.

The concepts of genotype and phenotype help in understanding Jensen's argument. Genotype refers to the gene structure of an individual—his fixed genetic make-up. Phenotype refers to the actual physical, anatomical, physiological, and psychological characteristics of a person and always reflects a combination of genetic and environmental influences. Jensen attempted to determine the relative proportion of genetic structure and environmental influences that determines the phenotypic trait we call intelligence. He estimated that environment accounts for approximately 25 percent of the variability in IQ and genetic factors account for the remaining 75 percent. He made his case with statistics derived from studies of identical twins reared apart and of unrelated children reared together.

Jensen's views stirred up a cyclone of controversy that has not yet died down. Many psychologists condemned his findings on the grounds that his statistics were faulty, his evidence inadequate, and his conclusions illogical. In an attempt to demonstrate the error in Jensen's logic, Whitten and Kagan (1969) used the example of height. They point out that there are genetic determinants of a person's height and that the more closely related two people are, the more similar their stature. Now consider the fact that children living in the rural areas of most Central or South American countries are much shorter than children who live in the urban areas of those countries. If we were to apply Jensen's logic, we would conclude that the shorter stature of the rural children must

Most of the experimental children were married and had children—all of whom had normal or above average intelligence. Only two of the control-group children were married. Almost all of the experimental group children had completed high school and several had gone on to college, but only one child in the control group had gotten through high school. Thus, 30 years after these children had been "mothered" by the oldest retardates, they were healthier, happier, better adjusted, and more productive than those who had not had the advantage of such human contact.

In very much the same manner, it has been found that placement in a good home tends to raise the IQ of the adopted child beyond what would have been predicted from the IQ of the biological parent (Skodak and Skeels, 1949). Thus, the importance of environment cannot be underestimated in the development and improvement of IQ.

---

be due to a different genetic constitution. The shorter stature of the rural children is, according to available evidence, not due to heredity but to disease and environmental malnutrition. As a matter of fact, the heights of children in most areas of the world, including the United States, have increased substantially during the past 20 years because of better nutrition and mass immunization against disease during the first five years of life. Even though height is largely hereditary, the increase in stature is a result of change in environment—not of changes in genetic structure.

Those who dispute the importance of Jensen's findings also note that the IQ test is a cultural invention—not a biological characteristic—and it is not very likely that genes would influence an IQ score in any simple manner. Moreover, 15 or 20 percent of our population of children change their IQ scores by at least 15 points, and some children change by as much as 60 points between six and ten years of age (Whitten and Kagan, 1969).

While the IQ battle was still raging, Richard Herrnstein added fuel to the controversy with his ideas about a *meritocracy*. Herrnstein backed up Jensen's view that intelligence is hereditary. When all social barriers to education are removed, he reasoned, the weak environmental determinants of IQ would be eliminated, and everyone would succeed in life according to his hereditary gift of intelligence. Thus we would have hereditary classes or castes, based on real merit in job performance. This in turn would be based on inherited differences in intelligence. According to Herrnstein, the class system

would thus become more rigid by strengthening its already existing association with superior or inferior biological endowment.

The major reason for opposition to Jensen's and Herrnstein's arguments can be best summed up with a statement prepared by the Society for the Psychological Study of Social Issues (a division of the American Psychological Association). In response to one of Jensen's articles, the statement read as follows.

As behavioral scientists, we believe that statements specifying the hereditary components of intelligence are unwarranted by the present state of scientific knowledge.

The evidence points overwhelmingly to the fact that when one compares Negroes and whites of comparable cultural and educational background, differences in intelligence test scores diminish markedly; the more comparable the background, the less the difference.

A more accurate understanding of the contribution of heredity to intelligence will be possible only when social conditions for all races are equal and when this situation has existed for several generations. Social inequalities deprive large numbers of black people of social, economic, and educational advantages available to a great majority of the white population. The existing social structures prevent black and white people even of the same social class from leading comparable lives. In light of these conditions, it is obvious that no scientific discussion of racial differences can exclude an examination of political, historic, economic, and psychological factors which are inextricably related to racial differences.

THE CHITLING TEST

The sociologist Adrian Dove constructed the Counterbalance General Intelligence Test (The Chitling Test)—"a half-serious idea to show that we're just not talking the same language." Some of the 30 items included would make the white, middle-class child feel "culturally deprived."

For example: A "handkerchief head" is: (a) a cool cat, (b) a porter, (c) an Uncle Tom, (d) a hoddi, or (e) a preacher. Which word is most out of place here: (a) splib, (b) blood, (c) gray, (d) spook, or (e) black. A "gas head" is a person who has a: (a) fast-moving car, (b) stable of "lace," (c) "process," (d) habit of stealing cars, or (e) long jail record for arson. Bo Diddley is a: (a) game for children, (b) down-home cheap wine, (c) down-home singer, (d) new dance, or (e) Moejoe call. If a pimp is up tight with a woman who gets state aid, what does he mean when he talks about "Mother's Day"? (a) second Sunday in May, (b) third Sunday in June, (c) first of every month, (d) none of these, or (e) first and fifteenth of every month. T-Bone Walker got famous for playing: (a) trombone, (b) piano, (c) T-flute, (d) guitar, or (e) ham-bone. (The correct answers are: c to the first five items and d to the last.) Copyright Newsweek, Inc. 1968, reprinted by permission.

Social Class and IQ

A study by Lesser, Fifer, and Clark (1965) looked at the effects of race and social class in 320 first-grade children in New York City. The study included equal numbers of Puerto Rican, Chinese, Jewish, and black children. In each group of 40 boys and 40 girls, half were from lower-class families, and half were from middle-class families. Four different kinds of tests (verbal ability, number facility, space conceptualization, and reasoning) were used to measure patterns of abilities in the groups, and each child was tested individually by a trained examiner of the child's own ethnic group who also spoke the language used in the child's home.

The researchers discovered that social class clearly makes a difference in the test scores, and in each of the four ethnic groups, middle-class children performed better than lower-class children. The performance of blacks revealed a greater separation between classes than any other racial or ethnic group, but the pattern of scores is much more affected by ethnic group membership and race than by social class. Jewish children of both classes do their best on the verbal test, and Chinese children of both classes do better in number facility, space conceptualization, and reasoning than in verbal ability. Black children consistently do better in verbal than in numerical tests. In general, Jewish and Chinese children perform better than black and Puerto Rican children. On the verbal test, the rank order is Jewish, Chinese, black, and

Puerto Rican. On the spatial tests it is Chinese, Jewish, Puerto Rican, and black. Obviously, we cannot assess intelligence by race or social class alone since intelligence reflects the influence of both.

A great many studies on social-class differences lead to the general conclusion that the average intelligence-test performance of children from upper-class and middle-class families is better than that of children from lower-class families. Such differences exist in almost all the studies, regardless of the tests and groups used. As Tyler (1965) stated: "From the early days of the intelligence-testing movement to the present, one investigator after another has reported consistent differences between the average IQs of groups at different socioeconomic levels" (p. 333). Coleman and his colleagues (1966) have reported that children of lower socioeconomic status score below the national averages on both verbal and nonverbal tests at all grades tested.

When social-class distinctions are erased, it makes a marked difference. The equal opportunity structure of the Israeli kibbutz and the great diversity of the cultural backgrounds of its members present an opportunity to examine what can happen to IQ if social factors are equalized. Outside the kibbutz, Jewish children of European parents have a mean IQ of 105, but the mean IQ of children born to first-generation, "Oriental" Jews (from African countries such as Morocco and Libya) is only 85. Some would suspect that the difference is genetic. However, when children of both groups are raised for four years in the kibbutz nursery, they achieve exactly the same mean IQ scores—115 points. Garcia (1972) asked whether the Oriental home inhibits intellect or whether the kibbutz environment stimulates it. He concluded that it was far more likely that the Oriental home developed facets of intellect that were "invisible" to IQ tests. The environment of the kibbutz made the child test-wise.

These observations refer primarily to persons within the normal range of measured intelligence. When we examine the social situation of persons who are less favored intellectually, the problems increase in number.

The Retarded

The size of the challenge of retardation in our society is enormous. Hormuth (1963) estimated there must be nearly six million mentally retarded children and adults in America. This means there are only four seriously disabling conditions that are more prevalent than retardation—mental illness, cardiac disease, arthritis, and cancer. There are twice as many retarded persons as the combined number of persons afflicted by polio, blindness, rheumatic heart disease, and cerebral palsy.

Technically, degrees of retardation are determined by performance on a standardized intelligence test. In fact, however, an implicit judgment is made of the degree to which the retardate will be able to manage self-care and live in a technologically advanced society. In common use are the labels or categories of persons known as idiots, imbeciles, and morons.

TWIN IQ AND BIRTH WEIGHT
Differences in measured intelligence of identical twins are puzzling since their hereditary endowment is identical and their life experiences at least similar. One clue was provided by Churchill (1965) who discovered that the smaller twin usually had a lower IQ than its identical sibling. His explanation was that both body size and brain maturation may be stunted before birth as a consequence of unequal sharing of nutrients in the placenta. Willerman and Churchill (1967) rechecked the observation of differential IQ by birth weight in both white, middle-class identical twins and in lower-socioeconomic, racially mixed twins. They found these results held true even when the birth weight difference was small.

LIKE FATHER, LIKE CHILDREN?
If you administer a science exam to four high-school students—the sons of a clergyman, a lawyer, a physicist, and a writer—which would you guess would be most likely to score the highest? The most logical choice, of course, would be the physicist's child. Werts and Watley (1972) conducted a survey of 127,125 students entering four-year colleges and universities. They found that sons and daughters tend to excel in the particular skills that the father uses in his occupation.

Fathers who were highly verbal types (clergymen, actors, school administrators, teachers, lawyers, and politicians) tended to have highly articulate children. Sons and daughters whose fathers were in positions of leadership possessed leadership skills, and artistic gifts also seemed to be passed on to the next generation.

This little boy is performing one of the tasks on the Wechsler Preschool and Primary Scale of Intelligence.

Degrees of Retardation

The *idiot* is the most severe degree of subnormality (5 percent of the retarded population), but these persons make up nearly 30 percent of hospitalized, mentally deficient patients since they are usually permanently hospitalized. On standardized intelligence tests, idiots show IQ scores no higher than 20 or 25 and cannot be expected to exceed the mental age of a normal two- to three-year-old child. This means they will be unable to protect themselves from most of life's dangers, may never learn bowel or bladder control, and some will never be able to feed or dress themselves.

The category *imbecile* contains only 11 percent of the retarded, but they make up 50 percent of those confined to institutions. Imbeciles have IQs ranging between 20 and 50 and attain mental ages of about three- to seven-year-old children. Persons at the high end of the imbecile IQ range can be trained to manage themselves, can be taught to do routine housekeeping, to be responsible for some degree of self-care, and to communicate in a limited manner. Few of them can manage the independent, self-supporting lives of normal citizens without support and social shelter.

Persons called *morons* make up 85 percent of all retardates and 20 percent of the population in institutions for the mentally deficient. Morons score between 50 and 70 on IQ tests and eventually reach mental ages equivalent to those of the average eight- to twelve-year-old. Morons develop more slowly than the average child, but those at the higher end of the intelligence range (60 to 70 IQ points) are required to attend school. Their intellectual limitations soon become apparent, however. In adult social life, they may come into conflict with our laws and social norms because of poor judgment, inadequate impulse control, or failure to anticipate the full consequences of their actions. But most of them can and do adjust on a reasonable, if limited, basis.

The categories of idiot, imbecile, and moron are not very useful for educators who must train or educate the child. For them, the categories approved by the American Association of Mental Deficiency are more useful—borderline, mild, moderate, severe, and profound retardation. For purposes of education, the educable have an IQ from 50 to 75, and trainable persons have an IQ from 30 to 50.

About 2 percent of the population of school-age children are the educable retarded who will be capable of performing at about the level of fourth- or fifth-grade children. Many of them will be removed from regular classrooms following several years of academic failure and placed in special classes with a scaled-down curriculum.

Theories of Retardation

In the first decade of this century, scientific explanations of feeblemindedness considered it to be an arrested development of the intellectual capacity of the mind manifested in subnormal intelligence. The chief cause was thought to be the absence of cells in some layers of the cerebral cortex ("lack of gray matter"), and for most feebleminded individuals this defect was assumed to be an hereditary condition. The feeling then was that feeblemindedness was irreversible (Bucklew, 1969).

The Organic Hypothesis.   The controversy about the relative influences of heredity and environment is still evident in various "expert" estimates, which state that heredity is involved in anywhere from 30 to 90 percent of the cases of retardation. According to Verville (1967), there are at least 200 possible causes of retardation.

In general, the organic view of retardation groups the causes under three major headings: (1) genetic, or inherited; (2) prenatal environmental influences; and (3) physical damage during birth.

Few of the genetic puzzles of retardation have been solved. Two exceptions are *Down's syndrome* which is apparently produced by either of two chromosomal abnormalities, and PKU *(phenylketonuria).* PKU is a relatively rare hereditary metabolic disorder that can be brought under control by establishing a proper diet early in life. If the condition is not detected in the first days of life, the victim will probably become a custodial case severely limited in intellectual development.

WILD CHILDREN
There have been several cases in which wild children are reported to have been reared by animals. In most cases the reporting is less than trustworthy. Stories of wild children reared by wolves, leopards, or cattle, portray these children as walking on all fours, being unable to speak, and having developed particularly acute senses of smell, taste, sight, or hearing. They are reported to have animal-like habits such as sharpening their teeth on bones and smelling food before eating it. These children can be classified as retarded, but we still don't know if they become so as a consequence of their exposure only to an animal environment or if they were abandoned by their parents when it became evident they were already retarded.

THE SEARCH FOR LABELS
In 1877 the Association of Medical Officers of American Institutions for Idiotic and Feebleminded Persons was founded. This professional group became the American Association for the Study of the Feebleminded during the years 1918 through 1940 and then changed its name to the American Association on Mental Deficiency. During these years the label mental subnormality *was suggested as a catch-all term, but it never caught on. Some professionals (Sarason and Gladwin, 1958) have also tried to differentiate* mental deficiency *and* mental retardation *by limiting the former term to cases where there is neurological pathology and the latter to cases where there is no clear evidence of organic damage. No fully satisfactory system of description yet exists.*

Gifted Children

"It was more than 40 years ago that Dr. Lewis M. Terman undertook his monumental study of gifted children, and scattered rather widely throughout the world today are close to 1,400 more or less middle-aged people who have one thing in common: in 1921–1922 they were selected as subjects in the Terman Study of the Gifted. The only requisite for inclusion in this group was an intelligence rating that placed the student in the top 1 percent of the school population as measured by a standardized test of intelligence. The purpose of the study was to discover what gifted children are like as children, what sort of adults they become, and what some of the factors are that influence their development.

"The most recent follow-up brings the records up to 1960 when the subjects averaged approximately 50 years of age. Thus it is now possible after close to 40 years of continuous follow-up to give a definitive answer to the question: 'What sort of adults do they become?' All the evidence indicates that with few exceptions the superior child becomes the superior adult. He maintains his intellectual ability . . . [and] his mortality rate is lower than most of the general white population of like age; his physical health, according to his own opinion and substantiated by the field worker reports and other sources of information, is good or very good (so rated by approximately 90 percent of subjects). The incidence of serious mental illness and personality problems appears to be no greater, and perhaps less, than that found in the general population; and crime is practically nonexistent."
Source: Oden, 1968

Under prenatal environmental influences we find: (1) damaging infection (German Measles in the first three months of pregnancy produces mental defects in 20 to 70 percent of exposed children); (2) metabolic defects (a disorder of carbohydrate metabolism called galactosemia); (3) endocrine disorders (hypothyroidism that produces a form of retardation labeled cretinism); (4) a variety of toxic agents (radiation, alcohol, excess vitamin D, addictive drugs); and (5) a number of physical traumas such as automobile accidents, falls, and so forth.

The infant's birth also may be hazardous since brain damage can occur as a result of inappropriately administered anaesthesia, hypertension in the mother, prolonged delivery, asphyxia (lack of oxygen), or damage resulting from mechanical instruments (forceps) used to assist a difficult delivery. Estimates of brain damage occurring during the birth process are as high as 6 percent of all cases of retardation (Tredgold and Soddy, 1956).

The Learning Hypothesis. Retardation, for the behavioral therapist Bijou (1966), can exist for an exceptional variety of reasons. The child may be unwanted, unattractive, or hated by the parents. Perhaps the infant was reared in isolated, unstimulating circumstances, which meant that the child did not learn to use the intellectual capacities with which he was born. As Ullman and Krasner (1969) indicate, the history of a retarded child may include several forms of neglect or punishment. Parents might not reinforce certain behaviors that are part of the learning process, or they might reinforce the wrong behavior (such as being very quiet all the time), or they might inflict punishment which is so severe that the child stops doing all sorts of other behaviors as well.

Pursuing these theoretical notions, behavior theorists have used operant conditioning to get responses from extremely vegetative, low-grade mental defectives (Brownfield and Keehn, 1966; Friedlander et al., 1967; Fuller, 1949; Rice and McDaniel, 1966; Rice et al., 1967; and Whitney and Barnard, 1966). They have taught some of these persons to respond to the environment at a very simple level such as that of toilet training (Giles and Wolf, 1966; Kimbrell et al., 1967). A variety of self-help behaviors such as feeding and dressing have been taught to persons once thought unteachable (Cook and Adams, 1966; Kerr, Meyerson, and Michael, 1967; Straughan, Potter, and Hamilton, 1965).

Using positive reinforcement (in the form of token rewards that can be exchanged for various privileges) has produced some striking results in the retarded. Girardeau and Spradlin (1965; Spradlin and Girardeau, 1966), for example, worked with institutionalized girls with IQs ranging from 20 to 50 and trained them to acquire the skills needed to live successfully in their home community. The researchers used bronze tokens (which could be traded for candy, pop, fancy underwear, cosmetics, records, and so on). The girls were reinforced when they displayed desirable behavior (making their bed, setting their hair, showering properly, being on time). And they were mildly punished for disapproved behavior—for a fixed period of time they were not allowed to earn tokens. The program not only succeeded with the girls but also provided a tremendous boost to the morale of the staff members at the institution since they could see clear evidence of positive progress in their charges.

Brothers and Sisters of Retarded Children

Grossman (1972) explored the way brothers and sisters were affected by living with their retarded sibling. He recruited 83 college-student volunteers who had a retarded brother or sister. One-half of this sample was selected from a highly competitive, expensive eastern college (Private U), and half came from a much less expensive, local college (Community U). Grossman and his co-workers found that a number of students apparently benefited from the experience of growing up with handicapped siblings, but they also identified a number who had been harmed. Those who seemed to have been harmed often manifested bitter resentment for the family situation. They had guilt about the rage they felt toward their parents and the retarded sibling, and they had feared that they themselves might be defective. Often they had been deprived of the personal attention they needed because so much family time and energy had to be given to their handicapped sibling.

For the Community U students, lack of money was often a serious limitation that affected their manner of caring for the retarded child. The parents were often poorly educated and, in the eyes of their children, unable to cope with the burden of a retarded child. The primary goal of many of these families was simple financial survival. As each child became old enough to help out, he was expected to share the burdens of family life. Overall the effect of a retardate in the family was much the same on brothers and sisters in Community U as on those in Private U. There was, however, a significant difference in the role of girls in well-to-do families and in poorer families. The young women whose financial circumstances were modest had been expected to assume a major share of responsibility for handicapped siblings. From an early age, they spent enormous amounts of time with the retarded child. In the well-to-do families, affluence removed some of the burden of direct care from the sisters.

The Retardate in Society

The mentally deficient child, despite his intellectual handicap, is still a sensitive human being who experiences anger and resentment as well as love and acceptance. He can also sense the mood of the people he depends on. McKinley and Keele (1963) reported that severely retarded boys responded positively to extra attention from others. If the retarded child has an accepting and supportive environment during his growing years, he may become a well-adjusted member of society. In studies of the graduates of special-educational classes (Boboroff, 1956; Dinger, 1961; Johnson, 1957), researchers found that high-level retarded persons get employment, can be married, and can become productive members of society. These studies fit the observations of Weaver (1946) who studied 8,000 mental defectives (IQ below 75) in the United States Army. In his sample, 62 percent of the females and 56 percent of the males were able to make satisfactory adjustments to the limited demands of military life. Of the remaining persons, there was a high proportion of symptoms of psychological disorder accompanying the mental limitations.

All retardates do not make an easy adjustment. Lee, Hegge, and Voelker (1959) discovered, for example, that only 61 percent of the graduates of special classes made even a limited adjustment to adulthood. Many of them failed to abide by laws, and many of the girls became sexual delinquents. Delp and Lorenz (1953) also reported that most of the 84 subjects they studied with an IQ of less than 50 still live with their parents late in life. These subjects were able to manage the simple tasks of shopping and going to the movies; but only ten were ever employed, and only two were working full time.

At the moment, only 4 percent of retarded cases are institutionalized. The institutionalized cases are the products of broken homes, homes that could not provide for them, and homes legally judged to be grossly inadequate (Benda et al., 1963). Whatever the degree of their retardation, few of these children receive visitors or gifts during their years of hospitalization (Zigler, 1967). It seems that some parents respond to retarded children, not as the "infants of God" as in the Middle Ages, but as the "infants of the Devil" as in the times of the Protestant Reformation.

Summary

1. A study of scores on intelligence reveals that educational attainment is directly related to intelligence. The use of intelligence tests, however, has been criticized on the grounds that they select for the wrong talents, that they are unfair to minorities, that the scores are used too rigidly, and that such tests are an invasion of privacy.

2. A number of definitions exists for the word *intelligence,* but the generally accepted version is that intelligence is "whatever intelligence tests measure."

3. When a test is standardized, it is administered to a large sample that is representative of the kind of people who will eventually take the test. The results of the sample tests provide norms for interpreting future scores.

4. The first intelligence test, the *Binet-Simon,* was designed to point out those children in French public schools who needed special instruction. Binet designed a number of tasks and assigned each item a *mental age* according to the lowest age at which a child could be expected to perform the task.

5. In the actual intelligence test, a child receives a mental-age score according to the hardest task he or she can perform successfully. The IQ or *intelligence quotient* is the ratio of mental age to chronological age. The formula is $\frac{MA}{CA} \times 100 = IQ$.

6. L. M. Terman modified the Binet-Simon test by focusing it primarily on scholastic intelligence, rather than on general intelligence. The *Stanford-Binet* test, as the American version was called, was standardized on white, English-speaking children.

7. Charles Spearman proposed that there was such a thing as a general-intelligence factor, and he labeled this *g.* It contributed in various degrees to every intellectual task a person did, but differences in performance between tasks were accounted for by *s* factors—that is, specific talents for different kinds of tasks.

8. Thurstone elaborated on Spearman's idea by designating seven primary mental abilities that contribute to intelligence. Although Thurstone thought that each of these abilities was independent of the others, it was later discovered that these abilities were highly correlated. If you were good at one, you would probably be good at the others.

9. The *Wechsler Adult Intelligence Scale* (WAIS) was designed to measure the IQ of adults. It consists of ten subtests, which are scored individually. The overall IQ is arrived at by using equal contributions of the scores on each subtest.

10. Evidence for the role of heredity in IQ comes from the fact that IQs of parents and their natural children are more highly correlated than the IQs of parents and their adopted children. Also, the IQs of identical twins (who share identical heredity) are more highly correlated than the IQs of fraternal twins.

11. The importance of environment in developing or improving IQ was demonstrated by a dramatic study in which the IQs of institutionalized children improved significantly after they received human contact and love, even though this attention came from retarded individuals. Moreover, orphans placed in good foster homes often develop IQs that are higher than those that would be predicted from the IQs of their biological parents.

12. In general, the findings regarding race and social class indicate that children of middle-class families have higher IQs than children in lower-class families—in all races. Although some suspect that this difference is a result of genetic endowment, a study of high- and low-class children placed together in a kibbutz indicated that removing social-class barriers can equalize intelligence.

13. In 1969, Arthur Jensen argued that the 15-point difference between the IQs of black and white children could be attributed primarily to heredity. Jensen's ideas have been criticized by other psychologists because he did not take into account the effects of environment and discrimination.

14. Individuals with IQs under 70 are considered retarded. The most severely retarded are labeled *idiot*. Less severe cases are called *imbecile;* and the retardates with the highest IQs are called *morons.* In general, only morons can be taught to lead independent lives. Another way to distinguish among the retarded is by noting those who are educable (IQ of 50 to 75) or trainable (IQ of 30 to 50).

15. The organic hypothesis points out that retardation can be caused by any of a number of complications, of which the three major organic causes are (1) genetic, (2) prenatal environmental influences, and (3) physical damage during birth. The learning hypothesis stresses that retardation can result from any early childhood environment that lacks love or stimulation, or from improper reinforcement and punishment that generalize to intellectual behaviors.

16. Behavior modification techniques, particularly those using positive-reinforcement token economies, have been able to get some severely retarded individuals to respond to their environment.

PSYCHOLOGICAL ISSUE

Education

At the turn of the century, educators believed the mind was composed of faculties that could be strengthened through exercise, much as you strengthen your muscles. This doctrine of formal discipline was used to keep Latin, Greek, and other topics in the curriculum. The argument was that these subjects provided the discipline necessary to train "the reason, the powers of observation, comparison, and synthesis." This doctrine of formal discipline was abandoned when experiments proved that, though some transfer from subject to subject takes place, it is quite limited. It depends much less upon formal mental training than it does upon learning to use the specific thing learned for a specific purpose. The study of Latin may improve the understanding of English words with Latin roots, but it does nothing to improve the understanding of words of Anglo-Saxon origin.

In contrast to this early approach to education, psychologists and educators alike have fallen in love

Anxiety and the College Student.   The effect of anxiety on the academic achievement of college students has been demonstrated by Spielberger (1966) with selected groups of high-anxious and low-anxious freshmen. Both groups were subdivided by levels of scholastic ability based on their College Entrance Examination scores. Spielberger then assessed the joint effects of anxiety and scholastic ability on the grade-point average at the end of the freshman year and the dropout rate due to academic failure by the end of the senior year.

In the middle range of ability, high-anxious students got poorer grades than low-anxious students. At the high and low extremes of ability, anxiety had little effect on academic performance. The able students did well, and the poor students did poorly, regardless of their anxiety level.

Those who became dropouts due to academic failure provided an even clearer illustration of the effect of anxiety on school performance. More than 20 percent of the high-anxious students left college because of academic failure, but fewer than 6 percent of the low-anxious students left for this reason. It is apparent that, given the ability to succeed in college, some fail to do so because of the effects of anxiety.

The Great School Legend.   Colin Greer (1972) notes that it is fashionable these days to talk of the decline of the public school—as if there were a time in some golden past when schools made equal opportunity available to children of every economic and social class. The truth is that our public schools have always failed the lower classes—both white and black. Current educational problems stem, not from the fact that the schools have changed, but from the fact that they continue to do precisely the job they have always done.

Blackboard Battlegrounds.   Armed robberies, assaults, and purse snatchings occur with depressing regularity in many of the nation's city schools. Principal Sid Thompson of Los Angeles declares: "For teachers and students alike, the issue unfortunately is no longer learning but survival." His own high school is known as "Fort Crenshaw" because of its steel mesh fence, armed guards, and classroom doors that lock from the inside. New York recorded 541 attacks last year—almost double the 285 reported in 1971. Detroit averages 25 assaults on teachers every month. The result is that many teachers are afraid of their students and incapable of imposing the discipline needed for teaching. Far more often, however, the students themselves are the victims. School officials have blamed most of these incidents on intruders or dropouts who return to prey on their former schoolmates. [*Time*, February 19, 1973]

with modern technology and are looking to the computer and the teaching machine to solve our persistent educational problems.

Teaching Machines   The newest wrinkle in education is the teaching machine developed nearly 50 years ago by Pressey (1926). Using Pressey's marvelous machine, the student could read a question and press a button corresponding to his chosen answer. If he were correct, the next question then appeared in the slot. If he were wrong, the question wouldn't move until he pressed the right button. Then B. F. Skinner (1954) developed several different kinds of machines that proved to be models for the computer-assisted instructional systems that followed.

In some sophisticated computer teaching-machine systems, the student sees a visual display, hears a message, and is required to make a response by operating a typewriter keyboard or by writing on the surface of a cathode-ray tube with an electronic pencil. If the student's response is correct, the computer feeds him the next instructional item. If he is wrong, the computer examines the error and then transmits remedial material to reteach the lesson. The computer thus simulates the human tutorial process, providing individualized instruction and adjusting instruction to the student's particular needs.

Computer instruction has been used at the college level. Students who were taught first-year Russian by computer did significantly better on final examinations than did a control group in the regular Russian class

(Suppes and Morningstar, 1969). As it turned out, however, computerized instruction proved to be an exceptionally expensive program for education, and the machine can actually be no better than the educator who programed it. If the programs were inadequate, so was the teaching. In short, teaching machines have been an interesting but premature development.

A Poverty of Expectations   The problem of learning may rest not so much with the child as with the expectations the teacher has for him. The young learner may fail to absorb what is being taught because of his *teacher's* reactions to his ethnic, cultural, or economic background. Rosenthal and Jacobson (1968), for example, suggest that teachers may themselves produce failure by expecting that certain students will not be good learners and by teaching in a way that makes these expectations come true.

Rosenthal and Jacobson explored the concept of the *self-fulfilling prophecy* in which the teacher's expectations for a pupil always seem to be confirmed, whatever the child's actual capacity for learning. In an experiment, they led teachers to believe (at the beginning of a school year) that certain of their pupils could be expected to show a marked academic improvement during the year. These pupils were called "late bloomers." The teachers assumed these predictions were based on tests administered to the student body during the preceding school year. They did not know that the children designated as potential "spurters" were chosen at random from the class. Intelligence tests administered after the experiment had been in progress several months then revealed that these "spurters" had indeed improved more than other children—evidently because their teachers expected them to.

The same kind of effect was produced in the laboratory when Rosenthal carried out experiments using rats designated as either bright or dull. In one experiment, twelve students in psychology were each given five laboratory rats of the same strain. Six of the students were told that their rats had been bred for brightness in running a maze. The other six were informed that their rats, for obscure genetic reasons, would probably be poor at running a maze. When the two groups of students taught the rats to run the maze, the rats believed to be good at maze running actually turned out to be better performers. Expectations alone, it seems, can produce positive changes in "learning" ability.

Hilda Taba (1964) defined the problem with exceptional clarity:

As the percentages of the age groups attending school increase, school also draws increasingly from the "bottom of the pile." The able, the adjusted, and the motivated, the upper 30 percent in ability, have always been in school. Extension of school attendance can only add students from the lower end of the span: the emotionally and the physically handicapped, the less willing and able, and the less motivated, those less able to cope with the school culture and its expectations. [p. 147]

Schools in Crisis. "The first thing to say—and it cannot be said too often—is that the school is not in crisis just because it is suddenly doing worse. Today's school does no poorer a job than it did yesterday; the school has simply done a terribly poor job all along. But what we tolerated in the past we no longer can tolerate.

"That yesterday's school was a place that children loved and in which they learned is sheer delusion. There is scarcely one autobiography of the last 300 years in which school years are years of happiness. School was a place of misery, of boredom, of suffering, where, as every schoolmaster knew, only one of every ten students learned anything at all. The rest were dunces." [Drucker, 1972, p. 86]

We expect today that most, if not all, students will really learn something. It is because this is such a novel demand that the school is in crisis today.

If you as a teacher are convinced your students are mostly educational "losers," this poverty of expectations is likely to be fulfilled. For these and a great many other reasons, there has been a growing public dissatisfaction with the learning process in our society's schools. We can look at some of these criticisms now.

The Criticism of Learning

In recent times, the assault on education has escalated. According to Sava (1968), however, the attack on our teaching methods may be focused at an age that is too late in the human life span. Research on the learning process suggests that early childhood education by the parents may be more important and more demanding than any later instruction. Evidence shows that half of the level of intellectual capability a person will achieve by age seventeen is determined by the time he is four. Another 30 percent is predictable by seven years of age. Thus, we may need radical alternatives to the idea of "school" itself (Reimer, 1971).

Most "modern" advances in education were invented and applied 100 years ago or more. In 1848 we invented the one-teacher-per-grade pattern. In 1862

we experimented with ungraded elementary schools, and in 1873 there were separate tracks for brighter students. In 1888 instruction was "individualized"; pupils were promoted to higher grades all during the school year in 1895; and talented students were given "enriched" curricula in 1898. Work-study-play programs (1900), ability grouping (1919), and team teaching (1930) are only a few of the innovations we reinvent every half-century.

Educators operate the schools as if they knew all the fine details of man's capacity to learn. And, when students don't learn, teachers look to see what is wrong with the *children* rather than the *school* (Schwebel, 1968). The critics look elsewhere for the source of the problem, and a brief sample of their comments may help define the issue.

The Critics Speak   What the schools teach reflects, directly or indirectly, our concepts of the good life, the good man, and the good society. But, Silberman (1970) sadly observes:

It is not possible to spend any prolonged period visiting public school classrooms without being appalled by the mutilation visible everywhere—mutilation of spontaneity, of joy in learning, of pleasure creating, of sense of self. . . . Because adults take the schools so much for granted, they fail to appreciate what grim, joyless places most American schools are, how oppressive and petty are the rules by which they are governed, how intellectually sterile and esthetically barren the atmosphere, what an appalling lack of civility obtains on the part of teachers and principals, what contempt they unconsciously display for children as children. [p. 10]

Worse yet, Silberman is convinced that a great deal of what is taught is not worth knowing for children, let alone adults.

Postman and Weingartner (1969) emphasize that our educational system is a poor guide for leading the young into the future. The educational establishment is not daring or vigorous enough to furnish ideas for a new approach to education. It needs a kind of shock therapy if it is to abandon the "veneration of crap"

What the "Free Schools" Are "Into." " 'We're into a new thing,' I hear the high-school students say. 'We're into ecology,' or 'into women's liberation,' or 'into communes.' It isn't that each of these items might not be a thing worth being 'into.' The trouble is the fantasy these students have: (a) that they are freely choosing each thing they go 'into'; (b) that to be 'into' something only for the length of time it takes to try and fail is of any real worth to other human beings.

• • • • • • •

"We meet, within the free schools, extraordinary numbers of young people who seem to be able to take up, exploit, relish, and reject new books, new notions, and new allies with almost the same rapidity and ease with which they would take or drop new college courses. The type of serious, well-intending, but inconstant men and women I now have in mind—hip in appearance, radical in words, but desperately well-programmed in behavior—discover each year the work of someone new, read it with relish, digest it with delight—but then make use of this new ideological appropriation as a persuasive reason to move on." [Kozol, 1972, pp. 10 and 12]

it has so long practiced. Schools need to teach children to think, to learn, and to educate themselves now as well as later in life.

The institution we call "school" is what it is because we made it that way. If it is irrelevant, as Marshall McLuhan says; if it shields children from reality, as Norbert Wiener says; if it educates for obsolescence, as John Gardner says; if it does not develop intelligence, as Jerome Bruner says; if it is based on fear, as John Holt says; if it avoids the promotion of significant learnings, as Carl Rogers says; if it induces alienation, as Paul Goodman says; if it punishes creativity and independence, as Edgar Friedenberg says; if, in short, it is not doing what needs to be done, it can be changed; it must *be changed.* [Postman and Weingartner, 1969, p. xiv]

Summerhill   The late A. S. Neill (1960) felt the book *Summerhill* had its impact because it was voicing what so many of the young had felt but had not been able to put into words. The theme of the book was freedom

With pipe in hand, A. S. Neill stretches out during a Sunday evening discussion with young people at Summerhill School in Leiston, England. The photographer, Joshua Popenoe, who was a student at this original "free" school for four years, reported that "There is much active participation in these discussions, partly because of Neill's habit of making some outrageous statement in order to get the participants to react heatedly."

in education for all to grow at their own pace, freedom from indoctrination, and freedom for children to live in their own community making their own social laws. Neill would abolish nearly every school subject in favor of only creative pursuits such as art, music, and drama.

Writing in a foreword to Neill's book, Erich Fromm described this radical approach to education and child rearing in terms of these principles:

• A firm faith in the essential goodness of children.

• A belief education must be both emotional and intellectual and must have happiness as its aim.

• A conviction punishment creates fear and fear creates hostility.

• A declaration that freedom does not mean license.

• A belief education must help the child cut his primary ties to parents and other authority figures, if he is truly to become an individual; and

• Dedication to rearing children to become happy human beings rather than to fit into the existing social order.

Neill's Summerhill children were not required to do things they did not wish to do. And they were allowed to do almost anything they wished, as long as they did not infringe upon the rights of others. They are radical notions indeed about what tomorrow's schools should be like, and others have a different vision.

School Tomorrow? Facsimile reproducers, tele-printers, electro-writers, flashbacks-by-wire, and similar inventions may one day render the classroom obsolete and substitute sound systems and videotapes for lecture halls. The ultimate outcome of school reform may be the possibility described by Schwitzgebel (1969). The school child of the twenty-first century may "spend part of his school day in a nine-foot opaque spheroid 'learning center' at home. Inside the spheroid will be a two-way TV set, a teaching machine with a typewriter connecting the student to the school's computer center, food and token dispenser, 360° color-variable lighting, temperature regulator, microfilm encyclopedia and reference library, tactile communication pad, and ste-reophonic speakers" (p. 45).

According to Oettinger (1969), this may be no more than a revival of the teaching-machine dream as an educational panacea. If so, these devices will again gather dust in a classroom corner once the enthusiasm has subsided. Again, as before, the greatest obstacle to the rapid and effective introduction of technology into the schools may be the incredible capacity of the American school system to resist *any* kind of change or progress.

The Non-Best Seller.   When A. S. Neill's *Summerhill: A Radical Approach to Child Rearing* was published in 1960, not a single bookseller in the country was willing to place an advance order for even one copy of the book. Ten years later, Neill's book was required reading in at least 600 university courses. And the number is still growing. During the year 1969, the sale of the book increased 100 percent over 1968, and there are now translations in French, German, Italian, Spanish, Portuguese, Japanese, Hebrew, Finnish, Norwegian, and Danish.

Have We Outgrown the Schools?   "Not many years ago a child obtained most of his information from direct experience. It was information restricted largely to his family, neighborhood, and community. It was supplemented by a few windows to the outside world that he had opened by reading at home or in school. . . . Schools as they now exist were designed for an information-poor society, in part to give a child vicarious experience through books and contact with a teacher. Obviously that function is altered radically by television, radio, and other media outside the school." [Coleman, 1972, p. 72]

Summary

1.   The educational system has recently undergone a barrage of criticism, but the problems facing the school system have always been around. Critics point to the lack of spontaneity, the petty rules, teachers'

dislike for their students, and the teaching of worthless information as liabilities of our public schools.

2. One attempt to solve the educational dilemma was to implement computerized teaching machines, which allowed the student to have individualized instruction and immediate feedback. However, these turned out to be too costly, and they still relied on the abilities of the programer.

3. A teacher's expectations may greatly affect how well her students do in school. Studies have demonstrated that, regardless of the child's intellectual abilities, if a teacher expects him to do poorly, he will indeed achieve less than a child who is expected to perform well.

4. Many college students do poorly in school because of high levels of anxiety about doing well. Moreoever, the majority of students who leave college are those who had high anxiety about doing well and failed to achieve.

5. One solution to the stagnant educational system is schools like Summerhill, an innovative project in which children lived and learned together. The children were allowed to learn what they wanted, at their own pace. They made their own rules about social conduct and generally were allowed to do as they wished. A. S. Neill's assumptions about children's desires and capacities to learn are certainly more optimistic than those underlying our current system of education.

EXPERIENCING THE WORLD

As we experience the inner and outer world of sensation and perception, we become aware that we *exist*. We realize that we have a unique kind and quality of human consciousness. Most animals have a sensory apparatus similar to (and often superior to) our own, but the messages they receive are used immediately for survival in their environment. When man is deprived of sensory stimulation, a variety of disturbances of perception and consciousness characteristically results. He can hallucinate sensory experiences that don't really exist, or he can become delusional about the meaning of sensations that *do* exist. Under different circumstances, some men and women also believe that they have the power of ESP—the ability to perceive events that reach consciousness through no known sensory pathway.

In many respects, we are incredibly magnificent sensing and perceiving organisms. We have used our intelligence to expand our senses, perceptions, and consciousness by inventing new ways to transmit and receive information. Television, radio, telephone, and X-rays are a few examples. We are also experimenting with a number of ways (such as hypnosis and meditation) to alter our state of consciousness. In addition, man is a drug-taking animal who has invented an infinite variety of chemicals that will alter his mood, distort his sensations and perceptions, and speed up or slow down the functioning of his brain and nervous system. It has been suggested that the next great step in human evolution will be the elevation of sensation, perception, and consciousness to a new state that is beyond our present imagining.

Sensation

A man may see how this world goes with no eyes. Look with thine ears. —Shakespeare

Sense organs are the sensitive tissues that enable us to discriminate among the stimuli in our environment. These channels of information let us experience the sights, sounds, and odors that surround us. Detecting these stimuli is essential to our survival since we must have information about the changes which occur around us.

Understanding how the sensory mechanisms monitor the stimuli of sight, sound, touch, and taste will help us in understanding human behavior. These include vision, hearing, smell, taste, touch, pain, cold, warmth, kinesthesis, and the vestibular or balance sense.

When we say we "sense" things (see, taste, hear), what is actually happening is that we are experiencing activity taking place in our nervous system—in our spinal cord and brain. Physical energy strikes us in various forms of stimulation, and this energy must be transformed by the sense organs into a code that can be transmitted to the brain. To do this, each sensory system includes receptor cells, nerve fibers which connect the receptor cell to the central nervous system, and the communications network within the central nervous system. *Receptor cells* respond to particular forms of energy, depending on which sensory system they are attached to—for example, the energy may be light (as in vision) or sound waves (as in hearing). The method by which the receptor cells convert physical energy into electrical impulses is called *transduction*. After the energy is converted, the impulse goes along the nerve fibers to the central nervous system, and eventually to the appropriate area of the cerebral cortex. Man is sensitive to a wide range of stimuli, and

THE ELECTROMAGNETIC WORLD

The world is filled with waves of energy called electromagnetic radiation. Radio and television waves are types of electromagnetic energy. Other types are ultraviolet light rays, X-rays, cosmic rays, infrared heat rays, sound waves and radar. Sound waves are measured by their frequency (cycles per second) and the distance from the crest of one wave to the crest of another. Some radio waves have wave lengths of 20 miles or more. Cosmic rays have a wave length of approximately 1 zillionth of an inch and occupy only a small part of the total electromagnetic energy spectrum. Light waves vary from 16 millionths of an inch (the blue end of the spectrum) to 32 millionths of an inch (the red end of the spectrum).

the complexity of our responses is based in part on the varied inputs we receive.

Although this chapter concentrates on the major sensory systems and the physical mechanisms involved in them, we need to keep in mind that sensations are not isolated phenomena. For example, we rarely experience just one sensation at a time. At almost every moment we are being bombarded with a multitude of stimuli—we are feeling, seeing, hearing—and we are interpreting these stimuli. Complex experiences have been defined as *perceptions* to distinguish them from the simpler experiences, but the distinction is somewhat arbitrary. The point is that our perceptions depend largely on our sensory experiences, and before we delve into some of the fascinating data on perception in the next chapter, we need to consider the way information comes to us from the outside world.

Sensory Thresholds

The minimum amount of stimulus energy necessary for an awareness of sensation is called the *absolute threshold* or *limen*. Thresholds differ for each sense and for each individual and are influenced by conditions in the environment. After the absolute threshold is reached, the *difference threshold* can be measured (the smallest detectable change in stimulus intensity). The difference threshold also varies from situation to situation. If, for example, you are lifting small weights, you can usually tell when 2 percent more weight is added or subtracted. Like the absolute threshold, the difference threshold is defined in statistical terms as the amount of change in physical energy necessary for a subject to detect a difference between two stimuli 50 percent of the time.

There is also a *threshold of maximum intensity*. This threshold is the maximum amount of stimulation that you can perceive. Unusually strong light or sound, for example, can be painful. This threshold, then, marks an intensity level above which normal sensory response changes to pain.

Two approaches to determining thresholds are the *method of limits* and the *frequency method*. The method of limits presents a series of stimuli (of different magnitude) one at a time for the observer to judge. While following the stimulus dimension in either direction, the subject reports whether each stimulus is detected or not. The average stimulus value that marks a change in the observer's responses defines the threshold. If, for example, I hold a watch to your ear and slowly walk away until you can no longer hear it and then walk back until you hear it again, I can measure (using the method of limits) the range, in feet, of how well you can hear. Since the results of different tests will vary slightly, I may arrive at an average of the different distances at which the sound disappears or reappears.

Frequency methods of threshold determination use a range of stimuli thought to contain the threshold point. As each stimulus is presented, the subject judges the presence or absence of the stimulus. If I know a ticking watch can be heard at 20 feet under quiet conditions, I can save time by using the frequency method of threshold determination. Rather than start

SENSORY THRESHOLDS

Vision	*A candle flame seen at 30 miles on a dark clear night.*
Hearing	*The tick of a watch under quiet conditions at 20 feet.*
Taste	*One teaspoon of sugar in two gallons of water.*
Smell	*One drop of perfume diffused into a three-room apartment.*
Touch	*The wing of a bee falling on your cheek from a distance of about half an inch (Galanter, 1962).*

with the watch at your ear and then move 50 feet away, I would simply go 18 feet away and ask you if you can hear it. Working only at a distance of 18 to 22 feet away from your ear, I could quickly determine the average threshold.

It must be noted that *sensory adaptation* can occur. Individual thresholds are always changing, but their changes are not entirely random. Sensory adaptation refers to (1) the reduced sensitivity to a stimuli that continues over time and (2) the increased sensitivity that follows a lack of stimulation. This is a familiar phenomenon. When you have been in sunlight, your eyes become less sensitive. If you then enter a dimly lighted room, you cannot see much until your eyes have adapted. A room that feels hot to someone coming in from the cold may feel cold to someone who has just left a steam room or sauna.

With these general rules of sensory stimulation in mind, we can now examine the primary senses which man uses to learn about events in the outside world. In general, all our sensations are multiple in form, and each of our senses adds some information to fill out the details of perception. We can begin our sensory exploration by considering vision—the world as we see it.

Vision

The human eye evolved from a few primitive light-sensitive cells. As more advanced forms of life developed with more complex nerve pathways and brain areas, a more complex perception of patterns became possible. In almost all predator birds and mammals, as well as in monkeys and man, the eyes moved to the front of the head and binocular vision became possible.

About two-thirds of all you know about the outside world comes to you through your eyes. Indeed, vision dominates your life. Even though the visual system makes up less than 10 percent of the brain, we know more about sight than we do about the rest of our sensory world.

The Eye

In many ways the human eye is like a color television camera. It admits light through a small hole and passes it through a lens that focuses an image on a photosensitive surface. In the eye, light first passes through the *cornea,* which is a transparent protective coating over the front part of the eye. Light next passes through the *pupil,* which can be widened or narrowed to let more or less light in by contractions in the muscles of the *iris,* the colored part of the eye. Inside the pupil, light passes through the *lens,* which can be adjusted to bring near or far objects into focus. The light is focused through the lens on the inner lining of the back of the eyeball, the *retina,* where it stimulates receptor organs that will transmit the information to the brain.

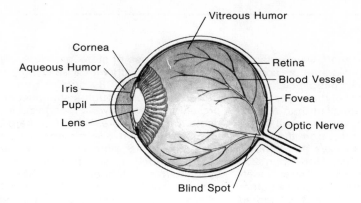

Cross section of the eye.

Rods and Cones. More than 6 million cones and 100 million rods are distributed on the retina of the eye. Rods are slim nerve cells. Cones are thicker with a cone-shaped tip at one end. Both contain chemicals that are sensitive to light. When light strikes a rod, it causes the breakdown of a chemical called *rhodopsin* (visual purple), which in turn starts the rod firing to signal the brain. The cones contain different photosensitive chemicals that break down when struck by other light waves. These processes in the rods and cones trigger neural activity.

Unlike cones, the rods are colorblind and are located mainly in the edges of the retina. The cones are the color receptors and are packed together in the center of the eye. The *fovea,* which is the depressed spot on the retina directly behind the lens, is packed with millions of cones, but no rods. A few cones are mixed together with the rods all the way to the outer edges of the retina, but the center of the eye is most sensitive to color.

When you first go into a dark movie theater, you stumble around barely able to make out the shapes of people or seats. After you have been there for a while, you are able to see quite well. As you go from bright to dim light, the rods and the cones adapt to the change in illumination. In dim light, the chemicals in the rods and cones are built up by the eye faster than they are broken down by light stimulation. The greater the concentration of these chemicals, the lower is your visual threshold. Thus, dark adaptation is a matter of building up a surplus of rhodopsin in the rods and other chemicals in the cones.

The cones adapt quickly in the dark (ten minutes or so), but the rods adapt slowly and are still adapting after 30 minutes or more of darkness. When completely adapted, the rods are much more sensitive to light than the cones. Thus, if you want to see a dim light in pitch darkness, do not look directly at it since the center of the eye contains only the less sensitive cones. If you look away from the object, its image will fall on the edge of the eye where the rods are. You will be much more likely to see it in this manner.

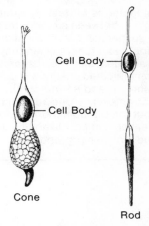

Greatly enlarged cone and rod from the retina of the eye.

The Eidetikers

Certain individuals have reported that sharp visual images persist for many seconds or even minutes after the source of the image has been removed. These people claim that the image is projected in space in front of their eyes. They maintain that the image is far more detailed than normal memory permits—almost as if the original were still there.

Such images have been called *eidetic,* from the Greek *eidetikos.* People who are thought to have this "photographic memory" are called *eidetikers.* More than 200 experiments and studies have been published about eidetic imagery, yet some question still remains as to whether or not the phenomenon exists. In 1969, Haber studied 20 children who were thought to be eidetikers. Haber felt that methods for testing eidetic imagery really didn't distinguish between superior memory and projected images. He suspected that the children might have been trying to fool researchers when they said they saw images. And he also felt that the researchers' questions might have communicated their own desire for the children to see an image, and so the children reported doing so.

Stromeyer is one researcher who is not so skeptical about the phenomenon of eidetic imagery. He studied an eidetiker named Elizabeth, using tests that couldn't depend on memory and were not easily faked. The tests involved the use of stereograms. A stereogram consists of two cards, each with a seemingly random pattern of approximately 10,000 dots. When the two cards are viewed together through a stereoscope, with one pattern presented to each eye, a recognizable figure emerges in depth. Stromeyer presented one card of the stereogram to Elizabeth's left eye for one minute. The other was presented to her right eye for the same time. He then asked Elizabeth to superimpose the image of the right eye pattern over that of the left. When Elizabeth did this, she was able to describe the image that one normally sees only when the two cards are viewed together through the stereoscope. Elizabeth also saw the image in three dimensions, a phenomenon which only occurs when each eye sees a different image.

Elizabeth could often recall an eidetic image several days after it was first presented to her. She could also recall one eidetic image among several at will. Even more unusual, Elizabeth could reproduce the *Land color phenomenon.* That is, she could combine images of a red-tinted picture and a green-tinted picture to see an image with the real color patterns.

Source: Charles F. Stromeyer, III, "Eidetikers," *Psychology Today,* November 1970.

The eye will also respond to forms of stimulation other than light waves. Pressure on the eyeball or the passing of an electric current through the head will produce the sensation of light. Thus, light is actually a quality produced when the eye is stimulated in any of a variety of ways.

Visual Acuity. *Visual acuity* is the ability to discriminate the details in the field of vision. One way this ability can be measured is by using the familiar eye chart. Standard perfect vision is often called 20/20 vision. If you stand 20 feet from a standard eye chart and see the material on the chart clearly, you are seeing normally. If you do not see normally, some of or all the material may be blurred. If you are standing 20 feet away, but see only what a person with normal vision could see at 50 feet, you have 20/50 vision. If you have 20/10 vision, you see things 20 feet away as sharply as the person with normal vision sees them at 10 feet.

Part of your eye, your "blind spot," has zero visual acuity. This spot where you see nothing at all is the point at which the nerves of the eye converge to form the optic nerve. The optic nerve exits through the back wall of the eyeball and connects the eye to the brain. You are not usually

You can determine where your blind spot is by closing your right eye and staring at the X. Now move the book closer or further away until the circle "disappears." At this point, the image of the circle is falling on your blind spot.

aware of the blind spot because you compensate for this empty spot in your vision.

Color Vision. We cannot see ultraviolet rays, X-rays, radio and television waves, or radar waves. But we can see the *spectrum* of color that occurs when we pass sunlight through a prism. This converts light into bands of red, green, yellow, and blue.

We now believe there are three types of cones—one sensitive to red, one to green, and one to blue. Each cone contains a single type of photosensitive pigment and, in combination, they give us the experience of color.

About 5 percent of the people in the world cannot see one or more colors. Most of these partially colorblind persons are men since color vision is an inherited, sex-linked characteristic. What the colorblind individual sees is a mixture of two basic colors. Some people with partial colorblindness have a red-green deficiency, and some have a blue-yellow deficiency. With one type of red-green blindness, you will see the world almost entirely in blues and yellows. A red fire engine will appear dull yellow, and grass will be blue. If you are blue-yellow blind, you will see a world of reds and greens. The most common type of color blindness is *dichromatic.* Color vision is normal in two of the three primary colors but deficient in the third. Dichromats will confuse purples, blue-greens, reds, and yellow-greens—the various shades in the red-green area of the visible spectrum.

WHAT COLOR IS IT?
A colorblindness test called the Holmgren wools consists of sorting strands of wool into various piles according to color. If you are red-green blind, you will sort all the reds and greens into one pile. While growing up, you would learn to compensate for this deficiency, however. Even though you may not be able to tell one color from the other, you would learn that grass is "green" and roses are "red."

Visual Defects

Quite a few distortions stem from physiological problems with the eye itself. The chances are one in four that you either wear glasses or should wear them. For the most part, problems result from slight abnormalities in the shape of the eyeball. If your eyeball is too long, the lens focuses the visual image *in front of* your retina rather than directly on it. Under these circumstances, you would see near objects rather clearly, but distant objects would appear fuzzy and blurred. The condition is known as *nearsightedness.* If your eyeball is too short, the lens focuses the visual image *behind* the retina rather than directly on it, making close objects indistinct while distant objects are in clear focus. Such a condition is known *farsightedness.*

If you watch carefully in the next movie you attend, you may notice something like the following. A man sitting close to the camera is talking with a woman on the other side of the room. When the man is speaking, the camera focuses on his face, which you see clearly. But the image of the distant woman is blurred and fuzzy. This is the way the nearsighted person typically sees the world. Now, when the dialogue continues and the woman begins to speak, the camera shifts focus, and suddenly the man's face (close to the camera) becomes blurred while the distant image of the woman sharpens and becomes distinct. This is the way the farsighted person typically sees things in the world around him or her.

As you grow older, your lenses gradually become brittle, and you cannot focus as readily on near objects. This condition is called *presbyopia.* Since everyone becomes more farsighted as he or she grows older, the nearsighted individual may actually find his or her vision improving somewhat with age. Farsighted people have by far the worst of the lot, since their vision not only deteriorates with age, but they also are subject to severe headaches if they misuse their eyes. The nearsighted person generally does not suffer as much from headaches caused by eyestrain.

If you have no cone cells, you will be completely colorblind. A person who has *achromatic* colorblindness sees nothing but black, white, and shades of gray.

We all have some experience of a world without color, as in black-and-white movies and television. But it is not easy to understand what it means to be truly colorblind. If you are totally colorblind, there is no color experience and, of course, no memory of color.

Hearing

Your ears are surprising organs. They are not as magnificent or delicate as your eyes, perhaps, but they are nonetheless fascinating instruments. The ears can almost detect the molecules moving in the air, and they can also withstand the shock of rock music and jet planes.

The stimuli that produce the sensation of hearing are the changes in air pressure produced by vibrations or movements of the sound source. The dimensions that describe sound stimuli are *intensity, frequency,* and *complexity.* These dimensions of the sound stimulus give us the experience of loudness, pitch, and timbre.

Pitch means the high or low quality of a sound. It is determined by the frequency of wave vibrations. *Loudness* is the amplitude of the sound wave—in other words, the amount of expansion and contraction of the pressure changes that form a sound wave. When you turn up the volume of a radio, you increase the amplitude of the vibrations, and therefore the sound is louder. *Timbre* is the sound quality produced by two instruments playing the same tone. A note played on a violin will not sound exactly like the same note played on a bassoon.

To understand this *vibratory sense,* imagine throwing a stone into a pool of water. What happens? Wave after wave of ripples circle out from the center. The waves strike the edge of the pool and then bounce back.

Structure of the ear.

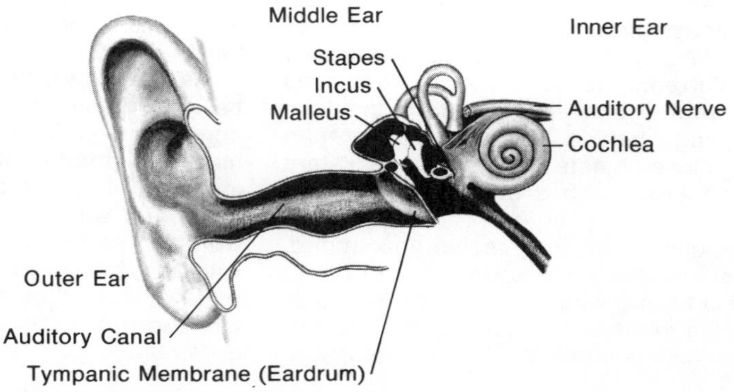

Middle Ear

Inner Ear

Stapes
Incus
Malleus

Auditory Nerve
Cochlea

Outer Ear

Auditory Canal

Tympanic Membrane (Eardrum)

Similarly, whenever any object is struck, it tends to vibrate. As it does so, the molecules of air around it are pushed away from it—just as a stone thrown into a pool pushes water molecules away from it. If you threw a number of stones into the pond, you would set up a series of waves on the surface of the water. If these were waves in the air, they would reach your ear and set your eardrum moving back and forth in rhythm with the vibrating object. These waves become patterns of neural energy that go to your brain so you can hear.

The ear receives and amplifies the vibration movements of the air in order to give information to the nervous system. The structures of the ear that do this are the outer, middle, and inner ears. The *outer ear* is composed of an inch-long canal and the *tympanic membrane* (the eardrum). Changes in air pressure are channeled to this flexible membrane, which moves in response to the pressure changes. The *middle ear* is composed of three bones: the *malleus,* the *incus,* and the *stapes.* These bones make up a mechanical system that conducts sound waves to the inner ear. In the *inner ear* the vibrations are transmitted to the fluid inside the *cochlea,* a snail-shaped structure. Finally, the sound waves reach the receptor cells for the sense of hearing and are translated into nerve impulses, which travel to the brain by way of the *auditory nerve.*

Your ears are far enough apart to allow you to locate the position of a sound source. If a noise is two or three feet away from your left ear, it will reach your left ear a fraction of a second before it reaches your right ear. The sound will also be louder in your left ear than in your right ear. The time lag and difference in loudness allows you to localize the sound as being on your left. To properly locate a sound, both ears are necessary.

Deafness

There are various kinds of deafness. Causes of deafness may be malfunction of the inner ear, damage to the inner ear, or damage to the auditory nerve. If you are affected by nerve deafness, you will have greater difficulty hearing high-frequency sounds than lower-frequency sounds. If there is total destruction of the auditory nerve, you may be fully deaf on the side where the damage took place.

A more common kind of hearing damage is called *conduction deafness.* This results from an injury or defect in the sound-conducting mechanism of the middle or outer ear. If you suffer from conduction deafness, you may not be able to hear normal conversation, and you may not be able to distinguish between similar words. If the conducting mechanism of the ear is injured or stopped up by wax deposits, or if a cold has affected the auditory channels, sounds of every frequency are usually affected. Conduction deafness can be remedied by mechanical devices such as hearing aids. These help amplify sounds and assist in conducting sounds through the middle ear.

Intensity of Some Common Sounds

Human Whisper	30
Normal Conversation	60
City Traffic	80
Subway Train	95
Farm Tractor	98
Motorcycle	110
Rock Band (Amplified)	114
Jet Airplane	135
	to
	150

The column on the right shows the decibel intensity of some common sounds. A decibel is the smallest difference in intensity of sound that the human ear can detect. The scale is logarithmic; a difference of ten decibels represents a doubling of sound intensity. Compiled from *Medical World News,* June 13, 1969, pp. 42–47, and other sources.

In extreme cases, it is necessary to operate surgically on the ear to make another small opening that can function as a path for sound conduction. In the past, this *fenestration* operation (making a new sound window) has produced some unwanted side effects such as an increased frequency of ear infections. It is now being replaced by new, more sophisticated methods.

The Skin Senses

The importance of the skin senses is reflected in our everyday language. As Montagu stated:

> We speak of "rubbing" people the wrong way . . . "a soft touch." . . . We get into "touch" or "contact" with others. Some people have to be "handled" carefully ("with kid gloves"). Some are "thick-skinned," others are "thin-skinned," some get "under one's skin," while others remain only "skin-deep." . . . Some people are "touchy." [1971, p. 5]

The sense of touch is actually a combination of at least three senses: pressure, pain, and hot and cold. If you unbend a paper clip and probe an area of your skin lightly, you will report a feeling of pressure at certain points where the wire contacts your skin—but not at *every* point. If you do the same

---

Skin Language

What kind of language can the skin understand? Well, most people would say, the skin can understand the "language" of texture—the rich, complex, unmistakable feels of silk, velvet, or tweed. Or the "language" of hot and cold, the "message" of the insect's sting, the language of warning, the affectionate touch on the shoulder, or the small number of pokes and jabs which can mean anything from, "Shhh—the boss is coming" to "Isn't that the most ridiculous thing you've ever heard?" But what about language in a narrower sense—can skin receive and understand a complex impersonal system of symbols like Morse, semaphore, or even English? [Geldard, 1968, p. 43]

Geldard explored the idea of "body English" with a language called *vibratese* consisting of 45 separate signals with three intensities (weak, medium, strong) and three durations (short, medium, long), delivered to five different spots on the chest.

He found that the vibratese alphabet could be mastered in a few hours. Before long two- and three-letter words could be introduced and then short sentences. He has begun experimentation with vibratese scattered all over the body and the skin may soon have a language all its own.

thing with a cold wire, you will feel cold at various specific points. If you probe your skin with a warm wire, you will feel warmth at various points. A pin point will produce spots of pain. It is apparent that different points on the skin are serviced by receptors that are sensitive to different kinds of energies.

Your skin is made up of several layers of tissue. These layers insulate you when it is cold and release water to cool you by evaporation when you get too hot. Skin stretches if you gain weight and shrinks when you diet. Nearly all of the skin on your body has hair, except for the palms of your hands, the soles of your feet, your lips, and your eyeballs.

The experience you have when you are touched lightly with a single hair is called either pressure or touch. The amount of pressure required to produce this experience varies for different parts of the body. The tip of the tongue, the lips, the fingers, and the hands are the most sensitive areas. The arms, legs, and body trunk are less sensitive. You experience pressure, not only when an object touches the skin, but also when hairs on the body are slightly moved.

Temperature

The number of cold-sensitive spots on your skin is greater than the number of warm-sensitive spots. A square centimeter of skin surface usually contains 13 cold spots and 2 warm spots. Since warmth and cold sensitivities are much greater along the trunk of your body, your hands and feet can withstand greater extremes of cold or warmth than can your bare back. It is easy to experiment with the decreased warmth and cold sensitivities in the hands and feet. Place one hand in a bucket of cold water and the other hand in a bucket of warm water. In a little while you will be aware that the feeling of warmth or cold comes only from the area where the hand meets both water and air. Now, put both hands in a third bucket of lukewarm water. This water will feel warm to the hand that was in cold water and cold to the hand that was in warm water. The sensation from the hand depends on the temperature to which the skin was previously adapted.

The experience of *hot* is different. A hot stimulus excites both warm and cold receptors. The cold receptors respond to temperatures that are cooler than the body as well as to those that are much warmer than the body. The warm receptors, however, respond only to stimuli that are warmer than the body. Try twisting two coils of tubing together. Pass a warm solution through one coil and a cool solution through the other. Now hold on to the two intertwining coils. The simultaneous stimulation of both warm and cool sense receptors yields a hot sensation. This is called *paradoxical heat*. Thus, "hot" and "cold" are relative terms that are always related to the temperature of the skin. Anything you touch that is colder than your skin will be perceived as cool. Anything you touch that is hotter than your skin will seem warm.

THE SKIN
"The skin, like a cloak, covers us all over, the oldest and the most sensitive of our organs, our first medium of communication, and our most efficient of protectors. Perhaps, next to the brain, the skin is the most important of all our organ systems. The sense most closely associated with the skin, the sense of touch, 'the mother of the senses,' is the earliest to develop in the human embryo. When the embryo is less than an inch long from crown to rump, and less than eight weeks old, light stroking of the upper lip or wings of the nose will cause bending of the neck and trunk away from the source of stimulation. At this stage in its development, the embryo has neither eyes nor ears. Yet its skin is already highly developed."
[Montagu, 1971, p. 1]

How We Feel (Or Don't Feel) Pain

Acupuncture has been practiced for centuries by Chinese physicians to relieve pain and discomfort. As paradoxical as it may seem, the insertion of needles into various sites on the body surface relieves pain either in the surrounding areas or in body regions quite distant from the needle site. Western physicians have a hard time understanding how acupuncture works because it does not follow their *specificity theory* of pain. This theory states that there are specific pain receptors in our body, which relay signals of pain directly to the brain. A person should therefore feel pain exactly where the stimulation occurs, and the amount of pain felt should depend on the amount of stimulation at the pain site. The ability of acupuncture to relieve pain in distant sites by the insertion of needles clearly contradicts the specificity theory of pain.

It is difficult for westerners to accept the Chinese theory of how acupuncture works. The Chinese believe that the body has forces known as *yin* (spirit) and *yang* (blood). At times yin and yang fall into disharmony. When this happens, pain results. The insertion of needles into certain sites causes the forces to come into harmony again.

Searching for a more scientific explanation, Melzack and Wall came up with a new theory of pain that would account for the effects of acupuncture (Melzack, 1973).

These researchers maintain that the transmission of pain signals depends on "gate-control mechanisms." These mechanisms permit or block the transmission of pain signals to the central nervous system. They suggest that the stimulation of certain areas will open the gate to allow pain signals to pass. The stimulation of other areas will close the gate, so that pain signals from any part of the body cannot reach the pain reception area in the brain. They also note that the cortex of the brain is involved in controlling the gate. It has long been known that anxiety heightens the sense of pain, and the cortex is the center of anxiety. If anxiety is reduced, pain should also be reduced.

In the case of acupuncture, Melzack and Wall suggest the following. The reassurance given to the individual lowers his anxiety. He therefore does not feel the stimulation of the needles as pain. The needles themselves are inserted at the sites which activate the reticular formation of the brainstem—one of the gate-control areas of the nervous system. The pain signals coming from the site of surgery, wherever it is, are therefore blocked before they reach the brain, and no pain is perceived.

Source: Ronald Melzack, "How Acupuncture Works," *Psychology Today,* June 1973, pp. 28–37.

Pain

Interestingly, pain can arise from extreme stimulation by any kind of stimuli. Very bright lights, loud noises, high or low temperatures, or great pressures all yield pain sensations. In relation to the skin senses, the pressure sensitivity is generally greater toward the end of a limb, whereas the pain sensitivity is decreased. Psychologists are still arguing whether pain is a separate sense with its own nerve structures or whether it results from a pattern of intense stimulation from any of a number of receptors. Pain seems to be received by a variety of nerve endings. It also seems to be transmitted to the brain by a number of different pathways. These pathways lead to wide areas of the brain rather than to a specific center as in some other senses.

McMurray (1950) reported a case of a person who never experienced pain.

At no time had she ever reported any form of ache or pain such as headache, earache, toothache, or stomachache. . . . The hands, legs, and feet showed multiple scars which had been produced by cuts, bites, and scratches, many of which were unnoticed. After a day on the beach she had to inspect her feet carefully for cuts. It is also interesting that she reported never having felt the sensation of itch. [p. 161]

For most of us, pain serves to warn us of tissue destruction. Most internal organs of the body do not experience pain and are unable to inform us when they are in trouble.

Melzack and Scott (1957) conducted some research on the response to pain. They used two groups of dogs. One group was raised in a normal environment, and the other was raised in an isolated, pain-free environment. All the dogs were then placed in a situation where they might be hit by an electrified toy car. Dogs raised in a normal environment received an average of only 6 shocks. Those raised in an isolated environment received an average of 24.7 shocks. The dogs reared in isolation could not learn to avoid shock. This experiment suggests that perceiving and responding to pain requires a background of early experience with pain.

Kinesthesis and Equilibrium

Close your eyes and raise your hand. You still know where your hand is. Now touch your nose with your finger. You know where both parts of the self are. The sense that tells us the positions and movements of our muscles and joints is called *kinesthesis*. Some kinesthetic receptors are embedded in the muscles and send information to the brain about the load on the muscle and its state of contraction. Other receptors are in tendons and joints. With these sensors you can detect a movement of one-third of a degree in the shoulder and wrist. In the ankle more than a full degree of movement is needed for detection.

The kinesthetic senses provide information about active body movement. Thus, you can tell the relative weights of objects by lifting them. You can walk along the street without watching what your legs are doing. And you can talk without thinking about moving your tongue and jaw.

Kinesthesis is extremely important to daily life. When kinesthetic sensitivity is destroyed somewhere along the spinal cord, impulses coming into the spinal cord below the point of damage cannot find a path to the brain. If this happens to you, you will sway and have trouble keeping your balance with your eyes closed. You may not be able to lift your foot onto a curb without first looking at the foot, and you will walk with a peculiar gait.

The balance senses work in conjunction with kinesthesis. These senses pertain to body motion and body position in relation to gravity. The sense organs for equilibrium are in the inner ear. The semicircular canals in the inner ear lie on three different planes. The canals are filled with a fluid that moves when the head rotates. This fluid movement allows perception of the body's movement. If movement is extreme, you get dizzy.

EQUILIBRIUM
If you lost all your other senses, you could still tell whether you were right side up or upside down, falling or rising, spinning or standing still, or moving forward or backward. You would know these things through your sense of equilibrium. In outer space where there is no gravity, this sense would be almost useless. A ride on a roller coaster, however, will give you some of the various sensations experienced when the body is moved about in space.

Smell

When our simian ancestors took to trees, their noses left the ground, and the smells that were once so important to living lost their prominence. From an evolutionary viewpoint, smell is one of the most primitive of the senses. Indeed, smell has a more direct route to the brain than any other sense.

Most of what you smell comes from gaseous chemical molecules that are heavier than air. These molecules tend to collect on the floor or ground. When you stand erect, your nose misses most smells. Human beings now have to sniff when they want to smell things. Breathing through your nose increases the number of molecules that can hit the olfactory membrane where they are detected.

Molecular action also accounts for how a male dog can tell at a distance when a female dog is in heat. The female dog in heat secretes a special odor, and a mere whiff of this smell will sexually excite the male dog. Fortunately for dogs and humans, we adapt even to the most powerful smells. Since our noses are mostly used to detect changes in the environment, they will eventually stop sending urgent messages to the brain and ignore even a persistent smell.

According to some theories, there are four basic odors: acid, fragrant, burnt, and caprylic (like limburger cheese). Other theories hold that there are six odors: fruity, flowery, burnt, spicy, resinous, and putrid. Most often, in fact, we describe smells as being "like" some similar, familiar odor. We say "it smells like burning rubber," or "it smells like a locker-room."

Taste

It may be hard to believe, but steak has almost no taste at all—if taste is limited to the message your tongue can send to the brain. It may smell good, look good, and have an interesting chewy texture, but these experiences have nothing to do with the taste of steak which is neither salty, sweet, sour, nor bitter. If taste were the only sensation you got from steak, it would hardly be worth paying for.

Your taste buds are scattered across the upper surface and sides of the tongue. They respond to four basic taste qualities: sweet, sour, bitter, and salty. The number of taste receptors on your tongue is limited, and your taste experiences are mixtures of these four basic qualities. All in all, our sense of taste is a quite restricted sensory experience.

The number of taste buds you have decreases with age. Older people are less sensitive to taste than are children. In general, sensitivity to sweet is greatest at the tip of the tongue. Sensitivity to salt is greatest on the tip and the sides. Sour is detected on the sides, and bitter is detected at the back of the tongue.

To a great extent, taste depends on smell. If you could not smell food, you could not tell what you were eating. After the first bite of food, you no longer perceive flavor in the same degree as when you first began eating. If you pause long enough between bites, however, the taste returns.

Summary

1. The receptors through which we experience the world are called *sense organs*. Sense organs receive physical energy from the environment and transform it into electrical impulses that are then sent to the brain. Each of our sense organs is specialized to receive a particular type of energy.

2. The *absolute threshold* is the minimum amount of energy necessary to produce a response in an organism. The *difference threshold* is the smallest amount of energy change necessary for a person to notice a difference in the stimulus. The *threshold of maximum intensity* is the level above which stimulation is perceived as pain.

3. Sensory adaptation occurs when the stimulus persists so long you stop being sensitive to it. After adaptation the absolute threshold rises. A higher level of stimulation is needed before you will again respond.

4. Vision is the dominant sense in man. Light passes through the pupil into the eye, where it stimulates receptor cells called *rods* and *cones* on the retina. These cells in turn transmit electrical impulses to the brain.

5. Rods are slim nerve cells on the edge of the retina. Cones are thicker and located in the center of the eye. *Rhodopsin,* a chemical in the rods, breaks down when struck by light, causing the rod to fire messages to the brain.

6. Until the rhodopsin builds up again, the eye loses some of its sensitivity to light. This means that if you come from bright light into a dark room, you won't be able to see until the rhodopsin has built up again. The more rhodopsin, the more sensitive your eyes are to light, and the less light you need to see.

7. The cones are responsible for color vision. It is believed there are three types of cones, each containing a photosensitive pigment. These pigments are sensitive to either red, green, or blue light. When the cones are stimulated in combination, we experience color.

8. In colorblindness, one or more of the three types of cones is not responsive to its primary color. Colorblindness is a hereditary, sex-linked characteristic, found almost exclusively in men.

9. The optic nerve carries impulses from the receptors in the eye to the brain. The place where the nerve fibers meet to form the optic nerve is the *blind spot*.

10. We describe sound according to its *pitch* (how high or low), its *loudness,* and its *timbre* (quality). These dimensions of sound result from the physical dimensions of the sound wave's frequency, amplitude, and complexity.

11. The ear converts changes in air pressure into electrical impulses that are interpreted by the brain as sound. The movement of the eardrum in response to vibration is converted to impulses by the inner ear.

12. Deafness can be caused by malfunction of the auditory nerve (nerve deafness) or damage in the ear (conduction deafness). Conduction deafness can be aided by mechanical devices or surgery.

13. There are actually three senses the skin receives: pressure, pain, and hot and cold. Different points on the skin have receptors sensitive to different kinds of energy. The amount of pressure needed for the experience of touch differs for various parts of the body.

14. The experience of temperature will be relative to the temperature of the body. There are two types of temperature receptors in the skin: warm and cold. One spot on the skin may send messages of warmth to the brain when it encounters objects a few degrees warmer than the skin. A different area will respond only to objects colder than the body. The experience of hot, however, comes when both warm and cold receptors are activated.

15. Extreme stimulation of any sense can cause pain. Psychologists are uncertain whether pain is a sense in itself, or merely a result of the intense stimulation of any receptor. Pain seems to be received by a variety of nerve endings and transmitted along a number of pathways to the brain.

16. In an effort to understand the effects of acupuncture, some psychologists proposed that the perception of pain can be mediated by certain parts of the nervous system, rather than being a result of the stimulation of specific pain receptors connected directly to the central nervous system.

17. Kinesthesis is the sense that tells us about body movement. Receptors for this sense are located in the muscles, tendons, and joints. Working with kinesthesis is the sense of equilibrium, located in the semicircular canals of the inner ear.

18. We experience smell when gaseous molecules pass the olfactory membrane of the nose. We experience taste when receptors on the tongue respond either to sweet, sour, salty, or bitter—or a combination of these qualities. Actually, it is the sense of smell that provides much of our eating enjoyment because the taste receptors adapt very quickly.

PSYCHOLOGICAL ISSUE

Sensory Deprivation

Most of us think we have a firm grip on consciousness. We know who we are, and we can tell the difference between fantasy and reality. Psychological researchers, however, have suggested that our sense of self and our identity may not be as strong as we think. If we are deprived of normal sensory stimulation, our grasp of reality may quickly disappear.

Confusion about what we mean by *sensory deprivation* is apparent in the terms researchers and theorists have used. You may have heard of isolation, perceptual isolation, reduced sensory input, interference with reality contact, and deafferentation. These terms testify to the elusive and complex quality of the phenomena (Kubzansky and Leiderman, 1961). Input from the environment can easily be reduced by cutting down on sensory stimulation, by reducing the patterning of sensory stimuli, or by making the sensory environment monotonous. Experimenters using different varieties of these methods are certain to reach different conclusions about the critically important feature of the environment. They are also certain to disagree about what needs to be removed in order to achieve a state of sensory deprivation.

Bexton, Heron, and Scott (1954) confined subjects for several days and nights in a small, soundproofed room. The subjects wore frosted goggles. Their ears

A soundproof chamber similar to the one used by Bexton, Heron, and Scott to test the effects of sensory deprivation.

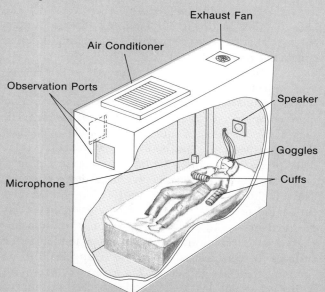

Exhaust Fan

Air Conditioner

Observation Ports

Speaker

Goggles

Microphone

Cuffs

Sensory Deprivation in Aviation. Sensory deprivation may play a part in reducing the efficiency of some pilots flying modern aircraft. The clouds below and the sky above are monotonously the same, hour after hour. If this is so, the problem may become even more acute with the supersonic aircraft of the future (Bennett, 1961). Aviators' emotional reactions can be summarized. Most pilots who experience unusual sensations at high altitudes feel their reactions are normal. Other pilots experience a greater degree of apprehension and may, for this reason, seek medical advice because of a fear that they will err in handling an aircraft. A few pilots are unable to expose themselves more than once to the isolation of great altitudes. Still others find that their experience at high altitude precipitates anxiety.

were covered by a sponge-rubber pillow containing speakers. And cylinders were used to cover their hands and forearms. After several days, the subjects began to hallucinate. They were unable to concentrate, and a significant loss appeared in their performance on an intelligence test. Subsequent experiments (Bliss and Clark, 1962) demonstrated that as little as one or two hours of sensory deprivation could produce such hallucinations. Other experiments (Heron, 1961; Ruff, Levy, and Thaler, 1961; Zubeck, Pushkar, Samson, and Cowing, 1961; Zuckerman and Cohen, 1964) made it clear that patterns of sensory stimulation are an important part of psychological life. We are quickly disorganized when our normal range of sensory input diminishes.

In addition to reduced sensory input, the deprivation situation can also involve a reduction in information input. Jones (1966) suggested that people need information about their physical and social environments. When information is withheld, you will seek information to reduce uncertainty. Thus, information can serve as an incentive to an information-deprived person, in much the same way as food is used as an incentive for a hungry or food-deprived person.

City Boys, Country Boys

Haggard (1964) suspected that sensory disturbances might occur more often when the experience of perceptual isolation is quite different from daily stimulation. An experiment was performed using two diverse groups of young men (Haggard, As, and Borgen, 1970). One group had grown up in rural areas, and the other group had been raised in an urban center. All subjects were told to lie quietly for five hours with their eyes open in a soundproofed room where light and noise levels were constant.

The country boys displayed fewer and less intense disturbances than did their urban counterparts. In contrast to the rural subjects, the urban men experienced hallucinatory sensations and perceptual distortions such as moving walls, colors that changed intensity, or objects that changed size. The rural men occupied their minds with thoughts about work they planned to do on the farm. The urban men found it impossible to concentrate or think coherently and spent their time in fantasies, daydreams, and confused reveries.

Boredom

If you have to work for long periods of time at repetitive tasks, you will probably complain of being bored and dissatisfied with your job. To test the effect of boredom on people, Heron (1957) paid male college students $20 a day to lie on a comfortable bed in a lighted cubicle 24 hours a day for as long as they would stay. There was, of course, time out for meals and going to the toilet. In addition, the subjects had to wear translucent plastic visors, which transmitted diffuse light but didn't allow any visual patterns. Gloves and cardboard cuffs were worn to restrict perception by touch, and auditory perception was limited both by a U-shaped foam rubber pillow and the continuous hum of air-conditioning equipment.

The volunteer students reported that they were unable to think clearly about anything for any length of time. They also saw "images," had waking dreams, and hallucinated.

The hallucinations usually began with simple forms. The subjects would start to see dots of light, lines, or simple geometrical patterns before the visions became more complex. Next, "true hallucinations" were seen, such as a procession of squirrels with sacks over their shoulders marching "purposefully" across the visual field, prehistoric animals walking about in a jungle, or processions of eyeglasses marching down a street. These hallucinations were uncontrollable and the picture could not be changed. Worse yet, when subjects emerged from several days of isolation, the room appeared to be in motion. There was a tendency for surfaces to seem curved, and objects appeared to be changing their size and shape. These results correspond with Zuckerman and Cohen's (1964) classification of

Sensation-Seeking Volunteers? Zuckerman (1969, 1971) developed a Sensation-Seeking Scale (SSS) to assess individual differences in optimal levels of stimulation. The need for change and intensity of stimulation is apparent in various behaviors. Behaviors labeled thrill seeking, social sensation seeking, visual sensation seeking, and antisocial sensation seeking were identifiable in males. Sensation seeking tends to correlate positively with asocial or psychopathic tendencies (Blackburn, 1969) and with the "need for change" (Pearson, 1970). The point to be made is that volunteers for sensory deprivation experiments tend to be persons who are high in sensation seeking (Zuckerman, Schultz, and Hopkins, 1967). These volunteers, therefore, possibly compose an unrepresentative sample.

two types of hallucinations: one being meaningless flashes of lights, spots, and lines; and the other being more meaningful scenes of people or objects.

Prolonged exposure to a monotonous environment impairs thinking, causes childish emotional responses, disturbs visual perception, and changes brain-wave patterns. These phenomena are bound to suggest that we have no more than a finger-tip hold on our sanity. Any or all of us could "lose our mind" simply by being deprived of stimulation. Let me reassure you, however, that it is not quite so simple. For one, these research subjects cooperated with the experimenters and did nothing to compensate for the reduction of stimuli. Only in rare cases, as we will see, is the psychological disorientation severe or long lasting.

Psychedelic Effects and Sensory Overload. Much research has been done on sensory deprivation, but little work has been done on sensory overload. Preliminary results of a study indicate that, "approximately 24 percent of 46 normal subjects exposed to sensory overload (consisting of increased light and sound stimulation) reported a variety of subjective 'psychedelic' effects. These effects pertained to perceptual distortions, disturbances in sense of time, 'otherworldly' feelings, feelings of loss of control, somatic effects, and diminished reality testing." [Ludwig, 1972, p. 114]

Sensory Deprivation and Psychosis

Curtis and Zuckerman (1968) reported a case of one young male subject who developed an acute psychotic reaction during an eight-hour sensory deprivation experiment. His delusions lasted several days, and severe anxiety and depression lasted several weeks. This was the third reported case of such a prolonged reaction, and the only case in which the subject was *not* a psychiatric patient prior to sensory deprivation.

During the postisolation interview, the subject was angry and almost incoherent. He accused the experimenter of putting drugs into his sandwiches, giving him a spinal anaesthetic, and piping some kind of gas into the room. One month after the experiment, the subject still experienced uncontrollable waves of anxiety and depression.

The odds for such an outcome are very small. Techniques like isolation can induce change for a short period of time, but maintaining these changes is extremely difficult. The healthier you are both physically and psychologically, the less effect isolation will have on you. People with stable personalities, clear-cut value systems, and an understanding of their own strengths and limitations are much more likely to resist no matter where or how they encounter influence. People who are inexperienced, psychologically naive, or confused about who they are and where they are going in life are much more susceptible to change.

Summary

1. By making the environment monotonous, cutting out sensory input, or eliminating information input, one can conduct experiments in sensory deprivation. Such experiments indicate that sensory stimulation is essential to proper functioning of the brain.

2. Persons undergoing sensory deprivation have been known to hallucinate. During and after the experience, their thinking is disorganized and confused. Interestingly, the more accustomed to intense sensory stimulation one is, the worse the disorganization caused by such deprivation.

Perception

Genius, in truth, means little more than the faculty of perceiving in an unhabitual way.—William James

The pieces of information we receive from the outside world do not come one at a time. Messages from several senses arrive at the brain simultaneously and must be sorted out, identified, and interpreted. To do this, the brain has to select certain messages from the jumble of sensory impressions and decide which message to pay attention to. Obviously, these decisions are important to our survival.

Developing perception requires the discrimination of objects and the features that differentiate one object from another. In this process, we must discriminate among colors, textures, shapes, and even more complex structural variables (Gibson, 1969, p. 15).

Attention

Attention is the psychological process of selecting certain stimuli while suppressing reactions to others. If we could not do this, we would be helplessly distracted by sensory overload. *Distractions* are demanding stimuli that you cannot ignore. They interfere with work efficiency, but after prolonged exposure we tend to become accustomed to them and tune them out.

Mech (1953) studied the effect of noise on students who were solving mathematics problems. Students were studied under either a quiet condition or a noisy one. One group was told that they would actually do better in the quiet situation. Another group was told that they would get better results in the noisy situation. A third group was given no information at all. The

Our perceptual development appears to depend, to a large degree, on our experiences and motor activity. In one experiment designed to show that visual stimulation was not sufficient in itself to develop perceptual ability, Held and Hein (1963) used the apparatus shown here. They raised two kittens in the dark (to prevent them from having visual learning experiences) until they were ten weeks old. Then they hitched one kitten in a harness that was connected to a basket in which the other kitten was confined. Both kittens saw the same things, but only the one kitten was free to move about. Within ten days, the active kitten was behaving normally—he would put out his paws when carried toward a table and blink at approaching objects. The confined kitten did not display these behaviors.

SPEED PERCEIVERS

Although advertisements for speed-reading courses sound like scientific reports on a major advance in human education, the ads are closer to science fiction (Carver, 1972). They claim that an average person can triple his reading speed with no loss in comprehension. But the evidence suggests that we cannot increase reading speeds without affecting comprehension.
Speed-reading courses do not increase your reading speed. They teach you to skim or scan material—to control what you attend to. Most of us read between 150 and 300 words per minute with complete comprehension of the written material. Researchers have shown that an intelligent individual reading very easy material cannot comprehend most of it at rates above 500 to 600 words per minute.

group given no instructions showed no differences in performance between the noisy and quiet conditions. In the other groups, it was found that subjects will either tune out noise or not tune it out depending on the instructions given.

We evidently *learn* to pay attention. As infants, it is hard for us to maintain attention for very long. One study of ten infants showed, however, that attention span can be prolonged and the onset of sleep delayed by making the infant's environment stimulating (Wolff, 1965). Interestingly, female babies reportedly could sustain attention longer than male babies (Kagan and Lewis, 1965).

Attention sets a limit on how many things we can do effectively at one time. It also limits our perception of the world about us. We can compare attention with using a flashlight on a dark night. When the beam of light is focused on one object, all the other objects seem to disappear in the dark. If you sweep the flashlight back and forth very rapidly, you will catch a glimpse of a number of objects, but none of them will register very clearly in your consciousness.

Each of us has learned to attend to certain stimuli and not to attend to others. This ability to be attentive and inattentive at will is an important feature of our perceptual system. We each learn to filter stimulation so it doesn't confuse us and thus destroy the perceptual organization that lets us comprehend what's happening. Our perception is indeed organized, and there are a number of theories about how this happens.

Subliminal Perception

In the fall of 1957, public concern was aroused by an "experiment" conducted in a New Jersey movie theater. During the showing of a regular film, the messages "Eat Popcorn" and "Drink Coca-Cola" were reportedly flashed alternately on the screen every five seconds for one-three thousandths of a second. Because of brief exposure, the stimuli were below the threshold of perception, and the viewers were unaware that such messages were being projected. Nevertheless, the "subliminal" message got across. James Vicary, the man who developed the experiment, claimed that, during the six weeks that this procedure was followed, the sale of popcorn rose 57.7 percent and that of Coca-Cola rose 18.1 percent. The phenomenon of subliminal perception produced excited comment in the popular press. Soon the press painted pictures of a nation of robots whose behavior could be controlled without their knowledge.

A number of articles denounced Vicary for having invented a new method of "mind control," but the ad agencies saw exciting possibilities. What if subliminal television commercials were flashed on the television screen almost continuously during all programs? The TV viewer would never complain because he or she wouldn't be aware that the ads were there. Still, viewers would be seized by irresistible urges to go buy things. It was imagined that politicians could sway millions of voters against their wills. Law enforcement agencies could fill TV and movie screens with hidden messages that commanded the viewer to "Support Your Local Police."

Psychologists invested a great deal of time and effort trying to determine just how subliminal perception might occur. Bach and Klein (1957), for example, showed one group of students a simple line drawing of a human face and asked the students to guess whether the face was angry or happy. Actually the face had been constructed to look neither happy nor angry. The first group of students were evenly divided in their guesses. The experimenters then showed the same face to a second group of subjects, but they simultaneously flashed the word *angry* so that the subliminal word was superimposed over the drawing of the face. A significantly greater number of students in this group reported that they thought the face was "angry." A third group saw the same face, but they had the word *happy* flashed over the drawing. A significantly greater number of these subjects said the face was "happy." None of the students in the second or third group reported seeing the words *angry* or *happy*.

Despite experimental evidence that perception can take place without awareness, its use for evil purposes seems unlikely. Shortly after the "popcorn experiment," a number of radio and television stations tried the technique. When a man named Pirie first ran the mile in less than four minutes, the British Broadcasting Corporation (BBC) flashed the message "Pirie Breaks World Record" on television screens at a very rapid speed. No one seemed to get the message, except for a few people with apparently superb vision who called up to ask why the BBC was flashing the message so rapidly (Mannes, 1957). A television station in Minneapolis, perhaps hoping to inspire the University of Minnesota football team, projected the slogan "Beat Michigan" subliminally on TV screens the week prior to the 1956 Michigan-Minnesota game. Michigan won easily that year. A radio station on the West Coast had someone whisper softly "Don't watch TV" during all their broadcasts, but television viewing didn't decline at all. These and other attempts to manipulate people's minds have produced highly unspectacular results. At least, we are safe for a while.

Perceptual Organization

In ancient times, it was thought that objects transmitted copies of themselves that traveled to the mind. We now know that objects do not emit copies. Rather, we see the light waves that are reflected by an object. The energy of the light strikes our eyes and causes chemical changes inside them. These changes in turn activate neurons and nerve impulses that travel to the brain. At the end of this chain, perception occurs in the brain and tells us about the objects in the outside world. The process of perception is, thus, a coding operation. Information from patterns of energy outside us are translated into

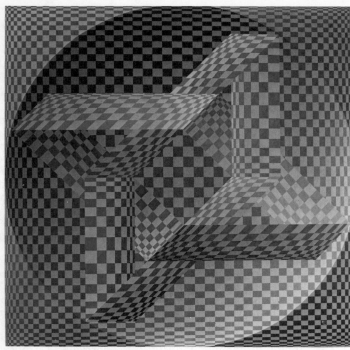

A primary aim of *op art* (the term comes from *optical art*) is to "stretch" vision by producing visual sensations that are not actually present in the painting. One such work is *Equivocation* by Ben Cunningham, in which you perceive depth and roundness even though the surface is flat.

nerve impulses which the nervous system codes and sends to different parts of the brain.

We also know there are principles that organize our perceptions. We see things as unified, meaningful wholes—not just as unrelated bits and pieces. This is particularly true of the illusion of movement. Take for example, the familiar theater marquee. Rows of lights give the impression of a light starting at one end and moving along until it reaches the other end of the marquee. When stimuli change together in the same direction like this, we tend to group or organize them into a unit. This principle of organization is called *common fate*.

Hastorf, Schneider, and Polefka (1970) described five characteristics of the perceptual experience. These are: (1) *immediacy* (perceptual experience occurs at all times); (2) *structure* (we perceive things as organized wholes rather than as separate elements); (3) *stability* (objects appear to remain the same despite changes in their position or illumination); (4) *meaningfulness* (we perceive in terms of our experience with objects and in terms of their orderly relationship to other objects); and (5) *selectivity* (we tend to note only certain stimuli and objects out of all possible stimuli we could perceive at any moment). Here, we shall be concerned with how we organize what we see into meaningful perceptions.

We organize stimuli by grouping them into meaningful patterns. There are several ways to do this. One way is to group by *likeness* or *similarity*. Objects of a like appearance will be grouped together. Dissimilar objects will not be grouped. We also group stimuli by *nearness* or *proximity*. Objects closest to each other appear as a group. A third way to group is by *symmetry*. The more symmetrical, the more likely that contours will be perceived as a figure. *Continuation* is still another way to group. We group stimuli that make the fewest interruptions in contour. Finally, we can use *closure,* which means the "closing" of incomplete lines in order to see a symmetrically whole object.

Since few stimuli occur in isolation, these ways of organizing our perceptions can be tied together. We almost always perceive stimuli surrounded by other stimuli. What we perceive is relative to what has gone before and what else is happening at that moment. Our perceptions are formed in these contrasts between various stimuli. But, of course, in the process of forming perceptions we also frequently misperceive.

The pointillism of Georges Seurat is an artistic illustration of the closure principle. The tiny dots or "points" of paint in a picture such as *Sunday Afternoon on the Island of La Grande Jatte* appear as a whole—much like the dots in a newspaper picture.

The Misperception of Reality

If you have ever stood in a "mystery room" at an amusement park, you know how easy it is to get confused about sensory cues. Perhaps, you perceived yourself as standing at an angle when you were actually standing upright. The trick is that the *room* is tilted so that all the visual cues you get suggest you must be standing at an angle when actually you are not. The message going to the brain from your eyes contradicts the less powerful message of gravity from the muscles and tendons of your body. Your eyes win.

One of the best known illusions is the *Necker cube* that many of us doodle. As you look at the cube it will reverse its direction, appearing one way and then another. A *fatigue theory* is said to explain it. That is, the central nervous system becomes fatigued with one position and alternates to the other. The fatigue hypothesis has also been used to explain other forms of indecision (Orbach, 1963). Shopland (1964) suggests that our eye is given

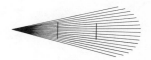

Above, the Ponzo illusion, where the lines appear to be unequal in length. Below, the Necker cube.

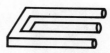

Top, the Müller-Lyer illusion Middle, a reversible figure-ground drawing. Bottom, the "impossible" figure, which appears impossible because of the conflicting visual cues in different parts of the total figure.

two perceptions at the same time, either one of which can be correct. The eye then alternates between them. Thus, if you put your hands on a physical model of the Necker cube, visual reversals are sharply reduced. Touch reinforces what the eye is seeing.

Another illusion is called the *Müller-Lyer illusion*. The two lines are of the same length but the "arrow" line looks shorter.

Your attention is usually focused on fewer than a dozen elements, but when there are many stimuli you can attend to all of them at once if you group them to achieve organization. One way to do this is to separate the perceptual field into two parts called *figure* and *ground*. The most basic organization of sensations is the distinction between a figure and the ground it appears against. A figure may be distinguished by its shape, its color, or its closeness. When the contrast between figure and ground does not give us enough cues to determine which is figure and which is ground, we have a *reversible figure*. More important to the perceptual process is how we see three-dimensional space.

Depth Perception

The image falling on the retina is curved to conform to the curvature of the eyeball, much like a bent photo. Since no depth is added to the image by the curvature of the surface of the eye, the question is: How do we perceive three dimensions when the image on the retina registers only two?

The explanation for our ability to "see" depth largely depends on the fact that we have two eyes. If you have vision in only one eye, you still have most of the visual experiences of someone using two eyes. You will see colors, forms, and space relationships. But with vision in both eyes, you have an advantage. You have the benefit of *binocular vision* in which the two eyes cooperate to give solidity and distance to objects.

Seeing depth also depends on the positioning of the two eyes. The position of our eyes provides us with *retinal disparity*. This means that your right and left eye each get a different (disparate) image of the object you

Would you believe that the two balls in the illustration on the left are actually the same size? The construction of the Ames room is such that when we look through the observation window the visual cues we receive make the room appear rectangular. The diagram at the right shows, however, that the room is trapezoidal. Since the ball at the right is closer to us, it appears larger than the other one.

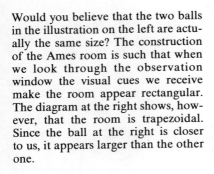
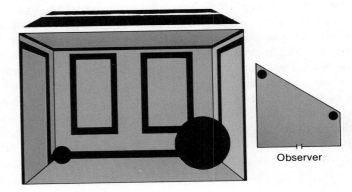

Observer

are looking at. If you cover your right eye and then cover your left eye, you will see an image slightly to the left and then see it slightly to the right. These two disparate images produce depth perception. The closer the object, the greater the disparity. A faraway object will produce only slight retinal disparity.

Binocular disparity is not the only factor in depth perception. If you lose vision in one eye, you are still able to perceive depth. As we know, painters portray depth using only the horizontal and vertical dimensions of their canvases. Our experience with objects during a life time of seeing and perceiving can make us perceive depth even when the sensory cues to depth are absent.

An infant, however, is an inexperienced perceiver. How does it know near from far or deep from shallow?

The experimental setup of the "visual cliff."

The Visual Cliff

For many years there was serious question about the existence of an inborn ability to perceive depth. The *visual cliff* experiment was designed to answer this question.

The experimental setup utilized a table which had a sheet of thick glass placed on top of it. The glass extended beyond the edge of the table, and a checkerboard pattern was laid down immediately under the glass. The same pattern was also fixed to the floor (three and one half feet below the glass) in a way which made the design seem continuous when viewed from above. Human infants were then placed on the glass surface and allowed to crawl about. In one experiment only 8 percent of the human infants ventured onto the "deep" side (beyond the table edge) even when urged (Gibson and Walk, 1960). When babies from six to fourteen months old were placed on the table and encouraged to crawl off the table over the fake cliff, they would not go beyond the perceptual "edge" of the "cliff" (Gibson, 1960; Gregory, 1966). Like many animals, the human infant has the beginnings of depth perception, which is later improved with learning.

Perceptual Constancy

When certain aspects of the environment appear stable and unchanging, we refer to them as *perceptual constancies*. The fact that our perception stays the same even though our senses are reporting drastic changes suggests that we are also using information and experience which already exist in the brain. As Gregory (1968) stated:

Perception seems to be a matter of looking up information that has been stored about objects and how they behave in various situations. The retinal image does little more than select the relevant stored data. The selection is rather like looking up entries in the encyclopedia: behavior is determined by the contents of the entry rather than by the stimulus that provoked the search. [p. 75]

We seem to be born with some part of our perception, and another part seems to be learned over the years. The relative contribution of each is a scientific question that has yet to be settled. It is worth examining briefly those aspects of perception that seem to remain constant for us. The sizes of objects in our environment seem to remain remarkably constant.

Size Constancy

If someone is 60 feet away from you, the image on your retina is exactly half the size of the retinal image you receive when he is 30 feet away. But you perceive him as being the same size whether he is 30 or 60 feet away. This *size constancy* helps us keep our world of sensory images straight.

We rely on our experience to tell us the true size of objects. If we lack other cues, our knowledge of the actual size of an object helps us judge its distance. Turnbull (1961) tells of the Bambuti Pygmies who live in the forests of the Congo and are not familiar with wide open spaces. Turnbull took a Pygmy to a vast plain, and when the Pygmy looked at a herd of buffalo several hundred yards away, he asked what type of insect they were. He refused to believe they were buffalo. The Pygmy had to learn to take distance as well as retinal image into account since he rarely looked at distances greater than a few yards.

The studies of Zeigler and Leibowitz (1957) indicate that eight-year-old children do not show the same degree of size constancy that adults do. Adults tend to perceive objects at their real size as far as 100 feet away. Eight-year-olds perceive the same objects as smaller than life size at this distance. This suggests that size constancy develops as a result of learning.

Our size perceptions represent compromises between *perceived* size and *actual* object size. How well our size constancy operates depends upon the presence of distance cues and upon our familiarity with the object. As regards distance, we perceive *apparent* distance and *real* distance. The more information available about the real distance of the object, the more the *perceived* size approaches the *actual* size. When distance cues are eliminated, the perceived size approaches the size of the retinal image, unless we are

---

The Moon Illusion

Sometimes our perception of stimulus objects is faulty. We perceive things as larger, smaller, brighter, or darker than they really are. These instances of misconception are called *illusions,* and they are of interest to psychologists because they tell us about the nature of our perceptual processes. The moon illusion is an example of this. The moon appears larger when it is near the horizon than when it is higher in the sky—despite the fact that its image on the retina is the same size. Rock and Kaufman (1962) account for this illusion with the *apparent-distance theory.* An object that is far away appears smaller to us than it does when it is closer. We compensate for this by assuming that an object that is far away is actually larger than it appears. Most people perceive the horizon as being further away than the sky directly overhead. Therefore, when the moon is on the horizon, they compensate for its apparently greater distance by perceiving it as larger than it appears.

Another theory for the moon illusion is that the size of an object depends on its surroundings. When the moon is high in the sky, it is surrounded by vast space, and so it appears rather small. When on the horizon, however, the moon is surrounded by much less empty space, and so it appears relatively large. Whichever theory turns out to be correct, the reason for the moon illusion will provide psychologists with a better idea of the processes that are influential in the way human beings perceive objects in their environment.

familiar with the object. Related to size constancy is *object constancy*. This is perceiving an object as being the same object regardless of a change in its position or illumination.

Brightness and Color Constancy

Brightness constancy exists because the brightness of an object is judged in relation to its surroundings. The amount of light reflected by a piece of black cloth in bright sunlight is greater than the light reflected by a piece of white cloth in the shade. Yet, the relative brightness (the percentage of available light reflected by an object) is the same regardless of the degree of illumination. Thus, the white cloth will reflect a certain percentage of the light striking it regardless of the intensity of the light.

Hans Wallach (1963) observed that the actual lightness or darkness of an object depends on the amount of light reflected by its surface. A patch of gray on a dark background will look light because its background gives off little light. On a light background, the gray patch will look dark because its background gives off more light. Thus, the perceived brightness of a surface depends on the brightness of the object compared to its background.

Brightness constancy allows us to perceive objects as having an unchanging brightness regardless of the intensity of light. A white fur in the shade appears brighter than a gray fur in the sunshine even though the light reflected from the gray fur is greater than that from the white fur.

Color constancy occurs when the apparent color of objects remains unchanged even when dark sunglasses are used. We tend to see familiar objects as retaining their original color under a variety of lighting conditions. This holds true even when objects are illuminated by colored light, provided there are sufficient contrasts and shadows. Information concerning the nature of the illumination and the color of surrounding objects are also clues to color constancy.

When these clues are eliminated, color constancy diminishes or disappears. If you look at a red object through a straw so that you do not know the nature of the object or the source or kind of illumination, the object will appear blue, brown, or some other color depending upon the color of light shining on it.

Much of our perception is based on the visual sense. But what if we were without sight? How would we perceive our world?

Blind Perception

Senden (1960) has reported that persons who were blind from birth but who have had their vision restored by surgical means when adults become confused by visual stimuli. They are able to distinguish figure from ground, fixate figures, scan them, and follow moving figures. (These abilities appear to be innate.)

Our perception of how light or dark an object is depends on the amount of light reflected by its surroundings. Here, the black line appears darkest in the bottom part of the illustration. whereas the white line appears lightest in the middle.

THE INVERTED WORLD
To learn how a reversal of sensory perception affects us, psychologists have worn special lenses that reverse the images of the outside world. Köhler's (1967) subjects wore such lenses for weeks, and observations were made on how they adapted. At the beginning, they were very clumsy and would bump into people and things. After a while they adapted, and the world began to look normal. Köhler reported that subjects had to go through an adaptation period to adjust to a "new" environment when the lenses were removed.

Signs in an English botanical garden are written in Braille in an attempt to help blind individuals feel part of the society of "normal people."

But they cannot identify objects that had been familiar only from the sense of touch. They cannot distinguish a triangle from a square, unless they count the number of corners or trace the outline. Neither can they tell which of two sticks is longer without feeling them. It sometimes takes them several weeks of training to identify simple objects. A white triangle may not be recognized when it is turned over to its red side, when viewed under altered illumination, or when turned upside down. They can distinguish between colors but they do not know which name to attach to the color.

Auditory Perception

Hearing provides cues that enable us to perceive the distance and direction of objects. Some of these cues may be obtained with one ear (*monaural*), and other cues require two ears (*binaural*). Monaural cues are enough for auditory perception of distance. Binaural cues are needed for directional localization of sound.

We estimate the distance of a sound primarily by its loudness. Loud, clear sounds are perceived to be nearby. Weak or muffled sounds are heard as being far away.

Since our ears are on opposite sides of our heads, a sound wave coming from either side will reach one ear before it reaches the other ear. Although only a split second is involved, the time differential between the sounds permits the hearer to gauge the direction of the sound source.

Wallach (1940) indicated that the time lag between the register of a sound in our two ears can tell us whether a sound comes from our left or our right. But it can't tell us whether a sound comes from above or below since the time lag for sounds from those directions is the same. In the same way, the time lag cannot even tell us whether a sound comes from directly in front or in back of us, since time lags for sounds from these directions are the same. Thus we often make head movements while listening to help us localize sounds. If we tilt our head to one side, we can tell whether a sound comes from below or above.

It has long been known that blind persons are able to detect obstacles in their paths. When asked how they do it, blind people do not give consistent answers. Some of them can't tell how they do it. To study this, Supa, Cotzin, and Dallenbach (1944) used four young adults. Two had been blind from early life, and two had normal vision. The experimenters wanted to find out whether blind persons were actually better at obstacle perception than were sighted persons.

Each blind subject was placed in a long hall and asked to approach an obstacle. The subject was asked to report when he first perceived the obstacle and when he was close, but not touching it. The subjects were fitted with blindfolds to equalize the amount of facial area exposed to air currents.

The blind subjects successfully detected the obstacle on every trial. The sighted subjects failed on the first 8 or 9 trials and took 40 or more trials to accumulate 25 successes each. Their performances continued to improve, and by the third experiment they were doing almost as well as the blind. If both blind and sighted subjects approach an obstacle while walking without shoes on a soft carpet, the accuracy of their judgments decreases.

In another experiment, the skin of each subject was completely covered by a heavy felt veil and leather gloves. The subject could still hear, but was not able to feel air currents. The subjects were still almost always successful in perceiving the obstacle either from a distance or up close. However, if the skin were left exposed and the ears were plugged, the subjects regularly collided with obstacles. The conclusion which the experimenters reached is that hearing is critically important for obstacle perception.

Perception and Human Needs

Your perception can be influenced if you *expect* to perceive something. Siipola (1935) demonstrated this by studying individuals' responses to words. He told one group of people they would be shown words that referred to animals. He then showed them combinations of letters that really did not spell anything (*sael, dack,* or *wharl*). Most of the group perceived the letters as the words *seal, duck,* and *whale.* He told a second group he was going to show them words pertaining to boats. He showed this group the same combinations that the first group saw. This group saw the words *sail, deck,* and *wharf.* They perceived what they expected to perceive.

Similar alterations of perception resulted in a study where subjects were asked to estimate the size of coins. The subjects were in two groups: one of children from poor homes and one a group of rich children. The poor children consistently overestimated the size of the coins and this was interpreted to mean that money had much greater value for the poor children (Bruner and Goodman, 1947).

Our *perceptual set* makes us ready to perceive or interpret the environment in a specific way. Perceptual set is determined in part by past experiences, which determine the meaning or significance of what you perceive. An object may have different meanings for different persons. As one psychiatrist says: "Think of your mother. If you and I see her at the same time, we certainly see very different persons. I, of course, do not know what you see; but I may see an attractive, mature woman just designed for a pleasant evening, or a fat, frowsy, old bore, or an interesting example of some obscure skin disease" (Preston, 1940, p. 45).

We develop expectations which lead us to perceive aspects of the environment that others don't perceive. We find in our environment the things we are looking for, and we overlook or avoid things that do not fit our interests.

Witnesses

Every lawyer or judge has a story about the unreliability of witnesses as perceivers of reality. Despite this fact, our trial process is based on the assumption that witnesses can see and hear accurately. If they do not testify accurately on direct examination, it is further assumed that cross-examination will straighten them out. Evidently neither of these assumptions is very accurate.

In the Warren Commission report on the assassination of President John F. Kennedy, there was conflict as to the number of shots fired, the direction from which they were fired, the size of the bag in which Oswald carried the rifle, and so forth (Marshall, 1969). Experiments have also shown how inaccurate we all are at estimating the speed of a car, particularly when it is coming toward us or going away from us. Color, body style, and noise of a car have been found to influence a witness's estimate of speed. Some highway patrolmen *expect* bright-colored sports models to exceed the posted speed limits.

When a situation involves danger and stress, the inaccuracy of perceptions is increased since such pressures tend to distort time and distance. In addition, when things happen quickly, as in a 10-second automobile accident, it is unrealistic to expect people to estimate distances, speeds, or even the sequence of events accurately.

In conversations, few people hear every word that is said. If parts of a conversation are not exactly recalled, we tend to fill in the blanks with what we would expect to hear in such situations. In general, better educated witnesses testify more correctly than other witnesses, but they also make a greater number of inferences. Marshall (1969) also points out that when a lawyer interviews witnesses before trial, the mere suggestion that other witnesses have seen things differently tends to induce a witness to adapt his perceptions accordingly.

Summary

1. *Perception* is the way in which we create meaningful patterns out of the sensory information we are constantly receiving. Perceptual processes combine the immediate information from our senses with the previous experiences that exist in the brain.

2. *Attention* is the process of noticing certain sensory input while ignoring the rest.

3. We tend to organize sensory information into unified wholes, rather than accept it in bits and pieces. The grouping of stimuli may be done according to a number of different principles. Our response to any one stimulus, therefore, will depend on the context in which we encounter it.

4. Perceptions of social situations can be influenced by colors and sizes of objects. Our accuracy in perceiving social situations is also affected by danger and stress and by our tendency to fill in blanks with our own expectations. Reliance on eyewitnesses in courts of law may not be such a good idea.

5. Because attention limits the number of things we can respond to, we can deal with more stimuli if we perceive them as parts of larger units. This happens when we group a variety of objects into *figure* or *ground*.

6. *Binocular vision* is responsible for our ability to see things in three dimension. Each eye sees the object slightly differently (retinal disparity), but when the images come together in the brain, they give the sense of depth.

7. *Visual cliff* experiments conducted on babies indicate that depth perception is innate but improves with learning. Depth perception is, therefore, not necessarily lost when we lose the sight of one eye. Prior experience may make us perceive depth anyway.

8. *Perceptual constancies* indicate that we use information stored in the brain to help us deal with new sensory data. Perceptual constancies allow us to see the environment as unchanging, even though our senses tell us that it is somehow different.

9. Objects that are far away appear smaller than those that are close. Because we know how far away the object is, however, we perceive it at its normal size. This is *size constancy*.

10. The accuracy of size constancy will depend on relevant cues such as distance or familiarity with the object. If we misjudge distance, then we will misjudge the object's size.

11. *Brightness constancy* is the ability to perceive objects as having the same brightness, regardless of the amount of light shining on them. This is due to the fact that no matter how bright the

light, an object will always reflect the same percentage of the light falling on it. We can best judge brightness when the object is seen against a background. The relative brightness for both object and its background will be the same no matter how bright the illumination.

12. *Color constancy* is the ability to perceive the real color of familiar objects even when lighting conditions send contradictory messages to the eye.

13. People who have been blind from birth and have their sight restored later on have difficulty performing tasks that require perceptual organization. Such difficulties demonstrate the extent to which our interpretation of the world depends on prior experience.

14. The distance of a sound is judged by its loudness. The direction can be judged by the split-second difference in the times at which the sound is heard in each ear.

15. It has been found that blind people are much better than blindfolded, sighted persons at avoiding obstacles in their paths. Experiments have shown that hearing is critically important for obstacle perception.

16. Perceptions can be influenced by the psychological disposition of the perceiver. *Perceptual set* is the readiness to perceive or interpret the environment in a specific way. Set may depend on past experience, values, or information given to the perceiver about the sensory stimuli.

17. When stimuli are presented below the threshold of awareness, they may still have an effect on the organism. The ability to be affected by stimuli without awareness is called *subliminal perception.*

Perception and Parapsychology

Wayne Sage (1972) remarked: "Forty years of experiments in the telepathic, clairvoyant, and precognitive capacities of the human mind have left us no more certain, or uncertain, that such abilities even exist" (p. 56). Sage has observed that with ESP you either believe it or you don't. It depends on what you are willing to accept as proof. Correctly or incorrectly, this form of "perception" has thus far failed to be accepted as legitimate by most American psychologists.

The status of *extrasensory perception* (ESP) is somewhat different in the Soviet Union. After Krippner and Davidson (1972) traveled there to observe some of the research of Russian parapsychologists, they reported:

Perhaps the most striking discovery we made during our stay in the Soviet Union was the difference between American and Russian approaches to parapsychology. In America the thrust of research is on simply proving the existence of ESP. . . . In the Soviet Union, however, there is little emphasis on the experimental, statistical approach or on proving the existence of ESP. . . . The Russian parapsychologists seem to harbor no doubts about the existence of parapsychological phenomena. Instead, they are seeking practical applications and an understanding of how these phenomena operate. [p. 56]

The American psychological establishment has not devoted much effort to parapsychology and extrasensory perception. The fact remains, however, that a large number of people believe they can receive impressions of distant realities which do not reach them through their sense organs. They report catching impressions of catastrophes that involve distant loved ones, or they have had curiously exact premonitions of future events (Murphy, 1961).

The study of parapsychology includes *clairvoyance* (where extrasensory perception allows you to know about an object or event without employing the usual senses), *telepathy* (being aware of another person's thoughts without communicating through the usual sensory channels), and *psychokinesis* (the ability to influence a physical object by a sheer exercise of will). Here, we shall focus on extrasensory perception.

The Closed Mind.

The psychologist Helmholtz (1821–1894) stated many years ago a sentiment that still seems evident among present-day psychologists. When asked in the late 1800s what evidence would convince him of the reality of extrasensory phenomena, he said that not even what his own eyes recorded would convince him of telepathy. He held that it was manifestly impossible. ESP has never lost this stigma of scientific "unrespectability." The few psychologists who are believers have had to fight the prejudice against them throughout their professional careers.

ESP

Jonas and Klein (1970) suggested that ESP is related to some unknown quality of brain tissue that is just beginning to emerge as human beings plod slowly along the path of evolution. In the search to understand ESP, a great many avenues have been traveled.

The parapsychologist can expect little support or recognition from fellow psychologists, however. Warner (1952) concluded, in a survey made more than 20 years ago, that fewer than 3 percent of psychologists felt ESP was an established fact, and a much higher percentage (10 percent) believed ESP was impossible. There is little likelihood that the attitudes of psychologists have changed drastically since then. As Gertrude Schmeidler (1969) recently noted: "A glance at the Psychological Abstracts indicates that by the criterion of number of published articles, parapsychology is only a minor topic; and ESP is only one of its subtopics" (p. 1).

Those most firmly set against ESP insist it is an illusory phenomenon that is no different from the superstitious beliefs of primitive and nonliterate people. They believe that scientific inquiry into its nature is of no more value than the ghost hunting that has occupied unscientific man for centuries. The disbelievers point out that discovering dependable ESP subjects is rare. Between 1938 and 1954 (despite active research in the field) no such subject appeared in America (Soal and Bateman, 1954). In England researchers credited only three persons with the capacity to maintain their ESP ability over a sustained period of time. Even this sustained ability was often a marginal one.

To understand why psychologists are skeptical, let us consider an experiment performed in J. B. Rhine's laboratory at Duke University (Rhine, 1942). Rhine was trying to determine whether a subject might, through some combination of ESP and willpower, influence the positions of cards in a mechanical shuffler. In all, 50 persons predicted the order in which cards would come out of the mechanical shuffler. The experiment was performed carefully. In more than 50,000 trials, the results were at chance level. Further statistical analyses were then made, but they failed to yield significant results. Finally, a fourth analysis (based on a complex statistic called a covariance of salience ratio) produced a better-than-chance effect. As one team of researchers stated: "When belief in bizarre effects is carried this far, it is no wonder that the unconvinced scientist begins to question the statistics, even though all the computations are accurate" (Hilgard, Atkinson, and Atkinson, 1971, p. 158).

Long-Distance ESP.

Moss, Chang, and Levitt (1970) attempted extrasensory perception across great distances. They arranged for a group of persons in Los Angeles to "transmit" their reactions to various emotional episodes to "receivers" in Los Angeles, New York, and Sussex, England. The most startling example of such experimentation with extrasensory perception was the attempt of astronaut Edgar Mitchell to send mental messages back to Earth during the Apollo 14 moon flight. Long-distance experimentation with ESP is not new. It was first attempted in 1933 in the Pearce-Pratt Distance Series of ESP tests.

The statistical argument is a futile one according to Crumbaugh (1969). It starts with the premise that ESP exists, and its proof relies on some demonstration

The Think Tank and the Magician. The Stanford Research Institute (SRI) is one of America's largest and best-known think tanks. Its staff of 2,600 specialists conducts research and solves problems in nearly every field of human endeavor for both government and private industry. In addition to its other projects, the institute has been investigating the psychic powers of an Israeli named Uri Geller. Geller claims to be able to communicate by telepathy, detect and describe objects hidden from view, and distort metal implements with his psychic energy.

News of the unusual activity reached the Department of Defense (DOD), and investigators were soon on the scene. Included among them was Ray Hyman, a psychology professor from the University of Oregon who is frequently employed by DOD as a consultant. Another was George Lawrence, a member of DOD, who was accompanied by psychologist Robert Van de Castle, a long-time researcher in parapsychology from the University of Virginia. Although Van de Castle concluded that Geller was "an interesting subject for further study," neither Lawrence nor Hyman was impressed. Hyman said that he could spot "loopholes and inconclusiveness" in each of Geller's feats of ESP and psychokinesis (the ability to move or bend objects without touching them). Hyman also said he caught Geller in some outright deceptions.

Geller, for instance, asked Lawrence to think of a number between one and ten and write it down, as large as possible, on a pad. While Lawrence wrote, Geller made a show of concentrating and covered his eyes with his hands. But Hyman, carefully observing Geller, noticed that the young man's eyes were open and visible through his fingers. Hyman concluded that Geller was able to see the motion of Lawrence's arm as he wrote and could therefore correctly identify the number. In another case, Geller caused a compass needle to turn about five degrees. Lawrence, noting that Geller had moved his body and vibrated the floor, did the same, and the needle deflected even more.

Despite the skepticism, Geller volunteered to demonstrate his powers to the editors of *Time* magazine. After Geller performed his feats, a professional magician named James Randi duplicated each one. In its story on Geller, *Time* called the psychic a fraud.

Only a few days after the *Time* article appeared, however, SRI reported its findings on Geller to a physics symposium at Columbia University. Their report described some of the feats Geller had performed in foolproof laboratory tests at SRI. Although they did not claim that Geller had psychic powers, the researchers stated: "We have observed certain phenomena . . . for which we have no explanation. All we can say at this point is that further investigation is warranted."

Some of the feats Geller had accomplished included:

Passing his hands over a sensitive laboratory balance covered with a bell jar, Geller caused it to deflect with a force up to 100 times that which would have been caused by jumping on the floor or by striking the bell jar.

Geller correctly guessed the number that would come up on a die shaken in a box eight out of eight times. The odds against him were a million to one.

By passing his hands over a row of ten identical film canisters, Geller was able to select the one can which contained an object. He performed this task 12 times with different objects, and without any errors.

The researchers admitted that Geller might have the ability to make micromanipulatory movements, but none of these was detected while Geller accomplished these feats, nor in the hundreds of feet of film the researchers took of his performance.

of a human capacity to violate the laws of mathematical expectancy. Crumbaugh feels that the critical problem is the failure of experimenters to produce an ESP experiment that can be replicated in a laboratory with the same results. In Crumbaugh's experience, only 25 to 50 percent of the experimental replications attempted in parapsychological experiments have been successful. In his own research in parapsychology, he reports meeting with almost constant negative results. Over the years, he was startled to learn that the published reports that made the most convincing case for ESP were conducted by researchers who had less than trustworthy reputations among working parapsychologists. Crumbaugh concluded it is impossible for scientists to decide the merits of the case for ESP solely on the basis of published reports.

Sheep and Goats. An unsettling observation stems from the work of Schmeidler and McConnell (1958). They separated research subjects into two categories: "sheep" (believers in ESP) and "goats" (nonbelievers in ESP). They found that the sheep regularly scored beyond chance expectation in experiments. The goats consistently scored at only chance expectation or a little below. This discovery led to a furor of scientific criticism and analysis during the late 1950s. To the many goats among professional psychologists, these research findings suggested that the study of ESP had always been unwittingly biased in its design, because it has traditionally been conducted almost exclusively among sheep.

ESP may well exist, but it has still to be demonstrated according to the rules of established science. If ESP does exist, it will enter the halls of science, but it must "play by the rules" established for the demonstration of all other kinds of phenomena.

Summary

1. While American psychologists have mostly declined to conduct experiments establishing the existence of extrasensory perception (ESP), Russian psychologists are studying its practical applications.

2. Extrasensory perception is defined as the ability to perceive objects or events without using the usual senses. ESP is the main concern of parapsychology, the study of *clairvoyance, telepathy,* and *psychokinesis.*

3. Some researchers suggest that ESP is related to an unknown quality of brain tissue that is only in the beginning of its evolutionary stages.

4. The validity of ESP experiments is continually challenged. So far, ESP experimenters have not been able to prove the existence of the phenomenon according to the rules of scientific research.

5. Among the shortcomings of ESP research, opponents point out that there are few reliable ESP subjects. Those who have been found demonstrate only marginal abilities. Further, research subjects who perform better at ESP tasks tend to believe that the phenomenon exists. Results from such subjects may be biased.

Consciousness

*Happiness lies in the consciousness
we have of it.*—George Sand

The human brain allows us to achieve a consciousness unique among the species on this planet. Psychologists have probed man's intelligence, his ability to think, create, learn, and remember, and his motives and intellectual perceptions at great length. There has also been much interest in states of consciousness brought on by sleep, dreams, meditation, hypnosis, and drugs.

At one time, consciousness was believed to be easily available to observation. In time we learned that normal waking consciousness is only one of several states of waking awareness. Others include fatigue, delirium, intoxication, and ecstasy.

The study of consciousness was considered "unscientific" for many decades. This lack of scientific respectability was due to the fact that the "data" being studied were, finally, the introspective reports of the subjects. Such studies seemed to be too easily filled with error and bias.

All of us have certain experiences we simply cannot put into words. The scientist studying consciousness realizes these limitations to experimentation. Take, for instance, the problem of communication between those who have taken LSD experimentally and those who had never taken it. How could such persons discuss, with mutual understanding, the effects of LSD on consciousness? An altered state of consciousness can also be an altered state of suggestibility. It is difficult, therefore, to untangle the conscious experience from what one *expects* to happen in the state of altered consciousness.

Sleep

When we are awake, we are constantly thinking and planning. During most of our waking hours, we talk silently to ourselves about our plans. Even when we are doing nothing at all, our minds are active and not empty of thought. We spend about one-third of our lives in the altered state of consciousness called sleep. (By age 60, you will have slept the same 20 years that Rip Van Winkle slept.) Yet, human beings do not sleep very well compared with other species.

When you say you didn't sleep a wink last night, it is almost always a sympathy-seeking exaggeration. You are seldom aware of the exact moment you slip into sleep, and you rarely know how long you have slept. You can't judge by how rested you feel or how alert you are when you wake up. If you sleep too long, you may feel even more tired than before, and you will perform poorly on tasks requiring alertness (Taub, 1969).

If you *really* go without sleep for a long time (say 48 hours), it takes a tremendous effort to stay awake. When you do go to sleep, you don't have to make up all the lost sleeping time. Even after many days of no sleep,

FEELING GOOD AND
FEELING BAD

"A man at 10 A.M. is not the same man at 4 P.M. or midnight. Indeed, the same man is radically different at 2 A.M. One of the obvious signs of this daily rhythm is the body temperature. It varies about two degrees in 24 hours. With great regularity the body temperature rises during the day and falls at night, dropping to its lowest point between 2 and 5 A.M.

"Ordinarily a person will feel at his best during the hours when his temperature is high, and if he is awake when it falls to its low point he will feel frankly terrible. This is the time when night workers and railroad people have most accidents, the time when a doctor will receive the most calls reporting night coronaries." [Luce and Segal, 1966, p. 199]

it takes only about 12 hours of sleeping to get even. If you go without sleep for 100 hours or more, you will drag around physically and start to lapse every so often into moments of lost awareness called *microsleep.* If you stay awake much longer, you will begin to hallucinate.

As you know, the world is populated by both long sleepers and short sleepers (Hartmann, Baekeland, Zweilling, and Hoy, 1971). Short sleepers average five and one-half hours of sleep per night. The long sleepers average slightly more than eight and one-half hours of actual sleep, even though they usually spend at least nine hours in bed.

Short sleepers are described as efficient, hardworking, and very active. Long sleepers are more often described as anxious, depressed, and withdrawn. Interviews with long sleepers uncovered a great variety of psychological and social problems. They tended to be shy and showed considerable anxiety in interviews. Almost all of them showed evidence of some inhibitions in sexual or aggressive functioning. They reported more minor medical and psycho-somatic problems, and they more frequently complained about things like occasional noises in experimental sleep rooms. Watching research subjects sleep made it clear that long sleepers do not sleep as well as short sleepers. They spend more time awake during the night, wake up more often, and generally don't sleep very deeply.

We don't really have much choice about sleeping since it seems to be an automatic behavior necessary to our survival. The amount of sleep we need does not vary greatly with the amount of mental work we do. Hard thinking does not make one sleepy. In fact, the lack of mental activity —boredom—is what makes you sleepy.

Is nightly sleep nothing but a habit? Insofar as we know, people all over the world sleep 5 to 8 hours in every 24 hours and generally do so at night. If this pattern were totally habit, we might expect to find some groups that get along on short naps during different parts of the day. But so far, no such cultures have been reported, not even in the northernmost regions of Canada, Norway, and Russia where winter means months of uninterrupted night and summer brings unending daylight.

There is probably no absolutely necessary relation between when people sleep and the day-night cycle. Lower animals, like humans, can also reverse their typical cycle in response to a change in environmental conditions. Physiologist Nathaniel Kleitman (1939) concluded that there are really two kinds of wakefulness. One, called *wakefulness of necessity,* is controlled by subcortical brain centers. The other, *wakefulness of choice,* is superimposed on the sleep cycle and is controlled by the brain.

The hypothalamus appears to be the portion of the brain that controls sleep. When one section of the hypothalamus is surgically destroyed (the sleep center), the test animal will remain awake until it dies of exhaustion. When another section (the wakefulness center) is destroyed, the animal will sleep almost constantly.

THE RHYTHM OF LIFE
"Plants and flowers move their leaves in a daily rhythm, which will persist even when they are transplanted into deep caves of unchanging darkness and temperature. It is almost impossible to find a living creature whose activity does not subside for at least one period a day. Lobsters become immobile. Clams breathe less vigorously. Butterflies fold their wings at night, attach themselves firmly to a blade of grass and refuse to budge until a civilized hour in the morning. Frogs, lizards, turtles grow still for long periods. Birds and mammals sleep." [Luce and Segal, 1966, p. 198]

CIRCADIAN RHYTHM
Humans tend to observe a 24-hour cycle of sleep and wakefulness known as a circadian rhythm *(from the Latin* circa diem, *meaning "about a day"). During this period, body temperature, activity of the brain, and muscular activity vary at different hours. Each person has his own personal rhythm, and even Siamese twins sharing a single blood circulation have separate rhythmic cycles. These rhythmic patterns can be influenced by learning. A day worker will reach the high point of his body temperature during the day and his low point during the night. When a worker is moved to the night shift, he is usually irritable and restless for the first few weeks because his bodily activity does not correspond to his past rhythmic cycle.*

Insomnia

The incidence of insomnia is rather common. In some cities insomniac clubs have been formed, and, as you might expect, meetings are held late at night when no one can fall asleep. Psychologists do know something about insomnia, although they still do not know enough.

To begin with, there is more than one kind of insomnia. Some of you may turn and toss restlessly until you get to sleep, but then you sleep well the rest of the night. Others seem to sleep and wake up and then sleep and wake up all night long. There is also a type called "postdormitional insomnia." With this, you wake up at some ungodly hour of the early morning, and, try as you may, you can't go back to sleep again. Most insomniacs are females. Only 10 percent of males have this problem.

Why can't you fall asleep? The answer depends on which psychologist you ask. Some will explain it as a "sleep phobia." You are afraid of what will happen when you go to sleep. You might have a nightmare, or an emergency might arise when you have lost consciousness. Other psychologists will identify the cause as anxiety or fear. You may die while asleep. Or, it may be depression and worry that wakes you up too early and won't let you go back to sleep (Karacan and Williams, 1971).

You may not really be an insomniac, of course. You might only have "imaginary insomnia." Most so-called insomniacs get a lot more sleep than they think they do. With daytime naps they get as much sleep as the rest of us.

You may have learned your sleep patterns from your sleepless parents. Or you may not be able to sleep because you are emotionally stimulated just before bedtime. A high level of mental activity and the alertness produced by such activity are incompatible with sleep and can delay the onset of sleep. If an insomniac tries to go to bed while stimulated, he will become even more emotional and have much greater difficulty getting to sleep.

In one experiment, insomniacs were given placebo pills to take a few minutes before going to bed. Some subjects were told that the pills would cause arousal (arousal condition). Others were told that the pills would *reduce* arousal (relaxation condition). As predicted, arousal subjects got to sleep more quickly than they had on nights without the pills. Presumably they attributed their arousal to the pills rather than to their emotions. As a consequence, they were less emotional. Also as predicted, relaxation subjects got to sleep less quickly than usual. Presumably they assumed that their emotions were unusually intense. Their arousal level was seemingly high even after taking a relaxing agent (Storms and Nisbett, 1970).

Beating Sleeplessness

You *can* do something about insomnia, if you really want to. If you practice relaxing your mind and muscles before going to bed, you will be amazed

WHO NEEDS AN ALARM CLOCK?
Some of us claim we can wake up at a predetermined time just by setting the "alarm clock in our head." Believe it or not, it's true. In one experiment, subjects were sent to bed with a target time to wake up. They were offered a pay bonus if they could hit the target (give or take 10 minutes). They found they could do it, no matter what stage of sleep they were in before waking. They didn't do it by "sleeping with one eye open." They slept as deeply during the night as they usually did (Zung and Wilson, 1971).

at how fast you fall asleep. If you get rid of tension, you will sleep like a log just as you always wished you could. But, you also have to stop napping in the afternoon. If you do, you will go to sleep quicker even though there will be no change in how deeply you sleep. If all else fails, you can apply for relaxation training to help you get sleepy.

Some researchers suggest that a high level of muscle tension keeps you awake. If so, then you ought to be able to avoid insomnia by learning how to relax. Kahn, Baker, and Weiss (1968) tried this idea on students at Yale a few weeks before final exams. The method used was simple (Schultz and Luthe, 1959). The subjects were instructed to lie comfortably on mattresses with their eyes closed. They were supposed to visualize themselves in a peaceful situation such as lying on a beach, while thinking the words, "I am at peace." This was alternated with another repetition such as, "My right arm is heavy." For 30 to 45 seconds, the leader repeated the instructions aloud: "I am at peace; my right arm is heavy. My right arm is heavy; I am at peace." The subjects were then asked to say the same thing silently for an additional 30 to 45 seconds. Next, the subjects were asked to practice the technique at home three times a day, using three one-minute trials, with short breaks in between. They were also asked to use the technique for five or ten minutes after going to bed. When these instructions were followed, nearly all people in the experiment reported clear improvement in sleeping. In a follow up study nearly a year later, the improvement still continued.

Perchance to REM

Approximately every hour and a half during sleep, our eyes dart and roll around under their lids in what is called REM (rapid eye movement) sleep. The REM periods are easily visible to anyone who looks at the closed eyelids of a sleeping person. An hour or so after going to sleep, the first REM period of the night usually starts and lasts for about 5 to 10 minutes. Later in the night, REM periods as long as 25 minutes will occur.

During most of the night, the eyeballs are still or roll slowly from side to side. This non-REM (NREM) sleep occupies about 75 percent of our sleeping time. We may dream during this period, but dreams seem to occur more often during REM sleep. The presence of rapid eye movement, then, seems to signify dreaming. These observations and the hypothesis of the connection between REM sleep and dreaming were made 75 years ago. Kleitman and his colleagues (Aserinsky and Kleitman, 1953), however, were the first to test the hypothesis systematically. They concluded that during REM periods the sleeper was looking at the various visual components of his dream.

Various stages of altered consciousness occur during sleep:

Stage 1 is falling asleep. This is a very short stage, usually occurring a few minutes after bedtime. Brain waves become irregular. The heart rate

NIGHTMARES AND NIGHT TERRORS
A bad dream in the form of a nightmare is pretty bad, but night terrors are even worse. Night terrors scare hell out of most people. When you are caught in the middle of one, your heart rate may speed up from 64 beats a minute to as high as 152 beats every minute. When such terrors visit you in your sleep, they often arrive early in the night, sometimes as soon as 45 minutes after you drop off to sleep.

Nightmares raise your heartbeat only slightly (10 to 16 beats a minute) and may be forgotten with the morning light. A full-blown night terror, however, propels you into a wide-awake state directly from the deepest stage of sleep. Such terrors are actually massive anxiety attacks, which also include rapid increases in breathing rate and calls for help. Scientists are not fully certain what triggers these attacks.

begins to slow, and muscles relax. The person in stage 1 is easy to wake and may not realize he has been asleep if awakened.

Stages 2 and 3 are deeper stages of sleep. In stage 2, brain waves show bursts of activity called "spindles." In stage 3, these disappear, and brain waves become long and slow (about one wave per second). At this stage, the sleeper is hard to wake and unresponsive to stimuli. Heart rate, blood pressure, and temperature continue to drop.

Stage 4 is the deepest stage, called *delta sleep*. In young adults, delta sleep occurs in 15- or 20-minute segments (interspersed with lighter stages) during the first half of the night. Delta sleep lessens with age.

In addition to these stages, there is stage-1 REM sleep, called *paradoxical sleep*. This resembles regular stage-1 sleep. The brain-wave patterns are much the same, and the muscles are relaxed. The sleeper is hard to awaken, however, and this is the stage of dream sleep.

REM sleep and NREM sleep are different in more respects than the occurrence of rapid eye movements. Some physiological processes that are connected in the normal waking state appear to be disconnected during REM sleep. Although most muscles are relaxed, some muscles show a good deal of spontaneous twitching. In addition, the brain is very active in REM sleep. The discovery that most dreaming occurs in stage-1 REM sleep stimulated further study of dreaming.

Dreaming

The need to dream appears to be as basic as the need to sleep. People dream about two hours a night on the average—whether or not the dreams are remembered. In one experiment, people were consistently awakened for five consecutive nights just as the periods of REM sleep began (Dement, 1965). These people became anxious, irritable, hungry, and had difficulty concentrating. Some began to hallucinate. There seems to be a strong need to compensate for dreaming time that has been lost (Dement, 1960). People who lose dreaming time because of illness or worry say they compensate by dreaming more intensely. Often they have nightmares when their worries have passed.

The longer you sleep the more likely you are to remember a dream. Since the later stages of sleep are light, you may be partly awake and become aware of the fact you have been dreaming (Taub, 1970). Although many people do not recall their dreams in the morning, they appear to dream as often as those who remember. It is of interest that those who cannot recall dreams also have difficulty in such recall when awakened just after a REM period.

When we are very little, we can't tell the difference between what is real and what we dream. We finally learn the difference, of course, and the stages of this learning have been described by Piaget (1950). In the first stage a child does not know what a dream is and doesn't understand the

BLIND DREAMING

Sighted persons might follow dreams with their eyes because their dreams are strongly visual. But people who have been blind for a long time do not use their eyes in this way. Many of them report their dreams are not visual in content. If rapid eye movements serve only the purpose of following dream activity, such movements should be absent in persons who have been without sight for many years. Berger, Olley, and Oswald (1962) found rapid eye movements were present during dreams for only those subjects who had been blind less than 15 years. Measurements taken with instruments attached directly to the eyelid (Gross, Burne, and Fisher, 1965) revealed that tiny movements do occur even in the blind. REM therefore seems to be a universal phenomenon in sleep, even when visual dreaming does not occur.

distinction that adults make between real and unreal. Young children will report that a dream is in the bedroom where everyone can see it. Or they will say the dream disappears when the lights are turned on or if one hides under the covers. Before long, the child begins to think of the dream as being inside his head, very much like a tiny TV show. If you could look inside, you would see it too. Eventually, the child achieves an adult understanding of the difference between dreams and reality. He does this because we keep telling him which is which.

Freud and Dreams

The most influential theorist of dreams was Sigmund Freud. Freud presented his theory in *The Interpretation of Dreams* (1900). There, he stated that unconscious impulses were responsible for dreams and that the aim of the dream was the gratification of some drive. The real meaning of the dream (its *latent* content) is not expressed directly but appears in disguised form. What is remembered in this disguised form is the *manifest* content of the dream.

Freud declared that dreams represented pent-up emotional stresses and basic desires that we repress or deny. In sleep, with the "social censor" off guard, these repressed forces thrust to the surface as dreams. We can see, then, why psychoanalysis attaches such great importance to the content of dreams. According to psychoanalytic theory, dreams are clues to a person's true personality (Evans, 1967, p. 42).

To Freud, much of our impulsive life centers around sexual wishes that are associated with taboos. Since these sexual wishes are suppressed, we can expect them to be symbolized in our dreams. Freud also thought that the dream was the guardian of sleep. Dreams got rid of unfulfilled impulses which might otherwise disturb sleep. The disguise was necessary so that the disturbing impulses would not perturb the sleeper. If the meaning of the dream became known to the dreamer, he might wake up to rid himself of such unacceptable thoughts. In Freudian theory, a nightmare is a dream that has been unsuccessful. The sleeper awakens because his thoughts have become so dangerous that conscious defenses must be brought into play to keep them under control.

DAYDREAMS

Although psychoanalysts have long used patients' daydreams in diagnosis and therapy, psychologists have devoted surprisingly little effort to these waking fantasies. Daydreaming is more than just an escape from reality. It is our way of exploring possibilities and rehearsing what reactions we might have to them.

Men and women daydream equally, but there is a difference in their fantasies. Women's daydreams may show an interest in fashions, whereas men are enthusiastic about heroics and athletics. The frequency of fantasies changes as people grow older. The peak of daydreaming seems to be in midadolescence and then it falls off gradually into old age (Singer, 1969).

MODERN
CHEMISTRY

The chemists of our Brave New World have made enormous strides in developing new substances to alter our consciousness. As Farber stated: "Believing, as we do, that we should be able to will ourselves to be calm, cheerful, thin, industrious, creative—and, moreover, to have a good night's sleep—they simply provide the products to collaborate in such willing. If the satisfactions turn out to be short-lived and spurious and if their cost in terms of emotion, intellect, and physical health is disagreeable, these scientists are ready to concoct new drugs to counter this discomfort. In other words, they offer us always new chances—virtually to the point of extinction—to will away the unhappiness that comes from willing ourselves to be happy." [1966, p. 261]

Drug-Altered Consciousness

Throughout history human beings have taken chemical substances to change their mood, perception, and thought processes. The urge to use chemical methods to alter the mind has spread to modern times with a vengeance (Evans, 1971). Observers of the contemporary drug scene can imagine a future time when chemicals will cushion all of us against headaches, frustration, and self-doubt. Whenever our tranquillity is threatened, we may simply swallow the pill of our choice and enjoy a brief, but satisfying, hallucination.

Drugs alter the state of consciousness in a number of ways. Some of these are: (1) disturbances in thinking (altered attention, memory, and judgment); (2) a changed sense of time (time may speed up, slow down, or seem suspended); (3) feelings of loss of control (helplessness, as in a nightmare when you run but never seem to get anywhere); (4) alteration of emotional expression (unexpectedly intense or primitive emotional outbursts); and (5) distortions of perception (illusions, hyperacute perceptions, or hallucinations) (Ludwig, 1966).

Drugs may also produce changes in the meaning or significance of events. They may bring on a sense of profound insight or discovery of ultimate truth, and this may trigger a sense of rejuvenation or renewed hope. There may also be a feeling of depersonalization. The usual perception of the body image is distorted so that parts of the body seem shrunken, enlarged, or seem to be floating. There may also be bodily symptoms in the form of numbness, weakness, dizziness, tingling, and the like.

Although a heroin user may at first feel an overwhelming sense of euphoria, he often ends up in a nightmarish world where his addiction controls his life.

Why Chemical Moods?

There is a long list of reasons why some people choose to try drugs and others abstain. The possibilities listed by Lipinski and Lipinski (1970) are:

- Curiosity.
- The feeling of missing something or not being "with it."
- A need to prove one's intellectual depth and emotional maturity (particularly for shy people who don't relate easily to others).
- A search for meaning (failing to find a clear answer in the outside world, the quest turns inward).
- Escape from feelings of inadequacy (the hope for a magical cure for personal, emotional turmoil without the embarrassment of revealing "weaknesses" to others).
- An end to isolation (drugs may give the feeling of greater closeness with others).

In addition to these possible motivations, there is a clear relationship between adolescent and parental drug use. When Smart and Fejer (1972) assessed use among 8,865 Toronto students, a positive association was found between parental use of psychoactive drugs, alcohol, and tobacco (as reported by students) and student use of psychoactive and hallucinogenic drugs. The relationship was strongest when students and parents both used psychoactive drugs. The data suggest that adolescents model their drug use according to parental use. To reduce adolescent use, parental use would also have to be reduced.

Four Levels of Psychedelic Experience

The psychedelic experience is different for everyone, but the quality of the experience may be similar. Masters and Houston have distinguished four levels of psychedelic experience that individuals may reach. Each is more profound—and therefore, harder to attain—than the one before it. Masters and Houston believe that a competent guide is crucial to reaching the highest levels.

Level I, Sensory: This is the most common level of psychedelic experience and is achieved by most individuals who take hallucinogens. The alteration and enhancement of sensation is the primary experience at this level. Colors may appear more brilliant and take on new values. Audio and tactile sensations also take on new qualities.

Level II, Recollective-Analytic: The individual experiences strong feelings about himself, which may relate to particular personal and psychological difficulties. This level of psychedelic experience can be quite profitable in helping the individual resolve his psychological conflicts, especially if therapeutic guidance is given.

Level III, Symbolic: This level is difficult to reach without a guide. The individual's thoughts, feelings, and actions are related more to man's collective history than they are to the drug user's individual one. His experiences may symbolize evolution or rites of passage. He may be left with greater insight into the underlying nature of man.

Level IV, Integral: Experiences at this level are mystical and religious. The individual may experience a form of death and rebirth. He may confront God and become united with Him or with the entire cosmos. The integral form of experience is the most profound of the four levels and is rarely reached.

For whatever reason our society chooses to alter its mood with drugs, we need to understand the consciousness-altering function of drugs. Perhaps, this will help us comprehend why recent history has been marked by widespread dissatisfaction with ordinary conscious life. It would be impossible to discuss all the drugs that are available, but LSD and the amphetamines can be used as illustrations.

LSD

LSD has been called a "Utopiate" by Blum (1964) and a "Nightmare Drug" by Louria (1966). LSD-25 (lysergic acid diethylamide) produces a profound alteration of sensory, perceptual, cognitive, and emotional experiences. Louria (1966) has described such experiences in these terms:

They [colors] swirl around the individual with great vividness. Fixed objects fuse and diffuse; there is often a perpetual flowing of geometric designs and one sensation merges into another and one sense into another so that the individual may say he can taste color; touch sound. The body image is distorted and ordinary sounds increase profoundly in intensity. There is a sense of intense isolation and depersonalization so that "me" as an individual disappears and the user feels he is fused with all humanity and with his environment. Time stands still, and many give themselves up to what they describe as an experience of inexpressible ecstasy. [pp. 45–46]

The term *hallucinogenic* implies that the characteristic effect or action of the drug is to produce hallucinations. *Psychotomimetic* is a similar term implying that the drug imitates or mimics psychosis. The terms *psychedelic* and *consciousness expanding* imply that the person who takes the drug can expect a positive, creative mind-expanding experience (Fort, 1970). No one of these terms is precisely accurate since the effects of the drug depend to a great extent on the personal characteristics of the user. The effect also depends on the setting in which the drug is taken and the purity of the product that is swallowed.

LSD was originally used in research on social problems. It was tried with alcoholics to help them stop drinking and with autistic children to increase their contact with people in the real world (Ungerleider and Fisher, 1970). LSD has also been used by persons dying of cancer in an effort to produce greater pain tolerance and a calmer acceptance of death. For some it produces a dramatic improvement, and for others it only makes things worse. LSD not only eases pain, but for some it also relieves depression, anxiety, and a sense of psychological isolation. Pain relief itself may be a sufficient justification for its use. Terminal cancer patients find that severe pain becomes the entire focus of their consciousness.

There are other substances that produce similar psychological effects. *Peyote* (a Mexican cactus) is made up of alkaloids (one of which is mescaline)

For one complete hour, Eva had been looking at the hamster with the greatest fascination, incapable of uttering one word. When she came out of her trance, she whispered, "I thought he was my brother. . . ."

that produce intense color awareness and hallucinations. Reflexes seem heightened; time is overestimated; and spatial perception is altered. Hearing and sight seem intensified, and ideas flow rapidly (Nabokov, 1969). Some Indian tribes have used mescal buttons (from the peyote cactus) for centuries in religious ceremonies. Another drug, *psilocybin,* is derived from mushrooms that have been used in Indian religious rites since pre-Columbian times. Psilocybin is not nearly as potent as LSD, but similar hallucinogenic effects are produced.

No psychedelic retains its popularity for very long. Certainly, no drug can provide a packaged answer to the complex riddle of being human. In recent times the most popular drugs are mood-changers of a different sort.

The Amphetamines

In 1887 a German pharmacologist synthesized Benzedrine, but he was not interested in exploring its pharmacological properties and put the project aside. In 1932, the Benzedrine inhaler was made easily available to the public in

 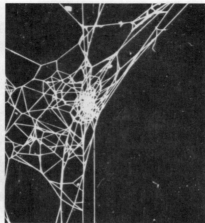 

The effect of dextro-amphetamine (speed) on the web-building of an adult female spider is shown in these three photographs. The web on the left is the control web, built on the first day of observation in about 20 minutes in the early morning hours. At 4 P.M. that afternoon the spider drank about 0.1 milliliter of a drop of sugar water which contained 1 milligram of dextro-amphetamine. The second web was built about 12 hours later by a severely disturbed animal. It shows some remnants of a hub, a few irregular and frequently interrupted radii, and some erratic strands of sticky spiral. The last web was built 24 hours after the second one and shows signs of recovery, but it took several more days for the spider to again build a web similar in perfection to the control one.

THE COPILOT

Grinspoon and Hedblom (1972) report that some of the early slang names for amphetamines originated among truck drivers, who called them "cartwheels," "coast-to-coasts," "West-Coast turnarounds," "truck drivers," and "copilots." "The last term presumably was derived from the now legendary accident that occurred when one exceedingly lucky driver, who had stayed behind his wheel for more than two days on speed, decided to take a brief nap in his sleeping berth while moving at 60 miles per hour. When finally extricated from his totally demolished vehicle, he stated that he had been sure that his assistant was competent to handle the truck in broad daylight. The "copilot," however, was an amphetamine-induced illusion; the driver had been alone for the entire forty-eight-hour period." [p. 38]

drugstores across the country. The American Medical Association gave this new drug the generic name *amphetamine,* from *a*lpha-*methyl-phethyl-amine.* The only caution at that time was that "continued overdose" might cause "restlessness and sleeplessness." Physicians were assured that no serious reactions had been observed. By the end of World War II, at least seven different inhalers containing large amounts of amphetamine were on the market. All of them could be purchased without a prescription.

As Grinspoon and Hedblom (1972) note:

World War II probably was responsible for spurring both the legal medically authorized use and the illegal black-market abuse of the amphetamines. When German Panzer troops overwhelmed Poland, then Denmark and Norway, and drove through Belgium and France, they were taking huge doses of methamphetamine to eliminate fatigue and maintain physical endurance. But the Wehrmacht was by no means the sole large-scale consumer of amphetamines during World War II; Japanese soldiers and factory workers used as much or more. Nor was use of these stimulants confined to the Axis powers. According to British war statistics, seventy-two million standard-dose amphetamine tablets were distributed to the British armed forces alone. [p. 36]

The drug proved to be so popular that by 1958 the legal U.S. production of amphetamines each year had risen to 3.5 billion tablets—enough to supply

LSD and the Terminal Patient

DR. PAHNKE: *What else happened during the day?*
MRS. PROCTOR: *I died.*
DR. PAHNKE: *What was that like?*
MRS. PROCTOR: *Beautiful. It sounds vindictive, but it was beautiful. (Chuckles.)*
DR. PAHNKE: *How can that be?*
MRS. PROCTOR: *I don't know. I felt like I was dying . . . I don't know how I came back. I don't remember that. I think I called for you—did I?*
DR. PAHNKE: *What does it feel like to die?*
MRS. PROCTOR: *You're just like the thin air, that's it. You have no pain. No fear.*
DR. PAHNKE: *Did that scare you?*
MRS. PROCTOR: *No. No fear at all. Very relaxed. If it's unusual maybe it's me. I don't know. Is it?*
DR. PAHNKE: *What?*
MRS. PROCTOR: *Unusual to feel that way?*
DR. PAHNKE: *That it's relaxed to die? Other people have said the same.* [p. 56]

Hooked up to a variety of life-preserving machines, the terminal cancer patient is often kept alive as long as possible. In the last weeks and months of the patient's life, doctors attempt to ease the physical pain with drugs, radiation, and surgery. Yet little is done to ease the psychological anguish of the patient surrounded by reminders of his impending death.

Fortunately, physicians have become more and more concerned with the psychological condition of the terminal patient. Although still in its experimental stages, one of the most promising procedures for helping such individuals is psychiatric counseling in combination with guided use of the psychedelic LSD.

One of the greatest obstacles to successful therapy with terminal patients is getting them to admit the likelihood of death. When he has admitted this, he is then guided through one or more experiences with LSD. Patients are given doses of LSD that are three to four times more potent than the doses taken by illegal users of the drug. The LSD experience lasts from 8 to 12 hours, but the residual effects of the experience may persist far longer.

For many patients, the LSD experience is one of dying and rebirth. The individual may go through an unpleasant period of experiencing himself, or his surroundings, as ugly and repulsive. He then comes up from these depths into a world that is peaceful and beautiful, and he may be left with a more serene outlook on life—and death. Some people find themselves rising higher and higher, with an increasing feeling of spirituality and unity with the universe. This state is called "transcendental awareness."

Here, for example, is the experience of one person. It is interesting that he had such visions even though he did not understand that LSD was anything more than a pain reliever.

MR. CASE: *I was in a junkyard. Everything got thrown together: skeletons, cans, whatall. Then everything got burned, destroyed, by a big ball of fire . . . I felt I was goin' in it too. I felt all my bones was in amongst all those other things. Like you said, you had to let it bypass you, or let it know it didn't get the best of you.*
DR. GROF: [In your session] *you mentioned Jehovah.*
MR. CASE: *That's when the preachin' was goin' on—how your soul is saved when you come back to earth you'd be another—er—ah, person, or whatever you'll be when you come back, why that's what you'll be. Whether it's an animal, or what. You could be something different. Sometimes, in a dream you may think like you're gonna be your own self, but you ain't, to my knowledge you won't. You'll be something else. Just take what comes in life.*
DR. GROF: *Some of these feelings are new, aren't they? I didn't hear you talking like this before.*
MR. CASE: *This is through this* [experience]. *This is what I feel through all this other stuff that was goin' through me. . . . That you'll be living, in other words that your* soul *will be livin',* your soul will be with you all the time, but yet you don't know what you'll be on the next earth. [p. 63]

Not all patients reach the state of transcendental awareness. But even for those who don't resolve psychological conflicts, the LSD experience leaves them with a serenity and warmth that eases the psychological distress. It is also suggested that because pain is usually tied to previous unpleasant associations and the anticipation of future discomfort, LSD's propensity to focus on the present may contribute to its pain-relieving effects.

Source: Jerry Avorn, "Beyond Dying." Copyright © 1973 by Harper's Magazine. Reprinted from the March 1973 issue by permission of the author.

every man, woman, and child with about 20 standard doses. Less than ten years later, the drug industry admitted it was producing enough amphetamine tablets per year to supply every living American with 35 to 50 tablets. By 1970, legal amphetamine production had risen to above 10 billion tablets. In 1971 it rose again to more than 12 billion.

Abuse of the addicting and dangerous amphetamines has reached frightening proportions. According to Grinspoon and Hedblom (1972), of the more than 12 billion standard-dose amphetamine tablets produced in 1971, an estimated 50 percent were diverted to the black market to supplement huge amounts of "home-cooked speed."

HOME-COOKED SPEED

". . . the manufacture and sale of "home-cooked" speed is thought to exceed the legal pharmaceutical production by a factor of between three and ten. Although the street dealers habitually proclaimed that their product was "100 per cent righteous pharmacy speed," it invariably contained more dilutants than amphetamines. These substances included lactose, Epsom salts, quinine, baking powder, monosodium glutamate (Ac'cent), photo developer, insecticides, ether, and even strychnine." [Grinspoon and Hedblom, 1972, p. 38]

When Speed Slows Down

When the amphetamine high is over, the physical and psychological effects are exceptionally uncomfortable. There may be extreme lethargy, fatigue, anxiety, terrifying nightmares, severe depression, disorientation, bewilderment, and confusion. The user may become extremely irritable and demanding. He may lose self-control or act out aggressive impulses. As Grinspoon and Hedblom put it: "His head aches, he has difficulty in breathing, he sweats profusely, and his body is racked with alternating sensations of extreme heat and cold and with excruciating muscle cramps. He characteristically suffers violently painful gastrointestinal cramps" (1972, p. 40).

The amphetamines can also lead to psychosis-like episodes called *amphetamine psychosis*. Snyder (1972) has described this state as follows:

> *Signs of amphetamine psychosis first develop while the speed-freak is under the influence of the drug. . . . The harbinger is vague fear and suspicion*—What was that? I heard something. Is somebody trying to get me? *Soon the paranoia centers around a specific delusion—for example, that the FBI is out to get him. An amphetamine party may begin with everyone very elated and talkative and may end with each person stationed silently at a window, peeking through the curtains for signs of the police. . . . Acting on his delusions the speed-freak may become violent*—to get them before they get me. *It is in this sense that the slogan SPEED KILLS is most accurate: more persons die from senseless and brutal violence associated with amphetamine delusions than from overdoses of the drug itself. . . . Another unique feature of amphetamine psychosis is compulsive, stereotyped behavior that the victim repeats hour after hour, apparently without fatigue or boredom.* [p. 44]

The New Drugs

Seconals, Tuinals, Quaaludes, and Sopors have become the new drugs used and abused by those in the drug culture. In the past, the drugs that dominated the drug scene were psychedelics (LSD, mescaline), amphetamines, and opiates

Truth Drugs

Drugs with sedative or hypnotic effects have been used to stimulate patients to talk. The technique, sometimes called *narcoanalysis,* proved useful to physicians who confronted large numbers of emotional casualties in the armed forces during World War II and the Korean War. In the twilight state induced by sodium pentothal and other drugs, even the usually uncommunicative patient talks easily and uninhibitedly. This helps speed up treatment by supplying the therapist with diagnostic material that might not otherwise have been forthcoming or might have taken a long time to uncover.

The use of chemical assistance in interviews began in 1922 when it occurred to physician Robert House that scopolamine might be employed in the interrogation of suspected criminals. He tried it by interviewing two prisoners who had received injections of scopolamine and he enthusiastically reached the conclusion that the patient under the influence of scopolamine "cannot create a lie . . . and there is no power to think or reason." This experiment and his erroneous conclusion attracted wide interest, and the myth of the truth drug became popular.

The theory behind using truth drugs was that, by stripping away the conscious controls of behavior, the "truth" would come out. It is not quite as easy as that, as Freedman (1970) reports in an experiment on sleep at the Yale Medical School. He injected the "truth drug" sodium amytal very slowly into a large number of volunteer medical students. Previously, he had attached electrodes to their heads and chests in order to take measurements related to sleep cycles. Since he was concerned with getting them to sleep, he simply informed them of what he was doing. But the method and rate of injection were otherwise identical with the technique regularly used for psychiatric interviews. He recalls that in only one instance was there any talking, and the subject revealed no spontaneous "truths" about himself or his experiences.

Limitations in the use of truth serum became apparent in the case of the Boston Strangler, who killed 13 women during the early 1960s. In the frantic search for a guilty party, one man who was innocent of the crime was put under a "truth" drug and made a very elaborate confession—which later was discovered to be entirely false (Frank, 1966).

The drugs now used most often in psychiatric interviews are sodium amytal and sodium pentothal because they are the most easily administered, have the fewest toxic side effects, and give the most predictable results. This technique has been used most extensively by Grinker and Spiegel who realistically concluded that in almost all cases they could have obtained essentially the same material and emotional release *without* the drugs.

Even more destructive to the "truth drug" myth was an experiment where sodium amytal was administered to volunteers after they had revealed shameful, guilt-producing episodes of their past and had then invented false stories to cover up the episodes. Under the influence of the drug, they were subjected to cross-examination of their cover story by a second investigator. The results suggested that normal individuals with no overtly pathological traits could stick to their invented stories. On the other hand, some neurotic individuals not only tended to confess more easily but also tended to substitute fantasy for the truth, confessing to offenses never actually committed.

These experimental and clinical findings indicate that only individuals with reasons for doing so are inclined to confess under the influence of drugs. Of course, if you *think* it is a "truth" drug which is impossible to resist, you may confess because you are convinced there really isn't any point in trying to protect yourself.

(heroin). Now, downers (barbiturates and other soporific drugs which act as depressants) are rapidly surpassing these drugs and becoming the nation's number one abused drug.

Most popular among the downers are the short-acting barbiturates (secobarbitol and pentobarbitol) and much newer soporifics such as Quaaludes. Users seem to prefer short-acting downers because they take effect in only 15 to 30 minutes and last from two to four hours. The immediate effect is that of a heavy, euphoric rush which can be sustained for some time, if the urge to fall asleep is successfully fought off.

The change to these newer drugs seems motivated by the bad side

effects produced by drugs like LSD and amphetamines. With LSD, even a simple experience can become difficult to handle. With amphetamines, physical and mental activity are accelerated to the point of exhaustion. The newer drugs are cheap, available, and bring on a much pleasanter, uninhibited euphoria similar to that of alcohol.

Apparently, there is no end to ways of achieving drug-induced consciousness alteration. This has led some observers to suggest that our society should abandon attempts to legislate how individuals treat or mistreat themselves.

The psychiatrist Thomas Szasz (1972) suggests that in an open society the government has no business regulating which drugs a person puts into his body. According to Szasz, all drugs should be legalized and unrestricted if we are to be consistent with the principles of personal liberty. At the moment, we reserve that liberty for the familiar drug alcohol. As Szasz noted:

Our present practices with respect to alcohol embody and reflect this individualistic ethic. We have the right to buy, possess, and consume alcoholic beverages. Regardless of how offensive drunkenness might be to a person, he cannot interfere with another person's "right" to become inebriated so long as that person drinks in the privacy of his own home or at some other appropriate location, and so long as he conducts himself in an otherwise law-abiding manner. In short, we have a right to be intoxicated—in private. [1972, p. 77]

There is no easy answer to the drug problem. It is evident that the drug issue is deeply implicated in the direction our society will take in the future. The argument rages not about the issue of altering consciousness but on the question of which methods are acceptable and which are not.

Meditation

The search for the meaning of life and for some way to cope with its pressures is as ancient as mankind itself. Recently, this quest has led to a widespread interest in meditation as a possible answer.

The simpler forms of meditation can be learned quickly. In an experiment conducted by Maupin (1965), college students volunteered to concentrate on the natural process of breathing. They were told to relax and then focus their attention on their breathing and the movement of their belly. They were to avoid being distracted by other thoughts or stimuli. Not all subjects were equally good at the task. In a two-week period, however, a group of "high-responders" reported reaching a deeply satisfying state of altered consciousness. They described it in terms of extreme detachment from the outside world, intense concentration, and pleasant bodily sensations.

MEDITATION IS . . .
"Meditation has been described as a process of calming the ripples on a lake; when calm, the bottom, usually invisible, can be seen. In another metaphor meditation is likened to the night: stars cannot be seen during the day, their faint points of light overwhelmed by the brilliance of the sun. In this image, meditation is the process of "turning off" the overwhelming competing activity that is the light of the sun, until . . . the stars can be seen quite clearly." [Naranjo and Ornstein, 1971, p. 214]

Meditation has been described as a deep passivity combined with awareness—a suspension of the usual rat race of mental and physical activity in order to *experience* things rather than *do* them. In Maupin's words, it is practice in the skill of being quiet and paying attention to the internal as well as external world. Usually, your mind bounces from one idea to another, reacting to every sensation, thought, or stimuli. But in order to reach new and unusual experiences, you must learn how to ignore the usual, familiar stimuli.

Learning to Meditate

Every new skill seems difficult and complicated until you learn it so well that it becomes automatic. Remember how hard it was simply to learn how to tie your own shoelaces? At first it seemed that you would never learn it, but now you do it without even being aware of it. Meditation is like that.

The position used in meditation is important. It should let you relax, yet not allow you to fall asleep. The cross-legged, "lotus" positions used by some meditators are very difficult and quite uncomfortable for most beginners. They are not absolutely essential to the meditative state. You can meditate while sitting up straight but relaxed in a regular chair. In that position you practice concentrating and eliminating distractions. You don't fight to prevent them. You just bring your attention back again to the object of your meditation every time it wanders. If you try too hard to prevent distractions, you can get distracted by the very task of preventing distractions.

Meditation ought to be like taking a vacation. You take a rest from the regular way you deal with the outside world. When you come back, your familiar world ought to look new and different to you. Most meditators sit alone or with a small group in a special room set aside for meditation. An attempt is usually made to reduce sources of stimulation to a minimum. Some meditators burn incense to give a consistent odor to the place of meditation and to mask other odors that might break concentration. Typically, meditation is practiced for a half-hour, twice a day.

In psychological terms there are two general kinds of meditation. One kind involves restriction of awareness by focusing attention on an object or repeated word. The other type involves opening up awareness to experience everything in greater depth. To achieve these goals, various meditative exercises are practiced. You may decide to concentrate on your breathing, focus on one part of your body, or stare at an object without blinking. In each instance, the goal is to keep your attention from wandering. It is not easy to do.

When simple meditative control is achieved, you then might try concentrating on a *koan* (a riddle or a question that has no answer). Two examples of a koan are: "If a tree falls in a forest when no one is listening, does it make any sound?" and "What is the sound of one hand clapping?" The point of meditating on such matters is the *concentration* itself. No answer is correct,

MANTRA
One form of meditative practice uses the mantra. *A mantra is a series of words that is used as the focus of awareness. The mantra is repeated over and over, aloud or silently, while all other thoughts and stimuli are excluded. "Mantra are sonorous, mellifluous words, which repeat easily. An example is OM. This mantram is chanted aloud in groups, or used individually in silent or voiced meditation. Another is OM-MANI-PADME-HUM."* [Naranjo and Ornstein, 1971, p. 150]

or every answer is correct. And all answers are irrelevant. The processes of concentration and self-control are the important things.

Meditation and Body Control

For a great many years psychologists dismissed the claims made in favor of meditation as unscientific and mystical. In recent years, however, research has proved that meditators can alter their bodily metabolism and even the electroencephalographic patterns of their brain waves.

Wallace and Benson's (1972) study of the metabolic changes that occur during transcendental meditation, for example, found that powerful metabolic changes were produced. These changes were different from those produced by either hypnosis or sleep. While meditating, less oxygen is consumed; the heart beat is slowed; respiration is retarded; and brain waves change. Various bodily measures indicated that the meditators were highly relaxed but awake. Wallace and Benson suggested meditation might prove to be a valuable tool for maintaining psychological health for those caught up in the bustle of industrial society.

Practicing yogis have made much more fantastic claims of body control. It is said that they can be buried alive or walk on hot coals. Until now, such actions have been considered impossible since the yogi would have had to control parts of the nervous system traditionally thought to work only on an automatic basis. We have known for some time, of course, that the mind can produce incredible and mysterious changes in the body. The fact is now evident that yoga masters, with years of practice, can accomplish astonishing control over what happens to their bodies. We don't know what limits are really possible. We can only guess at the final effect that meditative experience will have on psychology and the study of consciousness.

THE BLUE VASE
To study the phenomenon of meditation, Deikman (1963) had a research subject practice staring at a blue vase. The subject was told not to analyze the different parts of the vase but rather to try to see the vase as it existed in itself. The subject was supposed to exclude all other thoughts, feelings, or sounds of body sensations. As the experiment progressed, the subject reported an increasingly intense perception of the vase, a more rapid passage of time, less distractibility by outside events, and the achievement of a pleasant, rewarding new state of consciousness.

Summary

1. The study of consciousness was long considered unscientific because early work in the field was based on subjective reports open to error and bias. We have learned, though, that there is variety of states of conscious life.

2. Sleep is an altered state of consciousness which appears to be universal. The human propensity to sleep at night also appears to be instinctive.

3. If one goes without sleep for more than a few days, one begins to experience brief losses of awareness called *microsleep*. Longer periods without sleep will result in hallucinations.

4. Short sleepers seem to sleep better and wake up more refreshed than long sleepers. Each type of sleeper appears to be associated with a particular personality type.

5. The *hypothalamus* is the portion of the brain responsible for the sleeping and waking mechanism. One area of the hypothalamus controls waking, and another controls sleep.

6. Most living things, including humans, follow a 24-hour cycle in which internal processes vary at different hours. Each person has his own *circadian rhythm,* but one's rhythm can be altered through learning.

7. The problem of insomnia may result from a number of causes: fear of what will happen while you are asleep, worry or depression, or sleep patterns learned as a child. Arousal before bedtime also prevents sleep. A good way to beat insomnia is to learn to relax before going to bed.

8. Each nightly session of sleep involves several levels of altered consciousness, each associated with its own brain-wave pattern. The deepest part, called *delta sleep,* occurs only during the first part of the night.

9. Rapid eye movement (REM) is usually a signal that the sleeper is dreaming. Most dreaming occurs during stage-1 REM sleep. This resembles regular stage 1 sleep with the exception that the person is difficult to wake. In REM sleep the brain is very active, sometimes causing relaxed muscles to twitch.

10. Everyone dreams, even though they may not recall the content. It appears, in fact, that there is a real need to dream. People prevented from dreaming soon become anxious, irritable, and have difficulty concentrating.

11. Sigmund Freud proposed that dreams fulfilled the need to express unconscious, forbidden impulses. The expression is disguised, however, so the sleeper won't be disturbed. Freud maintained that many dreams contained symbols representing sexual organs and acts. Freud also thought that nightmares were unsuccessful dreams, which allowed forbidden wishes to become too explicit.

12. Drug-altered states of consciousness differ from ordinary consciousness in a number of ways. Sensory experiences and perceptions change, and one's relation to one's body becomes distorted. One may experience strong emotional feelings or interpret events in a way that leads to new insights about oneself or society.

13. The use of drugs results from a variety of motivations, not the least of which is a need to find meaning in a chaotic existence. There is also a strong relationship between drug use in parents and in their children.

14. Psychedelic experience, such as that achieved with LSD, may be primarily sensory, or it may take more profound forms. Masters

and Houston have distinguished the levels of experience as: *sensory, recollective-analytic, symbolic,* and finally, *integral.*

15. LSD has been used to help alcoholics and autistic children. It also appears to be successful in relieving the physical and psychological pain of dying patients.

16. Although *amphetamines* (speed) have been available to the public for several decades, only recently have physicians realized their dangerous effects. Amphetamines can lead to psychosis-like episodes of hallucinations and paranoia. Violence associated with amphetamine delusions and overdoses of the drug have caused death.

17. Amphetamines also have unpleasant aftereffects, including severe depression, terrifying nightmares, loss of self-control, and bodily pain. Speed and LSD have lost their popularity and have been replaced by depressant drugs, or downers, which give a more pleasant euphoric state.

18. In meditation, one experiences a detachment from the outside world, intense concentration, and pleasant bodily sensations. The new levels of experience associated with meditation result from one's loss of interest in the mundane stimuli of everyday life.

19. In the meditative state, one's physiological mechanisms undergo changes different from those in other states of altered consciousness. These changes—which involve a slowing down of functions—are highly beneficial to health. Meditators also show remarkable abilities to regulate bodily mechanisms that psychologists have long believed unsusceptible to voluntary control.

Hypnosis

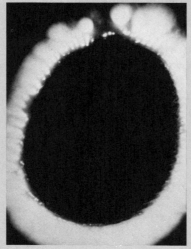

The phenomenon you see in these two pictures—which some call corona discharge or bioplasma—was captured on film by radiation photography. The top picture is of a subject's fingerpad before he was hypnotized; the bottom one was taken after hypnosis. There is no really satisfactory answer to why the corona (or crown) around the fingerpad changes after hypnosis, or why it changes at all, or even what the corona is—but there are researchers in this country and in Russia who are determined to investigate the phenomenon intensively.

Don't look up while you are reading this. There may be someone whose piercing eyes are waiting to catch your attention, hypnotize you, destroy your willpower, and make you a slave. At least that's what you might believe if you watch too many second-rate TV programs. The mystery that surrounds hypnosis was inevitable since it can produce so many unusual phenomena. Naturally you have some questions about this unusual state of consciousness, and we can try to answer a few of them for you.

Franz Anton Mesmer (1734–1815). The "father" of modern hypnosis was Franz Anton Mesmer. In his medical dissertation, "The Influence of the Planets," Mesmer attempted to reintroduce to medicine the study of the bodily effects of the gravitational forces exerted by the planets. He was especially interested in the influences of the sun and the moon, which at that time were called planets. Mesmer believed that magnets could cure disease by producing "an artificial ebb and flow" in the body. This motion would supposedly correct "the unequal distribution of the nervous fluid and its confused movement." It would produce a "harmony of the nerves."

The magnetism Mesmer spoke of was confusingly described. It was "like light" and could be "reflected by mirrors." It was also said to be "like sound that can be communicated," or like energy that can be accumulated, stored up, and carried from one place to another.

Mesmer abandoned the use of magnets by 1775 when he found that, by passing his hands over his patients' bodies, he could produce the same convulsions and peculiar sensations and behavior. In the end, Mesmer was driven from Paris as a charlatan and fraud, but he stimulated interest in what we now call hypnosis. [Pattie, 1967]

What Is the Power of Suggestion?

The power of suggestion often involves nothing more than focusing your attention on sensations you were not attending to before. Do you feel thirsty? Is your throat dry? Does it tickle a little? Does it feel scratchy? If I keep making these suggestions, you will eventually

notice things about your throat that you hadn't paid attention to before. The power of suggestion can also work at a much more complicated level.

How Is Hypnosis Done?

As the old joke goes: "Where does a 500-pound gorilla sleep? Anywhere he wants to." It's the same with inducing the hypnotic trance. You can do it anywhere you want to. The usual methods of focusing attention on an object or telling people they are getting sleepy are helpful, but unnecessary. The point is to get the subject to relax, use his imagination, attend closely to what is said, and stop fighting it. The rest is up to the hypnotic subject and his willingness to go along with the suggestions.

Can You Be Hypnotized?

Probably. Most people can. But it is easier for some and harder for others (Kroger, 1961). The difference seems to be a question of personality and the learning that takes place as you grow up (Hilgard, 1965; Hilgard, Atkinson, and Atkinson, 1971). If you want to be hypnotized and you feel the hypnotist has mysterious powers and can easily dominate you, then it probably won't be hard to hypnotize you. It helps if you have a vivid imagination or if you have been taught habits of automatic, unquestioned obedience to others. Remember, hypnosis is not something done to you by the hypnotist. It is an altered state of consciousness you produce for yourself.

Can You Hypnotize Yourself?

Some people can, with training. *Autohypnosis* may give you greater self-control, but self-discipline of this kind can be achieved in many other ways such as meditation and yoga. There is no real reason to believe one method is much better than another.

Can Hypnosis Get Rid of Pain?

Yes and no. The pain will still be there, but your response to it can be controlled (Sacerdote, 1966). The same thing can happen, however, with a simple sugar pill.

Hypnosis and Warts. Doctors from the Departments of Psychiatry and Dermatology at Massachusetts General Hospital in Boston recently used hypnosis to "suggest away" 31 warts on the hands and face of a nine-year-old fourth-grader. Her classmates had taken to calling her "warty face." When traditional methods failed, *hypnotherapy* was tried. The doctors found that the results were immediate. The warts began to fall off after the first session. [Surman, 1972, p. 25]

Will Hypnosis Give You Mystic Powers?

Hypnosis won't let you see the future, read people's thoughts, have ESP, or gain control over others. Attempts to acquire mystic powers through hypnosis have been tried for years, but nothing has happened so far. The most that can occur is a deepening of your *belief* that you have magic capacities. Again, you don't need hypnosis to achieve this end.

Can Animals Be Hypnotized?

Yes and no. They can't be hypnotized as people can, but they can be immobilized for short periods of time. *Animal hypnosis* or immobilization can be produced in a variety of animals such as chickens, frogs, and rabbits (Ratner, 1967). Research suggests that animal hypnosis is most often produced by threat to the animal. When it struggles to escape and cannot, all that's left is to play dead. This is what resembles the hypnotic state.

Will You Do Something Immoral While Hypnotized?

It depends on the condition your morals are in, of course. If you don't have criminal tendencies, hypnosis won't make you kill or rape any more than you usually do. In cases where "hypnotic influence" is said to account for criminal acts, the hypnotist and victim are found to be deeply involved with each other.

Can Hypnosis Make You a Better Student?

You won't become an academic superstar, but for some people hypnosis can be used to produce a state of general relaxation that increases the ability to learn. If you can hypnotize yourself into doing your homework regularly and carefully all during the semester, you won't need to be hypnotized to relax for the exam.

Is Hypnosis Necessary?

Not according to Theodore Barber (1969, 1970). He says that both the popular and professional literature have created the mistaken notion that a unique condition called the "hypnotic trance" exists. Barber claims there is no scientific support or reliable test for it. He insists that, anything you can do while hypnotized, you can do in a wide-awake state, if you are properly motivated.

Summary

1. Hypnotism is an altered state one brings upon oneself. Hypnotism may be nothing more than the effect of suggestion given to a properly relaxed and motivated person.

2. Experiments demonstrate that hypnotism can control the perception of pain and can increase self-discipline. However, other methods of suggestion seem to be equally powerful.

3. No one has proved that the "hypnotic trance" actually exists. There are no physiological correlates which differentiate an individual in an hypnotic trance from one in a normal state of consciousness.

Hypnotic Life Saving. The psychiatrist James R. Hodge hypnotized one of his suicidal patients. He gave her a posthypnotic suggestion that she would sink into a deep trance and call him for help if she was ever tempted by suicide again. It has worked. Hodge feels it is no guarantee against suicide and may be only symptomatic treatment. But when a life hangs in the balance, these arguments shrink in importance.

RELATING TO ONE ANOTHER

HUMAN BEINGS ARE RELATING CREATURES who form attitudes, beliefs, and opinions about other people and events in order to make sense of the world. It is the complexity of the act of relating that distinguishes the human species from other forms of life; and it is relating that produces joy as well as unhappiness for all of us. In many respects we are what we believe, think, and feel—the attitudes we hold toward life.

In this unit we will explore the impact of the communications that impinge on us from the outside world. We will consider how such persuasions shape our view of ourselves and examine how the style of our relationship with others is fashioned. The human capacity to sense, perceive, think, learn, remember, feel emotion, and be motivated all join together when we relate to the world and our fellow beings.

Although we usually think of human behavior as disorganized, irrational, and highly changeable, in reality our patterns of reaction are quite organized and, to a fair extent, predictable. If you watched the overt behavior of any stranger over a period of time, you would observe the consistency with which he seems to relate to people, objects, events, and ideas. By watching his behavior, you could probably tell a good deal about him. All of us relate to the world with a great deal of consistency because of the attitudes we have. Attitudes serve several important functions, the most important of which is providing us with ways of evaluating and handling each new event, object, or person we encounter; we don't always have to start from scratch. Be it a question of buying the right cleanser, choosing the best candidate, finding friends, or deciding whether to go along with the crowd, our attitudes often make the difference in how we relate to ourselves and the world around us.

Psychologists consider the study of attitudes and attitude change crucial to the understanding of man. They have spent a good deal of time and effort trying to figure out what influences the formation of our attitudes, what changes them, and what makes us do things despite our attitudes. McGuire (1966) estimates that 25 percent of the material in social psychology textbooks is devoted to the topics of attitude and attitude change. Some people feel that the research in this area is overdone, but when you consider how much of our behavior is based on our attitudes and how much effort goes into the change of attitudes, this really may not be the case.

Relating to Life

Being shipwrecked on an uninhabited island might make life a lot simpler for you. Of course, you would have to worry about running out of mangoes or coconuts. But the thoughts uppermost in your mind would be the possibility of rescue and the desire to get in touch with people again. All of us are addicted to the sights and sounds of civilization, even though life with others means withstanding a constant assault on our thoughts, our beliefs, and our attitudes.

An attitude has three major components—*beliefs* about an object, *feelings* about an object, and a *tendency to behave* in certain ways toward an object. Beliefs involve facts, opinions, and general knowledge. Feelings include hate, love, like, dislike, and related sentiments. And the tendency to behave in certain ways makes our actions predictable. The emotional factor distinguishes feelings from beliefs. If you believe that tall people make better basketball players than short people, that belief may have no emotion attached to it; it may simply be a matter of fact that you are neither for nor against. Beliefs or opinions are judgments you have made with the available facts. The addition of new facts may easily change your mind, however.

Attitudes are learned reactions most often formed in interaction with others. Many of the attitudes most basic to our life are acquired from our parents. And, even though attitudes change with new experiences, they do not change very markedly. Attitudes tend to be astonishingly persistent. If you learned prejudicial attitudes as a child, you are likely to retain them when you are old. For every person who significantly changes his or her attitudes, undoubtedly there are thousands who cling tightly to their emotionally held beliefs.

The Functions of Attitudes

The psychological theorist Daniel Katz (1960) argues that we form and maintain attitudes simply because they serve some useful purpose for us. They

How You Learned What You Feel

We speak about having attitudes, using them, and keeping them for a long time. But where do attitudes come from? Usually, they come from other people. As children we learn attitudes from our parents, and as adolescents we learn them from our peers.

When you were little, you may have been punished for talking back to your mother. No doubt you learned from this and similar experiences to respect your elders. Whether or not you agree with their methods, your parents were attempting to socialize you. They wanted to instill in you the attitudes that they and most of society value highly. When youngsters are rewarded for expressing the appropriate attitudes or punished for expressing wrong ones, they learn to hold certain attitudes. Through this socialization process, you probably learned many of the attitudes you still hold today.

Children often learn attitudes from their parents even when the adults make no attempt to teach them. By identifying with their parents, children often use their parents as models for behaviors and attitudes they should hold to. For example, if you are five years old and your mother wears lipstick, you will probably be tempted to try some yourself. You may also come to believe that make-up is a necessary part of a woman's attire. Whether the process be modeling or socialization, most children usually acquire only the emotional aspect of attitudes. That is, they like what they have learned is good and dislike what they have learned is bad. Only later do they acquire the beliefs to support these feelings or gain information that changes the attitude entirely.

As children become adolescents, the socializing agent switches from parents to peers. Once again, holding the right attitudes is reinforced, and holding the wrong ones is punished (often by the loss of approval of friends). The child at this point has begun to identify with the peer group, and thus the group provides new sources of behaviors and attitudes that can be imitated. To a large extent these attitudes are now incorporated into the per-

sonality. Before this, however, they may be more critically evaluated, because they must somehow be reconciled with attitudes that the child has already acquired.

are functional in daily life. Attitudes can serve a variety of functions and often fill several purposes at the same time. The following paragraphs deal with some of the functions Katz believes attitudes perform.

Utilitarian.   Attitudes get us what we want in life and keep us from experiencing unpleasant events. Because we acquire positive attitudes toward those people, objects, and events which are rewarding, and negative attitudes toward those which are punishing, we use attitudes in seeking pleasure and avoiding pain.

Ego-defensive.   Attitudes allow us to distort reality. They allow us to deny an unpleasant reality or "explain away" parts of reality we do not care to grapple with. In this way, attitudes function similarly to unconscious defense mechanisms. If your attitude toward the business world tells you that it is composed of stuffy, conservative people who make you do dull work, then it will be much simpler for you to drop out of society in search of a life which requires less self-discipline and provides immediate gratification of impulses. If your attitude is that people in trouble deserve what they get, you can justify not helping them. In both cases, your behavior may not be acceptable to others, but it will not damage your view of yourself.

Value-expressive.   Attitudes allow us to express our decisions about what is valuable and desirable or what is ugly and useless. Our values may not be shared by most others in the culture, but it is important that our chosen values form a consistent attitude. We must also be able to express these attitudes toward others. A great deal of interaction with others really amounts to communicating attitudes. As we will see, liking and disliking other people depends very much on how well our own attitudes match the attitudes of those others.

Knowledge.   Attitudes help you understand the world by allowing you to package the world in identifiable compartments or units. If you are liberal, you can quickly reach conclusions about the meaning of conservative proposals, and vice versa. You make sense of your acquired information by filtering it through an enormous number of attitudes accumulated throughout your lifetime.

As you study attitudes, it will be helpful to keep in mind that the functions of attitudes are not mutually exclusive. If the experimental research findings on attitudes appear confusing and sometimes contradictory, it will help to remember the functions which attitudes perform in giving order to a chaotic world. It might also be helpful to make a brief inventory of the attitudes which are important to you. Ask yourself what functions these attitudes are serving for you.

The Chicken or the Egg?

Over the years psychologists have assumed that your attitudes will determine how you behave toward the objects you interact with. In recent years, Bem

The Persistence of Attitudes

In the early 1960s, Theodore M. Newcomb did a follow-up study on a group of women whose attitudes he had previously examined in the 1930s. These women were from upper-class, conservative families and were students at Bennington College, an exclusive women's college in Vermont. When the girls had entered Bennington in 1935, most of them held the conservative attitudes. But by the time they graduated, their attitudes had become much more liberal because of the liberal faculty and the new ideas and opinions they were being exposed to. Newcomb wondered whether his former students still retained these liberal attitudes more than 20 years later, or whether they had returned to more conservative attitudes.

These young women, Newcomb discovered, remained liberal minded, unlike most young liberals even 20 years after graduation from college. Newcomb accounted for this persistence of unconservative political attitudes, in large part, by pointing to the men the women had married. Even though most of these men also came from upper-class, conservative homes, the Bennington girls had selected "husbands of generally nonconservative stripe who helped to maintain for them an environment that was supportive of existing attitudes" (Newcomb, 1963). It would seem, then, that attitude persistence and attitude change could be a function of whom you choose as a marriage partner.

(1967, 1970) has suggested this notion should be revised. He believes attitudes do not cause behavior as much as behavior causes attitudes. To Bem, we most often learn what is happening inside people by watching their behavior, and we estimate what others are feeling by noting their actions. We do the same when relating to ourselves—we measure our own attitudes by the way we behave. Bem suggests that we may like a club because we have already joined it; but we do not necessarily join because we like it beforehand.

An experimental exploration of this idea was carried out by Bandler, Madaras, and Bem (1968). They paid subjects to undergo a series of electric shocks. Before the shocks, some subjects were told that it would be better for them to escape the shock by stopping it when it came on. Other subjects were told to withstand the shock, even though it was up to them to decide whether to take the shocks or not. After each shock, the subjects rated how uncomfortable it was on a seven-point scale. (Actually all the shocks were equally intense.)

Bem (1970) found that the results of this experience supported his theory. The shocks were rated significantly more uncomfortable by the subjects who were told not to withstand them. The behavior of either ending or enduring the shocks produced different attitudes toward the discomfort caused by the shock.

Bem (1970) has cited another example of how his theory works. He reminds us that many whites are opposed to desegregation before it happens, but after it occurs their attitudes become more favorable. This attitude change happened, for example, in infantry units in World War II. In the early 1960s surveys repeatedly showed that Americans felt blacks were "pushing too hard" and that militant behavior would only hurt the cause of human rights. Today we know that, in spite of the disorders and perhaps because of them, attitudes about integration have become more favorable than ever before. It is nearly impossible to sort out cause and effect in such a complex social issue, but it is reasonable to conclude that favorable attitudes toward desegregation follow, rather than precede, the fact.

However our individual attitudes are formed, our primary concern in relating is to change the attitudes of others to conform more closely with our own view of life. In this respect we are all calculating persuaders of others.

The Calculating Persuaders

Remember the last time you had a Coke? I am sure it seemed like a simple, uncomplicated transaction—you were thirsty and you got something to drink. Right? Wrong, according to the advertisers who spend millions shaping your attitude toward their product. Knowing how much you enjoy music, for example, they taught you a song to sing; they suggested you would "like to teach the world to sing in perfect harmony" and that you would "like to buy the world a Coke and keep it company." They not only sold you a Coke; they also sold you a sense of community to combat anxiety over the modern, strife-ridden world.

Or, maybe you recently had a Pepsi—not so much because you were thirsty, but because you are "young in heart." You have "a lot of living to do" as a member of the Pepsi Generation (Nietzke, 1972). You could have had some trouble deciding between Coke and Pepsi, since advertisers make you choose between "coming alive" or getting "the real thing." The "real thing," of course, is supposed to remind you of how much better life was in the past (it wasn't) when nothing was plastic, chemical, or imitation.

AS I DO, NOT AS I SAY

In 1934, LaPiere did a classic study of differences between attitudes and behavior. In the company of a Chinese couple, LaPiere drove approximately 10,000 miles around the United States stopping in hotels and restaurants. Only once were they refused service; yet when LaPiere sent a questionnaire to each place visited during the journey, 92 percent of the restaurants and 91 percent of the hotels replied that Chinese would not be accepted as guests. In this case, it was easier to declare a privately held attitude than it was to back it up with behavior by denying service to the "white man" and the Chinese couple.

The Unconscious Shopper

Advertisers, using "consumer psychology," try to exert their influence on you no matter what you buy, and they may succeed since they know things about you that you may not know yourself.

Consider buying a new car. As everyone knows, you should be concerned about price, speed, design, gas mileage, safety, handling, wheelbase width, horsepower, equipment, and so forth. Not so, according to Smith and Engel (1968). Actually, the most important factor may be whether beautiful girls were used in the advertising copy. To test their observation, Smith and Engel constructed an ad that included a female model clipped from *Playboy*. She was a young redhead clad in black lace panties and a sleeveless sweater; she had been rated by 15 male observers as attractive and erotic. One hand rested on her hip and the other held a spear. Obviously, she had nothing to do with the features of the car. A control ad contained the identical automobile minus the female.

Experimental and control groups of men were then asked to rate the design of the car on a five-point scale from "excellent" to "poor." They were supposed to estimate the list price with standard equipment and the top speed of the car. Also they were to rate the car as appealing–not appealing, lively–dull, youthful–not youthful, high horsepower–low horsepower, safe–unsafe, easy to handle–difficult to handle, wide wheelbase–narrow wheelbase. I think you can guess the outcome of the experiment.

The experimental subjects who saw the ad with the girl in it rated the vehicle as more appealing, lively, youthful, and better designed. They also tended to rate the car as costing about $340 more than the price estimated by the control group. They thought it was about 7.3 mph faster, was less safe, and had a wider wheelbase. It is particularly interesting to note that in later interviews men in the experimental group not only denied the girl had any influence on them but also barely acknowledged any awareness of her.

Shopping for Fun

A pretty girl and a pretty car may logically fit together, but what about ordinary shopping? Do we go shopping just to get something we need or want? Some marketing experts suggest that we go shopping for a lot of reasons other than buying. When we say we are "going shopping" for groceries, this activity may really be a way of fulfilling what is expected of us in our social role of mother, housewife, husband, or student.

Since grocery shopping is a customary activity of the housewife, attempts to eliminate "food shopping" through home delivery and telephone order have never been very successful. Going shopping offers the housewife a diversion from her daily routine and thus is a kind of recreation. She can go to a store when she is bored or feels lonely. Now and then all of us go to a store to buy "something nice" when we feel depressed. "Just looking" keeps us informed about the latest trends. We are stimulated simply by handling the merchandise, listening to the sounds, and looking at the people. Occasionally, we will run into friends and have a chance to renew social contacts. In other words, "going shopping" is a complex social and psychological activity. A considerable portion of the energy and resources of Madison Avenue advertisers is expended on ways to induce you to buy goods you would otherwise never have dreamed of getting.

As the consumer psychologist Emanuel Demby (1972) asserts, we may well be getting only what we richly deserve. "Like small children, members of the affluent society demand immediate satisfaction of their needs. Sales of instant coffee, instant breakfasts, instant puddings, and instant dinners are on the rise. We no longer have to wait for television tubes to warm up—the commercials are there in full color at the touch of a knob" (p. 75).

The Attention Getters

Since so many similar products compete in the barrage of advertisements that drown us each day, the ingenuity of the consumer psychologist is focused on how to get and hold our attention. Thus, the methods of social science research have been used to study how the features of an ad make it noticeable.

An astonishing amount of effort has been invested in discovering various "facts" about advertising. For example, doubling the size of an ad will not quite double the frequency with which it is noticed; doubling its size again will yield an even smaller increase in readership. A colored ad surrounded by other colored ads is not necessarily better than a black-and-white ad in the same colored surroundings; a well-done black-and-white ad placed between colored ads may be a more effective attention getter. An ad placed just inside the covers is more often noticed than an ad placed anywhere else in a magazine. Consumers don't notice the old—only the different. If you are wondering whether this aspect of consumer psychology truly serves a useful social function,

The Year of the Lunar Watch

Vantage

we can say that, happily, there are consumer psychologists concerned with more weighty matters.

Earning and Spending

It is getting harder to do every year, but every so often consumers acquire more money than they need for simple survival purposes. This is called "discretionary" income since the consumer has a choice between spending and saving his money.

George Katona (1964) of the Survey Research Center at the University of Michigan has been polling consumers for many years in order to predict such consumer behavior. Each year his research group asks respondents about their personal finances. Respondents are asked to give their impressions of the economic picture for the coming year and for five years in the future and to tell whether it is a good time to buy cars, appliances, houses, and so forth. Using these data, Katona can demonstrate that fluctuations in an index of optimism or pessimism about our society's economic situation are related to nationwide consumer purchases made six to nine months later. Measuring the consumer's attitudes and predicting his behavior in this way is of considerable value not only to business firms but also to governmental agencies who must chart economic trends in order to make plans that are appropriately responsive to the moods of the consumer. It is important, for example, to know that people do not simply spend money as fast as they get it. Rather, they spend if they are convinced that their personal fortunes are on the rise, and they save if they anticipate bad times. This aspect of human spending has its somber side, of course. Loan companies regularly report that their best customers are those optimists whose ability to spend exceeds their ability to earn.

Consumer psychology is only one among many practical applications of the psychological study of human attitudes and behavior. Many observers have recently suggested that our society needs some means by which the diverse members of our culture can easily convey the current state of their attitudes and preferences to their elected governmental representatives in order to produce greater responsiveness to the will of the people. If this comes to pass, we will see the birth of a specialty which might be labeled political consumer psychology.

Political Consumer Psychology

The word *propaganda* suggests that someone is attempting to fool people or manipulate them. But, ironically, the leaders we most admire and respect regularly use propaganda to convince people of the correctness of their plans or policies.

Propaganda has to be subtle to be effective. The textbooks you read, for example, may reinforce the basic principles of capitalism by utilizing math problems which deal with buying, selling, renting, investing, and compounding interest. You learn more than math when you must calculate the yearly profit a supermarket chain can make if it marks up its meat prices 1 percent to cover the cost of trading stamps. You would learn a different lesson if you were asked to figure out how many food stamps a migrant worker's family would need every year to prevent his children from malnutrition. Propaganda is not always a deliberate intention of our educational system, but being an integral part of society, education is bound to reflect the society's value system and subtly reinforce it rather than alter it. Students reading textbooks make a nearly perfect captive audience. In the real world, it is not so easy. Or is it?

The Problem of Exposure

People in show business know the importance of proper public exposure to their careers. Politicians are painfully aware of how little political information is absorbed by the average citizen. Certainly, the level of our ignorance is remarkable. Everyone knows who the president is, but slightly more than half of the populace can name even one of their senators. Fewer yet can name both senators. And about the same percentage knows the name of their congressman. Most of us are at least familiar with the United Nations or the Peace Corps, but very few can explain what the Common Market is or how it works. Television has helped the exposure problem a little, but public affairs programs are still avoided by most viewers.

If propaganda or persuasion is your game, you must also contend with the fact that the small audience you attract may be composed of the wrong people. You may attract the people who already agree with you—not the people you want to persuade.

Democrats listen mostly to other Democrats. Republicans listen to other Republicans. And ethnic groups attend programs performed by their own ethnic group. Even psychologists tend to read articles in favor of psychologists. And you might read ads only pertaining to the items you've just bought. This selective exposure can be effectively eliminated only when the persuader can control all the media. Any dictator worth his salt will first take over the radio, television, and newspapers of the society he wishes to control.

The Propagandist's Handbook

Propaganda is effective to the degree that it relies on the basic principles of human motivation, perception, and learning. Some of the propagandist's rules of thumb are mentioned in Krech and Krutchfield (1948) and Goodwin Watson (1966). If you are trying to persuade others, be sure your message includes the following points:

"CLEAN FOR GENE"
In the scramble for the presidential nomination in 1968, those students who campaigned for candidate Eugene McCarthy voluntarily cut their hair and dressed in conventional clothing. This event was described as being "clean for Gene."
As every politician knows— but as psychologists have only recently demonstrated—there is an important relationship between the appearance of campaigners and the effectiveness of their communication with others.
Darley and Cooper (1972) tried experiments in which deviant, "freaky" campaigners handed out leaflets in a shopping center; the "freaks" had fewer takers than did more conventionally dressed campaigners. The conclusion reached was that the appearance of deviant campaigners triggered a negative attitudinal reaction in the voters they were trying to influence with leaflets. When questioned, those who were offered leaflets by "freaky" campaigners ascribed more radical opinions to the deviants' candidate than to the candidate supported by more conventionally dressed campaigners.

When Leon Trotsky wanted to persuade his audience, his intensity was apparent not only in his voice but in every gesture he made. Trotsky had been an important official in Lenin's government following the Russian Revolution, but he was defeated by Stalin in a contest for control of the Community party after Lenin died in 1924. This photo was taken in Copenhagen in 1931—two years after the revolutionist had been expelled from Russia.

1. Meets your listener's needs. "Food prices are too high. The greedy supermarket owners are at fault. I promise to roll back prices to those that existed a year ago." If no real need exists, create one. "You are not aware of it but all over the country they are planning to poison us by adding fluorides to our water."

2. Fits existing attitudes. "The income tax favors the rich, penalizes the poor, and destroys the great American tradition of rugged individualism." "Americans can never accept a peace without honor; we have never lost a war." "Day-care centers are communistic and will erode the strength of the American family."

3. Is positive rather than negative. "I can bring peace, prosperity, and pride back to America." "Buckling your seat belt says I love you." "Life insurance is for the living." "Give until it feels good."

4. Is simple, clear, and repeated. Tell them you are going to say it; say it; tell them you said it; and say it again. You hate ads you have seen a thousand times, but you remember them. Don't let the listener draw his own conclusions; tell him the answer.

5. Identifies the speaker with the listener. "I was a coal miner and I know how you feel." "My door has always been open to the working man." "I am just an average housewife who hates to do laundry."

6. Presents both sides of the issue. "I want to be fair so I will say my opponent has tried to solve this problem and I am sorry he failed." "There are a lot of good detergents, but only one is best." "Saving our natural resources will be expensive, but it will be worth it in the long run."

The list of rules to be followed when trying to change people's attitudes could be lengthened interminably. But the propagandist is often willing to settle for changing opinions if he cannot alter attitudes. We therefore need to take a brief look at this part of our belief system.

What's Your Opinion?

Probably everyone is aware of public-opinion polling as a means of assessing attitudes even though no one seems to know anyone who was ever polled. Opinion polls may use either open-ended or fixed-response questions. Open-ended questions allow you to make any response you wish. In fixed-response questions, you must select one response from a fixed set of answers. Frequently pollsters will have a small sample of people respond to open-ended questions and then use their answers to fashion fixed-response questions for the final poll.

Polls or Propaganda?

Opinion polling was first designed primarily to serve the needs of radio advertising in the 1920s. These polls were used to analyze the coverage and impact of commercials. The founders of polling—George H. Gallup, Elmo Roper, and Archibald Crossley—have been referred to as "those market researchers turned pollsters."

Although pollsters still earn their keep by gathering data on consumer preferences and habits, in recent years the use of surveys in the political process has increased enormously. Before nearly every election, the results of poll after poll appear in the newspaper, many times with conflicting results. Sometimes it seems that every candidate authorizes his own poll to offset a poor showing in the polls of his opponents. Although many people ignore the polls because they often disagree, the possibility remains that undecided voters may be swayed by poll results. Unfortunately we have yet to determine whether this is the case. Should the election favor the poll leader, it would be difficult to prove whether the poll made the difference or whether it was simply right all along.

The use of polls by politicians in elections and in supporting their positions might not be so bad if we could be sure the polls were really accurate. Many times they are not. For one thing, biased or incomplete samples can throw the results of a poll way off base. What is worse is that the polls may be worded so that the person answering the questions may not be able to express his opinion accurately. This is especially the case with polls that give various alternatives on questions of economics or foreign policy. Sometimes, none of the choices fits the individual's real opinion. Take, for example, the following questions on Vietnam, which could have appeared on a congressman's poll of his constituents.

In regard to the fighting in Vietnam, I think we should:
(a) employ massive bombing efforts in addition to guerrilla fighting,
(b) employ small-scale bombing and guerrilla fighting,
(c) use no bombing and continue guerrilla fighting,
(d) withdraw all troops immediately.

What would you have answered if you had received this poll five years ago? At that point, few people believed that it would be safe to withdraw troops immediately, but many wanted the war to end and the soldiers brought home. But there was no alternative for this opinion. In all probability, most liberal-minded individuals who felt the war was bad would have been forced to give answer c, "continue fighting." And a politician discussing the results would not have to mention what the alternatives were. All he would have to report is that the majority of his constituents thought it best to continue the war. Moreover, if it is true that behavior can affect attitude, how many opinions might have been changed by these polls of people who felt they had to check c instead of d?

This example may seem extreme, but there is no doubt that many polls are not as fair or objective as they are said to be. Says Schiller (1972): "Polls have served democratic ends not just poorly but disastrously. They have cultivated a deceptive guise of neutrality and objectivity. They have fostered the illusion of popular participation and freedom of choice to conceal an increasingly elaborate apparatus of consciousness manipulation and mind-management."

Big Brother, it seems, is everywhere.

The important fact is that no matter how carefully prepared a question may be, the meaning and trustworthiness of the answer depends on how adequate the sample of persons polled happens to be. A classic example of how sampling errors can distort the results is the sad story of the political poll conducted by the *Literary Digest*. The magazine predicted that the Republican candidate Alfred M. Landon would win the 1936 presidential election. The poll was conducted by selecting the names from lists of persons who had telephones. Today it might work, but in 1936 only half of the families in the United States had telephones. Further, those who did have phones were richer than the average citizen. Since high-income families tend to vote Republican, the *Literary Digest* polled a biased sample of voters and misread the results. Franklin D. Roosevelt, a Democrat, won the election. Not surprisingly, the magazine went out of business shortly after this public error.

Attitude- and opinion-polling methods have become more sophisticated (and cautious) in the years since the *Literary Digest* fiasco. A more expensive but less biased method of choosing a sample is *area sampling*. A geographical area is divided into blocks (in a city), and a certain number of dwelling units in each block are selected at random. Then the interviewer is instructed to interview the people who live in the specific units selected—and no others.

Although not as reliable as area sampling, another method is the *quota sample*. The persons selected for questioning are chosen so as to reflect the same proportions of similar persons in the total population. Interviewers are instructed to question a certain percentage of people in a given group, but they are free to interview whomever they like within the designated group. The problem with this technique is that interviewers, when given a choice, tend to question people of slightly higher income and social status, and this biases the results.

How to Brainwash

The word *brainwashing* suggests not only an image of the brain being washed, replanted with new thoughts, then hung out to dry. It also conveys a mixture of science and mysticism that is slightly scary. But the techniques of brainwashing are neither mysterious nor new. They are classic ways of inducing attitude change. When the word *brainwash* was coined by an American journalist in 1951 (Hunter, 1951) it was a translation of the Chinese expression *hsinao* ("wash brain" or "cleanse the mind"). The term described the process by which someone is reeducated and old beliefs replaced by new ones in "thought reform" programs for intellectuals who attended revolutionary colleges established just after the communist takeover of China. Observers of this phenomenon described it as *"an induced religious conversion,* as well as *a coercive form of psychotherapy"* (Lifton, 1961). It was a means of "coercive persuasion" to control men's minds (Schein, Schneider, and Barker, 1961).

Brainwashing involves three basic steps: unfreezing, changing, and refreezing. In other words, the individual you are about to brainwash must be led to doubt the ideology he believes in. He must be helped to see the merits of a new position. And he must be made to see the new position as the sensible and reasonable one. Based on their knowledge of attitude formation and change, psychologists (Walker and Heyns, 1967; Sampson, 1971) have made some suggestions about the steps involved in brainwashing someone effectively. If you want to do it, here's how.

Break down the old attitudes. Isolate the individual from all of his normal contacts with others. Keep him away from all the usual social supports for the attitudes he holds (other people, books, television, and so forth). Do everything you possibly can to see to it that the individual has no confidence left in his own position.

Institute the new. Arouse some need or needs in the person. Offer him a goal that will resolve that need, but make sure the goal involves conformity to your position in some way. The first conformity step should appear highly valued, but it should not be at a level too far from the starting point of the individual. (In other words, he will probably not sign a confession the first time you make him thirsty.) As you proceed, move the conforming behavior closer and closer to the behavior or attitude you wish to produce.

Walker and Heyns (1967) warn: "Be absolutely certain you know what you want and that you are willing to pay an enormous price in human quality, for whether the individual . . . is aware of it or not, the result will be CONFORMITY" (p. 000). But despite this ominous warning, only in rare cases does a person permanently change his opinion as a result of brainwashing. It is simply not that effective in changing attitudes (Brown, 1963). In most cases, brainwashing must compete against decades of training and against a society that holds the original values—not the newly acquired ones. Permanent change is, therefore, unlikely in the brief period of time used for brainwashing.

Polls and polling methods are always interesting, but let us now look at the larger problems of changing and influencing human attitudes.

Changing Attitudes

It would be nice to report that psychologists have discovered a simple, foolproof way to change people's attitudes, but the truth is that the human race clings stubbornly and often irrationally to its attitudes. Human beings tend to argue with even the most carefully designed and persuasive communications. Smokers, for example, keep on smoking even when they acknowledge that it is harmful to their health. Certainly, each one of us has a complicated collection of ways to protect our attitudes against any assault by facts or logic.

On Guard

People usually do not trust other persons who try to influence them. Allyn and Festinger (1961) demonstrated this experimentally by comparing the effect of messages delivered in various ways. A message was delivered by a person who was obviously trying to persuade the subject. The same message was also "accidentally" overheard from a "private" conversation. When the results of these messages were compared, the "accidentally" overheard message was markedly more effective in producing attitude change.

When you know in advance that someone is going to try to change your attitude, you tend to resist. Freedman and Sears (1965) told one group of teen-agers, ten minutes beforehand, that they were going to hear a talk titled "Why Teen-agers Should Not Be Allowed to Drive." Another group was not told about the talk until just before the speaker started. Those who were warned were less influenced by the talk than were the others. Apparently, if you are going to be persuaded, the persuasion must not be obvious. One way of softening you up for persuasion might simply be to pass out Cokes while you are getting the message. When this was tried by Janis and his colleagues (1965), it became apparent that, even though the Coke had nothing to do with the content of the message, those who got Cokes tended to be influenced more than those who didn't.

Scare Tactics

We often react negatively if we think a persuader is trying to scare us into adopting a new attitude. We know, for example, that traffic and health officials cannot resist trying to change our attitudes and behavior by arousing fear. If we are frightened enough, they think we will change our attitudes or behavior. But it happens that such persons don't know much about human psychology. Strong appeals to fear may backfire. If an appeal to fear is laid on too thick, it may not even be effective in getting us to brush our teeth

BRAINWASHING TODAY
Brainwashing is a part of modern behavior, according to Dr. James McConnell (1970). He is convinced that, "Somehow we've got to learn how to force *people to love one another, to* force *them to want to behave properly." Speaking of psychological force, McConnell suggests there are only two means of educating people—rewarding them for doing the right thing or punishing them for doing the wrong thing. Behaviorist McConnell recommends brainwashing for criminals and foresees the day when the worst criminal can be converted "into a decent, respectable citizen." He sees behavioral psychologists as the architects of the Brave New World of tomorrow.*

properly (Janis and Feshbach, 1953). In one experiment, 200 high-school students were divided into 3 experimental groups: a "strong-fear" group, a "moderate-fear" group, and a "minimum-fear" group. There was also a control group. The strong-fear group heard a lecture that attempted to arouse anxiety by portraying how decayed teeth and diseased gums could result from poor brushing habits. The moderate-fear group got a less frightening lecture. And the minimum-fear group heard a talk that was not very frightening at all. A control group of students heard a lecture on an entirely different topic. Before the lecture, the students filled out a questionnaire about their attitudes toward dental care, and the average attitude scores of all groups were about equal. After the lecture there were clear differences. Surprisingly, the minimum-fear group changed the most in attitudes toward tooth brushing (36 percent). The moderate-fear group was affected only slightly more than the control group (8 percent and 0 percent). The group presented with the most frightening pitch apparently disregarded the message since it seemed inconsistent with other things they had heard.

In the 20 years since that early experiment, theorists have come to the conclusion that fear will motivate you to change your attitudes and behavior, within reasonable limits. Dabbs and Leventhal (1966), for example, set up an experiment urging college students to get inoculations against tetanus. The experimenters described the disease in great detail, pointed out how serious it can be, and stressed how easy it is to catch. The evidence clearly demonstrated that, under most circumstances, arousing fear increases the effectiveness of persuasive communications—providing you don't arouse too much fear. If the listener is too threatened, he will dismiss the danger and reject the motive to change.

The Prestige Appeal

Beautiful settings, famous people, and cuddly animals are used to reinforce messages that tell us how to feel and what attitudes to hold. The athlete who says he shaves with a particular razor helps the sales of that razor by associating himself with it. The viewer might reason that athletes actually know very little about razors. But if he admires the player, his admiration will also be associated with the razor. Even though it is common knowledge that athletes do such commercials for the money, the appeal still seems to work.

We feel confident in believing that "doctors" recommend a product, since we assume that they are experts who know what they are talking about. To reinforce our preconceptions, commercials often feature a sincere, dignified, grey-haired man in a "doctor's" white coat. Again, the prestige of the association between doctor and product seems to work.

An interesting study was performed by Walster, Aronson, and Abrahams (1966) who examined how an audience reacted to a talk by a convicted

criminal. When the convict argued in favor of more individual freedom and against greater powers for the police, he produced almost no attitude change in the audience. When he argued for the opposite point of view (a stronger police force), he produced a great deal of attitude change. Thus, even a low-prestige communicator can have a considerable influence if he argues for a position that would hurt him rather than benefit him. His position somehow becomes more persuasive, since he does not appear to be arguing for his own advantage.

Carl Hovland (1959) noted some years ago that, in the artificial environment of a research laboratory, it is fairly easy to produce change in practically any attitude you wish. Advertisers, politicians, and other propagandists are painfully aware, however, that what works in the lab is not nearly as workable in real life. They know it is extremely difficult in a short period of time to produce any sizable change in people's opinions on important issues. Despite the millions of dollars that are spent in election years, most Americans know early in May how they are going to vote in November—and not much that happens will change their mind. Elections would be boringly predictable if it were not for undecided voters who do not form opinions about the candidates until the last moment.

Thus, there may be a great deal of smoke and not much fire in the area of attitude change. If you examine your own recent history of forming and changing attitudes, you can judge how often it happens to you in real life. Probably most of us seldom change our attitudes about important aspects of life. When our attitudes do change, it may most often be because we ourselves have caused an alteration that will bring them in line with our overt behavior.

Cognitive Dissonance

The phrase *cognitive dissonance* describes the match that lights the fuse of attitude change. Psychologically, human beings apparently need to achieve a kind of balance or consistency between their attitudes and their behavior. If you told lies to everyone you met, it would be difficult for you to see yourself as an honest person. The fact is that most of us do lie a lot. But, we call them "little white lies" and justify our dishonesty by pointing out that it is more important not to hurt other people's feelings. As we all know, the truth often hurts more than it helps.

Sometimes, facing the truth is painful because it means that you have lived a lie for years—that everything important in your life has been untrue. In such a case you would search desperately for another way to deal with the "truth"—a way to distort it and make it consistent with what you have always believed. Researchers have uncovered two striking cases that demonstrate this principle, and they are worth considering in some detail.

The End of the World

Leon Festinger and his colleagues (1956) studied a religious sect which believed that the end of the world was coming and that, as true believers, they would be saved by a spaceship sent from outer space. When the fateful day came and passed without world destruction, the group members were quite disturbed.

Their mistaken judgment did not cause them to abandon their beliefs, however. To justify all the effort they had put into the plans and preparations for the day of cataclysm (they had sold their possessions, moved to assembly points, left their friends), they concluded that the day had been put off temporarily but that the end of the world was still coming soon. To reassure themselves of the accuracy of this new conclusion, they stopped avoiding publicity and actively began to recruit converts to their cause—arguing that their faith had postponed the end of the world. The activity demonstrated the great faith they had in their beliefs. The more seriously they were taken, the more reassured they were that their ideas made sense.

Hardyk and Braden (1962) reported a similar instance which demonstrates how we deal with "facts" that don't sensibly fit the pattern of our behavior. One year a group of 135 men, women, and children left their homes in a small southwestern town leaving only a note on the door of their church. The note read: "Gone for two weeks, camp meeting."

For months they had secretly been building and stocking underground fallout shelters in response to prophecies of a forthcoming nuclear disaster. Obeying what they believed to be a command from God, they went to their shelters and awaited the nuclear catastrophe for 42 days and nights. From their interpretation of portions of the book of Revelations, they expected that one-third of the population of the earth would be wiped out by nuclear warfare and that injuries and sickness would be widespread among those who survived. They also expected that they would receive special powers from God so they might perform miracles of healing following the disaster.

When the prophecy failed, a great deal of dissonance was produced between the belief and the nonoccurrence of the predicted event. The group was unable to give up its strongly held beliefs and unable to deny that the world had not ended. As would have been predicted by the theory of cognitive dissonance, the believers became even stronger in their conviction and made powerful attempts to convert others to their cause. The group members decided they had simply misinterpreted God's purposes. They were convinced that God was using them to warn the world, and they continued to believe that an attack would come soon. In so doing they demonstrated the "balance model." The major point of the theory of cognitive consistency is that people have a tendency to move from a state of cognitive imbalance toward a state of balance to avoid the discomfort of believing one thing but living another (Fritz Heider, 1958).

Dissonance as a Drive

Cognitive dissonance is a motivating state of affairs. Just as hunger impels a person to eat, so dissonance impels a person to change his opinions or his behavior (Festinger, 1962).

The state of cognitive dissonance produces discomfort which must be

Cognitive Dissonance at the Supermarket

The idea behind making an "introductory low-price offer" is to get customers interested in buying a new product. The price is initially reduced and then raised to its regular level after a few weeks. According to the theory of cognitive dissonance, this is not a very smart bit of psychological merchandising. If the product were sold at the regular price right from the start, customers who buy it at that price will reduce dissonance by convincing themselves that it is a good product. But if the product were initially sold for a lower price, the bargain-hunting customer does not have to convince himself that he is buying a superior product.

To test this theory Leonard Doob and his fellow experimenters (1969) convinced several stores to sell a number of common products (mouthwash, toothpaste, aluminum foil, and light bulbs) either at the regular price or at an introductory low price for two weeks before raising the price to its regular level. What happened to mouthwash can be used as an illustration. At first sales were higher for the low-priced mouthwash as customers looked for bargains. However, when the price went up to its originally intended level, sales quickly dropped in stores where the initial price had been low. Thus, introducing mouthwash at a lower initial price resulted in lower total sales than would have been obtained by selling it at the regular price from the beginning.

The problem is not so much selling the product as getting people to continue buying it.

reduced by the individual to maintain consistent relations among his cognitions of himself, his behavior, and the world about him. To achieve this, the person may have to change his beliefs about himself. For example, the rejected college applicant may come to believe that he did not really want to go to school anyway. A person may also achieve consistency by changing his behavior. Thus, someone who believes he talks too much may practice keeping his mouth shut more often. Another means would be for a person to change his perception of reality. If others criticize him he may convince himself that they are doing so because they are jealous and envious.

An interesting example of how behavior can work to alter attitudes is the case of the "twenty-dollar liars" and the "one-dollar liars." In a study conducted by Festinger and Carlsmith (1959), each subject spent one hour in an extremely boring experiment where he made repeated judgments of the comparative heaviness of weights. At the end of the hour the subjects were told that the real purpose of the experiment was to see whether people would perform better if told beforehand that the experiment was interesting or if told nothing in advance. One group of subjects was then asked to tell the next group of subjects that the experiment was interesting and fun. They were paid one dollar for the lie. Another group of subjects was asked to tell the same lie but they were paid twenty dollars each. After the lies were told, each subject was asked by another experimenter to rate how interesting the weight-judging experiment had actually been for him. The experimenters predicted that the one-dollar liars got so little for their lie that they would have to justify their behavior to themselves; they would thus have to convince themselves the experiment was really interesting. The twenty-dollar liars, however, would not have to distort reality since they were well paid for what they did. There would be little dissonance if they knew they lied for pay.

These predictions were correct. Those who were paid twenty dollars for telling the next subject that the experiment was interesting rated the experiment accurately as boring and unenjoyable. The one-dollar liars rated it as significantly more enjoyable.

Tom Sawyer used this principle years ago when he had to whitewash a fence. He knew it would not be hard to convince his friends that painting fences was fun, and he knew that when they finished painting they would have to think it was even more fun.

These experiments are interesting and they demonstrate one way in which we deal with discrepancies between what we believe and what we do. A better test of the relationship between attitudes and behavior is in the real-life situation of smoking. The psychological issue of smoking illustrates how we relate to life and how we fashion our attitudes and behavior.

Summary

1. An attitude is a readiness to relate to objects, events, or other people in a consistent manner. Attitudes contain three components: beliefs, feelings, and tendencies to act toward the object in certain ways.

2. Attitudes serve to: (1) organize our world so that we can evaluate new experiences; (2) prevent us from dealing with unpleasant things; (3) keep our self-images intact; and (4) provide a basis for communicating with, and even liking, others.

3. Many of our attitudes are learned from others. As children we acquire attitudes through positive and negative reinforcement and identification with our parents. As we get older, our peer group is the source of our attitudes. Attitudes learned early in life are hard to change, but new attitudes may persist with proper social support.

4. Attitudes may also be formed in response to behavior. If we behave a certain way, we develop attitudes to go along with that behavior. This may be why forced desegregation works.

5. Consumer psychologists spend a great deal of time determining what consumers want and deciding what will convince them to buy. Some psychologists focus on what type of advertising will change attitudes toward products, whereas others attempt to predict when people are likely to spend their money.

6. A communication to persuade others to your point of view will be most effective if it: (1) meets the listener's needs; (2) presents both sides of the issue; (3) fits existing attitudes; (4) has a positive outlook; and (5) is simple and clear.

ANYONE FOR GRASSHOPPERS? OR, DISSONANCE OVER LUNCH

Zimbardo and his colleagues (1965) performed an experiment in which subjects were persuaded to eat grasshoppers. In one experimental condition, the experimenter was a pleasant, relaxed, and friendly person who presented his arguments in an attractive manner. In the other condition, the experimenter was cold, aggressive, distant, and came across as unpleasant. Some subjects in each group agreed to eat the grasshoppers. After they had done so, they rated how much they liked them. Those who had the unpleasant experimenter said they liked grasshoppers more than those who had the genial experimenter. The need to reduce dissonance was greater for those who believed they performed this distasteful act at the behest of an aggressive jerk!

7. Communications are also very effective when the speaker is prestigious, identifies himself with the audience, and/or appears to have no personal interest in whether others take his side.

8. Because people like to listen to communications they want to hear, even the most effective message may fall on ears that are already convinced. Communications will also lose their effectiveness when the audience is aware that you are trying to persuade them or when you frighten them so much that they refuse to listen at all.

9. Opinion polls are ways in which psychologists, market researchers, and politicians learn about the public's attitudes. But the accuracy of the polls may be under question if the sample is biased toward a particular subgroup of the population.

10. Polls may create as many problems as they solve. Choices given to individuals may not reflect the full range of alternatives. The results of opinion polls may often conflict, or they may sway undecided individuals.

11. Although laboratory research has isolated a number of variables that can lead to attitude change, in real life most important attitudes are extremely difficult to alter.

12. Most of the time, attitudes change because we ourselves bring them into line with our behavior. When attitude and behavior are not consistent, we experience an uncomfortable state called cognitive dissonance. Cognitive dissonance is a motivating force that causes either a change in behavior or an alteration in attitudes.

13. Brainwashing is really just an application of attitude-change techniques. It involves weakening a person's beliefs and then substituting new ones. Attitude change via brainwashing is not long lasting, unless you continue to keep the individual away from all sources of support for his previous belief.

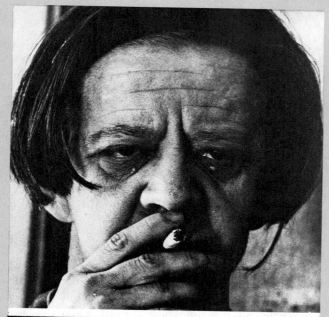

SMOKING
IS VERY
GLAMOROUS

AMERICAN CANCER SOCIETY

Smoking

The Surgeon General of the United States happily announced that 10 million Americans have quit smoking cigarettes in the last four years and that antismoking campaigns have kept another 30 million from starting the habit. But there are still more than 44 million of us who continue to smoke after years of health warnings. Cigarette sales are higher than ever (544 billion cigarettes in 1971—up 2 percent from the previous year), and there are indications that the number of teen-agers just beginning to smoke is rising again after a ten-year decline. Between 225,000 and 300,000 persons smoke themselves to death every year. We are not ignorant of the links between smoking and lung cancer, heart disease, emphysema, chronic bronchitis, and other ailments, but it just doesn't seem to make much difference to us in terms of how we treat ourselves.

It is startling that we can do so little about attitudes toward smoking, but psychologists have been trying. Since some people smoke and others don't, researchers looked first to the possibility that personality differences accounted for this apparently destructive way of dealing with our needs.

NO SMOKING!!! You have seen a great many no-smoking signs. And, of course, you always obey them and refrain from lighting up. Well, not quite. In an experiment to test the effect of such signs and posters, the number of cigarettes smoked by college students and staff members at a state mental health treatment center was compared in rooms with and without warning signs. There wasn't any difference. So much for the theory that posters prevent puffing!

The Smoker Personality

One researcher laid it on the line when he described persons who try to quit smoking but fail. These "losers" are said to be defiant, impulsive, danger-seeking, constricted, guarded, socially isolated, exaggeratedly self-reliant individuals who try to deny they need other people. Men, he suggested, may also fear that giving up the habit will somehow make them meek, passive, and less masculine. Smokers who cannot quit don't sound too charming, do they? In contrast, those who do manage to give up cigarettes were described as more likely to be better educated, better informed about the hazards of smoking, less strongly committed to smoking, and more likely to have others in their family who set an example for them.

Smokers never come off well in studies of their personality characteristics. When a safety research team divided 1,025 male auto-insurance applicants into three groups on the basis of their driving records, only 17 percent of those in the no-accident group were smokers. In the average-accident group, the figure was 29 percent. In the high-accident group, 47 percent were smokers. McGuire (1972) interpreted these findings to suggest that smokers may share personality characteristics which are conducive to having accidents—characteristics such as feelings of inadequacy, excessive anxiety, emotional restrictions, lack of independence and, among teen-agers, fits of restlessness, impulsiveness, or adventurousness. Similarly, Brackenridge and Bloch (1972) found that smokers are more neurotic, restless, extroverted, and anxious than are nonsmokers.

Finally, the heavy smoker is said to be one who feels he received minimal warmth, protection, and affection while growing up; to compensate, he has developed a style of life in which he does not need to rely on others (Jacobs and Spilken, 1971). Thus, as far as personality research goes, the conclusion seems to be that many people smoke, not only because they want to, but because they need to; and they cannot stop even when they fear they are damaging themselves. It may not be the fault of personality alone. Parents help.

Like Parent, Like Child

Both the scientific and popular media have been telling us that the example of parental smoking may lead children to take up the habit. Parents who smoke naturally wish their children would do as they say rather than as they do, but the truth is closer to "like parent, like child."

A significant relationship apparently exists between how often the parent smokes and the incidence of smoking in the child. In general, sons and daughters tend to imitate the smoking behavior of their same-sex parent more than their opposite-sex parent (Wohlford, 1970).

The Pregnant Smoker. The U.S. Public Health Service has suggested one more hazard of cigarette smoking—a significantly increased mortality rate among the fetuses and infants of women who smoke during pregnancy. Some 4,600 stillbirths each year in the United States can probably be attributed to women's smoking habits. In one study, pregnant women who smoked had a 30 percent higher rate of stillbirths than those who did not. Pregnant smokers also experienced a 26 percent higher rate of infant mortality within the first few days after birth. If the mother quits smoking by the fourth month of pregnancy, she will run about the same risks of child loss as do nonsmokers. Cigarette smoking is particularly dangerous in the last six months of pregnancy when the central nervous system of the fetus is still forming.

Baer and Katkin (1971) conducted a survey asking two questions: "Do you limit the amount you smoke?" and "Do you believe you smoke too much?" These two questions were given to four groups: (1) sons and daughters whose parents both smoked, (2) sons and daughters whose fathers smoked, (3) sons and daughters whose mothers smoked, and (4) persons whose parents were nonsmokers. In the group where the mother was the only smoker, sons tended to put no limits on their smoking but felt guilty about smoking too much. In the group where the father was the only smoker, the sons tended to limit their smoking and felt less guilty about it. With daughters, the influences were reversed. If the father were the only smoker, then the daughter smoked all she wanted but felt she was overdoing it. Thus, the effect of the smoking or nonsmoking parent is not a simple one. But, what if you want to quit—despite your personality or your parents?

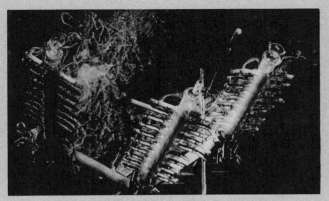

How much do you like being around smokers? If the smoker were this "smoking robot," you probably wouldn't like it at all. The American Cancer Society provided funds to develop the device, which provides a controllable means of collecting smoke residues. When the trapped tars are painted on the backs of mice, cancer results.

How to Stop Smoking

Psychologists have invented many ways for us to quit smoking, and what follows is only a small sample of the possible approaches. All of these methods can be made to work for certain people, but of course each person must find the one method suited to him.

The Hard Way   Resnick (1968) had his research subjects double or triple the number of cigarettes they smoked each week. He then checked how much they were smoking at periods of two weeks and four months later. It worked. Whether the number of cigarettes smoked or the number of persons who quit entirely were counted, percentages of decreased smoking were higher among those who doubled or tripled their smoking than for those who continued to smoke normally. Doubling your smoking is as effective as tripling it if you smoke about one pack a day. There is a catch, though. All of Resnick's subjects had wanted to quit and had previously made at least one unsuccessful attempt to give it up. Their attitude toward smoking was already clearly negative.

Cut Down Gradually   There are a couple of ways to do this and a couple of devices that can help. Two methods of gradual reduction in smoking were compared over a three-month period. The subjects in one group were required to smoke at preset random times using a signalling device to tell them when to light up. Those in another group were allowed to smoke any time they wished, provided they used a mechanical counter to regulate the number of cigarettes smoked each day. More subjects in the group using the mechanical counter finished the program, but the subjects using a signaling device to tell them when to light were more successful in eliminating smoking. The greatest difficulty in either method appears when you cut back to a level of 12 to 14 cigarettes a day. Both groups had trouble getting past that point and reported that "withdrawal" symptoms began to appear (Levinson, Shapiro, Schwartz, and Tursky, 1971).

Smoke Till You Can't Stand It   The psychologist Edward Lichtenstein (1973) has devised a variation of "the hard way" method. Lichtenstein gives a lighted cigarette to a smoker and seats him in front of a box. A metronome ticks away, and every six seconds the smoker is told to take a drag on the cigarette; meanwhile puffs of heated cigarette smoke blow into the smoker's face from an opening in the box. The combination of rapid smoking and blown smoke causes the subject's eyes to water and his nose and throat to burn. He shortly begins to cough and feel sick but he keeps smoking until he cannot force himself to take another drag. As soon as he quits, the metronome and the smoke machine stop. After a short rest and discussion of his reactions, he must light another cigarette and begin again. In two of Lichtenstein's studies, all but 1 of 58 hard-core smokers stopped smoking; 34 of the 58 were not smoking six months later.

Get Electric Shock   With this method you smoke in your normal way in the lab, but every so often you unexpectedly receive a painful electric shock. It may come while you are smoking, lighting up, or opening the pack—anytime during the smoking ritual. The problem with this method is that you stop smoking in the lab but go right back to it when you get outside. At least you stop in the lab.

Equality for Women. Women are catching up to men in the incidence of unexpected death from heart attacks—an increase that seems to be primarily related to a higher rate of cigarette smoking. In the decade between 1949 and 1959, the ratio of men to women dying of coronary heart disease was 12 to 1. In the years between 1967 and 1971, however, this ratio dropped to 4 to 1. The evidence now indicates that women who smoke heavily die younger. Among nonsmokers who unexpectedly died of heart disease, the average age at death was 67; for those who smoked more than 20 cigarettes a day, the age was 48.

Role Playing Elms (1966) took subjects who were heavy smokers and had them play the role of a non-smoker who must convince a smoker to quit. He found that the smokers developed attitudes favorable to quitting smoking simply by playing the role; they were also able to reduce the amount they smoked. Another, more grisly version of this approach is to ask smokers to play the role of someone who has just been told he has lung cancer (Janis and Mann, 1965).

Get a Medical Degree Physicians have been most successful in giving up the habit. Eighty-two percent of the doctors who ever smoked have tried to give it up, and 68 percent made it. Those who specialized in internal medicine were better than most at quitting, but radiologists were the best of all. It is easy enough to understand why these physicians would succeed where others have failed. I'd quit too if I spent all day dealing with lung cancer, chronic bronchitis, emphysema, and heart disease related to smoking.

But Don't Be a Psychiatrist On the basis of their psychological awareness, you might expect psychiatrists to be the most successful of all in ridding themselves of harmful behavior. But psychiatrists, of all physicians, smoke the most and have the least success in quitting. Only 39 percent of psychiatrists who smoke cigarettes have been able to quit. Since the nature of psychotherapy usually requires the psychiatrist to spend many hours of each day sitting in silence, he may experience a strong need to continue smoking as one of the few ways he can reduce tension (Tamerin, 1972). Psychiatrists are also much more likely to smoke in front of their patients since they don't feel they must be a model of proper behavior in the same way a cancer specialist feels he must be.

Does Any Method Work?

All methods seem to work at first, but this is followed by wholesale backsliding (McFall and Hammen, 1971). The particular method does not seem to make a truly significant difference (Keutzer, Lichtenstein, and Mees, 1968). In general, all subjects are able to cut down significantly at first. When the treatment is completed, smoking tends to drop to 30 or 40 percent of what it was at the start, but it then goes back up to 75 percent four to six months later. Subjects tend to be unable to go below 10 cigarettes a day, and only about 13 percent are able to quit entirely (Ober, 1968).

Sometimes the absence of a program works. One clinic simply met with volunteers who wished to stop smoking and urged them to use self-control, to monitor their own smoking, and to report their progress regularly. This nonprogram produced about the same results as did more elaborate programs.

Smoke Gets in Your Eyes. Spokesmen for the tobacco industry insist that the vision of most researchers has been clouded by emotion and that cigarettes are not getting a fair scientific shake. They point out that people have thousands of differences other than their smoking habits. Smokers live in different places, work at different occupations, come from different backgrounds, eat different foods, and breathe differing degrees of polluted air. Any one of these differences, they say, may be the critical factor that produces the disease and death rates attributed to cigarettes. Smoking may also be a feature of personality; nervous people smoke and nervous people may also have cancer and heart attacks. Smoking, they suggest, may be an effect rather than a cause.

What About the Antismoking Campaign?

Antismoking campaigns have no real chance to compete against the 80 million dollars spent by the cigarette industry each year for advertising. Good taste, fun, excitement, social status, and a desirable personal flair are associated with smoking in these ads. Thus we banned cigarette commercials from television and radio only to find that the effect of antismoking commercials may have been seriously overestimated (McRae and Nelson, 1971). A survey conducted in Florida showed that those who thought the antismoking commercials were effective were generally nonsmokers, had already quit, or had only recently taken up the habit. In other words, the commercials had their greatest effect on those who smoked the least. The two- and three-pack-a-day smokers said the commercials did not affect them at all.

The mass media do transmit information which makes us react to the inconsistency between what we believe (cigarettes are not good for you) and what we do (smoke). The problem is that we keep on smoking figuring that, if we enjoy it so much, it's worth it. Or, we fear that stopping will endanger our health by allowing us to get fat. Considering the daily barrage of warnings about things that are hazardous to our health, some have decided that being alive is dangerous in itself, and smoking can't make it very much worse.

Summary

1.   Smoking provides an example of a behavior that is inconsistent with the attitude that it is bad for us. Many smokers shrug off the dangers of smoking to make attitude and behavior consistent.

2.   Smokers who can't quit or smoke heavily are known to be impulsive, socially isolated, and, on the surface, extremely self-reliant. They have more car accidents than nonsmokers and are said to have the personality characteristics conducive to accidents.

3.   Most heavy smokers received little affection or warmth while growing up. Most had parents who also smoked.

4.   Methods for kicking the habit vary from excessive smoking to cutting down gradually. Some individuals go to a laboratory where they receive shocks while smoking. The role-playing technique applies the theory of cognitive dissonance. By pretending to be nonsmokers who had to convince smokers to quit, individuals may attempt to reconcile this new attitude with their behavior by giving up cigarettes.

5.   Just as the effect of cigarette ads seems to have been overestimated, antismoking campaigns seem to have had little effect on heavy smokers. Antismoking messages through the media seem to motivate smokers to develop some sort of consistency between the knowledge that smoking is dangerous and smoking itself. In most cases, it is the perception of the danger that changes, not the behavior.

Relating to Others

*Life teaches us to be less severe
with ourselves and others.*—Goethe

It was suggested in the early days of psychology that we relate to our fellow human beings because grouping together, *gregariousness,* is one of man's instincts—the same kind of instinct that causes ants to form ant colonies, elephants to herd, or baboons to establish bands with elaborate social structures. Humans, it was suggested, huddle together without consciously deciding or thinking about it. Whereas it may not be true that there is an instinctive drive to be gregarious, it is at least clear that humans congregate in order to survive. Helpless for some time after birth, the human infant must depend on the mother for security and satisfaction.

Growing up in the company of other human beings makes us dependent on their presence, and being forbidden interaction with them becomes a punishing experience. Our need to affiliate with others becomes crucial to our sense of psychological well-being. We consider other humans important features of our environment. When we want something, other people can provide satisfaction. When we are upset or anxious, our needs for affiliation with others may become particularly acute and pressing.

In 1959 Schachter demonstrated the manifestation of such affiliative needs among anxious female college students. In his experiment, some of the women were frightened by being told that they would receive a series of painful electric shocks. Others were told they would enjoy the experiment. Schachter tested to see if the frightened group had a stronger desire to be with other people by informing each of them they would have to wait ten minutes for the experiment to begin. They could choose to spend this time alone or with others. Only about 33 percent of the less anxious subjects wanted to wait with other persons, whereas nearly twice as many of the anxious subjects preferred to have company while waiting for the experiment to begin. Misery, Schachter concluded, likes company.

And, the company it prefers, according to Zimbardo and Formica (1963), is people anxious about the same things. Anxiety can be relieved, in part, when comparisons are possible with others. To compare yourself with others, you must affiliate with them to learn how frightened you are in contrast. Thus, social comparison is one motive for affiliation. The need for such comparison increases with the degree of uncertainty you are experiencing (Gerard, 1963).

Liking Others

We don't relate to others just to reduce fear. Most often, as we all know, we interact with people because we like them and they like us. It sounds simple, doesn't it? It isn't. Who likes whom and the reason why we call it "liking" are complicated psychological problems.

Beautiful Is Better

It may be only skin deep, but beauty has an important impact upon our lives. Its influence may begin surprisingly early. One study has noted that nursery-school teachers rank their pupils by appearance. Boys judged by their teachers to be relatively unattractive are not as well liked by their classmates as the more attractive boys (Berscheid and Walster, 1969). Unattractive boys are more likely than are attractive boys to be described by their classmates as aggressive and antisocial. When the children are asked to name the one person in their class who scares them, they were more likely to nominate an unattractive classmate than an attractive one. Physical attractiveness may thus contribute substantially to the social development of the child. It affects his self-concept and his first social relationships.

Later in life, when it is dating-and-mating time, physical attractiveness may still be the single most important factor in determining popularity. In a series of studies of blind dates, Berscheid and Walster (1969) found that the more physically attractive a date was, the more he or she was liked. Having an exceptional personality or intelligence made less difference than physical features in determining who liked whom.

These observations were put to the test in a "computer dance" sponsored by the researchers for some college students. The researchers obtained rough estimates of social attributes and ratings of each student's physical appearance. They then matched dates on an almost random basis, except that they were careful that the man was taller than the woman. In interviews after the dance, they discovered how much each person liked his or her date. Again, the degree

IS LOVE PATHOLOGICAL?
Magazines, movies, and television constantly tell us of the joys of love, and psychotherapists insist that the ability to love is a sign of mental health and maturity. Yet, anthropologists tell us of societies in which love is unknown. Such evidence may lead to the conclusion that love is a learned emotion. The more a person satisfies us, the more likely we are to love that person. We love because of our needs for security, sexual satisfaction, and social conformity (Casler, 1969). Defined in this way, love sounds very much like a pathological event rather than a joyous and unique emotion. The question is: Can you distinguish between the symptoms of "love" and the symptoms of "neurotic need"?

What's So Funny?

Humor is both a form of social perception and a form of communication that is apparently quite important to most people. Allport (1961) found that 94 percent of his research subjects rated their sense of humor as equal to or above average. Just what makes things funny has never been fully understood, although many writers have tried to come up with a unifying principle of humor by studying jokes and individual differences in humor appreciation. Although there is no one overall theory to account for different kinds of humor experiences, a few theories seem at least partially correct.

One theory suggests that humor permits us to express superiority, aggression, or sexuality in a socially acceptable fashion. Thus, when one laughs at the discomfort of a disliked or hated person, institution, or practice, one is actually expressing superiority, derision, or contempt. This may account for why we find ourselves laughing at the accidents of others.

Another theory suggests that incongruity is the core of humor.

Incongruity means that the parts of a situation are somehow not "fitting." What we call "fitting" depends partly, of course, upon our past experience. The fact that we sometimes find the unusual customs, or clothes, or manners of people in foreign lands a source of humor is due to the element of incongruity. . . . But it is not the novelty that is responsible for humor. There is nothing funny about seeing a completely new thing; what is required is that we see old things in new and unexpected relations. [McGhee, 1971, p. 254]

We are not born with a sense of humor, of course. Also, our social perception of what is funny changes with age. Wolfenstein (1954) argued that the purpose of humor in children is to overcome distress and frustration. As children develop, Wolfenstein suggests, they become increasingly aware of the restrictions placed on expressing sexual or hostile impulses. The child learns to use the joke as a means of expressing these impulses.

In adult life, humor may serve a variety of purposes. One purpose is communication. In the research reported by Davis and Farina (1970), male experimental subjects were confronted by a very attractive female experimenter whose dress and demeanor were sexually stimulating. They were asked to rate the funniness of a series of cartoons, some of which were clearly sexual in nature. The hypothesis of social communication would predict that subjects would try to convey their interest in the experimenter with increased appreciation of the sexual cartoons. Indeed, the sexual cartoons were rated by the

Some kinds of humorous experiences are difficult to verbalize. If you described the above photo to someone who hadn't seen it, do you think the incongruity would come across?

subjects as being funnier than the nonsexual cartoons.

These experimental results demonstrate that social variables will influence humor appreciation. The results also show that a principal role of humor can be communication with another person. Humor may serve this purpose, for example, when two strangers meet. Neither party knows what the other is willing to talk about. One way of dealing with this problem is to avoid all possibly offensive topics. Another way is to broach a potentially taboo subject by using it in a joke. As Davis and Farina state: *The listener, by providing or withholding laughter, may then indicate whether the topic falls outside the range of topics acceptable to him. This indirect method clearly smooths the process of designating limits, since in this way the listener may reject the offered jest on the pretext that it is simply a poor joke. Had the taboo remark been made openly, it would have been more difficult for the listener to reject the remark without rejecting the speaker at the same time.* [pp. 177–78]

IS LOVE A MISUNDERSTOOD PHYSIOLOGICAL AGITATION?
Psychologists still despair of the study of love because it is an emotional condition that seemingly defies definition and measurement. Two adventuresome researchers, Wolster and Berscheid (1969), have explored this uncharted region. They reached the startling conclusion that, if you are aroused physiologically and choose to call it love, then love is what it is (Wolster and Berscheid, 1971). Love exists when you say it does. Passionate love, according to Wolster (1970), may only be a misnomer for an agitated emotional condition. As he says: "As long as one attributes his agitated state to passion, he should experience true passionate love. As soon as one ceases to attribute his tumultuous feelings to passion, love should die." [p. 10]

of liking depended, to the largest degree, on the attractiveness of the date.

Males, more than females, place a high value on physical attractiveness even though both sexes *claim* that attractiveness is less important than intelligence, friendliness, and sincerity. This does not indicate a discrepancy between belief and behavior, however, since students think good-looking people are generally more sensitive, kind, interesting, strong, poised, modest, sociable, outgoing, and exciting than less-attractive people. For better or worse, most of us seem to like beautiful people more than those who are less favorably endowed. Yet, in a case where you are stranded with just one other person, your liking of that person may depend merely on his or her nearness or availability.

The Nearness of You

If you live in New York and I live in Michigan, it is not likely we will become friends, or like each other, or even get to know each other. In fact, if we lived only ten blocks apart, it would be considerably less likely that we will become friends than if we lived next door to each other. Distances affect contact, which in turn affects liking and our need for one another. Differences of only a few seconds in walking time can be important. If you live in an apartment, for example, the people you know well and the people you like are determined by the distance they live from your apartment door (Festinger, Schachter, and Back, 1950).

A careful study of nearness as a factor in liking was conducted by W. H. Whyte (1956) in a homogenous suburban residential community. Almost everyone had moved into the suburb at about the same time. Whyte read the social column in the newspaper and kept a careful check on who gave parties, who was invited, and who was friendly with whom. At baby showers, for example, almost everyone attending lived within a few blocks of one another. The same held true for other kinds of parties. After a few years most friends lived near one another.

Obviously, people who are close are more available than those who are farther away. But the phenomenon of liking is more complicated than that. Since you anticipate continued interaction with people who are close to you, you tend to exaggerate their positive traits and ignore or play down their negative ones. In a sense, you decide ahead of time to like people who are going to be close to you anyway. You anticipate that getting to know them will be pleasant, and your behavior toward them helps the relationship develop in a mutually satisfactory manner.

Nearness, of course, is not the only factor which affects liking. As you know, people do not always like their next-door neighbors, and roommates often do not like each other. Certainly, not all of our friends are people who live near us. Liking a person also depends on how similar that person is to you.

Peas in a Pod

If you have ever heard of computer dating you know that people are matched on the basis of similar interests and characteristics. Characteristics such as nationality, religion, politics, social class, education, age, sophistication, and skin color are matched in the belief that people who are similar tend to like each other more.

In an experiment in which I participated as an experimental "confederate," Ted Newcomb (1961) took over a residence at the University of Michigan and ran it as an experimental dormitory. The students who lived there agreed to take part in the study. Newcomb controlled room assignments and, on the basis of tests and questionnaires, he assigned some roommates who were similar and others who were dissimilar. The effect of similarity was particularly powerful. The similar roommates generally liked each other and became friends. The dissimilar roommates tended to dislike each other and did not become friends. Newcomb concluded that similar people find it easier to get along because the possibility for reward and mutual reinforcement is increased. Similar values enable them to avoid conflict and behavior that will be upsetting or annoying to each other.

THE ROMEO AND JULIET EFFECT

You are in love, but your parents disapprove. How does their interference affect the love relationship? According to Brehm's (1966) theory of reactance, such parental interference will be interpreted by you as a threat to your freedom, and it will deepen your feeling of romantic love. Driscoll, Davis, and Lipetz (1971) agree. They checked with dating couples and reported that those who felt the greatest parental intrusion also felt they were more deeply in love. Shakespeare, it appears, was a better psychologist than most parents.

If You Like Me, I Like You

Beauty, nearness, and similarity determine part of your decision to like or dislike a person. But a more important element is that you like people who also seem to like you.

Aronson and Linder (1965) staged a fascinating psychological experiment to demonstrate exactly how this works. They had subjects interact with a confederate and then let the subject overhear an interview in which the confederate gave his impressions of the subject. There were four of these "overheard" conversations. In one, the confederate was quite flattering throughout, saying he liked the subject. In another, the confederate was critical. He said he was not sure whether he liked the subject. He described the subject in fairly negative ways and didn't change his opinion from the beginning to the end of the experiment. In the two remaining "overheard" conversations, the confederate began on a positive note and became critical as the conversation continued, or he started out negatively and gradually grew more positive by the end of the discussion.

Have you figured out the results? When the subjects were asked how much they liked the confederate, they said that they liked him when he liked them. They disliked the confederate when he disliked them. The confederate who was liked the most was the one who began by making negative statements and became more and more positive in his descriptions. The confederate who liked a subject at the beginning and continued to like him was also liked, but not to the same degree.

To explain this peculiar twist in our choice of whom we like most, Aronson and Linder suggested that there is a gain-loss effect. Overhearing negative comments about yourself produces anxiety, self-doubt, and other painful feelings which are reduced when appraisal gradually becomes more positive. Hearing good things about yourself is rewarding, but when it also relieves previous painful feelings, it seems to be doubly rewarding. Even if you don't trust or like another person, you will like him more than before if he says something nice about you.

You can, if you wish, conduct a liking experiment of your own. Introduce strangers to each other after privately telling each person that the other is his or her secret admirer. If all other things are equal, they should become friends.

The Dimensions of Liking

Elliot Aronson (1970) examined the host of studies psychologists have done on the liking process and tried to summarize the many forces that affect how we feel about other people:

Nearness. We like those who are physically close to us more than other people because it takes less time and effort to get gratification from persons nearby.

THE BRIGHTEST AND THE BEST, BUT NOT PERFECT
If we have no other information about a person, we like the one who is intelligent, able, and competent more than we like the one who is not (Stotland and Hillmer, 1962).

There may be limits to this relationship, however, (Bramel, 1969). People who are exceptionally competent may make us uncomfortable by being too perfect. Aronson (1970) recalls that a Gallup Poll taken just after the failure of the Bay of Pigs invasion of Cuba showed that President John F. Kennedy's personal popularity had increased rather than decreased. This may have been a sympathetic response to his defeat or, as Aronson sees it, a reflection of how human fallibility in a high-ability person makes that person even more attractive.

Similar values, beliefs, and personal traits. We like people who agree with us more than those who disagree with us, and we like persons who are like us in personal style.

Complementary needs. We like persons who can satisfy our needs and whose needs we can easily satisfy in return.

High ability. We like able and competent persons more than incompetent ones, partly because we expect to gain more through association with them than from others less able and competent.

Pleasant or agreeable behavior. We like persons who are nice or who do nice things for us.

Being liked. We like persons who like us.

In short, even though it doesn't sound very flattering, we like people who give us maximum gratification at minimum expense to ourselves.

Obeying Others

People comply or obey for a variety of reasons. They may be afraid of the consequences if they do not comply. They may be seeking rewards if they do. Or they may feel internal obligations that can be paid off by complying. Every propagandist, door-to-door salesman, and advertiser knows that part of the secret of getting people to comply with your wishes is to induce him or her to agree first to a small request. Once a salesman has his foot in your door, you are much more likely to agree to some larger request. The special no-obligation offers you get in your daily junk mail ask you to react in some way to a product, even if it only amounts to sending back a postage-paid card saying you don't want to take the magazine but you do want to be entered in the sweepstakes.

It would seem that the whole idea of asking for a response with no purchases would be an incredible waste of money, but a study by Freedman and Fraser (1966) suggests that advertisers know what they are doing. To demonstrate how this compliance technique works, experimenters went from door to door pretending to represent a "committee for safe driving." They asked each housewife to sign a petition to be sent to California senators urging the legislators to work for laws that would encourage safe driving. It was hard to resist such a reasonable appeal and almost all the women agreed to sign. Some weeks later other experimenters returned and asked the women to put a large, ugly sign in their front yards saying "Drive Carefully." Would you do it? Over half of the women who had previously agreed to sign the petition agreed to post the sign. In contrast, among women who had not previously complied with the little request, less than 17 percent agreed.

The simplest way to get people to comply, of course, is to exert pressure on them with threats or rewards. But if you are not ready to play rough, there is another way. You can simply put people in a highly managed or controlled situation that exerts subtle pressure by making a refusal very

EYEPATCHES AND COMPLIANCE
Most of us change the way we behave when we interact with persons who are physically handicapped. A surprising number of us don't prefer handicapped persons as companions, don't interact as long with them as we do with nonhandicapped people, and experience some uneasiness around those with a visible handicap. Doob and Ecker (1970) arranged a test of these general observations by asking housewives to fill out a questionnaire and return it through the mail. More housewives agreed to fill out the questionnaire and more actually did so, when the investigator appeared to be handicapped by wearing an eyepatch.

difficult. It becomes very hard not to comply when a person feels he is expected to do so, when the experimenter depends on him, when any other possibility is not very realistic, or when a refusal would be commensurate with breaking a contract. These are the kinds of conditions Stanley Milgram (1963) set up in his controversial study of obedience.

Milgram's Shocking Machine

Milgram was deeply concerned about the submissive, obedient manner in which millions of Jews passively walked to their slaughter in Germany in World War II. He wanted to probe the "obedience to orders" that allowed so many Germans to cooperate in the massive human exterminations that took place from 1933 to 1945. "Gas chambers were built, death camps were guarded, daily quotas of corpses were produced with the same efficiency as the manufacture of appliances. These inhumane policies may have originated in the mind of a single person, but they could only be carried out on a massive scale if a very large number of persons obeyed orders" (p. 371).

Milgram constructed a shocking machine which had an instrument panel with 30 switches set in a horizontal line. Each switch was clearly labeled with a voltage designation ranging from 15 to 450 volts. The ranges of possible shocks were also labeled: Slight Shock, Moderate Shock, Strong Shock, Very Strong Shock, Intense Shock, Extreme Intensity Shock, Danger: Severe Shock. The last two switches were marked XXX. The machine was so convincing that no subject suspected it was a fake.

Thinking they were being paid to take part in a learning experiment, the obedience subjects were instructed to shock the learning "victim" whenever he gave a wrong answer. The subjects were supposed to increase the shock level by 15 volts each time this happened. Each of the subjects was also given a sample jolt of 45 volts. The victim of these procedures, of course, was a paid confederate who never really got any electric shocks at all. He was trained to pretend he was being shocked, and he was instructed to make errors in a controlled sequence that would be the same for each of the subjects in the experiment. When the 300-volt shock was administered, for example, the paid confederate pounded on the wall of the room where he sat strapped to the electric chair. The subject was able to hear his pounding. For shocks greater than 300 volts, the learner's answers no longer appeared on the panel.

When the pounding began, subjects ordinarily turned to the experimenter for advice. The experimenter instructed them to treat the absence of a response as a wrong answer and to shock the victim as previously instructed. When shock reached 315 volts, there was only silence in the room where the victim sat. At this point, if the subjects wanted to stop, the experimenter responded with a sequence of "prods." He used as many prods as necessary to bring the subject into line. These were:

IN THE NAME
OF SCIENCE?
In his book The Rise and Fall of the Third Reich, *William L. Shirer (1960) describes experiments conducted by Dr. Sigmund Rascher on human guinea pigs in Germany during World War II. Rascher's inhumane experiments involved studying the effects of sudden decompression at high altitudes and freezing at subzero temperatures. At the infamous Dachau concentration camp, hundreds of prisoners were dumped into a deep tank of ice water until they died of exhaustion. The horror we feel today about this casual torture and slaughter of innocents was evidently not felt by the German scientists of that era. In October 1942, German scientists met in Nuremberg and discussed the results of these death experiments, and not one protest was voiced. The accounts of these horrors fill the most shameful pages in the history of man.*

Prod 1:   *Please continue, or please go on.*
Prod 2:   *The experiment requires that you continue.*
Prod 3:   *It is absolutely essential that you continue.*
Prod 4:   *You have no other choice; you must go on.*

Before the experiment was actually conducted, it was predicted that only an insignificant number of subjects would go all the way and administer 450 volts to a victim who had stopped answering and ceased pounding on the wall. The results of the experiment, of course, confounded all the predictors. No subject stopped prior to administering Shock Level 20. Of 40 subjects, only 5 refused to go on. Two subjects broke off at the 330-volt level. One stopped at 345 volts, one at 360, and one at 375 volts. A total of 14 subjects defied the experimenter. But, 26 obeyed the orders of the experimenter to the very end, punishing the victim until the most potent shock available on the shock generator was reached. At that point, the experimenter stopped the experiment. Although obedient subjects continued to administer shocks, they often did so under extreme stress. Some were reluctant to administer shocks beyond the 300-volt level. They displayed fears similar to those who defied the experiment, but they obeyed anyway.

There were, of course, substantial pressures on the subjects to obey. The experiment took place in the prestigious laboratories of Yale, and it was apparently designed to advance the case of science. Both the subjects and victims were volunteers. They were being paid to do what the experimenter ordered. And the subjects had been told that the shocks were painful but not dangerous.

Subject and victim were also strangers to each other. In a later experiment, Zimbardo (1970) demonstrated that, if subjects administering shocks cannot be identified (some subjects met their victims while wearing hoods over their heads), they will administer shock with greater aggression to both "nice" and "obnoxious" victims.

As we look back on Milgram's experiment, we must admit that the all too human reactions of his subjects make some sad psychological sense. As we all know from personal experience, most of us comply and obey when we relate to others even though we might wish we hadn't later on. It seems that one of the hardest lessons for humans to learn is how to say no to other people.

The Ethical Storm

Milgram not only contributed some exceptionally provocative knowledge to the field of psychology, he also triggered among psychologists an ethical storm that has yet to subside. We are still arguing whether any contribution to science can justify the use of this degree of deception and trauma with experimental subjects. New rules and safeguards have been drawn up with regard to the humane use of human subjects in research, and I don't think anyone could "get away with" Milgram's experiment today. At the University of Michigan, for example, experimental subjects can choose never to be involved in any experiment that requires deception in any form.

One of the harsher critics of Milgram's work was Baumrind (1964). She believed the study was unethical, and she also contended that it told us very little about obedience in the real world. She objected strenuously to the fact that the subject's rights were not protected. Health examinations were not given to the subjects before the experiment to determine whether some psychological maladjustment or physical condition might exclude them from participation. No prior permission was obtained from the subjects to allow the experimenters to place them in a distressful situation. Baumrind pointed out that there could have been long-term effects. The subjects may have lost trust in the credibility of future experimenters or science in general.

Before the experiment the subjects probably saw themselves as gentle persons who would not inflict pain upon another person if they could help it. After the experiment, they might have been painfully forced to reevaluate themselves. Ethically and morally, we must also ask how far we can go in the name of research. Do we really have a right to set up an experimental situation where some subjects "sweat, stutter, tremble, groan, bite their lips, and dig their fingernails into their flesh"? Milgram also reported that "full-blown, uncontrollable seizures were observed for three subjects" (1963, p. 375).

Finally, psychologists raised objections to the "superficial" debriefing given to the subjects when the experiment was over. Milgram stated: "After the interview, procedures were undertaken to assure that the subject would leave the laboratory in a state of well being. A friendly reconciliation was arranged between the subject and the victim, and an effort was made to reduce any tensions that arose as a result of the experiment" (1963, p. 374). This comment was not very reassuring, however, since some found it hard to believe that such extreme tension could be erased by a quick debriefing procedure. Milgram reported (1964, 1968) that follow-up interviews indicated no long-term bad effects on the subjects. But even this did little to pacify his angry fellow psychologists.

Ethical or not, Milgram's work taught us something about human nature. It taught us that obedience is much more usual than any of us had suspected. It also taught us that the matter of how we relate to one another is an area which richly deserves deeper exploration by psychologists.

Perceiving Others

Accurate perception of the people around us, and their accurate perception of us, is necessary for the fulfillment of a great many of our psychological and social needs.

Body Language

We all are "people watchers" who hope to learn about the personality, emotions, and thoughts of others through their gestures, posture, and facial expressions—their body language. Linguists, anthropologists, psychiatrists, and psychologists have all tried to crack the code and transcribe body motion into meaningful communication. But so far decoding has been less than adequate. According to Duncan (1969), nonverbal communication includes: *kinesic behavior* (body motions, gestures, eye movement, posture, and facial expression), and *proxemics* (the use and perception of social and personal space).

A classic example of how body language works was reported by Fast (1971). While a young woman was telling her psychiatrist that she loved her boyfriend very much, she shook her head from side to side in subconscious denial of what she was saying. To understand the messages being given by another person, body language and spoken language must be considered together. Spoken language alone will not give us the full meaning of what a person says, nor for that matter will body language alone. If we listen only to a person's words, we may get as much distortion as we would if we listened only to the body language. As Birdwhistell warns: "No body position or movement, in and of itself, has a precise meaning." Such naive interpretations of kinesics are more suited to parlor games or cocktail conversation than to serious attempts to understand interpersonal communications.

Everyone in our society learns eye management (Fast, 1971). We do not stare at another person as we stare at art, scenery, or animals. A prolonged gaze, however, does signify love and attraction. But long gazes can also be aggressive, depending on the situation and the rest of the facial expression. Sunglasses pose a problem, because you can't tell if a person is staring, gazing, or even looking at you at all. The sunglasses wearer, on the other hand, feels protected, as if by hiding his eyes he can also mask his thoughts.

If we are having a conversation, how do you know when I am through speaking and it is your turn? According to Kendon (1967), when I finish speaking, I will look at you and will continue to look at you until you begin speaking. As you begin your reply, you will look away from me, and return your eyes in my direction when you have finished. If you don't look at me to signal the end of your statement, I may delay my response, or I may even remain silent. Kendon also noted that we speak more fluently and more rapidly if we look at the listener. If either of us hesitates while speaking, we most often will look away from the listener. Without the benefit of specific teaching, we learn the looking signals proper to each role.

How we position our body in relation to other human beings is another way to send messages. Where a person sits in a classroom, how close he stands when talking to others, or how he defends or yields his "personal space" at a party, are all *proxemic communications*.

One of the earliest experimental attempts to invade personal space on a systematic basis was undertaken by Williams (1963) who wanted to learn how different people would react to excessive closeness. After classifying students as introverts or extroverts on the basis of a personality test, he placed each individual in an experimental room and then walked toward the person telling him to speak out as soon as he came too close. He then reversed the condition by starting at a very close point and moving away until the person reported that he was too far away for comfortable conversation. His results showed that introverts keep people at a greater conversational distance than do extroverts.

Edward T. Hall (1967) described various sets of distances. *Intimate distance* is the space between full contact and 18 inches apart. *Casual-personal distance* is 18 inches to 48 inches, and *social-consultative distance* is between 4 and 12 feet. *Public distance* extends from 12 feet to the maximum carrying distance of the voice. These distance sets do not apply to all cultures, however. Arabs, for example, prefer closer contact than Americans. They may stand close together, stare into each others' eyes, and breathe into each others' faces when talking—all of which might be disturbing to someone not used to this much closeness.

People form extensive impressions of others on the basis of very limited information. If you see someone (or even his picture) for only a few minutes, you tend to make judgments about that person's intelligence, age, background, race, religion, educational level, and so on. Newcomb, Turner, and Converse (1965) listed a series of factors that are important in forming our interpersonal impressions. One important factor, called *primacy,* is the information we get

WHAT LARGE EYES
YOU HAVE

Hess (1965) reports that magicians doing card tricks can identify the card a person is thinking about by watching his pupils enlarge when the card is turned up. Chinese jade dealers supposedly watch a buyer's pupils to know when he is impressed by a specimen and is likely to pay a high price. Pursuing these clues, Hess constructed an apparatus whereby the subject peers into a box and looks at a stimulus picture projected on a screen. The apparatus is arranged so that the size of the pupil of his eye can be photographed as he views the stimulus picture.

In a series of pictures shown to a group of 20 men, Hess and his coworker Polt included two photographs of an attractive young woman. These two slides were identical except for the fact that one had been retouched to make the woman's pupils extra large, and the other had been altered to make her pupils very small. The average response to the picture with large pupils was more than twice as strong as the response to the picture with small pupils. When the men were questioned after the experimental session, however, most of them reported that the two pictures were identical. No subjects noticed that one picture showed larger pupils than the other.

about a person in the early stages of contact. This information tends to be remembered and also influences our future impression of the person. Another important factor is *vividness,* whereby an outstanding characteristic tends to be important in determining impressions. Also *frequency,* or characteristics that appear often, is influential in determining impressions.

The characteristics of the observer make up another factor that influences the impressions he forms of others. Temporary *motivational* or *emotional states* can influence our impressions of others. We are more likely to see others as sad if we are sad ourselves. Our impressions of others are also shaped by our own *attitudes.* If you have strong political opinions, you are particularly likely to notice the political opinions of others. *Preconceptions* are one more influence on our impressions. Stereotypes are an excellent example of this type of thinking. One final source of influence is *persistent personality characteristics.* Bossom and Maslow (1957) segregated students (on the basis of a test) into a "secure" group and an "insecure" group. Both groups of students looked at 200 photographs and judged each as "very warm," "cold," or "very cold." The "secure" group made a significantly greater number of "warm" judgments than did the "insecure" group, demonstrating that personality characteristics have a significant effect on our impressions of others.

Asch has researched the so-called *central traits,* which produce the tendency to assume from the presence of one human trait that a person also has other related traits. Knowing that someone is inconsiderate leads most people to expect that person to be boastful, cold, and hypocritical as well. But as Bruner, Shapiro, and Tagiuri (1958) point out, these inferences are not derived logically from the given trait. They are based on the individual's assumptions about personality. Asch (1946) theorized that our impression of another person is not simply the total of all the information we have about that person. Instead, the process of forming an impression is a dynamic event in which some pieces of information are important enough to modify the whole impression. One central trait that can affect the organization of our impressions pertains to the warm-cold dimension. When Asch used the adjective *cold* in a list of experimental stimulus words, only about 10 percent of the subjects said that the person so described would also be *generous* or *humorous.* When the adjective *warm* was used (instead of *cold*), about 90 percent of the subjects described that person as also being *generous.* More than 75 percent described the person as *humorous.*

Familiarity is an even more subtle influence on our judgment of other people. Zajonc (1968, 1970) conducted a series of experiments to demonstrate that familiarity leads to a positive perception. One study used pictures of faces. Some faces were shown to subjects as many as 25 times, whereas others were shown only once or twice. Subjects were asked how much they liked each face and how much they thought they would like the person in the picture. Familiarity appeared to have a significant effect. The more often the subjects had seen a face, the more they liked it.

Judging Others

Taft (1955) reports that people who are good judges of others tend to have high intelligence, good emotional adjustment, esthetic and dramatic interests, and to specialize in the physical sciences rather than in psychology. This last item is certainly not pleasing to psychologists. Cronbach (1955) and others explain, however, that as a judge you will usually be more accurate if most of your judgments are in the middle of the range of possibilities, since most individuals actually are in that middle range. If you make many extreme judgments, you are more likely to be mistaken. Cronbach suggests, in other words, that psychologists may be oversensitive to individual differences and make too many extreme judgments.

When judging others, we sometimes make errors because we assume the other person is more like ourselves than he actually is. This may be a problem that starts in early childhood. In a study by Dornbush and his colleagues (1965), every child at a camp was asked to describe every other child. These descriptions were then analyzed. What was interesting was that each child tended to use the same characteristics no matter whom he was describing. The campers differed among themselves as to which characteristics they used. But each child had favorite characteristics he considered important, and he used them for almost all his descriptions. If our childish perceptual habits persisted into adulthood, we obviously would be poor judges of others.

Bumper Stickers and Perception

In 1969 the members of the Black Panther Party complained of harassment by law enforcement officers. They had received so many traffic citations that some were in danger of losing their driving privileges. As it happened, all of them drove automobiles with Panther Party signs glued to their bumpers. Heussenstamm (1971) decided to assess the truth of their charges by selecting 15 research drivers (five black, five white, and five of Mexican descent) for an experiment. Each group included three males and two females.

All participants in the study had model driving records and were assigned cars ranging from a "flower-child," hippie-type van to standard American makes of all kinds. Then, stickers in day-glo orange and black with a menacing panther and the words **BLACK PANTHER** in large letters were attached to the rear bumper of each car. *The first student received a ticket for making an "incorrect lane change" on the freeway less than two hours after heading home in the rush hour traffic. Five more tickets were received by others on the second day for "following too closely," "failing to yield the right of way," "driving too slowly in the high-speed lane of the freeway," "failure to make a proper signal before turning right at an intersection," and "failure to observe proper safety of pedestrians using a crosswalk." On day three, students were cited for "excessive speed," "making unsafe lane changes" and "driving erratically." And so it went every day.*

One student was forced to drop out of the study by day four, because he had already received three citations. Three others reached what we had agreed was the maximum limit—three citations—within the first week. Altogether, the participants received 33 citations in 17 days, and the violations fund was exhausted. [Heussenstamm, 1971, p. 33]

The conclusion seemed obvious. Certainly, it was statistically unlikely that so many previously "safe" drivers could amass such a collection of tickets. Evidently, then, there was a real bias by police against drivers who were perceived as Black Panther supporters.

What do you see in this picture? Depending on your social orientation, you might perceive a beautiful young woman or an ugly old one. Can you see both? Look closely—if you need a clue, let the choker be a mouth, the earring be an eye, or vice versa.

Groups and Perceiving Others

The effect of groups on what we perceive and how we behave was demonstrated by Muzafer Sherif (1936). He seated students individually in a completely darkened room and asked them to judge how far a tiny point of light had moved. The fact was that the light was stationary, and movement was only apparent. This apparent movement is called the *autokinetic effect* and happens when there is no anchoring point in perception. Initially, each subject had varied perceptions of how far the light seemed to move. Before long, a unique range was established for each subject, and all of his later guesses were made within this range. After each subject had individually performed three sessions of judgments, he was brought together with one or two other students. Each person was again asked to say how far he thought the light moved. The subjects' initial judgments were generally at odds with one another, but gradually their estimates began to converge about a range that was unique to each particular group. The people in one group, therefore, influenced one another to create a group norm regarding the apparent movement of the light. This norm then influenced their individual perceptions of the apparent movement.

When studying group influence on perception, we have to ask whether a small minority can influence the majority enough to create new norms. Evidence suggests this can happen and probably does happen frequently in real life. In one experiment, 32 groups of coeds were told that they were participating in a study on color perception. Each group was made up of four naive subjects and two confederates. A given hue was projected on a screen, and the subjects were asked to name the color and give it an intensity rating. In some groups, when a blue color appeared, both confederates would consistently call it "green." In other groups, the confederates would call the color "green" but only on two-thirds of the trials. When the confederates consistently disagreed with the majority, 32 percent of the subjects followed their lead. But only 1 percent of the subjects followed the lead of the confederates when they were inconsistent in their judgment. Right or wrong, a vocal minority can have an effect on what we perceive (Moscovici, Lage, and Naffrechoux, 1969; Faucheux and Moscovici, 1967).

The Face of the Enemy. How and what we perceive can be affected by a phenomenon called *perceptual filtering.* Jerome D. Frank (1968) performed an experiment with a device that simultaneously showed a different picture to each eye. When looking through this device, one eye would see a picture of a baseball player, and the other eye would see a bullfighter. Frank asked one group of American teachers and one group of Mexican teachers to use the viewer. He reported that an overwhelming proportion of the Americans "saw" the baseball player, just as an overwhelming proportion of Mexicans "saw" the bullfighter. What these teachers saw was mostly determined by their cultural filters. They saw what they were accustomed to seeing and what they expected to see.

The behavior of nations and their perceptions of each other can also be distorted by their cultural filters. If Russian and American self-images are examined by reading materials published in each nation, it will be found that nearly 100 percent of the articles from both countries describe the adversary's goal as one of international domination or expansion. Both Americans and Russians perceive the other country's *leaders* as being the real villains. It is mutually supposed that the masses in the other nation are discontented and would overthrow their leaders if they could. In this way, the leaders become the visible devils on whom hostility and hatred are focused.

It is also known that our social perceptions can shift (Frank, 1968). In polls taken in 1942, the first three adjectives chosen to characterize the Germans and the Japanese were: *warlike, treacherous,* and *cruel.* Not one of these adjectives was among the top three used to describe Russians (our allies then). By 1966, all three of these adjectives had disappeared from descriptions of the Germans and Japanese, and the Russians were seen as "warlike" and "treacherous." Predictably, by 1966, the Communist Chinese had also become "warlike" and "treacherous" and "cruel." In 1973 the social perception of the People's Republic of China began to shift again as did our views about the North Vietnamese. There seems to be no limit to how our social perceptions can change. As Frank reminds us, the American image of the German people has flipped four times in less than half a century.

What *others* think and do—especially those others who are closest to us—obviously affects what *we* think and do. Let's look now at the role *conformity* plays in making other people so influential in our lives.

Conformity

To most of us, *conformity* is a dirty word evoking images of robot-like acceptance of the attitudes, opinions, and beliefs of others. It makes us think of controlling our thoughts and behavior so that others will accept us and approve of us. Buckling under to group pressure suggests that we are too weak to think for ourselves. Our heroes are the nonconformists of the world who march to the sound of a different drummer. As individuals we all may resent having to conform to the majority even though we understand it is the price of living in social groups without anarchy and chaos.

Cultural Conformity

There are cultural expectations to which we all conform without really being aware of it. The foods we eat and enjoy in our society may be repulsive to those in other cultures. Indeed, most aspects of how we relate to one another in business, dating, marriage, and friendship differ from culture to culture. Cultural norms exist to make our behavior predictable and to make day-to-day life much simpler.

You can test the truth of this observation if you visit a culture markedly different from our own. You will find it takes time to learn a new set of rules to fit all the behaviors you so automatically performed at home. In Thailand, for example, you might not know what to think when you see men walking down the street hand in hand. You might not understand why people are offended when you point your feet at them while sitting in your customary comfortable position. In India, you might persist in arguing with someone who keeps shaking his head "no." In fact, he is nodding "yes" or indicating that he is paying attention.

Conformity is often a pattern of behavior that oils the gears of social relations. It allows us to communicate with one another in an unambiguous manner. In a sense, it is like having a mutual answer to a problem so each one of us doesn't have to solve the equation over and over again. Uniformity in behavior is not the same as conformity. There may be general agreement about proper behavior in a society without social pressures as its source (Krech, Crutchfield, and Ballachey, 1962). Still there is a difference between conventions that require us to drive on the same side of the street and conformity that involves bowing down before every social breeze that comes along. Compliance to social demands is not the same as conformity. Einstein did not conform to the thinking of his fellow physicists or to the dress code of most professors, but he also did not devote his life to fighting such conventions.

Personal Conformity

At first it seems obvious that everyone knows what it means to be a conformist. But Kiesler (1969) reports that the meaning of *conformity* may range from

What some have labeled the "unisex" look is not just a phenomenon in the San Francisco Bay Area or other urban centers in the United States. This couple was photographed on the streets of London.

simply going along with a group to changing your attitudes or beliefs in response to group pressure. Conformity has many dimensions. Not too long ago, for example, the students at my university went on strike to support demands for admitting a greater percentage of minority students to the university. In discussions with students in my classes, it became apparent that some conformed (stayed away from classes) because they supported the movement. Others conformed despite the fact that they privately felt it was wrong to close the university. They didn't want to risk disapproval of their peers. In much the same way the "nonconformists" who continued to attend classes consisted of some who were against the strike and some who supported it, but feared they would lose their scholarships or incur parental disapproval.

Being independent also has many dimensions. Some of us form private beliefs and attitudes which we are simply unwilling to change when confronted by others who disagree with us. But it is hard to distinguish the independent person from the individual who rejects group pressure just because he or she is rebellious. We all know people who are always, on principle, opposed to the majority opinion. Such people will regularly be against anything the rest of us agree on. It seems to be "their thing" to appear to be an independent thinker, uninfluenced by the views of others.

Seeing Is Not Believing?

A classic experiment in conformity was conducted by Asch in 1951. Asch firmly believed that people are more independent than we believe them to be, and he designed an experiment to demonstrate that they would stand by their beliefs and perceptions even in the face of unanimous disagreement. He assembled subjects to participate in an experiment in visual judgment. The subjects sat around a table and judged lines of various lengths.

Only one member of each group was a geniune subject. All the others were stooges who deliberately exaggerated the length of the lines when reporting their judgments. The task was easy, and there were no disagreements at first. As the group judgments became more frequently and obviously wrong, the one real subject was faced with a difficult choice. He had to disagree with a unanimous majority or give an answer he knew was incorrect. The results reversed Asch's predictions. The subjects conformed to the false group consensus on about 35 percent of the trials.

In the various experiments, some subjects never conformed, and some conformed all the time. Overall, the conforming response was given about one time in every three. When subjects were interviewed later, most admitted that they didn't really believe the lines were that long. Their behavior clearly demonstrated how one is tempted to go along with the crowd, at least for a short time.

The pressure to conform works for almost any other absurdity you would care to use in an experiment. When you are faced with a unanimous group opinion, even if incorrect, the pressure of the majority is powerful enough to produce a fair degree of conformity. People conform to other people, even if it means going against their own perceptions of the world. They may not accept what the others are saying as the truth, but when asked to respond, they will give the same response that the others give. This is the basic definition of conformity.

To Conform or Not to Conform

To an astonishing degree, the decision to conform or not to conform in each situation in your life depends on how willing you are to be a social deviant. Thus, if you want others to like you and accept you, you will regularly be tempted to agree with them because by now you have learned what happens to deviants.

More than two decades ago, Schachter (1951) demonstrated how an experimental group reacts to deviants in its midst. He coached three stooges as follows: One was told to take a position consistently deviant from the group. Another was told to begin by being deviant and then change. And the last was told always to take the same position as the other members of the group. When the experimental "plants" did as they were told, the

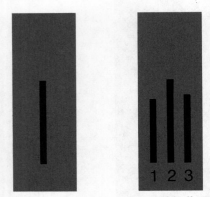

How good is your perceptual discrimination? Look first at the line on the left, then match it with line 1, 2, or 3 on the right. In one trial of Solomon Asch's experiment, much to the agitation of the one true subject, Asch's confederates insisted that line 1 was closest to the line on the left. How do you think you would react if everyone around you was giving what you believed to be a wrong answer?

Growing Independent

From preadolescence to adolescence the amount of conformity to external social pressure increases. It then seems to decline steadily after adolescence and into early adulthood. Developing a pattern of conforming behavior parallels the socialization process. In the early years we are not fully aware of social pressures to conform to the standards of our peers. The young child does not feel threatened by standing alone in thought or behavior, but this changes with pubescence. At about this time, the child becomes sharply conscious of his peers and begins to rely on them to determine his own behavior patterns. Uncertainty about personal judgment may produce slavish imitation of peers. This stage passes as experience teaches us that there are times and situations for conformity and times when independent action is proper. For most of us the day comes when we know we must make our own decisions despite the unanimous majority of peers that may oppose us (Costanzo and Shaw, 1966).

behavior of the other group members shifted so as to bring about greater conformity in the deviants.

If the deviant maintained his position, the others stop communication with him. They decided he was beyond hope, and they then ignored him. They also reported that they liked him less than those who agreed with the group. The group effectively rejected the deviant. When it came to assigning jobs, the deviant was never elected to important posts and was never chosen the leader. Rather, he was often assigned the worst jobs.

It is not necessary to coach confederates to produce this group action. If group members don't know one another and you tell them that one member of the group is different from the others (even if you don't tell the group exactly how he is different), this deviant will be mistreated, in a variety of ways, by the "nondeviants" (Freedman and Doob, 1968). The perils of nonconformity are clear, but the pressures to conform vary from situation to situation. Thus, you are much more apt to conform to group norms if the group has, in your eyes, a particularly high status. You will also tend to conform if you feel very close to the group, if you enjoy being a member of it, and if you like your fellow members. The more you care about being a member of a group, the more you will fear rejection. By the same token, if you feel secure and accepted by the group, you are more comfortable when disagreeing with its members. You know such disagreement will not jeopardize their feeling for you (Dittes and Kelley, 1956).

Nonconformity also loves company. A unanimous group is particularly difficult to defy. But if just one person, of either high or low status in the group, does not go along with the rest, it makes it much easier for a second person to disagree with the others.

It is important to point out that, if you are truly confident of your own judgment and willing to rely on it come hell or high water, you are much more likely not to conform. In an ambiguous situation, your own uncertainty is more likely to tempt you to go along with group opinion. As a series of studies has demonstrated, being male or being female also makes a difference in your readiness to conform (Julian et al. 1966, 1967). Simply put, women conform more than men do in almost every circumstance—not drastically more, but significantly more. This finding appears again and again in a variety of different studies. Obviously, our society rewards conformity for women (and they learn the lesson well), while it encourages nonconformity (within certain limits) for men. How we relate to others reflects how each of us solves the conformity-nonconformity puzzle.

Summary

1. It has been suggested that humans instinctively desire the company of other humans. Whether or not this is actually true, psychologists are fairly certain that we learn to value affiliation with others because they provide things we need.

2. Humor appreciation can be influenced by our social surroundings. Humor may result from noticing incongruity in the relations of elements, or it may result from a need to express forbidden feelings or taboo subjects. Humor is often used as a safe means of communication.

3. Many studies, as well as our daily lives, have demonstrated that beautiful people are more popular, whereas uglier ones tend to be disliked. Physical attractiveness may be valued in and of itself, but most individuals also associate positive personality traits with good-looking people.

4. We tend to like and become more friendly with people who live close to us. This is not only because we see them more often but also because our anticipation of having to deal with them frequently makes us look for their best traits.

5. People who are similar tend to like each other. They find it easier to get along because similar attitudes and behaviors make it likely that they will reward each other in interactions.

6. Even if you dislike a person initially, the fact that you think the person likes you means you will like him or her in return.

7. Psychologists are still puzzling over what makes individuals comply with the demands of others. One of the best ways of assuring compliance is to get the person to comply to a small request at first and then slowly increase the size of your demands.

8. The controversial shocking experiment conducted by Stanley Milgram illustrated how most humans will conform to requests to hurt another human being if they are placed in a situation that makes refusal difficult.

9. The Milgram experiment caused a storm in the psychological world because of the stress it placed on college student subjects and the possible long-term effects it might have had on subjects who discovered they were willing to inflict pain on helpless individuals. Other critics complained that the experiment did little toward explaining obedience in the real world.

10. There are two parts to body language: *kinesics* (movements, gestures, eye contact, and posture); and *proxemics* (the way we use space between ourselves and others). One can judge the meaning of body language only in relation to the entire behavior pattern. A particular movement in body language does not always convey the same message. Movements may contradict the spoken message, support it, or add new information.

11. People form extensive opinions of others from minimal information. We form our impressions by focusing on information we gather in early contacts (primacy); outstanding characteristics of the person (vividness); and characteristics which appear often (frequency).

12. Our impressions of others may also be influenced by our emotional state, our own personality characteristics, or our preconceptions. If we have strong attitudes about certain events or ideas, we will also be sure to notice them in others.

13. Because our information about others is limited and often gathered in bits and pieces, we may organize our ideas about people's personalities from only a few traits. Characteristics that carry enough weight to organize or modify our impressions are called *central traits.*

14. Perception of others will also depend on how often you interact. Familiarity does not necessarily breed contempt. Usually it leads to more positive judgments.

15. In general, a person who is oversensitive to individual differences is not as good at judging others as a less sensitive person might be. A more sensitive person tends to make judgments that are too extreme.

16. One reason why our impressions of others may be wrong is that we assume people are similar to ourselves. This, of course, is not always true. We also tend to use the same dimensions in describing all people. This tendency is especially seen in children.

17. Group pressure can also influence the accuracy of our judgments, particularly when the stimuli are ambiguous. Further, this pressure need not come from a majority of the group members. A consistent minority opinion will also alter our impressions.

18. Our collective perceptions as a nation are often as distorted as our individual views. Moreover, distortions usually depend on whether another country is an enemy or friend.

19. Conformity to cultural norms is usually necessary to make everyday life simpler and smoother. Most of us conform to society's expectations without really thinking of it as conformity.

20. Conformity to social pressure is at a minimum when we are very young, becomes much greater in adolescence, and declines again as we near adulthood.

21. Often you cannot tell why a person conforms to the expectations of others. Some people conform because they actually believe in their actions. Others conform because they fear disapproval from members of their peer group. By the same token, some people refuse to conform because of their beliefs or attitudes, while others merely wish to appear rebellious.

22. The results of the classic conformity study by Asch were surprising at the time because the experimenter did not think as many people would conform to group pressure as they did. In his line-judging experiments, Asch found that most people agreed with the rest of the group, not because they accepted the judgment as accurate, but because they wanted to keep in line with their peers.

23. Whether or not you will conform to a group attitude or behavior depends on how highly you value the group, how willing you are to suffer the fate usually accorded deviants, or how sure you are of your acceptance by the group even when you express deviant opinions.

Encounter

Relating to other people didn't seem to be a difficult psychological problem in generations past. The observation that relating seems to be a problem now is supported by the unprecedented growth of encounter groups on the American scene. One psychologist estimates that more than six million people have by now participated in some kind of encounter. These have mostly been middle-class Americans including students, lawyers, policemen, clergymen, housewives, businessmen, teachers, and doctors. Encounter has become a kind of revolution in interpersonal relations.

The seed was planted more than a quarter of a century ago by Kurt Lewin, the founder of Group Dynamics and creator of the first T-groups (training groups) in 1947 (Egan, 1970). About the same time Carl Rogers and his associates developed a theory of intensive group interaction. A group of strangers could become close personal companions, if only briefly, provided they could be left to their own devices. Ideas such as these flowered as the social times grew ripe. Today, as Sampson stated: "The housewife who finds little intimacy in her relationship with her husband, the salesman who finds little that is fulfilling in his work, the student who remains puzzled by the empty promises of his university, all come flocking to the T-group seeking a sense of belonging and a momentary closeness to other human beings. . . . In a real sense, then, the T-group movement is like a new religion for these persons" (1971, pp. 280–81).

What Happened to Society?

Eleanor Hoover (1972) suggests that the encounter movement mirrors the stresses and strains in the American personality. Encounter groups are answering pressing social needs which have not been met through the efforts of social scientists. Ruitenbeek (1970) says our enthusiasm for the encounter-group experience is due to the fact that contemporary society no longer provides its people with the natural qualities that enable them to satisfy their needs in a spontaneous, unstructured manner.

Carl Rogers says that in the highly mobile, high-density society of the future, the ability to make short-range, strong, effective relationships and the ability to relinquish them easily will be one of the preconditions of psychic survival (Back, 1972b). If structured encounter groups are indeed the wave of the future in human relations, we need to take a closer look at their dimensions.

Encounter—All Shapes and Kinds

The encounter movement encompasses an enormous range of variation. There are groups involved with sensory awareness, expressive movement, environmental awareness, social-emotional expression, problem solving, creativity, social sensitivity, social competence, and mystical experience (Mann, 1970). It is not possible here to catalogue the incredibly explosive variations in helping people relate to one another. We can choose just a few examples to give the flavor of group encounter, however.

Buyer Beware. Shostrum (1969) lists a series of "nevers" that apply to selecting an encounter group:
1. Never respond to a newspaper ad for group experiences.
2. Never participate in a group of fewer than six persons.
3. Never join a group on impulse or as a fling.
4. Never join a group whose members are already close associates of yours.
5. Never be overimpressed by fancy settings or surroundings for the group sessions.
6. Never stay with a group that has a theoretical ax to grind.
7. Never participate in a group whose leaders do not have professional connections or credentials.
This advice has increased in value in recent years as the variety of encounter groups has expanded beyond belief.

Marathon   Marathon groups sometimes seem to their participants to amount to endurance contests. The sheer elapse of time forces participants to put aside their social masks, hopefully to reveal the real self.

The rules of marathon are fairly simple (Lamott, 1969). Everyone stays until the end, and only the therapist is allowed to take naps. Physical assault is forbidden, but brutal frankness may be encouraged. No alcohol or drugs are allowed. Openness and intimacy are the watch words, and behavior in the group itself (not prestige and status in the outside world) is all that matters. Each marathon has different rules. In general, however, marathon regulations are designed to force intense personal contacts which are "real," rather than "polite" human interactions. Marathon groups are designed to help persons find an immediate breakthrough in some particular crisis of living (Shepard and Lee, 1970).

Bioenergetics   Bioenergetics emphasizes bodily contact and physical encounter as ways of liberating our bodies from the artificial controls we impose on them. The theory of structural integration called *Rolfing* is prominent in bioenergetics. Since Rolfing assumes that your attitudes and feelings are visible in your bodily movement, massage by a Rolf practitioner is used to correct the structural integration of the muscles and ligaments of the body. This frees the body of bad habits accumulated during childhood and allows an emotional release that could be the beginning of a new you (Keen, 1970).

Naked Encounter   The naked encounter is a deliberate attempt to divest us of the disguise our clothing provides. Shedding your clothes reveals also the inner self to others. In a recent innovation, for example, video tapes are made of the naked participants during sessions. Each person is then given several opportunities to view his behavior and physical appearance through video tape playbacks. The tapes include facial closeups, shots from the waist up, and full body profiles, as well as shots of walking, standing, turning, sitting, and talking.

Part of the purpose of this public encounter with the self was described by Blank (1969), who noted that the human body and our feelings about it are vital dimensions of our view of the self and of the world. Our body image is our idea of how our own bodies

You Take Your Chances. One out of 10 people who get involved with an encounter group is liable to become a "casualty," says psychologist Bruce L. Maliver. A casualty, he says, is "someone who, six months later, has a symptom or problem of serious, measurable psychiatric proportions that he did not have when he went into the group." And the lay person is in no position to determine ahead of time whether he or she will be among the unfortunate 10 percent or whether the group will be of the "casualty-inducing" type.

At present there are about 180 growth centers in the country, and the encounter industry takes in about $35 million a year. In his opinion, the 750,000 to 1,000,000 people who get involved with encounter groups each year are not getting their money's worth.

First of all, there is no screening in encounter groups. In group therapy you have a diagnostic procedure whereby the therapist interviews the individual to decide whether he belongs in therapy, whether he belongs on medication, or whether he needs no treatment at all.

The next critical difference is that there is no sustained follow-through in encounter groups. Nobody takes responsibility for developing and continuing a treatment plan. Nobody stays around to pick up the pieces if you have difficulty later.

appear to others, and this image often does not agree with the images that others hold of us.

Whatever the method employed to achieve an altered way of relating to others, the aim of encounter is to bring people closer together psychologically and emotionally. The idea is to open new vistas of thought and feeling, to expand our sense of mutual trust and openness, and to increase our sensitivity to one another (Morgan and King, 1971).

The Critics Speak

Kurt Back (1972a) has been a most vocal critic of encounter groups. He insists that it has become increasingly true in sensitivity training that one is either in it or out of it. Further, the attraction to it has had the nature of a religious experience. "The paradox of much of sensitivity training [is] . . . that it is an anti-intellectual movement in the name of science . . . the followers of the movement are quite immune to rational argument or persuasion. The experience they are seeking exists, and the believers are happy in their closed system which shows them that they alone have true insights and emotional beliefs. . . . Thus it wants . . . to become a cult, a new religion of the age of Aquarius" (pp. 30–31).

William Blanchard (1970) is even more blunt. He says that "ecstasy without agony is baloney," and growth centers have become pawns in a race for prestige.

Growth centers compete with one another to sign up leaders with the most prestige and to billboard the most impressive-sounding seminar titles. There is a rush to invent new and different awareness-enhancing techniques. . . . William Schutz at Esalen began with a rather modest promise of "Joy," following it with "More Joy." Herbert Otto . . . introduced "Peak Joy." . . . Then the Elysium Institute at Los Angeles countered with "Cosmic Joy" and "Advanced Cosmic Joy," for which the "Awakening Seminar" is a prerequisite. Any day now we can anticipate a program on Super Advanced Cosmic Joy. Like the makers of Tide, Bold and Ivory soap, the seminarists are always improving their product. [p. 8]

Professionals in therapeutic fields are equally, but less dramatically, cautious about this recent social development. They say a cult is spreading—a cult that preaches sensitivity, humanism, and openness while cloaking itself in an aura of pseudopsychotherapy. They remind potential consumers of encounter that almost every form of psychological therapy assumes that lasting psychological change must change the way you habitually handle your fears and your unconscious problems. It is difficult to believe that the complexities of human psychology can be reduced to the shot-in-the-arm treatment of brief group encounter. Psychological insight, they say, is not achieved that easily or quickly. They point to the fact that reunions of group members a few weeks or months later are notoriously badly attended despite the fact that tears and avowals of undying love are common at the first parting. Critics accept Back's (1972b) observation that, one way or another, protection for the consumer must come since sensitivity training is at the end of an era. "Its ideas are no longer new. The glamor has faded. Social scientists are waiting for hard-research results, and even the popular media are abandoning the wide-eyed picture of the breakthrough in human relations" (p. 34).

Traditional therapists are most bothered by the idea that encounter groups have only recently moved from the psychological laboratories into the outside world. They have yet to calculate the cost, in human terms, of such a venture (Cashdan, 1970). Critics are demanding standards of training and preparation for group leaders to protect the public from bad group theory and questionable group practices (Lakin, 1970). Kenneth Goodall (1971) reported that the casualty rate from group encounters may be as high as 10 percent. Campbell and Dunnette (1968) also indicated that the evidence of the ability of groups to induce lasting behavioral changes is questionable since accounts are often no more than individual testimonials.

My personal conclusion about the encounter group experience is that no method of interaction between human beings will affect all persons equally. No approach will be effective in all homes later on. We need to know which part of the process affects which life situation and how it is effective. T-group outcomes need to be compared with other forms of influencing human beings. The exact nature of the individual's experience and his interaction with the group needs to be explicit and measurable before we can draw trustworthy conclusions. We need to answer questions about the structure of T-groups, the time period, the setting, and the participants. When we finally do appraise the encounter group, I think it will prove to be valuable. I also believe it is not and never was intended to be a solution to all human problems.

Summary

1.   The aim of encounter groups is to bring people together to increase trust, openness, and sensitivity. The idea is to make individuals aware of the thoughts and feelings that they have not recognized before.

2.   Carl Rogers, one of the founders of the encounter group movement, believes that the ability to make effective, short-term relationships will be a major factor in psychic survival in the future. He believes that encounter groups are the way to develop this ability.

3.   Some theorists criticize encounter groups because the participants accord them almost religious significance and do not evaluate them rationally. Others find it hard to believe that complex psychological problems can be eliminated in a brief experience such as the encounter group.

4.   Some critics feel encounter groups are not only ineffective, but actually harmful. Unlike group therapy, there is no screening in encounter groups to determine whether the individual belongs in the group, requires different treatment, or perhaps medication. Nor does anyone take responsibility for what happens to participants after the encounter session is over.

WHEN RELATING FAILS

WHEN OUR RELATIONSHIPS WITH OTHERS FAIL, we are motivated to find out why. We explore the dimensions of psychological disorder to discover the most frequent causes of such failure. In the chapters that follow, we shall look first into the history of psychological abnormality as a reminder that psychopathology is certainly not the invention of the modern era. Disorder in human behavior can be traced to ancient times through various Biblical accounts of abnormality. We shall also see that the labels *normal* and *abnormal* are not the possessions only of Western, industrialized civilization. All cultures follow a number of norms, and thus they create their own definition of what is considered normal.

Each age and culture also creates its own categories of mental disorder. In these chapters, we will examine and differentiate among various types of neuroses and psychoses, remembering that individuals do not conform neatly to the labels that are created for them. Whereas the neurotic person is unhappy and cannot deal effectively with the problems in his everyday life, he does not suffer from the incapacitating alterations of behavior that plague the psychotic personality. With psychosis comes a severe distortion of perception and sensation that leads to gross disorders of one's motivation, emotion, thought, and action.

Various forms of psychotherapy have been developed to combat the distressing effects of neurotic and psychotic behavior. Although the numerous therapies are based on just as many theories about man's psychological abnormalities, the two dominant, competing explanations are the psychodynamic view and the behavioral view. In the last chapter of this section, we shall review the objectives and underlying principles of the behavioral and psychodynamic therapies. Present theoretical conflicts are very much in evidence, and thus far no single therapy can be said to be the right "solution" for every person or problem. Undoubtedly, the abnormal psychology of tomorrow will be a blend of today's various bodies of thought.

History of Abnormality

It is a common calamity; we are all mad at some time or another.
—Johannes Baptista Mantuanus

Searching the history of psychopathology is helpful only if it puts our modern views of emotional disorder in perspective. The history of human psychopathology can be subdivided in numerous ways, but for convenience we shall arbitrarily organize history into the primitive and ancient, golden, medieval, and modern eras.

Primitive and Ancient Man

Primitive and ancient man are not the same. Some quite primitive peoples live today in areas isolated from the surrounding modern world; ancient man lived thousands of years ago in a world which had no alternative style of life. In about the year 1000 B.C., Homer assumed that emotionally disturbed persons had offended the gods and were being punished as they well deserved. In the societies of both primitive and ancient man, treatment of emotional disorder included *trepanning*— an operation in which part of the skull was chipped away to allow evil spirits to escape. In some cases, this operation was surprisingly successful. In ancient times, evil spirits and demons were thought to exist, and strong medicine was called for to rid the patient of unwanted spirits (Kiev, 1966). Various cultures have used prayer, sacrifice, fumigation, starvation, fire, fear, bloodletting, catharsis, and scapegoats to recover lost souls.

When primitive man needs help in handling the emotions, thoughts, and feelings that distress him, he has to treat his body and his mind by

MANIA AND DEPRESSION
Near the end of the first century
A.D., *Aretaeus concluded that people who were irritable, violent, and easily given to joy and pleasurable pursuits were prone to the development of manic excitement. On the other hand, he felt that those who tended to be serious were more apt to develop melancholia. Aretaeus was the first to describe the various phases of mania and melancholia, and to view these different pathological states as expressions of the same illness.*

GALEN
Galen (130–200 A.D.*) was a physician who dominated Western thinking until the eighteenth century. Galen added psychic functions to the brain. He divided the causes of mental illness into physical and mental. Among the causes he named were injuries to the head, alcoholic excess, shock, fear, adolescence, menstrual changes, economic reverses, and disappointment in love.*

ASCLEPIADES
In 124 B.C., *the Roman physician Asclepiades distinguished between illusions, delusions, and hallucinations. He also noted the difference between acute and chronic mental illnesses and invented various devices designed to make patients more comfortable. One of these was a suspended hammock-like bed, the swaying of which was considered beneficial to disturbed patients.*

whatever means he can. He has cured his minor troubles "through various intuitive, crude, empirical techniques: he [has] cooled his injuries with saliva, alleviated his fevers by lying in cold water, extricated foreign matter from his skin as best he could with his fingers, rubbed his wounds with mud, [and] sucked snake bites to rid himself of venom" (Alexander and Selesnick, 1966, p. 7).

The Bible is our earliest recorded history of disordered human behavior; like Freud working many centuries later, it makes a number of references to sexual abnormalities. In the book of Genesis, for example, there is the story of Onan, from which is derived the term *onanism*—masturbation. The Bible also tells of kings pretending madness to escape the wrath of their enemies. "And it came to pass when the evil spirit from God was upon Saul, that David took a harp and played with his hand: so Saul was refreshed, and was well, and the evil spirit departed from him" (I Samuel 16:23).

The Golden Age

Greek civilization altered our vision of man. Hippocrates' notions of therapeutic treatment, for example, recommended a regular and tranquil life, sobriety, abstinence from all excesses, a vegetable diet, exercise short of fatigue, and bloodletting, if indicated, in the treatment of melancholia. He thought hysteria was limited to women and produced by the wandering of the uterus to various parts of the body. As a medical man, he described postpartum psychosis, severe phobias, and deliria associated with tubercular and malarial infections. He also favored the notion that the brain was the central organ of the intellect and that mental illness must be due to some sort of brain disorder.

Some of the later Greek and Roman physicians developed medicine to a high level, and the temples dedicated to Saturn were first-rate sanatoriums with pleasant surroundings where patients enjoyed entertainment, walks in the temple gardens, rowing along the Nile, and musical concerts. The priests of the temples even practiced a form of dream interpretation (Mora, 1967). Greek and Roman physicians also used a wide range of therapeutic measures, such as dieting, massage, gymnastics, hypnotism, bleeding, and mechanical restraints.

For six hundred years there was a Golden Age of rationality (in comparison to the primitive era from which it evolved). Then the Romans conquered and enslaved the Greeks. Concerned as the Romans were with the practical matters of warfare, architecture, road building, and law, they simply borrowed the Greek insights into madness. When the Roman Empire was overrun with plague and devastated by conquering barbarian hordes, the stage was set for the Middle Ages in which the advances in thought were to be discarded for a new religious demonology. Civilization shifted, and men retreated to a less rational view of humanity.

The Middle Ages

The Middle Ages reflected a psychology which upheld the belief: "Whom the Gods will destroy, they first make mad." Madness was the will of God, and its cure was religious ritual. Persons who exposed others supposedly marked by the devil were blessed, so witch hunts characterized the times. Treatment for emotionally disturbed persons consisted of *exorcism*—a process of casting the evil spirit out of the body. Typically treatment included prayer, incantation, noisemaking, flogging, starvation, and other unpleasant measures.

Epidemics of mass madness and religious hysteria reached a peak during the fifteenth and sixteenth centuries. An epidemic known as *tarantism* began in the thirteenth century and spread through parts of Italy and southern Spain. It apparently originated in the south of Italy where the symptoms were thought to be caused by the sting of a spider, the tarantula. Thinking they were infected, people would suddenly jump up, run out of their houses, and start dancing in the streets. They might have been joined by others, and all of them would participate in this frenzied affair until completely exhausted. The peasants believed that after being bitten the poison from the spider bite would remain in the system and be reactivated from time to time, especially when the weather was extremely hot.

During the latter part of the fifteenth century, the belief that psychological disturbance was the work of the devil became an "official" church position. By the close of the fifteenth century, the mentally ill were treated as witches. Following a papal bull of Pope Innocent VIII, the clergy were ordered to leave no stone unturned to detect those who were in league with the devil. To guide them in the witch hunt, a treatise, *The Witch's Hammer: Malleus Maleficarum,* was written by two German monks, Heinrich Kraemer and Johann Sprenger. Their book explained that bewitched individuals had been deprived of their reason by Satan. Satan could not enter the soul directly, but he could enter the body and the head and thus affect one's reason and sanity.

The *Malleus* told of six ways the devil could injure humanity: Satan could induce an evil love, plant hatred for another person, bewitch a man so he could not perform sexually, cause some disease, take away life, or deprive one of reason.

Certainly these were very bad times for the mentally ill, since a "devil psychology" dominated the thinking of doctors, lawyers, philosophers, and the ordinary citizen well into the seventeenth century.

Johann Weyer, a sixteenth-century physician and man of letters, was deeply moved by the scenes of imprisonment, torture, and burning of those accused of witchcraft. As a result, he published a book pointing out that a considerable number of those persecuted were actually sick mentally. This theory received the approval of a few outstanding physicians and theologians of his time, but it was more commonly met with vehement protest and condem-

The trepanning operation to rid a person of "evil spirits" in the Middle Ages is depicted here by the painter Hieronymus Bosch (1460–1516). The man in the chair is getting a hole drilled in his head to allow the spirits an exit.

WEREWOLF
In some isolated rural areas there were outbreaks of lycanthropy—*a form of emotional disturbance in which the patient imagined himself a wolf and imitated its actions. In 1541 a case was reported in which the lycanthrope confessed to his captors that he was really a wolf, but his skin was smooth on the surface because all the hairs were on the inside (Stone, 1937). To cure him of his delusions, his extremities were amputated; he died, still unconvinced.*

nation. Father Spina, the author of a polemical book against Weyer, stated: "Recently Satan went to a Sabbath attired as a great prince, and told the assembled witches that they need not worry since, thanks to Weyer and his followers, the affairs of the Devil were brilliantly progressing" (Castiglioni, 1946, p. 253). The church proceeded to ban the works of Weyer and his efforts were hidden in obscurity until the twentieth century.

"Abnormal" behavior in the American colonies was frequently punished by sending the offending person to the pillory. Anyone who deviated from society's norms—which were determined, for the most part, by what the religious leaders considered appropriate—was viewed with suspicion, or worse yet, as an instrument of the Devil. In this old drawing "witches" are being submitted to public ridicule. Others were put to death because those in power decided that the society could not tolerate deviancy.

The Modern Era Begins

Eleven years before the French Revolution a young doctor, Philippe Pinel, arrived in Paris. He was to revolutionize mental health care by freeing his patients from their chains and instituting humane methods of treatment. Pinel's student, Esquirol, became one of the first to apply statistical methods to the study of patients. Esquirol tabulated what he thought were the psychic causes of disorders (disappointment in love, financial loss, and so forth) and was instrumental in establishing new mental hospitals in France.

While Pinel and Esquirol were reforming mental health care in France, an English Quaker, William Tuke, established a pleasant country house called the York Retreat where mental patients could live and rest in a religious atmosphere. A beginning was being made, even if it was a small and isolated one.

Assessment

Certain types of psychological tests have been devised to help psychologists and psychiatrists determine the problems bothering patients who come to them.

Personality inventories are aimed at measuring a great variety of traits, including interests, emotional adjustment, social relations, attitudes, and values. An inventory is a collection of statements or questions to be answered in categories such as agree-disagree, like-dislike, and so on. Answers to several items taken together make up a scale by which a particular trait can be measured.

The Minnesota Multiphasic Personality Inventory (MMPI), for example, was a test originally constructed from 550 items based on the cues usually used by clinical interviewers to describe personality. The test originators hoped that the MMPI would be a reliable diagnostic device saving a great deal of professional time. Although it did serve this purpose in a sense, before long its primary use became that of a general personality inventory.

One difficulty of the self-descriptive personality inventory is that the person taking the test tends to respond in a way he thinks is socially desirable. This "social desirability" pattern of response has raised questions about the validity of many personality tests (Edwards, 1957).

Freudian psychoanalytic theory posed problems for personality theorists since observable behavior had to be treated as the surface reflection of events in the unconscious. But how could unconscious events be observed, especially if the person being tested was unaware of them? Because, as Freud suggested, the most potent forces of personality might be obscured by the patient's defenses, what the individual says may not be significant information as much as an unwitting attempt to keep unacceptable feelings, impulses, wishes, and conflicts hidden. Thus a number of devices were designed in an attempt to get the individual to express unguardedly the thoughts, feelings, attitudes, and impulses of which he is either unaware or is unwilling to disclose.

Perhaps the best known of the projective tests are the interpretive ones, where the individual is asked to react to pictures or inkblots. One such interpretive test is the Thematic Apperception Test (TAT) designed by Henry Murray in 1938. Murray thought a person's behavior could be understood in terms of the themes that were important or recurrent in his life. He designed a series of drawings portraying a few people, individuals in group situations, or landscapes in which no human figures are present. Some of the pictures were designed for women or girls, some for men or boys, and some for both sexes and any age group. The pictures were designed to reveal themes,

This is a drawing similar to those used in the Thematic Apperception Test. The instructions ask the person to tell a story for each of the pictures—to describe the themes that occur to him. What would you say about these two women?

conflicts, moods, or conflictual relationships common to most of us.

Another interpretive test is the Rorschach (1942), which consists of ten inkblots printed on cards. Five are black on a white background, two have red areas in addition to the black, and three are multicolored. These inkblots were originally produced by placing ink on a folded sheet of paper and pressing the halves of the sheet together. The ten blots that make up the set were selected from a much larger number. Since they were not designed to resemble actual objects, they can be interpreted to be whatever the person wants them to be.

Clinical analysis of the responses seeks answers to questions such as: How did the person behave toward the examiner and the testing material? Where in the blot did the person see the objects he reported? How much of the blot was used in the response? What features of the blot produced the response? What was the content of the responses reported? And, how accurate are the reported perceptions?

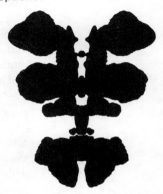

"New suspensory treatment for nervous atoxia, at the Salpétriêre Hospital, Paris." So reads the caption for this nineteenth-century engraving.

The nineteenth century witnessed the first marked changes in psychological theory and practice. Dorothea Dix, for example, devoted half of her life to the reform of hospitals for the emotionally disordered in America. As she worked for the establishment of humane, professionally run mental hospitals, she unwittingly encouraged a type of isolated mental hospital in which psychotics, criminals, and mental defectives were all confined together in a hopeless jumble.

During the latter half of the nineteenth century, the asylum ("the big house on the hill"), with its high turrets and fortress-like appearance, became a familiar landmark in America. Dix solved one social problem but unintentionally created another for the generations yet to come (Foucault, 1965).

In a book famous in the early 1900s, *A Mind That Found Itself,* a Yale graduate named Clifford Beers described his own mental collapse, the bad treatment he received in three typical institutions, and his eventual recovery in the home of a friendly attendant. The public storm stirred up by the book launched the *mental hygiene* movement to educate people in the understanding of mental illness.

The modern psychological era has established a firm foothold, partially because medical and biochemical advances have converted Bedlam into a place of order and reason. The medical and psychological sciences have stimulated new progress in the diagnosis and treatment of mental disorders. Twentieth-century therapists have come almost full circle and are now discussing the advantages of open hospitals and home care for those with psychotic disorders. This psychological era is one of optimism and hope—hope that the scientific method will finally solve man's most burdensome problem (Freedman and Kaplan, 1967).

For the first time we are questioning some of the beliefs that have characterized the study of abnormal behavior for so long. For one thing, we are beginning to admit that abnormality is very difficult to define and that each culture defines it differently. Moreover, we have begun to question the historical belief that physical illness is the proper model for viewing emotional disorder. This questioning is very important, for much of the current language and framework for talking about mental disorder comes from the medical model of abnormality. Even though the way in which we have viewed and dealt with emotional disorder might change enormously, psychologists realize that they must confront these issues if there is to be better understanding and treatment of what we call abnormality.

Defining Abnormality

The words *normal* and *abnormal* are labels that are defined by the era in which you are born and the society in which you live. There are many definitions of *normal* and *abnormal,* and they will undoubtedly change in your lifetime.

The Statistical Approach

If *abnormal* were used in a strictly literal sense, statistical norms would be sufficient to define it. Any deviation from the majority would be abnormal: geniuses, the mentally retarded, members of the radical left and right would all be declared abnormal. This definition of the word *abnormal* would be accurate but useless if we want to distinguish between desirable and undesirable deviations. Indeed, a statistical definition suggests equating mental health with conformity.

Most people have average intelligence because the majority of IQ scores fall into the middle section of a distribution of all scores. Only a few people have high intelligence; fewer yet have *very* high intelligence; and geniuses are rare indeed. The statistical model works well if we wish only to portray relatively uncomplicated traits or simple biological measurements, but it cannot describe the subtle complexities of human personality or emotional disorder.

The Adequacy Approach

Adequacy and *inadequacy* are relative rather than absolute terms since judgments of adequacy clearly depend on who is judging. Such standards themselves are relative to the cultural norms for one's age, sex, role, and status in every society. Using adequacy as a criterion has a number of limitations (Buss, 1966).

Inefficiency.   When the performance of everyday functions is regularly impaired by disabling behavior, then inefficiency in role performance may be used to judge the existence of abnormality. Whereas inefficiency is hardly grounds for hospitalization, the accompanying personal distress is considerable.

Efficiency can be assessed by comparing an individual's actual performance with his potential capability. Thus, a person with a high score on the Scholastic Aptitude Test could be expected to do very well in college. If he flunks out, we might consider this a breakdown in efficiency.

There are other possible measures of efficiency. We can, for example, compare a person's performance with the social, intellectual, or organizational demands of his role. Some social roles make few demands, and an inefficient individual may go undetected since we tolerate minor disorganization in any role performance. Some roles require a high level of organizational skill and therefore expose inefficiency much more quickly. The criterion of inefficiency, then, is limited to the level of efficiency demanded by the role.

Personal Discomfort and Distress.   Disturbed persons experience acute feelings of distress or unhappiness. When these feelings are sufficiently intense, he may classify himself as a disordered person even though his symptoms may not be apparent to others. Psychological discomfort may lead to physical

Straightjackets have long been used to restrain violent mental patients. This etching stems from an 1838 drawing done in Paris for *Des Maladies Mentales.* Today, even though tranquilizers and other drugs provide alternatives to physical restraint, the straightjacket has not been abandoned.

complaints, and people may try home remedies or see a physician. But these physical symptoms may not be related to any known medical disease. There is a twilight zone between medical disorders and psychological symptoms involving bodily complaints since neurotic symptoms may imitate the symptoms of organic disease.

Worry and apprehension are other forms of distress which may lead to depression lasting long after the initiating event. When depression seems unrelated to events which would obviously produce sorrow, the depressed behavior is judged to be abnormal.

Being Bizarre. When someone appears to be out of contact with reality, displays behavior inappropriate to his environment, or interprets the stimuli in his environment in an unusual way, he is considered deviant. Bizarre behavior may include delusions, hallucinations, serious memory loss, bodily tics, phobias, or compulsive rituals. Being bizarre is socially defined since the community decides which behaviors are minor or major departures from the normal standard.

The Cultural Model

However you choose to define it, abnormality means one thing for you and members of your society, and something entirely different for other people. Although almost all societies can distinguish between abnormal and normal behavior, their norms, or boundary lines are most certainly different from ours. Why? Because the idea of abnormality is based on the fact that each culture follows a number of norms approved by the greatest number of people in that culture. If most people have a common type of dance, manner of speech, or way of behaving, those actions are declared normal. If you behave in a way that does not follow the norms of your society, your actions will be labeled abnormal. Since abnormality is culturally defined, abnormal behavior in one society might be approved in another. Also, when a society's norms change, what was once said to be abnormal behavior might now be called normal.

The example of homosexuality shows how the dividing line between normal and abnormal is a continually shifting one. Our society considers homosexuality abnormal, but at some times and places homosexual behavior has been treated as normal. The Bible says, "If a man also lieth down with a man as he lieth with a woman, both of them have committed an abomination. They shall verily be put to death." Yet, in ancient Greece, homosexuality was tolerated and even encouraged. Our society is also repulsed by the thought of adult-child sexual relations. Yet, in certain parts of the world, it is "normal" for men to engage in sex with eight-year-old girls. We are against sexual play between children; but again, in many societies such play is a matter of little parental concern.

Disorders in one culture may have no exact counterpart in another culture. There are reports (Benedict and Jacks, 1954), for example, which suggest a high incidence of pathological aggression, assault, and hostility among members of some nonliterate societies, with a corresponding, infrequent occurrence of depression and self-blame. In technologically less-advanced societies, pathology may take the form of action and explosive irrationality. In our culture, the same problems would be expressed as thought disorders. In other words, we are more likely to remain rational and become depressed rather than attack others. Anthropologists have reported emotional disturbances of far-ranging varieties. Arieti and Meth (1959) recall that "among the islanders of Dobu (Melanesia), no sane woman leaves her cooking pots unguarded for fear of being poisoned. To us this behavior would indicate paranoia. Among some Eskimo tribes, the mother accepts the killer of her son in her son's stead. Among the Pupuans it is traditional for an uncle and nephew (mother's brother and son) to practice homosexuality" (p. 560).

Anthropologists have also reported kinds of disturbance that do not correspond to those in our culture. In Amok (Malaysia), for example, the victim suddenly goes berserk and assaults or kills anyone in his path (hence, the idiom "to run amok"). Rarely in our culture does the schizophrenic destroy innocent bystanders in a sudden outburst of rage. Further, such behavior would not have the understanding or implied social sanction it has in other cultures. *Latah* is most often an affliction of middle-aged and elderly women in Malaysia who become seclusive and unusually fearful after a sudden fright. They may also mimic and pantomime the words and actions of others, even if the other persons are irritated to the point of retaliation. A host of other disorders peculiar to a particular society include *piblokto* (a convulsive disorder

seen among Eskimos living in polar regions), *ufufunyane* (attacks of shouting, loss of vision, and loss of consciousness among some South African tribes), and *windigo* psychosis among Algonquin Indians (a starved man believes he is being controlled by some supernatural being that has an insatiable craving for human flesh).

It is quite apparent that what is considered normal is closely connected to the society's definition of good behavior. Order and disorder in human life cannot be understood without reference to the surrounding culture. A study by Broverman et al. (1970) reports that clinicians in our society seem to have different concepts of mental health for men and women; further, these differences parallel the sex-role stereotypes that are widespread in our culture. This double standard of mental health stems from the acceptance by some clinicians of the idea that mental health consists of a good adjustment to one's environment. For a woman to be considered psychologically healthy, she must accept the behavioral norms for her sex and adjust to her role even when this requires her to be a dependent, docile, unambitious, or childlike person.

The existence of such different values for males and females can be traced to Freud's view of the female of the species. Freud described women as envious, insincere, secretive, masochistic, and lacking in a sense of justice and honor. Freud's theory of sexuality is based on a masculine model in which the male is the norm and the female is an incomplete or deficient version of that model.

The Problems of Classification

Throughout this part we will be using diagnostic categories and labels to talk about maladaptive behaviors. This system of diagnosis will probably remind you of the way medical doctors talk about an illness and, indeed, the use of this classification system for mental disorder comes from the historical view that abnormal behavior is some sort of illness. We will discuss the problems connected with this view of disorder in the psychological issue, but we must acknowledge that the medical framework is the dominant view at this time. Nonetheless, we can use it to our advantage, if we heed a few warnings.

It is important to remember that a label is merely a name—and not an explanation—for a particular type of behavior. The diagnostic categories are useful because they allow psychologists to communicate in an agreed-upon fashion about abnormal behavior, but psychologists are the first to admit the many limitations of such classification.

For one thing, people do not fall neatly into diagnostic categories. A person labeled schizophrenic, for example, does not necessarily display all the symptoms we will discuss under schizophrenia. He would also be quite likely to display symptoms that could be classed in other diagnostic categories. For example, Zigler and Phillips (1961) examined case records of 793 manic-depressive, schizophrenic, neurotic, or character-disordered patients to determine how frequently any of 35 symptoms occurred. What they found was that the same symptoms appeared in many of the categories, and that the relationship between individual symptoms and a particular category was actually quite small.

Although the symptoms belonging to each diagnostic label are supposedly agreed upon by most psychiatrists, in practice diagnostic agreement among psychiatrists leaves much to be desired. In a classic study by Schmidt and Fonda (1956) the diagnoses of 426 patients admitted to a state hospital during a six-month period were analyzed. The researchers found that the overall agreement rate on diagnosis was about 85 percent. Residents agreed with the major diagnostic category used by the chief psychiatrist in 92 percent of the organically caused cases, 80 percent of the psychotic cases, and 71 percent of the character-disordered cases. Even worse was the fact that agreement occurred in only half the cases invoking a specific subtype of disorder, such as paranoid schizophrenia, and agreement was nearly absent in cases of personality and psychoneurotic disorders.

In a study by Ward et al. (1962), several sources for this type of disagreement were cited, including the fact that a patient may give different information to two different interviewers, and that the diagnostician may be inconsistent in his use of interview techniques, weighting of symptoms, or interpretation of the same interview data. But nearly two-thirds of the error was attributed to the inadequacies of the categories in the classification system.

Even if the diagnostic system were made more accurate, many psychologists object to it because it does little to improve our understanding of the causes and treatment of abnormal behavior. Perhaps one of the greatest dangers of the use of diagnostic categories is the risk of self-fulfilling prophecy; that is, if a person is labeled schizophrenic, it is highly likely that he will develop the behaviors associated with schizophrenia—even if he did not have them at first. Being told he is schizophrenic—or anything else—causes the individual to perceive himself as such, while his therapist and family may unconsciously treat him in such a way as to bring about their expectations. We have seen how an experimenter's expectations can influence the result of his experiment, and the same thing is likely to occur when the therapist places his expectations of abnormal behavior on his client. Kelly (1955) made this position clear when he observed that ". . . in comparing the complaints of psychologically sophisticated people with those of the psychologically naive, there was a definite tendency, once a person had chosen a psychological name for his discomfort, to display all of the symptoms in whatever book he had read, even if he had to practice them diligently. It suggested that psychological symptoms may frequently be interpreted as the rationale by which one's chaotic experiences are given a measure of structure and meaning" (p. 366).

As early as 1859, mental health workers suggested that progress in the field would be impossible until all classification systems were overthrown, since naming illnesses only comforts doctors, impresses relatives, and has little to do with treatment. Hundreds of names have been applied to the same psychological events over the centuries, but we seem not much nearer to the underlying truth.

Summary

1. Although the Greek civilization had a highly enlightened view of human psychopathology, the Middle Ages believed madness was caused by possession by the devil. For centuries, mental health reformers have battled against the effects of this demon psychology.
2. In the late eighteenth century, an enlightened doctor named Philippe Pinel instituted humane methods of treating mental illness. An additional source of help was the fact that physicians had begun

to suspect that mental disorder was a result of organic brain disorder. Although the theory has long since been discredited, the medical model of mental illness remains highly influential in our view of psychopathology today.

3. One of the results of the medical model was the use of diagnostic categories. Although the use of this system provides a convenient way of talking about mental disorder, it must be remembered that a classification is a label, not an explanation, and that most individuals do not fit perfectly into any particular category.

4. Psychologists often used psychological tests to diagnose the problems of the people they are asked to help. One such test is a personality inventory, in which the individual is asked to respond to questions about himself with words like "disagree or agree," "like or dislike." One problem with such self-report tests is that the individual may not answer honestly, either responding in a way to get social approval or because he is unconsciously defending against his real feelings.

5. Projective tests were designed to dig under the conscious surface and get the individual to express aspects of his personality that he may be unaware of, or reluctant to admit. The Thematic Apperception Test and the Rorschach inkblot tests are both projective tests.

6. Differentiating between abnormal and normal individuals is often quite difficult, and many approaches have been suggested. It must be remembered, however, that abnormality is always defined according to the norms of society, and closely related to what the society considers good and bad behavior.

PSYCHOLOGICAL ISSUE

The Myth of Mental Illness

The notion that abnormal behavior is a result of mental illness became popular around the middle of the nineteenth century. Great advances in the field of medicine during the past century had convinced many physicians that some form of organic disorder was responsible, not only for physical ailments, but for emotional difficulties as well. This view that individuals exhibiting uncontrollable antisocial behavior were "sick" was a great reform for the mental health movement. Up until this time, "insane" persons had been sent to prisons or chained and forgotten in asylums. With the acceptance of the medical view of psychopathology, these same individuals were instead sent to hospitals for treatment.

Although it soon became apparent that many persons who deviated from socially acceptable behavior did not acutally have any organic impairment in their brains, the medical model continued to exert its influence, creating the framework by which we view abnormal behavior even today. Behaviors are classified into diagnostic categories much as we diagnose a runny nose, fever, and chills as a cold. Terms like *symptom, cure,* and *treatment* are a standard part of clinical vocabulary. The notion that mental "illness" is something one has, rather than something one does, still dominates the thinking of most mental health workers. But it is important to remember that such views are merely the result of a certain *model* of psychopathology.

In recent years, the medical model has undergone attack by many theorists, including both psychologists and medical men. They have argued that the rigid classification system set up by the medical model is not particularly useful in dealing with behaviors that result from inappropriate learning or the inability to cope with stress. Such labeling procedures are not only inadequate but actually quite harmful. They can cause damage to the already shaken self-image of many individuals experiencing emotional difficulties.

Chief among the opponents of the medical model is psychiatrist Thomas Szasz, who claims that mental illness is a "myth." The individual is not actually sick; he merely has difficulty coping with the stresses of his everyday life. By assigning the cause of his problems to some external force like illness, rather than to the individual's own inappropriate behaviors, mental health professionals encourage the individual not to take any responsibility for his actions, when in fact it is his avoidance of his problems that has brought him to this state originally. This lack of responsibility is made worse by hospitalization, where the individual immediately falls into a "sick role," exhibiting the behavior patterns of a classic neurotic or psychotic (as he was diagnosed), rather than learning to cope with his problems effectively. Szasz's idea that abnormal behavior is a result of "problems in living" suggests that therapy should consist primarily of learning how to deal successfully with one's life and one's environment.

The idea that mental disorder is not a disease that someone else will cure, but rather something for which the individual is responsible, has serious implications for our view of the causes and treatment of psychopathology, and the relation of abnormal behavior to society as a whole. One of the most important considerations is the legal use of the term *mentally ill*. A person so judged is usually relieved of all responsibility for a criminal act, primarily because of our general belief that emotional disorder is an illness, and therefore something over which a person has no control. Yet, if in fact most of the people we say are mentally ill do not have brain tumors or central nervous disorders, but have simply failed to behave according to the rules of our society, how can we continue to "let them off" on the grounds that they have no responsibility for their acts?

Summary

Psychiatrist Thomas Szasz, who has opposed the medical model, says that mental disorder is not a disease, but a result of problems in living. Diagnosing patients as if they were ill destroys their sense of responsibility for learning to cope with their environments effectively.

The Neuroses

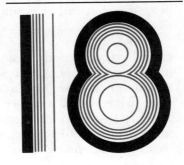

Though this be madness, yet there is method in't. —Shakespeare

The neurotic lives in an uncomfortable world where he may not be incapacitated but is too distressed to enjoy life. Neurosis prevents us from becoming what we might have been while making us miserable with what we are. Ideally, each of us should be able to handle the frustrations of life by working out a rational plan of action. The neurotic, however, seems unable to deal productively with conflict and responds, instead, in a manner that intensifies the problem.

At the outset, a distinction should be made between a symptom neurosis and a neurotic personality. *Symptom neuroses* involve the display of anxiety, phobia, obsessive-compulsive behavior, or some other reaction type. The term *neurotic personality* refers to a collection of personality traits and interpersonal difficulties. A symptom neurosis may or may not evolve from a neurotic personality. For example, the individual who tends to be compulsive may at some time develop severe obsessions and compulsions or may simply continue to have compulsive traits that never go much beyond the ordinary.

Neurotic personalities often do not express anger or hostility directly; instead they frustrate and hurt others by passive stubbornness, clinging overdependence, or indirect and displaced aggression. They have mixed feelings about other people, and their interpersonal attitudes may combine hostility, fear, and a need for affection. They may also want to feel loved but cannot easily love in return. They may withdraw from people or try to saddle a stronger person with their own psychological burdens.

THE NEUROSES
Anxiety neurosis
Hysterical neurosis
  Conversion type
  Dissociative type
Phobic neurosis
Obsessive compulsive neurosis
Depressive neurosis
Neurasthenic neurosis
Depersonalization neurosis
Hypochondriacal neurosis

The Psychodynamic View of Symptomatic Neurosis

There is broad agreement among psychodynamic theorists about the core of neurosis, the factors which bring on a neurotic breakdown, and the sequence of events that leads to neurotic symptom formation. Most theorists agree that the need to escape from anxiety through psychological defenses is a central aspect of the many different patterns of neurotic symptomatology. The most direct statement of psychodynamic theory is that, in childhood, a neurotic nucleus forms in which anxiety is not managed by conscious problem-solving processes, but rather is fought off by psychic distortions called *defense mechanisms.*

An apparently well-balanced, adult person may "come apart at the seams" when a poorly managed threat or conflict of childhood reappears (the angry, demanding boss whose behavior is like that of the feared father). Because of sickness, exhaustion, or other energy-depleting events, defenses which once worked very well can be weakened and cease to be effective. *Neurotic breakdown* can occur when frustration, conflict, and threat mount so high that the defensive structure must be reinforced: the cost of such "buttressed defending" is too great and does not leave enough energy to meet life's other problems.

Symptom patterns may be astonishingly varied, but they reflect a set of psychological characteristics common to most persons afflicted with neurosis. Coleman (1970) lists the following characteristics.

1. A basic feeling of personal inadequacy and low toleration for stress (feeling inadequate, the neurotic perceives more threat than others and is less capable of meeting it).
2. An anxious and fearful outlook on life.
3. Unusual tension and irritability (mobilized to meet life's many threats, the neurotic overreacts with great tension).
4. Disturbed interpersonal relationships (tense, irritable, and defensive, the neurotic is painfully aware of himself to the exclusion of others).

It is this egocentricity that dims the neurotic's perception of the feelings of others. It also hides how he himself helps to make his interpersonal relationships unsatisfying.

Anxiety and Neurosis

Psychodynamic theorists suggest that the manner in which an anxiety is managed becomes fundamental to the development of a neurosis, since the psychic techniques employed to avoid anxiety determine the pattern of neurotic symptoms. Anxiety becomes a signal of future danger. This warning allows the individual to take protective action and master excitation. If the excitation

THE EXISTENTIAL NEUROSES
The existential neuroses are thought to produce cognitive, effective, and behavioral symptoms. The symptoms may include an inability to believe in the importance of study, work, or play. Further, the existential neurotic may be weary of exercising choice about what he does or does not do. Meaninglessness, apathy, aimlessness, and doubt predominate.

is more than the ego can handle, the anxiety will trigger panic.

Freud spoke of three kinds of anxiety: reality anxiety, neurotic anxiety, and moral anxiety. Each kind of anxiety functions as a warning signal to escape, evade, or build up defenses. If these moves are not possible, anxiety will sooner or later disintegrate the personality and produce serious emotional disorder. The anxiety of everyday life is "realistic" *(reality anxiety)*. We usually refer to this type of anxiety by the word *fear*.

Moral anxiety is usually experienced by the ego in the form of guilt or shame and develops out of the superego or conscience. The conscience is ever ready to threaten or punish the ego for some action that violates the learned ideals. Moral anxiety owes its origin to the fear of punitive parents; but once parental standards become part of the self in the developed superego, moral anxiety becomes part of the mental apparatus. Unlike reality anxiety, moral anxiety cannot be escaped since it is a vital part of the self.

Neurotic anxiety issues from perceived, internal danger. It is a fear of what would happen if defenses fail and instinctive (forbidden) urges find expression in behavior. In the anxiety neuroses, maintaining a steady state of alertness and vigilance becomes distressing to the ego. Tension and anxiety narrow the victim's perceptual and cognitive range and restrict his ability to act. This odd mixture of childhood and adult motivations does not prove appropriate for solving either adult problems or childhood longings. The anxious person does things he knows he does not want to do—and this behavior makes him a less effective adult.

This brings into focus the primary neurotic problem—the maladaptive behavior of a full-grown human being who continues to react with self-defeating patterns of behavior. It was once said that a neurotic goes through life with a single LP phonograph record looking constantly for new stereo sets on which to play it. This may be the most characteristic pattern of neurosis —repetitive, unintelligible behavior that provokes irritable, retaliatory, rejecting responses from others.

We have described the core of the neurotic problem. Now let us turn to what psychodynamic theorists say about the mechanisms that form symptoms.

The Defense Mechanisms

Parents require children not only to control their behavior but also to make their thoughts and impulses coincide with behavior. An example which illustrates the defensive process is the management of love and hate while growing up. The child is spanked, deprived, and interfered with. During his suffering, he hates his mother and would angrily destroy her if he could. Such hostile feelings are usually forbidden in the mother-child relationship; if the child is to be accepted and loved and feel worthwhile as a person, he must rid himself of these negative emotions.

REPRESSION
Freud described repression as a mechanism that rejects impulses from consciousness and keeps them unconscious. Since repressed material continually exerts pressure to escape into consciousness, steady counterpressure is needed to prevent it. Thus, the person who relies on repression to manage life's problems can be anxious without being able to explain why, since the anxiety may be produced by impulses, thoughts, and urges striving to regain their original conscious status.

There is the source (himself) of the feelings, the impulse (hate), the object (mother) toward which it is directed, and the aim (kill) of the impulse. Alteration of any one of these aspects will produce a formula which is no longer threatening to his self-esteem or to the esteem others have for him. He can, for example, change the source *in some fashion and not tamper with the other elements; now* he *doesn't hate his mother and want to kill her. Or he can alter the* impulse *so that he* loves *his mother, not hates her. The* object *can be transformed so that he hates* school *but not his mother. Another compromise that will solve his dilemma is to admit that he hates his mother but merely wishes to* reprimand *her rather than kill her. In each instance, a slight change in his perception of the reality of hating his mother cleans up the thought and makes it presentable. In extreme circumstances the whole thought must be changed, leaving no element unaltered; in less threatening situations it is necessary only to reduce the intensity of each element of the sequence.* [McNeil, 1969, pp. 210–11]

These perceptual moves are designed, of course, to escape the pain of anxiety. The trouble is that after sufficient practice they may become habitual, characteristic patterns of reaction to conflict; indeed, they may become permanent character traits. In any event, the employment of defense mechanisms to deal with anxiety and conflict is a costly affair.

Selecting a Neurosis

The "choice" of a symptom pattern is not, of course, a conscious matter, nor is it a sudden event. Rather, it emerges out of a broad personality pattern which has developed over the years. It may be that the neurotic person,

---

Another View: The Behavioral Theory of Neurosis

The psychodynamic theorists explain neurosis as a defensive behavior designed to alleviate the anxiety caused by an unconscious conflict. This view implies, therefore, that the neurotic behavior is merely a symptom of an underlying difficulty which must be resolved before the neurotic behavior disappears.

The behaviorists, on the other hand, postulate no unconscious causes of neurotic behavior. To the behaviorists, neuroses are simply bad habits, developed and maintained in the same way other behaviors are learned. The difference is that the neurotic has either learned the wrong behavior, or has failed to learn the appropriate one.

How do such maladaptive behaviors come about? Through learning (either deliberate or accidental), an individual comes to find that a particular situation is anxiety provoking. Rather than dealing directly with the stress, the individual may try to avoid it altogether by performing some behavior that prevents the situation from occurring again. The relief of anxiety caused by this avoidance behavior is reinforcing. So is the attention, and perhaps even the control over others, that neurotic behavior brings. Furthermore, avoidance behaviors are extremely difficult to extinguish because the individual never gives himself a chance to learn that the threat he is avoiding no longer exists. The reinforcing properties of the avoidance behavior, coupled with the fact that the individual believes the threat is still present, makes neurotic behavior extremely persistent—no matter how self-defeating.

In this chapter we have discussed the psychodynamic reasons for several symptom neuroses. Can you explain them in behavioral terms?

following a traumatic experience at birth, becomes particularly susceptible to anxiety. It has not been possible, however, to obtain adequate evidence that this kind of crisis is significantly more frequent in the histories of neurotic patients. Something like a lower threshold of anxiety or a reduced capacity to defend against anxiety might exist, but again it is impossible to determine if this is a consequence of birth trauma or of exposure to emotional stress in childhood.

Psychodynamic theory, especially the orthodox psychoanalytic view, describes neurosis selection in terms of crises that may be experienced at oral, anal, or phallic stages. These crises result in the fixation of feelings or behavior which belong to the particular stage involved. The fixations establish the focal point for later regression. In other words, when a person is faced with anxiety and responds by regressing, he reacts in terms of earlier behavior patterns appropriate to some stage of development. The neurosis chosen reflects the particular "stage of crisis" in the individual's life.

The Hysterical Neuroses

Subsumed under this category are conversion and dissociative types of hysteria. Anxiety remains the cornerstone of these symptoms.

Conversion Type

The word *hysteria* originates in the Greek word *hystera* (uterus). Ancient Greek physicians believed that the uterus wandered about the female body until it reached a resting place where it would produce symptoms.

The symptoms of *conversion hysteria* are startling since they have no "real" physiological or anatomical basis. Nevertheless, patients may suddenly become blind, deaf, or unable to feel or speak. When a complete physical examination and extensive clinical tests are made, it appears impossible that the symptoms could take such forms. For example, a hand may become totally insensitive from the wrist down (glove anaesthesia)—even though physiologically this is an impossible event. Evidently, the patient unconsciously imitates diseases that affect the muscular or sensory systems.

According to psychoanalytic theorists, the bodily symptoms of hysteria represent impulses which are not allowed conscious expression. Because of anxiety, these impulses are converted (diverted) into sensory or motor channels to block the functioning of some organ system. Exactly how this occurs is a matter of considerable speculation. It is most interesting to note, however, that the response of conversion hysteria is often closely related to perfectly normal events common to most of us in daily life.

The symptoms of conversion hysteria may include mutism (inability to speak), aphonia (inability to speak above a whisper), tremor or tics (spasmodic jerking of a group of muscles), or a variety of anaesthesias. These

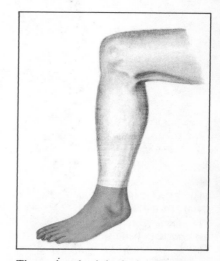

The only physiological explanation for stocking anaesthesia (as for glove or any other form of anaesthesia) would be for all the neural connections of the limb to be severed. But it is extremely unlikely that all the nerves leading into the foot or the hand would be destroyed in the right combination to duplicate symptoms reported by the neurotic.

If you saw the movie *Black Orpheus,* you will be familiar with the Macumba rituals that still take place in Rio de Janeiro, Brazil. The participants in this religion manage to accomplish a deliberate, self-induced dissociative state. For thousands of years dissociation from reality has been achieved with and without drugs. The women shown here go into a trance-like state by smoking cigars and dancing frenetically to the beat of drum-filled music.

symptoms seem bizarre and unusual, but they are, in a way, exaggerations of normal processes.

Conversion neuroses have become increasingly rare in recent times. Such hysterical phenomena were easily observed by Freud working in Austria at the turn of the century, and by the French psychiatrists Charcot and Janet. But hysteria is known to change its form from one historical period to another and seems to decrease as education and medical sophistication increase.

Conversion hysteria has not totally disappeared, however. Weinstein, Eck, and Lyerly (1969) report that in one mental hospital serving the Appalachia district of Virginia and West Virginia, nearly 25 to 30 percent of admissions displayed some conversion-type hysteria. The assumption is that this relatively isolated, poorly educated, superstitious population of patients is still reacting to emotional distress in ways characteristic of previous historical periods.

The symptoms of conversion hysteria have been labeled the "craft neuroses" or "craft palsies" because the physical symptoms "chosen" effectively prevent the individual from participating in a conflict-laden situation. Under the duress of combat, for example, pilots may suffer visual disturbances (night vision failure, distortion or loss of depth perception), or infantrymen may find their trigger finger stiff and unbendable. Writers get writer's cramp; violinists develop anaesthesia of the hand; and artists go blind. Interestingly enough, such paralyzed patients may move their hands or limbs when asleep or hypnotized. The conversion symptoms, in short, unconsciously provide an "out" for the suffering individual.

THE BEAUTIFUL INDIFFERENCE
The classic feature of conversion hysteria is la belle indifference. *This is "the beautiful indifference" a patient displays despite the seriousness of his symptoms. Such paralyzed hysterics have been labeled "hobbling heroes" (Nemiah, 1961). They awake one day to discover that the lower half of the body is paralyzed, and they take to crutches with a cheery display of fatalistic accommodation to this new state of affairs—that's the way the old ball bounces!*

Dissociative Type

The *dissociative type* of hysterical neurosis is characterized by gross personality disorganization which, according to psychodynamic theorists, is a consequence of repressed impulses returning to consciousness. The defensive measures used in dissociative reactions are denial and further repression. The range of symptoms in this diagnosis includes amnesia, somnambulism (sleepwalking), multiple personality, and depersonalization (West, 1967).

Sleepwalking. The dreamlike dissociative conditions called sleepwalking, trances, or twilight states reflect brief periods in which one's fantasy life dominates reality. A normal regression occurs when we go to sleep; in this regressed state unconscious conflicts emerge, and an attempt is made to solve conflict while asleep. Sleepwalkers, in an abnormal regression, are not actually asleep; they are dissociated from reality. Sleepwalking, in fact, is surprisingly like being partly drunk. The semi-sloshed drinker knows what the realities of his situation are but chooses to deny them and express other impulses.

The sleepwalker may be unable to recall what transpired in his dissociated state. In other words, he may suffer a memory loss similar to that in amnesiacs. Somnambulism is usually limited to adolescence, since it is most commonly a response to the turmoil of leaving childhood and becoming an adult. But as Sandler (1945) reported, sleepwalking is not always an isolated symptom.

Amnesia. Amnesia includes various kinds of pathological forgetting such as that produced by old age, brain injury, psychological disorder, or drugs. The central feature common to each of these forms is the loss of personal identity. When you can no longer recall who you are, where you live, or the direction of your life, we would assume that you have discarded the symbols of your identity and are trying to deal with some sort of mounting conflict in your existence.

The amnesia victim has been described as an immature, dependent, suggestible, egocentric person. Unable to cope with life, he takes flight psychologically when troubles mount. The amnesiac's "new" personality is no more mature than the abandoned one, but he is making a last-ditch effort to deal with problems. When all other resources fail, he forces his own identity out of his memory.

Multiple Personality. You are not likely to encounter a person with multiple personality in the everyday course of your life. Taylor and Martin (1944) searched many decades' worth of literature and could report fewer than 100 cases.

For a few persons, dissociative reactions similar to amnesia occur early in life, distort personality development during the formative years, and produce an adult whose psychic structure contains more than one distinct personality.

Once this second personality has become a separate self, the individual may begin to function as two individuals. Today he is one person; tomorrow he may be another. Further, each of the personalities may have no awareness of the other. Confusion is, of course, inevitable when one self must account for the unknown actions of the other.

Each of us experiences diverse aspects of our different personalities at various times. Some of us have life styles that are dramatically different in different situations and periods of our life. Some who are reputed to be exceptionally moral or straight may have secret lives diametrically opposed to the public image. Indeed, very few among us do not experience shifting moods and feelings or create fantasy "selves" to impress others. But the key to distinguishing between normal and pathological forms of multiple personality is whether there is an unconscious dissociation of one personality from the other.

Depersonalization Neurosis.   Suppose you returned home tonight and suddenly felt you were in the wrong house. The furniture looks different; the pictures on the wall seem new to you; the others who live with you don't seem to react in predictable ways. Nothing seems right. What would you do? How would you react? Would you begin to doubt your sanity?

When the feeling of estrangement or depersonalization is focused on one's body, it may be even more frightening. This is an experience similar to those reported by psychotic persons. Suppose, for example, parts of your body no longer seem to belong to you. Your arm begins to feel like an alien object attached to your shoulder; your eyes begin to scan the environment in a way that suggests they are operating independently from your conscious will. In such instances, part of the self seems to be lost. The determination between self and not-self, which is made in early childhood, comes unglued, and nothing seems real anymore.

We lack a great deal of information about the precise nature of the depersonalization reaction. It is considered a neurotic rather than psychotic reaction, however, because even though it is distressing it does not totally disorganize the habits of daily living.

The Psychophysiological Disorders

When we speak of *psychosomatic* events, we refer to how an individual manages anxiety. The relationship between physiological reactions and emotional stimulation has been described by Levitt (1967): "The physiological responses to emotional stimulation are *autonomic*. The function of an autonomous response is to make an automatic, internal adjustment in the body without a conscious or voluntary effort by the individual" (p. 91).

Unlike the symptoms of conversion hysteria, the psychophysiological reactions involve actual changes in the anatomical structure or physiological functions of the body. An hysteric activates response in organ systems that can be manipulated by voluntary control. The psychophysiologic reaction, by contrast, involves organ systems that are under the control of the autonomic nervous system. In other words, such organs cannot normally be triggered voluntarily. Consideration of all organ systems is beyond the scope of this chapter, but we can use one example—that of bronchial asthma—to indicate how our emotions and our bodily functions become psychologically entangled.

Respiratory Reactions

The relation between emotional states and asthmatic attacks has been demonstrated in a classic case where a patient allergic to roses suffered an attack when confronted with a papier-mâché rose. Similar cases have been recorded where the predictability and regularity of attacks made emotions—rather than allergens—the suspected causal agent. What begins as an allergic response may also have a learned or conditioned aspect impressed upon it so that the psychological cue is enough to trigger the physiological response (Turnbull, 1962).

In bronchial asthma, the bronchioles of the lung are physically constricted, and choking, gasping, and wheezing are commonplace. Not all bronchial asthma is caused by psychogenic factors, of course. Some asthmatics respond to real physical allergens in the environment. Indeed, there is no logical reason to interpret *all* physical disorders in psychogenic terms.

In bronchial asthma emotional forces may play a predominant part, however. With or without some inherited inclination to asthmatic reaction, individual emotional conflicts are known to contribute to the disorder. For Witthower and White (1959), the fundamental psychodynamics include: (1) an inordinate need for maternal dependence and love, (2) an ambivalent attitude toward the mother, and (3) fear of losing or destroying the mother. Exploration of these psychodynamic postulations has, unfortunately, been based on too few cases and too little reliable experimental evidence.

A usual clinical explanation of recurrent asthma traces it back to childhood and the nature of the parent-child relationship (Fitzelle, 1957; Margolis, 1961). Clinicians who deal regularly with asthmatic cases describe several types of "asthmatogenic mother":

STRESS AND RESPONSE

Lacey, Bateman, and van Lehn (1953) found that stressful situations produce the same symptoms of psychosomatic disorders in the same persons. That is, under stress, people show the same specific bodily response from situation to situation.

Subjects were tested under four different stress situations. During these stresses, measurements were taken of each subject's palmar skin potential and heart rate. The results showed that the pattern of bodily response was generally the same for each subject. Those who showed a greater change in heart rate than in palmar skin potential under one situation also showed a greater change for heart rate under all stress situations.

THE UNCOMMON COLD

A woman who caught colds every winter went into psychoanalysis after an unhappy marriage. She slowly became aware that she had spent most of her life denying her feelings of rage, grief, jealousy, and sensuality. At the end of her treatment, she also realized that she had not caught one cold during the last year of psychoanalysis. Perhaps, the best ways you can prevent the common cold are not to punish your mind and body by forcing yourself to go to work if you feel ill, and to know yourself and your emotions. How you feel psychologically may determine how you will feel physically (Freeman, 1973).

1. The "deprived" mother who is anxious, self-pitying, and has only meager personal resources to offer her child.
2. The "achievement"-oriented mother who has high personal aspirations for herself and equally high goals set for her child.
3. The "assertive" mother who is impulsive, controlling, and oriented toward using power.

In clinical-experimental work exploring these "types" of mothers (Block, Harvey, Jennings, and Simpson, 1966), evidence was uncovered only for the "deprived" mother.

The Obsessive-Compulsive Disorders

Obsessive-compulsive disorders make up approximately 12 percent of all neurotic disturbances. Its victims are usually brighter than average persons (Laughlin, 1967), and some theoreticians have suggested that a greater number of first born or only children are subject to this kind of personality disorganization (Kayton and Borge, 1967). This may be due to the exclusive exposure of the child to adults without the relief of siblings or because of the higher expectations parents have for first born or only children. The deterioration of obsession into severe depression is common; but the risk of suicide, alcoholism, or drug addiction is less than usual (Rosenberg, 1968).

Normal Obsessions

Most of us have a number of little rituals and modest obsessions. Sometimes, tunes or snatches of song will continuously run through one's head. In a study of persons under stress, Berg (1953) reported that each subject had experienced this phenomenon when under pressure. They reported being irritated by the continued presence of a tune, but they were unable to drive the tune from their minds. It is suggested that such tunes are both a temporary distraction from problems and a psychological return to more pleasant circumstances. Indeed, the experimental subjects reported that the insistent songs brought associations of happier moments.

All of us have been frustrated by a bureaucrat who behaves in a ritualistic, rule-bound, obsessive-compulsive manner. He might insist on the letter-perfect adherence to "rules" while refusing to examine the logic behind the rules. In this respect, much of the modern protest against the "system" is a reaction against preserving meaningless, arbitrary, inflexible policies which have outlived their relevance.

The Obsessive-Compulsive Way of Life

David Shapiro (1965) proposed looking under the surface in obsessive disorder to find some psychological patterns that will help us understand this neurotic

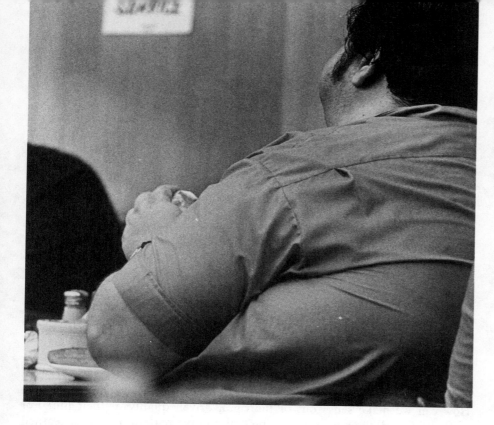

Compulsions take many forms— including compulsions for food. As we saw in the issue on overeating in Chapter 8, there is no simple explanation for why some people are obsessed with the thought of food and feel compelled to eat even when they're not hungry.

style of life. Obsessive-compulsive persons have a rigid approach to life; this rigidity may include pursuing an absurd course of action or dogmatic, opinionated style of thinking. Cognitive rigidity is coupled with an unusual involvement in activity. An obsessive is a busy person, but his busyness is strained and driven. He may be "trapped" in work whether it interests him or not. The deadline set for completion of every task becomes a fixed, rigid, absolute dictum; he frets about meeting the deadline and is disappointed and angry when he fails. Once he becomes caught up in a task, he is no longer free to stop it or do less than a perfect job. He imposes standards on himself which compel him to labor mightily on each and every assignment that comes his way. Naturally, it would be difficult for such persons to enjoy the rest and relaxation of vacations. Vacations would be as meticulously organized as any other serious assignment.

The indecisiveness of obsessive-compulsive persons is legendary. After every possible factor and force has been carefully measured and weighed and a decision finally seems imminent, some new possibility occurs, and the decision is once again delayed. In this manner, the obsessive engages in psychological acrobatics trying to avoid a decision that might later prove wrong. If a decision *must* be made, the obsessed person is happiest when he can invoke a policy, rule, or logical principle. The physical and psychological effort—the sheer energy expended in decision making—is enormous.

Ritual and Compulsion

Compulsive actions may become ritualized in the effort to assure one's own psychic safety. The victim of compulsion feels he has to count, touch, wash his hands, or endlessly repeat certain behavior patterns even if these actions seem absurd. The comfort such actions provide is sufficient justification for the behavior. It simply feels better to perform the ritual.

The exactness of the ritual—every move is made precisely as it was in the past—has a magical quality. In Kolb's words:

> . . . the defensive patterns of the compulsions resemble penance, atonement, and punishments, or serve as precautions, prohibitions, and restrictions. In many ways, they are closely allied psychologically to the ceremonies and taboos that primitive people devise as protections against demonological and other supernatural forces. [1968, p. 485]

The neurotic individual is trapped in a pattern of his own defensive making; he must act as he does or suffer anxiety. He decides to act out his rituals to feel comfortable, and he learns to live with their senselessness.

The Defenses

We all know persons who suffer varying degrees of obsession or compulsion. How can we make sense out of the rigid, driven quality of their life? For Sigmund Freud, the answer was to be found in the pattern of defense learned early in life. Freud described the defense mechanisms used by obsessive-compulsives as isolation, undoing, and reaction formation.

Isolation. Our thoughts generally contain both an idea and our own emotions or feelings about the idea. When these two aspects of thought are separated (when emotion is dissociated from thought), our experience resembles that of the obsessed person. We may have an objectionable thought without the emotion that would usually accompany it. An obsessed person, for example, might be plagued by a fantasy that all the members of his family are dead or horribly mutilated. He is aware of these thoughts but reacts to them in a neutral (unemotional) fashion, since the full meaning of such thoughts is hidden from him.

Undoing. When isolation proves to be an inadequate defense against anxiety, a new maneuver is called for to undo, or cancel out, the hostile, forbidden impulses. In a classic form of such a defensive behavior, a patient suffering from the nagging fear that he has accidentally killed his family by leaving the kitchen gas jets turned on, reassures himself by checking, rechecking, and checking again to be sure the gas jets are fully turned off. The problem with actions designed to undo is that each action is another stimulus triggering again the obsessive thought which the person needs so much to deny. He is caught in a vicious circle of action, reaction, and action again.

Reaction Formation.   Reaction formation (doing the opposite of the repressed wish or impulse) is a defense which aims at organizing a fairly permanent character trait rather than simply defending against anxiety provoked by each new situation. Behavior based on reaction formation may appear exaggerated and inappropriate to others, but it provides a kind of permanent protection from anxiety that isolation and undoing seem unable to achieve. The lives of some persons are systematically organized "like clock-work" to assure a dependable, predictable world. For some persons, excessive cleanliness, kindness, and concern for others may mask the urge to express opposing patterns of behavior—to soil, be self-seeking, and injure others. If the denied impulse is intense, the degree of reaction formation may have to be equally intense.

Summary

1.   The neurotic is an adult who is unable to deal effectively with the problems of everyday life. His behavior is self-defeating and merely intensifies his problems.

2.   The characteristics of a neurotic are: Feelings of inadequacy, low toleration for stress, a fearful outlook on life, irritability, and disturbed personal relationships.

3.   A neurotic personality displays certain odd personality traits and has interpersonal difficulties. A symptom neurosis is a clear-cut pattern of symptoms such as phobia, obsessions and compulsions, or anxiety. A neurotic personality need not develop a symptom neurosis, although it is possible he will.

4.   In the psychodynamic theory, neuroses are mechanisms by which an individual escapes anxiety. The anxiety is caused by childhood frustrations that have not been resolved.

5.   The neurotic lives in a state of constant tension, afraid that his defenses will fail and his anxiety will overwhelm him. This state of tension prevents the neurotic from dealing effectively with the rest of his environment.

6.   All of us use defense mechanisms to some extent, but some individuals continue to use them in situations where they will not work. Among the defense mechanisms Freud postulated are repression and rationalization. Repression is an attempt to keep forbidden impulses from reaching consciousness. Rationalization is an attempt to substitute comforting reasons or interpretations for the real ones.

7.   According to behaviorists, neuroses are learned habits which persist because the reduction of anxiety and the accompanying attention and care are both reinforcing.

8. The existential neurosis occurs when an individual who has failed to resolve his own identity is confronted with stress.

9. Among the symptom neuroses, there are the hysterical neuroses—conversion hysteria and dissociative states. Psychodynamic theory views both of these as attempts to prevent forbidden impulses from entering conscious expression.

10. In conversion hysteria, the individual may mimic some form of paralysis, although there is no anatomical basis for the illness. Such symptoms are interpreted as repressed material gaining expression in bodily disorder and also as attempts to avoid the source of anxiety.

11. Dissociative neuroses are characterized by gross personality distortion; the individual performs forbidden behaviors of which he remains unaware. Included in this category are amnesia, somnambulism, multiple personality, and depersonalization.

12. Psychophysiological neuroses are the result of the body's responses to emotional problems. Like conversion hysteria, these symptoms are a means of managing or avoiding anxiety, but the two are different in that psychosomatic illness has a real physiological basis.

13. Obsessive-compulsive disorders are characterized by ritualistic behavior and repetitive thoughts over which the individual has no control. According to Freud, these disorders result from an attempt to control anxiety using the defense mechanisms of isolation, undoing, and reaction formation.

PSYCHOLOGICAL ISSUE

The Prevalence of Disorder

The seriousness of emotional disturbance in our society became particularly apparent during World War II when one out of every five of our young men (nearly five million) was rejected for military service because of mental illness. Of one million additional men accepted for service but later discharged with a disability, 43 percent had neuropsychiatric problems.

The frequency of emotional disturbance in our culture was even more dramatically demonstrated in the Midtown Manhattan Study conducted by Srole and his colleagues (1962). In this research, residents in a section of New York's East Side were randomly sampled. Over 1,600 persons filled out a detailed questionnaire concerning the severity (absent, mild, moderate, or serious) of their past and present physical and mental symptoms. They were also asked to indicate the degree to which these symptoms interfered with their adjustment. The researchers found that fewer than one in four persons was "well" and nearly one in five was "incapacitated" by emotional disorder. Indeed, if so few of us are free of symptoms, the problem of defining mental illness and mental health is magnified. It seems reasonable to conclude that anxiety and emotional difficulties are the price that must be paid to participate in modern, civilized society.

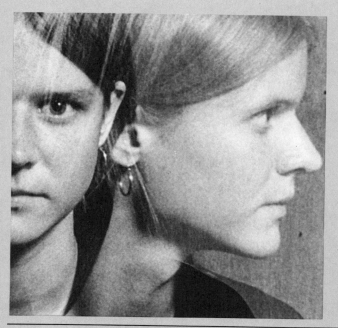

Disorder, Now and Then

Since 1880 our population has increased more than four times, and the number of hospitalized mental patients has multiplied 18 times. This steady increase has more than matched the expansion of hospital facilities, and today we calculate the size of the problem in the many millions.

The conclusion one might reach is that technological civilization is costing us our sanity. According to Goldhamer and Marshall (1949), however, this does not seem to be the case. They concluded that, aside from an increase in the number of people over 50 (made possible by increases in life expectancy), admission rates have been remarkably stable throughout various periods of history. There is no clear evidence that the pressures of modern life are destroying us psychologically.

The frequency and kinds of symptoms we see today are, of course, not identical to those of the past. The members of our society are better educated, less restricted in sexual and other expressive outlets, and more sophisticated about psychological disorder. Our society has evolved and changed, and so have the psychological symptoms we display.

Estimating the Problem. Conservative estimates indicate that at least one person in every ten (20,000,000 in the United States) will some time during life have a mental or emotional illness that could benefit from professional help. On any one day, there are three quarters of a million persons under psychiatric care in hospitals. Mental illness occurs at all ages. Estimates of the number of mentally ill children range from 500,000 to as many as 1,000,000. About 473,000 children under 18 years of age received some service in a psychiatric facility in the United States in 1966.

Our Present Problem

The occurrence of new cases of emotional disturbance during a fixed period of time (incidence) and the total number of active cases in the population at any one time (prevalence) must not be confused. Thus, figures on *prevalence* may remain the same over a two-year span of time. This would hide the fact that, in any one year, there may be a great many new cases but also an equally high rate of cure.

It is difficult to decide which estimates of *incidence* (or the frequency of mental disorder) are the most reliable. Some years ago Lemkau and Crocetti (1958) estimated the probable incidence of disorder. They set the lower limit at 50 cases per 100,000 and the upper limit at about 250 per 100,000. The median figure was 150 cases per 100,000 in any one year. Their estimate of prevalence was 290 cases per 100,000 persons with approximately 150 of these hospitalized. They suggested: "It is probable that for each 1,000 children born, between 14 and 20 will be hospitalized . . . within their lifetime" (p. 80).

An "official" view provided by the U.S. Department of Health, Education, and Welfare (1967) reports that there has been an overall drop in total patient population. This is a consequence of an increase in release rate despite the growing admission rate.

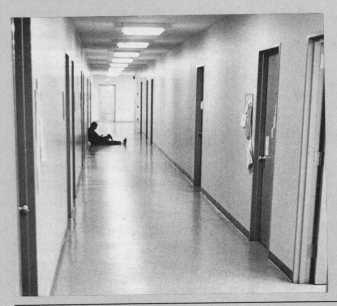

Disorder and Social Status

Incidence and prevalence figures tell only a small part of the story of psychological disturbance. Who you are socially may have a dramatic effect on when and if you will be distressed by life and what form the disturbance is liable to take. As an illustration, Meyers and Roberts (1959) reported on the kinds of symptoms shown by 25 neurotics and 25 schizophrenics selected from different social classes. Even when these patients had the same diagnosis, middle- and lower-class patients behaved quite differently. The symptoms of the middle-class group were expressed by inhibited actions; none was in trouble with the law. By contrast, lower-class patients tended to "act out," to be aggressive, rebellious, violent, and self-indulgent. Thus, 60 percent of the members of the lower-class group were in legal trouble because of their symptoms. Middle-class symptomatology reflects self-depreciation, failure, and guilt, whereas lower-class patients tended to blame someone else for their difficulties, were suspicious, and ready to assault others.

Another widely cited study is that of Hollingshead and Redlich (1953) who examined the pathology and social class structure of New Haven, Connecticut, and surrounding towns. Five classes were identified: Class I were wealthy business and professional men; Class II were managers and lesser ranking professionals; Class III were white-collar workers, proprietors, and skilled laborers; Class IV were semiskilled workers; and Class V were unskilled laborers and factory workers. A census was taken to determine which residents were getting psychiatric care. Both the psychiatric group and the control group of normal persons were categorized by social class. A clearly significant relationship was found between social class and psychiatric care. Fewer members of the higher classes (I-IV) were under psychiatric care than would have been predicted by the number of such persons in the population. A greater than expected number of people under psychiatric care came from the lowest social class (V). Class V, for example, made up 17.8 percent of the general population, yet had 36.8 percent of its members under psychiatric care. Diagnoses were also significantly correlated with social class. Upper class persons (I and II) were most often diagnosed as neurotic; psychosis seemed to be reserved for the lower classes (IV and V).

This does not mean that members of the lower socioeconomic classes are more disturbed than the more privileged and affluent. Rather, it implies that the symptoms of mental disturbance regularly tend to be associated with the style of life appropriate to one's social class. One conclusion is evident. The fate of psychological disturbance is not completely an individual matter. It is, rather, a matter of one's relatedness to the larger society.

Summary

1. Although the current rates of hospitalization for mental disorder are much higher than they were 100 years ago, most psychologists agree that the increased incidence is not a result of pressure of modern life. They believe a larger population and more individuals who live to the ages of senility account for the increase in mental illness.

2. A correlation does seem to exist between the prevalence of disorder and social class. Studies show that the lower classes have more people under psychiatric care than do the upper classes. It is assumed that this is not because lower-class people are more disturbed but because upper-class people are likely to receive help early. Also, higher mental illness rates could result from a more insecure environment.

3. Another interesting correlation between class and disorder is that lower-class people tend to act aggressively when mentally disturbed, whereas middle-class patients tend to be inhibited. It is assumed that middle-class patients blame themselves for their predicament, while lower-class individuals blame others.

4. Although classification of mental disorder into categories is useful in describing sets of symptoms, the limitations of the current classification system must be kept in mind. In addition to being inadequate, the use of such a system may be dangerous in perpetuating the disease model of mental disorder and in encouraging patients to take on the role that is expected.

PSYCHOLOGICAL ISSUE

Drinking

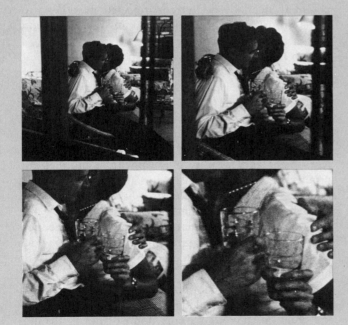

Alcoholics are most often classified as persons suffering from personality disorders or disturbances. Men and women with personality disturbances adopt a "style of living" which, unfortunately, inflicts discomfort and misery on innocent others as well as on themselves. Although they do not suffer from the same kind of irritating or tension-producing symptoms which neurotics face, their attempts to cope with life are all too often destructive and self-defeating.

An estimated 96 million Americans drink alcohol, and an astonishing 9.6 million of them are alcoholics. Alcohol may shorten your life span anywhere from ten to twelve years. It is blamed for half the highway deaths each year, and problem drinking drains the economy of $15 billion a year. So, why doesn't everyone stop drinking? We don't stop partly because we like it and partly because it is one of the few drugs that can be used as a thirst quencher, as a way of gracious living, a social lubricant, a food, a medicine, an intoxicant, a psychedelic agent, a symbol of being grown up, and a way to defy authority.

Alcohol alters your psychological state in an odd manner. In small amounts it is a depressant that reduces the effective expression of your impulses, needs, and anxieties. It relaxes the guards that watch your behavior, but after that point it scrambles your sensations and perceptions. How fast this scrambling effect takes place depends how much you weigh, how much you move around when drinking, what kind of mood you are in, and what you had to eat before you started bending your elbow. You will get drunk quicker when you are celebrating than when you are trying to forget. And you will fall over faster if you haven't eaten all day.

Once you discover that liquor will bolster your self-confidence and ease the pain and tension of daily living, you have taken the first step toward alcoholism. The next step involves drinking more heavily and now and then having "blackouts" where you can't remember all the details of what you did or said at the party. Before long, you may be hoisting your glass until you find you can't say no to the next drink. You go on "benders" that last days or weeks. You are hungover all the time. You don't eat much anymore since it tends to kill off the blurred state you have been in for some time, and you don't give much of a damn about what people are telling you. Without a few shots, you don't feel normal. By now you care about booze more than anything else, and you are near the end of the line.

Theories of Alcoholism

A lot of us drink, but only some of us are alcoholics. Although psychologists have hammered out a variety of theories to explain the difference, we still haven't been able to explain it (Buss, 1966). Biological theorists have looked for something wrong in the brain, the glands, or the body's metabolism, but no reliable evidence has been found to support this idea. Cultural theorists are fascinated by the fact that there are national and racial differences in alcoholism. They feel differences in style of life must account for the variations.

Psychodynamic theorists view alcoholism as an exceptionally complex problem with as many patterns of drinking as there are individual alcoholics. To them, alcoholism can be a symptom of any number of psy-

---

The Bottom of the Barrel.   When you think of an alcoholic, you are most likely to picture the classic derelict wino described by Regestein and Howe [1971]: The dirty, unshaven, bleary-eyed, vulgar, stumbling wino who is crushed like a grape between his feelings of loneliness and his terrible fear of being hurt by people. Only when drinking can he tolerate interpersonal relationships. He staggers through life shy, guilty, ashamed, hostile and fearful toward authority. He is most often in his early 50s. He quit school by the tenth grade, was dishonorably discharged from the army, has been in and out of jails like a yo-yo, has dropped out of Alcoholics Anonymous, and has lost track of his family. Not a pretty picture. But, he makes up only a tiny percentage of the estimated 9 million alcoholics in the country.

The Executive Lush.   If you are a corporate executive and you regularly have so many martinis at lunch that you are wiped out for the rest of the afternoon, you may qualify as an executive lush. Do you miss a lot of days on the job? Do you have the status symbol of a built-in bar in your office? Do you come to work hungover and in pain? Congratulations! You *are* an executive alcoholic.

You will cost your company a small fortune in lost time, botched deals, bad decisions, and inefficiency, but if you get a loyal executive secretary to cover for you, the company won't fire you for a long time. According to the National Council on Alcoholism, 45 percent of the alcoholics in this country have professional or managerial positions. The typical alcoholic has been at his job 12 years; he's between the ages of 35 and 54; and his alcoholism has been present but unrecognized for years.

---

chological disorders. Psychodynamic theorists suggest that the psychological histories of alcoholics may have certain features in common. These might include:

An Inability to Handle Tension in a Mature Manner   The potential alcoholic easily feels rejected by others, retreats from conflicts, avoids making decisions, and cannot tolerate tension for long periods of time.

A Deep Dependency on Other People   Since others seem more capable or stronger, alcoholics retreat to passivity and seek to be cared for and protected by others. If situations that demand independence cannot be avoided, they use alcohol to escape tension.

A Severe Unexpressed Hostility to Close Friends   When the need to be dependent on others goes unfulfilled, resentment and hostility may appear in indirect and disguised ways. Consciously, the alcoholic insists that he loves those who are closest to him. Unconsciously, his behavior indicates the opposite is true.

Egocentricity   The immaturity and self-centeredness of the alcoholic is most apparent in the degree to which he feels sorry for himself and thinks people pick on him.

To the learning theorist, you learn to drink as your parents do. Heavy-drinking parents raise heavy-drinking children. If your parents don't drink at all, it is probable you won't either (Chafetz, 1967). The behaviorist believes, however, that what is learned can be unlearned.

Conditioned reflex therapy, or aversion therapy, is credited with success among alcoholics. The association of avoidance responses (via drugs) with alcohol connects drinking with unpleasant consequences. When a patient who has taken Antabuse drinks alcohol, he experiences headache, dizziness, chest pain, nausea, air hunger, and vomiting within minutes. The problem remains though that the dedicated alcoholic will simply stop taking the drug once he is comfortably seated in a bar.

. . . And a Scotch and Coconut for My Friend. Young chimpanzees can be used for research on alcoholism since they will drink enough to produce symptoms of withdrawal when the supply is cut off. Mild to severe symptoms of physical dependence are observed when the chimp bar is closed after 6 to 10 weeks of steady drinking. Chimps also seem to build up a tolerance for alcohol and keep it in their bloodstream when they have been drinking for a while [Pieper, 1972]. No one asked the chimpanzees if they were interested in learning to hold their liquor "as good as any man in the bar," of course.

The Family

When you think of the wife of an alcoholic, what words come to mind? Victim of circumstances? Long-suffering? Martyr? Brave? Courageous? You are probably pretty close to describing how the wife sees herself—someone who, through no fault of her own, is made miserable over and over again by her husband's irresponsible drinking. In some cases this certainly is an accurate picture, but in an incredible number of instances a closer look suggests that it takes two to make an alcoholic marriage. The "innocent" wife has an important part to play in her husband's drinking. Thelma Whalen (1953) has described some of the roles and personality types she observed among the wives of alcoholics:

• *Suffering Susan* is the wife who needs to punish herself by choosing a husband who makes her life miserable.

• *Controlling Catherine* has a distrustful, resentful attitude toward men in general, and a more adequate male would have been too threatening to her own psychological needs. She needs a man who will be inadequate or inferior in some way.

• *Wavering Winifred* is the person who needs someone who needs her so she chooses a husband who is

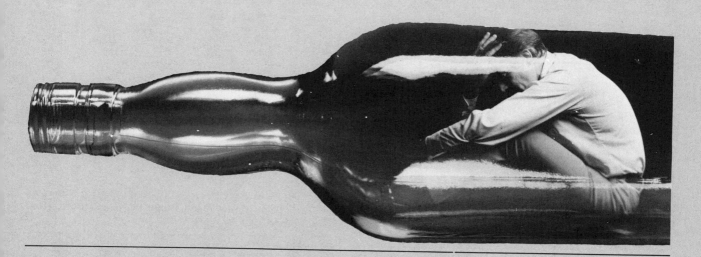

weak and unlikely *not* to need her. She is secure only as long as she can be sure her man cannot get along without her.

• *Punitive Polly* is rivalrous, aggressive, and envious. She would only marry a vulnerable man she can punish in the same way a mother does her very small boy who has been very naughty.

Whatever the personality structure of the wife, in most cases she knew the husband drank before they got married, even though his alcohol intake was usually within socially acceptable limits.

Of course, men are not alone in their alcoholism. There are alcoholic mothers as well as alcoholic fathers and husbands who have to contend with wives who drink. The female alcoholic, however, reports more depressive symptoms, has a higher incidence of depressive episodes, and makes more suicide attempts than the male heavy drinker. She usually becomes alcoholic around the age of 30 (eight years later, on the average, than her male counterpart), but both males and females are first hospitalized for alcoholism about age 40. She suffers a broken marriage in almost half the instances, has an alcoholic spouse about one-third of the time, and frequently complains of sexual dissatisfaction in her life.

Joan Jackson (1956) describes the stages of family life that often follow the realization of an alcoholic parent.

Stage 1. Attempts to Deny the Problem Although excessive drinking only happens occasionally at first, it begins to put strain on the marriage, and both try to pretend these drinking episodes are normal. ("Everyone gets drunk once in a while.") Situations in which it might happen again are avoided. ("Let's stay home this New Year's Eve.")

Stage 2. Attempts to Eliminate the Problem The family begins to withdraw from social contact to keep the drinking problem from becoming common gossip. The truth is kept from the children and the boss. An all out attempt is now made to control the drinking, but it doesn't work.

Stage 3. Disorganization "What's the use?" describes this stage as the problem appears permanent. The family starts to come apart and stops trying to understand the alcoholic or to keep the drinking a secret.

Stage 4. Attempts to Reorganize in Spite of Problems This is the stage at which the family becomes stabilized. The wife takes over her husband's role, and he is treated like a difficult child who simply won't behave himself. This reorganization is almost impossible to maintain for long. The husband's drinking escalates, and he may be fired from his job, put in jail, or hospitalized. In the reverse case, of course, the husband assumes the maternal duties and tries to cope as best he can.

Stage 5. Efforts to Escape the Problem The decision to give up leads to divorce once the spouse can face feelings about deserting a sick person. The decision is made easier if the husband has become abusive, destructive, or violent.

Stage 6. Reorganization of the Family If successful, this stage allows the family to sort itself out, redivide responsibilities, and begin a new pattern of living together.

It is unnecessary to add gruesome detail to the story of excessive drinking. The destructiveness is apparent. Therapeutic attempts of great variety have been used to eliminate problem drinking, but, on the whole, they have met with only modest success. The best known approach to helping those who can't handle alcohol is Alcoholics Anonymous.

Items for a Lull in the Conversation

• Unlike other things you drink, alcohol is not digested. It is absorbed directly into the blood stream where it travels to the brain.

• Men drink three times as much as women, and alcoholics drink 11 times as much as others.

• Some experts estimate that every tenth car approaching you on the highway may be driven by an alcoholic.

• Drinking to excess is geographic. The citizens of California rank highest with those in New Jersey, New Hampshire, and New York close behind.

Alcoholics Anonymous

The basic principles of Alcoholics Anonymous are that only an alcoholic can help another alcoholic, that psychiatric and other treatment is usually unsuccessful, and that alcoholics can manage to lead relatively normal lives by banding together in a spirit of mutual help and understanding. Most important, an alcoholic must never again take even one drink. Abiding by these rules, they maintain that 50 percent of all alcoholics coming into AA get sober and stay that way. Twenty-five percent have one or two slips before they see the light, and the other 25 percent are either psychotic or not alcoholic at all.

These statistics are probably generous estimates of the success of AA, but the fact remains that this idea has worked where other approaches have failed. AA branches are found in prisons, hospitals, and towns of all sizes. The only requirement for membership is a desire to stop drinking.

AA members assert that there's nothing wrong with alcoholics except alcohol, and all the alcoholic has to do is to stay away from that first drink. They regard alcoholism as a physical disease, not a mental one, even though their sessions resemble a mixture of revival meeting and public confessional. Psychotherapists part company with the AA program when it insists that the alcoholic is free of emotional problems and that the drug is a *cause* rather than a *symptom* of deeper problems. Therapists insist that alcoholics will be cured only when they gain insight into why they can't control their drinking in the first place. Perhaps AA works very well for some people, but it doesn't work at all for others. Half of those who come to the meetings drop out of the program in the first month. We must suppose that those who stop attending and keep on drinking would be classified by AA as either psychotic or not alcoholic at all, but such classification is of doubtful accuracy.

Psychologists have pondered the problem of alcoholism for a great many years but have yet to solve it. Alcoholics Anonymous works for some people, and until social scientists can find a better approach we must be thankful we have something that works at all.

Summary

1. One-tenth of all Americans who drink alcohol are alcoholics, and those who abuse alcohol may shorten their lives by ten to twelve years.

2. In small quantities alcohol is a depressant. In larger amounts it starts to confuse one's sensations and perceptions and may cause "blackouts." It is not digested, but travels directly into the blood stream and then to the brain.

3. There are different theories about alcoholism, but no one has yet been able to explain why some of us drink and are not alcoholics while others of us are. Psychodynamic theorists list traits they see as characteristic of alcoholism—inability to handle tension, excessive dependency, unexpressed hostility, and egocentricity. There is a high correlation between heavy-drinking parents and heavy-drinking children.

4. The idea of an "innocent" spouse in an alcoholic marriage is not always supported by fact. Often, women choose men who have alcoholic tendencies because they want to punish themselves.

5. The amount of female alcoholism is somewhat hard to measure because many housewives hide their problem by drinking during the day when their husbands and children are away. But whether the father or mother (or both) is alcoholic, the disruptiveness caused by abuse of alcohol pervades the whole family situation.

6. Alcoholics Anonymous attempts to combat drinking by having alcoholics help other alcoholics. The most important rule of AA is "never take another drink."

The Psychoses

*The mind is its own place, and
    in itself
Can make a heaven of Hell, a
    hell of Heaven*
            —John Milton

Severe psychological disorders called psychoses and schizophrenias represent
serious alterations of motivation, perception, sensation, emotion, behavior,
or thinking. Distortions of these basic components of human life produce
the symptoms of psychotic disorder.

Disorder in the motivational system may paralyze an individual's urge
to act—he may cease to make voluntary movements or decisions about life.
Or, he can make decisions but only with an accompanying doubt that his
decisions might not be the correct ones. The motivation to act may also be
marred by excess at the other extreme. The individual may overreact or react
too strongly.

When perception and sensation are distorted, the individual can no
longer understand his world. Imagine the effect of a sudden increase or
decrease of your sensory capacities. Suppose you lost your sense of touch
or you saw that the objects and people closest to you were changing their
shape, form, and outline without rhyme or reason. Hallucinations represent
such distortions in the senses. Nothing is more disconcerting than to experience
sensations for which there are no appropriate physical stimuli.

Emotion, behavior, and speech can all become disordered. When one
is excessively happy or sad, or when emotion takes a form that does not
fit the social definition of the situation, the behavior is labeled abnormal.
Schizophrenics, for example, may experience emotions of a degree and kind
unlike those usually felt by "normal" persons. Any disturbance of verbal
behavior severs communication with the rest of society, as does behavior which

Are Neurotics Just "Better" Psychotics?

The pattern of behavior we call psychosis is much more serious and disabling than neurosis. Although the neurotic's ability to cope with his problems and to function effectively in society is somewhat restricted by his self-defeating behavior, the psychotic's ability to function at all is severely impaired.

The basic distinction between the two is that while the neurotic is acutely aware of his environment, the psychotic has lost a great deal of contact with reality. Often he cannot tell the difference between his own fantasies and reality. Unlike the neurotic whose thought processes are relatively intact, the psychotic suffers from delusions, hallucinations, and loss of control over thoughts, feelings, and actions.

The boundary between neurosis and psychosis—like the boundaries between various classes of pathological behavior—is not always clearly defined, and some psychologists argue that psychosis is merely a more extreme form of neurosis, marked by increasing personality decompensation. They point to the fact that many psychotics display neurotic behavior patterns before and after psychosis, and that some neurotics occasionally experience mild delusions. However, only a very small number of clear-cut neurotics actually become psychotic, and most psychologists believe that, rather than being phases of the same continuum, neurosis and psychosis are two unique pathologies which differ not in degree but in the nature of the disorder.

CHILDREN OF
SCHIZOPHRENICS
Schizophrenic parents seem to have no harmful effects on the intellectual development of their children. The IQ's of 262 children of schizophrenics were compared to the childhood scores of their 129 schizophrenic parents. The children's IQ's were significantly higher than those of their parents. Children with schizophrenic mothers performed better than children with schizophrenic fathers, however (Lane, Albee, and Doll, 1970).

does not conform to socially accepted actions. If thoughts are too extreme or distant from average thought, then again, the thinker is declared a deviant.

Disorder in systems of motivation, perception, sensation, emotion, behavior, and thinking are severely threatening and stressful to the victim. As the disorder mounts, defensive attempts to escape anxious feelings begin to crumble and something called decompensation may occur.

Part of what happens in psychosis can be described by this process of *decompensation*. When most of us try to solve problems and defend against anxiety, we make a number of adjustments such as altering our patterns of thinking, feeling, and behaving. We compensate for the pressures we are experiencing. If the stress becomes too great or our defensive maneuvers prove to be insufficient to the task, we too may be forced into deviant forms of behavior. Our alteration of psychic and biological energy is marked first by heightened tension, agitation, and alertness. These patterns of behavior may be quite deviant from past behavior and may provoke concern among those who know us.

Suppose you are an actor and that you've been psyching yourself up for a major performance for the past several hours. You have been compensating for the extra effort by visualizing yourself as a magnificent performer and by mentally rehearsing the part you will play. Just as you go onstage, a terrific explosion occurs right behind you. The explosion would be the "last straw." The stress would be too much and you would, in effect, come apart at the seams. At that moment, you would be experiencing disorganization and deterioration of coordination, attention, and concentration. So it is with the average person who marshals all his or her resources for a special task only to have everything go awry when something unexpected happens.

Physical decompensation may add additional stress to the burden the victim is already carrying. Psychological and biological decompensation swell together to produce the characteristic symptoms and patterns of behavior recognized as psychoses.

The Schizophrenias

The schizophrenias are a particular kind of psychosis. The Belgian psychiatrist Benedict Augustin Morel described a condition which he labeled *demence precoce* as an hereditary disease leading to psychological deterioration after its first appearance in the adolescent years. The German psychiatrist Emil Kraeplin later gathered thousands of case histories and developed a system of classification which distinguished three kinds of *dementia praecox:* hebephrenia, catatonia, and paranoia. Eugene Bleuler added a fourth form, dementia (the simple type) and coined the term *schizophrenia* to describe the disease. In more recent times new distinctions have been added to our understanding of schizophrenia.

THE SCHIZOPHRENIAS
Simple type. *Seldom hallucinations, delusions, or intellectual impairment. Marked by general apathy or social withdrawal.*
Hebephrenic type. *Hallucinations, delusions, inappropriate emotion, wild or "silly" behavior.*
Catatonic type. *Stupor or excessive agitation with visible motor disturbance.*
Paranoid type. *Fragmentary, unorganized delusions often accompanied by auditory hallucinations.*

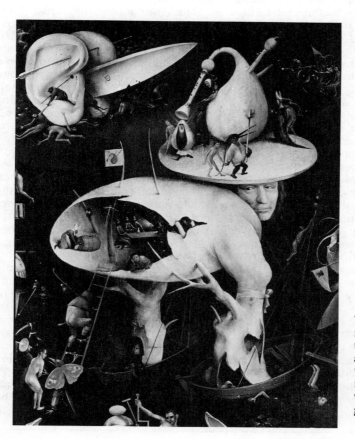

This nightmarish scene of burning ruins and fantastic instruments of torture represents Hell, some critics assert. But no one knows for sure what its enigmatic creator Hieronymus Bosch had in mind. It might well reflect Bosch's ideas of the anguish suffered by the mentally ill.

Process and Reactive Schizophrenia

Process schizophrenia develops early in life. The patient has a long history of disturbed behavior and has seldom experienced any precipitating events of a decisively traumatic nature. Rather, there is apparently a gradual shift from a moderately withdrawn state to a schizophrenic condition. In contrast, *reactive schizophrenia* develops suddenly, often after a dramatic event or some combination of events. The patient suffers from intense anxiety, guilt, and confusion; he has vivid hallucinations, bizarre delusions, or intense fears of dying. The reactive schizophrenic often seems more disturbed than the process schizophrenic, but the reactive patient is much likelier to recover.

Ain't It Great To Be Crazy?

"The process of entering into *the other* world from this world, and returning to *this* world from the other world, is as natural as death and giving birth and being born. But in our present world, which is both so terrified and so unconscious of the other world, it is not surprising that when 'reality,' the fabric of this world, bursts, and a person enters the other world, he is completely lost and terrified and meets only incomprehension in others." (Laing, 1967, p. 125)

Such is the view of schizophrenia proposed by R. D. Laing, the British existential psychiatrist known for his "celebration" of the schizophrenic. Laing believes that some schizophrenics are on the path to higher sanity, while the normals of the world remain less than sane in an insane world. According to Laing, most individuals are alienated from themselves. They have set up a dual personality: the outer self, set up to meet the outward demands of society, and the inner self, the true self. Unfortunately, the inhuman society continually makes demands which conflict with the real, or inner, self, while the outer self complies. Eventually the inner self has slipped away, and the outer self is all that is left. Thus Laing says: "What we call 'normal' is a product of repression, denial, splitting, projection, introjection and other forms of destructive action on experience. It is radically estranged from the structure of being" (p. 27).

Laing sees schizophrenia as a natural and understandable reaction to an insane world filled with unresolvable conflicts. But more than this, schizophrenia is a process by which the individual explores his inner self in an attempt to bring the split personality back together again. At the end of the voyage through inner space, the individual returns saner than he ever was before the onset of psychosis. For this reason, Laing feels that schizophrenia is a process that would benefit each of us, and society as well.

The schizophrenic needs help, Laing agrees, but traditional psychotherapy only interferes with the "natural healing process" that is schizophrenia. Indeed, most therapy for psychotics is aimed at an adjustment to our view of normality and the restoration of previous personality structure, which, as Laing points out, is far from healthy. Moreover, the individual may be driven truly insane by the chemicals, surgery, or mental hospitals which he is subjected to as a "psychotic." Because he is a product of our society, the schizophrenic feels lost and afraid in the inner world he hardly knew existed—and which others condemn—and it is psychiatry's role to guide him through the exploration of this inner space and help him find his way back. The guide must be someone who has been there before. "Psychiatrically," says Laing, "this would appear as ex-patients helping future patients go mad" (p. 128). Laing's ideal is a multiplicity of places like Kingsley Hall, a community, which he helped establish in 1965, where therapists and patients live together and patients are free to go mad.

"Perhaps we will learn to accord to so-called schizophrenics who have come back to us, perhaps after years, no less respect than the often no less lost explorers of the Renaissance. If the human race survives, future men will, I suspect, look back on our enlightened epoch as a veritable age of Darkness. They will presumably be able to savor the irony of this situation with more amusement than we can extract from it. The laugh's on us. They will see that what we call "schizophrenia" was one of the forms in which, often through quite ordinary people, the light began to break through the cracks in our all-too-closed minds." *Source:* Laing, 1967, p. 129.

Research suggests that the relevant causal factors are different for each type of patient. According to Higgins (1972), the mother is implicated in process schizophrenia; she is usually described as dominant, carping, punitive, and a generally unpleasant person. The father is usually weak, ineffectual, and submissive; he does little to protect the process schizophrenic from the on-slaughts of the mother. The child learns to adopt docile, obedient, and submissive behavior (like his father's) as a way of escaping the mother. The process schizophrenic is always a good boy; he never gives his mother any trouble.

The history of the reactive schizophrenic is different. The father is described as harsh, aggressive, and demanding, while the mother is weak and submissive. The father—though distant, feared, or hated—nevertheless provides an assertive identification model. The child learns to respond forcefully to his physical and social environment. Higgins suggests that the reactive's history often appears to be "supernormal." He may have a wide circle of friends, participate in group activities, have academic or vocational success, and, sometimes, a good marriage.

When stressful events occur (the death of a loved one, financial disaster, or crippling illness), the reactive schizophrenic finds himself defenseless and suffering from enormous anxiety and acute emotional and cognitive disorganization. When he is removed from the stressful situation, he will, in time, reorganize his defenses and return to the kind of life he led before his breakdown.

It should be noted that the patterns of human behavior called schizophrenic are subdivided into a number of types without regard for the process-reactive distinction. Also, Sarbin (1972) contends, the disease called schizophrenia is largely a myth: "Contemporary researchers have a choice. They may persevere in the search for that elusive factor that will reliably distinguish schizophrenics from normals. Or they may question the disease model of schizophrenia itself, and try to find a better, truly explanatory paradigm. Continuing with the old paradigm is—for 'schizophrenics' and researchers alike—an exercise in futility" (pp. 18 and 27).

Simple Schizophrenia

Between 3 to 7 percent of hospitalized schizophrenic patients are diagnosed as *simple schizophrenics*. They are described as apathetic and seclusive and have minimal social contact with other human beings.

When the patient stops communicating with others, becomes noticeably sloppy in his personal habits, and excessively absorbed in fantasy or day-dreaming, he may come to the attention of authorities. The qualities of dullness, indifference, absence of motivation, and scattered attention may then be discovered. The simple schizophrenic may appear retarded or seem unable to cope with the complexities of modern life.

For some simple schizophrenics, the path of least resistance becomes an aimless wandering from place to place. Hobos, tramps, bums, or prostitutes are often simple schizophrenics seldom detected or diagnosed since they live lives of minimal responsibility. Our prisons also contain a fair number of simple schizophrenics.

The early form of simple schizophrenia is marked by shyness and hypersensitivity; its victims typically display a poor sexual adjustment and an unaggressive personality. In general, the age of onset of the symptoms ranges from 12 to 40 years of age with its first appearance around age 17. When simple schizophrenics come to the attention of social and legal authorities, it is most often the result of the appearance of deviant sexual behavior (child accosting, rape, voyeurism, prostitution), assault on others, destruction of property, or some other form of antisocial behavior.

Hebephrenic Schizophrenia

From the Greek word meaning youthful mind, *hebephrenic schizophrenia* is what most people associate with stereotyped concepts of insanity or "craziness." Hebephrenic behavior appears at an earlier age than simple schizophrenia and represents a more severe disintegration of the personality. Its appearance may be sudden, but most often it runs an insidious course of development. The symptoms include incoherent speech punctuated with inappropriate giggling, smiling, or open laughter; intense delusions and hallucinations; strange grimaces, odd posturings, unusual mannerisms and gestures; and alterations of voice and speech rhythms.

The degree of psychic distortion suffered by the patient is revealed by the bizarre quality of his delusions and hallucinations. He may be convinced that he is a famous person, that he is dead and can still walk, that he has X-ray eyes, or that he is invisible. He may lose bowel and bladder control, indulge in obscene and exhibitionistic behavior, smear urine and feces, or act like an infant. In general, the chances that he will get well are very slim.

The hebephrenic's symptoms may begin early in childhood: he may demonstrate a certain oddness and an increasing preoccupation with the self and seclusion from others. Hebephrenics become the "old timers" in every mental hospital—the patients who live most of their lives in a hospital setting.

Catatonic Schizophrenia

Catatonic schizophrenia is marked by motor disturbances that are not evident in the other schizophrenias. The catatonic may be stuporous, retarded in movement, mute, and unreactive. He may express passive aggression by refusing to cooperate with social demands, and this may be the sole indication that he is aware of the world outside his own fantasy life. At times he can become assaultive, and some patients alternate unpredictably between inhibition of movement and sudden, aggressive response to stimulation. The catatonic's inhibition is an active, forceful controlling of the self—a willful erecting of an uncooperative facade. The catatonic may fear making a mistake that would jeopardize his already dangerous situation. These patients can maintain for hours a stuporous, malleable posture (waxy flexibility) which requires some force of will on their part. If the rigidly held position is painful or exhausting, the expenditure of physical energy is extraordinary. The catatonic is often the victim of active hallucinations and delusions of a mystical or persecutory nature. In short, he is preoccupied with an invisible world that fully absorbs his attention and energy.

Paranoid Schizophrenia

The *paranoid schizophrenic* appears the most normal and least disturbed patient on the ward. On closer contact, his delusions and hallucinations become apparent. Such patients make up more than half of all first admissions for schizophrenia, and they remain hospitalized for so long that they form the majority of all hospitalized schizophrenics.

The paranoid schizophrenic lives with fear, suspicion, and fragile interpersonal relations for many years before his delusional system becomes fixed and visible to others. Even when his schizophrenic deterioration becomes massive, he may maintain a reasonable orientation to reality in most phases of his life. He may make a marginal social adjustment for a number of years and may escape detection until his late twenties or early thirties.

The paranoid schizophrenic reacts to life as if he were a hunted animal.

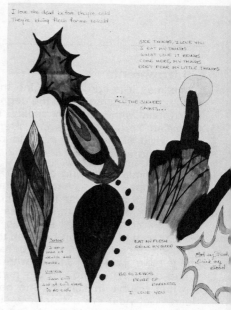

Art done by schizophrenic persons often reveals more about what takes place in their inner worlds than numerous therapy sessions.

THE THREE CHRISTS OF YPSILANTI

Delusional systems may be maintained by persons despite contradictory evidence (Rokeach, 1964). At the Ypsilanti State Hospital in Michigan, three male paranoid patients, each claiming to be Jesus Christ, were transferred to adjacent hospital beds; they were assigned to the same dining table, given jobs together, and regularly seen together by a social psychologist. These continuous direct confrontations did not result in the disappearance of their delusions. The two older men remained essentially unchanged, while the third only showed some changes in his delusional thinking.

Schizophrenia

Sometimes it is hard to imagine the inner world of the schizophrenic person, and the degree to which he or she may totally withdraw from reality. In her novel *I Never Promised You a Rose Garden,* Hannah Green provides some vivid examples of a world called *Yr* which both haunts and comforts a 16-year-old schizophrenic girl.

For a time—how long by Earth's reckoning Deborah did not know—it was peaceful. The world made few demands so that it seemed once more as if it had been the world's pressures that had caused so much of the agony in Yr. Sometimes she was able to see "reality" from Yr as if the partition between them were only gauze. On such occasions her name became Januce, because she felt like two-faced Janus—with a face on each world. It had been her letting slip this name which had caused the first trouble in school. She had been living by the Secret Calendar (Yr did not measure time as the world did) and had returned to the Heavy Calendar in the middle of the day, and having then that wonderful and omniscient feeling of changing, she had headed a class paper: NOW JANUCE. The teacher had said, "Deborah, what is this mark on your paper? What is this word, Januce?"

And, as the teacher stood by her desk, some nightmare terror coming to life had risen in the day-sane schoolroom. Deborah had looked about and found that she could not see except in outlines, gray against gray, and with no depth, but flatly, like a picture. The mark on the paper was the emblem of coming from Yr's time to Earth's, but, being caught while still in transition, she had to answer for both of them. Such an answer would have been the unveiling of a horror—a horror from which she would not have awakened rationally; and so she had lied and dissembled, with her heart choking her. Such a danger must no more be allowed aloud, and so that night the whole Great Collect had come crowding into the Midworld: gods and demons from Yr and shades from Earth, and they had set up over their kingdoms a Censor to stand between Deborah's speech and actions and to guard the secret of Yr's existence.

Over the years the power of the Censor had grown greater and greater, and it was he who had lately thrust himself into both worlds, so that sometimes no speech and no action escaped him. One whisper of a secret name, one sign written, one slip of light could break into the hidden place and destroy her and both the worlds forever.

[It was this terror, this fear that the other world of Yr would destroy her if she did not obey its demands, that finally found Deborah in a psychiatric ward. Her struggle

toward sanity was a long one, and there were deep retreats sometimes when she felt she had revealed too much to her psychiatrist. In the following passage Anterrabae is the Falling God of Yr, whose hair is fire.]

Yr was massed against her when she got back to the ward. Sitting on a hard chair, she listened to the cries and screams of the Collect and the roaring of the lower levels of Yr's realms. *Listen, Bird-one; listen, Wild-horse-one; you are not of them!* The Yri words sounded an eternity of withdrawal. *Behold me!* Anterrabae fell and said, *You are playing with the Pit forever. You are walking around your destruction and poking a little finger at it here and there. You will break the seal. You will end.* And in the background: *You are not of us,* from the cruel-jawed Collect.

Anterrabae said, *You were never one of them, not ever. You are wholly different.*

There was a long, profound comfort in what he said. Quietly and happily, Deborah set out to prove the distance across the yawning gap of difference. She had the top of a tin can, which she had found on one of her walks and picked up, both knowing and not knowing what she expected of it. The edges were rippled and sharp. She dragged the metal down the inside of her upper arm, watching the blood start slowly from the six or seven tracks that followed the metal down below the elbow. There was no pain, only the unpleasant sensation of the resistance of her flesh. The tin top was drawn down again carefully and fastidiously following the original tracks. She worked hard, scraping deeper, ten times or so up and back until the inside of the arm was a gory swath. Then she fell asleep.

Source: From *I Never Promised You a Rose Garden* by Hannah Green (Joanne Greenberg). Copyright © 1964 by Hannah Green. Reprinted by permission of Holt, Rinehart and Winston, Inc.

He survives through alertness and carefully designed defensive measures to ward off attack by others.

He is grandiose and egocentric in his belief that everyone is watching him, plotting against him, and trying to get something from him. Beneath these feelings of persecution lies a grandiose belief that only talented or important persons would be so hounded by others; the justification for such persecution is that others are jealous of his superior ability, talent, or knowledge. Persecution is therefore simultaneously painful and gratifying, frightening and reassuring.

Mania and Depression

Even though the history of manic-depressive disorders reaches back to the days of Homer and Hippocrates, it took centuries for clinicians to discover that the two conditions are faces of the same disorder. About one half of today's manic-depressive patients have just one encounter with the disorder; the other half experience several attacks over a period of years (Grinker et al., 1961). The initial attack usually occurs between twenty and thirty years of age and afflicts women more frequently than men. (About 70 percent of hospitalized manic-depressives are female.) Fewer than 15 to 25 percent of all manic-depressive patients display the alternation between mania and depression that was once characteristic of the disorder. The attempt to solve personal problems through mania or depression usually does not bring on a total break with reality as in schizophrenia. Of the 20 percent of schizophrenic patients admitted to mental hospitals each year, 14 percent will be labeled depressive or manic.

CROSS-CULTURAL DIAGNOSIS
In a study in which American and British psychiatrists were asked to make diagnoses on the basis of videotaped doctor-patient interviews, the patients were more likely to be classified as schizophrenic by the Americans and as psychotics with mood disorders by the Britishers. Patients showing disorders of both thought and mood were labeled schizophrenics by the Americans and diagnosed as suffering from an affective disorder by the British psychiatrists (Mosher and Feinsilver, 1970).

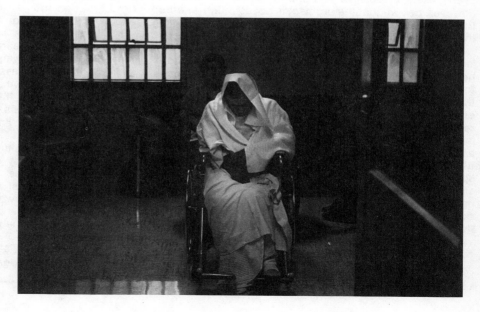

Mania

About 30 percent of all patients admitted to hospitals with mood and emotion disorders will display *manic* symptoms in varying degrees. Three degrees of manic activity are usually used to describe the intensity of excited behavior. These are: hypomania, acute mania, and hyperacute mania.

Hypomania.   In the *hypomanic* (least excited) stage, it is difficult to distinguish the disorder from the kind of excitement that is usual for someone having a good time. Since our society has always admired the "go-getter" and hard worker—the model of energy, drive, and activity—hypomania will be reinforced when it results in community progress, problem solving, innovation, and change. Hypomanics may be widely admired, not so much for their effectiveness, as for the stimulus value they provide to others who actually get the work done. The hypomanic may be considered a cultural hero in a bustling, active society.

Why Are We Depressed?

Depression remains a major puzzle to psychologists of nearly all theoretical persuasions. The psychodynamic view suggests that depression is a result of rejection—real or imagined—in childhood; in this way, losses in adult life are particularly traumatic because they bring a rebirth of the childhood crisis. The common behavioral view postulates that the life of the depressed individual has been absent of positive reinforcers. Some behaviorists, however, believe that the problem is not so much whether the reinforcements are positive or negative, but whether they are appropriate to the situation.

Martin E. P. Seligman has proposed that depression is the result of an individual's belief that nothing he does has any effect on his life situation. The individual comes to such a conclusion, Seligman believes, because negative and positive reinforcements come to him independent of his actions. Thus a famous actress who is always receiving attention and affection because of who she is—rather than what she does—is as prone to depression as the man who works hard but can't seem to hold down a job. The same thing may be responsible for the widespread depression that has been reported among college students. They have received "goodies from the sky"—material rewards—without having earned them by their own actions. In all these cases, reinforcements have little or nothing to do with the way the individual behaves. No wonder an individual begins to feel that things are out of his control.

In support of his theory, Seligman compares depression to learned helplessness—a phenomenon produced in experimental subjects in the laboratory. Dogs are placed in a harness and given shock from which they cannot escape. Later the same dogs are placed in a shuttlebox and shocked again, but this time they can terminate the shock by jumping over a barrier in the box. Naive dogs have no trouble learning the escape routine. But those dogs that have been given inescapable shock howl first and then sit passively, taking the shock. The experiments have been repeated with other animals, and with human subjects as well. Depressed patients and subjects who have learned that they are helpless commonly show similar symptoms: passivity, loss of appetite, lack of outward aggression, and an inability to learn that one's responses do make a difference. Moreover, depressed people say things that seem to describe the feeling of helplessness: "I'm a born loser," "I can't do anything right," or "I'm blocked no matter what I try to do."

Seligman's theory indicates that therapists can help depressed patients by showing them that their actions do make a difference. Moreover, individuals could be "inoculated" against depression in adulthood if they have childhoods in which positive and negative reinforcements are delivered contingent to their actions. If Seligman is right, maybe you can have "too much of a good thing."

Source: Martin E. P. Seligman, "Fall into Helplessness," *Psychology Today*, June 1973, pp. 43–48.

When hypomania signals the beginning of a manic attack, the patient's mood shifts, his level of activity rises, behavior becomes more spontaneous and outgoing, and he experiences an increased alertness in sensory perception and thought processes. The rate of speech increases, and a "pressured" quality is added to it. The patient bounces from idea to idea and is hard to interrupt.

Hyperactivity, increased alertness, an expanded sense of well-being, and self-confidence appear as the hypomania deepens. When the outer limits are reached, his ideas begin to be questioned by his associates, and his enthusiasm turns to anger and resentment toward those who now seem to be interfering.

Acute Mania.   When mania becomes *acute,* its victim resists criticism, restraint, or domination by others even though he becomes an increasing nuisance to his friends and the general public. By now he may be absolutely convinced of his superior judgment and ready to launch a far-out scheme that will prove he was right all along (Schwartz, 1961). He is likely to become aggressive, vulgar, and insensitive to how others view him; he might abandon his previous habits of grooming since he no longer cares what others think of him.

Hyperacute Mania.   *Hyperacute* or *delirious* mania is the final stage. The patient is by now close to delirium, confused, wildly excited, unresponsive to others, violent when crossed, disoriented, and incoherent. By this time, he may be hallucinating, and his agitated behavior may continue until a state of total exhaustion is reached. Manic actions are an attempt to manipulate, push, and force life. Filled with doubt and fear, the manic makes a last desperate attempt to avoid the depression he feels is about to close in on him.

Depression

Depression and mania would seem to be opposite and unrelated, but the manic is apparently running away from depression by plunging into so much activity that it drowns out the intimation of on-coming depression. Like mania, depression is described according to its severity: it can be simple, acute, or hyperacute. In addition, a special category includes agitated depressions where the patient is hyperactive and upset by the delusional content of his thinking; he may fear, for example, that the end of the world is soon coming (Kraines, 1957).

Simple Depression.   The simple phase of depression resembles the way most of us feel when we get dejected or discouraged. The simple depressive is without his usual energy or motivation, and his physical activity and thinking slow down measurably as he devotes himself to feelings of worthlessness, sin, or punishment. The sense of hopelessness increases as he becomes less active and is perpetually preoccupied with internal miseries. Before long,

THE MOVING DEPRESSION
Weissman and Paykel (1972) declare that the stressful effects of American geographical mobility have been underestimated and that moving often places stress on the individual. A group of depressed women were studied. In most cases, the women did not relate their illnesses to recent moves, but their depressive symptoms resulted from faulty adaptation to the stresses and changes created by moving. The women did not associate their symptoms with moving, since it is an accepted part of American life which is almost taken for granted.

communication with the outside world gets severed; habits of eating and sleeping are disturbed; and he may think about suicide as a well-deserved punishment or the only way out of his many problems.

Acute Depression.   As the depression becomes more acute, his self-accusations increase, deepen, and become less oriented to reality. His world now appears distorted, alien, and delusional. Bodily symptoms may also appear. The patient is withdrawn from the outside world and has only his internal bodily experience as the focus of his attention. The depressed patient's body does, in fact, change as it becomes inactive—there may be severe constipation, loss of sexual impulse, or interruption of menstrual periods. These bodily changes increase the patient's worries, and 75 percent of acutely depressed patients begin to think of death or suicide (Arieti, 1959).

Hyperacute Depression.   By now depression has made the patient stuporous and unresponsive. He may have to be fed or be bedridden; he is confused and totally absorbed with delusions of sin and death. In some instances the symptoms take a different direction, and increasing agitation rather than hyperacute depression is the outcome. An agitated depression, like a retarded depression, is marked by a mood of sadness and despair; and the patient is obsessed with ideas of suicide, imminent destruction, and catastrophe. These patients are acutely aware of dangers that other people seem to ignore. They pace the floor restlessly and are too distracted to sleep or eat. They may devote all their energy to giving warnings, complaining about the condition of the world, or crying over their terrible fate.

Agitated Depression.   Agitated depression is an exaggerated form of the normal behavior of a person who is under severe pressure but unable to work out life's problems. In normal life, these periods of agitation are brief; for the agitated depressive, it is a prolonged part of existence. To him the world appears ready to collapse; his internal experience is one of hopelessness and failure.

The Organic Disorders

Acute Brain Disorder

Acute brain syndromes are biochemical changes in brain functions that produce a sudden onset of delirium, stupor, or coma. The patient in this stuporous condition is brought to full, normal consciousness only with great difficulty, and he can remain alert only for very short periods of time. The severity of the symptoms correlates roughly to the amount of damage the central nervous system has sustained. If the disorder is acute, the prognosis is good since the usual healing mechanisms of the body will remedy or compensate

SEVERE DEPRESSION
Mrs. K. was brought to the clinic by her husband after having taken an overdose of sleeping pills. He admitted that she had been "a little" depressed for some time, but he had simply encouraged her to "snap out of it." Mrs. K. spoke in a barely audible voice; she sat, unmoving, with her hands in her lap. After much encouragement and urging, she would only comment, "I wish I'd died—nobody cares—All against me—all—everybody—my husband —poisoned their minds—my kids—turned 'em against me—don't want to talk—let me alone. . . ."
[*Strange, 1965, p. 346*]

for this breakdown of its functions. When drug intoxication is relieved, a high fever reduced, or nutritional deficiency remedied, the nervous system and the brain may again become dependable organs.

Chronic Brain Disorder

Brain lesions, infection, or the normal physiological degeneration that comes with age can all produce chronic brain damage—damage that cannot be reversed. The victim of chronic brain disorder suffers progressive decay of intellectual, cognitive, and emotional functions; he may also have impaired concentration, memory, ability to deal with symbols, or ability to differentiate one object from another. Behavior ceases to be rational because the nervous system fails to integrate internal and external stimuli properly. With very aged patients, a mixture of hardening of the cerebral arteries and senile brain disease accounts for 30 percent of first admissions to mental hospitals (Fishbein, 1962). The advances made by medicine have kept us alive but have also altered our psychotic problems.

As with the use of the straightjacket, this method of restraining violent mental patients is not as prevalent as it was before the advent of "miracle" drugs.

Senile Brain Disorder

One of the costs of growing old is the increased risk of senile psychotic disorder. The psychoses of senility are most frequent in Western industrialized society since the advances of medical technology have extended the *average* life span (Burgess, 1960). With age, unfortunately, comes not only physical but psychological disorder as well (Arnhoff, 1961; Himwich, 1962).

For some patients, senile brain disorder will produce simple deterioration without any psychotic patterns of behavior. In senile deterioration, the patient begins to forget essential facts, loses the capacity to deal with symbols and abstractions, and has troublesome memory lapses.

As cells of the brain and central nervous system die and are not replaced, the controls which were once used over the emotions may become ineffective. Senile persons may then display shocking behavior; sexual, aggressive, greedy, or inconsiderate thoughts may appear which may also involve the person in distasteful encounters with the law. The two most common brain syndromes of the aged are senile brain disease (atrophy and/or degeneration of parts of the central nervous system) and cerebral arteriosclerosis (the thickening of arteries in the brain). These produce nearly 80 percent of the brain disorders of the aged (Marks, 1961).

Syphilis and Brain Damage

One of the most dramatic instances of damage to the brain is produced by cerebral syphilis. If syphilis is not treated, it kills or maims. Syphilis has existed for centuries, and its spread across the planet could well have been due to the great voyages of Columbus and Vasco De Gama. This infection has been the camp follower of every army in history. Sex, war, and exploration spread syphilis to the four corners of the earth.

The syphilis spirochete is extremely virulent and can penetrate the defenses of the body with startling ease. The modern miracle of penicillin and antibiotic drugs should have banished this disease long ago, but man has stubbornly refused to learn about it. Thus we have a rising rate of infection and the formation of newer, more resistant strains of the spirochete.

Somewhere between 10 to 30 years after infection, the syphilis spirochete takes its toll on the brain and central nervous system. If the blood vessels and heart are its target, death is sudden. If the nervous system is its focus, the victim has *paresis* (a paralytic disorder of the central nervous system). Only a small percentage of those with untreated syphilis suffer paresis, but an untreated case is regularly fatal.

When general paresis occurs, the patient may experience manic expansiveness and euphoria, or severe depression. Either emotional extreme may be marked by disorientation, delusions, hallucinations, or destruction of intellectual and cognitive capacities. With treatment, about 50 percent of syphilitic patients show improvement or recovery; a small percentage die during treatment; and a slightly greater number show little improvement.

The physical incapacity of organic damage is sometimes compounded by a breakthrough of psychotic processes. Psychosis following brain damage may emerge as inappropriate extremes of emotional response (mania or depression), cognitive or perceptual deviation (hallucinations and delusions), suspicion and hostility (paranoia), or withdrawal from reality and retreat into fantasy (the schizophrenias). In such cases, the damage to the brain does not "cause" the psychosis. It simply makes a nonpsychotic adjustment less possible for those who had been reasonably free of distress in the past.

Summary

1. Psychoses are severe psychological disorders characterized by gross distortions in motivation, perception, sensation, emotion, thought and behavior. Unlike neuroses, psychoses usually involve a loss of contact with reality and thought disorder involving either delusions or hallucinations. It has been suggested that psychoses are a much more severe form of neuroses, but many psychologists believe that they are distinct disease entities.

2. The process of psychotic breakdown involves decompensation. When usual coping patterns begin to fail, the individual may attempt to use exaggerated and inappropriate defenses which appear as psychotic behaviors.

3. Schizophrenia is a form of psychosis marked by distortions of thought, perception, and behavior. Schizophrenia may develop

slowly over time (process) or be a result of sudden events (reactive). Personal histories of these two types of schizophrenic individuals are quite different, and the reactive is more likely to recover.

4. Schizophrenia is classified into four subtypes: simple, hebephrenic, catatonic, and paranoid. Each type is known for a particular pattern of symptoms, but individuals often display behaviors belonging in more than one category.

5. Mania and depression are classified as affective disorders because they involve a change in mood. Psychologists believe that mania and depression are actually two forms of the same disorder. The manic is only trying to run away from depression by his intense activity.

6. Mania is characterized by greater and greater levels of excitement, an expanded sense of self-confidence, and agitated behavior. Depressive individuals are marked by a sense of hopelessness, feelings of guilt and failure, inactivity, and thoughts of suicide.

7. The psychodynamic theory of depression is that fear of rejection in childhood is brought back by adult loss or failure. Behaviorists believe that depression is due to a lack of positive reinforcement, or perhaps even any type of reinforcement that is inappropriate to an individual's behaviors.

8. Acute brain disorder, which causes delirium or stupor, is a result of biochemical changes in the brain. If the problem can be corrected, chances for recovery are quite good. Chronic brain disorder, however, is a result of lesions, infections, or degeneration that cannot be reversed. Its effects include a progressive worsening of concentration, memory, and cognitive functions. Syphilis and senile brain disorder are two forms of chronic brain damage.

9. Psychosis may sometimes follow organic brain damage, even if the damage is corrected. It is a result of the fact that the individual cannot cope with the stress he has undergone.

10. Those theorists who believe schizophrenia is inherited point to studies which show a relationship along blood lines in the incidence of the disorder. However, others point out that such studies involve very small numbers and that environmental factors have not been ruled out.

PSYCHOLOGICAL ISSUE

The Psychotic Disorders of Childhood

A little more than a quarter century ago, few theorists or clinical workers were much concerned about the psychoses of childhood. It was then, as it is now, a rare event most often misdiagnosed as mental retardation or organic disorder. Since the late 1930s, however, the scientific literature devoted to this condition has increased by about tenfold each decade.

Childhood Psychosis

Some researchers deny that childhood psychosis exists at all. Others treat it as a rough equivalent to adult schizophrenia. Whereas some report that manic-depressive psychosis occurs in childhood, there are others who insist that this cannot occur in children between seven and seventeen. A psychotic child is said to be seclusive, to live in a fantasy world, to have abnormal reactions to ordinary stimuli, and to suffer extreme difficulty in communication. The psychotic child, however, seldom hallucinates or is delusional, and his difficulties with reality seem to stem from misinterpretations of the stimuli around him rather than from the creation of his own world.

Infantile psychosis usually refers to children with profound abnormalities of language development, a variety of ritualistic and compulsive symptoms, and a collection of stereotyped mannerisms beginning in infancy. Mutilative behavior (head-banging, biting, scratching, or hairpulling) directed against the self has been reported in as many as 40 percent of schizophrenic children (Green, 1967). Children who are able to use language to communicate show less of this self-mutilative behavior than do nonverbal children (Shodell and Reiter, 1968).

The psychotic child seems incapable of adequate social reaction since he uses fantasy to cope with conflict. These fantasy productions are not the same as the normal child's wishful thinking. It is unquestionably an understatement to say, as Yates (1970) did, that the literature of childhood psychosis is in a hopelessly disorganized and confused state. We began by believing that schizophrenia was a young person's disorder, and this belief made it unlikely, on theoretical grounds, that the same disturbance could occur in very young children. We thought then that children suffering from a schizophrenic disorder differed from schizophrenic adults only because of the incomplete maturation of the child.

Theories of Childhood Psychosis   There is a strong theoretical conviction that severe disorder in childhood might be traced to a constitutional or genetically determined abnormality in the child. Genetic/constitutional theorists argue that there must be some as yet undiscovered biological insufficiency that predisposes the child to maladjustment.

The most popular dynamic theories have implicated the mother as a prime source of disturbance in childhood. The mother is described as either detached or overprotective; or, at the very least, the mother's personality is in some way abnormal. Mothers of psychotic children have been described as rigid, restrictive, punitive, impersonal, overprotective, overpossessive, anxious, and domineering. In other studies, mothers were described as obsessive, rejecting, and cruel. These characteristics are used to define the "schizophrenogenic" mother who unwittingly produces pathology in her child. Other experts believe that childhood schizophrenia is not a single disorder and, therefore, cannot be attributed to a single cause. There is no essential conflict between psychodynamic and behavioral

theorists in tracing the source of psychosis to what the child learns and is exposed to. There is disagreement, however, about the details of how psychic disruption occurs.

Schofield and Balian (1959) have suggested that the personal life history of seriously disturbed individuals does not always support the assumptions of the dynamic theorists. In a life-history study of a matched group of schizophrenics and normals, it was difficult to demonstrate the warped personal history we have so long assumed must have been present. The parents of both schizophrenics and normals were described as affectionate; schizophrenic children were not reported to display unmanageable behavior in school; and it

The Human Machine. The psychiatrist Bruno Bettelheim [1959] has reported the case of Joey, a boy who saw himself as a machine. Electrical power helped Joey live and machinery helped him eat, defecate, and sleep. When his "machine" was turned off he sat quietly inert. Joey had been ignored by his parents; he was an unwanted and unloved baby; and when he cried his parents would not comfort him or satisfy his needs. His toilet-training was strict and at a very early age. Joey retreated into the world of machines, where he could be safe from human feelings. Through treatment and understanding, Joey finally abandoned his machinelike world to become human.

was difficult to distinguish in general between the personal histories of the two groups.

Autism

Leo Kanner's paper on *infantile autism* prompted the first important differentiation among children labeled childhood schizophrenics. In 1943, Kanner described a small sample of children who displayed behavior patterns that resembled, but did not exactly duplicate, those of childhood schizophrenia. Kanner considered this a rare form of disorder since he could discover only 150 such cases out of the approximately 20,000 disturbed youngsters he had encountered. Following this report, autism became a fashionable diagnosis, since its newness freed it of the social stigma attached to childhood schizophrenia or childhood psychosis.

The Symptoms of Autism   The principal difficulty displayed by the autistic child is his inability to relate to others. The autistic child is most often male. He is aloof from interpersonal contact shortly after birth; he fails to use language to communicate; and he seems more attached to objects than to people. The child is aware of the environment, and some autistic children get seriously upset if any detail of their surroundings is altered. Deeply immersed in an "autistic aloneness," the child is disconnected from his fellow human beings and may accumulate a series of eccentric patterns of behavior. An autistic child may survive by eating only one kind of food; he may eat only when the food is

---

Depriving the Deprived.   Maier (1970) described the treatment of a five-year-old psychotic boy whose disability fitted most of the criteria of the infantile autism syndrome. The child was placed in a small, barren, dimly lit room for a period of some 74 days with the hope that this would force a significant reorganization of the child's personality. During this time, he was fed and visited twice daily by a therapist at irregular times. The result was a significant improvement of the boy's ability to relate to other people and adapt to his environment.

---

cut or arranged in a particular way; or he may drink only from special containers.

Autistic children usually look like other children; they move quickly and easily, have normal coordination, and make few demands on parents. But, they also fail to imitate the gestures of others, reach out to them, or react to their overtures. There is so little response to others (in contrast to their deep involvement with objects) that, when speech is acquired, it is likely to be limited, sparingly used, or parrot-like. As some autistic children grow older, a few may overcome these psychological handicaps and display remarkable mental abilities. Most autistic children end up in institutions, but the brilliant exceptions make this disorder even more puzzling.

When infantile autism and adult schizophrenia are compared, the differences are quite clear. To begin with, autism is much more common in males, whereas schizophrenia is about equally common in both sexes. In addition, the social class of the parents of autistic children often differs from that of the parents of schizophrenics; the parents of autistic children tend to have above-average intelligence and high socioeconomic status (Lotter, 1967). Studies of infantile autism have also indicated that adult schizophrenia rarely appears in the parents or brothers and sisters of autistic children. Delusions and hallucinations are common symptoms in schizophrenia, but they seldom occur in autism.

It is true that the symptoms of childhood schizophrenia overlap with many of those attributed to autism. Reversion or regression to primitive forms of behavior, distorted thinking, seclusiveness, emotional blunting, idiosyncratic speech, repetitive movements, negativism, destructiveness, apathy, and strange mannerisms have all been found in schizophrenia. Regression is probably the single event which is typical of schizophrenia but not of autism. Infantile psychosis might, then, be an appropriate label for autism, while childhood schizophrenia could be limited to cases where personality disintegration takes place after five years of age.

The Causes of Autism?   A disorder as mysterious and loosely defined as this is bound to be attributed to as many causes as there are theories. When Kanner first described this disorder, he thought autism was an inborn disturbance that made emotional contact with others impossible. This "inborn" statement led organic theorists to suggest that the source of autism is the malfunctioning of the reticular formation in the brain stem, an excess of oxygen administered in early infancy, or constitutional defect. Bender (1947) proposed the concept of a diffuse encephalopathy, and Knobloch and Pasamanick have stressed the possibility that brain damage may have originated in difficulties during pregnancy or birth (Knobloch and Pasamanick, 1962; Pasamanick and Knobloch, 1963).

Kanner later stressed the emotionally cold and obsessive characteristics he detected in the parents of autistic children (Kanner and Eisenberg, 1955; Eisenberg and Kanner, 1956). He decided that, while the children probably had some inborn defect, the disorder might better be described as due to the lack of affection from the parents. He considered autism a psychogenic disorder caused by "emotional refrigeration."

Bettelheim's (1967) view is that autism develops as a response to extremely negative feelings on the part of the parent—feelings so marked that the child abandons hope for love. Bettelheim explains the abnormality of the child's response by citing the critical periods in development (in the first six months when real object relationships begin; at six to nine months when language and locomotion appear; and at eighteen to twenty-four months when the child can shape his relations with the environment).

Behavioral psychologists have added the hypothesis that autism is environmentally determined and that this maladjustive behavior is the result of differential reinforcement given the child. Autism is due to faulty learning in which the autistic child has not been conditioned properly by the parents (Ferster, 1961). Autism, to the behaviorist, is the result of faulty conditioning.

This view is based, in part, on the response of some autistic children to operant conditioning methods of treatment. These techniques have had success, but there have also been failures. We also know from past experience that it is exceptionally hazardous to argue about the causes of a problem by referring to the type of therapy which is effective in resolving it. It is conceivable that autism develops because of faulty conditioning, but there is no evidence that such abnormalities in environmental reinforcement existed during the child's early years.

Summary

1. Childhood psychoses usually involve abnormalities in language development, rituals, compulsions, stereotyped mannerisms, and the lack of response to others. Unlike adult psychoses, childhood disorders seldom involve hallucinations or delusions.

2. Among the possible causes of childhood psychosis, trauma at birth, constitutional defects, schizophrenogenic mothers, and the learning of maladaptive behaviors have all been suggested. In comparing the life histories of normal and schizophrenic children, however, no clear-cut differences emerge.

3. Many of the symptoms of autism and childhood schizophrenia are quite similar, but the two can be distinguished because of the autistic child's inability to react to others, insistence on sameness in surroundings, highly developed motor skills, stable home, and younger age.

4. In the past, theories of the cause of autism have centered on the parents, who were said to be cold and unresponsive to their children. Unfortunately, there is no systematic proof of this idea. However, behaviorists point to the successes of behavior therapy in dealing with autistic children as possible evidence that the cause of the disorder is environmental and a product of bad learning.

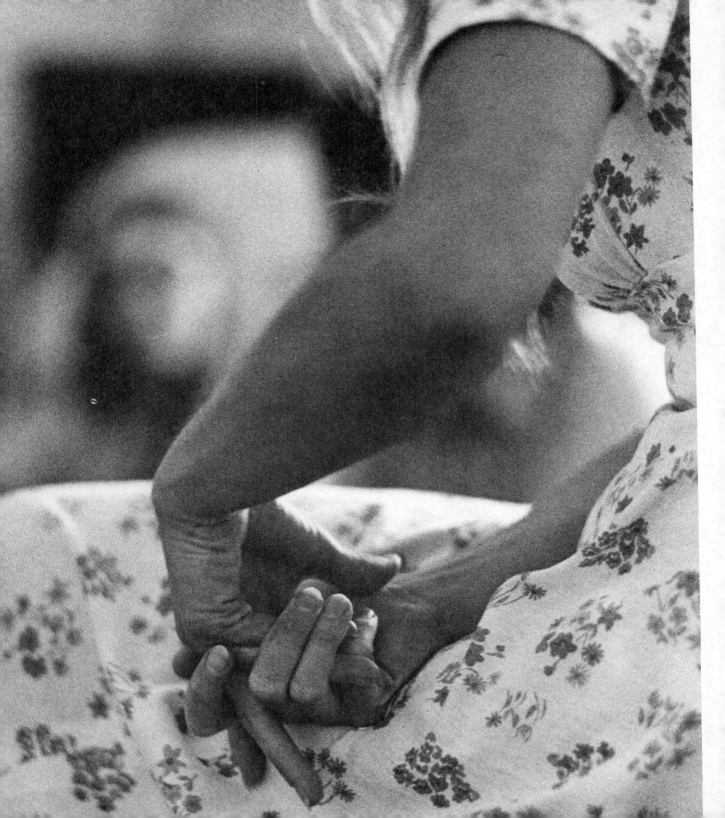

Therapy

20

"The current psychotherapeutic scene is a bewildering panorama of schools and methods, practitioners with all sorts of backgrounds, and patients with an enormous variety of woes and ills. . . . No single therapy holds a monopoly. Paraprofessionals, subprofessionals and nonprofessionals, some with no training at all, compete with orthodox psychologists" (Frank, 1972, p. 22).

Despite this bewildering array, all forms of psychotherapy have in common certain features. For one, every successful therapy establishes a relationship in which the patient has confidence in the therapist's competence and desire to help. The setting in which therapy takes place is usually distinguished from the setting of daily living. The features of the setting identify it as a sanctuary and a place of healing. In this sanctuary, the patient is encouraged to let himself go, express forbidden thoughts, release pent-up emotions, and try out new ways of behaving.

Furthermore, all psychotherapies are based on a theory that explains the cause of distress, specifies goals, and prescribes procedures for attaining the goals. The ability to name, clarify, and explain symptoms is, in itself, powerfully reassuring.

Frank (1973) proposes that persons seeking therapeutic help are all suffering from a condition he calls *demoralization*. That is to say, they are conscious of having failed to meet their own expectations or the expectations of others, and they feel powerless to change either the situation or themselves. Their life is constricted, and they cling to habitual activities, avoid novelty and challenge, and are reluctant to make long-term plans. In short, they seem to be cowering in a psychological corner.

RENT-A-FRIEND
Schofield (1964) has made the interesting observation that many clients are paying a psychotherapist's fee to purchase the commodity of friendship. In this "purchased" friendship with a therapist, a patient may feel free to reassess his values, thoughts, feelings, and behaviors. Buying a friend is better than having no friend at all, when you find yourself in psychological trouble.

Demoralization may be no more than brief uneasiness caused by some passing problem, or it may be so severe that the patient must be hospitalized. Any therapeutic procedure thus performs two interrelated functions: it combats the patient's demoralization, and it treats his specific symptoms. Sometimes patients feel no need for further therapy, despite persistence of symptoms, once they have recovered their morale (Sifneos, 1972).

WITCHDOCTORS

"Witchdoctor is a term that arose out of the eighteenth century exploration of Africa. The world was simpler then, and the newly discovered cultures were quickly assigned their proper status in The Order of Things. We were white, they were black. We were civilized, they were primitive. We were Christian, they were pagan. We used science, they used magic. We had doctors, they had witchdoctors. The term witchdoctor, then, is a vestige of imperialism and ethnocentrism."
[Torrey, 1972, p. 69]

Witchdoctors and Therapists

Torrey (1972) is one of the few psychiatrists who have examined what Western psychotherapists can learn from witchdoctors. As a psychiatrist, Torrey insists that he uses the same mechanisms for curing patients as do witchdoctors and gets about the same results. The common features of curing used by doctor-healers all over the world include the following principles.

The Principle of Rumpelstiltskin. According to the Grimm brothers' fairy tale, there is magic in the right word. The therapist's act of naming what is wrong with his patient is in itself therapeutic. It may make the patient feel that someone understands. Since the doctor-healer is a person of considerable social status, the patient's anxiety is reduced even further. A problem understood by someone is a problem that can be cured. Indeed, this principle works in every culture.

Personal Qualities of the Therapist. Psychiatrists, as well as witchdoctors, use their personal qualities to help cure their patients. These common qualities—empathy, warmth, genuineness—are important in effective psychotherapy, and the therapist who possesses them gets better results than one who does not.

Existential Therapy

In a world plagued by alienation, the impersonality of computer-run bureaucracies, and the breakdown of traditional institutions and sources of values, the philosophy behind existential therapy holds much appeal. Existentialists believe that the meaning to life, the source of fulfillment, is not to be found in outside institutions but in man himself. Even in a hostile environment, the existentialists say, man retains the freedom to choose what he is and what he shall do. Unfortunately, man often forfeits this freedom. The goal of existential therapy is to help the individual take responsibility for who he is; to heighten his sense of being in charge of his life; and to help him make conscious life choices and accept their consequences, whether they involve pleasure or pain.

Because each individual has his own unique way of "being in the world" (social interaction), existential therapists vary in the techniques they use. However, fundamental to the process is an authentic relationship between the therapist and his client. The therapist does not just mirror his client's thoughts (as in psychoanalysis and client-centered therapy); he actually expresses his own opinions and feelings as a person.

As in other humanistic therapies, the therapist stresses the importance of being fully aware of one's feelings and the experiences of the here and now, but the existential purpose is to make the individual aware of the choices he is making at each moment. Then he can begin to recognize the freedom he does have in making these choices.

The Patients' Expectations. One way to increase a patient's expectations of cure is to use an impressive setting for the healing. In Western culture, psychotherapists smoke pipes, dress differently from other medical professionals, have beards, and so forth—much like the face paint and mask used by therapists in other cultures. If the patient believes the therapist has special mystical power, so much the better.

Torrey has clearly pointed out that we "cure" with "scientific" methods in our society, just as witchdoctors "cure" with ritual chants and dances in other cultures. The differences between "sophisticated" and "primitive" practices may be less significant than we would like to believe!

Psychotherapeutic Goals

The general goals of psychotherapy include: (1) relief from anxiety, symptoms, and conflict; (2) establishment of personal maturity, feelings of adequacy, and integration of the different parts of the self; (3) the improvement of interpersonal relationships; and (4) assistance in making a satisfactory adjustment to the culture and the society (Watkins, 1965). Differing therapies may emphasize one or more of these goals to the exclusion of others, but the great bulk of traditional approaches to psychotherapy are derived from the theoretical principles espoused by Freud, the father of psychoanalysis.

The psychotherapeutic relationship is usually a unique experience in the patient's life; he will openly confess his most intimate feelings, thoughts, and reactions to a professional helper who analyzes behavior but does not criticize or condemn it. What is disarmingly simple about therapy is that it is essentially one person talking to another until the emotional, cognitive, or behavioral disorder disappears. Traditional psychotherapy focuses on the expression of the patient's feelings and attitudes and on recognition and interpretation of these by the therapist.

Redlich and Freedman (1966) describe what can be called "common-ground" analytic psychotherapy. This is the method most often taught in

DOES THERAPY WORK?
Metzoff and Kornreich (1971) have some kind words to say about therapy. They point out that:
"There are two frequently quoted and contradictory legends about the outcome of psychotherapy. One maintains that one third of treated patients get better, one third remain the same and one third get worse. The other asserts that two thirds of neurotics get better on their own, without treatment. Neither belief is supported by acceptable evidence. No one has established a reliable rate of cure for persons who have therapy or a rate of recovery for persons who have not had it. Nevertheless, contrary to prevailing beliefs, adequately controlled, fully scientific experiments have demonstrated repeatedly that psychotherapy does bring about positive changes" [p. 61].

Client-Centered Therapy

You consider yourself a generous person, but when a friend describes a recent trip to Europe, you refuse to listen because you are jealous. Or perhaps you consider yourself a mature and rational individual, yet a silly movie makes you cry. How do you explain the inconsistencies between your behavior and your self-concept? "That's not me," you say.

Everyone experiences inconsistent feelings now and then, but when these alien behaviors continue to occur, many people begin to realize that they really don't know what the real "me" is. Others have trouble accepting who they are when they actually find out. According to humanistic theories, maladjustment is a result of denying all those feelings and behaviors that do not conform to one's image of oneself, even though the image is often false. Rather than correcting the self-image, however, the individual continues to evade the contradictory experiences. When these attempts fail, the inconsistency brings intense anxiety and this anxiety becomes increasingly difficult to resolve.

According to Carl Rogers, who developed client-centered (or Rogerian) therapy, no experience should be considered alien to an individual. Indeed, experiencing a wide range of thoughts and behaviors is essential to the process of self-realization. Thus the aim of client-centered therapy is to help the client realize and become his true self by allowing him to test out the feelings that, until now, he has refused to admit are part of his life. How does the therapist do this? Not by teaching or modifying specific behaviors, or by delving into his client's unconscious motivations, but by offering the client unconditional positive regard. In other words, the therapist continues to respect the client no matter what he does or says. This is exactly what the client needs, because he has spent his life behaving and thinking according to others' wishes. Now he feels free to try out new experiences because he knows he will not be rejected.

Although most of the responsibility for the progress of therapy appears to rest with the client, the therapist plays a crucial role not only in providing an atmosphere conducive to trying out new selves, but also in helping the client discover which thoughts or behaviors he has eliminated from his life. During the therapy session, the therapist will often rephrase his clients' statements in such a way as to highlight the things the client seems to be suggesting, but will not admit in so many words. Through this process of discovery and trial, the client comes to realize what his true self is.

THE DOCTOR THINKS THAT "NO WELL-REGULATED INSTITUTION SHOULD BE UNPROVIDED WITH THE CIRCULATING SWING." 1818.

training centers, and, along with chemotherapy, it is what most neurotic or psychotic patients will get as treatment in most institutions in America. As Sundberg and Tyler (1962) indicate, most current methods of psychotherapy concentrate on "bringing about *a sufficient lowering of the patient's level of anxiety so that he will be able to permit himself to explore the painful areas of his experience*" (p. 293). Thus, privacy, confidentiality, and freedom from interruption are valued by all forms of therapy.

Somatic Therapy

The somatic therapies utilize chemical or electrical treatments. These treatments seem to work despite theoretical arguments about why they produce the psychological effects they do.

Chemical Shock

If enough insulin is injected into a patient's bloodstream, a lowered blood sugar (hypoglycemia) results, and the patient slips into a coma-like state. Psychiatrists had difficulty explaining why certain psychotic symptoms decrease

This woman, whose hands you see in the photograph at the beginning of the chapter and who also appears in a picture a few pages from here, is the leader of a group therapy session. When she was shown these photos, she was amazed, saying she had no idea she had been "wringing her hands." Therapy is a difficult and often strenuous procedure for everyone involved—and that does include the therapist.

following this coma, but they soon began to apply chemically induced shocks to patients with all kinds of symptoms.

Electroshock

Electroshock is another means used to produce convulsions in mental patients. This involves the injection of a muscle relaxant to soften the severity of the seizure and to prevent fractures during the convulsion. Electrodes are then placed at both temples of the skull, and from 70 to 130 volts are applied for about 0.5 seconds to induce a seizure lasting slightly less than one minute. Treatments may range from 5 to 30 or more in number. After shock, there is a loss of memory and the ability to learn, but this clears up after a short time. Persisting brain damage is rare. Research on modifications of electroshock has focused on the spacing of treatments (Sargant, 1961) and on combining treatments with varied tranquilizing and antidepressant drugs (Cannicott, 1963; Wittenborn, Plante, Burgess, and Livermore, 1961).

Electroshock has been most effective for the depressions. Improvement is dramatic and rapid in retarded or agitated depressive patients. Results are almost as good for manic patients. Improvement, of course, is not cure, and

THERAPISTS TREAT, NATURE CURES
Many years ago Myerson (1939) said: "The neuroses are 'cured' by Christian Science, osteopathy, chiropractic . . . bromides, benzedrine sulfate, change of scene, a blow on the head, and psychoanalysis, which probably means that none of these has yet established its real worth in the matter. . . . Moreover, since many neuroses are self-limited, anyone who spends two years with a patient gets credit for the operation of nature" (p. 641).

it does not indicate a complete remission of symptoms. It does mean that better contact can be established with the patient during the time for intensive treatment (McNeil, 1970).

Psychosurgery

Surgical alteration of the brain still causes heated argument among therapists today. When the various shock therapies came into vogue, a Spanish neurologist, Egas Moniz, suggested that the bizarre ideas of some patients circulated in a cyclic fashion in their diseased brains and produced mental disorder. To short-circuit this reaction, Moniz surgically disconnected the frontal lobes from the rest of the brain in psychotic patients.

This surgery calmed some agitated patients, but it also made vegetables of others—they walked, and talked, and looked like human beings, but they were without ambition, tact, imagination, or consciousness of self (Greenblatt, 1967). When a part of the brain tissue is destroyed, it will not replace itself and the person that once was is also destroyed. This is indeed a chapter in treatment history that should not be forgotten by future generations. Certainly, it was a savage surrender of therapy to surgery. It spread rapidly across the world and left in its wake an untold number of damaged human beings (McNeil, 1970).

Psychopharmacology

The psychoactive chemicals have been widely used in therapy primarily to bring symptomatic relief to patients and to produce a state in which the patient is better able to work out his problems.

For convenience, the various chemical compounds are often described in terms of their intended effect, as for example, tranquilizers and energizers. Since we cannot always predict that tranquilizers will bring tranquility, such treatment still relies on trial and error. The most common tranquilizers, for example, have both sedative and tranquilizing effects, and it is not easy to distinguish one effect from the other (Holliday, 1965).

The chemical group called phenothiazines most frequently used bear trade names such as Mellaril, Sparine, Compazine, and Thorazine. These make up the major tranquilizers. Miltown, Equanil, and Librium are minor tranquilizers and produce only moderate tranquilizing effects. These chemicals are used to calm anxious patients or at least make them indifferent to their emotional problems. In some patients, for example, obsessive thoughts and compulsive actions continue to exist, but the thoughts are less vivid and the actions less vigorously pursued.

The sedatives such as Amytal, Nembutal, and phenobarbital are used to reduce the restlessness and agitation that accompany personal problems. Sedatives are faster acting than tranquilizers and can take effect quickly, whereas tranquilizers must be ingested for some weeks before a stable state of tranquility is achieved.

The energizers (or antidepressants) are used to alter the mood of the patient by stimulating an increase in the general level of behavior. They bring on an increased appetite, less awareness of fatigue, and increased speed of action and reaction. By chemically triggering the brain to a new state of alertness, the depressed person is helped to reinvolve himself in life. Antidepressant drugs have proved to be particularly useful for patients who are both depressed and anxious about the way life is going. The psychostimulants most used are Benzedrine, Dexedrine, and Ritalin.

It should be pointed out that these energizing, tranquilizing, and sedating drugs do not change the fact that the effect of neurotic behavior on loved ones and on children may continue to exist whether the patient is tranquil or not. Eventually, the therapist must return to dealing with the causes of neurosis rather than with its symptoms.

The Placebo

In America we are apparently addicted to placebos. A *placebo* (which is the Latin word meaning "I shall please") is any medicine that works psychologically but has no physical effect. Medically, placebos are no more than "sugar pills," but the placebo effect is more complex since physical reactions are always interlaced with psychological responses. The placebo effect is likely to be prevalent in any sort of therapy—with or without drugs.

The "power of suggestion" has been easily demonstrated by research in medicine. The method of administration, for example, may be an important factor in determining one's response to a placebo. One doctor found that a placebo administered in a bright red, gelatin capsule brought favorable results in 81 percent of the cases tested. There were favorable results in only 49 percent of the cases when the placebo was administered as a tablet, and in 69 percent of the cases when it was administered as a liquid. Hypodermic injections are usually more effective than tablets but somewhat inferior to capsules. Blue or green solutions bring better results if they are applied externally, whereas liquids are more effective if they are colored in warm tones of red, yellow, or brown and if they have a bitter taste (Leslie, 1954).

When drugs used for mental disorders were administered to "normal" pharmacy students, the effect was quite clear. Forty-five students took a capsule at 8:30 A.M. thinking that its maximum effects would appear in about two hours and would disappear by the end of the experiment at 12:30. Fifteen of them were told their capsule was a stimulant; another fifteen were told that it contained a tranquilizer; and the remaining fifteen were told that it was only cornstarch. Sixty percent of the subjects reported feeling the effects they were *supposed* to feel. Seventy-three percent of the "stimulated" subjects reported feeling the effects compared to only 46.7 percent of the "tran-

IMPLOSIVE THERAPY

In implosive therapy, every effort is made to arouse as much anxiety in the patient as possible. Implosion therapists believe it is necessary for the patient to experience a full anxiety reaction without suffering any harm. The therapist describes an extremely frightening situation relating to the patient's fear and urges the patient to imagine himself in it and experience it as intensely as possible. This is said to produce an internal explosion (implosion) of panic, but as the patient goes through it again and again, the outcome should be a diminished fear of the situation—his fear response should be extinguished.

quilized" subjects. The pulse rates of the "stimulated" group rose when a reading was taken during the supposed time of maximum effect and fell again by the close of the period. Pulse rates in the "tranquilized" group fell and then rose again by the close of the period (Brodeur, 1965).

It sounds remarkable, and it is. Now you need only imagine how much more effective it would be for a confident, inspiring, sincere, dedicated "therapist" to tell you that good things are certain to follow the therapeutic "treatment" he prescribes.

Behavior Therapy

Behavior therapy was at first heralded as a much needed breakthrough, but its views were hardened too rapidly; it chose its enemy (psychoanalysis) with too much haste and defended its successes with more enthusiasm than objectivity.

Behavior therapy has insisted that a learning cure rather than a talking cure for disorder is called for. In his treatise on learning theory and behavior therapy, Eysenck (1959) contrasts this approach with traditional psychotherapy. Eysenck maintains that psychotherapy is based on an inconsistent theory that has never been properly postulated in testable scientific form and that uses impressionistic evidence, as for example, a personal experience not subject to experimental demonstration.

The Delancey Street Foundation in San Francisco is a new approach to the concept of therapeutic communities. Located in fashionable Pacific Heights, this "extended family" is made up of over 200 people (including many ex-convicts and ex-drug addicts). Although rich neighbors have protested their presence, founder John Maher asks, "Where do you expect a guy to kick 'horse'? In the ghetto?" Encounter groups and therapy sessions are part of the overall program, which also includes several enterprises—a moving service, a Volkswagen repair shop, a restaurant on chic Union Street. In its family

Behaviorists assume certain biological drives such as sex, hunger, thirst, and body contact are common to us all. These are considered *deficit motivators*—we are stirred to action when we are hungry, thirsty, sexually aroused, or isolated from our fellow man. The behaviorist claims that if he could control the conditions under which all our physiological needs are met, he could also control all behavior of the organism. If aggression and exploration are the means by which we satisfy our needs, these behaviors can also be brought under control. Thus, behaviorists assert that, once they analyze what is sustaining unwanted behavior or inhibiting wanted behavior, they can set up a remedial program.

There are a number of widely used techniques available to the behavior therapist: desensitization, relaxation, extinction following negative practice, avoidance learning, aversive conditioning, and operant conditioning. These may be used alone or in combination, depending upon the problem to be solved.

Behaviorists believe that they can account, theoretically, for virtually any behavior by using some combination of learning-theory concepts along with special applications of reinforcement to produce inhibition or enhance discrimination. This, they feel, can be done without any reference to hypothetical personality structures inside the individual.

Behavioral therapy frequently deals with "models" that serve as examples for the younger members of our society. Modeling can be used to shape

THE CONFORMING CURE
One criticism of therapeutic control is that it may teach human values that reach beyond the therapy situation. For example, if reward is given for surface behavior and conformity to what someone else decides is "good," the individual may be taught to value outer appearance, blind conformity to the socially accepted norms, social approval at the expense of self-approval, and action at the expense of thinking or feeling (Grossman, 1968).

concept, Delancey Street provides something extremely valuable for people trying to "drop back in"—others who care about them. Every member feels some responsibility for correcting the behavior of others who deviate from the social norms or for assisting those who need help in an emergency. In this respect, the goal of the foundation is similar to that of community mental health programs—to *prevent* mental illness and to *promote* mental health for *all* people in a community. And mental health can only be possible when the physical, social, and economic facets of a person's life are also healthy.

Gestalt Therapy

German for "whole," the term *gestalt* accurately describes this innovative therapy, whose aim is to put the individual in touch with his entire self. According to Fritz Perls, advocate of this form of therapy, individuals tend to block out awareness of aspects of themselves and their experience, looking at only part of who they are or what they are doing. The therapist's job is to make these individuals whole again by helping them recognize all the facets of their personalities and experiences. The individual is made aware of his feelings, thoughts, and actions as they occur together.

Like client-centered and existential therapy, the goal of gestalt therapy is self-actualization and acceptance of responsibility for one's personality and one's life. (These humanist therapies differ mainly in technique.) Gestalt therapy frequently takes place in groups, although the emphasis is always on the individual. The therapist will point out all aspects of a person's behavior—tone of voice, eye movement, gestures—which the individual usually ignores. He challenges the client to confront his feelings about certain situations and to recognize sensations from his body of which he is usually not aware. Because dreams are a part of personality, and therefore each person's responsibility, the therapist will often ask the client to determine the meaning of his dreams by acting out the

roles of objects and people in the dreams, rather than by introspection. In addition, clients are encouraged to take care of "unfinished business"—that is, to resolve problems from the past which affect current behavior. To do this, the individual plays the role of himself and his adversary and acts out a dialogue concerning the conflict or tension he is experiencing.

behavior initially. Or, when applied appropriately, consistently, and with the proper timing, it can be used to reorganize or eliminate abnormal behavior. The methods of reinforcing certain behaviors while extinguishing less desirable ones can be applied by persons who have not had the prolonged training of traditional psychotherapists.

Behavior therapy is considered more scientific than psychotherapy by its supporters; indeed, its abandonment of concepts such as repression, the unconscious, defense mechanisms, interpretation of symptoms, symbols, and dreams is regarded as a scientific breakthrough.

Desensitization

Desensitization therapy is based on the theory of Dr. Joseph Wolpe, who feels that the goal of therapy is to recondition the patient to associate pleasantness rather than anxiety with certain feared objects or events. Dr. Wolpe suggests that two opposite reactions to a situation cannot exist at the same time; thus, he attempts to replace anxiety by its opposite—relaxation.

Wolpe begins at a very basic level: the patient is instructed to think of something that makes him mildly anxious. When he gets a mental image of this mildly anxiety-producing situation, he is trained to relax, thereby associating the feeling of relaxation with the mildly anxious situation. Next the patient thinks of something that produces greater anxiety, and again he learns to relax. These sessions continue until the patient is able to imagine one of his most feared situations and still associate it with relaxation (Wolpe and Lazarus, 1966).

There is some question as to whether relaxation really inhibits anxiety or whether the expectation of cure is enough in itself. One difficulty with the relaxation method is that the patient has to be able to relax in the first place; some cannot do this long enough for the therapy to be effective (Glick, 1970).

In one experimental study, several different behavior therapy techniques were used to eliminate fear of snakes (Bandura, Blanchard, and Ritter, 1969). The subjects were young adults whose snake phobias were severe enough to restrict their activities in various ways. Some, for example, could not participate in gardening or hiking for fear of encountering snakes. After testing the subjects to determine how close they would come to a harmless king snake, they were divided into four matched groups according to their degree of fear. One group watched a film in which children and adults played with a large king snake and appeared to enjoy it. The subjects in this group were told to stop the film whenever a particular scene provoked anxiety; they were to reverse the film to the beginning of the sequence that bothered them and practice relaxing while watching it. This procedure was labeled "symbolic modeling."

A second group was gradually guided in touching a live snake, first with a gloved hand, then with a bare hand; they then began to hold the snake and let it coil around their arm, and finally they let the snake loose, caught it, and let it crawl over their bodies. The procedure was called "live modeling with participation."

Subjects in the third group were given a standard desensitization experience and taught to relax as they imagined scenes of snakes. The fourth group served as a control and received no special training.

All three treatment groups improved more than the control group, but the group that had live modeling combined with guided participation showed the greatest gain. Almost all the subjects in this group completely overcame their fear of snakes, and a follow-up some time later revealed that the snake phobias were still gone.

Token Economies

A growing number of mental hospitals in this country are using "token economies" as part of the therapy program. Patients are rewarded for engaging in socially constructive activities such as keeping clean, getting to meals on

RECOVERY
In an attempt to shape complex socially oriented behaviors in a group of chronic neuropsychiatric patients, a behavior-milieu therapy ward was formed in conjunction with another chronic ward which served as a control. The goal of the treatment program was to restore the patients to their communities. The treatment program consisted of a combination of (a) behavior therapy, (b) token economy, (c) attitude therapy, and (d) ward government. A total of 478 patients passed through the treatment program over a period of 35 months. Sixty-eight percent of the patients were returned to their communities with only 14 percent of them returning to the hospital (Head, Boblitt, Moore, and Hord, 1970).

Therapy, as we have seen throughout this chapter, takes many forms. Here women are engaged in work therapy at the psychiatric day hospital of Velp in Holland. Mentally disturbed patients, referred usually by private psychiatrists, participate in a daily program which also includes sports and recreation activities, and regularly held group discussions with a psychologist.

time, and performing assigned tasks. Payment consists of tokens (such as poker chips) which may be used later to "purchase" luxuries such as increased television time, private sleeping accommodations, weekend passes, and the like.

It is necessary to start gradually, but token economies can be effective in producing desired behaviors even among severely disturbed patients. Patients may get tokens just for moving close to nurses or other patients. Through a process of shaping, it is then possible to encourage them to strike up conversations; they may eventually be rewarded for quite complex forms of interpersonal interaction.

One such token economy was established for an entire ward of 86 chronic schizophrenics whose average length of hospitalization was almost 25 years. Social behaviors and first attempts at recreational and vocational activities were most highly reinforced. Token fines as well as rewards were used in an effort to eliminate activities disruptive to the ward. Before long, instances of breaking hospital rules dropped sharply. Patients took a more active interest in their surroundings. One patient, in fact, left the hospital for the first time in over 40 years (Atthowe and Krasner, 1968).

Summary

1. The basic ingredients of most successful therapies are: (1) a therapeutic relationship in which the client has confidence in the therapist; (2) a therapeutic situation in which the individual feels safe and quite apart from everyday life; and (3) a theoretical basis for the therapy which specifies the cause of distress, the goals of therapy, and the procedures for attaining them.

2. It is interesting to note that certain characteristics are common to success in a variety of situations: (1) the therapist's ability to

GIVING
PSYCHOLOGY AWAY
". . . the secrets of our trade need not be reserved for highly trained specialists. Psychological facts should be passed out freely to all who need and can use them. . . . There simply are not enough psychologists, even including nonprofessionals, to meet every need for psychological services. The people at large will have to be their own psychologists, and make their own applications of established principles." [Miller, 1969, p. 68]

name the ailment, (2) the therapist's warmth and empathy, and (3) the patient's expectations for being healed.

3. In psychodynamic therapies, the patient talks to the therapist, and the therapist interprets what the patient says. The object of therapy is to lower the individual's anxiety enough so that he can feel free to explore the underlying conflicts troubling him.

4. In somatic therapy, physical agents such as electroshock, chemical shock, surgery, and drugs are used primarily to improve contact with the patient, or to lower his anxiety so that he can work out problems in life.

5. Psychologists have found that, to some extent, administration of any form of treatment will produce results according to the patient's expectations of symptom removal or cure. This is known as the placebo effect and has been repeatedly demonstrated through the administration of false medications.

6. The objects of behavior therapy are (1) to teach individuals skills they have never learned, (2) to extinguish those behaviors that are incorrect, and (3) to break up incorrect associations that have been made. According to behavior therapists, treating unconscious causes, if there are any, is irrelevant to permanent cure.

7. Behavior therapy employs a wide variety of techniques, but they are all based on principles of learning theory. Even individuals who have not gone through the long training required for traditional psychotherapy are still capable of using these methods with clients.

8. In the technique of desensitization, developed by Joseph Wolpe, the individual is made to relax while the therapist describes situations that make the client anxious. The situations are presented in order from the least anxiety provoking to the most. Almost opposite to desensitization—but still a method of behavior therapy—is implosive therapy, where the individual imagines a very frightening experience as intensely as possible so that he will learn that there is no danger.

9. Several hospitals have begun to use an application of operant conditioning known as token economies. Patients receive rewards for performing socially desirable functions.

10. Therapies based on humanistic-existential theories are aimed at helping the individual achieve self-actualization and take responsibility for his life. Many individuals with no specific symptoms of disorder are involved in some form of gestalt, existential, or client-centered therapy. The often hazy theoretical differences between the humanistic theories of personality formation are pointed up by differences in these three techniques.

Variations in Psychotherapy

When the final history of psychotherapy is written, it will refer to the 1960s and 1970s as the decades of variation—variation in technique, method, approach, theory, and practice. The "discovery" of new solutions to man's ancient psychological problems has accelerated so rapidly that today's therapeutic miracle shortly becomes a forgotten flash-in-the-pan. We have become the consumers of the therapy-of-the-month, which is due, in part, to glamorization and exaggeration by the popular mass media. (The inventors of sure-fire new therapies make interesting guests on TV talk shows.) Further, we are a society which increasingly seeks quick and simple solutions to the difficulties of being human.

Every "new" therapy works for some of the people some of the time, but no one therapy works for very many of the people very much of the time. In addition, our society has developed a large group of seekers who enthusiastically attend every new circus that comes to town. Having recently completed transactional analysis, they are now "into" biofeedback and are looking forward to visiting Esalen groups, and trying primal scream therapy when they can work it into their schedule.

There is, unfortunately, a cult-like quality to each of these innovations in therapy. Each declares itself to be the sole owner of truth; each disparages all other forms of therapy; and each claims to have produced miracles for its believers. Before we sample these recent therapeutic variations, it may be wise to consider the tempered views of Jerome Frank.

Profusion and Perspective

Frank (1972) notes that the current psychotherapeutic scene displays such a profusion of methods, practitioners, and patients that any systematic description is impossible. "Psychotherapy is offered for an almost unbelievable diversity of human ills—psychoses, marital disharmonies, addictions, sexual deviations, school phobias, to mention just a few" (p. 27).

Frank attributes the sudden flood of new therapies to the current upheaval in contemporary society. He

Mass Therapy. Herschelman and Freundlich (1970) have described group therapy meetings involving 35 to 45 patients and 10 or 11 therapists. Their limited goal was to reduce tension on the ward. This goal was not only achieved, but it was also possible to accomplish meaningful exploration of individual emotion-laden areas despite the size of the group. The multiple-therapist technique was found to be a significant improvement over the traditional ward meeting or patient-staff conference.

accepts Rollo May's (1968) observation that when traditional values and institutions become discredited, they lose their power to unite members of the society and to provide a meaningful view of the world. As a result, members of the society cast about for new ways of preserving a sense of security and significance. One of these ways is psychotherapy. If the quest for help is itself intense, then any of a number of methods may work.

The Primal Scream   The Primal Institute in Los Angeles is well stocked with teddy bears, baby bottles, cribs, punching bags, isolation chambers, and life-size photographs of patients' parents There is even a birth simulator, made of inner tubes, where patients can relive the trauma of birth—if that is their problem. When therapy is going on, there may be as many as 40 or 50 patients on the floor writhing through what are called *Primals,* while several therapists circulate among them giving comfort and aid to those having difficulty releasing their feelings.

Primal therapy began in 1967 with a 22-year-old patient whom Janov was treating. When the patient was told to call out for his parents he reluctantly did so at first, and then became upset, writhed on the floor, and began to breathe rapidly. Finally an agonized scream convulsed his whole body. When he calmed down, he felt "cured" by having released feelings pent up for a lifetime. Primal therapy was born, and Janov began to ask other patients to call out for their missing parents. Unfailingly, there was a trauma, a scream, and a rebirth of feeling.

Janov's therapy centers on the idea of pain. For him, neurosis is frozen childhood pain. Each time a child is not held when he cries, not fed when he is hungry, or ignored when he needs attention, it contributes to a "Primal pool of pain" which, when deep enough, can produce neurosis as a way of life. As the neurotic child grows into a neurotic adult, he often becomes involved with persons who perpetuate his childhood patterns; through them, he tries to achieve symbolically what he was deprived of long ago. The child who had a cold mother grows up and marries a cold wife hoping to warm her up and prove at last that he can win his mother's love. The child whose father never loved him may become homosexual seeking to get from men the affection his father refused him as a child.

According to Janov, if the patient can successfully reexperience this original pain, he can be free for the first time and become a superior human being. While the data from his physiological studies are incomplete, Janov suggests that post-Primal man is so free of ten-

The Monologue. The monologue is an approach to therapy that employs television with adolescent users of dangerous drugs. It is a short videotape experience in which the patient is in a room all alone talking to a television camera. Remaining alone, he then watches the replay of his monologue. The video tape is next examined by the doctor and patient together. Adolescence is a time of ego identity crises and self-consciousness. The monologue, as part of the videotape experience with its immediate playback, is an effective new form of therapeutic experience (Wilmer, 1970).

sion and defenses that he may well live longer and be prey to fewer diseases than his non-Primaled fellows (Keen, 1972).

If you can believe the testimony of satisfied patients, the results of Primal therapy are nearly miraculous. "Ulcers, arthritis, epilepsy are cured; flat-chested women require larger brassieres. Many a man feels that he has added a cubit onto his stature; intelligence increases, eyesight sharpens, coordination improves" (Keen, 1972, p. 88). On the other side, critics have called Janov a "dangerous, publicity-seeking charlatan."

Transactional Analysis Transactional analysis is about the "games people play" and the catchy names Dr. Berne has attached to them. Berne talks of the "con," the "gimmick," and the "payoff." If, for example, a woman courts a compliment and receives it gratefully, it is nothing more than a harmless social pastime. But if she asks for reassurance, receives it, and then tries to show that the compliment was undeserved, she's played "Yes, but." Her payoff was not simply the massaging of her vanity, but the chance to prove her partner stupid and feel superior at his expense (Langouth, 1966). Such games are harmful because they involve emotional deception—the con—in relating to others.

The principles of Script Analysis also evolved from Transactional Analysts. "We have evidence, that between the ages of three and seven, a child develops a 'script' for his future—i.e., a story-line blueprint that determines how he will live the rest of his life—par-

ticularly his important relationships, his feelings about himself and his achievements, and the outcome that he will experience as 'success,' 'failure,' 'I almost made it,' or 'at least I tried' " (English, 1973, p. 48).

The way in which a child acquires feelings about himself and others as he grows up establishes his "position." Berne lists four of these.

1. I'm not O.K.—You're O.K.
2. I'm not O.K.—You're not O.K.
3. I'm O.K.—You're not O.K.
4. I'm O.K.—You're O.K.

Psychosurgery. Dolores Katz has described the scene vividly. "The angry, anti-social child is laid upon a table and put to sleep. A hole is drilled into his brain; a silver probe searches briefly, and then a portion of the child's brain is carefully destroyed. The child will be 'better' now. He will not upset his parents or society anymore with his strange rages, his anti-social behavior. He will be quiet.

"The chilling scenario . . . has been enacted some 30 times at the University of Mississippi Medical School, where Dr. Orlando J. Andy has operated on the brains of pre-teen children judged to be behavior problems." [Katz, 1972, p. 16]

The Fright Cure.   Some state hospitals have undertaken the use of "the fright drug." This breath-stopping, paralyzing chemical—succinycholine—has been coupled with behavioral, aversive therapy for some violent patients. Patients experience "a vivid fear of imminent death" while a "therapist" sits nearby castigating the patient for his violent behavior. The experience has been described as one of "suffocating" or "drowning." It seems we have discovered the first of a host of many chemicals, unfortunately, capable of making deviation more painful and frightening than conformity.

The basic element of Transactional Analysis (T.A.) is analyzing the "transactions" between people. Transactional analysts believe there are three "ego-states" within each of us—the Parent, the Adult, and the Child (P-A-C)—and each of these interacts with different people in different situations.

Lamott (1972) uses the example of a married couple—John and Barbara—having fun at a party. The transaction of having fun together involves the Child ego-state of both partners. When John suggests they have another drink and Barbara answers, "You always drink too much at parties," she has moved into her Parent state. John can respond by staying in his Child state and saying, 'Aw, come on, sweetie, let's have fun." Or, John may decide to respond by saying, "You know very well that I don't *always* drink too much at parties, and furthermore you said you'd drive us home, and furthermore if I'm hung over tomorrow, it's my hangover and not yours, and anyway it's Sunday." He has shifted into his Adult—the data-gathering, rational, problem-solving state; and his remarks are addressed to Barbara's Adult, although it is fair to guess that Barbara's Adult isn't listening (p. 132).

In terms of P-A-C, the healthy personality is one in which the rational Adult is in control, but is indulgent toward the Child (who likes fun and sex), and resistant toward the Parent (who keeps trying to enforce ancient rules that tend to get in the way as the personality develops).

According to Berne, the point of this human game playing is that these transactions allow people to exchange "strokes." A stroke is a unit of recognition; the term reminds us that the infant derives his primary vital recognition through physical handling and stroking. After infancy, we symbolize. We register strokes from smiles, frowns, and from words.

"Positive" strokes can be physical caresses, smiles or words of acceptance. Blows, frowns or verbal criticisms give us "negative" strokes. . . . Young children need many strokes for sheer survival. They lap up whatever kinds they get—positive, negative or crooked—and they become conditioned to that mix. Their Child Ego-State concludes that the particular diet of strokes they were raised on is the only kind worth getting. Thus, people who grow up on a diet consisting mainly of negative strokes continue to crave them. Often they become delinquent or addicted to drugs in order to keep receiving the negative strokes they mistakenly believe they need. [English, 1973, p. 47]

Different strokes for different folks, I guess.

Summary

In recent years, several new therapies have gained almost cult-like popularity because of man's need to find meaning in life. Among these new therapies are Janov's Primal Scream and Transactional Analysis.

The Mental Hospital

Public misconceptions of what mental institutions look like and of how they care for their patients are two of the problems which face administrators of state and private facilities. Does this photograph conform to your stereotype of an "institution"? It is the canteen of Napa State Hospital in Imola, California.

In the last decade, there has been an increasingly vigorous assault by professionals and laymen alike on the multitude of flaws in the traditional idea of the "mental" hospital. These complaints were dramatically brought to light by Rosenhan (1973) who conducted a field experiment in which eight "normal" persons were admitted to 12 mental hospitals. The eight people were instructed to abandon their pretended symptoms once they became "patients." From then on, they were told to behave "normally." Their task was to get discharged from the hospital by convincing the staff they were really sane.

The eight "patients" were three women and five men of different ages and different occupations—a psychology graduate student, three psychologists, a psychiatrist, a painter, and a housewife. Rosenhan himself was one of the pseudopatients.

The settings were similarly varied. In order to generalize the findings, admission into a variety of hospitals was sought. The 12 hospitals in the sample were located in five different states on the East and West coasts. Some were old and shabby, some were quite new. Some were research-oriented, others not. Some had good staff-patient ratios, others were quite understaffed. Only one was a strictly private hospital. All of the others were supported by state or federal funds or, in one instance, by university funds. [Rosenhan, 1973, p. 251]

At the time of admission, names and occupations were altered but the details of personal life history were presented just as they had actually happened. The "patient" was always cooperative (except the medicine was never swallowed). When asked how he was feeling, he always replied "fine" and reported that his symptoms had disappeared.

Despite their sanity, the pseudopatients were never detected. Admitted with a diagnosis of schizophrenia, each was discharged with a diagnosis of schizophrenia "in remission." At no time during hospitalization had any question been raised about possible pretense, nor were there any indications that the "patient's" status was suspect.

Length of hospitalization ranged from 7 to 52 days,

with an average of 19 days. The pseudopatients were not very carefully observed during this time. Interestingly, it was quite common for the other patients in these hospitals to detect that a pseudopatient was not really one of them—an observation that was not made by the hospital staff.

The experience of being a psychotic patient was far from a pleasant one. As Rosenhan describes it,

Powerlessness was evident everywhere. . . . His freedom of movement is restricted. He cannot initiate contact with the staff, but may only respond to such overtures as they make. Personal privacy is minimal. Patient quarters and possessions can be entered and examined by any staff member, for whatever reason. His personal history and anguish is available to any staff member (often including the "grey lady" and "candy striper" volunteer) who chooses to read his folder, regardless of their therapeutic relationship to him. [p. 256]

Even more startling to these experimenters was the medical care they received as pseudopatients.

All told, the pseudopatients were administered nearly 2,100 pills, including Elavil, Stelazine, Compazine, and Thorazine, to name but a few. (That such a variety of medications should have been administered to patients presenting identical symptoms is itself worthy of note.) Only two were swallowed. The rest were either pocketed or deposited in the toilet . . . the pseudopatients frequently found the medications of other patients in the toilet before they deposited their own. [p. 256]

After the experiment was completed and the results presented to other professionals, an unexpected obstacle was encountered—disbelief. Thus, to see if the tendency toward diagnosing the sane as insane could be reversed, Dr. Rosenhan arranged a second experi-

Women and Madness. "In 1960 the membership of the American Psychiatric Association totaled 11,083, of whom 10,100 were men and 983 were women. In 1970 their membership increased to 17,298 of whom 14,267 were men and 1,691 were women. Thus 90 percent of all psychiatrists during the last decade were men. It is important to remember that psychiatry is the most powerful of the mental illness professions, in terms of prestige, money and *ultimate* control over psychiatric policies, both in private practice and in mental hospitals. Psychiatrists, both medically and legally, decide *who* is insane and *why; what* should be done to or for such people; and *when* and *if* they should be released from treatment." [Chesler, 1972, p. 62]

"As early as the sixteenth century women were 'shut up' in madhouses (as well as in royal towers) by their husbands. By the seventeenth century, special wards were reserved for prostitutes, pregnant women, poor women, and young girls in France's first mental asylum, the Salpétrière." [p. 32] "Traditionally, the psychotherapist has ignored the objective facts of female oppression." [p. 110]

ment. Staff members at a research and teaching hospital who had heard and disbelieved the results of the first experiment were told that, at some time during the next three months, one or more "fake" patients would seek admittance to their hospital. Each staff member was therefore on his guard to detect any person posing as a patient. In fact, no "fake" patients attempted to gain admission to the hospitals. When the staff members recorded their opinions about 193 new admissions, 41 persons were thought to be fake patients by at least one staff member; and 23 patients were considered suspect by at least one psychiatrist.

The discoveries in Rosenhan's dramatic experiment are self-evident. Rosenhan is, of course, not denying that anxiety, depression, and psychological suffering exist. Rather, we must devise better ways to decide who should or should not be hospitalized.

The Happy Hospital

There are two sides to every story, of course. Oddly enough, in every mental institution there are many chronic patients who don't want to leave. The patients and staff often learn to relate to one another in a mutually satisfying, if somewhat distorted fashion, so that long-term patients develop an almost child-like dependency (Rosenberg, 1970). A convincing research effort by Benjamin and Dorothea Braginsky (1973) illustrated the extent to which patients will act "rationally" to protect their position in the mental hospital. The Braginskys were impressed with the fact that every mental hospital contains patients who perform demanding, complex jobs within the hospital, live cooperatively with their fellow residents, and participate regularly in community activities.

The Braginskys assert that mental patients have been able to "manage" their status in the hospital by using a variety of strategies. Patients in a series of experiments ". . . used ingratiation strategies to stay on the 'good side of the staff,' selectively censored information on psychological tests to create symptoms of either mental illness or mental health (whichever served their best interest), and manipulated psychiatric interviews to avoid unpleasant outcomes or to gain desirable ones. . . . Clearly, when it served their purposes to remain in the hospital, the patients convinced the three psychiatrists that they were disturbed and in need of hospital care. When this same portrayal would lead to the locked wards, they avoided it, presenting instead images of 'healthy' mental patients." (Braginsky and Braginsky, 1973; p. 24)

Mental patients revealed in a survey that they knew very well how the hospital worked and where all the pleasurable facilities of hospital life were located. The same awareness was not evident for those facilities most relevant to their therapeutic well-being (the location of the social worker or the nurse's office in their building).

The conclusions reached in the Braginskys' study of the mental hospital system are startling.

The hospital and its formal functions is a fiction maintained by the staff and the outside world. In reality, the patients in the open wards live in a resort. . . . Both settings [the ward and the resort] *impose minimal external demands, offer similar physical facilities (swimming pools, dances, movie theaters), do not expect the residents to be productive, allow the residents freedom to choose how they will spend their time, and are installations designed explicitly to refresh and refurbish the residents. Both settings are meant to reduce stress and tension.* [p. 32]

The Law and the Patient

Too many of us are convinced that the emotionally disturbed are more dangerous than normal persons despite a mountain of statistical evidence to the contrary. A common misconception is that mental "illness" requires long-term hospitalization. It is obvious, of course, that thousands of persons in our mental hospitals would not have to be there in the first place had they received adequate treatment early enough. In fact, Seymour Halleck (1969) is convinced patients would not resist hospitalization if they expected they would shortly be released back to society. As it is now, the present system allows friends or family to commit patients to hospitals simply if they prove to be too irritating or too disruptive.

Halleck (1969) maintains that it is hard to imagine a more frightening experience than that of being removed from your home and locked up in an institution without knowing precisely why you are being confined or how you can obtain your freedom. He recommends that, at a minimum:

An individual hospitalized against his will has a right to argue his case in the courts. He must be informed at every step in the commitment process of exactly what

The Half Way House. Newly released mental patients can be organized to function effectively outside the hospital. Fairweather and his colleagues (1969) demonstrated this in an experimental program in which a lodge was founded in the community where patients could live as a group. At first there was a research staff member present but he was later replaced by a lay person. The patients were given full responsibility for regulating each other's behavior, for operating the lodge, purchasing and preparing food, and earning money. They set up a handyman service business that produced an income of over $50,000 in three years. They disbursed this money among themselves according to each patient's productivity and responsibility. Three and a half years after their discharge, this group was compared to another group of seventy-five patients who had been released at the same time but had not had this experience. The members of the half way house were better able to hold income-producing jobs, to maintain satisfactory levels of adjustment, and to achieve meaningful lives in the community. And it cost the taxpayer only $6 a day per lodge (Rausch and Rausch, 1968).

Don't Go on the Weekend.   Mendel and Rapport (1968) examined clinicians' decisions on whether to hospitalize patients. They found that (1) social workers tended to hospitalize fewer patients than did psychiatrists or psychologists; (2) hospitalization was related to the patient's previous hospital history rather than to the severity of current symptoms; and (3) patients seen during evenings and weekends were twice as likely to be hospitalized as patients seen during the normal work day! The clinicians were unaware that their decisions were influenced by this "weekend" impulse to hospitalize patients.

---

is being done to him and he must also, if he wishes, have an attorney. . . . Once committed, the patient should know what steps will restore his freedom. Certainly any patient should have at regular intervals the right to petition the court for release. And the law must provide for continuous review of the confinement of anyone who is hospitalized for more than a few months. [p. 51]

It is reasonable to conclude that the traditional mental hospital is an imperfect device for care of the mentally disturbed and it seems imperative to develop a variety of more effective alternatives. Wishing is not having, of course, and until such alternatives are available it is not unreasonable to insist that greater safeguards be furnished to those inmates of our asylums.

Summary

1.   The inadequacies of mental hospitals in dealing with mental illness were pointed out by an experiment conducted by David Rosenhan in 1973. Several normal individuals were admitted to mental hospitals across the country. These pseudopatients went undetected, and they had difficulty getting out although they were voluntarily committed. They also reported that the environment of the mental hospital was not really conducive to cure but rather designed to make patients totally powerless.

2.   Despite the poor conditions of most hospitals, mental patients often find these institutions secure havens from the stress-filled outside world. Unfortunately, the design of most programs in mental hospitals promotes a dependency on the staff and the willingness among patients to remain in the hospital rather than return to the outside world.

HUMAN SOCIAL ISSUES

WOMEN'S LIBERATION, ASSASSINATION, race riots, prostitution, child abuse, discrimination, homosexuality, war crimes. We have been called a violent society, a racist society, a sick society, an insane society, and the overwhelming presence of these issues in each day's headlines seems to confirm these unfortunate labels. We argue about the causes, the merits, and possible control of these controversial matters, but no one seems to have the answers. As a student of psychology, you are probably wondering what the science of human behavior has to say about these social problems. Unfortunately, psychology is only in the preliminary stages of understanding the nature of violence, racism, and sexual problems because each of these is so complex, so difficult to isolate, and so wrought with emotion.

In this part I have presented a descriptive account of some of the issues that are plaguing our society and some of the attempts psychologists have been making to study and theorize about them. By now you have acquired many of the basic principles of being human and an understanding of scientific investigation. You are prepared to tackle the same problems that psychologists are currently puzzling over. It will be your job to draw from the information your own conclusions about the nature of violence, the effects of pornography, or the reasons for discrimination. Because the research is relatively new and because these phenomena are so difficult to study, you will find that the evidence is sketchy and the theories conflicting. But that is how all scientific progress begins.

This chapter is designed to let you try your hand at being a psychologist. Therefore, while you are reading these accounts you should keep in mind not only what other psychologists have observed or suggested, but also how you might study some of these issues—how you might test your own theories and apply your new-found knowledge to improve the human situation.

Being Violent

The violent by violence fall.
—Welsh Proverb

The timeless childhood chant, "rich man, poor man, beggarman, thief, doctor, lawyer, Indian chief" is a brief catalog of man's oldest "professions." To this, modern man has added the categories of skyjacker, Hell's Angel, soldier-slaughterer, and child batterer. Each is part of the puzzle of human violence. Bloomberg, taking a long, hard look at mankind, decided that we would be misleading ourselves to think that we could eliminate violence from human affairs. "We can only attempt to minimize the frequency, the duration, and the intensity of its manifestations. . . . If we try solely to suppress violence once it emerges, then we can be sure that it will appear frequently, be persistent, and reach great heights of .destruction" (1969, pp. 360–61).

New Faces of Violence

The Skyjacker

Some people have a soft spot in their hearts for the underdog who takes on the establishment, even when it involves dangerous and violent acts such as skyjacking. The saga of D. B. Cooper, who parachuted from a Northwest Airlines plane with $200,000 in loot, is an example. *Saturday Review* reported a bowling alley in Seattle that advertised a "D. B. Cooper Bowling Sweep-stakes" with cash prizes. Also, a "D. B. Cooper" T-shirt with the words "Skyjacking—the only way to fly" and a country-western song that gained brief popularity on the West Coast celebrated Cooper's venture (*Saturday Review,* 1972).

Not everyone saw D. B. Cooper as a folk-hero, but for a while most of us joked about skyjacking, treating it as a kind of lark which included free trips to Cuba. But, the skyjacker soon stripped his mask and began to show the violence and ugliness hidden behind it. He in no way resembled a modern Robin Hood. He became a desperate, frightened, dangerous man on the run, risking his own and everyone else's life in a frantic grab for money, political advantage, or brief fame. People were killed in airport shoot-outs; planes were held for ransom or blown up; and it stopped being funny. Our sobering national mood was reflected in a suggestion by a Los Angeles police chief that each airport have its own courtroom and gallows with which to try and then hang skyjackers.

The Hell's Angels

THE TRIUMPH OF
TECHNOLOGY
In the early days of televised slaughter catsup was used as a blood substitute for color movies and chocolate syrup made the scene bloody in black-and-white. Today, special effects experts have developed 'blood guns' that shoot pellets of synthetic blood and splatter realistic red blotches on the actor. Or, the victim can be rigged from head to toe with tiny explosive dye charges that can be triggered electronically to give a bloody effect. Dow PS-2 is a plastic that shatters on impact just like delicate glass. PS-2 bottles and glasses can be made so thin that stage glassware can be pushed into an actor's face as well as broken over his head without injuring him. (Field, 1972). One small step for Man, a giant step for TV.

Before the advent of skyjackers, Americans had already had a bitter love affair with the Hell's Angels. The organized, group violence of motorcycle gangs in the 1950s and early 1960s was celebrated in movies and songs before the public faced up to the fact that we were making heroes out of alienated, law-breaking dropouts who wanted no part of our civilized society. Amateur theorists speculated that the Hell's Angels bolstered their own feelings of self-worth through their noisy, powerful bikes; they roared through the countryside terrorizing citizens and defying the rules and limits of community life. Before long, they were described in the popular press as hostile, suspicious troublemakers who reacted violently to real or imagined frustration. They were said to be united by violent impulses and their common need to prove themselves fearless. They shared a contempt for the "squares" who kept interfering with their search for rough and ready pleasure at the expense of other human beings.

How can we explain the American fascination with such violent persons and violent acts? As the social psychologist Robert Kahn (1972) suggests, the problem is that many Americans buy the idea that some bloodshed is necessary and justifiable. In a nationwide survey, Kahn asked what should be done to handle disturbances involving a gang of hoodlums, blacks in a ghetto, or white students in a campus protest. In each case, people were asked what the police should do. Should they (1) let it go, not do anything; (2) make arrests without using clubs or guns; (3) use clubs but not guns; (4) shoot, but not to kill; or (5) shoot to kill? Kahn also asked how often each tactic should be used: almost always, hardly ever, or never.

The answers were surprising. The men who responded supported the use of guns by police; about two out of three said that, in handling hoodlums, the police *most always* or *sometimes* should shoot but not to kill. Almost as many men (61 percent) thought police should handle ghetto disturbances in this way, and 48 percent considered shooting a reasonable way to control student protest. Nearly one-third of this sample of American men thought the

Does TV Make Us Violent?

Murders, shoot-outs, kidnappings, fist-fights, lynchings: although most of us have never even held a gun, we participate in these events all the time—by watching television. For years, psychologists have wondered how all this television aggression affects our violent society, and in particular, our children. Does television increase aggression by giving youngsters a model for the expression of hostility? Or does television violence have a *cathartic* effect—that is, does it provide an outlet for aggressive impulses?

In experiments designed to answer such questions, children have been exposed to live or filmed aggressive scenes, then placed in a free-play situation with a variety of toys or other play materials. The results of these experiments have regularly shown that exposing young children to aggression produces a greater occurrence of activities such as punching inflated plastic clowns, popping balloons, striking stuffed animals, and operating mechanized "hitting dolls" (Liebert and Baron, 1972).

Critics of such experiments ask, however, whether televised aggression will increase the chances that a child might actually harm a *real* person (Klapper, 1968). Thus, real people have been used as targets of aggression in recent investigations. These studies suggest that showing young children films with aggressive behavior may lead these children to imitate what they saw and to aggress against fellow human beings (Hanratty, O'Neal, and Sulzer, 1972; Savitsky, Rogers, Izard, and Liebert, 1971).

A typical experiment used 68 boys and 68 girls between the ages of five and nine. The children in the experimental group watched the first three-and-a-half minutes of a program from the television series, *The Untouchables*. In these few minutes there was a chase, two fist-fighting scenes, two shootings, and a knifing. Children in the control group watched a highly active but nonviolent three-and-a-half minute videotaped sports sequence in which athletes competed in hurdle races, high jumps, and the like. When both groups of children were given a chance to help or hurt another child and then to play, the results were relatively consistent. There was evidence that a child's willingness to aggress may be at least temporarily increased just by watching aggressive television episodes.

In 1971, Feshbach and Singer designed a study to examine the role of television violence in a natural viewing situation extending over a six-week period. The subjects were boys, 10 to 17 years old, who lived either in a private school or in a detention home. Half of the boys in each institution were given a viewing schedule of predominantly

aggressive TV programs, and the other half received a schedule of mostly nonaggressive programs. They were told to watch no less than six hours of television a week, and no matter how much they watched, they had to choose all programs from the appropriate list. Before and after the experiment, all the boys in the study were given tests to measure their aggressive personality traits and fantasies. On each day of the study, they were also rated for aggressive behavior by their immediate supervisors.

The results of the experiment contradicted most of the previous laboratory studies on television violence. Subjects in the boys' home who had viewed aggressive programs showed much *less* aggression (both physical and verbal) than those who had seen the nonaggressive shows. In fact, the effect of television viewing was greatest with those boys who were especially aggressive at the start of the study. In the private school, on the other hand, the differences in television viewing had little effect on the boys' behavior. The researchers suggested that these boys had other means for the catharsis of aggressive impulses.

There is no simple answer to the question of TV violence. We can say that TV expands the imaginable range of violent acts. But the few carefully controlled studies undertaken, unfortunately, have not produced findings consistent enough to tell us what we ought to do. It is possible that television may cause children to get so used to violence that they exert less control over their aggressive impulses. Likewise, it might lessen their objections to violence in others. On the other hand, as one observer pointed out, the present generation of college and high school students was raised on television violence, yet they seem to be more opposed to war than their radio-raised parents.

police should shoot to kill *almost always* or *sometimes* in hoodlum disturbances or ghetto riots; about one-fifth voted for such violent action to deal with student protest.

From the study, we can conclude that the typical American accepts the idea of shooting and killing, when used to stop social disruption. The typical American also believes he has the right to kill if he is defending himself. Psychologically speaking, it is only a short distance from this position to admiration of the skyjacker or a brutal Hell's Angel. To understand how Americans got this way, psychologists have studied the relationship of frustration and aggression in producing violent human beings.

Frustration and Aggression

Parents teach their children the rules for expressing aggression in our society, but these rules and the manner in which they are enforced vary with each family. Sears, Maccoby, and Levin (1957) tried to find out whether the amount of aggression in a child's behavior is connected to how parents feel about and deal with aggressive behavior in child rearing. Their results indicated that very severe punishment for aggressive behavior results in passivity and inhibition (particularly in girls). The researchers also reported that, although parents must make it abundantly clear that aggression is undesirable, they should avoid punishing the child for his aggression.

One problem with analyzing the relationship between child-rearing practices and the aggressiveness of our citizens is that parents are made responsible for the kind of adults their children become. It would be easier for all of us if we didn't have to take the blame. Right or wrong, one way to avoid the responsibility is to blame our violence and aggressiveness on our animal instincts.

Our Animal Heritage?

Animals are much more peaceful than human beings and rarely engage in bloody fights for mates, territory, or dominance. Yet, we tend to describe all species as if they were prisoners of their instincts and unable to choose between aggressive or peaceful behavior. Recently, this instinct hypothesis has been discussed in a number of popular books such as Ardrey's *The Territorial Imperative* and Morris's *The Naked Ape*. As a result, the controversy over applying the instinct hypothesis to human aggression has flared to life again.

The critics of such theoretical notions (Berkowitz, 1970; Montagu, 1968) vigorously insist that the instinct theorists have based their claims on unjustified and inappropriate comparisons between animal and human behavior. A similarity between the behavior patterns of two different species does not necessarily imply identical underlying causes. It is true that territorial animals will

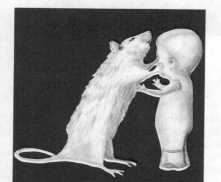

Displacement of aggression. This rat learned aggressive behavior because he was subjected to an electric current that was turned *off* when he attacked another rat. When the victim rat was removed and the current again was turned on, the rat attacked a rubber doll even though he had never been rewarded for this action before. He *displaced* his aggression by attacking a substitute. Have you ever seen a little boy hit his smaller brother when he was really angry with his big brother?

attack intruders trespassing on their territory, but an animal which is still searching for a suitable home base backs off when it meets an established owner (Tinbergen, 1968). Even animals follow rules with regard to violence.

It is my personal conviction that we won't learn much about the numerous forms of human violence by studying animals. Such studies do tell us something about the short period when we were infants without command of the language; but when we learn to speak we part company with our animal cousins and become part of a universe no animal can begin to comprehend. At the point when we are capable of understanding words like *liberty, freedom, equality, brotherhood,* and *love,* it is a whole new ball game for the human species.

This painting, *Guernica,* is Picasso's denunciation of the violence spawned by the Spanish Civil War, 1936–39. The Fascist powers bombarded an unarmed Basque city, and the famous painter captured on canvas the suffering and agony. The bull to the left standing over a mother and dead child represents the invader.

Frustration

Much, but not all, of human aggressiveness is thought to be directly related to frustration. Since the society demands that we satisfy our needs only at particular times and places and only in particular ways, it is inevitable that we will be frustrated in fulfilling our needs. This interference, however, is apparently necessary for civilized group living, since it makes the behavior of others at least partially dependable and predictable.

Some years ago at Yale, Dollard and his associates (1939) stated the principle reason why psychologists became interested in laboratory studies of frustration and aggression. They declared that frustration always leads to some form of aggression. After critics reacted to this statement vigorously, one of the researchers, Miller, amended the statement by suggesting that frustration produces any of a number of responses—one of which may be aggression. Interestingly, there was very little criticism of another portion of the statement, which suggested that aggressive behavior allows one to assume the existence of some sort of frustration beforehand. Although these statements about frustration and aggression were made more than 30 years ago, the scientific argument is still not settled.

Laboratory studies of frustration have limitations since what is gained in precision tends to be lost in naturalness. Since experimentally induced frustration is necessarily an artificial sample of the normal annoyances of life, laboratory conflict may only loosely match the subject's experiences in real life. Some of the confusing findings which issue from "staged" frustration experiments may be due to techniques which do not duplicate, or even approximate, frustrations in real life.

How we react to frustration is an exceptionally complicated event. Our actions depend on factors such as the setting, the intensity and duration of the frustrating experience, and our immediate capacity to deal with the frustration. It is important to ask what happens when we are unable to react aggressively toward the cause of our frustration. If the person bugging us is too powerful, too important, or simply out of town, we may take it out on someone or something else. In more than one case, this may be a reasonable explanation of riots and of the reactions of minority-group members in our culture.

Frustration and Catharsis

At one time or another nearly everyone has lost his temper and become violently aggressive in expressing angry feelings. Releasing pent-up anger in this way sometimes makes us feel a lot better, even if we are sorry afterwards. "Blowing off steam" as a means of emotional relief may resemble taking a drink of water to quench one's thirst. Violence should reduce the need to be aggressive, as water satisfies thirst. The complication arises when we feel anxious or guilty about losing our temper; we may suppress our aggressive needs because we dislike feeling guilty.

The theory of aggressive catharsis assumes that the world would be a less violent place if we all took time every day to scream, rage, or attend bloody movies. We would see to it that our children watched television programs which were loaded with violence. Though such suggestions have been made, the American public does not seem quite ready to adopt them. The principal objection to the catharsis theory is with the suggestion that each of us has a reservoir of aggression which must be allowed to spill over regularly if we don't want the dam to burst. This is at best a very sloppy approximation of the facts of human hostility. If a hostile way of life is learned in early childhood, it is theoretically possible for the hostility to be rooted so deeply that no attempt to drain it off could counterbalance the rate at which it is replenished from within.

Make-Believe That Turned Brutal

Results of an experiment at Stanford University illustrate how easily and quickly each of us can be transformed into a quite different person when the circumstances of our life are altered. Psychology professor Philip G. Zimbardo designed a two-week experiment in which normal, intelligent, educated, middle-class students at Stanford became—by the flip of a coin—either guards or prisoners in a make-believe jail. After six days, however, the game turned sour and had to be called off. The make-believe guards had turned brutal and half the college-student prisoners suffered acute emotional breakdowns. The make-believe prison was constructed in the basement of a campus psychology building, but even this unmistakably artificial setting did not prevent the appearance of a sadistic-masochistic, guard-prisoner mentality.

Three "prisoners" had to be released from the experiment within the first four days, because they were overcome by hysterical, traumatic reactions (crying, confusion, severe depression). The make-believe guards and prisoners couldn't avoid reacting psychologically to what was only an illusion—for them illusion became reality. The saddest aspect of this experiment was its demonstration of the degree of interpersonal savagery to which rational man quickly and helplessly descends when his life condition is drastically up-ended. For example: "Good" guards never interfered with the inhumane behavior of "bad" guards. Prisoners chose personal comfort over loyalty to fellow prisoners. And, in general, it became clear how powerful the effect of the social environment can be on the morals, ethics, values, attitudes, beliefs, and personal convictions of each of us. The results are not always pleasant to contemplate.

The frustrations of growing up can fashion human personality, and the frustrations of difficult life situations can produce human violence where we might least expect it.

The Soldier-Slaughterer

Every war has recorded instances when soldiers suffering from severe psychological frustration have lost self-control and have savagely begun to slaughter anything that moves—women, children, and even barnyard animals. Such wanton killing, reported throughout history, has not been done in panic, but rather, has been executed deliberately, coldly, and efficiently. Such slaughter certainly involves the dehumanization of the innocent victims (Gault, 1971).

For incidents such as My Lai to happen, the soldier must begin to feel that he can no longer tell the enemy from his friends. The enemy, moreover, begins to lose his human attributes. Because of our cultural differences and prejudices, the Oriental has been viewed as inscrutable or incomprehensible. The enemy is further dehumanized by names such as "dink," "slope," or "gook."

The individual soldier is under pressure to act swiftly and shoot first, despite his own fear of death or injury. Before long, he may begin to feel like only one insignificant part of the huge machine; he is only following orders, even though he carries and controls tremendous firepower. He also carries the desire to avenge the death or maiming of his buddies. To this recipe we need add only one ingredient—a restless, aggressive person who is without compassion for others and who believes "might makes right." Indeed,

Goya was another painter who used the canvas to protest the ravages of war. *The Third of May, 1808* commemorates the execution of a group of Madrid citizens by Napoleon's troops.

Riot squads are a relatively new development in our police forces, although confrontations between police and protest groups are age-old. One of the problems we face today is to figure out how to select and train enforcement people who will remain rational and retain their self-control in mob situations.

it takes an unusually aggressive individual to question prisoners while aloft in a helicopter and then push them out to their death if they are too slow in answering.

The questions now are: What will become of the men who have been trained in the slaughterhouse of Vietnam? Have we also lost some of our humanity watching the first televised war?

The Child Batterer

Newspapers occasionally carry articles about infants or small children who are hospitalized with so-called "accidental" injuries. In one such case an eight-month-old baby had two broken arms, a broken leg, a torn-off fingernail, and scars and bruises all over his body. The parents said the infant must have had "an accident" (Zalba, 1971). Such parents sometimes insist that their children were simply being punished for misbehavior, but it is hard to imagine how an eight-month-old infant could "misbehave." In many of these cases, X-rays reveal the existence of previous multiple skull fractures and broken bones.

It is not easy to identify the child batterer. The innocent parent tends

THE VIOLENT TUBE
In January 1972, the United States Surgeon General released the report of his advisory committee on television and children's aggression. The response was immediate and exceptionally confusing. The New York Times *headlined its account: 'TV Violence Held Unharmful to Youth'; on Long Island,* Newsday's *headline was: 'TV Linked to Violence in Young.' (Liebert and Neale, 1972) In view of the fact that the average child born today will, by the age of 18, have spent more of his life watching television than in any other single activity except sleep (Lesser, 1970), the problem obviously may be a serious one.*

Mothers Anonymous: The Last Resort

Mrs. J.H. of Redondo Beach, California, is a child-abuser. For four years, she explains, she struggled with an uncontrollable urge to severely punish her daughter. When she tried to obtain counseling, social agencies told her she "didn't fit into the right category" for treatment. One afternoon, she attempted to strangle her child; desperate, she confronted the local child-guidance clinic. If they didn't do something to help her, she threatened, they'd be guilty of her daughter's death. Finally, she was placed in therapy.

Her case is not unusual. Doctors say that child abuse continues to be a major problem in this country. When discovered by authorities, the battered child can receive special care. But, as Mrs. J.H. found, little help is available

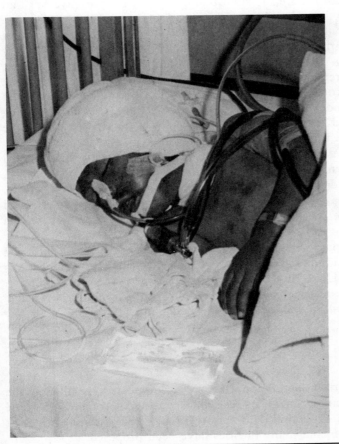

for the troubled parents. Often, these adults have grown up as abused children themselves, and they are continuing the child-beating cycle. Encouraged by her therapist, Mrs. J.H. developed an idea. "I decided," she explains, "that if alcoholics could stop drinking by getting together, and gamblers could stop gambling, maybe the same principle would work for abusers, too."

Early in 1970 she started running a series of newspaper ads: "Mothers Anonymous, for moms who blow their cool with their kids—call 379-6896."

More than 200 mothers called her and then joined M.A. Currently two groups meet in a church in Redondo Beach, another in Long Beach, and a fourth at Corona Women's Prison (for women not helped in time). Most abusers find that they can be rehabilitated in a short time: An M.A. psychiatric consultant says that almost all mothers can stop beating their children after three months with a group. Nevertheless, the mothers continue to attend meetings.

Although a professional counselor attends each meeting, the mothers do most of the talking. "What we have here," says Mrs. J.H., "is not a confrontation group, not sensitivity training, not Freudian analysis. I guess you'd call it laymen's reality therapy. We don't let people just moan about how they were beaten when they were three; we say, 'You're thirty-three now, the problem is to stop doing what you're doing to *your* children.'"

Members call each other whenever they're under stress, and receive instant help. "Want me to come over? Should I take your child for a few days?" In fact, the mothers say that swapping kids is one of their most effective methods of help. It's a quirk of the child-abuse syndrome that often only one child in a family serves as "whipping boy" (usually the one who reminds the parent of her own faults). When a mother starts losing control, it's urgent that this child be removed temporarily.

M.A. is expanding rapidly, steered by a board of directors composed of three social workers, two M.D.'s, three abusers, and one lawyer. New groups are forming in Santa Monica and Santa Ana, California, with plans for a group in Saint Paul, Minnesota.

M.A. has attracted considerable attention in recent months. Dr. R. E. Helfer, leading authority on child abuse, and author of *The Battered Child,* made a special trip to California to study the group. "It all makes me very proud," says Mrs. J.H., who admits with a smile that being proud is a brand-new wonderful feeling.

Source: Phyllis Zauner, "Mothers Anonymous: The Last Resort," *McCall's,* January 1972, p. 57.

to protect the abusive one by denying that the spouse was responsible for assaulting the child. If both parents were involved in the beating, then of course they may lie. In some cases, a seriously beaten child may be taken by the parents to a new hospital where no record of previous beatings would exist.

Child abuse, like other manifestations of violence, is as ancient as recorded history. In older times it was not unusual for infants to be killed, maimed, abandoned, or sold. In colonial times, they were often flogged for no reason other than to break their spirit. Only in recent years have we become deeply concerned about the human rights of children. It is now felt that the state should intervene when parents seriously injure their offspring.

Most of us, of course, were not battered by our parents when we were young, but nearly all of us can recall being painfully spanked or shaken to make us "shape up." As Steele and Pollock (1968) have observed, "The amount of yelling, scolding, slapping, punching, hitting, and yanking acted out by parents on very small children is almost shocking. Hence, we have felt that in dealing with the abused child we are not observing an isolated, unique phenomenon, but only the extreme form of what we would call a pattern or style of child rearing quite prevalent in our culture" (p. 332). Not every culture uses beating as a means to teach children, but Steele and Pollock's study of abusive parents makes it clear that in our society such parents come from every social, economic, and educational level. Also, mothers and fathers assault children in about equal numbers. Without exception, the child-battering parents they studied had been abused when they were children and were now doing the same thing to their own young.

Typically, these violent mothers and fathers have serious emotional problems of their own, and they tend to demand too much from their children. If the child doesn't do what the parent feels he should do (like stop crying), and if the parent happens to feel unusually inadequate, angry, or unloved at that moment, the accumulated rage and frustration is taken out on the helpless child.

Thus, the lessons learned about frustration and aggression while growing up are carried into adulthood and may appear in such diverse violent forms as the skyjacker, the Hell's Angel, the soldier-slaughterer, or the child-batterer. As we will see, these lessons may also lead to individual murder and suicide. The burning question is, when will we stop being violent?

Summary

1. The American fascination with violence appears to result from the fact that most Americans feel violence is necessary and justifiable in certain situations. The reason for this belief in violence is as yet unclear, but many theories have been proposed.

2. Aggression, according to some, results from the inability of parents to make it clear to their children that violence is frowned-upon. The problem with this theory is that it places the burden of societal interactions upon parental guidance, rather than on an individual's own behavior.

3. Robert Ardrey and Desmond Morris have each suggested that violence is a result of instinctual aggressiveness in man. Critics of the instinct theorists point out that their theories are based on inappropriate comparisons between animal and human behavior and the false assumption that similar behavior necessarily has the same underlying cause.

4. Another theory of aggression states that frustration, which occurs frequently in our lives, leads to some form of violent or aggressive behavior. Although laboratory studies have demonstrated a causal relationship between frustration and aggression, frustration may lead to behaviors other than aggression. Furthermore, the type of aggression displayed will depend on the setting, the intensity of frustration, and the ability to get back at the original cause.

5. According to the catharsis theory, violence is a way by which we drain off our aggressive impulses. This theory leads to the suggestion that if everyone could find some means of releasing aggressive feelings—physical or verbal violence or watching violent movies—the amount of violence in our society would be much reduced.

6. Early studies of the effect of television violence indicated that watching violent films increased aggression in children by providing a model. More recent research, however, suggests that violent television may provide an outlet for aggressive impulses.

7. Soldiers who kill innocent people in cold blood have usually dehumanized their victims to the point that killing no longer affects their consciences. This aspect of the soldier-slaughterer should make us worry, not only about soldiers returning from war, but also about those of us who watched the distant fighting without emotion in our own living rooms each night.

8. Parents who beat their children severely usually suffer from deep emotional problems and, in most cases, were victims of child abuse themselves. Some theorists suggest that child beating is not really a unique phenomenon but a more extreme form of our traditional pattern of raising children by spanking them.

9. Because of their theories of the nature of human aggression, many psychologists believe that violence is inevitable. Social-learning theorists, however, believe that violence can be minimized by providing children with the proper models and reinforcing only unaggressive responses to frustrating circumstances.

PSYCHOLOGICAL ISSUE

Homicide

A self-appointed judge and jury found John and Charles Ruggles guilty of killing Buck Montgomery in Redding, California in 1892—and lynched them.

Berkowitz (1962) maintains that persons who murder have usually had a long history of frequent personal frustrations. In interviews with the mothers of 51 male murderers, it became apparent that, when compared with their nonhomicidal brothers, the murderers had suffered many more physical and psychological frustrations such as illness, accidents, and harsh treatment by others. Berkowitz suggests that because of frequent frustrations these killers develop a special readiness to see and expect frustrations in the world about them; they tend to respond with intense anger when they are crossed and do not learn how to restrain their violent impulses. Any frustration may provoke them into an extreme reaction.

It would be a lot safer if we were able to spot potential murderers and either help them or simply steer clear of them, but it is not that easy. Even children sometimes have murderous impulses. Of course, murder by children is rare, and most of the cases we read about appear to be accidents rather than cold-blooded calculations. When children do kill it most often results from sudden anger.

Who Kills?

Being male will affect the odds that you will commit murder. About eight times as many males as females are arrested for assault, and seven times as many males are arrested for murder. It is interesting to note that women kill more than men do only when they destroy their own infant children. In most instances, the female of the species is not nearly as deadly as the male.

Age also makes a difference in our readiness to kill others. The most dangerous ages are between 20 and 39; the rate at which we kill one another drops quite sharply after that time. Nearly five times as many murders are committed by persons between 25 and 29 years of age as are committed by persons between 50 and 54. The rate of slaughter by the young is nearly 20 times greater than that by persons over 65.

To be on the safe side, then, you ought to be wary

Among the most notorious criminals this country has ever known are Clyde and Bonnie. Two young, amoral people with numerous personal hangups, they killed others with a wantonness that shocks the senses. They died as they lived—violently.

of young men. However, if you really want to be safe, be even more suspicious of those closest to you. As Wolfgang reported in 1969, 67 percent of the persons murdered personally knew their murderers. Twenty-five percent of the murderers were relatives; 28 percent were close friends; and 14 percent were acquaintances. In his study of 588 consecutive homicides in Philadelphia, Wolfgang found the following formula.

1. If you are under 16 years of age, your murderer will most likely be a parent or relative.

2. If you are a woman over 16, your murderer will most likely be a husband, lover, or relative.

3. Women are more likely than men to kill their mates.

4. When a man is killed, the killer is most likely to be his wife.

5. Spouse slayings are more violent than the average homicide.

6. The bedroom is the most murderous room in the house.

7. Men are in greatest danger of being killed in the kitchen; for women, the bedroom is the most dangerous.

We do not really kill the people we love, but we do kill those who are emotionally closest to us. We kill persons who are close enough to frustrate us by destroying our self-esteem. Insult, humiliation, or coercion provoke hostility, anger, and aggression.

Murder together with suicide is not an uncommon happening. When men kill themselves, they seem inclined to take a woman with them. Thus, the husband who commits suicide is ten times more likely than is a woman to kill his spouse before taking his own life. Love may be a "many splendored thing," but it can also be a very deadly affair.

Assassination   What were you doing on November 22, 1963? You will probably remember that was the day President John F. Kennedy was assassinated in Dallas, Texas. Two days later another assassination took place when Jack Ruby gunned down Lee Harvey Oswald. The murder was even recorded live on television. The fact is, many of you have grown up with the sound of gunfire ringing in your ears: Malcolm X was killed in 1965; Martin Luther King, Jr. and Senator Robert F. Kennedy were slain in 1968; and Governor George Wallace was seriously wounded in an assassination attempt in 1972. Like the rest of us, you will be shocked—but not really surprised—when the next political killing occurs. Indeed, the list of assassinations throughout history is so long that it numbers in the thousands.

Some of the more well-known assassinations in our society were those of Abraham Lincoln in 1865, John Garfield in 1881, and William McKinley in 1901. Certainly, the higher and more important the office, the more often its holders are attacked. One out of every five presidents has been the victim of assault, but only one out of every 166 governors, one out of every 142 senators, and one out of every 1,000 congressmen have been targets for such aggression. The safest job of all is that of vice-president—none has been attacked.

Does America have an abnormal tendency toward violence and assassination? Absolutely. According to the National Commission on the Causes and Prevention of Violence (*NCCPV Report,* 1969), the United States is the leader among stable democratic societies in rates of homicide, assault, rape, and robbery. The homicide rate in the United States (about 5 violent deaths per 100,000 people per year) is twice that of Finland, the world's second most violent nation. The homicide rate in Canada is 1.3 deaths per 100,000 people; in France the rate is 0.8; and in England the rate is 0.7 violent deaths per 100,000 people per year. In the vast majority of cases, however, the countries with a high level of development are the ones least prone to political assassination (Horowitz, 1972).

It should be easy to spot a potential assassin even if it is almost impossible to stop him. To begin with, the assassin is usually a man who is described as a "lonely misfit." He is hostile to his environment, unable to establish meaningful relationships with other people, and perpetually discontented. Further, he seeks a place in history as a "great man" (Donovan, 1970). Almost every assassin has suffered severe emotional disturbance, delusions of grandeur or persecution, and a history of loneliness and alienation (Weisz and Taylor, 1969).

Arthur Bremer—Assassin. The man who shot George Wallace kept a diary in which he wrote on April 24, 1972: "This will be one of the most closely read papers since the Scrolls in those caves. And I couldn't find a pen for 40 seconds & went mad. My fuse is about bernt. There's gona be an explosion soon. I had it. I want something to happen. I was sopposed to be dead a week & a day ago. Or at least infamous" [Bremer, 1972]. Bremer fit the mold of all American assassins—Caucasian, male, 24 to 40 years old, shorter than average, and owner of a handgun.

American assassins have killed for personal reasons as much as for political reasons. In older days political murder was designed to replace one leader with another, to get rid of a political tyrant, or to terrorize the population. What is disturbing is not only the fact that assassinations are so prevalent in America but also that we have such a casual attitude toward gun-barrel politics. In a recent national poll on political violence, 51 percent of the respondents agreed with the statement: "If people go into politics, they more or less have to accept the fact that they might get killed" (Crotty, 1972). This national feeling makes it unnecessary to look very far for an explanation of why men try to murder their political leaders.

People Kill People with Guns   With each new assassination the cry for gun control is heard again; yet the United States is the only advanced Western society without such controls. Observers calculate that the number of firearms in civilian hands in the United States increased from 2,100,000 in 1962 to 5,300,000 in 1968 (*NCCPV Report,* 1969). The rate of increase in the number of handguns was even greater—from 600,000 to 2,500,000 between 1962 and 1968. In the twentieth century alone, this appalling arsenal has killed something like 800,000 Americans—considerably more than have perished in all our wars (Kriss, 1972).

In contrast to the American scene, the British people have had stern gun-control laws for years, and a person who uses a gun to kill has been subject to hanging. In 1957 the law was revised so that a murderer who killed without using a gun could escape the death penalty. The number of gun deaths dropped at once, but the homicidal impulse still found an outlet in a substantial increase of killings by other means. By 1971 the British homicide rate started to climb back to its previous level, increasing by 42 percent over the previous year.

The issue to be resolved is whether we need gun control or control of our impulses. After all, few of the 100 to 200 million guns in our closets have ever been fired in anger for the purpose of killing another human being.

Summary

1. Statistics on homicide indicate that males under 39 are most likely to be murderers and that most people are murdered by someone they know. The reason for this is that people with whom we are intimate are in the best position to frustrate us and make us angry.

2. Assassinations in the United States usually result from personal, rather than political, motives. Assassins are lonely and disturbed individuals who believe that they will finally achieve recognition by committing the murderous act.

Suicide

In ancient times suicide was considered a heroic way of dealing with an impossible life situation. The Japanese hero faced with an intolerable "loss of face" committed Hari-Kiri, just as the Greek or Roman warrior fell on his own sword to save his honor. The social, religious, and legal reactions to suicide have changed over the years. At first it was accepted as a natural event; then it was condemned by the church; next it was defined as a criminal act; and finally it was described as a product of mental derangement. For centuries the suicide of religious martyrs was glorified as an example of man's dedication to the highest of principles. Later, there was an attempt to design a variety of "punishments." The dead person's property might be confiscated; he might be denied an honorable burial; or he might be hanged for the crime of suicide. In extreme cases, the body of the suicide might be dismembered; the offending hand was buried in one place and the body was buried in another to separate the "murderer" from his "victim."

The Measure of Suicide

It is difficult to find reliable body counts of suicides, and of course the rate at which people kill themselves differs from place to place and from time to time. Nonetheless, you can get some idea of the size of the problem by figuring that about 10 out of every 100,000 persons in America kill themselves each year. Using

The Deadliest Attraction. In the Western world, the single most attractive site for suicide is San Francisco's Golden Gate Bridge. Recently, it surpassed the Eiffel Tower in Paris as a way to end it all. The history of the bridge since 1937 lists close to 500 people who have plunged to death in the water below. In 1971, the average age of persons jumping from the bridge was 29.5 years; and three times as many men as women took the fatal dive. For a long time, San Francisco has had the highest suicide rate in the United States (30 per 100,000 population). Seventy-five percent of those who jumped had been residents of the San Francisco region.

this figure, you can calculate how many persons will kill themselves in your town. Keep in mind that for every successful suicide there are probably another ten suicide attempts that fail. This means that each year there are about 110 suicidal acts for every 100,000 people. It is also indicative of an inestimable degree of human misery for the families that are in some way affected by the suicidal tendency (Lester and Lester, 1971). Suicide ranks among the top ten reasons for death in this country; it is the second most usual cause

of death among college students and the third most frequent cause of death among teenagers. It ranks as the fourth cause of death in all males between 20 and 45 years of age (McGee, 1965).

Suicide statistics are notoriously unreliable not only because shame is attached to the act but also because people who successfully kill themselves have often tried and failed several times before. One survey of patients at a suicide prevention center showed that 60 percent of those who finally managed to kill themselves had made previous attempts (Wold, 1970). Also, what looks like an accident may actually be deliberate suicide. We know that more than 55 thousand of us die each year in automobiles, but no one knows how many of these drivers consciously or unconsciously set up the conditions for a fatal crash. When car accidents were carefully examined in one study, up to one-half of the dead drivers had numerous previous driving offenses; over half had also been drinking; and nearly half were suffering from depression. Such self-destructive drivers were characterized as reckless, risk-taking, impulsive persons who frequently got behind the wheel after a violent argument. Such "accidents" unfortunately also involve the deaths of innocent victims who have no desire whatsoever to end their lives.

A survey of known suicides gave this description of the conditions in which self-destruction is most likely and least likely to occur. Suicides are most likely to occur in the spring, in the late afternoon, on a Monday (for males), and at home (in 74 percent of all cases). Suicide is least likely in winter in the early morning (Maris, 1969). But these details tell only part of the story. The finger on the trigger or the hand fumbling with the bottle of sleeping pills varies according to sex, marital status, and race.

Male Supremacy   Maris (1969) studied the cases of more than 2,000 suicides in the Chicago area during a five-year period. His sample showed that men are more likely to commit suicide than are women. The excess of male over female suicides exists in every country of the world and goes from a low of 2.4 percent in Ireland to a high of 23.6 percent in Finland. In the United States the surplus of male suicides has averaged nearly 12 percent. Firearms and explosives accounted for twice as many suicidal deaths among males as among females, whereas five times as many females as males killed themselves with chemical substances, mostly barbiturates.

Wedded Bliss   The suicide rate of married persons is lower than that of single, widowed, or divorced persons. The rate is highest among divorced persons,

which suggests the possibility that in marriage the single relationship to the spouse might make all the difference. A widowed person has lost a relationship to a spouse but may have the compensation of happy memories or the companionship of sons and daughters. For the divorced person, a relationship which was once meaningful may have left only the pain and resentment of an unhappy affair. Without the help of relationship to others, the likelihood of suicide increases greatly.

For the divorced person, the rate of suicide doesn't level off with age as it does for the single, married, or widowed individual. Instead, the suicide rate increases from early in life and continues to grow even after 75 years of age.

White Death, Black Death   Suicide is not colorblind. Reporting on suicides in Los Angeles County during 1957, Farberow and Shneidman (1961) discovered that 95 percent of the suicides were white, whereas only 3 percent were black. Similarly, suicide among blacks in the South is only about one-fourth that of southern whites (Vitols, 1967). The lower suicide rate among blacks seems to be related to their generally lower social and economic status in society; if you are already at the bottom of the social class structure, there is less shame attached to not rising in the world. "It is often assumed, particularly by black persons, that suicide represents a white solution to white problems. As Dick Gregory once cracked, 'You can't kill yourself by jumping out of the basement.' And Red Foxx scoffed, 'Only three Negroes have jumped off the Golden Gate Bridge, and two of them were pushed' " (Seiden, 1970).

Times are changing, though, and recent research suggests that suicide among young, urban black men has soared in the last 15 years. Older blacks are not killing themselves in greater numbers, but the younger blacks seem to be. Seiden (1970) contends that, if you wanted to drive someone to the edge of despair, there is no better way to do it than by doing what we now do to young urban blacks. We see to it that they cannot feel capable, useful to others, or competent in making their own way. After a while they drop out, turn on

Doctor, Heal Thyself. The doctor you expect to preserve your life may be planning to take his own. More doctors die of self-inflicted wounds than are killed by automobile accidents, airplane crashes, drownings, and homicides combined. American doctors kill themselves at twice the rate of average American males and this seems to be the case in other parts of the world as well [Ross, 1971]. Surprisingly, of all doctors, psychiatrists are most likely to kill themselves; they are six times more likely to commit suicide than are pediatricians, for example.

to drugs, or pursue a criminal career until they kill themselves, are shot, or are locked up for life.

Death at an Early Age

"To be or not to be" has long been the question, and "not to be" increasingly has become the answer for some young people. A skyrocketing number of young people no longer believe they "have everything to live for." In the ten years from 1960 to 1970, for example, the suicide rate for women under 20 in Los Angeles jumped from 0.4 to 8 per 100,000 population. For young men of that age, the rate went from 3 to 10 suicides per 100,000. The city of Los Angeles is no exception to the national trend; other cities report similar increases. In the 15- to 19-year-old group, suicide is now the fifth leading cause of death (Jacobs, 1971).

The suicide rate among college students is exceptionally high—after accidents, the second cause of death. It is hard to understand why this relatively privileged group with the advantages of intelligence and educational opportunity would want to close the door on life. Seiden (1966) tried to answer this question in a study of 23 University of California students who committed suicide during the ten-year period from 1952 through 1961. Twice as many older students (over 25) as younger students killed themselves. These students were not in academic trouble (two-thirds of them were above the grade-point average), and they did not kill themselves during those periods when they might have been plagued by the stresses of final exams. The suicides usually occurred early in the semester—in the months of October or February.

This study convinced Seiden that the suicidal act was really a final dramatic gesture summing up a life-time pattern of inadequate adjustment. To their fellow students the suicide seemed to be doing well; but the suicide himself usually believed that his achievements didn't measure up to what he or others expected him to accomplish. The fundamental fact is that few of the suicide's fellow students knew him very well; he was typically asocial and withdrawn. "These particular students were uniformly described as terribly shy, virtually friendless individuals, alienated from all but the most minimal social interactions. Frequently they had compensated for their personal solitude by increased study and almost total absorption in school-work" (p. 410).

But before you begin to wonder if attending college may be hazardous to your health, consider the additional findings reported by the Los Angeles Suicide Prevention Center (*Trans-action,* 1971). They examined data on youthful suicides in 52 Los Angeles colleges from 1960 to 1968. They also studied a sample of nonstudents between the ages of 15 and 29. It turned out that the nonstudents had a suicide rate that ran from two to three times higher than the student rate. Like their student counterparts, these suicides had been solitary figures who communicated very little with anyone.

Becoming Suicidal

Some psychiatric theorists insist that about 90 percent of all suicides have serious emotional disturbances. Reconstructing the life of the deceased by studying all available evidence and records and by interviewing those who knew him best has led most American researchers to agree that suicide is a symptom of de-pressive emotional illness which produces feelings of helplessness, hopelessness, and worthlessness as well as a loss of interest in food, sex, work, friends, and everything else that normally makes life worth living (Blum, 1972). These depressions produce distinct physical symptoms: unusual fatigue, disturbed sleep patterns, and an inability or unwillingness to eat. Of all psychiatric conditions, depression is the most likely to be associated with suicide.

Most of us are unhappy some of the time, but it is not easy to understand how suicidal people get so deeply and disastrously depressed. We don't have all the answers yet, but the Los Angeles Suicide Prevention Center has outlined one do-it-yourself method for rearing a suicidally inclined child. They suggest that you begin by giving the child personal experiences which will produce feelings of being inadequate and unloved. The child should also be taught to develop a harsh, punishing conscience filled with powerful feelings of guilt and shame; further, he should be instilled with exceptionally high standards and have a compulsion toward intense self-criticism for failure to achieve. Society can help by teaching values which emphasize achievement, the accumulation of wealth, and an unrealistic view of love (Farberow, 1970).

Why are we so concerned about preventing suicide? Why not let each person decide for himself when he has had enough of living? One reason we try to prevent suicide is because these people, when prevented, often go on to lead happy, productive lives. In addition, suicide does not involve a single life; it affects the lives of all those connected with the victim. His family suffers not only sorrow but usually guilt; they blame themselves for not preventing the tragedy. Children, too, suffer from the social stigma attached to the suicide of a parent; frequently, they become fearful that they are destined to follow the parent's example. Considering that ten attempts are made for every successful suicide, we must believe that most people really don't want to die and would not kill themselves if there were any other solution to life's problems.

Summary

1.   Most people who commit suicide are depressed individuals who have learned early in life that they are unloveable. As children, they were taught exceptionally high standards for themselves in terms of educational achievement, wealth, and success in love. Each normal failure brings misery to the already weak self-concept.

2.   Married individuals have a lower rate of suicide than single, divorced, or widowed people. This statistic is attributed to the fact that married people have at least one other person in their life to provide some meaning for them and to help them snap out of suicidal tendencies.

3.   Suicide is the second highest cause of death among college students and is probably due to an individual's failure to live up to his own—usually unrealistic—standards.

Sex

Sweet lovers love the spring. —Shakespeare

The praying mantis is an insect several inches long that looks like a twig with a head and legs. During the mating season, when the hormone levels of the female mantis are high enough to inhibit her normal behavior patterns, she will allow the male to come close to her without immediately killing him. But hunger is a more immediate and powerful drive than sex, even during the mating season; so the male's best chance for sexual contact is to wait until the female has just caught an insect. At this moment he can safely sneak up on her while she is distracted by lunch. If he fails in his first amorous attempt, he may end up being her dessert. Even if he finds the proper position on his first try, his troubles are far from over if his head comes close to hers during lovemaking; she might very well bite it off. Interestingly, an insect can live for several hours without a head and can continue vigorous and effective love making "dead or alive."

The Relativity of Sexual Behavior

Human sexual practices are not quite as dramatic as those of the praying mantis, but they have varied exceptionally in different cultures during the course of human history. Our ideas about what is proper and improper are continually changing. Current patterns of sexual behavior do not match those of other eras, nor are such patterns necessarily "natural" or inevitable (Marmor, 1971). In the early Christian era, public nudity was no cause for shame; virginity was relatively unimportant; marriage was often a temporary arrange-

The mores and social attitudes of Victorian times provide a sharp contrast to how we think, dress, and act today. Some would call the change positive, others would say not enough has been accomplished, and still others would simply throw up their hands in horror.

ment; and sexual relations outside of marriage were taken for granted. In a few ancient societies, all the male wedding guests would copulate with the bride.

Monogamy does not occur in all human societies. Only 16 percent of 185 societies studied by Ford and Beach (1952) were monogamous; indeed, many societies permit and expect extramarital sex. In some tribes a man would not begrudge his wife to another, and women are free to chase sex objects as eagerly as men.

There seems to be no absolutely natural pattern of sexual behavior in man. Among human societies, there is no agreement on the age when sexual activity ought to begin; on the kind of partner who may be chosen; on the preferred time, place, or positions of intercourse; or on the moral or religious significance of various forms of sexual expression. What is psychologically healthy in one culture may not be so in another, and what is normal or deviant depends on the value systems of the society. What we once labeled "perversions" we now call "deviations," and these may eventually be described as mere "variations" in the choice of a sexual object.

The Sexual Revolution

For years the dominant sexual standards in the United States included abstinence from intercourse until marriage. Premarital intercourse may have been begrudgingly tolerated when the partners were in love or engaged. The standard for men—held by both men and women—tended to be more permissive in regard to sexual intercourse, either before marriage or when there was no love relationship. Among other things then, the sexual revolution implies a dramatic change in attitudes about premarital behavior. As Smigel and Seiden (1968) report, the double standard is tottering if it has not yet fallen. But reviewing the literature published since the early 1920s, these researchers concluded that—if there is a revolution—it has been progressing rather slowly. It started with the generation born in the decade from 1900 to 1909. The shift since then has been toward the transitional double standard—intercourse is acceptable for men under many conditions but acceptable for women only if they are in love.

America's supposedly changing sexual standards were studied by Reiss (1968) who concluded that the popular notion of an American sexual "revolution" is a myth. Reiss is one of the few behavioral scientists to make systematic investigations of racial as well as social class differences in sexual attitudes. His findings show the following:

"The Kiss." This simple physical act has been depicted in a myriad of ways by the world's artists. And the way the public views these works of art changes with time. Other generations would have been less than enthusiastic about Brancusi's sculpture. How do you view it?

> . . . [there are] large variations to the way whites and Negroes of precisely the same class view premarital sexual permissiveness. Among the poor, for instance, only 32 percent of white males approve of intercourse before marriage under some circumstances—compared with 70 percent of Negro males. The variation is even more dramatic among lower-class females; 5 percent of whites compared with 33 percent of Negroes. Generally, high-school and college students of all classes were found to be more permissive than those in the adult sample. But even among students there were variations associated with race. [Reiss, 1968, p. 26]

Thus to speak of a sexual revolution, we must specify the social class and race we are talking about.

Our most recent anxieties about sexual morality have focused on the attitudes and behavior of college students. If current college students now view love between partners as irrelevant to intercourse, then a dramatic change in principles has certainly occurred. Although attitudes about socially acceptable premarital sexual activity seem to have become significantly more liberal, the change may not be so dramatic as to justify the label "revolution." If there is indeed a revolution, then it is not going equally well in all parts of our country. A study published in 1970 reported that only 7 percent of the women at a white southern college found premarital sex acceptable, but 62 percent of the women at a liberal New York college found it acceptable (Kaats and Davis, 1970). Acceptance of premarital sexual behavior has

"Gay Liberation" has become a rallying cry for the many homosexuals who are, for the first time, openly declaring their sexual preferences. They disagree vehemently with the Establishment view that their way of life is ridiculous, pitiful, shameful, or degrading. They ask for toleration, if not acceptance, and they also ask that psychologists stop regarding homosexuality as a personality aberration.

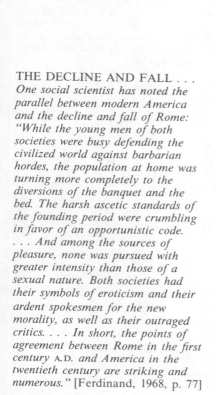

THE DECLINE AND FALL . . .
One social scientist has noted the parallel between modern America and the decline and fall of Rome: "While the young men of both societies were busy defending the civilized world against barbarian hordes, the population at home was turning more completely to the diversions of the banquet and the bed. The harsh ascetic standards of the founding period were crumbling in favor of an opportunistic code. . . . And among the sources of pleasure, none was pursued with greater intensity than those of a sexual nature. Both societies had their symbols of eroticism and their ardent spokesmen for the new morality, as well as their outraged critics. . . . In short, the points of agreement between Rome in the first century A.D. *and America in the twentieth century are striking and numerous."* [Ferdinand, 1968, p. 77]

changed markedly in some places, but most men still hold to a standard which allows greater sexual freedom for them and less freedom for women—particularly when the woman is a sister or potential marriage partner. In general, men and women still agree it is important that women be virgins at marriage; both men and women would lose more respect for a girl who engaged in sex without love than they would for a man who did so (Kaats and Davis, 1970).

Still some behaviors have shifted in modern times. Genital stimulation called "heavy petting" has increased significantly. Figures from studies completed in the 1960s reveal that 61 percent of the junior and senior college women had such experiences (Luckey and Nass, 1969; Packard, 1968). Most studies of college students report that between 35 and 50 percent of college women have experienced sexual intercourse. Groves, Rossi, and Grafstein (1970), studying first semester freshmen and juniors, noted that their reported rate of 36 percent intercourse among junior women is almost twice the 20 percent figure which Kinsey found for college women of the 1940s. Thus, while there seems to have been no significant change in the sexual activities of men since the year 1900, the picture has changed somewhat for women.

Gagnon (1967) evaluated the research evidence and suggested that the percentage of people engaging in premarital sexual activity has not changed markedly over the last four decades. Gagnon states that only 5 to 7 percent of American women have intercourse with five or more men before they marry. As for men, premarital intercourse has always been the case for 70 percent of college males, 80 percent of men with a high school education, and 90 percent of males with only an eighth-grade education. Considering this fact, it is difficult to see how much revolution could occur in the male sexual experience. Commenting on Gagnon's conclusions, McCandless (1970) stated that the reports of increased percentages of sexual activity should be considered simply that—increased percentages rather than a revolution.

The Swinging Scene

One sign of changing sexual practices is the "swinging" scene in America (Smith and Smith, 1970). Group sex and partner exchange have recently become fashionable topics in the popular magazines (O'Neill and O'Neill, 1970), despite the fact that the exchange of sexual partners has been standard practice for hundreds of years in some other cultures. It is important not to confuse "utopian" and "recreational" swingers. Utopian swingers practice sexual freedom in order to eliminate the psychological evils of possessiveness and jealousy. Recreational swingers do it just for the fun of it.

Bartell (1971) collected data on swinging couples in Middle America and noted that the scene is less swinging than you might imagine:

1. Blacks are not welcome as sexual participants.

2. Male homosexual activity is exceptionally rare and nearly always disruptive to the swinging party.

3. Nearly all women swingers engage in sexual activity with other women at some point in the festivities, and this is almost always a spectator sport for men.

4. Swingers seem obsessively preoccupied with personal hygiene and between sexual encounters showering seems to be a constant activity.

5. Swinging is inhibited by unspoken rules designed to limit emotional involvement among participants. In other words, there can be intense sexual interaction provided there is only superficial human interaction.

Charles and Rebecca Palson (1972) studied the swinging scene as anthropologist-participant-observers. They reported that swinging is initiated by the husband seeking sexual variety. It is accepted passively by the wife who wishes to please the husband. For the woman, the swinging sexual activity is a continuation of her need to please men rather than a search for personal pleasure. It is not all that perfect for the men either. Bartell (1971) reports, for example, that fewer than 25 percent of the males are able to "turn on" regularly at large-scale, multiperson, swinging parties. Swinging can only temporarily remove impotence.

This facet of the sexual revolution is not likely to become the sexual wave of the future. Swinging may be satisfying to some and necessary for others, but it will not take the place of a relationship that deepens over time between two persons who have been able to make an emotional commitment to each other.

The New Sex Therapy

Scientifically, we know a great deal more about the functioning of your heart, your liver, and your stomach than we know about the normal functioning

SOME NOTES ON CONTRACEPTION
Modern methods of contraception have separated sexual activity from the function of reproduction. This may allow greater sexual freedom, but it also creates psychological problems for both men and women. For men the ability to make babies is often tied to their feelings of masculinity. Vasectomies, and even their wives' taking pills, cause men to feel emasculated and become impotent. Although women no longer have to worry about getting pregnant, many now complain about the possibilities of being used because of their greater sexual freedom. Some people may forget to use birth-control methods because of unconscious desires for a child to cement a relationship. Others dislike using mechanical methods because it makes it necessary to recognize the intention to engage in intercourse.

SEX-CHANGE SURGERY

An estimated 500 persons have undergone surgical sex change in the last few years in this country. Male transsexuals—persons with the normal physical attributes of the male sex but with the emotional disposition of the female sex— undergo surgical transformation where the penis and testicles are removed and an artificial vagina is constructed with the sensitive skin of the penis. In some cases there is artificial breast enlargement. Changing the female transsexual to a male involves removing the breasts, removing the womb (hysterectomy), and constructing a nonfunctioning penis and testicles using sexually responsive tissue. These organs are decorative and do not function.

DIFFERENT SEX FOR DIFFERENT SECTS

Anthropological studies comparing two societies—one Polynesian and the other Irish—can set the sexual revolution in its proper cultural context. In Donald Marshall's (1971) account of Mangaia Island in Polynesia, copulation is the predictable outcome of social contact between the sexes, and sex happens before the development of affectionate feelings. Parents encourage their offspring to have varied sexual experience in order to find the most compatible mate. In sharp contrast is Messenger's (1971) study of an Irish island which is "the most sexually naive of the world's societies, past or present." Sex is never discussed in the home; most girls are unprepared for the first menstrual flow; and the female orgasm is unknown or considered a deviant sexual response.

of your sexual organs. Yet an astonishing proportion of the patients who walk into a physician's office could use guidance in sexual matters—guidance they are not likely to get since such matters are not part of the curriculum in most medical schools. But, something is being done about this situation. It began some years ago with the pioneering work of an Indiana University biology professor named Alfred Kinsey. Then, in the 1950s William Masters and Virginia Johnson made recordings of bodily reactions while women experienced various types of sexual arousal (chiefly masturbation). Later, they also studied the physiological changes that accompanied sexual excitement in males. They delayed public discussion of their work until 1962 when they presented their findings to an audience at the annual meeting of the American Psychological Association. Their research led Masters and Johnson to pioneer in new types of therapy for men and women who have various types of sexual problems. Using therapy teams composed of one male and one female, they treated people for such problems as premature ejaculation and impotence in males and failure to reach orgasm in females. Partner surrogates were screened and trained as part of the therapeutic team for single men who had no satisfactory sexual partner to bring to the therapy—a problem not faced by the few single women who were treated. The surrogates saw their partners during the two-week therapy session but did not continue contact beyond that.

One of the major goals in treating sexual maladjustments was to establish lines of communication between men and women so that each could gain a better understanding of the other. At most sex-therapy clinics, the early stages of treatment consist largely of exercises designed to focus on bodily sensation. The partners are instructed simply to stroke various parts of one another's bodies—carefully avoiding genital contact—to master the knack of giving pleasure in order to receive pleasure. Once the partners have begun to shed their inhibitions about physical contact, an advance is made to the breasts and genitals. Then, when the therapists feel the couple is ready, sexual intercourse is practiced with an emphasis on learning to communicate which kinds of sexual contact are most gratifying.

The Center for Marital and Sexual Studies in California has added innovations of their own to the Masters and Johnson formula. As a visual aid for their patients, they show video tapes of more skilled volunteer subjects in action. In an even more far out approach, one New York psychiatrist treats sexual hangups during nude encounter sessions.

Some critics argue that the sex therapists are merely treating symptoms without relieving the deep emotional problems that prompt them; the critics warn that relieving a sexual problem by such therapy could result in the patient's disturbance emerging in other, potentially more serious symptoms. Sex therapy is still new, and only time will tell how effective it is as a long-term cure. Masters and Johnson report that 80 percent of nearly 2,000 treated patients continue to have satisfactory sex lives five years after treatment.

Women's Liberation

The women's liberation movement resurfaced in 1963 when Betty Friedan published a book called *The Feminine Mystique*. In this book, Friedan tried to explain why the American housewife is universally in a state of deep personal distress (Decter, 1972). Young women were discovering that they had been betrayed and cheated by life. They were well housed, well fed, and well dressed; their children were healthy; and they were not abused or beaten by their husbands. Still, said Friedan, American women were miserable and resentful.

In the six years after the book appeared, the women's liberation movement took hold among radical students, young career women, and the daughters of the harried housewives Friedan wrote about. Some of the wives and mothers-to-be decided that housework was an endless, unfulfilling task and that the traditional male-female relationship in our society left a lot to be desired. Since for centuries there has been a remarkable persistence of male dominance in societies the world over, the women's liberation movement has a high hurdle to surmount (Howe, 1970).

Equal Pay for Equal Work?

Despite all the talk about women's liberation, the fact is that things really haven't gotten much better for women since the movement began. As the graph demonstrates, the gap between the incomes of men and women is getting larger—not smaller. It is not just that women are engaged in occupations that traditionally have low salaries; the fact is that women are paid less than men even when they do equivalent work. For example, in 1970, men in professional and technical work had a median income of $11,577; the median income of women in the same job category was only $6,675. Male clerical workers received a median salary of $7,965 a year; female clerical workers had a median income of $4,646. In every job category listed by the Bureau of the Census, women were paid less than men for the same work.

Of course, there have been some improvements in the position of women over the past few decades. In 1940, for example, 25.8 percent of the women in America were working, but in 1970 that figure had risen to 39.6 percent. (This still means, however, that twice as many men work as women.) The number of women in typically "male" occupations also seems to be increasing, although this rise is fairly small. In 1960 12.7 percent of all working women were engaged in professional or technical occupations; in 1970 that figure had risen to 14.8 percent.

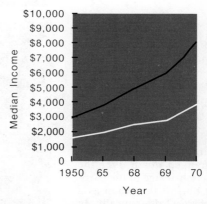

The discrepancy between male and female salaries is obvious in this graph. Black line, men; white line, women.

In 1960, 1.3 percent of working women were craftsmen or foremen; in 1970 the figure was 1.7 percent.

Sources: U.S. Bureau of the Census, *Current Population Reports,* series P-60; data appearing in U.S. Department of Commerce, *Statistical Abstracts, 1972,* p. 328; and U.S. Department of Commerce, *General Social and Economic Characteristics,* "United States Summary," 1970.

Men's ideas of "ladies' socials" may not have changed much over the years, but the self-image of the participants, and thus of the group as a whole, has changed dramatically. In the middle of the nineteenth century, the women in the top photo are attending a "DMC Club" meeting—DMC being a French form of crocheting. In the middle of the twentieth century, the women below are showing off their joint efforts at a quilting bee—an old-fashioned enterprise that's making a new-fashioned come back.

Machismo and Liberation

Machismo is a pattern of exaggerated masculine characteristics involving aggressiveness, virility, fearlessness, and the absence of sentimentality. To Aramoni (1972), machismo is also a destructive attempt by the man to overcome the humiliation of having been an ineffectual little boy. Feeling inadequate, the "machista" struts through life challenging and dominating others in order to deny his own weakness.

Machismo regards the woman as a toy to be played with; she can be abandoned without guilt since she is merely an object of conquest—a trophy. She is a further proof of masculinity rather than a person in her own right. If the woman is the macho's sister or mother, of course, he feels quite differently since her protection then becomes a matter of honor. It is absurd, of course, that the same men who demand respect for their own sisters and mothers show no respect for the sisters and mothers of others.

Classic cases of male machismo exist in our society, but most of us are more familiar with its subtler expression in the notions of male supremacy and female inferiority. Even five-year-olds are versed in society's sexist stereotypes—patterns which are perhaps ingrained for life. By that age every little boy and girl knows which are the proper professions for men and women. Two educators in Detroit surveyed kindergartners and discovered the children of both sexes saw men as all powerful. Men were considered twice as likely as women to perform the jobs of both sexes. The children were certain a man could handle an architectural draftsman's job; but the few children who believed a woman was capable of architectural work qualified their answers with statements such as, "if she had special training." The stereotyping was even more dramatic in the children's own career choices. Eighty-three percent of the girls and 97 percent of the boys chose occupations traditionally associated with their sex.

When the kindergarten girl has grown up and married, she must fulfill the male fantasy of the perfect wife. As one writer put it:

Have to go on a business trip? She will pack your suitcase with clean clothes which she washed and ironed or sent to the cleaners (after picking them up off the floor where you dropped them). Want to talk? She will listen eagerly. Woman. She will look like a goddess at the crack of dawn and stand in the door as you leave for work, and be standing there waiting when you come home. Above all, she is an animal who will become a willing, anxious, sex-starved beast any day or night you wish. [Lester, 1970, p. 31]

Despite the lopsidedness of this social arrangement, women's liberation is not liberation from men as much as it is liberation from the myths that have confined and enslaved women in their own minds (Limpus, 1970). The prison is as much psychological as it is cultural. According to Chessler (1971), the psychological prison may be in the form of female "neuroses." The symp-

toms women experience may not reflect mental illness as much as they reflect a natural reaction to the stress of being confined to a narrow sex-role stereotype.

The Movement

Groups within the movement vary in their demands and strategies, but the major goals include an end to job discrimination by sex, equal pay for equal work, free child care, an equal sharing of family responsibilities, the right to abortion, an end to all forms of sexual exploitation, and a restructuring of sex roles. Over the years, there has been a gradual increase in the number

Equal Rights Amendment

1. Equality of rights under the law shall not be denied or abridged by the United States or by any State on account of sex.

2. The Congress shall have the power to enforce, by appropriate legislation, the provisions of this article.

3. This amendment shall take effect two years after the date of ratification.

A constitutional amendment seeking equal rights for women has been introduced into every Congress since 1923, but in every case the amendment has failed. The Equal Rights Amendment (ERA) introduced in the 1972 Congress has also seen a storm of opposition—and much of it from women. What's all the fuss about? Although the wording appears rather harmless, the ERA could mean drastic alterations in many of the time-honored institutions and regulations all of us are accustomed to. Many women feel that, rather than improving their position, the amendment would abolish many of the legal safeguards which currently protect them. Here are just some of the changes that passage of the ERA would probably call for:

• Women would be eligible for the draft.

• Women would no longer have to take their husbands names upon marriage; the last name of their children would be a matter of the parents' choice.

• In case of divorce, alimony would be paid either by the husband or the wife, depending on financial status.

• Child-custody laws would no longer favor mothers; judges would have to decide custody in terms of where a child's welfare was best served.

• Unequal prison sentences for men and women would no longer be allowed.

• The age of marriage consent would be the same for both sexes.

• Statutory rape laws would probably be eliminated.

• Women could no longer be banned from jobs because of the possibility of pregnancy.

• Laws protecting women from physical exertion on a job would be illegal; jobs requiring physical exertion would be open to all men and women who are capable of performing the task.

Some laws would remain as they are, however, because they were made in regard to specific physical characteristics unique to one sex and therefore do not infringe upon the rights of the other sex. Thus, women would still be allowed maternity leaves; forcible rape would still be an offense; and separate restrooms could be maintained.

Sources: "Facing Equality for Women," *Time,* October 4, 1971; and "Trouble for ERA," *Time,* February 19, 1973.

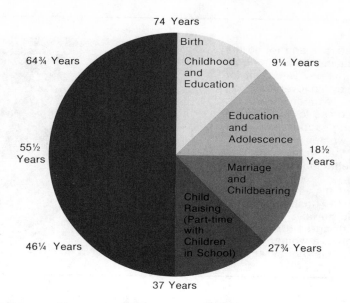

74 Years — Birth

Childhood and Education

9¼ Years

64¾ Years

Education and Adolescence

18½ Years

55½ Years

Marriage and Childbearing

Child Raising (Part-time with Children in School)

27¾ Years

46¼ Years

37 Years

It used to be that almost all of a woman's life was devoted to child raising. And there wasn't much question what a woman was going to do with her "later" years when she only expected to live to 35 or 40. The average woman, today, though, has about half of her life ahead of her after the kids are out of the house. How might these increased years psychologically affect women whose whole orientation has been to the home and the family?

of rights and opportunities afforded women (Kraditor, 1968).

Today's movement consists mostly of urban, white, college-educated, middle-class women—a group that is generally considered rather privileged to begin with (Brownmiller, 1970). The movement's activities have been many and varied. In consciousness-raising groups, for example, women assemble informally to talk with one another and to be heard perhaps for the first time. The groups provide an opportunity for friendship and a chance to relieve the woman's sense of isolation from her own kind. The groups try to increase awareness of the problem of oppression by the male. Women's crisis centers have also been established to provide personal counseling and information on services for women in the community. In these centers women can interact with other women in matters of education, legal aid, emergency medical assistance for rape or assault, self-defense classes, and the like. The outspoken feminist Germaine Greer (1971) suggests that such centers may counteract the artificial dependence, noncompetitiveness, self-sacrifice, and sentimentality thought for so long to be the essence of femaleness.

Counterattacks

Despite the endless masculine jokes made at the expense of women seeking liberation, counterattacks have been coming from various female quarters as well. Elizabeth Volar (1973) believes that our social situation is just the reverse of that described by militant feminists: "Men have been trained and conditioned by women, not unlike the way Pavlov conditioned his dogs, becoming their slaves." Volar insists that most work done by men is hard, whereas housework is easy. To Volar, it is the American male who is thoroughly

A RADICAL FEMINIST VIEW
Elizabeth Davis (1971) suggests that, contrary to the Biblical account, before man there was woman. "The first males were mutants, freaks produced by some damage to the genes caused perhaps by disease or a radiation bombardment from the sun" (p. 351). To Davis "The most wasteful 'brain' drain in America today is the drain in the kitchen sink, down which flow daily with the dishwater the aspirations and the talents of the brainiest fifty-nine and ninety-seven-hundredths percent of our citizenry—housewives whose IQ's dwarf those of the husbands whose soiled dishes they are required to wash" (p. 333). Ms. Davis takes a hard line indeed when she calls for a complete and total demolition of the social body.

Women's Lib and the Polls

The Roper organization polled Americans and found the following percentages of support for the women's rights movement. "Women should get equal pay with men for doing the same job" is accepted by an overwhelming majority of both women and men. "Women should be treated the same as men when it comes to applying for and getting jobs" similarly won strong support among 71 percent of men and 74 percent of women. Seventy-four percent of both sexes also agree that women who are pretty should not get better pay or better jobs than women who are not.

Still, only 16 percent approve of the idea that "If a woman can earn a better living than her husband, should she be the breadwinner and should he take care of the house and kids?" Women strongly disagree (68 percent) with the statement "In case of divorce, a woman should pay her ex-husband alimony if she has money and he doesn't."

This healthy, normal baby has a handicap.
She was born female.

manipulated by the female. He works incessantly to pay the price for sexual favors.

Helen Lawrenson (1971) is equally suspicious of the liberationists. She feels the liberationists are extremist freaks who respond to love as if it were a disease. She has described the movement as being "a hair-raising emotional orgy of hatred as vicious as it is ludicrous." It encompasses "the penis, the Pill, false eyebrows, brassieres, Barbie dolls, Freud, Dr. Spock [and] detergent advertisements" (p. 83).

Males have been more than a little cautious in making comments about the movement. Joseph Adelson (1972), however, suggests that the women of America don't care for the movement and are turned off by its assault on cherished values; they are irritated by the accusation that they are not free. Adelson states: "There is so much talk of self—of self-fulfillment, self-realization, self-determination—and so little of one's devotion and responsibility to particular others—I don't mean mankind; I mean particular others. Perhaps this accounts for the strange absence of the child in so much of the literature of the movement. With so little felt to be available to and for the self, what can be left to offer another?" (p. 98)

Any reform movement aimed at uprooting traditional social arrangements certainly has an overwhelming job to do, but perhaps in this century and in this sophisticated society more progress will be made than ever before. If the soaring sales of the liberationist magazine *MS.* is any indication, it seems obvious that there are a substantial number of persons concerned with the relationships between male and female. Time will tell whether tomorrow is to witness a war between the sexes or an evolution to less stressful relations between woman and man.

Summary

1. When talking about differences in sexual practice, it is important to remember that there is no absolutely natural pattern of sexual behavior. Throughout history, among different cultures, and across class lines, what is right for one group may be considered wrong for another group.

2. The answer to the question of whether or not there is really a sexual revolution depends on whom you talk to. Ideas about premarital permissiveness, for example, differ to a great extent between whites and blacks of the same social class. These standards also differ according to geographical region. In general, however, the sexual revolution appears to be a gradual change in the behavior as well as the standards of women.

3. "Swinging" is a form of group sex. Among married couples participation appears to be initiated by the husband, with the wife just going along to please him, and is performed for recreation. In utopian communities it is considered a means of eliminating possessiveness and jealousy.

4. Masters and Johnson pioneered many of the techniques of sex therapy designed to treat impotence, premature ejaculation, and inability to achieve orgasm. One of the major sources of sexual difficulties is the inability of partners to communicate with each other about sexual contact, and sex therapy aims at eliminating this problem.

5. The historical domination of women is associated with the idea of machismo—extreme pride in one's maleness, fearlessness, and the ability to use women unemotionally as objects. Most men who accept this pattern of behavior are actually covering up for their own feelings of inadequacy. Whatever the cause, the ideas behind machismo continue to infiltrate our society with stereotypes about male superiority and female inferiority.

6. The idea of liberation for women is not really liberation from men, but liberation from the stereotypes and myths that confine women to specific and sometimes unpleasant social roles. Among the demands of liberation are equal treatment under the law, an end to job discrimination, and equal pay for equal work.

7. Many women have rejected the women's liberation movement because of its often radical stands. Elizabeth Volar believes that, in reality, women have manipulated men throughout history in order to put themselves in a position of luxury. A number of men and women object to the movement because it deals so much with the ideas of self-fulfillment and ignores the importance of relationships with others.

Prostitution

Prostitution has always existed to deal with what society labels antisocial sex—in other words, sex between strangers and sex without marriage. Prostitution provides sex with a paid partner just as pornography provides it through imagined intercourse with a fantasy object (Polsky, 1967).

The Workaday World

The average full-time prostitute works six days a week and has an average of three clients daily. Every day nearly a third of a million men or about two million men every week use the prostitute's services. If the average price paid per visit is about $10, then it can be estimated that the combined earnings of full-time prostitutes is roughly $900 million a year. Working a six-day week, the average prostitute will gross about $10,000 a year, but she will get to keep only between $5,000 or $6,000 (Winick and Kinsie, 1971). This, of course, is a very conservative estimate of the actual revenue each year in the United States. Obviously, detailed records of such transactions are seldom kept.

Being a prostitute is no bed of roses. The job can be as routine and boring as any other; and if you are on the bottom rung of the professional ladder, the hours can be long and exceptionally dreary. Forced retirement is always waiting around the corner; the older you get, the lower is your pay, the worse the working conditions, and the less appetizing the task to be performed.

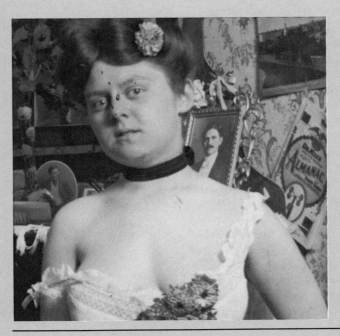

The Myth of the Happy Hooker

An old joke involves a client asking a prostitute how she—an honor graduate with a master's degree from an exclusive eastern university—happened to become a prostitute. Her answer was: "Just lucky, I guess." This joke reflects the persistent myth that the girl who has everything can happily become a prostitute; but the myth and the facts don't match.

In Greenwald's (1958) careful study of 20 call girls,

he reported that not one of them recalled growing up in a happy home with parents who got along well. In three-fourths of his cases, the girls' homes were broken before they reached adolescence. His girls all seemed to have doubts about who they were, and they searched for hints about what role they should play. With a poor sense of self, it was very difficult for them to achieve satisfactory relationships with other people; only 5 of the 20 girls interviewed had not attempted suicide.

Greenwald concluded that prostitution is a predictable outcome of an early environment marked by parental discord, neglect, and rejection. At a young age, these girls learned that sex was something you could trade for personal gain. Especially for very poor girls, the road to prostitution is an easy one to follow. The typical prostitute grows up in a slum neighborhood. She has had an unstable family life and may have been an illegitimate child, a school dropout, or a minority-group member. In addition, she is experienced with drugs. One study of women arrested for prostitution in New York City revealed that 8.5 percent of the first offenders, 25.5 percent of those with 5 arrests, 52 percent of those with 11 to 15 arrests, and 70.8 percent of those with 20 or more arrests were

The Oldest Profession. "In ancient Cyprus, each respectable woman was required to prostitute herself at least once to a stranger, in order to become eligible for marriage. The sexual union was consummated in the temple of Aphrodite or Astarte. Each Babylonian woman also had to yield once to the embrace of some stranger in the temple of Mylitta, and to dedicate to the goddess the fee she had so earned. The unattractive woman sometimes had to wait in the temple for years before encountering a willing male to free her from her obligation." [Benjamin and Masters, 1964, p. 36]

In ancient Greece most brothels offered sexual services for as little as three cents in today's currency. Girls employed in such brothels were slaves, and the "house" was operated by the state. The *Hetairae* were the aristocrats of Greek prostitution. Like the courtesans of the Italian Renaissance and the expensive call girls of today, the Hetairae were in contact with the most famous and distinguished men of their time and became important influences in politics, the arts, and other important areas of social life. [Benjamin and Masters, 1964]

Decor, dress, and mannerisms may change from generation to generation, but the basic principle behind prostitution remains the same. Men pay women money for sexual satisfaction that they are unable or unwilling to obtain elsewhere.

Although the madam and girl on the left are no longer plying their trade, others have replaced them. The call girl on the right was photographed in her madam's apartment in New York City.

When in Rome. In ancient Rome, male homosexual prostitutes were probably as numerous as their female heterosexual counterparts, and apparently no social disgrace was attached to consorting with them. A brothel would often have both homosexual and heterosexual prostitutes. The sexual exploitation of child slaves was commonplace, and there are records of six- and seven-year-old boys and girls dying of venereal infections. Even suckling babes were introduced into the brothels. The Roman Emperor Domitian was considered noble when he prohibited the prostitution of infants. [Benjamin and Masters, 1964]

narcotic addicts. Getting out of the life is more than a little difficult if money must be earned to support a drug habit.

If the typical prostitute is happy, it is usually only during those times when she interacts with her pimp or procurer. Her relationship with the pimp constitutes the only important human tie she seems able to maintain (Adler, 1955). Her hours of privacy are most often devoted to fantasies about girls who have "made good"—prostitutes who have left the life to become the happy wives of rich, famous men (McManus, 1960).

The Lesson of the Middle Ages. During the Middle Ages, special religious orders were established to assist ex-prostitutes in their rehabilitation. Some of the harlots were bored by the institutions; some seduced their keepers; lesbianism was rampant; and almost all of those who survived went back to the life when they gained their freedom. Prostitutes could not be rehabilitated because society was unwilling or unable to provide them with attractive alternatives. [Benjamin and Masters, 1964]

A Noble Calling

If you ask a prostitute to justify her nightly labors, she might make it sound like a noble profession indeed. She may insist that she fulfills a vital social function by servicing man's varied sexual needs and thereby protecting our social institutions from destructive dis-

cord. She may view herself as an unofficial sexual therapist who gives comfort, insight, and satisfaction to men who are too embarrassed, lonely, or isolated to get interpersonal gratification in other ways (Bryan, 1966). There is some contradiction in her frequent conviction that customers can and should be exploited, but she does not consider such actions any more immoral than the businessman who bilks his clients.

One study revealed that, out of 732 male clients, 574 were married, and only 158 were single. Seventy-eight percent of the clients said they went to prostitutes because they "got something different" when they paid for it. Ten percent said the difference was in the type of sexual act performed (Winick, 1961–62). Other studies have shown that every prostitute must learn quite early in her career that she will encounter a good share of customers who have "kinky" or "freaky" sexual requests (Murtagh and Harris, 1957).

Crime Without a Victim

Prostitution in America is mostly a criminal activity, but in each case the "crime" involves consent on the part of the "victim." There is no direct and clear harm inflicted by one person on another; thus prostitution is considered a victimless crime. For instance, the customer does not ordinarily file a complaint against the prostitute.

Without complainants, our laws against prostitution are often unenforceable since police must adopt ethically and legally questionable enforcement techniques. Because of the problem of obtaining evidence, techniques that come close to or constitute entrapment are widely used in these situations. We all know that it has been a common practice to use plainclothes policemen to impersonate potential "customers" of the prostitute or "prospects" for the homosexual. Certainly, our society has never been able to solve the psychological problem of prostitution, and it remains an important dimension of the "problem" of sex.

Our Founding Fathers.   You won't find it in most history books, but in 1676 the American colonies were described as the haven of all types of notorious vices. The Colonies were said to be a "Sodom of uncleanness and a pest-house of iniquity." As Benjamin and Masters stated: "White indentured servants who came to the Colonies were, for all practical purposes, slaves. The women were sexually at the disposal of their masters. Negro sexual slaves gradually and largely replaced Indians and whites in that capacity. The sexual use of Negro females . . . was a fact of everyday colonial life, and of American life for many years thereafter." [Benjamin and Masters, 1964, pp. 72–73]

Summary

1.   Although prostitution has been in existence almost as long as civilization, members of the "oldest profession" lead miserable lives. Their childhood memories are of parental discord, neglect or rejection. They have little sense of self, no meaningful relationships with other people, and are usually taking drugs in some form.

2.   Prostitutes insist that their profession fills the need of men to experience varied sexual practices without marital discord.

PSYCHOLOGICAL ISSUE

Pornography

Although the Supreme Court has had trouble settling on a workable definition of pornography, everyone else is sure that they know pornography when they see it. The difficulty is that what is obscene to you may not be so to me.

Due to increasing permissiveness in regard to sexually oriented plays, movies, books, and magazines, a United States Commission on Obscenity and Pornography was appointed. When it reported its findings to Congress in the fall of 1970, President Nixon denounced the Commission as "morally bankrupt"; the Senate rejected the Commission's report by a vote of 60 to 5. As we recount some of the Commission's findings you can make your own judgment.

There Is No Business Like the Porno Business

Approximately 85 percent of adult men and 70 percent of adult women in America have been exposed at one time or another to explicit sexual material in visual or written form. Obviously, there is an enormous audience for such material. To be completely accurate, it must be pointed out that only about 40 percent of

adult males and 26 percent of adult females have seen pictures of sexual intercourse during the past two years; the rate for both sexes is much higher before age 21, however.

Estimates vary, but it has been calculated that the porno industry sold 25 to 30 million paperbacks in 1969 at a retail price of approximately $45 to $55 million. Much of this money is pure profit; magazines which have a publication cost between 30¢ and 70¢ are usually sold for $2.00, $5.00, or even as much as $10.00. Paperback books are produced for less than 50¢ per copy but are usually sold anywhere from $2.00 to $10.00. When such books are in great demand, the price may rise to $20.00.

Pornographic films are also profitable mail-order items although fewer films are sold this way than books. Production costs average between $1.00 and $2.00 for black and white films and from $2.00 to $4.00 for color. These then sell for $15.00 to $25.00 for black and white and from $20 to $40 for color. Mail-order film advertisers almost always advertise a variety of still photographs as well, and these are usually priced in the $5.00-to-$10.00 range.

For Men Only.   The vast majority of ''adults only'' books are written for heterosexual males. About 10 percent are aimed at the male homosexual market, and an even smaller percentage is designed for sadists, masochists, or fetishists. Virtually none of these books is intended specifically for a female audience. [The Report of the Commission on Obscenity and Pornography, 1970]

With profit margins of this size, it is easy to understand why adult book stores flourish in our cities. Contrary to what you might guess, the patrons of these sex shops are not drooling sex deviants or young people looking for a cheap thrill. If you go to your local adult book store (for research purposes, of course), you are most likely to find that your companions are white, middle-aged, middle-class, married males dressed neatly in business suits. How does this fact affect your view of pornography consumers?

Pornography and Sex Crimes

A book about sex written at the turn of the century declared that one-half of the young people in our prisons and houses of correction started on their evil careers by reading dirty books. Such books were described as the "nicotine and alcohol of literature; they poison and burn . . . the head and heart as surely as their cousins do the stomach." Times have certainly changed. Books that were once smuggled from more permissive countries can now be borrowed from most public libraries; films previously seen only at all-male "stag" shows now play at your neighborhood movie theater.

The pornography problem arises from the concern of many parents, educators, and clergymen that exposure to erotic materials will lead to depravity and encourage sex crimes.

Kant and Goldstein (1970) conducted a research project which suggested not only that these fears may be groundless but also that some exposure to pornography may be helpful. They found, for example, that a sample of rapists had seen less pornography as teenagers than had a comparable group of normal adults; the same was true for child molesters. The steady customers of adult bookstores had also seen fewer "dirty books" as adolescents and, as adults, seemed to be making up for lost time by satisfying their curiosity later in life. "In fact, the normal adults . . . reported more experience with pornography as teen-agers than any deviant group we studied and, as adults, they continue to see more erotica than sex offenders do" (p. 59).

A sample of 60 deviants was studied in another attempt to find out whether there is a relationship between pornography and the development of normal or abnormal sexual behavior. These Caucasian males had been charged with or convicted of rape or child molesting. The researchers found that the deviant group had seen less pornography than had noncriminal members of the control group. The sexual deviants, no matter what their age, education, or occupation, had one thing in common—they had little to do with pornography when they were adolescents. It is reasonable to assume that a naturally high degree of sexual interest and curiosity exists among adolescents; we might also conclude that a less than average adolescent exposure to pornography might reflect either avoidance of heterosexual stimulation or response to a strict family atmosphere that did not allow normal encounter with the facts of sexuality.

In countries where there is virtually no censorship of sexual material (Denmark, for example), studies of the correlation between erotic materials and sex crimes indicate that the increased availability of explicit sexual materials seems to coincide with a decrease in the incidence of sexual crimes. Analysis of police records of sex crimes in Copenhagen during a 12-year period revealed that a dramatic decrease occurred; the decrease coincided with changes in Danish law which permitted the availability of explicit sexual materials.

The Final Word

The final conclusions of the Commission on Obscenity and Pornography made some high-placed government officials very unhappy. The Commission stated that research to date has simply found no evidence that exposure to explicit sexual materials plays a significant role in causing delinquent or criminal behavior among youth or adults. The Commission could not conclude that exposure to erotic materials is a critical factor in sex crimes or sex delinquency. The Commission, in fact, came to believe that much of the "problem"

It Depends on Who You Ask.   Surveys of psychiatrists, psychologists, sex educators, social workers, counselors, and similar professional workers reveal that large majorities of such groups believe sexual materials do not have harmful effects on either adults or adolescents. On the other hand, a survey of police chiefs found that 58 percent believed that "obscene" books played a significant role in causing juvenile delinquency. [The Report of the Commission on Obscenity and Pornography, 1970]

---

regarding so-called pornographic materials stems from the inability or reluctance of people in our society to be open and direct in dealing with sexual matters. In the past, we did not talk openly about sex to each other or to our children.

An interesting paradox to think about was pointed out by Berkowitz (1971). The President's Commission on the Causes and Prevention of Violence told us that media violence can induce persons to act aggressively; a majority of the members on the President's Commission on Obscenity and Pornography told us that the portrayal of sexual deviations does not seriously promote similar actions. Both of these statements about the influences on basic human impulses seemingly cannot be correct. The Commission on Violence suggested that the media influence is probably long last-

Ingres was well over eighty when he painted *The Turkish Bath* (1864). It is like a magnificent assembly of all the odalisques and bathers he had painted since his youth. Would anyone you know call this work pornographic?

Defining the Undefinable. In June, 1973, the Supreme Court set new obscenity standards by giving the individual states more leeway to ban pornographic movies and publications. This new opinion held for the first time that juries in state courts may measure prurient appeal by the standards in their own communities and not by a "national standard." The new guidelines eliminated the substance of a 1966 ruling on the subject, which said that to be obscene the material must be "utterly without redeeming social value."

ing; the Commission on Pornography, however, maintained that any effect is only short lived. The Commissions thus reached opposite conclusions, and no one can be certain where the truth can actually be found. It is important to note that one commission dealt with aggressive urges and the other commission with sexual impulses. The difference may be in the different drives being considered, of course, but this still leaves our society in a quandary about what to allow and what to prohibit.

Summary

1. The President's Commission on Obscenity and Pornography reported that there was no evidence to indicate that pornography plays a significant role in causing crime or delinquency.

2. Research on pornography indicates that normal adults see more pornography than do sex offenders. One study found that imprisoned sexual deviates had seen less pornography in the year before imprisonment than a normal control group.

3. In Denmark, the increased availability of sexual materials coincides with a decrease in the incidence of sexual crimes.

4. The pornography commission's conclusions seem to contradict those of the President's Commission on the Causes and Prevention of Violence, which reported that media violence induces individuals to act aggressively. As of the moment, neither point of view has won out; nor has there been a satisfactory combination of theories.

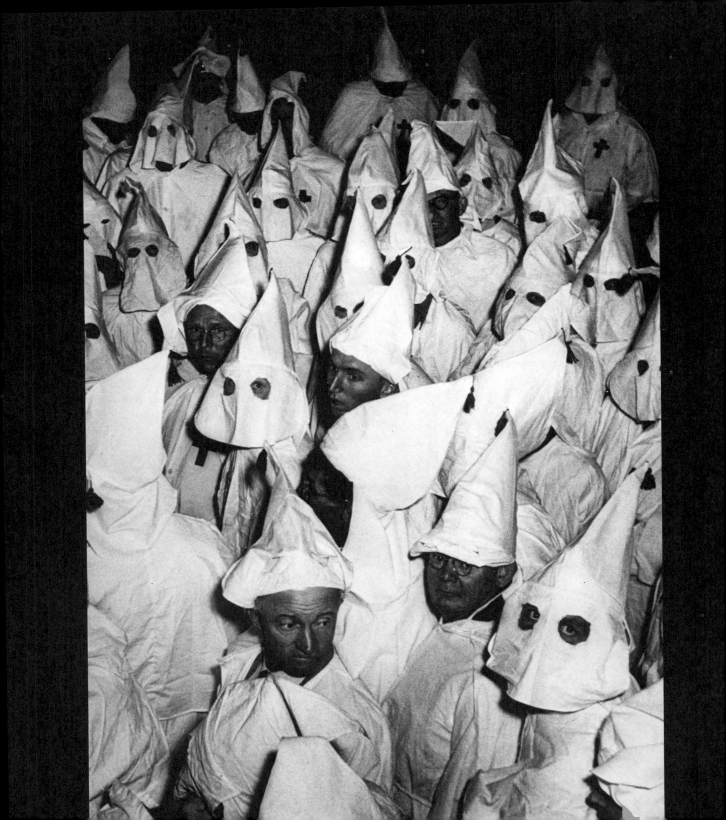

Prejudice

23

A great many people think they are thinking when they are merely rearranging their prejudices.
—William James

In our society it often seems *race* is only half a word—a word that is incomplete without adding words such as *prejudice* or *discrimination*. Before we consider the facts of racial differences among humankind, we first need to examine the patterns of psychological response that have made race a critical social issue.

Prejudice and discrimination are often closely intertwined, but they are distinctly different concepts. Prejudice refers to an attitude, whereas discrimination refers to behavior. If we were able to respond to every person as an individual we would be free of prejudices about blacks, long-haired students, or women. Prejudice ignores the particular qualities or characteristics of the individual and groups him with others who happen to have the same skin color, speak with the same accent, have the same type of name, or come from the same part of the country. It can also be said that people who are prejudiced against one group tend to be prejudiced against others as well. Thus, if you meet someone and learn he is prejudiced against Jews, Puerto Ricans, and blacks, you don't need to ask him how he feels about Chicanos.

In daily life we often prejudge; that is, we make decisions before all the information is in. This prejudgment turns to prejudice only if it is never revised or modified with further information. Discrimination is behavior which is unfavorable toward an individual or group. When individuals are denied equal treatment because of their membership in a racial group, they are being discriminated against. The action may be justified in many ways, but it is still discrimination.

IN 1858, ABRAHAM LINCOLN SAID . . .
"I will say then that I am not nor ever have been in favor of bringing about in any way the social and political equality of the white and black races. I am not nor ever have been in favor of making voters or jurors of Negroes, nor of qualifying them to hold office, nor to intermarry with white people; and I will say in addition to this that there is a physical difference between the white and black races which I believe will forbid the two races living together on terms of social and political equality. And inasmuch as they cannot so live, while they do remain together, there must be the position of superior and inferior and I as much as any other man am in favor of having the superior position assigned to the white race." [quoted in Silberman, 1964, pp. 92–93]

557

**THE RACIALLY
SUPERIOR ATHLETE**
*In recent years there has been an
overwhelmingly disproportionate
representation of black athletes on
all-star rosters and Olympic teams.
There is no question that black
society is contributing more than its
share of star athletes in sports. Is it
racial superiority or is it increased
motivation? Psychologists would
conclude that social conditions have
instilled a heightened motivation
among young black males to achieve
success in sports. Whereas whites
have access to a great variety of
means of achieving success, blacks
are left with one or two endeavors
open to them—sports, and to a lesser
degree, entertainment (Edwards,
1972).*

Prejudice and discrimination are usually associated—but not always. It is possible to be prejudiced and yet not discriminate; for instance, you may not care much for athletes, but you treat them with equal fairness if you come into contact with them. Prejudice can be learned through personal experiences with racial or religious groups, but we suspect that most often it is learned from others who already are prejudiced. Prejudices are formed in early childhood and often develop fully in the total absence of the object of prejudice. Some theorists have suggested that prejudice gives us feelings of superiority, and certainly many people apparently need to think they are better than others. Prejudice can allow the poorest, least educated, most unimportant person in our society to feel he is mentally, morally, or socially superior to someone else. Actually, prejudice is much more complicated than this, and its causes differ from one person to another. Remedies for prejudice must take into account how the attitudes developed in the first place.

Stereotypes

Once you have reached the conclusion all Cubans are "lazy," you will be much more likely to notice examples of "lazy Cubans." If you see a "lazy" Anglo, you will pay little attention, or else you will interpret it quite differently. (He must be resting after a hard day's work.) Without being fully aware of it, we all become skilled at perceiving only those events that are consistent with our prejudices. After a while, we amass a pile of evidence which assures us that our prejudices are justified.

The prejudiced person stereotypes other people by applying a common

The Authoritarian Personality

Although prejudice probably exists to some extent in all of us, psychologists have found that persons exhibiting a certain cluster of personality traits tend to be much more prejudiced than others. Such individuals are said to have "authoritarian personalities." Chances are that, if you know someone who displays this set of characteristics, he or she will be highly prejudiced.

The authoritarian personality:

• distrusts human nature and thinks that man is basically evil;

• is rigidly moralistic and conforms to conventional values and behaviors;

• is defensive; his fears, hostilities, and desires to perform unconventional behavior are projected onto others.

• admires authority and submits uncritically to it; believes others should also submit to authority without question; dominates inferiors and is most comfortable within a power hierarchy where everyone knows his place;

• selects friends because of their usefulness; his relationships with others are based on power differences;

• oversimplifies, overgeneralizes, and thinks in black and white terms, particularly in regard to other people;

• holds to the extremes of masculinity or femininity; and

• has little insight into himself or into the feelings and behaviors of others.

The authoritarian personality is thought to be a product of a home that discouraged emotion and demanded obedience at all costs.

Source: T. W. Adorno, E. Frenkel-Brunswick, D. J. Levinson, and R. N. Sanford, *The Authoritarian Personality,* New York: Harper, 1950.

label and attributing a set of characteristics to everyone in that category. Even when particular individuals do not fit the stereotype of a certain category, we simply treat them as exceptions to the rule and keep our stereotypes intact.

Some evidence shows that a person who holds stereotypes is actually rather good at recognizing members of the group he dislikes. Lindzey and Rogalsky (1950) found, for example, that anti-Semitic students were more accurate than unprejudiced students in distinguishing between photographs of Jewish and non-Jewish people. The prejudiced person apparently looks for oversimplified but specific characteristics that fit his stereotype of the out-group. He is also frequently wrong in his judgment, however, and incorrectly identifies in-group members as belonging to the out-group. Nevertheless, the prejudiced person is characteristically very confident in his judgments.

Of course, no one of us is totally free of prejudice, and all of us stereotype other people. But this becomes a critical social issue when our personal, economic, or social frustrations lead us to look for a scapegoat.

Scapegoat

The modern idea of a *scapegoat* comes from an age-old practice reported in the Old Testament. When things were going badly for a desert tribe, a special ceremony was held in which the sins of the tribe were symbolically transferred to a goat, which was then driven off into the wilderness. Thus, finding a victim to blame our troubles on is an ancient and familiar pattern. Frustrated students blame their professors for poor grades; businessmen blame labor unions for rising prices; and labor unions blame management for causing unemployment. In the 1930s Adolf Hitler convinced his followers that the Jews were responsible for most of Germany's economic and social problems.

In the book *ABC's of Scapegoating* (1944), Gordon Allport listed four characteristics of people who are made scapegoats: (1) they are easy to identify; (2) they are easy to get to; (3) they can't retaliate; and (4) they have been used as scapegoats before. Children learn, for example, that it is safe to be aggressive toward some people but not toward others. They discover early in life that the ideal scapegoat should be weak and powerless. The "acceptable" target depends upon which part of the society you belong to. In certain black subcultures, it appears that whites are now accepted objects of aggression.

Racism

In the book *Future Shock,* Alvin Toffler (1970) points out that books about current social issues are now obsolete before they can be printed and distributed. This is particularly true of racial relations in the United States. The only fact that has remained constant since the Civil Rights Movement is the apparent inability of blacks and whites to communicate meaningfully and reduce the mutual fear and suspicion which characterizes interracial relations.

PATRIOTIC LOOTING
"Rioting and looting in the black ghettos of America are held up as horrible examples of lawlessness on the rampage. Yet the history books enthusiastically tell of a group of patriotic white folks in Boston who dressed themselves up as Indians *no less, boarded that foreign ship, and dumped all the tea in the water. How can anyone who proudly remembers that moment in history have nerve enough to call black folks hoodlums? The lawlessness in the Boston harbor, for which white folks wanted Indians to take the rap, is honored in our national memory as the Boston Tea Party."* [Dick Gregory, 1971, p. 4]

Getting to Know You

Suppose all you knew about black people was what you learned from watching TV commercials or reading newspaper and magazine ads. According to a study reported in the social science magazine *Society* (1972), you might reach the following conclusions:

1. There are not many blacks in America. The number of advertising pages in which blacks appear did increase dramatically from 1965 to 1969 (from 2.2 percent to 8.6 percent of the total ad pages), but it dropped back to 4.1 percent in 1970. Blacks are underrepresented compared with their numbers in the general population.

2. Blacks in black magazines are mostly celebrities. An ad featuring Mrs. Nat King Cole selling Sears refrigerators may be used on ghetto billboards and in black publications but seldom appears in magazines circulated to the general society.

3. Blacks live and work in exotic places. Many ads portray blacks in foreign settings in service occupations such as servant, waiter, or entertainer; they are, for example, native bearers on a safari or servants in ads for Jamaica and British West Indies Airlines.

4. Blacks stay in the background in white crowds. Seventy-eight of 173 ads showing blacks in predominantly white groups placed the blacks in the rear of the crowd. In this way the product to be sold is never too closely identified with them.

5. Blacks are losers. Blacks are regularly overrepresented in appeals for the March of Dimes or the United Fund, despite the fact that these agencies serve a predominantly white public. Or, blacks are shown as redeemable failures who can be rehabilitated by job-retraining programs. Blacks are portrayed as losers because they seldom appear to have families, are almost never seen at work, and rarely are seen enjoying their leisure time in sports or hobbies.

If you wanted to learn more about blacks, it wouldn't help much to watch the news on television. Blacks see a lot of the white world—indeed, they can hardly avoid it—but communication flows only from white to black, seldom the other way. The one aspect of the black world you might see on TV would be rioting. Few whites see blacks except when the community is inflamed (Rivers, 1967).

How did this condition come about? It began in Colonial America when the slave was defined as chattel, not as a person. The slave was not entitled to social protection since property came under the slaveholder's absolute power (Pinkney, 1969). The slave trade was officially abolished in 1808, but our heritage from those days is modern racism.

The Commission on Civil Disorders labeled our nation racist. This does not mean that all of us are equally racist or that only the United States is populated by racists. But it does mean that our society has established a network of institutions which perpetuate racist attitudes; indeed, racism affects us all (Delany, 1969) through the assumptions we make about the world and the patterns of our social activities (Kovel, 1970). Sadly, it is nearly impossible to be white and to grow up without some degree of racial prejudice. Nor can a white man know what it means to be black in America.

The full extent of American racism was documented in 1968 by the Kerner Commission, which concluded that we are moving toward two separate and unequal societies—one black, one white. Segregation and poverty have created a ghetto environment unknown to most white Americans. White institutions created it; white institutions maintain it; and white society condones it.

MALCOLM X
The man called Malcolm X told how he abandoned a life of stealing, pimping, and dope peddling to become a leader in the black revolution. Brilliant, sensitive, "a giant in a sick world," he gave manhood, pride, and self-respect to blacks. In 1965, he was assassinated while making a speech in New York. It was a critical moment in the race struggle in America, and his death attracted world-wide attention.

White Social Science

It would be comforting to report that white social scientists have been willing to study, or even interested in studying, the black segment of our population; the truth of the matter, however, is closer to Billingsley's observation:

> *Students of human behavior, policy makers, and citizens who look to the body of knowledge about the human condition which has been generated and reflected by American social scientists will find no area of American life more glaringly ignored, more distorted, or more systematically disvalued than black family life. Thus, black families who have fared so ill historically in white American society have fared no better in white American social science, and largely for the same reason.* [1970, p. 127]

So far, social scientists have not only failed to meet the challenge of the black minority, but they also may have contributed misinformation which has in turn perpetuated a number of stereotypes and myths about black families. As Billingsley notes:

There are four tendencies in the treatment of black families in social science scholarship. The first is the tendency to ignore black families altogether. The second is, when black families are considered, to focus almost exclusively on the lowest income group of black families, that acute minority of families who live in public housing projects or who are supported by public welfare assistance. The third is to ignore the majority of black stable families even among this lowest income group, to ignore the processes by which these families move from one equilibrium state to another, and to focus instead on the most unstable among these low income families. A fourth tendency, which is more bizarre than all the others, is the tendency on the part of social scientists to view the black, low-income, unstable, problem-ridden family as the [cause of] *the difficulties their members experience in the wider society.* [1970, pp. 132–33]

These tendencies among social scientists are an accurate account of the past history of research on race. We can only hope that a new generation of psychologists will reverse the trend, that black psychologists will redirect future studies, and that social scientists will devote more of their energy to an objective appraisal of the rapidly shifting racial scene.

As Different as Black and White

We know a great deal about attitudes toward blacks. Indeed, there is too much to include in a brief account. In a representative study done by Campbell and Schuman (1968), the attitudes of 5,000 blacks and whites in 15 American cities were surveyed. They found that, when whites were asked about blacks, about 95 percent were in favor of equal-employment opportunities. About

---

Apartheid

About 17 percent of the population of South Africa is made up of 2.3 million white Afrikaners descended from early Dutch, French, and German settlers and 1.5 million English-speaking whites. There are also more than 15 million black Africans and more than 2 million people of mixed blood. Yet, those who are designated as black live in *apartheid* (Afrikaans for "apartness"), which is administered by the controlling whites.

Segregation of the races is total. Mixed marriages are not only illegal but also punishable. Africans may not stay overnight in white areas; and even park benches and post office windows are segregated. Africans are not allowed to hold meetings or form political parties; and they are jailed if they cannot produce their pass permits on demand.

In the year ending June 30, 1971, a total of 934,604 blacks were prosecuted, and even more were arrested, for apartheid violations which apply only to their race and which would not be crimes in most countries. Blacks, for example, can be "endorsed out" of a white area. To be endorsed out is to be deported from the main labor market to the tribal areas, where jobs and opportunities are almost nonexistent. The process often separates a man from his wife, or children from their parents.

The Black Panthers have created a new self-image for many of their brothers and sisters—and sometimes the white population looks at that new image with trepidation. Militant American blacks have borrowed heavily from Frantz Fanon, black psychiatrist and author. In *The Wretched of the Earth* his message was a call to arms to create a new history of man free from the inhumanities of white domination.

two-thirds approved of legislation to assure such opportunities. But, no more than 20 percent of these whites believed very many blacks were really discriminated against in the job market. Perhaps, it is predictable that one would not voice an opinion against discrimination, if he does not even recognize that discrimination really exists. The survey also revealed that only about half of the whites were in favor of open-housing legislation; and about the same percentage reported that blacks would be acceptable as neighbors.

The most hopeful sign in the survey was the fact that the younger you are (in your 20s or 30s) and the more education you have, the more favorable your attitudes will be toward blacks. But, this is still not enough. When asked why blacks had inferior housing, employment, and education, most white respondents continue to cite a lack of ambition in the blacks themselves, rather than the conditions produced by discrimination.

In the survey, blacks responded to the same questions. The difference in their answers was as "clear as black and white." Most blacks believed serious racial discrimination exists with respect to employment opportunities, and one-third reported they could testify to this from their own experiences. Even so, 80 percent of the blacks felt it was possible to get ahead "in spite of prejudice and discrimination." It was also interesting that about one-third of the blacks believed most whites have good intentions; another third thought whites are indifferent to the race problem; and a final third described whites as hostile and ready to suppress blacks. Obviously, one part of the "racial problem" is that, when blacks and whites look at the same events, they still interpret them differently.

THE DECLARATION
OF WHITE INDEPENDENCE
"I discovered that the founding fathers obviously made a mistake in writing their Declaration of Independence. Thomas Jefferson neglected to label it 'For Whites Only.' Without that label the Declaration of Independence becomes a dangerous document—in the black ghettos of America, on the Indian reservation, in the grape fields of California where Mexican-American workers are struggling for human dignity, in the Puerto Rican slums and ghettos; in short, wherever America's long train of abuses is most painfully felt."
[Dick Gregory, 1971, p. 2]

Rejecting the Self

Imagine that from the time you were a child, everyone has told you that you are worthless, stupid, insignificant, and ugly; there is no way you can amount to anything. Now imagine that everyone in your neighborhood believes much the same about themselves. If everyone you contact is uneducated, unskilled, poorly dressed, and often hungry and sick, you will probably try to do everything you can not to be like them; you will deny those features in yourself that are similar to theirs. You may change your name, get your nose reshaped, bleach your skin, straighten your hair, or lose your accent. If you are a child, you aren't able to do these things easily, but you still feel you are more worthless than others. You secretly wish you were someone or something else.

In 1958 research was done on black children aged three to seven (from both northern and southern schools). The children were asked to choose between white dolls and colored ones, and it was found that a white doll was most favored. Approximately 60 percent of the children saw a white doll as the "nice" one to play with and described a colored doll as one that "looks bad." When the youngest children were asked to select "the doll that looks like you," one-third of them selected a white one. This held true for one-fifth of those children with the darkest skin color (Clark and Clark, 1958). It is distressing to think that, at such tender ages, black children express a preference for being white. But the years since 1958 have witnessed a growing, changing self-image for blacks, and this message is being heard by their children.

In 1970, the same kind of experiment was repeated with both black and white public school children in Lincoln, Nebraska. The majority of children in each group indicated a preference for dolls of their own color. The difference between the results of these two experiments undoubtedly reflects the awakening of black consciousness. Hopefully, our youngsters—both black and white—may be the first of a new generation of children whose self-images have been improved and whose sense of pride in being human has been heightened.

Our Many Minorities

Despite the brotherhood weeks and the myth of the American melting pot, our society has an astonishingly shameful record of mistreating our many minority peoples. In particular, those who are racially different from the majority group have suffered most.

The Japanese

After the Japanese attack on Pearl Harbor in December 1941, the United States Army established military zones from which aliens had to be evacuated in the interest of national defense. All Japanese people were ordered to leave the West Coast, but there was no place to go since they were not wanted elsewhere. The state of Nevada, for example, warned that the large numbers of Japanese moving inland from California would be put in concentration camps. The logic was simple. "A Jap's a Jap!" snapped Lieutenant General John L. De Witt, Commanding General of Western Defense. "It makes no difference whether he is an American or not."

The day after Pearl Harbor, funds belonging to Japanese-Americans in California were frozen, and banks refused to cash their checks. Milkmen refused to deliver their milk; grocers refused to sell them food; and insurance companies canceled their policies. The state of California revoked their licenses to practice law or medicine and dismissed them from civil service jobs in city, county, and state offices. By August 1942, the Army moved over 110,000 West Coast Japanese to ten hastily built camps in Arkansas and the Rocky Mountains. In the following years 31,625 Japanese were resettled in other parts of the country, but the vast majority of them later returned to California.

It was quite different in Hawaii, where persons of Japanese descent made up about one-third of the population. Only limited restrictions were imposed on them, and no more than a few were interned. The Japanese in Hawaii were dealt with in the same way as the Germans and Italians were handled in mainland America.

The economic loss to the evacuated Japanese was enormous, but it didn't compare with the psychological impact of this racist act by the dominant white culture. Besides the disruption to families and the breakdown in group solidarity, imprisonment rendered the Issei generation powerless, and their

THE JAPANESE
The Japanese settled on the West Coast during a stable social and economic period; their mother country had already entered a period of technological development which permitted them to acquire the skills necessary for adjusting to American society. Californians decided that the Japanese were patient, clean, polite, and able to mind their own business (Lyman, 1973), and therefore they were welcomed as laborers. Before long, however, antagonism replaced these positive feelings, and the Japanese began to abandon the cities and turn to agriculture. Since they were markedly successful in this occupation, the white majority retaliated again by passing alien land-holding acts which prohibited the Japanese from owning land. The bewildered Japanese were forced back to the cities only to discover that, by then, many barbershops, restaurants, and hotels refused service to Orientals; and several large coastal cities had passed local regulations which kept the Japanese out of attractive neighborhoods. The worst, however, was yet to come.

THE JAPANESE-AMERICAN GENERATIONS

Issei—*Foreign born*

Nisei—*First American-born generation*

Sansei—*The second and later generations of native born. The grandchildren of Issei.*

Yonsei—*The fourth generation. The great-grandchildren of Issei.*

Gosei—*The great-great-grandchildren of Issei.*

Kibei—*Born in the United States of Issei parents, educated in Japan, and returned to America.*

Nisei offspring saw the necessity of becoming less Japanese and more American. Most of the generation to follow (Sansei, the children of Nisei) were yet to be born or too young to be affected by the imprisonment of World War II. They have grown up in homes where there is not a great deal of cultural difference from other American homes. Nor have today's young Japanese experienced the kind of demoralizing prejudice and discrimination felt by their parents. They have assimilated so well to the dominant culture that they have succeeded more dramatically than any other nonwhite citizens of America.

The Chinese

Conformity to Anglo-Saxon appearance, religion, language, and traditions has always been the critical factor in determining who is or is not considered an American (Hill, 1973). Throughout the history of the United States, nonwhite populations have been discriminated against, and the Chinese were no exception. From the beginning of the great Chinese immigration in 1848, there has been conflict. Even though they were not treated as slaves, the Chinese were restricted to certain categories of employment, denied basic civil rights, and not allowed to become citizens.

The Chinese were exploited as cheap labor and no one had to take responsibility for them when they were no longer useful. When the Chinese began to take jobs away from white miners, the white communities passed laws which forced the Chinese to leave mining camps. They were mistreated and exploited in a great variety of other ways. "For example, a license fee of $8.00 a year was demanded of one-horse laundry wagons. But those laundrymen who collected and delivered by foot (the Chinese) had to pay $60.00.

Especially galling to the Chinese was the so-called Queue Ordinance, which stipulated that criminals must have their hair cropped. For the Chinese this meant loss of their pigtails—a form of sacrilege. Eventually, all these ordinances were declared unconstitutional, but they caused much hardship during the years they were enforced" (Marden and Meyer, 1968, p. 48).

Unlike the Japanese, the Chinese reacted to these abuses in a passive manner; as long as they "stayed in their place," white America begrudgingly tolerated them. The Chinese were forced into their Chinatown ghettos, and for the next several decades their numbers steadily declined. They avoided Americanization and became isolated from mainstream America.

The Chicanos

Three hundred years ago, most of what is now called the American Southwest was part of the empire of Spain. Today, there are nine million persons of Spanish descent in this region. The Spanish-speaking people of the Southwest United States have designated themselves variously as "Latin Americans," "Spanish-speaking Americans," "Mexican-Americans," "Mexicanos," and "Hispanos" (Marden and Meyer, 1968). Recently the name Chicano has become popular.

Today 85 percent of our Mexican-Americans are American born, and half of them are third generation. The Mexican-Americans are a fast-growing population living in the five southwestern states. Mexican-American families differ from other American families in one important respect: Spanish is the predominant language spoken in the home even among those who have lived in the United States for three generations (Anderson and Johnson, 1971).

As a group, the Mexican-Americans are plagued with problems. They have an extremely low level of education and a high rate of unemployment. They are poor, and they are discriminated against. If they try to rent an apartment, they may be told that no apartments are available or to be quoted exceedingly high rents or fees (Johnson, Porter, and Mateljan, 1971).

In Arizona, California, Colorado, New Mexico, and Texas, Mexican-American children are still segregated from the whites. In Texas and New Mexico two-thirds of all Mexican-American students attend predominantly Mexican-American schools. Of course, only 4 percent of their teachers are Mexican-American.

Although more than 25 years have passed since the courts first outlawed discriminatory education, the United States Commission on Civil Rights reported to Congress that Mexican-Americans in the Southwest simply do not obtain the same benefits of public education as do whites.

The cry of Chicano power is now being heard across the land; like the Indians, the Mexican-Americans have learned from the blacks the importance of vigorously pursuing their civil rights.

THE CUBANS
Under a government-sponsored resettlement program, Cuban refugees were offered jobs and one month's free rent for agreeing to take up residence outside Florida. Now more than half of the 612,648 Cuban refugees in the United States have been resettled, but Florida still has about 261,200 Cubans living in the county that surrounds Miami and Miami Beach. The big resettlement centers outside Florida are New York, with 98, 479 Cubans; New Jersey, with 71, 233; and California, with 47,699.

Summary

1. Prejudice is an attitude held toward a particular group. Persons within the group are viewed not in terms of their individual merits but according to the general and superficial characteristics that make them part of the group.

2. Prejudices are usually acquired through contact with other persons who are prejudiced. Attitudes toward the out-group are based on insufficient information, but a prejudiced person does not change his attitude even when new and conflicting information is acquired.

3. Psychologists have identified those individuals who are usually highly prejudiced as authoritarian personalities. Such persons tend to overgeneralize and think in black and white terms; they are highly conventional, moralistic, and uncritical of higher authority.

4. Stereotyping is often related to prejudice formation. Individuals apply a label to persons of a particular group; even when members of the group do not conform to the stereotype, they are considered exceptions to the rule. Research shows that prejudiced people are better than unprejudiced persons at recognizing members of an out-group because they look for the stereotyped trademarks.

5. Another reason for prejudice is the need to find someone to blame our troubles on. Scapegoats are usually people who are easy to identify and who are unable to retaliate.

6. Discrimination is behavior that denies members of the out-group the same courtesies, privileges, or protection offered to members of all other groups.

7. One of the reasons racism is difficult to eliminate is that the media continually present information to the public that conforms to its stereotypes. Psychologists have also contributed to the misinformation about out-groups, particularly blacks. They have also failed to carry out meaningful research on racism and black problems.

8. Most whites do not recognize the amount of discrimination that exists against blacks; much of black failure is still blamed on a lack of ambition in blacks themselves.

9. Until recently, black people had difficulty accepting their blackness. In a research study done 15 years ago, black children preferred white dolls to black ones; in 1970, a similar study showed that black children now preferred black dolls, indicating that blacks are no longer rejecting their identities.

10. Despite our claims of being a melting pot, one glance at American treatment of immigrant minorities suggests that we only accept people of other races when they have assimilated to the American way.

PSYCHOLOGICAL ISSUE

The Indian

Imagine for a moment that you are an Indian, and think of the familiar song "My Country 'Tis of Thee." Remember how it goes? "Land where our fathers died. Land of the Pilgrims' pride." In reaction to this song, Indians have said: "Some of us broke out laughing when we realized that our fathers undoubtedly died trying to keep those Pilgrims from stealing our land" (Deloria, 1969). Certainly, most of us don't think of Indians as the real native Americans; in fact, we hardly think about Indians at all. In his classic study on poverty in 1962 Michael Harrington insisted that the rich simply do not see the poor; to the rich, poor people are invisible. But even in Harrington's book, Indians were not mentioned: How invisible can you get?

All of us have seen hundreds and thousands of Indians killed on TV and in the movies. We know that an Indian has high cheek bones, a prominent nose, reddish brown skin, and wears war paint and feathers. According to the Bureau of Indian Affairs, however, an Indian is a person who lives on a reservation or whose name appears on a "tribal roll." This person may be a pure blooded native, or he may have one-quarter, one-eighth, or even less Indian blood.

An Indian History

The confusion started when Columbus thought he had reached India and mistakenly called the natives of America *Indians* (Forbes, 1964). Estimates of the number of Indians in what is now the United States in 1492 range from 700,000 to 1,000,000. By the time Indians became official wards of our government in 1871, their population had been reduced to less than half a million (Marden and Meyer, 1968).

In the years from 1607 to 1778, English and Dutch settlers engaged in friendly barter and trade with the Indians, until the white men decided they needed Indian land. In 1754 the British Crown formulated a policy of protecting Indian land and when America became independent the policy was continued on

The massacre of Wounded Knee in 1890 stemmed from the Sioux's defiance of a government order prohibiting the Sun Dance and other religious rituals. Certain dances were later allowed, however, including this one "to restore an eclipsed moon," photographed by Edward S. Curtis in 1914.

paper; in actuality, however, the Indians were slowly forced off the land and pushed west.

On June 30, 1834, Congress passed *An Act to Regulate Trade and Intercourse with the Indian Tribes and to Preserve Peace on the Frontiers*. Indian country supposedly included all land west of the Mississippi but not within the states of Missouri and Louisiana or the territory of Arkansas. No white persons were permitted to trade in Indian country without a license, and none would be permitted to settle in Indian country (Brown, 1970). The act was to be enforced by the military, but before these laws could be put into effect, a new wave of white settlers swept westward to form the territories of Wisconsin and Iowa. The "permanent Indian frontier" had to be shifted further west.

The great Cherokee nation was one of the victims of this act. It had survived more than 100 years of the white man's wars, diseases, and whiskey, but now the Cherokees were to be moved west. When gold was discovered in their territory, it was decided that the Cherokees must be moved quickly. So, during the fall of 1838, General Winfield Scott's soldiers rounded them up and started them on the long winter trek westward. One of every four Cherokees died from cold, hunger, or disease on this march. A nearly similar fate awaited the Choctaws, Chickasaws, Creeks, and Sem-

inoles forced to give up their homelands in the South. In the North, what few members were left from the Shawnees, Miamis, Ottawas, Hurons, Delawares, and other tribes were sent west beyond the Mississippi.

The independent and undisciplined pioneer pushed farther into the Indian country. Reflecting the white man's aggressive society, he soon demolished the native culture (Sheehan, 1972). In 1871, Congress declared that all Indians were wards of the federal government, and from 1887 to 1914 their lands were reduced from 138 million acres to 47 million acres. Then, as a permanent solution to the "Indian problem," the children were sent to boarding schools to forget their language and Indian ways.

The Indian Today

The Indian of today is no longer the vanishing American. The Indian population has more than doubled in the past two decades (from 343,000 in 1950 to 792,730 in 1970). But the modern Indian must often wish he lived in the days when the Indians won a few battles as at Little Big Horn.

Being born Indian means a life expectancy of only 64 years rather than the 70.8 years common to other Americans; being Indian also means facing the prospects of 45 percent unemployment, an average

Dee Brown's book *Bury My Heart at Wounded Knee* sensitized many Americans to the plight of the real natives of this country. Thus, when young Indians in 1972 took over Wounded Knee, South Dakota, as a protest against the Bureau of Indian Affairs, many saw the confrontation with federal officials as symbolically avenging the Sioux who died in 1890.

family income of only $4,000 per year, and little chance of going to college (18 percent compared to 50 percent for other Americans). Among Indians, the incidence of flu and pneumonia is twice as great as in the general population, and the death rate from tuberculosis is five to seven times greater than the national average. More than 50 percent of the Indian population must still haul their drinking water from distances of a mile or more. They must go without indoor plumbing, and they die from accidents at a rate which is three times the national average. Being Indian means living in substandard housing, going hungry, having only one doctor for every 900 people, or having only one dentist for every 3,000 (Gregory, 1971).

Being born an Indian means that you are twice as likely as those in the general population to die by suicide. Why? One researcher who studied the Cheyenne reported that, when the Indians were free people, they had their own cultural ways of dealing with self-esteem, and suicide was rare. When a man felt he was losing the esteem of others, he organized a war party to raid an enemy tribe; he would either regain his self-esteem through some brave act or die in the attempt. When the Cheyenne were placed on reservations, these ways of handling aggression were forbidden. The Cheyenne men were also required to cut the long hair, which they valued as a symbol of

An Indian Lament. "Into each life, it is said, some rain must fall. Some people have bad horoscopes, others take tips on the stock market. . . . But Indians have been cursed above all other people in history. Indians have anthropologists.

"Every summer when school is out a veritable stream of immigrants heads into Indian country. . . . From every rock and cranny in the East *they* emerge, as if responding to some primeval fertility rite, and flock to the reservations.

" 'They' are the anthropologists . . . that infest the land of the free, and in the summer time, the homes of the braves." [Deloria, 1969, pp. 83–84]

strength. The loss of ways to deal with aggression and the declining sense of self-esteem were psychologically crippling in the extreme (Lester and Lester, 1971).

Summary

Perhaps the greatest crime of all has been white treatment of the American Indian population—the original occupants of this country. Indians live in poverty and are subject to high rates of disease, death, and unemployment. Suicide among Indians is twice that of white Americans, probably because the inhuman treatment of Indians has destroyed their self-esteem.

PSYCHOLOGICAL ISSUE
Being Poor

Below 20 percent of our old are working. Without work and without money, they fill their days with sitting, watching, and waiting.

One of the many problems of being poor in this country is having to contend with your "bad reputation." As one writer stated: "On the average, the poor in the United States have bad reputations. They are regarded as responsible for much physical aggression and destruction of property; their support is alleged to be a heavy burden on the rest of the community; and they are said not even to try very hard to meet community standards of behavior or to be self-supporting. Poverty, it is said, is little enough punishment for people so inferior and so lacking in virtue" (Haggstrom, 1971, p. 457)."

Who are these poor people? They are families with no wage earners, families headed by females, young males, and males over 65. Most have "poverty-linked" characteristics: little education (less than eight years), residence in rural areas, six or more children who are younger than 18, membership in a minority group, and residence in the South (Ornati, 1971). They are the "losers" in our society; they were born poor, and most likely they will die poor (Schorr, 1971). They will quit school, marry young, have children early, and take jobs with low wages and no prospects for advancement.

The poor are socially disadvantaged in every way imaginable. Crude estimates suggest that the poor make up about 15 to 20 percent of the population. They resemble one another in their poverty, but their racial or ethnic subcultures are different. The poor include about 20 million English-speaking whites, 8 million blacks, 2 million Spanish-Americans, 700,000 Puerto Ricans, and 500,000 American Indians (Hav-

Things. "Many things nappen around my way where I live. The people do so many things. They be in the hallway taking dope. And sometimes they die from dope. They go around and steal cars and sell them. And they beat on you if you talk about it. All this is done quick and a lot. I don't even bother to look no more." [Duva, 1972, p. 174]

ighurst, 1969). Though each group has substantial numbers of people who perform at average or higher levels of occupational status and whose children do well in school, poverty remains an anchor which keeps most from moving ahead in the world.

The Culture of Poverty

The idea of a culture of poverty is a notion advanced by social scientists who suggest that the behavior of the poor results from a system of values quite different from middle-class values. Supposedly, the poor have common characteristics wherever they may live (Allen, 1970). According to Oscar Lewis (1966), slum children have thoroughly learned the basic values and attitudes of poverty by the age of six or seven. Their values include a belief in luck, a search for immediate pleasures, impulsiveness, an inability to delay gratification or plan for the future, feelings of inferiority, and an easy acceptance of aggression as a way of life. If Oscar Lewis is right, then the poor will find their values regularly in conflict with the principal values of the controlling middle class. Further, there will be no simple ways to bring about fundamental changes in this life style. Confined to the slum culture, the child is limited in his learning environment; the poverty-stricken environment results in "cultural deprivation" wherein the child fails to develop the "intellectual skills" of the middle classes (Tulkin, 1972). Certainly, the problems associated with being poor are many in number, but, perhaps, the worst problem is welfare.

The Reluctant Welfare State

Welfare has been defined as the one social program nobody is happy about. In the psychological exchange of giving and getting, conflict, mutual resentment, and anger are generated. Welfare is no exception to the rule. The majority of Americans who see themselves as the givers view the poor in characteristic terms. According to one opinion survey, they most frequently feel that poor people: (1) lack thrift and knowledge of proper money management, (2) lack effort, (3) lack ability and talent, (4) have loose morals and tend toward drunkenness, and (5) suffer from sickness and physical handicaps (Feagin, 1972). Only after these opinions are given do the middle Americans mention factors such as prejudice, discrimination, failure of society to provide good schools, or low wages as reasons for poverty. If you hold a man responsible for his own

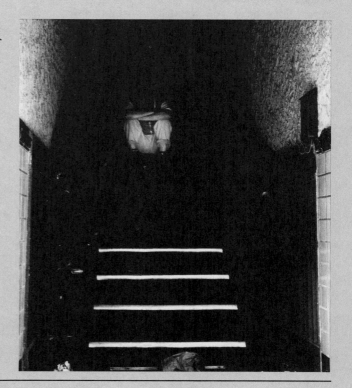

Someone Says

Someone says "look at her raggy clothes"

Someone else says "she can't afford no better"

You walk away,

Trying to believe in yourself.

—Charlene
[Duva, 1972, p. 55]

The Hall

When I was small,
I'd play in the hall.
Now I've grown tall,
And just walk through the hall,
Carefully.

There are dark hallways where I live. When you go in, you get scared. Voices scream stop stop. Then it's quiet again. You don't wonder what happened. You just know that you might be next, so you hurry upstairs.

—Darlene
[Duva, 1972, p. 168]

poverty, it then follows that you will have negative attitudes toward welfare programs or any new antipoverty proposals.

What we do to help the poor has always been a reflection of the beliefs we hold about poverty-stricken people. Some observers feel that many poverty programs have been sabotaged by these attitudes, which may be more prevalent among middle-class welfare administrators than we would care to admit (MacDonald and Majunder, 1972).

To relieve our feelings about public welfare, we usually make welfare recipients work for the money they get. During the depression of the 1930s, the first response of the government was to appropriate billions of dollars for direct relief payments; in a very short time, however, this was abandoned and work was invented to justify the giving of relief. The argument was that direct relief did little to renew personal pride or restore the dignity of a previous way of life.

In 1962 Michael Harrington announced in *The Other America* that there were some 40 million poor people in the richest country in the world. Two years later, President Johnson declared war on poverty, and by 1968 the number of people classified as poor had dropped to 25.4 million. Since then, we haven't made much progress; in 1971 the Census Bureau reported that 25.6 million people had incomes below the government's poverty line. The psychological difficulties of a life of poverty clearly affect an incredibly large number of Americans; yet we have never managed

to make more than a lukewarm, temporary dedication to the task of helping the poor.

Summary

1. The poor people of this country include families without wage earners and families headed by females, young males, and persons over 65. They are usually members of minority groups, live in rural areas, and have minimal education.

2. Oscar Lewis, among others, has suggested that the culture of poverty prevents these people from getting ahead. Children living in poor areas learn the basic attitudes of the poor by the age of six or seven. These include a belief in luck, an inability to delay gratification, and a feeling of inferiority.

3. A major obstacle to the success of programs to aid the poor is that most middle-class Americans believe that poor people are personally responsible for their plight. They blame poverty on an inability to manage money, lack of ambition or talent, loose morals, and a tendency to be drunkards. The idea that individuals should be made to work for welfare is based on the notion that direct relief does little to renew personal pride or to encourage returning to working life.

PART TEN

THE INDIVIDUAL AND SOCIETY

MANY OF THE BEHAVIORS AND ATTITUDES we think are basic to human nature are actually learned cultural norms and acquired social roles. We assume that males are naturally aggressive and that they always take the lead, whereas females are passive and primarily emotional beings. Such conceptions of "human nature" are disproven by studying the very different roles of male and female in other cultures.

The newborn baby arrives in a world that has already prescribed the patterns of behavior that will be used in caring for him. He is born into a *society,* a group of people who are dependent upon one another and who have developed patterns of organization that enable them to live together and survive as a group. These prescribed patterns of behaving and thinking, the products of behavior transmitted from generation to generation, are what we call *culture.*

Since so much of a person's behavior is determined by his relation to the society in which he lives, we can understand him only if we understand how his behavior fits into his society. Being born into a society of others sets standards for almost all aspects of our behavior and influences our behavior, perception, motivation, and thinking. The Tchambuli people believe that it is "human nature" for women to be rational, businesslike, hard-headed, and self-reliant. Men are supposed to be artistic, vain, and proud. Among the Arapesh people, both male and female are passive. American society encourages competition and material rewards for achieving goals and individual initiative. Yet, the Zuñi Indians of the Southwest are taught to be unaggressive and cooperative and to spend time on ceremonies rather than on individual achievement.

Psychology is concerned with individual behavior, but we live in groups and almost everything we do is influenced by others. This unit is specifically concerned with how our society functions and changes, and how we as individuals are affected by—and contribute to—the form our society takes.

Culture and the Individual

Man seeketh in society comfort, use, and protection.—Francis Bacon

Every one of us knows what it means to live as a cultural being in our American society. We know, at least, how to survive in one segment of our society, surrounded most often by others who are very much like us. We know how we as a people respond to disaster or to war, and we know something of the demands that group living makes upon us. We also are aware of how difficult it is to achieve a workable balance between cooperation and competition. We have a great many others to consider every time our personal needs come in conflict with the patterns of our culture. We, in fact, are so accustomed to living life in our particular cultural fashion that much of what we think, believe, feel, and do has become automatic and is no longer easily available for conscious examination.

Society is organized for several different purposes: (1) to maintain the biological functioning of individual group members, (2) to reproduce new group members, (3) to socialize new members into functioning adults, (4) to produce and distribute goods and services necessary to life, (5) to maintain order within the group and between the group and outsiders, and (6) to define the "meaning of life" and to maintain the motivation to survive (Bennet and Tumin, 1948).

The Quality of Life

Since the beginning of the twentieth century, the quality of American life has been increasingly dependent on how we react to urban life. We have become a city-dwelling culture, and our cities and suburbs have become

579

increasingly unsafe. Reporting on a 1971 survey of the quality of American life, Lear (1972) sums it up as follows:

Q. Is it safe to go out walking around here at night?
A. No. (Metropolitans 56 percent, suburbans 20 percent, rurals 14 percent)
Q. How important is it to lock your doors when you go out of the house for just an hour or two?
A. Very important. (Metropolitans 81 percent, suburbans 60 percent, rurals 37 percent)

In his 1919 painting *The City* Fernand Léger expressed what many of us associate with today's urban places—buildings, signs, people, and traffic crowding together in very little space.

The Unsafe Society

Those who can escape from our unsafe cities to the suburbs, whereas those who are left behind survive by developing a "stockade mentality." In the inner city, steel gates have replaced wooden doors, and Plexiglas barriers now enclose what were once open store counters. The city has become a bizarre habitat of fences, guards, alarms, and barricades. We have constructed an architecture of fear in which our homes are armed forts and the "extras" offered by landlords include trespass-proof apartments. One "dream" development offered an encircling wire mesh fence, two entrances flanked by guardhouses, ID cards for residents, and a private minibus to bring children to the regular school-bus stop at the front entrance (Clark, 1971).

As far back as 1961, Jacobs (1961) suggested that major American cities would come to resemble groups of stockaded villages with sentries posted along the walls and armed guards accompanied by patrol dogs. Despite the fact that we are prisoners of our own fences, we seem willing to pay this

price to gain back our lost sense of security. As Wideman (1972) put it: "Fear has reached the proportions of a debilitating psychic plague" (p. 103).

The Untrusting Society

Crime, drug use, declining morality, public protests, and various aspects of environmental pollution are cited by significant numbers of people as evidence that "things are getting worse" in America. When asked for their overall estimate of whether things are getting better, worse, or staying about the same, people are about twice as likely to say that things are worse. Some groups of Americans are far more critical of the quality of American life than others, and, surprisingly, it does not seem to be the old folks who are most disturbed. Those most alienated are much more likely to be young, well educated, metropolitan residents, and black.

Wrightsman and Baker (1969) reported some of the views of incoming

THE QUALITY ISN'T WHAT IT USED TO BE
"One-third of the adults in the nation are concerned over not being able to sleep at night. . . . About 25 percent feel too exhausted to get up in the morning, and about the same percentage lacks an appetite or feels unable to control it. A majority (52 percent) of the sample polled reports that they are 'lonely and depressed' some of the time, and 23 percent said that they have felt 'emotionally disturbed.' " [Nelson, 1968]

THE QUALITY OF SWEDISH LIFE

Sweden is in the midst of a quiet debate about the degree of freedom that her citizens actually enjoy. "Despite the trappings of sexual permissiveness and an avant-garde 'with-it' attitude toward subjects as diverse as marriage, women's liberation, the environment, and left-wing political causes, Sweden remains a rigid, deeply conformist society with narrow individual freedom." A homeowner must get permission from the local authority to paint the outside of the house in certain colors, since there are laws concerning color schemes. Every citizen has a six-digit personnummer *covering every aspect of his life—his social security, military, medical, police, tax, and motor record. The whole idea of dropping out and doing whatever you want to do doesn't quite enter people's minds (Weinraub, 1972).*

freshmen at Peabody University from 1954 to 1968. Trust (the extent to which people are seen as moral, honest, or reliable) decreased in questions having to do with national and international politics, the judiciary, and the mass media. There was also decreased trust in people. The students believed there was greater hypocrisy, self-seeking, and competitiveness.

Additional evidence of the loss of trust is revealed in the Detroit Area Study conducted by the Institute for Social Research. The questions posed in its 1971 interviews were the same questions asked in earlier years. The sample contained 1,881 persons aged 24 and older. The 1971 survey found a lower percentage of persons saying that our institutions were doing a good job. The greatest decline in trust related to high schools. In 1959, 45 percent of the respondents said high schools were doing a good job. In 1971, 29 percent felt this way. There were similar losses of confidence in other aspects of our society.

It is also apparent that people count on their leaders less and less. In a Harris Survey, a majority of the public could not say they felt "a great deal of confidence" in the leaders of most institutions. As recently as 1966, the majority of people expressed strong confidence in only half of those people running our key institutions. Even doctors are no longer immune to criticism. The number of persons who said they had a "great deal of confidence in the men running medicine" declined sharply from 61 to 48 percent in recent years.

The Psychological Impact

Psychologically, each of us is formed by the kind of society and culture in which we live. As pertains to modern American life, a number of social critics have suggested that the cost of our "civilized" existence can be measured in terms of alienation and dehumanization.

Alienation. The labels used to describe this condition are legion: estrangement, disaffection, anomie, withdrawal, disengagement, separation, noninvolvement, apathy, indifference, and neutralism. All depict a gap between man and his fellow man that daily grows greater. This growing sense of unrelatedness persists despite our technological gains and increased opportunities. As one pair of researchers stated: "Knowledge has spread, but it has not abolished war or fear; nor has it made all men brothers. Instead, men find themselves more isolated, anxious and uneasy than ever" (Josephson and Josephson, 1962, p. 10).

Alienation has been described as a sense of loneliness, personal isolation, apathy, powerlessness, rootlessness, and loss of a sense of self. It has caused some of us to abandon the goal of being an "integrated" person who is productively involved in society. And it seems to exist at every level of society. Surveys of elementary school children reveal that even at this tender age only 45 percent believe the President always told the truth about the Vietnamese war. Fewer than 31 percent believed he was doing the right thing in foreign policy. The attitudes of today's children will certainly be reflected in the quality of American life tomorrow. In addition to our children, cynicism among adults may also have reached unusual proportions. Nearly half of the persons interviewed during the 1970 elections felt that our government is run primarily to serve the interests of the few rather than the many. Several polls coincided in suggesting that people feel America, as a society, is on the wrong track and steadily losing ground. If the revelations about Watergate are any indication, we are in for a long winter of discontent with regard to the democratic political process and the psychological characteristics of our leaders.

We Americans live in what Brenton (1964) calls a Goldfish Age. The details of our private lives have increasingly become a matter of business and governmental concern. Our children may shortly be assigned birth numbers that will stay with them throughout life, and we may even be the first culture to become a "dossier society." As Miller (1971) commented, the dossier society started several decades ago when the federal government entered the taxation and social welfare spheres. Since then, greater and greater quantities of information have been elicited from individual citizens and recorded. Added to this are the enormous quantities of investigatory information gathered as an inevitable byproduct of the nation's emergence as a

Indifference, personal isolation, and even traces of fear can be seen in these two portrayals of the New York subway.

Crowding

The research on crowding is sparse. Most controlled experiments that have been conducted on crowding involved nonhuman subjects. Research done on humans has mainly involved statistical correlations between population density (number of persons in a given amount of space) and factors like crime rate, infant mortality, suicide, illegitimate birth, and mental breakdown. Whereas these studies initially found that indicators of societal breakdown were greatest in high-density areas, most of them did not take into account the fact that these same areas are usually the poorest as well. When the researchers statistically controlled for educational, economic, and racial factors, they found no relationship between population density and societal ills.

One of the few laboratory experiments with humans was conducted by Jonathan L. Freedman and Paul Ehrlich (1971). They decided that, if crowding were indeed stressful, it would interfere with the performance of subjects on complex tasks. So the researchers placed from four to nine subjects in rooms of various sizes, and they found that there was no effect of room density on individual task performance—i.e., no interference was observed.

In another part of the experiment, the researchers placed groups of subjects in either large or small rooms. The subjects interacted informally, made group decisions, and played games. Members of the male groups became more suspicious and combative and reacted more negatively toward other members of the group when they were in the high-density condition. Females, on the other hand, were friendlier and more positive in the high-density rather than low-density conditions. Interestingly, when the men and women were mixed, density had no effect.

Freedman and Ehrlich concluded that the psychological effect of "density per se is not particularly detrimental to human beings." However, its ecological effects—food shortages, pollution, and so forth—are still very much a danger. The psychological effects found in crowding research to date may be due to the absolute number of individuals who are forced to interact, rather than to the amount of space per person.

Source: Jonathan L. Freedman, "A Positive View of Population Density," *Psychology Today,* September 1971.

dominant world power. In no other society is so much counting, measuring, interrogation, testing, and record keeping done. Yet we passively accept this state of affairs.

Dehumanization. One effective defense against distressing emotions is to feel psychologically somewhat less than human. If we view others as nonhuman, inanimate objects, we ourselves become dehumanized as well as alienated from others. Bernard, Ottenberg, and Redl (1968) suggest that such dehumanization includes many factors. Aside from a failure to be horrified at man's inhumanity to his fellow man, there is: An increased emotional distance from other human beings, a diminished sense of personal responsibility for the consequences of one's actions, an obsessive involvement with bureaucratic problems to the detriment of human needs, an inability to oppose dominant group attitudes or pressures, and feelings of personal helplessness and estrangement.

The dehumanized and deindividuated citizen will join groups and act in ways he would never contemplate when acting alone. In fact, one reason for joining groups is to attain a state of deindividuation or anonymity where one does not feel singled out or identifiable (Festinger, Pepitone, and Newcomb, 1952). The larger the group, the easier it is to lose our identity. A group of rioters, for example, is stirred to violent excesses that occur only because each participant is a faceless, nameless member of a crowd.

Singer, Brush, and Lublin (1965) conducted experiments on subjects who were placed in identifiable or anonymous conditions. In the identifiable condition, each subject dressed in normal clothes and was called by name. In the anonymous condition, all the subjects put on identical lab coats, and the experimenter avoided using their names. The groups then discussed a variety of topics, including one in which the use of obscene language was required. Subjects in the condition of anonymity showed greater freedom in the discussions. There were fewer pauses in the conversation, more lively discussions, and a greater willingness to use obscene language. Subjects who were easily identifiable were more constrained and appeared reluctant to use the taboo words.

Positive Social Behavior

The consequences of alienation and dehumanization can best be illustrated in one aspect of the living laboratory of life in America—helping others. In March 1964, Kitty Genovese was brutally attacked as she returned home from work late at night. Thirty-eight of her neighbors heard her frantic cries for help, but none came to her assistance. No one even bothered to call the police during Miss Genovese's futile half-hour battle for her life. In a similar incident in Chicago, 60 persons ignored a uniformed policeman's cries for

IMPROVING OUR SOCIETY?
Efforts to remake people have proved exceptionally inefficient in the rehabilitation of criminals. We rely heavily on reeducational programs for prisoners, but out of every two inmates who are released, one will be rearrested and eventually returned to prison. Of the 151,355 inmates in state prisons on December 31, 1960, 49 percent had previously been committed at least once to adult penal institutions. Reformatories come off no better. A study of 694 offenders released by one well-known institution reported that 58.4 percent returned within five years (Etzioni, 1972).

The Law and the Good Samaritan

You are sitting on the edge of a pier eating a sandwich and watching the sunset when the fisherman next to you leans too far forward and falls in. He screams to you, "Help! I can't swim. Throw me a life preserver." You make no effort to get up to throw the life preserver hanging only five feet from you, even though you could do this with absolutely no danger to yourself and only the most minimal effort. Indeed you sit chomping away on your sandwich and now, along with the sunset, you watch the fisherman drown. [Kaplan, 1972, p. 214]

Under the law you are not responsible to the family of the fisherman you permitted to drown, nor would you be criminally liable in any way for his death. Most of our laws are concerned more with doing wrong rather than with *not* doing right. We are all well aware of how difficult it is to stop wrongdoing. Would laws promoting altruistic behavior have a better fate? Even if they did, enforcement would still be a problem.

The Good Samaritan laws now in existence protect you only from lawsuits if you make matters worse when you try to help. These laws aren't perfect and some risk is still involved. There are also laws that reward you for capturing criminals or providing information that leads to arrest and conviction, but there is some social stigma attached to them ("everybody hates a squealer"). Failing to design any more satisfactory way to encourage good citizenship, we might try, as one psychologist suggested, a lottery in which people who had done a service to others over and above what could be required will become eligible for "good-citizens" cash prizes (Kaplan, 1972).

If our society is going to find some effective ways for producing desired behaviors—as well as eliminating the undesirable ones—then it will have to abandon its trial-and-error methods for solving the dilemma. The psychological investigation of altruistic behavior is still in its early stages, but hopefully psychologists will soon come up with a set of principles that can be applied toward making more of us Good Samaritans.

assistance as he battled two youths. In Santa Clara, California, several motorists saw a taxicab driver being robbed, but none summoned the police. In San Pedro, California, other motorists drove by two policemen who were struggling to prevent a man from jumping off a bridge (Gross, 1964). Sadly, the list of such incidents grows longer every day.

Altruism

Since most of us are taught that it is good to be generous and to aid the needy, we might wonder how such shocking incidents continue to happen. What keeps us from being altruistic and responding with positive social behavior? Darley and Latane (1968) conducted a study in an attempt to answer that question. They placed subjects in a room that was connected by intercom to other rooms. The real subjects were supposed to carry on a group conversation by intercom. They were unaware that a confederate was also present in one of the rooms. At some point in the group discussion, the confederate became very ill and apparently began to suffer an epileptic seizure. Darley

Oil spills, such as the ones in the Santa Barbara Channel in 1969 and in San Francisco Bay in 1971, have stimulated community cooperation on a scale surprising to many observers. Spills are an alarming form of water pollution, and even people with limited environmental awareness respond when they see their beaches covered with the mucky, sticky substance. Volunteers have not only formed battalions to rake up the immediate mess, but they have worked for months afterward taking care of birds who otherwise would have died from the oil coating.

and Latane wanted to see how many people would leave their rooms to get help and how long it would take them to do so. The researchers were interested in determining whether the *size* of the group would have an effect on helping behavior. They found that subjects who thought that only they were aware of the epileptic seizure responded more promptly than did subjects who thought they were part of a larger group. One explanation for this unpredictable fact is that the subjects who were part of a "group" didn't feel that it was up to them to do anything, since responsibility was diffused equally to everyone.

In a related experiment (Darley and Latane, 1968), a room began to fill with smoke, but the subjects didn't react dramatically when others seemed unconcerned. The presence and conduct of other people clearly seems to change an individual's response to danger.

There are three things a person must do if he is to intervene in an emergency situation. First, he must *notice* that something is happening. He must then *interpret* that event as an emergency, and decide that he has *personal responsibility* for intervention (Darley and Latane, 1968). Even the first necessary ingredient, noticing, is complicated by the fact that Americans consider it bad manners to look too closely at other people in public. We are taught to respect the privacy of others, and we do this by keeping our eyes and ears to ourselves.

Of course, most of us don't practice what we will do in an emergency, and we are not always certain exactly what has happened, what we should do to help, or what we can do (Darley and Latane, 1970). People use a great many reasons to justify their reluctance to help in emergencies. Many of us simply don't want to become involved. We are inclined to deny that an emergency really exists when we have a direct personal responsibility for taking action. We tend to "adjust" our understanding of what is happening to justify avoiding the unwelcome pressure to take action. If the others fail to help, we may define an apparent emergency as a situation in which helping is not appropriate.

Nonetheless, our first conclusion that unconcerned, depersonalized citizens will impassively watch the misfortunes of others is far from accurate. It is more likely that the average witness to an emergency is an anguished individual in genuine doubt. He may want to do the right thing, but he is forced to make complex decisions under the pressure of stress and fear.

Justice and Guilt

All of us want to believe we get what we deserve and deserve what we get. Most of us care deeply about justice. We expect that good things should happen to good people and suffering should come only to bad people. Lerner (1971) reminds us, however, that we also like to think that people who fail or who are deprived deserve their fates because they were unable or unwilling to reach goals or avoid suffering.

HELPING OTHERS

Why people help one another in time of distress was demonstrated by Tilker (1970). In an experiment, observers watched while a "teacher" appeared to apply severe electric shock to a "learner" strapped in an electric chair. The observers were given different degrees of responsibility for the conduct of the experiment (no responsibility, ambiguous responsibility, or total responsibility). Tilker concluded: "Results supported the hypothesis that if a person is forced to 'get involved' or 'feel responsible' for the safety and well-being of another, and is receiving maximum feedback from that person regarding his condition, then he will be most likely to react in a socially responsible manner and attempt to alter the course of events" [p. 95]

Lerner pursued this theme of justice and how it affects the way people react to—and create—victims. In a series of studies, Lerner and his colleagues found that our desire to live in a just world can lead us either to help a victim or condemn him if we find that we are unable to help. If we can neither relieve his suffering or persuade ourselves that he deserved his fate, we may try to run away from the victim or, at least, alter our awareness of his plight.

The altruistic act of charitable giving is not much different. Krebs and Whitten (1972) describe a revealing study done in Cambridge, Massachusetts. In this study, a solicitor for an African relief fund approached students who were leaving the psychology laboratory after having participated in experiments as subjects. Some of the students showed an exceptional willingness to donate money and even agreed to solicit money for the fund in the future. The "solicitor" was, of course, an experimental confederate. The students were part of a study on altruism designed to produce feelings of shame or guilt. Almost without exception, students who had been made to feel ashamed were the most generous donors. If a subject gave money, he was asked to take over while the solicitor went on a coffee break. If he agreed to this, he was then asked to be a solicitor for the fund in the future. If he said yes to all these requests, he was next asked for a dime for coffee. The subjects who complied with all four requests were those who had been made to feel ashamed in the experiment. These same subjects also donated twice as much money as anyone else.

People are not only more likely to help others when they feel guilty, but it has been shown that they are also more likely to donate blood after being convinced that they have harmed someone. Investigators have concluded that we often act generously to alleviate feelings of guilt. Shame is also the frequent motive for charity.

This interpretation suggests that people attempt to maintain a realistic level of self-esteem by acting out particular images in front of others. When self-esteem is low, they act out positive images; when it is unrealistically high, they take measures to lower their images slightly. It follows, then, that when people are induced to behave in an unrepresentatively altruistic way, they would be less likely afterward to behave altruistically than people who have not. [Krebs and Whitten, 1972, p. 52]

Man Cooperating and Man in Conflict

The American competitive spirit has produced children who have been shown to act in systematically irrational ways. Ten-year-olds in Los Angeles participated in the experiments of Nelson and Kagan (1972) and repeatedly failed to get rewards they wanted because they competed in games that required cooperation. The children sacrificed their own rewards in order to reduce the rewards of their peers. This tendency toward irrational competition in-

Studies of disaster situations such as earthquakes indicate that the victims do not wander through the rubble dazed, disoriented, in shock and unable to cope—even though the media commonly reports such stereotypes. Actually, in a disaster morale goes up rather than down since the emergency—at least temporarily—dissolves differences in class, race, rank, and age. In the background of this photo, San Francisco burns after the Great Quake of 1906.

creases with age and produces adults whose drive to compete may override their self-interest. We find examples in athletics, business, politics, and universities.

Nelson and Kagan's studies show that the competitive spirit is not universal. Ten-year-old children in rural Mexico, for example, cooperated and got the prizes by avoiding competition. In contrast to urban children, rural children in all the cultures studied by Nelson and Kagan proved to be more cooperative in conflict-of-interest situations that require mutual assistance.

Stacey and DeMartino (1958), among others, have characterized our culture as competitive, noting that in our society all of our human relationships are molded by an outspoken competition. Those who see our society as too competitive point out that fierce competition has taken its toll in human maladies such as ulcers, heart attacks, suicides, and divorces. Young people are questioning the value of competition and are seeking escape from the rat race of our culture. There are still others, however, who wonder what would happen to our economic and technical achievements if we could restrain the competitive thrust of our society.

The fact that the competitive urge can be quickly aroused seems to be a key to understanding why the history of mankind is a continuous chronicle

The Risky Shift

It was said some years ago that "a camel is a horse designed by a committee." This wry comment has caused a great deal of discussion about the merits of group decision making. We have seen how men often change their behavior when they are part of a group. If this is so, then the question is: Who should make the important decisions in our society—one man or a group?

In the early 1960s, researchers initiated investigations on how people in groups behave when asked to make decisions regarding risky courses of action. Members of the group were asked to select the odds of success they would need before recommending the risky alternative. Each member of the group was first given the problem to resolve independently. Then the group was asked to discuss the alternatives and arrive at a consensus on the desired course of action. The object was to see whether individuals or groups were more likely to recommend risky courses of action.

Mr. G, a competent chess player, is participating in a national chess tournament. In an early match he draws the top-favored player in the tournament as his opponent. Mr. G has been given a relatively low ranking in view of his performance in previous tournaments. During the course of his play with the top-favored man, Mr. G notes the possibility of a deceptive, though risky, maneuver which might bring him a quick recovery. At the same time, if the attempted maneuver should fail, Mr. G would be left in an exposed position and defeat would almost certainly follow.

Imagine that you are advising Mr. G. Listed below are several probabilities or odds that Mr. G's deceptive play would succeed. PLEASE CHECK THE LOWEST PROBABILITY THAT YOU WOULD CONSIDER ACCEPTABLE FOR THE RISKY PLAY IN QUESTION TO BE ATTEMPTED.

___ *The chances are 1 in 10 that the play would succeed.*
___ *The chances are 3 in 10 that the play would succeed.*
___ *The chances are 5 in 10 that the play would succeed.*
___ *The chances are 7 in 10 that the play would succeed.*
___ *The chances are 9 in 10 that the play would succeed.*
___ *Place a check here if you think Mr. G should not attempt the risky play, no matter what the probabilities.* [Kogan and Wallach, 1964]

Contrary to expectations, the group decision on most items was *more* risky than the average decision of each member of the group before the discussion. Following the experiment, when group members were asked to list their own choices again, the private judgments showed a shift toward risk. Thus the change to greater risk taking involves more than a simple conformity to the group.

These findings triggered a host of "explanations" to interpret the meaning of the experiments. Roger Brown (1965), for example, suggested that we live in a culture that values risk. People want to think of themselves as risk takers. Each person enters the group convinced that he is more risky than the average, only to discover he is not. He must therefore preserve his self-image by moving in a more risky direction. Studies by Wallach and Wing (1969) and by Levinger and Schneider (1969) found that subjects see their peers as being less risky than they and that subjects admire decisions that are more risky than their own. Madaras and Bem (1970) also showed that risk takers were more admired than risk avoiders.

Other theorists favored the notion of "diffusion of responsibility" (Wallach, Kogan and Bem, 1964). Abandoning the risk-taking questionnaire used in earlier studies, they gave their subjects the opportunity to choose test items of increasing difficulty and increasing payoff. Thus, the group could try a hard item that they probably would not get correct but that would pay a high reward if they did. Or they could choose an easier item with a higher probability of solution and lower reward for being correct. The researchers found that risk taking was greatest when the group, rather than the individuals, reached the decision as to how hard a problem should be tackled. Evidently, people become relatively more risky when they all share in the responsibility for success or failure and a bit more conservative when they alone bear the responsibility.

Dorwin Cartwright (1973) made a careful, detailed examination of the massive research effort expended on the theory of "risky shift" in the last decade. He points out that researchers have steadfastly ignored the fact that some groups move in a conservative rather than risky direction. Until we can account for these "exceptions to the rule," we would be wise not to move rapidly in the direction of letting committees do the work of our society, or take the place of individuals working alone.

After ten years of research . . . we still do not know how the risk-taking behavior of "real-life" groups compares with that of individuals. Should the decision about nuclear war be assigned to a committee or to an individual? Should decisions about surgery be left to a group of surgeons? Is it better to have a jury or an individual decide whether a possibly dangerous person is to be set free? The answers to such questions are not much clearer now than they were ten years ago. The results of research on the risky shift do suggest, however, that there is probably no universal answer to these questions. [Cartwright, 1973, p. 231]

of conflict. Perhaps the most convincing illustration of the ease with which human beings tend to take sides, identify with their own in-group, and dislike the members of an out-group was demonstrated by Rabbie and Horwitz (1969). These two researchers divided experimental subjects into groups simply by flipping a coin. As they note:

> *What is striking in the present experiment is how little it evidently takes to move two randomly formed groups of strangers into mutual antipathy. Flipping a coin to decide the allocation of a scarce resource is commonly used in everyday social life in the effort to be fair. Yet this simple act triggered processes within the two groups of strangers that were far-reaching enough to affect the perception of personal traits. Although subjects had no prior experience with anyone in the room, the flip of a coin was sufficient to shape their views of out-group members as less friendly, less familiar, less considerate, and less desirable as associates than in-group members.* [Rabbie and Horwitz, 1969, p. 276]

You might assume that this would happen among strangers, however they are formed into groups. Yet one would not expect this to be the case among persons who know one another well and consider themselves friends. There is evidence that this expectation is *not* always true.

It is natural to assume that friends will be more cooperative than strangers. Exploring this hypothesis, Oskamp and Perlman (1966) used subject pairs who were best friends, acquaintances, people who disliked each other, or people who were complete strangers. These subjects were selected from two different colleges: one a small, friendly liberal arts college with a highly cooperative atmosphere; the other with a less cooperative atmosphere. Oskamp and Perlman found, of course, that pairs of friends were most cooperative. But this was true only for the subjects from the liberal arts college. Those from the less cooperative atmosphere were *least* cooperative when participating with their friends.

Oskamp and Perlman attribute these findings to the social standards encouraged by the two different schools. In the liberal arts college, there were pressures for students to cooperate, and this gave pairs of friends a history of cooperation. The college with a competitive atmosphere served to foster rivalry.

Waging Experimental War

Insight into the development and reduction of conflict between groups has been provided by a series of studies by Muzafer Sherif. Sherif studied the process of group formation in the development and reduction of intergroup conflict. His subjects were groups of preadolescent boys who did not know they were being studied while they attended a summer camp. The boys were strangers to one another and were described as normal preadolescents from roughly similar backgrounds. Three experiments were conducted in different years and in different locales, but the basic findings were much the same.

One experiment took place at Robbers Cave, Oklahoma, in the summer of 1954 (Sherif et al., 1961). In this locale, the behavioral scientists caused, conducted, and concluded a war between groups of well-adjusted, middle-class boys who had willingly come to the experimental camp.

The war was designed to have three successive stages:

Stage No. 1: Experimental In-Group Formation. During the first six days, two groups of boys were brought to camp and kept isolated geographically from each other while they solidified themselves into identifiable and meaningful groups. These "boy nation-states" came to be known, respectively, as the Rattlers and the Eagles.

Stage No. 2: Intergroup Relations—Friction Phase. During this week, the two groups were brought into contact in a series of competitive group activities and mutually frustrating situations that produced a high level of intergroup hostility.

Stage No. 3: Intergroup Relations—Integration Phase. This final phase was dedicated to the experimental reduction of the intergroup enmity by means of introducing superordinate goals. The attainment of these desirable and compelling goals could only be achieved through the mutual, cooperative efforts of the Rattlers and the Eagles.

A preliminary experiment was conducted just prior to Stage No. 3. Simple togetherness and the opportunity for contact was arranged between the groups. The experimenters set up a series of situations such as participating together in psychological experiments, attending a movie, and eating in the same mess hall. This mutual exposure produced jeers, catcalls, insults, a food-throwing fight, and similar outrages.

The concept of superordinate goals (goals requiring cooperation) was translated into action when the children were induced to interact in the following situations:

1. *The drinking-water problem.* In this situation, a water shortage was elaborately staged. (Valves were turned off far from the camp; faucets were plugged; and so on.) The help of all the children was "required" to track down the trouble and relieve the common problem.

2. *The problem of securing a movie.* The staff informed the children that an attractive movie could be obtained from town, but the camp could not pay the whole rental fee. The Rattlers and Eagles had to overcome this financial obstacle through intergroup negotiation.

3. *The camp-out problem.* The entire group was removed from the familiar camp setting and thrown together to perform the necessary tasks for an extended camp-out. A number of planned interactions occurred during this time. A truck, for instance, conveniently "stalled" and required mutual effort to restart. Throughout the trip the staff capitalized on similar spontaneous incidents.

This Integration Phase of the experiment was successful in reducing the existing tensions between the groups. The researchers attribute the outcome to the interpersonal experiences generated by cooperating to achieve super-ordinate goals. Hostility reduction was described as the *cumulative* effect of interaction since no single incident seemed to have turned the tide.

The experiment at Robbers Cave has been called an "unparalleled modern classic." Despite the elaborate praise it has received, we must be aware of its limitations. Obviously, the behavior of less than 22 carefully selected eleven-year-old boys during a three-week session at camp can be extrapolated to the larger scene only with considerable caution. Further, it has been suggested (McNeil, 1962) that a more appropriate model might be found by studying delinquent children for whom open hostility produces less guilt, the concept of "fair play" is less pressing, and the response to social criticism more contemptuous. With such raw material, the consequent experi-mental broth might resemble a devil's brew more than a cup of friendship. What if this experiment were to be repeated with children of Thailand, China, Paraguay, or Nigeria? Would the all-American happy ending have been the predictable outcome?

A more crucial criticism has to do with the selection of superordinate goals to resolve this test-tube, intergroup hostility. For instance, what if a suitably unappetizing common enemy had been conjured up to redirect the angry energies of the boys? What if our cultural need for individual achieve-ment had been allowed to ravage the internal cohesion of the groups (i.e., a powerful competition for prizes and awards within the group)? What if selected members of the Rattlers and the Eagles had been inspired to launch a hunger strike for peace? What if the two groups had been prevailed upon to establish a supernational agency to regulate the intergroup tension (Stagner, 1961)? The long list of possible "what if's" needs to be explored so we can judge the relative effectiveness of each and order them on some rough scale of usefulness.

It is interesting that the "common-enemy" approach to the reduction of intergroup hostility was attempted by these researchers in an earlier study (Sherif and Sherif, 1953). It proved to be a successful device, but it was an expensive one experimentally since the conflict was spread to an even greater number of combatants. This approach was like causing a war to drain off the feelings that lead to war.

Another alternative which was considered and abandoned was to disrupt the in-groups by emphasizing individual achievement and accomplishment. Even if such an all-American plan had succeeded, it seemed to promise little in the way of practical implications for the reduction of intergroup tensions in state-sized groups. The intrusion by an outsider into the leadership pattern of the group was rejected for similar reasons. The impossibility of "getting to" a leader in the real world seemed enormous.

The design of this experimental attempt to manipulate group hostility, by its very nature, rejects certain explanations of intergroup relations. Some of the causes of intergroup anger that were discarded are: Theories about national character; innate instincts of aggression; the superiority or inferiority of certain human groups; the effect of individual frustration; or the character of leadership. In this respect, the research was designed to explore a limited and select hypothesis.

At one point during the height of the hostile excursions the groups were making against each other, the Eagles raided and wrecked the Rattlers' cabin and then returned to their own quarters where they entrenched and prepared weapons (socks filled with rocks) in anticipation of retaliation by their victims. When the Rattlers discovered this atrocity, their leader labeled the Eagles (collectively) "communists." This spontaneous epithet no doubt evoked an adult smile, but its significance may have escaped the observers of this conflict in microcosm. It is the steady solidifying of hostility that sets an upper limit on the effectiveness of plans to restore peace by simply increasing contact between the various nations.

The Sherif work raised as many issues as it resolved, but international events have given a very urgent cast to what would otherwise have been considered theoretical research with little practical application. Ideally, a systematic plan of experimentation ought to be undertaken to explore the effectiveness of a variety of means for reducing intergroup hostility. We suffer from an abundance of speculation and a dearth of actual experimentation on such matters (McNeil, 1962).

Summary

1. Society is organized to insure both the physical and psychological well-being of its members. When the society begins to fail in providing meaning for life and order within the group, its members may experience a number of emotional difficulties.

2. Individuals in America, for example, no longer have as much trust as they once had in one another or in their leaders and institutions. The quality of life seems to decrease, while material gains increase.

3. The problems of our society—drugs, crime, declining morality, pollution, giant bureaucracies, and public disorders—are reflected in the increasing alienation and dehumanization of the citizens. *Alienation* is a feeling of not being connected with one's society or one's fellow man. *Dehumanization* is the feeling that one is merely a cog in the wheel rather than an individual, and that others are also inanimate objects.

4. *Deindividuation,* or a feeling of loss of identity, occurs when an individual becomes an anonymous member of a group. Deindividuation is often responsible for the violent excesses of large

groups because members feel they cannot be identified for their misdeeds.

5. Experiments on risk taking demonstrated that groups are more likely to make risky decisions than are individuals. It has been suggested that this is because risk is valued in our society. When one learns he is not more risky than the next person, he will feel compelled to preserve his self-image by taking more chances. Another explanation is that risk is greater in groups because responsibility for a poor outcome is diffused among a number of people.

6. Some people believe that alienation and dehumanization are responsible for the reluctance of our society's members to get involved with the problems of others. Experiments on helping behavior, however, indicate that the motives for not helping are much more complex.

7. When part of a larger group, persons may not help because they feel the responsibility for helping has been diffused among all the observers of the emergency. In addition, if others are not helping, one may assume that there is no emergency after all. Good Samaritans, therefore, are usually those people who notice the problem, interpret it as an emergency, and feel the responsibility for helping.

8. Our need to believe in justice and our need to alleviate guilt may both contribute to our attitudes toward helping others. Altruistic behavior may stem from feelings of guilt or shame. It may be used to preserve one's self-esteem. On the other hand, when one cannot help the victim, he may preserve his self-esteem and his beliefs about justice by persuading himself that the victim deserves his fate.

9. Most people will agree that the American way fosters a competitive spirit not found in a number of other cultures. While some insist that competition got us where we are today, others point out the psychological and physical casualties of the rat-race society.

10. Although few experiments have been conducted on the causes of conflict, those that have been done indicate that it is not difficult to provoke competition and conflict—even among friends.

11. The Robbers Cave experiment demonstrated that intergroup hostility could be produced among two groups of boys by placing them in competitive activities. The study showed furthermore that tension is not necessarily reduced through mere contact with the other group. The most successful technique for reconciling the groups was placing them together in situations that required cooperation.

12. Since the Robbers Cave study showed that hostility could be easily generated and then reduced in a group of young boys, the results seem to imply that innate aggressiveness, national character, leadership, individual frustrations, or feelings of superiority are not essential for conflict to occur. On the other hand, the experiment could not deal with how one might reduce conflict when such factors were present.

PSYCHOLOGICAL ISSUE
Psychoecology

Man, the contaminator and polluter, has made this planet unsafe for you, for me, and for every living thing. The issue of ecology is a psychological one. Strangling on strange chemicals or being crowded off the earth will happen only if we understand too little about human nature to prevent it or if we discover the environment has already been so altered that there won't be time enough to return it to a more healthy state. It is a psychological and social disease, for example, that prompts us to recycle throw-away bottles while allowing more than 50,000 deaths each year on our highways.

Too Many of Us?

The question is not how many people the earth can support but how many can live here happily (Krutch, 1962). At present, we simply don't know what the limits are. The best known research on the effects of crowding was done by Calhoun (1962) who used a population of wild Norway rats in a quarter-acre enclosure. With plenty of food and no natural enemies or disease, the rat population should have grown without limits. But in 27 months the population stabilized at 150 adults, even though 5,000 adults would have been a reasonable expectation.

What happened was that the females were unable to carry pregnancy to full term or died while giving birth. This crowding of the population also produced, among some males, either frantic activity or pathological withdrawal. Some of these rats would eat, drink, and move about only when all the other rats were asleep.

According to Kahn and Wiener (1967), animals are disorganized or destroyed by overcrowding. If man becomes as crowded on this planet as the rats were, we may not be able to adjust any better than the animals can. We already know that packing human beings together produces social, physical, and mental breakdown in the forms of crime, suicide, venereal disease, and illegitimacy. But we don't know why.

Here's to the Open Road.   There were only 78,000 cars in 1906, and there are more than 90 million today. These cars and the 800,000 businesses that are dependent on them have altered our way of life, rearranged our landscape, and triggered a mass exodus to the suburbs. We consume 26 million gallons of motor fuel every day (93 billion gallons a year). We pour 1 million tons of sulphur oxide, 12 million tons of hydrocarbons, and an additional 1 million tons of poisonous dust-like matter into our atmosphere each day, and kill one another with cars at a rate of more than 50,000 a year (Esposito, 1970). Americans make up only 6 percent of the planet's population, but we own half of its motor vehicles. Abandoning our beloved automobiles will be resisted to the bitter end—which may be sooner than most of us think.

The environmental condition of crowding seems to affect the way individuals learn their habits and values. As Ardrey (1966) proposed, the "territorial imperative" may be a powerful source of motivation in human behavior. He argues that human family loyalty and responsibility, as in lower animals, rests on joint attachment to a private territory. He suggests further that the willingness to make personal sacrifices for society probably would not exist in the human species without territory and property. This view promotes the idea that, as the world's population increases and available space decreases, territorial behavior will become an important consideration in human interaction. Calhoun coined the phrase *pathological togetherness* to describe the stimulus that lowered the rat fertility and shortened their lives. Psychologists must ask if this is to be the human fate.

Those who feared this possibility formed an organization called Zero Population Growth (ZPG). The San Diego branch of ZPG, for example, sponsored Mother's Day and Father's Day raffles in which the first prizes were a one-year supply of birth-control pills and a free vasectomy. One ZPG button carried the message: "Jesus was an only child" (Greene, 1972). Changing human attitudes toward these concerns may prove to be by far the most difficult challenge to psychology.

Psychological Ecology

Human ecology is the study of man adapting to the circumstances of his life—a task at which man has been exceptionally successful. As one writer stated, man "is the least specialized creature on earth: he is indeed the most adaptable. He can hunt or fish, be a meat eater or a vegetarian, live in the mountains or by the seashore, be a loner or engage in teamwork, function in a free democracy or in a totalitarian state" (Dubos, 1967, p. 19).

Some years ago two psychologists, Robert Barker and Herbert Wright (1954) collected ecological data about children and their daily lives. The researchers wanted to know where children go, what they do, what they say, and with whom they interact. For Barker and his associates (Barker, 1960; 1963), *psychological ecology* dealt with these behavioral events occurring in specific environmental settings or "natural habitats." From studies such as theirs, it has become apparent that it is almost impossible to establish hard and fast rules for human feelings and attitudes.

The Ecology Attitude   We seem to be the victims of a "psychology of more" (Looft, 1971). Americans are addicted to the concept of "supergrow"—the idea that our society can only be alive if it grows and expands constantly (DeMott, 1969). If it is newer and bigger, it is better. Our attitude that "more is good" is proving

The Crowded Japanese.   If you were to herd half of America's more than 200 million people into the state of California, you would produce the kind of crowding that exists in present-day Japan. In the major cities of Japan, you can witness an immense, flowing river of people who never seem to shove, cut one another off, bump, or elbow. Throngs of people stand shoulder-to-shoulder, but this closeness seems to bring comfort rather than anxiety. Fifty percent of Japan's 100 million citizens have learned to live with one another on only 1.5 percent of their land. They may feel uncrowded at densities that would produce intolerable feelings in Americans.

to be a major obstacle to social survival (Wagar, 1970). We need to invent a "psychology of enough" and alter existing attitudes before we can do much about preserving the environment for generations yet to come.

The psychoecologists must find a way to convince us that we need to know more about the impact of our technological innovations. Only then can we decide whether we're willing to pay the price. At least we need to move *toward* a physical environment that encourages human interaction and provides opportunities for individuals to assert themselves and get a sense of self-fulfillment (Howard, 1967, pp. 277–78).

As Margaret Mead (1971) observed, it is the human attitude that determines whether man will stop forests from being depleted, the soil from being washed into the sea, or the gene pool from becoming exposed to excessive radiation. It won't be easy, however. We have had a great deal of experience, for example, with the issue of fluoridation of our water to reduce dental decay. Even when experts agree about the benefits of this technological advance, 60 percent of the local referendums fail to support fluoridation (Crain, Katz, and Rosenthal, 1969). ·

Trash and Behavioral Psychology. Perhaps one of the clearest delineations of the fact that the trashing of our environment is a psychoecological issue is research reported by Leonard Bickman (1972). Examining the relationship of attitudes to actual environmental behavior, Bickman arranged some "planted" litter and studied the people who passed by it. He asked every fifth person whether it was everyone's responsibility to pick up litter. Of those asked, 94 percent agreed with the statement, but less than 2 percent actually picked it up. Talk obviously is cheap, and personal responsibility is harder to stimulate.

We have known for some time that man's urge to smother his environment with trash cannot effectively be curbed by passing antilitter laws or making trash cans "cute." A behavioral approach to the psychology of trash control is reported by researchers at the University of Washington in Seattle. The researchers stud-

The Baby Bust.   The 1970 census reveals we are now experiencing the greatest decline in the number of children five years old or younger in the last 120 years. The present population drop is nearly double that of the largest previously recorded decline during the Great Depression in the 1930s. Almost every decade since 1850 has registered an increase in preschoolers. Considering the fact that the number of young adults reached a new high during the 1960s, we must conclude that there has been a massive, unexpected reevaluation of the morality of bringing children into a troubled world.

ied two movie houses in Seattle during the Saturday afternoon children's matinees. They determined the relative amount of trash deposited in trash cans and then experimented with several approaches to discourage littering. Doubling the number of trash cans had no effect and showing an antilittering film before the regular movie increased the properly deposited trash by only 5 percent. Handing out personal litter bags raised the deposited trash from 19 to 31 percent, and this figure increased to 57 percent when it was combined with a special announcement about trash (Goodall, 1971).

The researchers then handed out litterbags and promised cash rewards for each bag of litter turned in after the show. The amount of trash turned in rose to 95 percent. Outdoor littering of our national parks and public beaches is a much more irritating problem than the typical child clutter at Saturday movies. It may well be that such behavioral modification techniques will be an important part of psychology's contribution to a new ecological balance for the planet.

Ecology as a Social Issue

If you believed every pronouncement made about the approaching ecological disaster, you would be tempted to give up the fight. Since the dramatic warnings emanate from high-level experts, they cannot always be dismissed as the work of alarmists. But, their tone is so pessimistic that their threats may be rejected because they evoke disbelief. If we as citizens become overwhelmed by this sense of urgency, we may become even less sensitive to our surroundings. Bombarded with too much crisis information, many people may stop reading the newspaper and reduce their public-affairs activities believing there is little they can do to solve a worldwide problem.

The language of ecology is also being increasingly used to keep the poor out of the suburbs. A conflict has developed between preserving open land or making that land available for housing the poor. The accusa-

---

Utopia and Ecological Reality. "We want to live in a small intimate community; yet we want to have all the amenities of the great metropolis. We want a dwelling with privacy, identity; yet we want the setting of a rich social life. We want to be near open country; yet we let the city spread endlessly. We want all the things suburbia has to offer; but we also want the amenities of the downtown area. What we really want is Utopia, but we are not clear about what Utopia is." [Safdie, 1967, p. 253]

---

tion has been that ecology is a middle-class fad designed to reeducate the poor so that they're not going to want what the middle class already has. It is very fashionable to oppose pollution of the air and water or destruction of the woodlands, but this fashion may only reinforce existing economic segregation of the poor from the rich.

Like every other social issue critical to the quality of life, ecology has become a political football. Some critics are convinced the ecology movement is a reactionary move that will increase the amount of social injustice for those not rich enough to overconsume. The poor will hardly benefit. They will simply pay more for every necessary commodity in life. The poor will not enjoy the clean lakes and pristine pure national parks they cannot afford to visit on annual vacations (Neuhaus, 1971).

The state of human ecology seems so basic to the quality of life that we may assume that everyone shares

---

Sailing the Ocean Blue . . . Federal scientists report that vast areas of the Atlantic Ocean, from Cape Cod to the Caribbean, are befouled by floating oil, tar, and plastics. Scientists aboard ships of the National Oceanic and Atmospheric Administration calculated that at least 665,000 square miles of water are covered by the substances. The sources of the debris appeared to be, at least in part, chemical factories and oil tankers. The largest area of pollution was found off the eastern coast of the Bahamas chain, running north and south about 300 miles and about 30 miles wide.

our environmental concern. The fact is that, in general, persons expressing such concern tend to be liberal, Democrats, young, well educated, and high in socioeconomic status. Most environmental activists (61 percent in one survey) agree the solution to current ecological problems will require "significant changes in the system." Twenty-five percent believe we must replace our institutions with a "radically different" social order. According to Dunlap and Gale (1972), the eco-activists seem to be "good liberals"—not just the same old radicals with a new cause. They may, in fact, be the only radicals most people like and tolerate as they proceed to make some fundamental changes in everyone's way of life.

Summary

1. The psychological concern with ecological problems is really a matter of how to change people's attitudes toward the environment.

2. Ecology has become a social issue as well. Many individuals believe that it can be used as an excuse to discriminate against the poor.

3. Experiments with rats indicate that overcrowding can lead to vast disorganization and pathological behaviors in a previously normal society. One reason for this may be what Ardrey calls the "territorial imperative"—that is, everyone needs some space he can occupy and call his own.

4. Numerous studies have associated high population density with increases in all measurements of social breakdown. However, some researchers have argued that this relationship is a result of the fact that high density areas are also those with a poorly educated and poverty-stricken population. One series of controlled experiments with humans indicates that density itself does not produce stress. Rather when a large number of people are forced to interact—regardless of the space they have—psychological difficulties occur.

Styles of Living

Style has no fixed laws; it is changed by the usage of the people, never the same for any length of time.—Seneca

When life is filled with satisfaction, most of us are content not to tamper with the winning formula. When the quality of life seems to worsen or does not promise to improve, we naturally begin to search for a pattern of living that may restore the joy we feel has gone out of our lives. Turmoil gives birth to invention, and those of us who are experimentally minded try new forms of living together.

Trying on new lifestyles for size is not limited to hippies and dropouts, even though newspapers publicize experimental communes and group marriages only when they involve social dropouts or deviates. Many lifestyle innovators do it privately. James W. Ramey (1972) of New York's Center for the Study of Innovative Life Styles completed a study of 80 upper-middle-class couples who explored the possibility of entering communal living or group marriages. Over 90 percent of the husbands and wives were in academic, professional, or managerial positions. Their ages ranged from 21 to the late 50s. The wives in the group were most concerned with the sense of isolation that can come, when raising children, with overdependence on their husbands for adult contact and insufficient use of their talent and training. Husbands were most concerned with financial security and getting relief from the rat race. More open sexual intimacy and friendships were also an important concern. Among the projects initiated were three group marriages and several active communes. There were also joint vacations, living together on weekends, partial exchange of sex roles when several adults lived together, and the purchase of a free school by several of the families.

PLATO'S UTOPIA

Plato's ideal city-state was populated by three classes of citizens: artisans, warriors, and a ruling class—the guardians. The guardians were selected from among the most intelligent, able, just, and powerful 50-year-olds in the society. These prospective rulers were educated in the art of temperance, goodness, and nobility from early life. Guardians deficient in the ability to learn science were drafted into the warrior ranks at age 20. The "draft" was the first hurdle in educational selection. At age 30, the student guardians were sorted into rough categories of "more" or "less" promising. At 35, the survivors were allowed to begin an apprenticeship in governing the Republic. Only at age 50 were guardians considered properly prepared to assume full responsibility for the lives of others.

THE PROMISE OF UTOPIA

The Old Testament is a lush garden of utopian ideas and ideals. Jeremiah described a promised land where young and old would rejoice together. Ezekiel dreamt of an age when property would be evenly distributed among all. And the little-known visionary Deutero-Isaiah described a millennium in which honest toil would get its proper reward and the gift of eternal life would be granted every man. From 200 B.C. to 150 A.D. the pessimistic writers of apocalyptic visions predicted utopia would come only on the heels of an awesome cosmic cataclysm which would destroy all evil leaders.

THE MILLENNIUM

At the beginning of the eighteenth century, a group of Pietists led by Magister Johannes Kelpius sailed to America to build a tabernacle in the wilderness. The brethren deeply believed the second coming of Christ was imminent, so they mounted telescopes on the roof of the tabernacle and looked to each meteor or comet as a sign that the time was near. The millennium was continually postponed, and even ardent believers began to drift away from the commune. Kelpius moved into a cave and became absorbed in astrological occultism, believing that the American Indians were one of the lost tribes of Israel and that he was destined to be immortal. Kelpius died at the age of 35, and the brotherhood finally dissolved completely in 1748.

Visions of a better way of life have long beckoned Americans to withdraw from the larger society in search of new paths to honesty, intimacy, and the sense of togetherness that gives meaning to life.

The Utopian Dream

Today's search for intimate community is a revival, not a discovery. Communal movements are as old as American history. In the mid-1800s Ralph Waldo Emerson remarked that every other person seemed to carry in his pocket a plan for the "perfect society." Indeed, Emerson's friends at Brook Farm had "gone back to the land," and New York newspapers were running columns for people interested in forming communal associations. Communal movements have been most prominent during times of social ferment like the 1840s and 1850s. Today, they tend to occur along with other radical movements such as feminism, black liberation, and mysticism. During the nineteenth century, more than one hundred communities with nearly 100,000 men, women, and children experimented with alternative social arrangements for living.

The early American experiments with alternative lifestyles were as deviant and daring as those today. In those days, the female liberationists were the Shakers and the Oneidans. They were women who abandoned the classic prescriptions for male-female relations and dared to define their role in new and unique ways.

The Shakers

The Shakers started as members of a Quaker revivalist sect who became convinced that the second coming of Christ would be in the form of a woman. Ann Lee, the illiterate daughter of an English blacksmith, was hailed as the Christ incarnate after she reported visions of a visit with Christ. In 1774, she founded a community which grew to 6,000 people by the time of the Civil War. Outsiders made fun of the emotional, gyrating, trembling form of worship of the "Shaking Quakers" and persecuted them for deviating from the "normal" way of life.

The Shaker creed included public confession of one's sins, celibacy, communal property, and withdrawal from the world. To the Shakers, God was bisexual. Lust was the basis of all sin, and women were considered more sinful than men (remember Eve and the apple). Contact between males and females was limited to such an extent that third persons were used to relay messages between them. Touching one another, working together, giving presents, passing on the stairs, or mingling of any sort was strictly forbidden. Shaker females were relatively freer than women in the outside American community of that time, but their absolute freedom was far less than that taken for granted by the adult female of the 1970s.

Representatives of two styles of living come in contact when four Amish visitors from Indiana exchange curious greetings with a surfer in Southern California.

The Oneidans

The Oneida Community of Perfectionists was not as well known as the Shakers, but they were much more controversial. John Humphrey Noyes, the leader of the group, was convinced that the second coming of Christ had already taken place in 70 A.D. He reasoned, then, that man had already been redeemed from sin and no longer needed to be repentant. He was soon declared a heretic by the traditional church. Faced with excommunication, he formed a communal society where each convert relinquished all claim to property and abandoned "selfish" possessiveness of other persons.

Any member of the group could freely have sexual relations with any other member. Females as well as males could take the initiative sexually. The young, at puberty, were given practical experience with sex by older members of the community, and, when children were born, they were raised communally. Considering the year was 1847, one is not surprised that Noyes and his group were soon run out of town. They finally abandoned the practices of free love, joint marriage, and community ownership of property. In 1881, the community came to a formal end. What is currently called the sexual revolution is less novel than most of us suppose.

The Modern Utopians

In 1966 there were about 100 "intentional communities" in the United States. Today there are about 3,000 communes, a third of which are in rural settings. It is important to keep in mind that no two communes are exactly alike. Some are anarchistic way stations for wandering drug freaks who are running from, rather than going toward, purpose and meaning in life. Some are "scientific" communities based on information and approaches drawn from the behavioral sciences. Others are religious or political communes dedicated to a totally new way of life.

Fairfield (1971) visited communes across America and described the basic ideals that pioneering utopians seem to hold in common. Those who reject conventional society to try another style of life are expressing a need to create an environment suited to their own tastes and preferences. They are searching for themselves by getting back to the land while getting emotionally closer to other human beings. For some modern communards, the story of utopian living described by B. F. Skinner a quarter century ago is still a model.

Walden Two

Psychologist B. F. Skinner's novel *Walden Two* (1948) got little public notice for 15 years after its publication. Then, in the 1960s, the book ran swiftly on the crest of a wave of renewed interest in utopia. Its message was heard

Divorce—1970s Style

Along with the changes in styles of living together come changes in *not* living together. Over the last few decades our styles of divorce have changed markedly. Alimony is becoming a thing of the past. Divorced women are increasingly supporting themselves by their own employment and do not depend on alimony (Bohannan, 1970). The spectacular extent to which this has become true in recent years is reflected in the rate at which women return to work after a divorce. In 1940, 25.7 percent; in 1969, 42 percent, and in 1967, 71.2 percent of divorced women (over 16) were in the labor force.

Perhaps the most significant change in divorce styles was the elimination of the adversary divorce. Before the idea of "no-fault divorce" became a reality, the law required that one party had to be accused of bad behavior,

and the other—usually the wife—proved blameless. This forced battle between innocent and guilty usually meant the couple had to make up or exaggerate their differences and make the long list of misbehaviors available to the public—and the gossips. The modern style of divorce takes the position that, if one or both persons cannot bear to live with the other, there is enough reason to dissolve the union. The details of why they cannot manage life together are private and no one else's business.

You can see, of course, how such changes in styles and attitudes of divorce have contributed to the increasing divorce statistics. With the legal hassles out of the way, however, the psychological problems involved in deciding to divorce are becoming more apparent. (See the box titled "The Psychology of Divorce.")

by a generation of young people discontent with the existing styles of living. Skinner's ideas of a community offered young people an alternative—a way to "start all over again the right way." The society was to be one in which human problems were solved by a scientific technology of human conduct—the forerunner of modern behavioristic psychology.

According to the plan, daily labor was to be rewarded with labor-credits rather than money. Since all goods and services were to be shared in common, only four hours of work would be required of each citizen each day. Babies were to be raised in climate-controlled Skinner boxes until their first year of growth was over. They would then be moved to group quarters with the other one- to three-year-olds. There, surrounded by child-sized furniture, they would be taught freedom from envy, jealousy, and other annoying emotions. Child training would be accomplished by behavioral engineering. For example, children would be taught self-control by standing patiently for five minutes before "steaming bowls of soup," even when they were ravenously hungry. After five minutes elapsed, a coin would be flipped. If "heads" turned up,

Started in the 1960s, the Lama Foundation in New Mexico is a religious group whose members practice Eastern meditation and live together in an ashram (religious retreat).

VISITING WALDEN TWO TODAY

A recently formed commune called Twin Oaks is attempting to use Skinner's Walden Two *as a guide to its evolution as a community. A resident of Twin Oaks observed there is a particular kind of visitor that makes the whole community uncomfortable, but they are invited because they bring in much-needed cash. These visitors are the psychology or sociology classes from nearby colleges who come with their professor to be shown around the buildings and farm. After a two-hour discussion, they go back home. The trouble with these people is that their interest in community is minimal. Twin Oaks is a field trip for them, generally taken after having read* Walden Two. *On two occasions the professors have been kind enough to show the Twin Oaks residents some of the students' evaluations. As one resident said: "We sit around the dining room tables reading them aloud to each other. Some of us laugh. Others just swear."*

the child would be allowed to sit down to eat. The "tails" meant five more minutes of self-control. This, and related exercises, would form the basis of ethical training for children. Reward would be the keynote, and punishment would be outlawed.

Women would marry young and bear children early. Sex would become a natural, pleasurable, honorable, and admired activity. Finished with child bearing by the age of 22 or 23, the women would still be young in mind and body and would be free to lead fulfilling lives. The classic form of the family would disappear in Walden Two, since there would be separate rooms for husband and wife. Simple friendship between the sexes would be encouraged. Trial marriage would be sanctioned; easy divorce provided; and children would be raised by the community rather than the parent pair.

Psychology usually deals with the internal psychic life of the individual and finds itself on alien soil when expected to answer questions about how man ought to live in community with other human beings. In *Walden Two,* B. F. Skinner made a first attempt at applying psychology to the whole man in a social environment. It is a significant comment on the state of psychological knowledge that no comparable scenario has been written by theorists of psychoanalytic, humanistic, or other psychological persuasions. As we will see, what René Dubos (1961) called the utopian "dreams of reason" involve a host of psychological problems. As he said of utopian experiments in the past: "Dreams of human harmony were soon dispelled in the heat of human conflicts and rivalries under practical conditions. Utopias invariably bring out the traits of human nature—and there are many obvious ones—that stand in the way of unselfish and stable relationships" (p. 47).

Today's Search for Eden

The communards and the communard-watchers have begun to write and publish in a flood of words (Atcheson, 1971; Diamond, 1971; Houriet, 1971; Mungo, 1971). In his review of several recent works, Bennet Berger (1971) notes: "Their image of the good life is one of friends as family always gathered round, possessing and consuming as little as they need rather than as much as they can be induced to want; the communal household set amidst green fields and hills and valleys—a household always full of people putting out good vibes, brothers and sisters living harmoniously with nature, spending their time together working, playing, eating, drinking, smoking, loving, rapping, hanging out" (p. 6).

This romanticized view of life is an image of a sheltered society in which the young never mature to play a significant or meaningful role in the conduct of human affairs. They never grow to reach beyond the pleasures and gratifications of the self. From the available accounts of current utopias, it is apparent no magical solution has been found. The unending procession of disturbing personal hassles still seems to be an inevitable accompaniment to any scene where humans try to live together in peace and deep understanding.

An additional problem is posed by the psychological composition of today's communal movement. As Philip Slater (1970) noted in his book, *The Pursuit of Loneliness,* it is ironic that young people who form communes seem bent on creating the same kind of narrow society in which they themselves were formed and from which they fled in desperation. Any community which subtracts old people, children, white-collar and blue-collar workers, and all variety of eccentric and conventional human types is no community at all—it is only a deformed version of the larger society.

The notion of a return to the nurturing land waxes bright in the romantic fantasies of white, middle-class, urban-born-and-bred young people. This is primarily because such a life is so distant from everything they have ever known. Dissatisfied with urban life, they declare concrete, glass, and stainless steel the cause of their unhappiness. Popular communal sentiment hopes that straight America will collapse because of its inherent hypocrisy and corruptness. But if this prediction were to come true, the existing communes (which often depend on the largesse of the surrounding culture) would topple with it.

The Commune and Tomorrow

The condition of American communes today might best be described as a weakening "holding action." Some have survived the past few years; others have disappeared completely. New communes are being formed no faster than old ones are disbanding.

The typical commune of a few years ago was an experiment in anarchy, held together by the hope that people could live in harmony without rules,

SELF-SUFFICIENCY
One goal that most communal groups consider—but abandon as unreachable—is self-sufficiency. The Jehovah's Witnesses, who believe that utopia is in the next world, have become self-sufficient at their international headquarters in Brooklyn, New York. Bethel houses 1,400 Witnesses in dormitory style in a group that combines the cooperative spirit of the commune with technological sophistication. Witnesses make their own ink; do their own dry cleaning; repair their own shoes; and run their own carpentry, machine, and electrical shops. They also build their own furniture and have their own surgeon, dentist, and nurses. The food they eat comes from self-sufficient Witness-owned-and-operated farms that grow grains, fruits, and vegetables; raise hogs, cattle, and chickens; and make cheese, jellies, and relishes.

leaders, or coercion. These notions left the communards vulnerable to problems created by their own middle-class conditioning, by hostile outsiders, and by disease. Not many communes are forming today, and not many early ones have lasted without changing and tightening up. History is seldom kind to the innocent or the dreamer.

Much more frequent today are religious communes. They are sexless, dopeless, and spotless Jesus people, yogists, Satgurujis, and Hare Krishnans. Their communes have considerable survival power built on the strength of their devotional energy and by their acceptance of hierarchical social structures.

What's happening now is mostly family farms and groups of couples dividing their collective meadows. They are not really communes, but still communities.

A betting man, at this point in history, would probably be willing to make good odds on the failure, within the next ten years, of most communes now extant in the United States. . . . The "smart money" is against the continued existence of most communes, hip, religious, or political. Communes are threatened both externally and internally; externally because communalists have little power in their dealings with the outside world and internally because of the possibilities of decay from within. [Roberts, 1971, p. 111]

The Psychology of Divorce

Being human, most of you will wind up married someday. And many of you will then get divorced. Before the turn of the century, there was one divorce for every 18 marriages. Following World War II, there was one divorce for each 3.8 marriages. The rate has remained quite stable since then.

Shifting social sentiments and changing social conditions have contributed to a more enlightened attitude about divorce, which in turn has led to the higher divorce rate in recent years. In a number of cases, for example, the divorce is no more serious than a drifting apart of persons who were once close to each other. Even so, the decision to divorce is complicated by the fact that at least half of the divorces involve children. The total number of children of divorce doubled between 1953 and 1966, and the average number per divorce increased by about one-third. There are now more than 6 million American "divorced" children under 18.

We know relatively little about the psychological effect that divorce has on the young. When Judson T. Landis (1960) questioned 3,000 college students, he did find that the children from broken homes started dating later than children from happy marriages, dated fewer persons, and dated less frequently. Of course, these findings are 15 years old and our more accepting attitudes about divorce may have alleviated such effects. Nevertheless, twice as many of the children from divorced or unhappy homes express doubts about the chances of having a successful marriage of their own. These fears are probably realistic since it appears divorce is more frequent among the children of divorced parents.

The degree of emotional shock experienced by a child of divorce depends on how the parents deal with each other before the divorce. Divorce can be an enormous shock to the child who once considered the home happy and the parents well-adjusted to each other. By the same token, the children of battling parents can feel relief when the conflict finally ends. Whatever the circumstances, however, divorce usually increases the emotional distance between father and child, and this is bound to alter some part of the pattern of growing up. In addition, divorce may create problems for the child as a consequence of (1) conflict created because of a deep attachment to both parents; (2) continuing awareness of the parents' marital problem (which the child may carry with him for the rest of his life); (3) the need to deal with the consequences of having had parents who could not agree on the proper balance of freedom and restraint; (4) the inevitable comparison of his own life with the lives of children from normal homes; (5) the development of emotionally disturbing attitudes toward his parents; (6) the possibility of becoming a stepchild; and (7) the strain of shifting between households with different sets of standards.

Our new attitudes toward divorce have led to the increasing realization that divorce is not just a psychological problem for the children—but one for the adults as well. Paul Bohannan (1970) points out that, because most of us are ignorant of what it involves, divorce is likely to be traumatic. The experience of separation is a complex happening. In each instance it involves: (1) the emotional problem of the deteriorating marriage; (2) the legal problems; (3) the economic problems of money and property; (4) the problems of custody, single-parent homes, and visitation; (5) the problems involving changes in friends and community; and (6) the psychic problem of regaining individual autonomy (Bohannan, 1970, p. 157).

The emotional divorce, in Bohannan's view, produces people who are likely to feel hurt and angry. The legal divorce makes them bewildered. The economic divorce may make them feel cheated, and the parental divorce causes them to worry about what is going to happen to the children. The community divorce may make them disenchanted with their friends, and the psychic divorce may reestablish fear and loneliness.

The idea of communes "working," flourishing, or succeeding is beside the point in the case of the communes now existing in America. The success or longevity of the enterprise itself is of no consequence. What is essential is the experience of a life of voluntary poverty or, at least, a life of modest means. The important aspect is the learning of uncompetitive, cooperative, neighborly sharing (Katz, 1971).

The collapse of attempts at communal life has been attributed to a variety of causes: too little advance preparation for the adventure, too little capital, too little screening of the motives of the members, too little experience with the agricultural basis of community effort, and too little recognition of the difficulties inherent in any social experiment surrounded by a larger alien society. The experiments that have succeeded in other societies have been essential parts of the culture—not angry rejections of it. One example of such success is the kibbutz.

The Kibbutz

The traditional American styles of family life and child rearing have come under attack by those who no longer think ours is a "natural" or particularly effective way to raise children. The critics of the nuclear family point to the kibbutz system in Israel as a model more suited to modern times.

In the kibbutz, children routinely relate to the group from early in life. From the beginning, the child learns to trust his environment and the people in it. Research indicates, however, that the psychosocial maturity of Austrian, Israeli, Polish, or Yugoslavian young people raised either at home or in group-care settings failed to differ significantly (Goldman, 1971).   n

The first wave of immigrants to Israel experimented with this new lifestyle. They banned marriage for the first five years of pioneering. When the first child was born, communal care was designed, and a new family pattern was initiated—a startlingly radical move involving an end to the traditional structure of the Jewish family. The traditional division of labor that confined women to the home and excluded them from social and economic life ceased to exist (Rabkin and Rabkin, 1969). The kibbutz offered women freedom and equality. Only childbirth remained an inescapable female assignment. In the kibbutz, husband and wife were treated as individuals with independent jobs and roles in society (Talmon-Garber, 1954).

Children were raised by community members assigned to this specific task. Children slept, ate, and studied in special houses, and each age group led its own life—a unique social arrangement. For the kibbutz child, a sense of "we" and "they" emerges early in life. Children support their group against others, exclude out-group members from play, and show concern when a member is absent. They share objects in the children's house, and the child who shares is praised lavishly. According to Rabkin and Rabkin (1969), the kind of young adult that emerges from this pattern of communal child rearing is a healthy, intelligent, generous, somewhat shy, but warm human being whose roots are both in his community and the larger Israeli society. He seems free of emotional disturbance and expresses satisfaction with communal living.

Some theorists try to relate the kibbutz experience to present-day America by suggesting that communal child rearing might be the answer to the problems of children who are exposed to disruptive broken families. Could such group socialization eliminate the psychological damage suffered by our disadvantaged young? Probably not. Communal child rearing is no panacea, and these socialization practices are not likely to be transported intact to the American scene until we are prepared to drastically overhaul the goals of our society. It is folly to release children into an individualistic, competitive society after rearing them collectively and teaching them to prize cooperation and responsibility for one's group rather than individual accomplishment. No extended communal child rearing plan has been tested in America, so we can only speculate.

The Communes of Europe and Asia

When a society decides the level of its productivity is a critical feature in survival, it eliminates the traditional family pattern. "To a certain extent, this has been the policy of all Western societies at war and most systematically of the Hebrew kibbutz and the Chinese commune" (Pitts, 1964). In China, the communal movement was designed to undermine traditional loyalty to the *Tsu* (the father's clan) and to substitute a new loyalty to the communist state. The commune successfully took over many of the family's functions (helping the family with wedding or funeral arrangements, coping with financial emergencies, schooling, and so forth). In both the Soviet Union and China, the economic revolution produced significant social change as it freed the woman from home drudgery and the care of small children (Yang, 1959).

In the Soviet Union, collective child rearing moved into a new phase with the expansion of nurseries and kindergartens and the introduction of boarding schools and "schools of the prolonged day." Soviet infants are placed in group playpens with six or eight children. Their later regime of training is described by Bronfenbrenner (1970): "Each child is on what a Western psychologist would view as a series of reinforcement schedules; that is, the upbringer spends a specified amount of time with him in stimulating and training sensory-motor functions" (p. 17). Children are taught to share in work and play and to evaluate and criticize one another for the good of the group in order to become "New Soviet Men and Women."

Soviet children, controlled by collective values and peer-group standards, grow up to be polite, considerate, well-behaved adults. But some observers suggest the New Soviet Man is also docile, conformist, and without creative originality. As Field stated: "I have often wondered why with such a wonderful upbringing, life and the people in the Soviet Union are so often gray and morose" (1970, p. 3). Field concludes that the Soviets have designed a pattern of child rearing geared to the requirements of both an authoritarian and industrial society—child rearing that produces adults who will fit smoothly and obediently into assigned social slots.

An American Commune

The Hutterian Brethren of the Great Plains region in America and Canada are singular examples of long-term, successful communes. These colonies have been in existence since 1874 and are still flourishing. More than 18,000 members of this Christian communal sect are organized in farm colonies of about 150 members each. Since they believe it is sinful to marry outside the sect, the present descendants all stem from the original 101 couples. When colonies get too large (population doubles about every 15 years), land is purchased, and a new colony is formed. The "cardinal principles of the Hutterites are pacifism, adult baptism, the communal ownership of all property, and simple living. Jewelry, art, and overstuffed chairs are regarded as sinful luxuries. Radio sets and the movies are taboo. Children are the only possessions to which there is no limit: the average completed family has more than ten" (Eaton and Weil, 1955, p. 439).

Hutterite children are trained from infancy to accept the social system and to suppress ambitions and material desires. At three years of age, children are shifted from family care to nursery schools to learn the Hutterite way of life. Between birth and age 12, the children are almost completely insulated from contact with the outside world. At best, youngsters may catch a quick glimpse of the "other civilization" during brief trips to nearby small towns.

It is a severe way of life, but it seems to eliminate a great many of the social problems we have in our society. The history of the Hutterites records no case of murder, arson, sex crime, severe physical assault, divorce, or family desertion. Members of the Hutterian Brethren do suffer emotional disorders and do have problems, but they seem comparatively freer of the difficulties that haunt the outside world.

Summary

1. When the quality of life is less than we desire, experimentation in living styles usually takes place either to escape or to make life more bearable. The search for communal environments has typically occurred in this country during times of social ferment. Change has occurred because of the radical movements of feminism, black liberation, and interest in the occult.

2. Several of the early American experiments in alternative living styles resulted from religious beliefs. The Shakers believed that a young woman was Christ incarnate, whereas the Oneidans believed that Christ had already returned in 70 A.D.

3. The Shakers believed that lust was the basis of sin and therefore eliminated almost all contact between the two sexes. Celibacy, communal property, and withdrawal from the world were part of the Shaker creed.

4. The Oneidans, in contrast to the Shakers, permitted free sexual relations between all males and all females in the community. They too believed in communal ownership of property.

5. Many of those individuals who have looked into communal living or group marriage arrangements are middle-class married couples. The wives are usually seeking ways to use their talents and overcome their isolation. The husbands are interested in financial security and leaving the rat race.

6. Individuals found in communes today are trying to live in an environment they can create and control themselves. They wish

to be close to nature and to other human beings and lead a life that is relatively hassle-free. Most American communes are based on the belief that the outside society is hypocritical and corrupt.

7. Many communal experiments fail because the individuals who come to them are not prepared for the hardships of living off the land and living with a number of other people. Today's communes also incorporate many of the faults they rejected in the outside society. They have, for example, often limited membership in their communities to young intellectuals from middle-class backgrounds.

8. Walden Two was a community envisoned by psychologist B. F. Skinner and based on the principles of behavioral psychology. It is the most complete picture of a utopia to come out of any psychological school of thought. A commune called Twin Oaks has been modeled after Skinner's ideal.

9. Although the majority of communes fail in a short time, the strongest seem to be those formed along religious lines. That may be because of the great devotional energy of the members and because these communes do not shirk from using rules and hierarchical structures.

10. The longest thriving American commune is the Hutterian Brethren of the Great Plains, founded 100 years ago. Members of the Hutterite commune are almost completely isolated from the outside world and have been taught the virtues of communal property and a very simple life. Despite its severity, Hutterite life is free of crime and family breakdown and has fewer emotional disorders.

11. The kibbutz of Israel are communes that function as an essential part of Israeli society, rather than being a rejection of it. Its most distinctive feature is communal child rearing that eliminates our conception of the nuclear family and leaves both husband and wife free to pursue their own interests on the kibbutz.

12. Children raised in the kibbutz have a strong sense of cooperation and group spirit and develop a great attachment to Israeli society. They appear to grow up without emotional difficulties.

13. Although some people argue that communal child rearing would benefit the United States, it would probably be disastrous unless many of our basic values—such as competition—were overthrown.

14. From their infancy, Soviet children spend most of their days with other children, learning cooperation in work and play. They also learn the importance of criticizing one another for the good of the group. Some people suggest that the Soviet method of child rearing creates people who will fit neatly into an authoritarian and industrial society.

15. Freedom to divorce has increased. Divorces now can be granted if both parties agree. The principle of alimony is slowly disappearing.

16. Divorce, however, creates problems if children are involved. Though the separation may be a relief from the conflict, children can still be upset by a number of aspects of their parents' split. These children may have less happier marriages themselves.

17. The divorce may be equally traumatic for the adults involved, especially if they are not aware of the many problems and life changes they are about to undergo as a result of severing the marriage bond.

PSYCHOLOGICAL ISSUE

Marriage

In times past, marriage was clearly a cooperative, legal arrangement. The men of the family brought in the harvest; the women canned and prepared it; and the children milked the cows or gathered eggs. The family unit was necessary for survival (Lederer and Jackson, 1968). In modern industrialized society, the traditional family unit and our notions of romantic love are both under assault by an increasing number of persons experimenting with new styles of living together.

Most young people today still marry persons pretty much like themselves. They marry people with whom they are in daily contact, and they view marriage in much the same way their parents do. Despite the progress women have made toward achieving freedom of choice in marriage, the fact remains that the single woman or the childless wife in our society are still considered social deviates (Dixon, 1970). The most popular single age for getting married is still 18 (one-fourth marry at this age), but, on the average, most women marry closer to the age of 21. The preliminaries to marriage have changed since the good old days, and even the style of courtship has been computerized. Young people may now register their needs, desires, preferences, and interests with a data bank that promises to match them with a suitable partner. Clearly, at this point in American history, there is an enormous number of new styles of living together.

Styles of Marriage

In all probability, marriage will exist longer than most of our institutions, but that doesn't mean it will always follow the same style. Even now, so-called ordinary marriages differ from couple to couple because each individual in a marriage requires something different from the partnership. Much of the experimentation in marriage styles—and the changes going on within existing marriages—result from each couple's need to deal with a number of issues that only recently have come into question. Indeed, most of the issues involve

Wedded Bliss? Full-fledged marital happiness is, apparently, difficult to achieve. In intensive interviews with married partners, only 45 to 50 percent of them described their marriage as successful (Young, 1962). In addition, Hunt (1971) reports that the ideal of being faithful to one's partner is not always fulfilled. It is not that the adulterers in our society are always unhappy with the wedded state. It is just that sexual relations outside of marriage may fulfill a variety of other human needs, such as reassurance about one's attractiveness, youthfulness, power, achievement, and acceptance. Still, theorists predict that monogamy, for all its limitations, will survive the experimental assaults on it (Rostow, 1970).

Single Bliss? A larger proportion of men and women under 35 are staying single than in the recent past. The U.S. Bureau of Census reports a 1971 survey showing that 56 percent of men and 45 percent of women under 35 were single that year. In 1960, only 51 percent of men and 37 percent of women were single. Census Bureau officials are uncertain whether the change reflects an increasing tendency to delay marriage until later years, or whether more of today's young people will remain single for their entire lives.

working out the relative amount of freedom allowed each spouse in a relationship that has been traditionally restrictive. The problem of whether the couple will live its own life rather than devote most of its time to child rearing is under scrutiny. Another problem is whether each individual should feel free to develop himself or herself fully and honestly, even at the expense of weakening the marriage bond. Will traditional male-female roles be taken, or will the woman work outside the home while her husband takes over some of the housekeeping responsibilities? Does the pairing relationship have a time limit, or is life-long commitment assumed? Are both spouses free to have other sexual relationships, or will traditional monogamy be the rule? Of course, these issues have always been implicit in marriage bonds, but only recently have couples begun to look into the alternatives to traditional marital patterns. And of course, the way in which they ultimately resolve these problems will greatly affect the styles of their marriage.

Interracial Marriage

In 1967, the U.S. Supreme Court overturned a Virginia law forbidding marriages between whites and blacks. The fact that Virginia and sixteen other states had passed such laws in the first place testifies to the hostility toward interracial marriages felt in some parts of society. Nevertheless, mixed marriages are increasing.

The Census Bureau reported a significant increase in interracial marriages between 1960 and 1970. The

The First Protest In 1848 the Women's Rights Convention insisted that the promise of obedience in the marriage contract was barbarian and should be abolished. This was the first time in history a mass meeting of women assaulted a major assumption of marriage—that women and children had to obey husbands and fathers in order to maintain the stability and welfare of families. Always, in the past, divorce was a male privilege. Now women initiate legal action in almost seven out of eight divorce cases in the United States (Fuchs, 1972).

1970 census showed a total of 16,419 black men who had married white women during the decade. In 1960, the census report showed only 7,534 such marriages over a similar time span. The number of white men with black wives during a ten-year period totaled 7,352 in 1970, compared with 6,082 in 1960. The total of all interracial marriages with black husbands and white wives was 41,223 in 1970 (compared with 25,476 in 1960). Marriages between white husbands and black wives totaled 23,566 in 1970 (compared with 25,913 in 1960).

The number of new, socially mixed marriages is not only increasing, but there is evidence that American society is becoming more tolerant—at least in terms of expressed attitudes given to public opinion pollsters. The polls report, on the average, about a 10 percent increase in approval over the last four years, but this leaves nearly 75 percent of our society still disapproving.

Ernest Porterfield (1973) reports that, "Almost one American in five has dated someone not of his or her own race, according to a 1971 Louis Harris survey. The figure rises to one in three on the West Coast and for young persons (21 to 25) across the nation. In the South, the figure falls below one in ten" (p. 71). In Porterfield's survey of 20 marriages between blacks and whites in a midwestern city, the parents and relatives of 12 of the 16 white brides opposed their marriages. For 11 of these couples, the white parents and relatives had not changed their attitudes, even after the pair had been married from one and a half to four years. Seven white brides reported having little or no contact with their families.

In sharp contrast, the relatives of all the black spouses gradually accepted the white partners, and only one of the four black brides encountered such family opposition. It was precisely this hostile reaction from their families that proved to be the most emotionally disturbing feature of some of these marriages. Porterfield observed that the wives could ignore most of the pressures from society, but their parents' rejection of

them and their children seemed to be devastating. Interestingly, the race of the husband seems to determine where an interracial couple will live. When the husband is white, the couple usually lives in a white neighborhood. If he is black, they live in a black neighborhood.

In a rapidly changing society, interracial marriage is just one aspect of our increasing experimentation with new and different styles of living. It is a form of experimentation that has increased noticeably following every war in which our young men are sent to live in societies with values differing from our own.

War Brides.   The American Dream can become a nightmare for Oriental war brides. Casework in Los Angeles on ten American-Japanese couples who had returned to this country after World War II found only three wives still living with their husbands. As long as the couple had stayed in the Orient, the stabilized relationship worked. The wives found security and happiness, and the husbands enjoyed the unquestioning respect, gratitude, and attention the wives gave them. Once in the United States, however, some husbands became disenchanted with their wives' total dependency and submission—qualities they had once valued. The husbands' complaints made the wives fear desertion, and the marriage relationship deteriorated rapidly.

After Experimentation, What?

When Leo Davids (1971) tried to imagine what form American marriage might take in the year 1990, he saw startling possibilities. For one, he saw an end to the myth that parenthood is "fun," accompanied by a more realistic conviction that it is a serious, trying, time-consuming task. He thinks giving birth will eventually come under community control; husband-wife roles will be equalized; and abortion and new forms of marriage will be commonplace. There will be parent licensing to screen out unfit parents. Courtship will be computerized. Marital option contracts will be popular. And childless trial marriages as well as compound marriages will become commonplace. The right to bear children will be regulated, and fewer than one-third of married couples will be allowed to propagate. Those permitted to bear young will undergo suitable testing, qualification, and intensive parent training beforehand, and male parents may be prohibited from working full time during a child's growing years.

How we get together and with what joy and pain we stay together or separate has been the subject of almost continual experimentation for mankind. The style of life suited to one era disappears as its particular crises ease and demands for new variations are heard. I think Margaret Mead summed it up best with her observation:

Whenever there is a period of upheaval in the world, somebody's going to do something to the family. If the family's being very rigorous and puritanical, you loosen it up. And if it's being very loose, you tighten it up. But you have to change it to really feel you're accomplishing something. If we go back into history we find over and over again, in moments of revolutionary change, that people start talking about family, and what they're doing to it, and what's wrong with it. They even predict it's going to disappear altogether. It is in fact the only institution we have that doesn't have a hope of disappearing. [1971, p. 52]

Summary

1. The majority of the American population still believes in traditional forms of marriage. Despite the fact that many individuals are marrying later or refusing to marry, the single people in our society are still regarded as social deviates.

2. Experimentation in marriage is primarily an attempt to confront issues that have not been questioned until recently. Changing social codes regarding sexual permissiveness, abortion, birth control, and women's rights have led couples to make deliberate choices about babies, length of marriage, roles of spouses, and individual freedom in the partnership.

3. Interracial marriages are increasing, and more people in our society seem to be accepting them. Most interracial couples state that their major difficulties stem from disapproval by parents—not by the larger society.

The World of Work

Work keeps at bay three great evils: boredom, vice, and need.—Voltaire

We are members of a culture that weans us on fierce individualism, independence, the myth of rags-to-riches, and a deep-rooted, absolute belief in a personal destiny limited only by imagination, enterprise, energy, self-denial, and "sticktuitiveness." At the very heart of these Christian virtues is the idea that a man can be defined by his work. As Thomas Carlyle told us in 1843: "Older than all preached Gospels was this unpreached, inarticulate, but ineradicable, forever-enduring Gospel: Work, and therein have well being."

The world of work is the adult arena in which we display competence, just as the school world is the contest arena for the child. In the life of men, working gives a feeling of being tied to the larger society, of having a purpose in life. When a sample of workers were asked whether they would stop work if they inherited enough money to live comfortably without working, an overwhelming 80 percent answered that they would continue to work anyway (Morse and Weiss, 1968). Whereas two-thirds of working men give positive reasons beyond need for continuing to work, one-third are certain that being without a job would make them feel lost, useless, and unable to decide what to do with their time. Thus, some of us work to ward off a sense of loneliness and isolation. We feel that we would "go crazy" if we didn't have a task to do each day.

Work is vital for most Americans, since the job becomes the organizing center of life. For the average man, work regulates his life activity, fixes his position in society and in his group, and determines many of his satisfactions and experiences" (Aiken, Ferman, and Sheppard, 1968). It is precisely this

THE PROTESTANT WORK ETHIC

The Protestant ethic states that if you work hard, life's rewards will come without fail. The ideal man in the Protestant tradition is one who is not distracted by activities unrelated to his work. He postpones the pleasure of prestige for the future. He conserves his assets for a time of need, and he uses surplus wealth to extend his economic enterprise even though it means self-denial. Because of this Protestant tradition of self-denial and hard work, "The standard work week in 1900 was 54 to 60 hours or more; a person steadily employed in a manufacturing plant thus worked about 3,000 hours per year. Today such a worker averages fewer than 40 hours a week and receives a paid vacation, putting in only about 2,000 hours a year" (Mack, 1967). Today the Protestant ethic is beginning to weaken. More value is accorded to being, as opposed to doing.

VACATION TIME

Members of the American upper middle class have an unusual view of the proper relation between work and play. An American businessman or professional man may apologize for taking a vacation by insisting it is only "to recharge his batteries"; he justifies rest or play primarily in terms of returning to do a better job. In contrast, the European seems to enjoy his vacation as a pleasure in its own right and deliberately works to be able to afford to play in better style. "For example, many Europeans seem to plan intensely, a year ahead, how they will spend their vacations. Once on vacation, they would resent any interruption for work—such as a business phone call—far more than any American would. It is the vacation that, at the time at least, deserves to be taken more seriously—not the work."
[Kahn and Wiener, 1967, p. 214]

emphasis on work that multiplies the importance of having a job in our society. A task to be done becomes an earthwork erected to ward off insecurity (Lerner, 1958).

Industrial Psychology

In America, the greatest rewards of money and power go to those who are successful in corporate leadership. For more than a century, business has been the most sought-after vocational field in America.

Early in the twentieth century, business and industry began to apply psychological techniques. The earliest contributions to industry from psychological laboratories involved learning curves for new tasks, attention, and fatigue. Efficiency experts were also produced to make time and motion studies. In more recent years, research into industrial accidents led to the discovery of accident-prone individuals and situations that cause costly errors and injuries.

"Engineering psychology" has covered such topics as systems design, automation, machines responsive to speech and handwriting, feedback signals, prosthetic devices for amputees, lighting problems, safety equipment, and legibility of type and of instrument scales (Fitts, 1958). Industrial psychologists have also been closely associated with processes of selecting and promoting workers. Using a combination of tests, life-history data, and interviews, psychologists can make a reasonably accurate estimate of whether an individual is likely to be happy and successful in a particular job, under a particular kind of supervision. One review (Ward, 1960) showed that about 60 percent of companies with 10,000 or more employees use psychological tests in the selection of salaried employees.

The Work Motives

When you do an activity solely for the pleasure of it, psychologists say you are *intrinsically motivated* since the activity is its own reward. If you do something for an outside reward such as money, good grades, or to avoid punishment, you would be described as *extrinsically motivated*. Edward Deci (1972) devised an experimental puzzle called Soma to explore intrinsic and extrinsic work motivation. He gave each subject four puzzle-problems to solve. After completing the four puzzles, each subject was left alone to do whatever he wished: read magazines, solve more puzzles, or whatever interested him.

If he spent his free time playing with the Soma game, this became a measure of intrinsic motivation for that activity. In one experiment, half of the subjects were told they would get a dollar for each correct solution to a puzzle, while the other half were not paid for getting the right answers. Deci discovered that money made a big difference. Subjects who were paid spent significantly less time with the puzzles when they were alone than did subjects who had worked the same puzzles for free. Intrinsic motivation decreased when subjects were given an external reward.

In other experiments, threats of punishment produced the same effect. An obnoxious buzzer would blast if the puzzle weren't solved within a time limit. But working to avoid this threat produced little intrinsic motivation. In much the same way, being paid for working on the puzzle whether or not correct solutions were reached showed no change in the degree of intrinsic motivation. It is apparent that, when a person works for no apparent reward, he is likely to explain his behavior in terms of *internal* motivation. If he works for reward or to escape punishment, he will attribute his behavior to *external* forces.

Interestingly, when experimental subjects were rewarded with praise for each correct solution, intrinsic motivation increased markedly. These subjects reported that they liked the puzzles more and also spent more free time working on puzzles than did subjects who were not praised. Deci concluded that an intrinsically motivated activity is one that provides feelings of competence and self-determination. Positive verbal reinforcement reaffirms the individual's confidence in himself and makes him feel more competent. Deci states:

> *If we want individuals to enjoy what they do, to derive joy and satisfaction from their work as well as their play, we must do two things. We must create more activities that are inherently interesting and gratifying; and we must not use extrinsic rewards in a way that will lower the interest level of those activities that are intrinsically motivated.* [1972, p. 92]

The Hawthorne Effect

In the late 1920s, Elton Mayo and his colleagues at Harvard became convinced that workers would work harder if they were happier. The problem was that no one quite knew how to make workers happy. A series of experiments were undertaken, the most famous of which was done at the Hawthorne works of the Western Electric Company near Chicago, Illinois. The original description of the results was reported by Roethlisberger and Dickinson in 1938. The subjects were women who assembled telephone equipment.

Before the Harvard group became involved in these studies, the company had explored the effects of lighting and discovered that increases in lighting improved work performance. A simple change in working conditions seemed to be the answer until the lighting was decreased experimentally and it was found that efficiency *didn't* decrease. Obviously, lighting itself was not the critical factor. The researchers then investigated how rest might affect performance. They moved a group of women to a special area called the "relay assembly room," where their performance could be closely measured. Increased rest produced greater efficiency, but this efficiency remained even when the rest periods were then reduced. These unpredictable findings could, of course, be attributed to the fact that experimental subjects often respond quite differently when they are in a nonexperimental setting. It was quite evident, for example, that the women developed very high morale during the experiment. They became extremely motivated to work hard and well. The reasons for this high morale were: (1) the women felt special because they had been singled out for a research role (showing that management thought they were important) and (2) they had already developed good relationships with one another and with their supervisor. They had been given considerable freedom to develop their own pace of work and to divide the work among themselves in a manner they found most comfortable. On a small scale, this research effort of the 1920s revealed a basic principle that remains applicable in today's highly industrialized society.

This principle, which has come to be known as the *Hawthorne effect,* refers to the effects on performance of participation in an experiment and emphasizes the importance of attitudes and interpersonal relations in work motivation. On the job, the actual working conditions may be less important to morale than the workers' feelings that management is concerned about their welfare.

In recent years, as new generations of workers have replaced their elders, other concerns have arisen. One of these is about the possible dehumanizing effect of labor in a totally man-made setting.

Humanizing Work

The industrial psychologist McGregor (1960) suggested that a theory of human nature, in the form of a set of assumptions, underlies most industrial organizations. These assumptions, which he called *theory X,* include the following. Everyone dislikes work and will try in every way to avoid it. This in turn

THE INVISIBLE BLUE COLLARS
Despite their numbers, young blue-collar workers—18- to 24-year-old men and women—may be the "forgotten people" of the 1970s. These young workers constitute the largest single group in the country whose needs have not been considered and whose consciousness remains remote from mainstream leaders. When most people discuss the 18- to 21-year-old voters, they tend to think of campus youth, even though 70 percent of the young people between 18 and 24 are not in school. There is dissatisfaction among blue-collar workers, but we hear about it only when young assembly-line workers foul up an automobile plant in anger at management practices.

forces the industrialist to find a way to coerce people to do their work. Further, the average person prefers to be directed and wants to avoid responsibility.

McGregor has an alternative set of principles which he calls *theory Y.* The assumptions of this theory of human nature are that the expenditure of energy is natural, that external control is not the only way to ensure good performance, that people like responsibility, that people are creative and that, under present industrial conditions, only part of the human potential is fulfilled.

It should be apparent that, if you are the manager of a business, it will make a great deal of difference whether you subscribe to theory X or theory Y. The current movement to humanize the nature of work makes a lot of sense to the Y theorist but seems like coddling workers to an X theorist. You might briefly suppose that the educational institution you are attending right now is the work setting and you are an employee. Are your professors X or Y theorists?

Making work more fitting for an adult to perform involves altering those tasks that damage, degrade, humiliate, exhaust, or persistently bore the worker. Interesting and satisfying assignments that utilize the skills of the worker must be substituted. In part this state of affairs can be achieved if we are willing to abandon some very ancient traditions. Robert Kahn (1973) suggests that, traditionally, we have fitted individuals into jobs. We have accepted the demands of the job without question and then sought persons who could best perform them. We have trained workers, assigned them to their roles, and counseled them into adjustment. All our efforts at recruitment, testing, classification, and counseling have assumed that the job is a fixed feature of work and that the right person must be discovered or fitted into the job requirements.

Kahn suggests that we start from the opposite end and seek to fit the *job* to the individual. He has designed a two-hour, time-and-task unit he calls the *work module.* Thus, a conventional job consists of four such modules per day (eight hours), five days a week, 48 or 50 weeks a year. Kahn observed that occupations in which workers make their own jobs are characteristically high in intrinsic job satisfaction. For example, professors, research scientists, and farmers are free to work independently much of the time. According to Kahn's view of work, these occupations need not be the only jobs in which freedom is possible. Take a stock man in a supermarket whose job it is to stamp prices on food containers and place the items on the shelves, for example. If all the work of the supermarket were broken down into two-hour modules, it would be possible for the stock clerk to choose to spend two modules a day stamping prices, one module at the cash register, and one module learning inventory control. Or, he might wish to change the time pattern of his work, by reducing the number of days per week and increasing the number of modules worked per day. In such a case, the nature of the job would be changed dramatically. It would be humanized.

PARTICIPATION

Alfred J. Marrow (1964) described two companies which were the same size and made the same product but differed in management style. The Harwood Manufacturing Company encouraged employee participation in planning, problem solving, goal setting, and decision making. The Weldon Company operated in a traditional hierarchy with direction from the top down. Comparing the two companies, social psychologists found Harwood superior in man-hour productivity, standards of performance, turnover, control of waste, and readiness to innovate. It was concluded that, when workers participate, they feel the resulting procedures and products are their own. "Our product" is usually regarded as better than that of others (Blake and Mouton, 1962).

Kahn notes that the probable causes of satisfaction and dissatisfaction at work revolve around the *status* of the occupation and the *job characteristics*. The higher the status of the occupation, the more satisfied are the persons who engage in it. For example, 93 percent of university professors, compared to 16 percent of unskilled auto workers, said they would seek the same type of work again. Job characteristics such as variety and autonomy also have strong effects on satisfaction and dissatisfaction. The assembly line prescribes the exact method by which a job is to be done and the speed at which it must be performed. Workers react negatively to such mechanical pacing and favor a self-determined, self-controlled pace of labor. In particular, the new generation of young people seems to be less tolerant of machine control than their parents were.

In addition, good supervisors, high pay, and high satisfaction with one's labors tend to humanize work. If you improve comfort, challenge, pay, and the opportunity for interaction with co-workers, you will increase the satisfaction workers get from their jobs.

The Crisis of Unemployment

Your parents know the meaning of unemployment from the personal experience of growing up in the Great Depression of the 1930s.

[The Depression] *marked millions of people—inwardly—for the rest of their lives. Not only because they or their friends lost jobs, saw their careers broken, had to change their whole way of living, were gnawed at by a constant lurking fear of worse things yet, and in all too many cases actually went hungry; but because what was happening to them seemed without rhyme or reason. Most of them had been brought up to feel that if you worked hard and well, and otherwise behaved yourself, you would be rewarded by good fortune. Here were failure and defeat and want visiting the energetic along with the feckless, the able along with the unable, the virtuous along with the irresponsible.* [Allen, 1952, p. 131]

From 1930 until the early 1940s, millions of people were unemployed. The psychology of being jobless became a critical feature of the work world. There were no industrial psychologists in those days, but those who went through this time of prolonged joblessness have vivid memories of the psychological impact of the experience.

The Psychology of Being Jobless

At the heart of a man's conception of himself as being capable, competent, able, and admirable is his job. When deprived of this outlet for self-expression and self-assessment, the male's inner security is lost, and deterioration of psychological well-being is inevitable.

THE WORK CURVE
Only a few highly disciplined people can work at the same pace over a long period of time. Work has its ups and downs. You probably do not study as well at the end of a long cram session as you did at the beginning, and you may not study as effectively at the very beginning as you do after a little while. All of us seem to need a kind of warm-up time to get going at any job. Once into the task we may feel an initial surge of enthusiasm, but this fades into a slower, long-distance kind of work pace. At the end of the day our enthusiasm rises again, and production increases much like the "final kick" of a runner approaching the finish line.

Dorothea Lange's striking photographs communicate some of the desperation of the Depression. In 1936, on the first day that social security payments were made available to the unemployed, men line up and wait in San Francisco. The picture on the previous page is also a Lange photo from the 1930s.

When unemployment strikes, the consequences are immediate. There is at once a reduction of contact with friends, since social obligations are expected to be returned in kind. This withdrawal from friendships also happens because the worker is deprived of social relationships in his daily work situation that once provided him with emotional and psychological support. The laborer might even lose contact with the union which gives him a sense of competence and control over his environment. Without a socially useful role, steady erosion of one's social identity begins to occur.

At first you are hopeful as you make the unending rounds of stores and factories looking for a new job. You are turned down but leave your name. Each contact with a potential employer is like buying an Irish Sweepstakes ticket that might—just might—be a winner. As the cold certainty filters into consciousness that it isn't going to be easy to get a new job, you become a little more frantic. You become less patient with the long lines of other hopefuls ahead of you. You are more irritable. Your shoes break down; your clothes become threadbare with wear; and a look of panic appears in your eyes. Laughing becomes a luxury as savings run out. Credit is extended to the breaking point, and relatives and friends can no longer lend you money. Your fear infects the family as you pawn everything of value and move to cheaper and cheaper quarters. Then, you go on relief. By now you are numb, resigned, hopeless, and almost beyond humiliation.

Bewilderment, hesitation, apathy, loss of self-confidence, were the commonest marks of protracted unemployment. A man no longer cared how he looked. Unkept hair and swarthy stubble, shoulders a-droop, a slow dragging walk, were external signs of defeat, often aggravated by malnutrition. Joblessness proved a wasting disease. What social workers called "unemployment shock" affected some men as if they were in a grip of panic, driving them to frenzied search for work by day, sleepless worry at night. To a few persons joblessness apparently brought a sense of personal importance—of being part of a national crisis, a front-page problem—but more universal was a mood of lost self-esteem, perplexity, or bitterness toward old employers and life in general. [Wecter, 1948, p. 32]

Attitudes and reactions shift over time to reflect one's stage of unemployment. If continued long enough, being jobless brings almost everyone to a final destination best described as apathy. The common response among the unemployed to the Great Depression was apathy and inaction. So many persons were chronically depressed during these hard times, that a pessimistic outlook on life seemed to be the norm.

One investigator studied men who were laid off work during the closing of a Detroit plant in 1965. A group of 54 men averaging 47 years of age were interviewed at the time of their lay off and reinterviewed 6, 12, and 24 months later. More than half of these men displayed a significant psychological or physiological change for the worse. There were seven deaths and one suicide during the time span studied—figures which were markedly out of statistical proportion to actuarial predictions for that age group.

The Unemployment Syndrome

Social scientists have for many years conducted studies dealing with the reactions of lower-class and minority workers to unemployment, but they have seldom researched the feelings and behavior of middle-class men facing the same perils of unemployment. Powell and Driscoll (1973) filled this information gap by studying what happened to a number of suddenly unemployed scientists and engineers. They determined that, when joblessness is prolonged, a series of symptoms or stages of psychological reactions are predictable.

Stage I: Period of Relaxation and Relief. Most of the men Powell and Driscoll studied initially reacted to unemployment with a sense of relief. It was seen as a chance to take a vacation at home, be with the family, sleep late, read, or pursue hobbies. The men considered themselves between jobs, and they were confident of finding work as soon as they were ready. Most of them made an effort to look for work at this stage, but this was done on a casual basis such as calling a friend or responding to an ad.

Stage II: Period of Concerted Effort. After about 25 days, the unemployed man begins to get bored with leisure and starts making a systematic, organized attempt to find work on a full-time basis. He is optimistic and

FUTURE FEAR
Unemployment leaves a legacy of fear, indelibly stamped in the consciousness of many of its survivors—a fear that can never be assuaged by any number of possessions. As one victim of the Great Depression reports: "Everyone was emotionally affected. We developed a fear of the future which was very difficult to overcome. Even though I eventually went into some fairly good jobs, there was still this constant dread: everything would be cut out from under you and you wouldn't know what to do. . . . I suspect, even now, I'm a little bit nervous about every job I take and wonder how long it's going to last—and what I'm going to do to cause it to disappear. I feel anything can happen. There's a little fear in me that it might happen again. It does distort your outlook and your feeling." [Terkel, 1970, pp: 485–86]

does not become depressed or anxious when he gets rejection letters from potential employers or no response at all. If he has savings to tide the family over, it helps in sustaining a positive, organized approach. Men who have been laid off before seem to adjust better than those who have never been out of work. Family relations during this period are good, and the wife often helps in the job search by giving moral support and encouragement.

Stage III: Period of Vacillation and Doubt. At this point the unemployed man has usually been out of work longer than ever before. He has to admit that the usual ways of finding a job are not producing results. Job-seeking behavior becomes sporadic and alternates with periods of intense activity and then none at all. At this time many men say they begin to doubt their judgment and think seriously about making a change in their careers. Increasingly, they develop a feeling of being past their prime and are convinced that being over 35 is a handicap that keeps them from finding a job. This conviction produces a deep moodiness as frustration builds and anger mounts.

Relations with others deteriorate, and family problems increase since these men feel they have become a burden on their family. After three to nine weeks, job-hunting activity comes to a virtual end.

Stage IV: Period of Malaise and Cynicism. If and when the unemployed scientist or engineer looks for a job, he may now be more concerned with protecting himself against the pain and disappointment of being turned down than in finding work. To protect his self-esteem, he may, for example, respond only to ads which ask applicants to send resumes but which don't require any personal contact.

These men now become apathetic and listless. They believe luck is more important in getting a job than anything they can do, and they stop feeling as upset and anxious as they did earlier. Now, they feel helpless. They limit social relationships to a few close friends and relatives. In the end, they give up and some stop thinking about ever returning to the working world. They can no longer see themselves in a working role.

Powell and Driscoll believe these reactions to unemployment and the frustrations associated with it are not peculiar to this specific group of individuals. Rather, these stages are typical of the sequence that goes from reduced competence and energy to listless discouragement. It is the personal tragedy of prolonged unemployment.

The Jobless Family

The impact of prolonged unemployment not only affects the internal psychological state of the unemployed individual but also alters his relationships with others. In particular, family members are the injured innocent bystanders, when the unemployed father suffers psychological disarrangement from no longer being king of the castle.

In some families, earning the money means power, prestige, and a margin of tolerance whereby male authority is never truly tested. Conflicts can often be managed by controlling the distribution of financial resources. Declining family finances force the male, often for the first time, to make choices. And, his decisions are not always considered fair and just. When the unemployed husband is home most of the day, it becomes evident that much of his authority has rested on his being away from certain kinds of family problems. His forced presence at home often brings out long-suppressed differences of opinion between husband and wife. Negotiating these differences often ends in an unaccustomed defeat for the husband. Unexpected disagreements may develop about child rearing and, as a result, unemployment inadvertently causes a great many families to experiment with new ways to raise children.

Most men do not relinquish their claims to authority without a struggle, of course. Many fight bitterly to retain their tottering thrones, despite the mixture of contempt and rebellion they experience in the family. Most react to the threat by arbitrarily escalating demands on their wives to respect them. For others, the psychological reactions assume a variety of guises. Some may display an increased "touchiness" and overemphasize authority. Issues which would have passed unnoticed in days gone by will be exploded. Increased stubbornness is another characteristic reaction. Beseiged husbands may select certain trivial strongholds for defense at any cost, even if it means loss in more fundamental realms of family life. A spiteful refusal to accede to a wife's reasonable suggestion is actually a desperate clinging to power in the family.

THE WIDENING GAP
There are 30 million women in the work force, and nearly two-thirds of them are employed as domestics, clerical, service, or sales workers. In 1968, a woman with four years of college training earned the same as a man with an eighth-grade education. Salaries of women workers have always been lower than those of men, and the gap is widening. A woman working full time in 1970 made only 57 percent of a man's income (down from 64 percent in 1955). In 1971, women with one to three years of college education still had lower incomes than men who had completed only eight years of school.

The psychological importance of work is made abundantly clear when work is not available. An incredible number of males in our society experience a substantial deterioration of personality, disintegration of emotional stability, breakdown of morale, and involvement in excessive drinking or promiscuity when they are unemployed. Some families, of course, draw closer together and "find themselves." In other families, unemployment precipitates a permanent sediment of disillusionment and bitterness. There are families that thrive only in the fat years, and others who gain something vital and important from periods of adversity.

Life Crisis and Sickness

The slings and arrows of outrageous fortune can make you sick and even kill you. Any major change in one's status or position in life can trigger physical illness. The effort to cope with such sudden, incomprehensible change depletes the store of energy usually available to resist the onslaught of disease. Clearly, the "dis-ease" which leads to physical illness is often psychological in nature.

When Holmes and Masuda (1972) interviewed 5,000 patients about life events that preceded physical illness, they uncovered an exceptional range of prior stresses and strains. These included the birth of a child, a visit by a mother-in-law, the death of a spouse, and a change in job status.

We did a study of patients who had colds and nasal infections, asking them, when they came in for medical care, to come back when they had recovered. As each returned to us, recovered, we measured the blood flow, the freedom of breathing, the swelling, and the amount of secretion in his nose. Then we began to talk with him about the event or events that had occurred before he became ill. After this conversation—about his mother-in-law, for example, or his new job—we repeated the measurements, and discovered that our talk had renewed the cold symptoms. . . . Biopsies of nasal tissue confirmed that we caused tissue damage by talking about psychologically charged events. (The mother-in-law example is not merely facetious, by the way. A person often catches a cold when his or her mother-in-law comes to visit. So many patients mentioned mothers-in-law so often that we came to consider them a common cause of disease in the U.S.) [p. 71]

Holmes and Masuda assembled a list of life events that most frequently preceded illness and attempted to identify which of these events had the greatest and which had the least physical effect. In order to establish a scale that would predict the onset of disease, they asked 394 persons to rate the degree of social readjustment demanded by each of 43 major life crises. The researchers then calculated a weight for each event. They soon discovered that the single most critical happening, in terms of necessary social readjustment, was the death of a spouse. The top ten life crises were as follows:

1. Death of spouse
2. Divorce
3. Marital separation
4. Jail term
5. Death of close family member

6. Personal injury or illness
7. Marriage
8. Fired at work
9. Marital reconciliation
10. Retirement

When these events were ranked in importance by persons of various ages, sexes, races, and incomes, it was clear that the impact of serious life changes is felt as early as adolescence. The correlation between life crises and physical illness was most visible when a series of such crises were piled one atop another at a single moment in time. A few mild alterations in life patterns had only a modest impact on health. In contrast, life crises that were rated moderate were statistically associated with 51 percent of recorded health changes. Major crises of living produced health changes in 79 percent of the patients studied in one year.

Of particular interest is the rank-ordering of life crises connected with employment and finances. These were:

Rank	Life Event
8	Fired at Work
10	Retirement
15	Business readjustment
16	Change in financial state
18	Change to different line of work
20	Mortgage over $10,000
21	Foreclosure of mortgage or loan
22	Change in responsibilities at work
26	Wife begins or stops work
30	Trouble with boss
31	Change in work hours or conditions

The sheer number of such concerns is noteworthy in any list of sickness-producing events.

High Risk, Low Risk

This relation of illness to life-crises was independently confirmed in scientific studies such as the detailed examination of 2,500 officers and enlisted men aboard three U.S. Navy cruisers. In this study, life-change data were gathered for six months and then health-change records were collected after the Navy men had spent six months at sea. In the first month of the cruise the high-risk group (those who had been exposed to severe life changes before embarking) had nearly 90 percent more illnesses than the low-risk group. And, the high-risk group reported significantly more new illnesses each month than their lower-risk fellow sailors.

The next obvious step was to inquire whether more serious crises would lead to more serious illnesses. So, researchers examined sports injuries among 100 college football players. They discovered that among those players who sustained multiple injuries a significant number were in the high-risk group. In fact, 50 percent of the members of the high-risk group suffered injuries during the season compared with only 10 percent of the players in the low-risk group. The lesson is obvious: those victimized by life suffer the most-serious consequences to their personal health. Human beings get sick during the struggle with life crises since it takes more than most of us have available to cope with a troubled environment. When life becomes too hectic and coping attempts fail, illness is the unhappy result.

Summary

1. For most people in our society, work is not just a means for making money. It is the way to define and prove oneself, and it is also the pattern along which we organize the rest of our life.

2. Industrial psychology attempts to apply psychological principles to make work pleasant and more productive. One of the main tasks of industrial psychologists has been to determine if potential employees will be happy and successful at their jobs.

3. When one does a job solely for the satisfaction of doing it, he is said to be *intrinsically motivated*. When he is given some kind of external reward for his effort, he is said to be *extrinsically motivated*.

4. Studies by Deci indicate that extrinsic rewards such as money or the avoidance of punishment can actually decrease intrinsic motivation. Praise as an extrinsic reward will increase intrinsic motivation.

5. Improving work conditions will improve worker satisfaction and, therefore, production. But the more important variable is that the workers think the management is interested in their welfare. The demonstrated importance of the employees' perceived attitude of management is known as the *Hawthorne effect*.

6. An employer's assumptions about why his employees are working will affect his policies toward them. Those who believe that all workers dislike working will probably use coercive measures to keep employees in line. Those who believe workers find fulfillment in their work and desire responsibility will do more to provide worker satisfaction.

7. Most professionals who make their own jobs report high satis-faction in employment. One way to humanize even low-status jobs, therefore, is to allow workers to select their own respon-sibilities and choose their own hours.

8. Job satisfaction can be affected by: Status, variety, autonomy, responsibility, good supervisors, good pay, and the opportunity to interact with other workers.

9. Because of the degree to which our lives and our conception of self-worth center around our work, unemployment is usually a devastating experience leading to the erosion of one's social identity.

10. As time passes, the jobless individual's outlook on life changes from one of hope, to panic, and eventually to cynicism and apathy.

11. Family life is often disrupted by unemployment, particularly if the male's power in the home rested on his bread-winning ability and minimal presence in the house. In order to retain his status, the male usually becomes insistent on his authority even in minor matters, and each dispute becomes another threat to his self-esteem.

12. Psychologists have found that any major life changes can trigger physical illness. This is probably because, regardless of an outward appearance of coping with stress, the body continually reacts to the crisis with emergency measures that drain away the energy normally used to fight illness.

Leadership

We have been puzzled for centuries about the qualities of human leadership, and the more leaders are studied, the more complicated the problem seems to become. Do leaders *inherit* their special characteristics? Do they *learn* the characteristics that allow them to rise to prominence? Or, do the *times* make the leaders and thrust them into leadership positions?

According to the first theory, some of us are certain to rise to the top because we are born with the right combination of the proper qualities. In the times of kings and nobility, it was believed that qualities of leadership were genetically determined. One was born to greatness and descended from a long line of great forebears. Today, we favor a democratic version of

this theory. We believe the qualities of leadership can be learned by anyone with the appropriate desire and adequate opportunity. A contrasting view of leadership suggests that leaders are created by special situations and patterns of human events. When leadership is necessary for the group, someone will acquire power and influence if he is in the right spot at the right time. Willing or not, someone will be thrust into the seat of power, since each crisis manufactures the leaders it must have.

The Leadership Mystery. "We spend at least several billions of dollars a year on leadership development and executive recruitment in the United States. Leaders are paid 10, 20, and 30 times the salary of ordinary workers. Thousands of books and articles on leadership have been published. Yet, we still know relatively little about the factors that determine a leader's success or failure." [Fiedler, 1969, p. 39]

In this regard, the only thing we can be certain about is that leaders differ from one another in about as many ways as all people differ from one another. Any attempt to find a standard set of traits which would characterize the universal leader has been useless. What would you look for in the way of personality traits that would assure you of effective leadership in student government, a combat marine platoon, a discussion group, your church, a sales team, or a food boycott? Could one person direct in each of these situations with equal effectiveness? Bales (1970) has concluded that, since one leader can rarely be all things to all group members, groups tend to subdivide leadership. One leader will be responsible for the completion of the group's task, while another tends to the psychological problems. Once in a while, the same person may serve both functions, but this is usually not the case.

Bass (1960) suggests that this division of roles may follow the distribution of personalities in the group. As a group approaches work to be done, some of the members will be task oriented; some will be interaction oriented; and others, self-oriented. Task-oriented per-

sons take pleasure and satisfaction from completing assigned tasks and focus their energy on the problem rather than on other people. In contrast, interaction-oriented persons enjoy talking, socializing with others, and prefer to work in a group rather than alone. Self-oriented individuals find working alone more rewarding and are more interested in their own needs than in the demands of the task or the needs of the group.

How to Be a Leader

Let us assume for a moment that leaders are made, not born, and that becoming a leader is your burning ambition. Although the problem of leadership is complex and no single recipe is possible, we are pretty sure of some clues to the puzzle.

Be Appointed Leader   It is simpler to become a leader if the appointment is hereditary as well as customary—like becoming king. In this way, you are surrounded and protected by tradition, and your actual personal characteristics will hardly be noticed. If your attributes are noticed, they will be interpreted as virtues rather than faults. In a similar fashion, the raiment of a priest or the uniform of a policeman are responded to with little knowledge of the man wearing them.

If you are a tyrant, your style of leadership may be hazardous, but you may still be effective, for a while. It is not necessary for your followers to feel loyalty to you, since you can control their lives by threat, torture, or death. It is important only to surround yourself with advisers who fear you and who are afraid to suggest contradictory ideas or defy you. You can then assume your subordinates are stupid, incompetent, and dependent on you, and they will act accordingly.

Be Active in the Group   By and large, the leaders most often chosen are active participants of the group. They are also dependable, persistent, verbal, self-confident, and popular. It helps if the group members are unsure about how to attain goals on their own. If they cannot cope with the problems facing them, they will turn to a leader. A number of studies indicate that groups are more likely to choose an assertive person than an unassertive one. The assertive person talks a great deal and advances a larger number of ideas. If he is not too arrogant or aggressive, his participation makes him visible in the group, and visibility counts.

Be Different, but Not Too Different A leader can be active and assertive, providing he is not *too* different from the group. Members like their leader to be one of them and expect him or her to make the choices that suit most of the group. The leader can innovate and initiate if the new ideas are not too different or pushed too rapidly. Deviates are not chosen as leaders. Right or wrong, members tend to choose someone who will maintain the status quo.

Recipes for leadership can contain a great many more ingredients than these few, of course, but these represent the basic components of the process. Another way to look at the concept of leadership is to examine the circumstances that surround the operation of the group.

The Least-Preferred Co-worker

Fred E. Fiedler (1973) has fashioned what can be called a *contingency theory of leadership*. His view connects leader effectiveness directly to the situation in which the group operates. Thus, the theory predicts that the leader's contribution to group effectiveness depends on both the characteristics of the leader and the favorableness of the situation. For Fiedler, there is no universally successful type of leader. Task-oriented leaders may be effective under some circumstances but not under others. Likewise, a permissive leader who stresses human relations may be successful in one group and fail in another.

As Fiedler observes, the leader used to have unquestioned authority, but today he must often be able to persuade those under him. In response to this shift, billions of dollars have been poured into programs designed to teach managers how to make their organizations more productive. This enormous investment has produced little in the way of measurable success.

In Fiedler's theory, effective group performance depends on the proper match between (1) the leader's style of interacting with his subordinates, and (2) the degree to which the situation gives control and influence to the leader. Fiedler uses an index of leadership style called the "Least-Preferred Co-worker" score (LPC) as a means of assessing this match. He asks a leader to think of all the persons he has ever worked with and then describe the one person he worked with least well. This co-worker is rated on a 16-item scale containing entries like the following:

Least-Preferred Co-worker (LPC)

1	2	3	4	5	6	7	8
Friendly							Unfriendly

1	2	3	4	5	6	7	8
Cooperative							Uncooperative

The person who describes his least-preferred co-worker in relatively favorable terms is thought to be primarily interested in good personal relations with his fellow workers. This person is relationship motivated. The person who describes his least-preferred co-worker in harsh and relatively unfavorable terms is interested primarily in performing well. He is task motivated.

Charisma. "The term *charisma* implies some sort of divine grace, miraculously bestowed . . . to inspire confidence and to demand sacrifice of even life itself from their followers. . . . In charismatic leadership we see the effects of something like hypnotic suggestion reinforced and magnified by social support. Often the leader's reputation for greatness reaches the followers in advance of their actual contact with him. They come to hear him, prepared to be awed. Stories of his achievements may run far beyond the facts—including such tributes as belief in his miraculous birth and precocious childhood. Even those who have come prepared to scoff find themselves powerfully influenced by the enthusiastic responses of their neighbors in the audience." [Watson, 1966, p. 155]

The Young Leaders.   Alexander the Great at 18 led the select Macedonian Cavalry to victory. William Pitt became Prime Minister at 24, and Senator Charles Percy was President of Bell and Howell at 29. None of these men was a highly experienced leader before he became successful (Fiedler, 1973).

John Maher, founder of the Delancey Street Foundation (see Chapter 20), was an ex-drug addict and ex-convict who "dropped back in" and decided to do something positive for society's outcasts. He has had remarkable success with his three-year-old project, not only because he understands the problems facing Delancey Street members, but also because he has the personal qualities that attract supporters to his cause.

Thus, whether a leader is task oriented or person oriented, he will be most effective when placed in the appropriate work situation. No amount of training, at present, will change one kind of leader into another. It is less expensive to change the leader's work environment than to tamper with his leadership style.

Who will become a leader and who will remain a follower has traditionally been defined in terms such as intellectual competence, emotional maturity, human relations skills, administrative competence, and so forth. Fiedler has added new characteristics to the list—*task orientation* and *person orientation*. As business and industrial operations increase in size and complexity, it is likely that new characteristics of successful

The Followers.   If leaders are to lead, they must have followers. They must also have some idea about what makes their followers tick. According to Edgar Schein (1965), leaders have basic assumptions about the motivations of man, and they use their assumptions to determine how to get their followers to perform effectively. Depending on which of the following theories of man a leader subscribes to, he will take the appropriate steps to motivate his workers.

Rational-economic man.   According to the rational-economic theory, man is primarily motivated by money. Rational-economic man has little motivation beyond getting the largest possible paycheck at the end of the week. The leader's task, then, is to manipulate and motivate the worker to perform as productively as possible, given what he can be paid.

Social man.   If the leader assumes man is a social creature, attention must be given to social needs. If the leader treats the follower as an unfeeling robot or ignores his need to socialize, he will lose his flock and be unable to produce the desired results.

Self-actualizing man.   The leader who sees his followers as individual, self-actualizing beings will make their labors personally meaningful and satisfying by giving them as much responsibility as they can handle. He will reward the acquisition of skill and responsibility by providing progressively greater challenge and responsibility. Self-actualizing man is viewed as intrinsically motivated by personal, internalized reasons for doing a good job. He takes pride in his work because it is *his* work.

Complex man.   If this assumption guides the actions of a leader, he will respond to his workers or followers as persons possessed of a great many motives, capable of learning new motives, and responsive to many different kinds of managerial strategies. Managerial strategy will vary with the individual since no single tactic will work for all men at all times. The complex view of motivation encompasses many of the features of rational-economic, social, and self-actualizing man, but it also makes more demands on the personality of the leader. Thus, it is the most difficult to accomplish successfully.

managers must emerge. A company's competitive standing in the future may well depend on two factors: the intelligence of leadership, and the mobilization of all the potential knowledge and insight among employees at every level.

Summary

1.   It is difficult to determine whether leaders are born with leadership qualities, or whether ordinary men are merely thrust into leadership positions by the circumstances.

2.   Because certain leaders perform well in one group situation, but not in another, it is almost impossible for psychologists to detect the set of characteristics that would indicate a person is a leader.

3.   In some cases, there is more than one leader in the group, and each is responsible for a different aspect of group behavior. For example, one would be responsible for production and another for morale.

4.   The easiest way to become and remain a leader is to be appointed through tradition. In other cases, leaders are chosen if they are active in the group and appear somewhat different, but not really deviant.

5.   One way to determine what type of leader you have is to ask him to characterize the coworker he least preferred working with in the past. From his description you can tell if he is *task oriented* or *person oriented*. For either type of leader to be successful, he must be placed in the appropriate work situation.

Appendix: Psychology and Numbers

Just being alive makes you a big-time gambler. Every moment of your life and with every move you make, you take a chance. We spend our mental lives juggling the odds on everything we do. If you get in your car and don't buckle your seat belt, you have just bet your life on the statistical probability of having an accident. You play the numbers game every time you shop in your local supermarket and try to judge whether the jumbo or family-sized box is ounce for ounce the best buy.

You need to know something about statistics if you want to become a sophisticated shopper in the psychological market place. Your daily newspaper is filled with statistics about the cost of living, rising crime rates, population trends, food prices, batting averages, and other numbers having to do with your personal well-being. Every time you turn on TV you are bombarded by statistical claims reported by "independent research laboratories" and various statistical "proofs" of the superiority of one product over another. In this day and age, there is no escape from numbers.

You may suspect someone is trying to sell you something (an idea, a conclusion, an interpretation, a point of view), but you need to know something about statistics to understand the most common "tricks of the trade." To begin with, you must know that most research of any kind has a limited generalization. In other words, it can be applied most meaningfully only to the group of subjects studied in that particular time and setting and with the specific methods used. Usually, every research provides only partial answers, and to understand how far these limited answers can be trusted, you need to know about statistics.

The "Laws" of Probability

The most familiar example of *chance, odds,* or *probability* is when you flip a coin a great many times and count how often heads or tails come up. Under ideal circumstances, it is probable, of course, that heads will turn up half the time and tails the other half. This does not mean that heads will come up next if tails appeared on the last toss. Coins do not have a memory, which means each toss is independent of the toss that went before. When four or five heads come up in a row, it is tempting to bet the next toss will be tails. But such thinking is called the "gambler's fallacy" since the odds on the next toss are exactly the same as those on the first toss—50/50. If you don't believe that odds, probabilities, and chance have a "lawful" regularity, do what Iverson (1971) and his colleagues did. Take some dice and throw them 4,380,000 times and count how often each number comes up. You will find some exceptions to the rules of chance, but you won't find that the "laws" are violated if they are honest dice.

The *laws of probability* were discovered simply by observing what occurs when events happen at random (are not influenced by special forces). As we will see, much research done by psychologists is reported in terms of the probability that such events would happen as they did. Most often, the significance or insignificance of research findings is expressed in terms of probability estimates that are familiar to you. We all talk about odds ("not one chance in a thousand," "a hundred to one") and, when psychologists speak of *levels of significance,* that's all they are talking about. At the .05 level (5 percent level), psychologists mean that on a chance, or accident, basis they would only get such research results 5 times in 100 (odds of 20 to 1). Experimental findings significant at the .01 level (1 percent level) would, similarly, only be expected to happen by chance 1 time in 100 (odds of 100 to 1).

Science uses such numbers to communicate because words are too imprecise. Imagine doing research in which you had to tell about your findings using only terms such as *quite a lot, not nearly as much, more,* or *a whole bunch.* It is hard to tell, scientifically, if *quite a few* is more than *pretty much.* Such terms have no precise meaning and, as the old saying goes, measures like *a long time* depend on which end of the branding iron you're on.

Descriptive Statistics

Descriptive statistics are simply numbers that describe other numbers. These statistics are necessary since what scientists start with, when they make a statistical analysis, are raw data—a jumble of numbers, measurements, and observations, which must be ordered in a meaningful way. For purposes of illustration, we can make up some numbers as raw data. Just so our numbers represent something close to your heart and important to your survival, let's take examination scores.

Suppose your class is given a multiple-choice exam consisting of 25 questions with 1 point for every correct answer and 0 points for each one you miss. The *range* of possible scores is 0–25. A perfect score (every question answered correctly) gets 25 points (an unlikely possibility unless the exam is idiot simple). The worst possible score would be 0 points (also an unlikely possibility, but now and then some clown wanders into the exam thinking it's his organic chemistry class). Let's suppose there are 36 students in your class, and the raw test-score data look something like this:

Distribution of Raw Scores

Exam Points Scored	Number of Students
25	0
24	0
23	0
22	1
21	2
20	3
19	4
18	5
17	6
16	5
15	4
14	3
13	2
12	1
11	0
10	0
9	0
8	0
7	0
6	0
5	0
4	0
3	0
2	0
1	0

Illustration #1 may be the usual system your teacher uses to array the test scores in order to do some statistical analysis of them. When your teacher organizes your test scores in this way, he is distributing them according to the frequency with which they showed up. He makes (or plots) a *frequency distribution* (how often is each score attained). If he likes pictures better than columns of numbers, he can make a *histogram* using the same raw data. He would simply make little "boxes" (each representing one test score) and see how high each pile of boxes becomes. Let's say six people scored 17 points on the exam. Thus, six boxes piled up on score 17 makes a picture or graphic out of the number 6. Histograms are constructed merely to make the numbers and their relationship to one another easier to visualize.

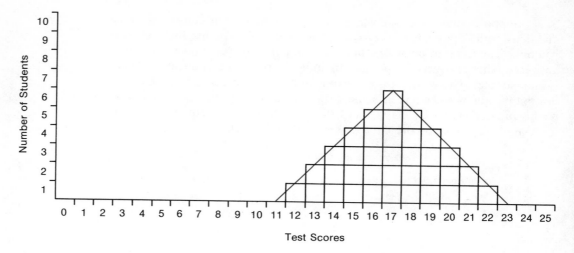

Another graphic portrayal can be in the form of a *frequency polygon.* This is the familiar graph often seen in magazines and newspapers to convey numerical information. The number of scores in each category (0–25) is indicated by a point and then the points are simply connected to make a kind of curve or graph.

Whether you prefer the frequency distribution in columns, as a picture, or as a frequency polygon, the statistical information you can get from it will be the same. You can determine the *mode* or *modal point,* for example, simply by looking to see which test score appears most often. In this case, six students got scores of 17 on the test. Thus the mode (or most "fashionable" score) would be 17 items correct. You can also find the *median,* or middle number. That would be the point below which one-half of the 36 students can be found and above which the other half would be found. In this case the mode and median are the same—a score of 17 points.

With some simple arithmetic, you can also figure out what is called the arithmetic *mean* (sometimes called the *average*) of the distribution. If you add up the different scores the 36 students got on the test (22, 21, 21, 20, 20, 20, 19, 19, 19, 19, 18, 18, 18, 18, 18, 17, 17, 17, 17, 17, 17, 16, 16, 16, 16, 16, 15, 15, 15, 15, 14, 14, 14, 13, 13, 12), you get a total of 612 points. Then if you divide by the number of students who took the exam (36), you discover the arithmetic mean is also 17 points on the exam.

By this time you should be suspicious that something fishy is going on. The *mode, median,* and *mean* have turned out to be the same number, and there is not much sense in learning three different ways to figure out the same answer. What's fishy is that, when I made up the imaginary test scores, I made them perfectly symmetrical or regular. The picture is like equally spaced steps going up one side and coming down the other side of the figure. I constructed an ideal or *normal* curve. If you have a large collection of random numbers or a very big stack of information, you will sometimes get this normal curve when you plot your data into a frequency distribution. In a class of only 36 students, however, this will rarely happen since the sample of students is pretty small. If the exam is a real "crusher" and hardly anyone can get many correct answers, the scores might be *skewed to the right*. In other words, everyone's test scores will pile up at the low end of the scale of scores.

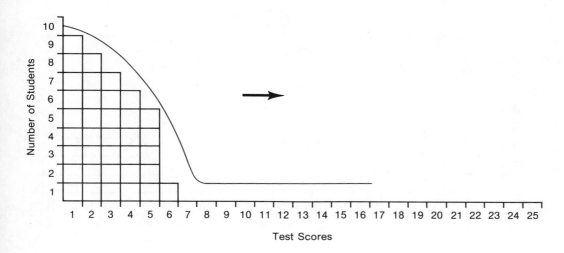

If the exam asks questions that your kid brother could answer, then everyone will do well on the test, and the frequency distribution might be *skewed to the left* as follows:

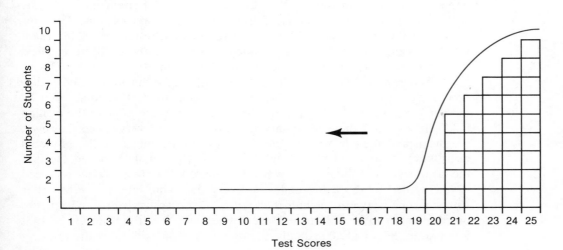

I know as you look at the illustrations it looks as if someone got the terms mixed. When all the scores are to the left side it is called *right skewed*, and when all the scores are on the right it is called *left skewed*. I think it's weird too. It is only a 'convention'—an arbitrary way to describe the curves.

Now, if half the class studied for the exam and half the class didn't bother, you might tally up the exam scores and get a *bi-modal* distribution.

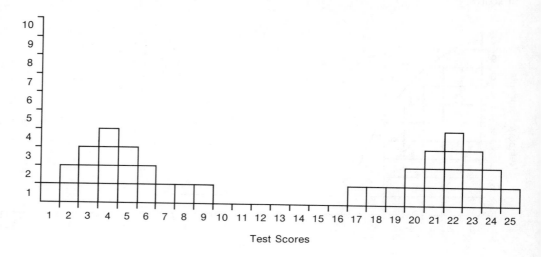

Test Scores

If I ask you which test score appeared most often you would have to answer that 3 points and 22 points appeared with equal frequency. You can now see why we use the other measures called *mean* and *median*. Let's calculate the mean and median for this bi-modal distribution and see what happens. The median divides the class into top and bottom halves so the point that divides the class in half falls somewhere between 12 and 13 points correct on the exam. Thus, if I told you the median test score on the exam was 12.5 points, you wouldn't have much information and could never guess the test scores would look like they do in illustration #5.

Where would you guess the mean would fall for this bi-modal distribution? If you add up all the test score points and divide that total (450) by the number of students (36), you will find the mean is the same as the median (12.5). If you shift these imaginary test scores around very much, however, the mean and median will no longer be the same. Think of the bi-modal distribution as a board with weights on both ends of it. You can see that the mean would be the point at which the board would be perfectly balanced if you wanted to slip a log under it. Every time you get on a teeter-totter with someone heavier or lighter than yourself, you adjust your weight (figure out the mean) to be able to balance it properly. When you decide to split a restaurant bill of $12.00 equally among four of you, without really thinking about it, you calculate a *mean* by dividing the total of dollars owed ($12.00) by the number of persons (4) and figure everyone owes $3.00. These statistical numbers—*mean, median,* and *mode*—give you a certain amount of information about numbers, events, measures, or observations. Each has its value to psychologists trying to tell you about their research. Further, each statistical measure gives you a slightly different view of a distribution of numbers. Which measure is used depends on what information you want to convey to others.

A familiar measure of your performance on an examination is the *percentile* which lets you compare your score with others who took the same test. The percentile score that corresponds to the raw score you got on the test represents the percent of all the raw scores of the other students that fall below it. Thus being in the 80th percentile means your test score is equalled or exceeded by 20 percent of the other scores in the group. Having a score that falls in the 10th percentile means you did better than only 10 percent of those in your class.

Statistical analysis of data is a fundamental research tool for psychologists, and this account of descriptive statistics only touches the surface of a very sophisticated technology used to explore human nature. As you all well know from experience, knowing about percentiles, means, medians, modes, and frequency distributions has little to do with the most important decision your psychology teacher makes about examination scores—in other words, the descriptive grades he assigns to these numbers.

Inferential Statistics

If there is one prominent feature in most psychological studies, it is the statistical relationship of one group of persons, scores, or measures to another group measured by means of the statistic called the *coefficient of correlation.*

The Coefficient of Correlation. Using the example of examination scores, let us suppose your teacher is heartless enough to give you another exam. Now there are two sets of scores, and statistical questions can be asked about the relationship between them. Being the truly super student that you are, you should be able to predict (with reasonable certainty) that, if you did well on the first test, you will do well on the second. If you got a terrible score on the first test and didn't study for the second exam, you can probably make an equally accurate prediction about what your second score will be.

If both tests are good measures of how much psychology you know and everyone in the class works about as hard on the second test as on the first, then there should be a *high positive correlation* between an individual's scores on the first and second tests. The high scorers on test #1 ought to be the high scorers on test #2, just as everyone else in the class will "hold his place" from test to test. The correlation between the tests will be high for everyone.

When such relationships between two sets of scores are converted (for convenience) into number form, the arbitrary designations + 1.00 *(perfect positive correlation),* .00 *(no correlation),* and −1.00 *(perfect negative correlation)* are used. Since perfect correlations are rare, you will find psychologists most often referring to fractional figures such as +.62, −.30. (Again, a .00 correlation is rare.) Thus, if the score you got on your first test bears absolutely no relationship to your performance on the second test, the correlation between the two test scores will be zero or close to zero. If all the high scorers on the first test bombed out on the second test, and all the poor scorers did beautifully the second time around, you might come close to a perfect negative correlation.

Correlation coefficients are just numbers—a shorthand way to communicate information as well as a way to summarize masses of other numbers. A correlation is a measure of the relationship between any two things. The higher the number of the correlation coefficient (whether positive or negative), the stronger the relationship. Still, even when you get a very high positive or negative relationship between two events or measures, all you know is that the two events vary together. You don't know anything about the *nature* of the relationship between the two. If I tell you there is a very high correlation between being punched in the nose and having a nosebleed, you would *infer* the punch caused the nosebleed—and you would be correct most of the time about cause and effect. But in the slightly more complicated and less obvious situations of psychological research, the correlation between two measurements won't tell you if there is a cause and effect relationship between them. For example, there is a significant correlation between a male's height and how well he will do, financially, in life. Taller people make more money, get promoted to positions of greater power, more often get elected to public office, become college presidents, and so forth. There is a correlation between these outcomes and height, but the correlation doesn't tell us why this is true. If you have a high correlation, you can make successful predictions more often, but you won't know why the predictions work.

Psychologists frequently make statements about the statistical significance of their findings. When the correlation coefficient is used, there is a crude rule of thumb you can use to gauge how strong or *significant* the relationship between the two measures may be. Correlations from .00 to .20 are generally insignificant. At about a correlation of +.30 or −.30 statistical significance begins. These are crude measures since every correlation depends for its significance on the size of the sample, the units of measurements, the amount of variability in the measures, and so forth.

Judging Statistics

At this point you have not learned enough about psychology and numbers to call yourself an expert, but you have learned enough to be cautious. Darrel

Huff (1954) wrote a fascinating book called *How To Lie With Statistics,* and in the final chapter he tells us how to look a phony statistic in the eye and win the staring contest. He suggests that, if you can get answers to just a few questions, you can make a pretty good guess about what to believe or not to believe.

He proposes you start by asking: "Who says so?" Most of us have already learned this lesson from television, of course. We have watched thousands of actors in white lab coats telling us what product "many" doctors recommend for "fast, fast, fast" relief from whatever ails us. If it is said to work in "minutes," you have to ask how many minutes is "fast, fast, fast." A deceptive commercial may not lie with its statistics. It may just not tell the truth or only tell part of the truth. Further, a clear bias may be evident since "who says so" is the company pushing the product and, certainly, they may not be impartial reporters of the truth.

The next question is: "How does he know?" If 1,000 doctors were asked to recommend the product and only 40 were willing to do so, it is not illegal to say "many" (after all, the commercial didn't say "most"). If soap X is said to get your jeans 10 percent cleaner than soap Y, you can chose not to believe it because you can easily think of several dozen ways in which the experiment can be rigged, misinterpreted, or the data selectively reported.

Remember the automotive glass company that showed you on television how little their glass distorted your vision? We all figured we knew how good it was through the evidence of our own eyes—until it turned out that the glass wasn't even in the commercial (the window had been turned down). You must also ask: "What's missing?" In this example the glass was missing, and the commercial was more than a little deceptive. If "who says so" tells you "how he knows" but leaves out parts of the raw data, be careful. Of course, statistics can be made to look better if some numbers are left out. If you see a graph or other picture representation of facts and notice there are no numbers telling exactly *how much,* don't believe it. TV research reporters love percentages. But "what's missing" may be the actual numbers that tell you whether "10 percent less polyunsaturated fat" is a lot or a little.

Look out, Huff warns, if someone changes the subject, statistically. When the FBI changed its form for reporting crimes, there appeared to be a sudden crime wave all across the country since crimes were counted that had not been reported on the previous form. When slipshod newspaper reporting compared past and present armed robberies, for example, it seemed as if half the population was sticking up the other half, when in fact the old statistics couldn't be compared with the new statistics.

A final question is whether or not it makes sense. This may be your only defense if you can't get at the actual numbers and see how the magic statistical trick was done. You always have the right *not* to make up your mind until you get the kind and amount of information you feel you need to make a trustworthy decision. Most psychologists aren't pushing soaps and automobiles. But psychologists are human beings, and it is possible for them to push their own point of view in research areas that are highly controversial ones. Knowing statistics is like knowing the rules of the scientific game—each of you can be your own umpire and call them as you see them.

Personality Assessment

In business and industry persons are selected for important positions in terms of their personalities as well as other factors. Personality assessment is done for research purposes to understand how and why personality changes.

A psychological test of personality is an instrument that evaluates you by comparing you with other people who have taken the same test. In other words, when you take the test, the results are compared with the scores from large groups of other people. These scores are used to determine whether you differ from the others, how much you differ, and in what ways you differ.

There are at least two central ways to predict behavior—the *clinical* and *statistical* (Meehl, 1954). *Statistical prediction* is based on information interpreted according to a formula that tries to eliminate personal impressions or hunches. Data about an individual, for example, may be collected and analyzed statistically rather than by guess.

In contrast, the psychologist using *clinical prediction* employs not only objective test scores and biographical data but also freely uses personal judgments and opinions and makes a prediction based upon his clinical experience with people. Thus, clinical prediction, for better *or* worse, clearly includes a "human element."

A number of researchers insist that statistical prediction is equal to or better than clinical prediction (Meehl, 1954; Gough, 1962). But it has been noted that most comparison studies put the clinician at a disadvantage by asking him to predict behavior in unfamiliar areas (McArthur, 1956). Which method is best depends on several factors including the nature of the event being predicted, the time allotted for the decision, the need for theoretical reasoning, and the expertise of the clinical psychologist (Lindzey, 1965; Meehl, 1965).

References

Adams, R. L., and Fox, R. J. Mainlining Jesus: The new trip. *Society,* February 1972.

Adamson, B. E., and Taylor, O. W. Functional fixedness as related to elapsed time and set. *Journal of Experimental Psychology,* 1954, **47**, 122–126.

Adelson, J. What generation gap? *New York Times Magazine,* January 18, 1970.

Adelson, J. Is women's lib a passing fad? *New York Times Magazine,* March 19, 1972.

Adler, P. *A house is not a home.* New York: Popular Library, 1955.

Adolph, E. F. The internal environment and behavior: Water content. *American Journal of Psychiatry,* 1941, **97**, 1365–1372.

Adorno, T. W., Frenkel-Brunswik, E., Levinson, D. J., and Sanford, R. N. *The authoritarian personality.* New York: Harper, 1950.

Aiken, M., Ferman, L. A., and Sheppard, H. L. *Economic failure, alienation, and extremism.* Ann Arbor: University of Michigan Press, 1968.

Alexander, F. C., and Selesnick, S. T. *The history of psychiatry.* New York: Harper, 1966.

Allen, F. L. *The big change: America transforms itself: 1900–1950.* New York: Bantam, 1952.

Allen, V. L. Theoretical issues in poverty research. *Journal of Social Issues,* 1970, **26**, 149–167.

Allport, G. W. *Personality: A psychological interpretation.* (2nd ed.) New York: Holt, 1961. (a)

Allport. G. W. *Pattern and growth in personality.* New York: Holt, 1961. (b)

Allport, G. W. The general and the unique in psychological science. *Journal of Personality,* 1962, **30**, 405–422.

Allport, G. W., and Vernon, P. E. *Studies in expressive movement.* New York: Macmillan, 1933.

Allyn, J., and Festinger, L. The effectiveness of unanticipated persuasive communications. *Journal of Abnormal and Social Psychology,* 1961, **62**, 35–40.

Altman, J. *Organic foundations of animal behavior.* New York: Holt, 1966.

Altus, W. D. Birth order and its sequelae. *Science,* 1966, **151**, 44–49.

Anderson, B. The effect of injections and hypertonic solutions in parts of the hypothalamus of goats. *Acta Physiologica Scandinavica,* 1953, **28**, 188–201.

Anderson, J. G., and Johnson, W. H. Stability and change among 3 generations of Mexican-Americans: Factors affecting achievement. *American Educational Research Journal,* 1971, **8**, 285–309.

Andrews, L. M., and Karlins, M. *Requiem for democracy.* New York: Holt, 1971.

Angelino, H., Dollins, J., and Mech, E. Trends in the fears and worries of school children as related to socioeconomic status and age. *Journal of Genetic Psychology,* 1956, **89**, 263–276.

Anthony, D. S. Graphology. In N. L. Farberow (Ed.), *Taboo topics.* New York: Atherton, 1963.

Anthony, D. S. Is graphology valid? *Psychology Today,* August 1967.

Appley, M. H., and Trumbull, R. (Eds.) *Psychological stress; Issues in research.* New York: Appleton-Century-Crofts, 1967.

Aramoni, Aniceto. Maschismo. *Psychology Today,* January 1972.

Ardrey, R. *The territorial imperative.* New York: Atheneum, 1966.

Arieti, S. Schizophrenia: The manifest symptomatology, the psychodynamic and formal mechanisms. In S. Arieti (Ed.), *American handbook of psychiatry,* Vol. I. New York: Basic Books, 1959.

Arieti, S., and Meth, J. M. Rare, unclassifiable, collective, and exotic psychotic syndromes. In S. Arieti (Ed.), *American handbook of psychiatry.* Vol. I. New York: Basic Books, 1959.

Arnhoff, F. N. Concepts of aging. In P. H. Hoch and J. Zubin (Eds.), *Psychopathology of aging.* New York: Grune & Stratton, 1961.

Arnold, M. Stress and emotion. In M. H. Appley and R. Trumbull (Eds.), *Psychological stress: Issues in research.* New York: Appleton-Century-Crofts, 1967.

Aronson, E. Who likes why. *Psychology Today,* April 1970.

Aronson, E. Some antecedents of interpersonal attraction. In W. J. Arnold and D. Levine (Eds.), *Nebraska sym-*

posium on motivation, 1969. Lincoln: University of Nebraska Press, 1970.

Aronson, E., and Linder, D. Gain and loss of esteem as determinants of interpersonal attractiveness. *Journal of Experimental Social Psychology,* 1965, **1**, 156–171.

Asch, S. E. Forming impressions of personality. *Journal of Abnormal and Social Psychology,* 1946, **41**, 258–290.

Asch, S. E. Effects of group pressure upon the modification and distortion of judgments. In H. Guetzkow (Ed.), *Groups, leadership and men.* Pittsburgh: Carnegie Press, 1951.

Aserinsky, E., and Kleitman, N. Regularly occurring periods of eye motility and concomitant phenomena during sleep. *Science,* 1953, **118**, 273–274.

Asher, J. John Ertl's neural efficiency analyzer: Bias-free test, or just a "neat gadget"? *APA Monitor,* March 1973.

Ashida, S. Modification by early experience of the tendency toward gregariousness in rats. *Psychonomic Science,* **1**, 343–344.

Asimov, I. *The new intelligent man's guide to science.* New York: Basic Books, 1965.

Asimov, I. *Is anyone there?* Doubleday, 1967.

Atcheson, R. *The bearded lady.* New York: John Day, 1971.

Atkinson, J. W. *An introduction to motivation.* Princeton, N.J.: Van Nostrand, 1964.

Atkinson, K., MacWhinney, B., and Stoel, C. An experiment on recognition of babbling. *Papers and reports on child language development.* Stanford, Calif.: Stanford University Press, 1970.

Atthowe, J. M., Jr., and Krasner, L. Preliminary report on the application of contingent reinforcement procedures (token economy) on a "chronic" psychiatric ward. *Journal of Abnormal Psychology,* 1968, **73**, 37–43.

Auger, T. J., Wright, E., and Simpson, R. H. Posters as smoking deterrents. *Journal of Applied Psychology,* 1972, **56**, 169–171.

Avorn, J. Beyond dying. *Harper's,* March 1973.

Ax, A. F. The physiological differentiation of emotional states. *Psychomatic Medicine,* 1953, **15**, 433–442.

Ayllon, T., and Michael, J. The psychiatric nurse as a behavioral engineer. *Journal of Experimental Analysis of Behavior,* 1959, **2**, 323–334.

Bach, M. *Strange sects and curious cults.* New York: Dodd, Mead, 1961.

Bach, S., and Klein, E. S. Conscious effects of prolonged subliminal exposures of words. *American Psychologist,* 1957, **12**, 397. (Abstract)

Back, K. W. The way of love and trust: The sensitivity encounter movement. *Society,* June 1972. (a)

Back, K. W. The group can comfort but it can't cure. *Psychology Today,* December 1972. (b)

Baer, D. M. Let's take another look at punishment. *Psychology Today,* October 1971.

Bakan, D. Psychology can now kick the science habit. *Psychology Today,* March 1972.

Bales, R. F. *Personality and interpersonal behavior.* New York: Holt, 1970.

Bandler, R. J., Madaras, G. R., and Bem, D. J. Self-observation as a source of pain perception. *Journal of Personality and Social Psychology,* 1968, **9**, 205–209.

Bandura, A., Blanchard, E. B., and Ritter, B. The relative efficacy of desensitization and modeling approaches for inducing behavioral, affective, and attitudinal changes. *Journal of Personality and Social Psychology,* 1969, **13**, 173–199.

Bandura, A., and Walters, R. H. *Social learning and personality development.* New York: Holt, 1963.

Baratz, J. C. A bi-dialectal task for determining language proficiency in economically disadvantaged Negro children. *Child Development,* 1969, **40**, 889–901.

Barber, T. X. *Hypnosis: A scientific approach.* New York: Van Nostrand Reinhold, 1969.

Barber, T. X. *LSD, marihuana, yoga and hypnosis.* Chicago: Aldine, 1970.

Barker, R. G. Ecology and motivation. In M. R. Jones (Ed.), *Nebraska symposium on motivation.* Lincoln: University of Nebraska Press, 1960.

Barker, R. G. (Ed.) *The stream of behavior.* New York: Appleton-Century-Crofts, 1963.

Barker, R. G., and Wright, H. F. *Midwest and its children.* Evanston, Ill.: Row, Peterson, 1954.

Barron, F. The creative personality akin to madness. *Psychology Today,* July 1972.

Barry, H., III, Bacon, M. K., and Child, I. L. A cross-cultural survey of some sex differences in socialization. *Journal of Abnormal and Social Psychology,* 1957, **55**, 327–332.

Barsley, M. *Some of my best friends are left-handed people.* Hollywood, Calif.: Wilshire, 1968.

Bartell, G. D. *Group sex.* New York: Peter H. Wyden, 1971.

Bass, B. M. *Leadership, psychology, and organizational behavior.* New York: Harper, 1960.

Baumrind, D. Some thoughts on the ethics of research: After reading Milgram's "Behavioral study of obedience." *American Psychologist,* 1964, **19**, 421–423.

Bavelas, A., Hastdorf, A. H., Gross, A. E., and Kite, W. R. Experiments in the alteration of group structure. *Journal of Experimental Social Psychology,* 1965, **1**, 55–71.

Beach, F. It's all in your mind. *Psychology Today,* July 1969.

Beecher, H. K. *Measurement of subjective responses.* New York: Oxford University Press, 1959.

Bellugi, U., and Klima, S. The roots of language in the sign talk of the deaf. *Psychology Today,* June 1972.

Bem, D. J. Self-perception: An alternative interpretation of cognitive dissonance phenomena. *Psychological Review,* 1967, **74,** 183–200.

Bem, D. J. *Beliefs, attitudes, and human affairs.* Belmont, Calif.: Brooks/Cole, 1970.

Benda, C. E., Squires, N. D., Ogonik, J., and Wise, R. Personality factors in mild mental retardation: Family background and sociocultural patterns. *American Journal of Mental Deficiency,* 1963, **68,** 24–40.

Bender, L. Childhood schizophrenia: Clinical study of 100 schizophrenic children. *American Journal of Orthopsychiatry,* 1947, **17,** 40–56.

Benedict, P. K., and Jacks, I. Mental illness in primitive societies. *Psychiatry,* 1954, **17,** 377–389.

Benjamin, H., and Masters, R. E. L. *Prostitution and morality.* New York: Julian Press, 1964.

Bennett, A. M. H. Sensory deprivation in aviation. In P. Solomon et al. (Eds.), *Sensory deprivation.* Cambridge: Harvard University Press, 1961.

Bennett, J. W., and Tumin, M. *Social life, structure and function: An introductory general sociology.* New York: Knopf, 1948.

Bereiter, C., and Englemann, S. *Teaching disadvantaged children in the preschool.* Englewood Cliffs, N.J.: Prentice-Hall, 1966.

Berg, I. *Education and jobs: The great training robbery.* New York: Praeger, 1970.

Berg, I. A. Observations concerning obsessiveness in normal persons under stress. *Journal of Clinical Psychology,* 1953, **9,** 300–302.

Berger, A. A. Dagwood in the American psyche. *Human Behavior,* January 1973.

Berger, B. M. The new stage of American man: Almost endless adolescence. *New York Times Magazine,* November 2, 1969.

Berger, B. M. The best things in life are free, or you can build them yourself. *New York Times Book Review,* November 1971.

Berger, R. J., Olley, P., and Oswald, I. The EEG, eye movements and dreams of the blind. *Quarterly Journal of Experimental Psychology,* 1962, **14,** 183–186.

Berkowitz, L. *Aggression: A social psychological analysis.* New York: McGraw-Hill, 1962.

Berkowitz, L. The frustration-aggression hypothesis revisited. In L. Berkowitz (Ed.), *Roots of aggression: A re-examination of the frustration-aggression hypothesis.* New York: Atherton, 1970.

Berkowitz, L. Sex and violence: We can't have it both ways. *Psychology Today,* December 1971.

Berlyne, D. E. Curiosity and exploration. *Science,* 1966, **153,** 25–33.

Bernard, V. W., Ottenberg, P., and Redl, F. Dehumanization: A composite psychological defense in relation to modern war. In R. Perrucci and M. Pilisuk (Eds.), *The triple revolution: Social problems in depth.* Boston: Little, Brown, 1968.

Bersheid, E., and Wolster, E. *Interpersonal attraction.* Reading, Mass.: Addison-Wesley, 1969.

Bettleheim, B. Joey: A mechanical boy. *Scientific American,* March 1959.

Bettleheim, B. *The empty fortress: Infantile autism and the birth of the self.* London: Collier-Macmillan, 1967.

Bexton, W. H., Heron, W., and Scott, T. Effects of decreased variation in the environment. *Canadian Journal of Psychology,* 1954, **8,** 70–76.

Bickman, L. Environmental attitudes and actions. *Journal of Social Psychology,* 1972, **87,** 323–324.

Bijou, S. W. A functional analysis of retarded development. In N. R. Ellis (Ed.), *International review of research in mental retardation,* Vol. I. New York: Academic Press, 1966.

Biller, B. Father absence and the personality development of the male child. *Developmental Psychology,* 1970, **2,** 181–201.

Billingsley, A. Black families and white social science. *Journal of Social Issues,* 1970, **26,** 127–142.

Binstock, J. Motherhood: An occupation facing decline. *The Futurist,* June 1972.

Birch, H. G. The relation of previous experience to insightful problem-solving. *Journal of Comparative Psychology,* 1945, **38,** 367–383.

Birch, J. D., and Veroff, J. *Motivation: A study of action.* Belmont, Calif.: Brooks/Cole, 1966.

Birven, J. E. The abuse of the urban aged. *Psychology Today,* March 1970.

Black, H. *They shall not pass.* New York: Morrow, 1963.

Blackburn, R. Sensation seeking, impulsivity, and psychopathic personality. *Journal of Consulting and Clinical Psychology,* 1969, **33,** 571–574.

Blake, R. R., and Mouton, J. S. The intergroup dynamics win-lose conflict and problem solving collaboration in union-management relations. In M. Sherif (Ed.), *Intergroup relations and leadership.* New York: Wiley, 1962.

Blanchard, W. H. Ecstasy without agony is baloney. *Psychology Today,* January 1970.

Blank, L. Nudity. *Psychology Today,* June 1969.

Bliss, E. J., and Clark, L. D. Visual hallucinations. In L. J. West (Ed.), *Hallucinations.* New York: Grune & Stratton, 1962.

Block, J., Harvey, E., Jennings, P. H., and Simpson, E. Clinicians' conceptions of the asthmatogenic mother. *Archives of General Psychiatry,* 1966, **15,** 610–618.

Bloomberg, W., Jr. American violence in perspective. In T.

Rose (Ed.), *Violence in America.* New York: Vintage, 1969.

Bloustein, E. J. Man's work goes from sun to sun but woman's work is never done. *Psychology Today,* March 1968.

Blum, R., et al. *Utopiates.* New York: Atherton, 1964.

Blum, S. Suicide. *Playboy,* November 1972.

Boboroff, A. Economic adjustment of 121 adults, formerly students in classes for mental retardates. *American Journal of Mental Deficiency,* 1956, **60**, 525–535.

Bohannan, P. (Ed.) *Divorce and after.* New York: Doubleday, 1970. (1971 Anchor)

Bossom, J., and Maslow, A. Security of judges as a factor in impressions of warmth in others. *Journal of Abnormal and Social Psychology,* 1957, **55**, 147–148.

Bowers, M., Jackson, E. N., Knight, J. A., and LeShan, L. *Counseling the dying.* New York: Thomas Nelson, 1964.

Brackenridge, C. J., and Bloch, S. Smoking in medical students. *Journal of Psychosomatic Research,* 1972, **16**, 35–40.

Brady, J. V. Ulcers in "executive monkeys." *Scientific Monthly,* October 1958.

Braginsky, M., and Braginsky, D. D. Mental hospitals as resorts. *Psychology Today,* March 1973.

Bramel, D. Interpersonal attraction, hostility, and perception. In J. Mills (Ed.), *Experimental social psychology.* New York: Macmillan, 1969.

Brehm, J. W. *A theory of psychological reactance.* New York: Academic Press, 1966.

Bremer, A. An assassin's diary. *Harper's,* January 1973.

Brenton, M. *The privacy invaders.* New York: Crest, 1964.

Bridges, K. M. B. Emotional development in early infancy. *Child Development,* 1932, **3**, 324–341.

Brodeur, D. W. The effects of stimulant and tranquilizer placebos on healthy subjects in a real life situation. *Psychopharmacologia,* 1965, **7**, 444–452.

Bronfenbrenner, U. The psychological costs of quality and equality in education. *Child Development,* 1967, **38**, 909–925.

Bronfenbrenner, U. *Two worlds of childhood: U.S. and U.S.S.R.* New York: Russell Sage Foundation, 1970.

Broverman, I. K., Broverman, D. M., Clarkson, F. G., Rosenkrantz, P. S., and Vogel, S. R. Sex-role stereotypes and clinical judgments of mental health. *Journal of Consulting and Clinical Psychology,* 1970, **34**, 1–7.

Brown, D. *Bury my heart at Wounded Knee.* New York: Bantam, 1970.

Brown, J. A. C. *Techniques of persuasion.* Baltimore: Penguin, 1963.

Brown, R. *Social psychology.* New York: Free Press, 1965.

Brown, R. *Unfinished symphonies: Voices from the beyond.* New York: Bantam, 1971.

Brown, R., and Hildum, D. C. Expectancy and the identification of syllables. *Language,* 1956, **32**, 411–419.

Brownfield, E. D., and Keehn, J. D. Operant eye-lid conditioning in trisomy-18. *Journal of Abnormal Psychology,* 1966, **71**, 413–415.

Brownmiller, S. The new feminism. *Current,* April 1970.

Bruner, J. S., and Goodman, C. C. Value and need as organizing factors in perception. *Journal of Abnormal and Social Psychology,* 1947, **42**, 33–44.

Bruner, J. S., Shapiro, D., and Tagiuri, R. The meaning of traits in isolation and in combination. In R. Ritagiuri and L. Petrullo (Eds.), *Person perception and interpersonal behavior.* Stanford, Calif.: Stanford University Press, 1958.

Bryan, J. H. Occupational ideologies and individual attitudes of call girls. *Social Problems,* 1966, **13**, 441–450.

Bucklew, J. The current status of theory in mental retardation. In N. H. Pronko (Ed.), *Panorama of psychology.* Belmont, Calif.: Brooks/Cole, 1969.

Buckner, H. T. Flying saucers are for people. *Trans-action,* May-June 1966.

Burgess, E. W. *Aging in Western societies.* Chicago: University of Chicago Press, 1960.

Buss, A. H. *Psychopathology.* New York: Wiley, 1966.

Buss, A. H. *Psychology: Man in perspective.* New York: Wiley, 1973.

Butler, R. A. Curiosity in monkeys. *Scientific American,* February 1954.

Butler, R. N. Age: The life review. *Psychology Today,* December 1971.

Button, A. D. *The authentic child.* New York: Random, 1969.

Calhoun, J. B. Population density and social pathology, *Scientific American,* June 1962.

Cameron, N. *Personality development and psychopathology.* Boston: Houghton Mifflin, 1963.

Campbell, A., and Schuman, H. *Racial attitudes in fifteen American cities.* Ann Arbor: Institute for Social Research, University of Michigan, 1968.

Campbell, J. P., and Dunnette, M. D. Effectiveness of t-group experiences in managerial training and development. *Psychological Bulletin,* 1968, **70**, 73–104.

Cannicott, S. M. Technique of unilateral electroconvulsive therapy. *American Journal of Psychiatry,* 1963, **120**, 477–480.

Cannon, W. B. "Voodoo" death. *American Anthropologist,* 1942, **44**, 169–181.

Carmichael, L., Hogan, H. P., and Walter, A. A. An experimental study of the effect of language on the reproduction of visually perceived form. *Journal of Experimental Psychology,* 1932, **15**, 73–86.

Carroll, J. B. *Language and thought.* Englewood Cliffs, N.J.: Prentice-Hall, 1964.

Cartwright, D. Determinants of scientific progress: The case of research on the risky shift. *American Psychologist,* 1973, **28**, 222–231.

Carver, R. P. Speed readers don't read: They skim. *Psychology Today,* August 1972.

Cashdan, S. Sensitivity groups: Problems and promise. *Professional Psychology,* 1970, **1**, 217–224.

Casler, L. This thing called love is pathological. *Psychology Today,* December 1969.

Casler, L. Death as a psychosomatic condition: Prolegomena to a longitudinal study. *Psychological Reports,* 1970, **27**, 953–954.

Castiglioni, A. *Adventures of the mind.* New York: Knopf, 1946.

Ceraso, J. The interference theory of forgetting. *Scientific American,* April 1967.

Chafetz, M. E. Addictions: Alcoholism. In A. M. Freedman and H. I. Kaplan (Eds.), *Psychiatry.* Baltimore: Williams & Wilkins, 1967.

Chesler, P. Men drive women crazy. *Psychology Today,* July 1971.

Chesler, P. *Women and madness.* New York: Doubleday, 1972.

Child, I. L., and Whiting, J. W. M. Determinants of level of aspiration: Evidence from everyday life. *Journal of Abnormal and Social Psychology,* 1949, **44**, 303–314.

Chomsky, N. A review of B. F. Skinner's Verbal Behavior. *Language,* 1959, **35**, 26–58.

Chomsky, N. Language and the mind. *Readings in Psychology Today.* Del Mar, Calif.: CRM Books, 1969.

Chomsky, N., and Halle, M. *Sound patterns of English.* New York: Harper, 1968.

Christie, R. The Machiavellis among us. *Psychology Today,* November 1970.

Christie, R., and Geis, F. L. (Eds.) *Studies in Machiavellianism.* New York: Academic Press, 1970.

Churchill, J. A. The relationship between intelligence and birth weight in twins. *Neurology,* 1965, **15**, 341–347.

Clark, K. B., and Clark, M. P. Racial identification and preference in Negro children. In E. E. Maccoby, T. M. Newcomb, and E. L. Hartley (Eds.), *Readings in social psychology.* New York: Holt, 1958.

Clark, M. Patterns of aging among the elderly poor of the inner city. *Gerontologist,* 1971, **11**, 58–66.

Clausen, J. A. Family structure, socialization, and personality. In L. W. Hoffman and M. L. Hoffman (Eds.), *Review of child development research,* Vol. 2. New York: Russell Sage Foundation, 1966.

Coleman, J. C. *Abnormal psychology and modern life.* Glenview, Ill.: Scott, Foresman, 1964.

Coleman, J. C. *Abnormal psychology and modern life.* Glenview, Ill.: Scott, Foresman, 1970.

Coleman, J. S. The children have outgrown the schools. *Psychology Today,* February 1972.

Coleman, J., Campbell, E., Hobson, C., McPartland, J., Mood, A., Weinfield, F., and York, R. *Equality of educational opportunity.* Washington, D.C.: U.S. Government Printing Office, 1966.

Comfort, A. *The nature of human nature.* New York: Avon, 1966.

Cook, C., and Adams, H. E. Modification of verbal behaviour in speech deficient children. *Behaviour Research and Therapy,* 1966, **4**, 265–271.

Cooper, A., Furst, J. B., and Bridger, W. H. A brief commentary on the usefulness of studying fears of snakes. *Journal of Abnormal Psychology,* 1969, **74**, 413–414.

Cooper, J. C. *Religion in the age of Aquarius.* Philadelphia: Westminster, 1971.

Coopersmith, S. *The antecedents of self-esteem.* San Francisco: W. H. Freeman, 1967.

Coppolino, C. A., and Coppolino, C. M. *The billion dollar hangover.* New York: Popular Library, 1965.

Costanzo, P. R., and Shaw, M. E. Conformity as a function of age level. *Child Development,* 1966, **37**, 967–975.

Crain, R. L., Katz, E., and Rosenthal, D. B. *The politics of community conflict: The fluoridation decision.* Indianapolis: Bobbs-Merrill, 1969.

Cronbach, L. J. Processes affecting scores on "understanding of others" and "assumed similarity." *Psychological Bulletin,* 1955, **52**, 177–193.

Cronbach, L. J. *Essentials of psychological testing.* (2nd ed.) New York: Harper, 1960.

Crotty, W. S. Presidential assassinations. *Society,* May 1972.

Crumbaugh, J. C. A scientific critique of parapsychology. In G. Schmeidler (Ed.), *Extrasensory perception.* New York: Atherton, 1969.

Curtis, G. C., and Zuckerman, M. A psychopathological reaction precipitated by sensory deprivation. *The American Journal of Psychiatry,* 1968, **125**, 255–260.

Dabbs, J. M., Jr., and Leventhal, H. Effects of varying the recommendations in a fear-arousing communication. *Journal of Personality and Social Psychology,* 1966, **4**(5), 525–531.

Darley, J. M., and Cooper, J. The "clean for Gene" phenomenon: The effects of students' appearance on political campaigning. *Journal of Applied Social Psychology,* 1972, **2**, 24–33.

Darley, J. M., and Latane, B. When will people help in a crisis? *Psychology Today,* December 1968.

Davids, L. North American marriage: 1990. *The Futurist,* 1971, **5**, 190–194.

Davidson, P. O. Validity of the guilty knowledge technique. *Journal of Applied Psychology,* 1968, **52**, 62–65.

Davis, E. G. *The first sex.* Baltimore: Penguin, 1971.

Davis, J. M., and Farina, A. Humor appreciation as social communication. *Journal of Personality and Social Psychology,* 1970, **15**, 175–178.

DeCharms, R., and Moeller, G. Values expressed in American children's readers: 1800–1950. *Journal of Abnormal and Social Psychology,* 1962, **64**, 136–142.

Deci, E. L. Work: Who does not like it and why. *Psychology Today,* August 1972.

Decter, M. *The new chastity and other arguments against women's liberation.* New York: Coward, McCann & Geoghegan, 1972.

Deikman, A. J. Experimental meditation. *Journal of Nervous and Mental Disease,* 1963, **136**, 329–373.

Delany, L. T. Racism and strategies for change. *Psychology Today,* August 1969.

Deloria, V. *Custer died for your sins.* New York: Avon, 1969.

Delp, H. A., and Lorenz, M. Follow-up of eighty-four public school special class pupils with I.Q.'s below fifty. *American Journal of Mental Deficiency,* 1953, **58**, 175–182.

Dember, W. N. Alternation behavior. In D. W. Fiske and S. R. Maddi (Eds.), *Functions of varied experience.* Homewood, Ill.: Dorsey, 1961.

Demby, E. H. Psychographics: Over-the-counter life-style. *Psychology Today,* April 1972.

Dement, W. C. The effect of dream deprivation. *Science,* 1960, **131**, 1705–1707.

Dement, W. C. An essay on dreams: The role of physiology in understanding their nature. In *New Directions in Psychology,* Vol. II. New York: Holt, 1965.

DeMott, B. *Supergrow.* New York: Dutton, 1969.

Dempsey, D. Learning how to die. *New York Times Magazine,* November 14, 1971.

Deutsch, M., and Brown, B. Social influences in Negro-white intelligence differences. *Journal of Social Issues,* 1964, **20**, 24–35.

Diamond, S. *What the trees said.* New York: Delacorte, 1971.

Dinger, J. Postschool adjustment of former educable retarded children. *Exceptional Children,* 1961, **27**, 353–360.

Dittes, J. E., and Kelley, H. H. Effects of different conditions of acceptance on conformity to group norms. *Journal of Abnormal and Social Psychology,* 1956, **53**, 100–107.

Dixon, J. J., deMonchaux, C., and Sandler, J. Patterns of anxiety: The phobias. *British Journal of Medical Psychology,* 1957, **30**, 34–40.

Dixon, R. B. Halleluja the pill? *Trans-action,* November–December, 1970.

Dollard, J., et al., *Frustration and aggression.* New Haven: Yale University Press, 1939.

Dollard, J., and Miller, N. E. *Personality and psychotherapy.* New York: McGraw-Hill, 1950.

Donovan, R. J. Does "typical" U.S. assassin start out as "lonely misfit"? *Detroit Sunday News,* September 24, 1972.

Doob, A. N., Carlsmith, J. M., Freedman, J. L., Landauer, T. K., and Tom, S., Jr. Effect of initial selling price on subsequent sales. *Journal of Personality and Social Psychology,* 1969, **11**, 345–350.

Doob, A. N., and Ecker, B. P. Stigma and compliance. *Journal of Personality and Social Psychology,* 1970, **14**, 302–304.

Dornbusch, S. M., Hastorf, A. H., Richardson, S. A., Muzzy, R. E., and Vreeland, R. S. The perceiver and the perceived: Their relative influence on the categories of interpersonal cognition. *Journal of Personality and Social Psychology,* 1965, **17**, 434–440.

Douglas, J. D. *Youth in turmoil.* Public Health Services Publication #2058. Chevy Chase, Md.: National Institutes of Mental Health, Center for Studies of Crime and Delinquency, 1970.

Driscoll, R., Davis, K. E., and Lipetz, M. E. Parental interference and romantic love: The Romeo and Juliet effect. Unpublished manuscript, University of Colorado, 1971.

Drucker, P. F. School around the bend. *Psychology Today,* June 1972.

Dubos, R. *The dreams of reason.* New York: Columbia University Press, 1961.

Dubos, R. J. Man adapting: His limitations and potentialities. In W. R. Ewald (Ed.), *Environment for man.* Bloomington: Indiana University Press, 1967.

Duncan, S., Jr. Nonverbal communication. *Psychological Bulletin,* 1969, **72**, 118–137.

Dunlap, R. E., and Gale, R. P. Politics and ecology: A political profile and student eco-activists. *Youth and Society,* 1972, **3**, 379–397.

Duva, N. A. (Ed.) *Somebody real: Voices of city children.* Rockaway, N.J.: American Faculty Press, 1972.

Eaton, J. W., and Weil, R. J. *Culture and mental disorders.* Glencoe, Ill.: Free Press, 1955.

Edwards, A. L. *The social desirability variable in personality assessment and research.* New York: Dryden, 1957.

Edwards, H. The myth of the racially superior athlete. *Intellectual Digest,* March 1972.

Egan, G. *Encounter: Group processes for interpersonal growth.* Belmont, Calif.: Brooks/Cole, 1970.

Eisenberg, L., and Kanner, L. Early infantile autism: 1943–55. *American Journal of Orthopsychiatry,* 1956, **26**, 556–566.

Elms, A. C. Influence of fantasy ability on attitude change through role playing. *Journal of Personality and Social Psychology,* 1966, **4**, 36–43.

Ellis, H. *A study of British genius.* (New rev. ed.) Boston: Houghton Mifflin, 1926. (Originally published in 1904 by Hurst and Blackett, London.)

Elton, C. F., and Shevel, L. R. *Who is talented? An analysis of achievement.* (Res. Rep. No. 31.) Iowa City, Iowa, American College Testing Program, 1969.

Emmons, W. H., and Simon, C. W. The non-recall of material presented during sleep. *American Journal of Psychology,* 1956, **69**, 76–81.

English, F. TA's Disney World. *Psychology Today,* April 1973.

Epstein, R., and Komorita, S. S. Self-esteem, success-failure, and locus of control in Negro children. *Developmental Psychology,* 1971, **4**, 2–8.

Ervin-Tripp, S. Language development. In M. L. Hoffman and L. W. Hoffman (Eds.), *Review of child development research.* New York: Russell Sage Foundation, 1966.

Esposito, J. C. *Vanishing air.* New York: Grossman, 1970.

Ettinger, R. C. W. *The prospect of immortality.* New York: Macfadden-Bartell, 1964.

Etzioni, A. Human beings are not very easy to change after all. *Saturday Review,* June 3, 1972.

Evans, D. R. An exploratory study into the treatment of exhibitionism by means of emotive imagery and aversive conditioning. *Canadian Psychologist,* 1967, **8**, 162.

Evans, W. O. Mind-altering drugs and the future. *The Futurist,* June 1971.

Exline, R. V., Thibaut, J., Hickey, C. O., and Gumpert, P. Visual interaction in relation to Machiavellianism and an unethical act. In R. Christie and F. L. Geis (Eds.), *Studies in Machiavellianism.* New York: Academic Press, 1970.

Eysenck, H. J. Learning theory and behavior therapy. *Journal of Mental Science,* 1959, **105**, 61–75.

Fairfield, D. Communes, USA. *The modern utopian.* Vol. 5, nos. 1, 2, 3. San Francisco: Alternatives Foundation, 1971.

Fairweather, G. W., Sanders, D. H., Maynard, R. F., and Cressler, D. L. *Community life for the mentally ill: Alternative to institutional care.* Chicago: Aldine, 1969.

Farber, L. H. Ours is the addicted society. *New York Times Magazine,* December 11, 1966.

Farberow, N. L. Self-destruction and identity. *Humanitas,* 1970, **6**, 45–68.

Farberow, N. L., and Schneidman, E. S. *The cry for help.* New York: McGraw-Hill, 1961.

Farson, R. E. Emotional barriers to education. *Psychology Today,* October 1967.

Fast, J. *Body language.* New York: Pocket Books, 1971.

Faucheux, C., and Moscovici, S. Le style de compotement d'une minorité et son influence sur les résponses d'une majorité. *Bulletin du Centre d'Études et Recherches Psychologiques,* 1967, **16**, 337–360.

Feagin, J. R. God helps those who help themselves. *Psychology Today,* November 1972.

Fenz, W. D., and Epstein, S. Gradients of physiological arousal in parachutists as a function of an approaching jump. *Psychosomatic Medicine,* 1967, **29**, 33–51.

Ferdinand, T. N. Sex behavior and the American class structure: A mosaic. In E. Sagarin (Ed.), *Sex and the contemporary American scene. The Annals,* 1968, **376**, 76–85.

Ferrare, N. A. Institutionalization and attitude change in an aged population. Doctoral dissertation, Western Reserve University, 1962.

Ferster, C. B. Positive reinforcement and behavioral deficits of autistic children. *Child Development,* 1961, **32**, 437–456.

Festinger, L. Cognitive dissonance. *Scientific American,* October 1962.

Festinger, L., and Carlsmith, J. M. Cognitive consequences of forced compliance. *Journal of Abnormal and Social Psychology,* 1959, **58**, 203–210.

Festinger, L., Pepitone, A., and Newcomb, T. Some consequences of deindividuation in a group. *Journal of Abnormal and Social Psychology,* 1952, **47**, 382–389.

Festinger, L., Riecken, H., and Schachter, S. *When prophecy fails.* Minneapolis: University of Minnesota Press, 1956.

Festinger, L., Schachter, S., and Back, K. *Social pressures in informal groups: A study of human factors in housing.* New York: Harper, 1950.

Feuer, L. *The conflict of generations: The character and significance of student movements.* New York: Basic Books, 1969.

Fiedler, F. E. Style or circumstance: The leadership enigma. *Psychology Today,* March 1969.

Fiedler, F. E. The trouble with leadership training is that it doesn't train leaders. *Psychology Today,* February 1973.

Field, M. G. The child as father to what kind of man? *Psychiatry and Social Science Review,* 1970, **4**, 2–6.

Field, R. The technology of TV violence. *Saturday Review,* June 10, 1972.

Fincher, C. *A preface to psychology.* New York: Harper, 1964.

Fine, R. The psychology of blindfold chess: An introspective account. *Acta Psychologia,* 1965, **24**, 352–370.

Fishbein, M. Statistics and the epidemiology of arteriosclerosis. *Postgraduate Medicine,* 1962, **31**, 311–312.

Fitts, P. M. Engineering psychology. In P. R. Farnsworth and Q. McNemar (Eds.), *Annual review of psychology,* Vol. IX. Palo Alto, Calif.: Annual Reviews, 1958.

Fitzelle, G. T. Personality factors and certain attitudes toward child rearing among parents of asthmatic children. *Psychosomatic Medicine,* 1959, **21**, 208–217.

Flacks, R. The liberated generation: An explanation of the roots of student protest. *Journal of Social Issues,* 1967, **23**, 52–75.

Flanagan, J. C. The definition and measurement of ingenuity. In C. W. Taylor and F. Barron (Eds.), *Scientific creativity: Its recognition and development.* New York: Wiley, 1963.

Flapan, M. A paradigm for the analysis of childbearing motivations of married women prior to birth of the first child. *American Journal of Orthopsychiatry,* 1969, **39**, 402–417.

Flexner, L. B., and Flexner, J. B. Intracerebral saline effect on memory of trained mice treated with puronycin. *Science,* 1968, **159**, 330–331.

Forbes, J. D. (Ed.) *The Indian in America's past.* Englewood Cliffs, N.J.: Prentice-Hall, 1964.

Ford, C. S., and Beach, F. A. *Patterns of sexual behavior.* New York: Harper, 1952.

Fort, J. The pleasure seekers. *Mind over matter,* 1970, **15**(1), 65–83.

Foucault, M. *Madness and civilization: A history of insanity in the age of reason.* New York: Pantheon, 1965.

Frager, R. Jewish mothering in Japan. *Sociological Inquiry,* 1972, **42**(1), 11–18.

Francoeur, R. T. *Utopian motherhood.* Doubleday, 1970.

Frank, G. *The Boston strangler.* New York: New American Library, 1966.

Frank, J. D. The face of the enemy. *Psychology Today,* November 1968.

Frank. J. D. The bewildering world of psychotherapy. *Journal of Social Issues,* 1972, **28**, 27–40.

Frank, J. D. The demoralized mind. *Psychology Today,* April 1973.

Frankl, V. E. *Man's search for meaning.* Boston: Beacon, 1958.

Freedman, L. Z. "Truth" drugs. *Scientific American,* March 1960.

Freedman, A. M., and Kaplan, H. I. *Psychiatry.* Baltimore: Williams & Wilkins, 1967.

Freedman, J. L., and Doob, A. N. *Deviancy.* New York: Academic Press, 1968.

Freedman, J. L., and Fraser, S. C. Compliance without pressure: The foot-in-the-door technique. *Journal of Personality and Social Psychology,* 1966, **4**, 195–202.

Freedman, J. L., and Sears, D. O. Selective exposure. In L. Berkowitz (Ed.), *Advances in experimental social psychology,* Vol. II. New York: Academic Press, 1965.

Freeman, J. Growing up girlish. *Trans-Action,* November-December 1970.

Freeman, L. *Your mind can stop the common cold.* New York: Peter H. Wyden, 1973.

Freud, S. Civilization and its discontents. In *Standard Edition,* Vol. 21. London: Hogarth, 1961. (First German ed., 1930).

Freud, S. *The complete introductory lectures on psychoanalysis.* James Strachey (Trans. and Ed.). New York: Norton, 1966.

Friedenberg, E. Z. Current patterns of generational conflict. *Journal of Social Issues,* 1969, **25**, 21–38.

Friedlander, B. Z., McCarthy, J. J., and Soforenko, A. Z. Automated psychological evaluation with severely retarded institutionalized infants. *American Journal of Mental Deficiency,* 1967, **71**, 909–919.

Fuchs, L. H. *Family matters.* New York: Random, 1972.

Fuller, P. R. Operant conditioning of a vegetative human organism. *American Journal of Psychology,* 1949, **62**, 587–590.

Gagnon, J. H. There is no sex revolution. *Bloomington* (Ind.) *Herald-Telephone,* January 19, 1967.

Galanter, E. Contemporary psychophysics. In R. Brown et al. (Eds.), *New directions in psychology,* Vol. 1. New York: Holt, 1962.

Gale, R. F. *Developmental behavior: A humanistic approach.* New York: Macmillan, 1969.

Garcia, J. IQ: The conspiracy. *Psychology Today,* September 1972.

Gardner, M. *Fads and fallacies in the name of science.* New York: Dover, 1952.

Garvey, C., and McFarlane, P. A measure of standard English proficiency of inner-city children. *American Educational Research Journal,* 1970, **7**, 29–40.

Gates, A. I. Recitation as a factor in memorizing. Quoted in J. Deese, *The psychology of learning* (2nd ed.). New York: McGraw-Hill, 1958.

Gault, W. B. Some remarks on slaughter. *American Journal of Psychiatry,* 1971, **128**, 82–88.

Gazzaniga, M. S. The split brain in man. *Scientific American,* August 1967.

Geldard, F. A. Skin language: Body English. *Psychology Today,* December 1968.

Gelder, M. G., and Marks, I. M. A controlled prospective trial of behavior therapy. *British Journal of Psychiatry,* 1966, **112**, 309–319.

Gelder, M. G., and Marks, I. M. Desensitization and phobias: A crossover study. *British Journal of Psychiatry,* 1968, **114**, 323–328.

Gelder, M. G., Marks, I. M., Wolff, H. H., and Clarke, M. Desensitization and psychotherapy in the treatment of phobic states: A controlled inquiry. *British Journal of Psychiatry,* 1967, **113**, 53–73.

Gerard, H. B. Emotional uncertainty and social comparison. *Journal of Abnormal and Social Psychology,* 1963, **66**, 568–573.

Getzels, J., and Jackson, P. Family environmental and cognitive style: A study of the sources of highly intelligent and of highly creative adolescents. *American Sociological Review,* 1961, **26**, 351–359.

Getzels, J. W., and Jackson, P. W. *Creativity and intelligence.* New York: Wiley, 1962.

Gibson, E. J. *Principles of perceptual learning and development.* New York: Appleton-Century-Crofts, 1969.

Gibson, E. J., and Walk, R. D. The visual cliff. *Scientific American,* April 1960.

Giles, D. K., and Wolf, M. M. Toilet training institutionalized severe retardates: An application of operant behavior modification techniques. *American Journal of Mental Deficiency,* 1966, **70**, 766–780.

Girardeau, F. L., and Spradlin, J. E. Token rewards in a cottage program. *Mental Retardation,* 1964, **2**, 345–351.

Glaser, B. G., and Strauss, A. L. Dying on time. *Trans-action,* May-June 1965.

Gleason, H. A., Jr. *An introduction to descriptive linguistics.* (Rev. ed.) New York: Holt, 1961.

Glick, B. S. Conditioning therapy with phobic patients: Success and failure. *American Journal of Psychotherapy,* 1970, **24**, 92–101.

Gmelch, G. Baseball magic. *Trans-action,* June 1971.

Goldberg, P. Are women prejudiced against women? *Trans-action,* September-October 1968.

Goldberg, S., and Lewis, M. Play behavior in the year-old infant: Early sex differences. *Child Development,* 1969, **40**, 21–31.

Goldhamer, H., and Marshall, A. W. *Psychosis and civilization.* New York: Free Press, 1949.

Goldman, R. K. Psychosocial development in cross-cultural perspective: A new look at an old issue. *Developmental Psychology,* 1971, **5**, 411–419.

Goldman, R., Jaffa, M., and Schachter, S. Yom Kippur, Air France, dormitory food, and the eating behavior of obese and normal persons. *Journal of Personality and Social Psychology,* 1968, **10**, 117–123.

Goldwyn, R. M. Operating for the aging face. *Psychiatry in Medicine,* July 1972, **3**, 187–195.

Golub, A. M., Masiarz, F. R., Villars, T., and McConnell, J. V. Incubation effects in behavior induction in rats. *Science,* 1970, **168**, 392–395.

Goodall, K. Casualty lists from encounter groups. *Psychology Today,* July 1971. (a)

Goodall, K. Litterbags and dimes for litterbugs. *Psychology Today,* December 1971. (b)

Goodall, K. Big brother and the presidency. *Psychology Today,* April 1972. (a)

Goodall, K. Shapers at work. *Psychology Today,* November 1972. (b)

Goplerud, C. P., and Miller, G. M. Drugs in pregnancy. *Journal of the Iowa Medical Society,* 1968, **58,** 707–708.

Gough, H. G. Clinical versus statistical prediction in psychology. In L. Postman (Ed.), *Psychology in the making.* New York: Knopf, 1962.

Grayson, R. R. Air controllers syndrome: Peptic ulcer in air traffic controllers. *Illinois Medical Journal,* August 1972.

Greeley, A. M. *Come blow your mind with me.* New York: Doubleday, 1971.

Green, A. H. Self-mutilation in schizophrenic children. *Archives of General Psychiatry,* 1967, **17**, 234–244.

Green, H. *I never promised you a rose garden.* New York: Holt, 1964.

Greenblatt, M. Psychosurgery. In A. M. Freedman and H. I. Kaplan (Eds.), *Psychiatry.* Baltimore: Williams & Wilkins, 1967.

Greene, W. The militant Malthusians. *Saturday Review,* March 11, 1972.

Greenspoon, J. The reinforcing effect of two spoken sounds on the frequency of two responses. *American Journal of Psychology,* 1955, **68**, 409–416.

Greenwald, H. *The call girl.* New York: Ballantine, 1958.

Greer, G. *The female eunuch.* New York: McGraw-Hill, 1971.

Gregory, R. C. *No more lies: The myth and the reality of American history.* New York: Harper, 1971.

Gregory, R. L. *Eye and brain: The psychology of seeing.* New York: McGraw-Hill, 1966.

Gregory, R. L. Visual illusions. *Scientific American,* May 1968.

Grinker, R. R., Miller, J., Sabshin, M., Nunn, R., and Nunnally, J. C. *The phenomena of depressions.* New York: Hoeber, 1961.

Grinspoon, L., and Hedblom, P. Amphetamines reconsidered. *Saturday Review,* July 8, 1972. (Special issue)

Gross, L. Who cares? *Look Magazine,* September 8, 1964.

Gross, M. L. *The brain watchers.* New York: Random, 1962.

Grossman, D. On whose unscientific methods and unaware values? *Psychotherapy: Theory, Research and Practice,* 1968, **5**, 43–54.

Grossman, F. K. Brothers and sisters of retarded children. *Psychology Today,* April 1972.

Groves, W. E., Rossi, P. H., and Grafstein, D. Study of life styles and campus communities: A preliminary report to students who participated. Johns Hopkins University, Department of Social Relations, 1970.

Guilford, J. P. A factor analytic study across the domains of reasoning, creativity, and evaluation: Hypothesis and description of tests. *Reports from the psychology laboratory.* Los Angeles: University of Southern California, 1954.

Guilford, J. P. *The nature of human intelligence.* New York: McGraw-Hill, 1967.

Gustin, J. L. The revolt of youth. *Psychoanalysis and the Psychoanalytic Review,* 1961, **98**, 78–90.

Haan, N., Smith, M. B., and Block, J. Moral reasoning of young adults: Political-social behavior, family background, and personality correlates. *Journal of Personality and Social Psychology,* 1968, **10**, 183–201.

Haber, R. N. Eidetic images. *Scientific American,* April 1969.

Haber, R. N. How we remember what we see. *Scientific American,* June 1970.

Hacker, H. M. The new burdens of masculinity. *Marriage and Family Living,* 1957, **19**, 227–233.

Haggard, E. A., As, A., and Bergen, G. M. Social isolates and urbanites in perceptual isolation. *Journal of Abnormal Psychology,* 1970, **76**, 1–9.

Haggstrom, W. C. The power of the poor. In L. A. Ferman, J. L. Kornbluh, and A. Haber (Eds.), *Poverty in America.* Ann Arbor: University of Michigan Press, 1971.

Haimowitz, M. I., and Haimowitz, N. R. (Eds.) *Human development.* New York: Crowell, 1960.

Hall, C. S., and Lindzey, G. *Theories of personality.* (2nd ed.) New York: Wiley, 1970.

Hall, E. T. Silent assumptions in social communication. In F. W. Matson and A. Montague (Eds.), *The human dialogue.* New York: Free Press, 1967.

Halleck, S. The reform of mental hospitals. *Psychology Today,* March 1969.

Hanratty, M. D., O'Neal, E., and Sulzer, J. L. The effect of frustration upon imitation of aggression. *Journal of Personality and Social Psychology,* 1972, **21**, 30–34.

Hardyck, J. A., and Braden, M. Prophecy fails again: A report of a failure to replicate. *Journal of Abnormal and Social Psychology,* 1962, **65**, 136–141.

Harlow, H. F. The nature of love. *American Psychologist,* 1958, **13**, 673–685.

Harlow, H. F. Love in infant monkeys. *Scientific American,* March 1959.

Harlow, H. F., and Harlow, M. K. A study of animal affection. *Natural History,* 1961, **70**, 48–55.

Harlow, H. F., and Harlow, M. K. The effect of rearing conditions on behavior. *Bulletin of the Menninger Clinic,* 1962, **26**, 213–224.

Harlow, H. F., and Harlow, M. K. The effect of rearing conditions on behavior. In J. Morey (Ed.), *Sex research: New developments.* New York: Holt, 1965.

Harlow, R. S. *A life after death.* New York: Doubleday, 1961.

Harrington, M. *The other America.* Baltimore: Penguin, 1962.

Hartley, R. E. Sex-role pressures and the socialization of the male child. *Psychological Reports,* 1959, **5**, 457–468.

Hartmann, E., Baekeland, F., Zwilling, G., and Hoy, P. Sleep need: How much sleep and what kind? *American Journal of Psychiatry,* 1971, **127**, 41–48 (1001–1008).

Hastorf, A. H., Schneider, D. J., and Polefka, J. *Person perception.* Reading, Mass.: Addison-Wesley, 1970.

Havighurst, R. J. *Human development and education.* New York: Longmans Green, 1953.

Havighurst, R. J. Minority subcultures and the law of effect. The Annual Edward L. Thorndike Award Lecture presented to the Division of Educational Psychology at the Annual Meeting of the American Psychological Association, Washington, D.C., August 31, 1969.

Hawkins, R. P. It's time we taught the young how to be good parents (and don't you wish we'd started a long time ago?). *Psychology Today,* November 1972.

Hayes, K. J., and Hayes, C. The intellectual development of a home-raised chimpanzee. *American Philosophical Society,* 1951, **95**, 105–109.

Hays, R. R. *The dangerous sex.* New York: Putnam's, 1964.

Hebb, D. O. *Textbook of psychology.* (3rd ed.) Philadelphia: Saunders, 1972.

Heckhausen, H. *The anatomy of achievement motivation.* New York: Academic Press, 1967.

Heckhausen, H. Achievement motive research: Current problems and some contributions towards a general theory of motivation. In W. Arnold (Ed.), *Nebraska symposium on motivation.* Lincoln: University of Nebraska Press, 1968.

Heider, F. *The psychology of interpersonal relations.* New York: Wiley, 1958.

Heilman, M. E., Hodgson, S. A., and Hornstein, H. A. Effects of magnitude and rectifiability of harm and information value on the reporting of accidental harm-doing. *Journal of Personality and Social Psychology,* 1972, **23**, 211–218.

Held, R. and Hein, A. Movement-produced stimulation in the development of visually controlled movement by selective exposure during rearing. *Journal of Comparative and Physiological Psychology,* 1963, **56**, 872–876.

Henry, J. *Culture against man.* New York: Random, 1963.

Heron, W. The pathology of boredom. *Scientific American,* January 1957.

Heron, W. Cognitive and physiological effects of perceptual isolation. In P. Solomon et al. (Eds.), *Sensory deprivation.* Cambridge: Harvard University Press, 1961.

Herschelman, P., and Freundlich, D. Group therapy with multiple therapists in a large group. *Journal of American Psychiatry,* 1970, **127**, 457–461.

Hess, E. H. Imprinting: An effect of early experience. *Science,* 1959, **130**, 133–141.

Hess, E. H. Attitude and pupil size. *Scientific American,* April 1965.

Hetherington, E. M. Effects of father absence on personality development in adolescent daughters. *Developmental Psychology,* 1972, **7**, 313–326.

Hetherington, E. M. Girls without fathers. *Psychology Today,* February 1973.

Heussenstamm, F. K. Bumper stickers and the cops. *Transaction,* February 1971.

Higgins, J. The concept of process-reactive schizophrenia: Criteria and related research. *Journal of Nervous and Mental Disease,* 1964, **138**, 9–25.

Hilgard, E. R. *Introduction to psychology.* (3rd ed.) New York: Harcourt, 1962.

Hilgard, E. R. *Hypnotic susceptibility.* New York: Harcourt, 1965.

Hilgard, E. R., Atkinson, R. L., and Atkinson, R., et al. *Introduction to psychology.* (5th ed.) New York: Harcourt, 1971.

Hilgard, J., and Newman, M. F. Anniversaries in mental illness. *Psychiatry,* 1959, **22**, 113–121.

Hill, H. Anti-oriental agitation and the rise of working-class racism. *Society,* January-February 1973.

Hill, W. F. Activity as an autonomous drive. *Journal of*

Comparative and Physiological Psychology, 1956, **49**, 15–19.

Himwich, H. E. Research in medical aspects of aging. *Geriatrics,* 1962, **17,** 89–97.

Hoch, E. L. Psychology today: Conceptions and misconceptions. In W. B. Webb (Ed.), *The profession of psychology.* New York: Holt, 1962.

Hochreich, D. J., and Rotter, J. B. Have college students become less trusting? *Journal of Personality and Social Psychology,* 1970, **15,** 211–214.

Hockett, C. F. The origin of speech. *Scientific American,* July 1960.

Hoffman, B. *The tyranny of testing.* New York: Crowell-Collier, 1962.

Hoffman, M. L. Father absence and conscience· development. *Developmental Psychology,* 1971, **4,** 400–406.

Hoffman, M. L., Mitsos, S. B., and Protz, R. E. Achievement striving, social class, and test anxiety. *Journal of Abnormal and Social Psychology,* 1958, **56,** 401–403.

Holland, M. K., and Tarlow, G. Blinking and mental load. *Psychological Reports,* 1972, **31,** 119–127.

Holliday, A. R. A review of psychopharmacology. In B. B. Wolman (Ed.), *Handbook of clinical psychology.* New York: McGraw-Hill, 1965.

Hollingshead, A. B., and Redlich, F. C. *Social class and mental illness.* New York: Wiley, 1958.

Holmes, T. H., and Masuda, M. Psychosomatic syndrome: When mothers-in-law or other disasters visit, a person can develop a bad, bad cold. Or worse. *Psychology Today,* April 1972.

Honzik, M., Macfarlane, J., and Allen, L. The stability of mental test performance between two and eighteen years. *Journal of Experimental Education,* 1948, **17,** 309–324.

Hoover, E. L. Alpha: The first step to a new level of reality. *Human Behavior,* May-June 1972. (a)

Hoover, E. L. The age of encounter. *Human Behavior,* January-February 1972. (b)

Hormuth, R. A proposed program to combat mental retardation. *Children,* 1963, **10,** 29–31.

Horner, M. Fail: Bright women. *Psychology Today,* November 1969.

Horowitz, I. M. *Assassination.* New York: Harper, 1972.

Houriet, R. *Getting back together.* New York: Coward, McCann & Geoghegan, 1971.

Houston, S. H. Black English. *Psychology Today,* March 1973.

Hovland, C. I. Reconciling conflicting results derived from experimental and survey studies of attitude change. *American Psychologist,* 1959, **14,** 8–17.

Howard, J. T. Some thoughts on the future. In W. R. Ewald (Ed.), *Environment for man.* Bloomington: Indiana University Press, 1967.

Howe, I. The middle-class mind of Kate Millett. *Harper's,* December 1970.

Huff, D. *How to lie with statistics.* New York: Norton, 1954.

Hunt, M. The future of marriage. *Playboy,* August 1971.

Hunter, E. *Brainwashing in Red China.* New York: Vanguard, 1951.

Hurlock, E. B. American adolescents of today: A new species. *Adolescence,* 1966, **1,** 7–21.

Iversen, G. R., et al. Bias and runs in dice throwing and recording: A few million throws. *Psychometrika,* 1971, **36,** 1–19.

Jackson, C. M. Some aspects of form and growth. In Robbins, W. J., et al., *Growth.* New Haven: Yale University Press, 1928.

Jackson, J. K. The adjustment of the family to alcoholism. *Journal of Marriage and Family Living,* 1956, **18,** 361–369.

Jacobs, J. *The death and life of great American cities.* New York: Random, 1961.

Jacobs, J. Adolescent suicide. New York: Wiley, 1971.

Jacobs, M. A., and Spilken, A. Z. Personality patterns associated with heavy cigarette smoking in male college students. *Journal of Consulting and Clinical Psychology,* 1971, **37,** 428–432.

Jacobs, P. A., and Strong, J. A. A case of human intersexuality having a possible XXY sex-determining mechanism. *Nature,* 1959, **183,** 302.

Janis, I. L., and Feshbach, S. Effects of fear-arousing communications. *Journal of Abnormal and Social Psychology,* 1953, **48,** 78–92.

Janis, I. L., Keye, D., and Kirschner, P. Facilitating effects of "eating-while-reading" on responsiveness to persuasive communications. *Journal of Personality and Social Psychology,* 1965, **1,** 181–186.

Janis, I. L., Mahl, G. F., Kagan, J., Holt, R. R. *Personality: Dynamics, development, and assessment.* New York: Harcourt, 1969.

Janis, I. L., and Mann, L. Effectiveness of emotional role-playing in modifying smoking habits and attitudes. *Journal of Experimental Research in Personality,* 1965, **1,** 84–90.

Jensen, A. R. Counter response. *Journal of Social Issues,* 1969, **25,** 219–222. (a)

Jensen, A. R. How much can we boost IQ and scholastic achievement? *Harvard Educational Review,* 1969, **39,** 1–123. (b)

Jersild, A. T., Markey, F. V., and Jersild, C. L. Children's fears, dreams, wishes, daydreams, likes, dislikes, pleasant and unpleasant memories. In A. T. Jersild, *Child psychology.* Englewood Cliffs, N.J.: Prentice-Hall, 1960. (Orig. pub. 1933)

Johnson, D. A., Porter, R. J., and Mateljan, P. Racial discrimination in apartment rentals. *Journal of Applied Social Psychology,* 1971, **1**, 364–377.

Johnson, G. O. A study of social inadequacy and of social failure of mentally retarded youth in Wayne County, Michigan. *Exceptional Child,* 1957, **24**, 136–138.

Jonas, A. D., and Klein, D. F. The logic of ESP. *American Journal of Psychiatry,* 1970, **126**, 1173–1177.

Jones, H. E. *Motor performance and growth.* Berkeley and Los Angeles: University of California Press, 1949.

Jones, M. C. The later careers of boys who were early- or late-maturing. *Child Development,* 1957, **93**, 87–111.

Josephson, E., and Josephson, M. (Eds.) *Man alone.* New York: Dell (Laurel ed.), 1962.

Jost, H., and Sontag, L. W. The genetic factor in autonomic nervous system function. *Psychosomatic Medicine,* 1944, **6**, 308–310.

Julian, J. W., Ryckman, R. M., and Hollander, E. P. *Effects of prior group support on conformity: An extension.* Technical Report 4, ONR Contract 4679. Buffalo: State University of New York, 1966.

Julian, J. W., Regula, C. R., and Hollander, E. P. *Effects of prior agreement from others on task confidence and conformity.* Technical Report 9, ONR Contract 4679. Buffalo: State University of New York, 1967.

Kaats, G. R., and Davis, K. E. The dynamics of sexual behavior of college students. *Journal of Marriage and the Family,* 1970, **32**, 389–399.

Kagan, J. The child: His struggle for identity. *Saturday Review,* December 7, 1968.

Kagan, J. On the meaning of behavior: Illustrations from the infant. *Child Development,* 1969, **40**, 1121–1134.

Kagan, J., and Lewis, M. Studies of attention in the human infant. *Merrill Palmer Quarterly of Behavior and Development,* 1965, **11**, 95–127.

Kagan, J., and Moss, H. A. *Birth to maturity.* New York: Wiley, 1962.

Kahn, H., and Wiener, A. J. *The year 2000.* New York: Macmillan, 1967.

Kahn, M., Baker, B. L., and Weiss, J. M. Treatment of insomnia by relaxation training. *Journal of Abnormal Psychology,* 1968, **73**, 556–558.

Kahn, R. L. Violent man: Who buys bloodshed and why. *Psychology Today,* June 1972.

Kahn, R. L. The work module: A tonic for lunchpail lassitude. *Psychology Today,* February 1973.

Kalish, R. A. The old and new as generation gap allies. *Gerontologist,* 1969, **9**, 83–89.

Kamiya, J. Conscious control of brain waves. *Psychology Today,* April 1968.

Kanner, L. Autistic disturbances of affective contact. *Nervous Child,* 1943, **2**, 217–250.

Kanner, L., and Eisenberg, L. Notes on the follow-up studies of autistic children. In P. M. Hoch and J. Zubin (Eds.), *Psychopathology of childhood.* New York: Grune & Stratton, 1955.

Kant, H. S., and Goldstein, M. J. Pornography. *Psychology Today,* December 1970.

Kaplan, J. A legal look at prosocial behavior: What can happen for failing to help or trying to help someone. *Journal of Social Issues,* 1972, **28**, 219–226.

Karacan, I., and Williams, R. L. Insomnia: Old wine in a new bottle. *Psychiatric Quarterly,* 1971, **45**, 274–288.

Kasper, A. M. The doctor and death. In H. Feifel (Ed.), *The meaning of death.* New York: McGraw-Hill, 1959.

Kastenbaum, R. Age: Getting there ahead of time. *Psychology Today,* December 1971.

Katona, G. *The mass consumption society.* New York: McGraw-Hill, 1964.

Katz, D. The functional approach to the study of attitude change. *Public Opinion Quarterly,* 1960, **17**, 69–78.

Katz, D. The chilling prospects of psychosurgery. *Detroit Free Press,* December 30, 1972.

Katz, E. *Armed love.* New York: Bantam, 1971.

Katz, I. Review of evidence relating to effects of desegregation on the intellectual performance of Negroes. *American Psychologist,* 1964, **19**, 381–399.

Katz, I. Some motivational determinants of racial differences in intellectual achievement. *International Journal of Psychology,* 1967, **2**, 1–12.

Katz, I., Epps, E. G., and Axelson, L. J. Effect upon Negro digit-symbol performance of anticipated comparison with whites and with other Negroes. *Journal of Abnormal and Social Psychology,* 1964, **69**, 77–83.

Katz, I., and Greenbaum, C. Effects of anxiety, threat, and racial environment on task performance of Negro college students. *Journal of Abnormal and Social Psychology,* 1963, **66**, 562–567.

Katz, I., Henchy, J., and Allen, H. Effects of race of tester, approval-disapproval, and need on Negro children's learning. *Journal of Personality and Social Psychology,* 1968, **8**, 38–42.

Kaufmann, H. *Introduction to the study of human behavior.* Philadelphia: Saunders, 1968.

Kayton, L., and Borge, G. F. Birth order and the obsessive-compulsive character. *Archives of General Psychiatry,* 1967, **17**, 751–754.

Keen, S. Sing the body electric. *Psychology Today,* October 1970.

Keen, S. Janov and primal therapy: "The screaming cure." *Psychology Today,* February 1972.

Kelly, G. A. *The psychology of personal constructs.* New York: Norton, 1955.

Kendler, H. H., and Kendler, T. S. Vertical and horizontal processes in problem solving. *Psychological Review,* 1962, **69**, 1–16.

Kendon, A. Some functions of gaze-direction in social interaction. *Acta Psychologica,* 1967, **26**, 22–63.

Keniston, K. The sources of student dissent. *Journal of Social Issues,* 1967, **23**, 108–132.

Kerr, N., Meyerson, L., and Michael, J. A procedure for shaping vocalizations in a mute child. In L. P. Ullman and L. Krasner (Eds.), *Case studies in behavior modification.* New York: Holt, 1965.

Kerry, R. J. Phobia of outer space. *Journal of Mental Science,* 1960, **106**, 1383–1387.

Kessler, J. W. *Psychopathology of childhood.* Englewood Cliffs, N.J.: Prentice-Hall, 1966.

Keutzer, C. S., Lichtenstein, E., and Mees, H. L. Modification of smoking behavior: A review. *Psychological Bulletin,* 1968, **70**, 520–533.

Keys, A., Brozek, J., Henschel, A., Mickelson, O., and Taylor, H. L. *The biology of human starvation.* Minneapolis: University of Minnesota Press, 1950.

Kiesler, C. A. Group pressure and conformity. In J. Mills (Ed.), *Experimental social psychology.* New York: Macmillan, 1969.

Kiev, A. Prescientific psychiatry. In S. Arieti (Ed.), *American handbook of psychiatry,* Vol. III. New York: Basic Books, 1966.

Kimbrell, K. L., Luckey, R. E., Barbuto, P. F., and Love, J. G. Operation dry pants: An intensive habit-training program for severely and profoundly retarded. *Mental Retardation,* 1967, **5**, 32–36.

Klapper, J. T. The impact of viewing "aggression": Studies and problems of extrapolation. In O. N. Larsen (Ed.), *Violence and the mass media.* New York: Harper, 1968.

Kleitman, N. *Sleep and wakefulness.* Chicago: University of Chicago Press, 1939.

Knobloch, H., and Pasamanick, B. Etiologic factors in "early infantile autism" and "childhood schizophrenia." Paper presented at the 10th International Congress of Pediatrics, Lisbon, Portugal, September 1962.

Kogan, N., and Wallach, M. A. *Risk taking: A study in cognition and personality.* New York: Holt, 1964.

Kohlberg, L. Moral development and identification. In H. Stevenson (Ed.), *Child psychology.* 62nd Yearbook of the National Society for the Study of Education. Chicago: University of Chicago Press, 1963.

Kohlberg, L. The child as a moral philosopher. *Psychology Today,* February 1968.

Kohlberg, L. The cognitive-developmental approach to socialization. In D. A. Goslin (Ed.), *Handbook of socialization theory and research.* Chicago: Rand McNally, 1969.

Köhler, W. Gestalt psychology. *Psychologische Forschung,* 1967, **31**, 18–30.

Kolb, L. C. *Noyes' modern clinical psychiatry.* (7th ed.) Philadelphia: Saunders, 1968.

Kovel, J. *White racism: A psychohistory.* New York: Pantheon, 1970.

Kozol, J. *Free schools.* Boston: Houghton Mifflin, 1972.

Kraditor, A. *Up from the pedestal: Selected writings in the history of American feminism.* Chicago: Quadrangle, 1968.

Kraines, S. H. *Mental depressions and their treatment.* New York: Macmillan, 1957.

Kramer, R. A fresh look at the only child. *New York Times Magazine,* October 15, 1972.

Krebs, D., and Whitten, P. Guilt-edged giving: The shame of it all. *Psychology Today,* January 1972.

Krebs, R. L. Girls: More moral than boys or just sneakier? *Proceedings of the 76th annual convention of the APA,* 1968, **3**, 607–608.

Krech, D., and Crutchfield, R. *Theory and problems of social psychology.* New York: McGraw-Hill, 1948.

Krech, D., Crutchfield, R., and Ballachey, E. *Individual in society.* New York: McGraw-Hill, 1962.

Krippner, S., and Davidson, R. Parapsychology in the U.S.S.R. *Saturday Review,* March 18, 1972.

Krippner, S., and Hughes, W. Genius at work. *Psychology Today,* June 1970.

Kriss, R. P. Gun control: A missed target. *Saturday Review,* August 26, 1972.

Kroger, W. S. *Childbirth with hypnosis.* New York: Doubleday, 1961.

Krutch, J. W. A naturalist looks at overpopulation. In F. Osborn (Ed.), *Our crowded planet.* New York: Doubleday, 1962.

Kubzansky, P. E., and Leiderman, P. H. Sensory deprivation: An overview. In P. Solomon et al. (Eds.), *Sensory deprivation.* Cambridge: Harvard University Press, 1961.

Labov, W. The logic of non-standard English. In F. Williams (Ed.), *Language and poverty: Perspectives on a theme.* Chicago: Markham, 1970.

Labov, W., and Cohen, P. Systematic relations of standard and non-standard rules in the grammar of Negro speakers. Paper presented at the 7th Project Literacy Conference, Cambridge, Mass., May 1967.

Lacey, J. L., Bateman, D. E., and Van Lehn, R. Automatic response specificity: An experimental study. *Psychosomatic Medicine,* 1953, **15**, 8–21.

Laing, R. D. *The politics of experience.* New York: Ballantine, 1967.

Lakin, M. Group sensitivity training and encounter: Uses and abuses of a method. *Counseling Psychologist,* 1970, **2**, 66–70.

Lamott, K. Marathon therapy is a psychological pressure cooker. *New York Times,* July 13, 1969.

Lamott, K. The four possible life positions:
1. I'm not O.K.–you're O.K.

2. I'm not O.K.–you're not O.K.
3. I'm O.K.–you're not O.K.
4. I'm O.K.–you're O.K.
New York Times Magazine, November 19, 1972.

Lancaster, E. *The final face of Eve.* New York: McGraw-Hill, 1958.

Landis, J. T. The trauma of children when parents divorce. *Marriage and Family Living,* 1960, **22**, 7–13.

Lane, E. A., Albee, G. W., and Doll, L. S. The intelligence of children of schizophrenics. *Developmental Psychology,* 1970, **2**, 315–331.

Langner, T. S., and Michael, S. T. *Life stress and mental health.* Glencoe, Ill.: Free Press, 1963.

Latané, B., and Darley, J. Group inhibition of bystander intervention in emergencies. *Journal of Personality and Social Psychology,* 1968, **10**, 215–221.

Latané, B., and Darley, J. *The unresponsive bystander: Why doesn't he help?* New York: Appleton-Century-Crofts, 1970.

Laughlin, H. B. *The neuroses.* Washington, D.C.: Butterworths, 1967.

Lawrenson, H. The feminine mistake. *Esquire,* January, 1971.

Lazarus, R. S. *Psychological stress and the coping process.* New York: McGraw-Hill, 1966.

Lear, J. Where is society going? The search for landmarks. *Saturday Review,* April 15, 1972.

Lederer, W. J., and Jackson, D. D. *The mirages of marriage.* New York: Norton, 1968.

Lee, J. J., Hegge, T. G., and Voelker, P. H. *A study of social adequacy and social failure of mentally retarded youth in Wayne County, Michigan.* Detroit: Wayne State University, 1959.

Lehman, H. L. *Age and Achievement.* Princeton, N.J.: Princeton University Press, 1953.

Lemkau, P. V., and Corcetti, G. M. Vital statistics of schizophrenia. In L. Bellak (Ed.), *Schizophrenia.* New York: Logos Press, 1958.

Lenneberg, E. H. On explaining language. *Science,* 1969, **164**, 635–643.

Lerner, M. J. All the world loathes a loser. *Psychology Today,* June 1971.

Lerner, M. *America as a civilization.* New York: Knopf, 1958.

Lerner, R. M., and Korn, S. J. The development of body-build stereotypes in males. *Child Development,* 1972, **43**, 908–920.

Leslie, J. Ethics and practice of placebo therapy. *American Journal of Medicine,* 1954, **16**, 854.

Lesser, G. S. Designing a program for broadcast television. In F. F. Korten, S. W. Cook, and J. L. Lacey (Eds.), *Psychology and the problems of society.* Washington, D.C.: American Psychological Association, 1970.

Lesser, G. S., Fifer, G., and Clark, D. H. Mental abilities of children from different social class and cultural groups. *Monographs of the Society for Research in Child Development,* 1965, **30**, 1–115.

Lester, D. Voodoo death: Some new thoughts on an old phenomenon. *American Anthropologist,* 1972, **74**, 386–390.

Lester, G., and Lester, D. *Suicide: The gamble with death.* Englewood Cliffs, N.J.: Prentice-Hall, 1971.

Lester, J. Women: The male fantasy. *Evergreen,* September 1970.

Leventhal, G. S. Influence of brothers and sisters on sex-role behavior. *Journal of Personality and Social Psychology,* 1970, **16**, 452–465.

Levinger, G., and Schneider, D. J. Test of the "risk is a value" hypothesis. *Journal of Personality and Social Psychology,* 1969, **11**, 165–169.

Levinson, B. L., Shapiro, D., Schwartz, G. E., and Tursky, B. Smoking elimination by gradual reduction. *Behavior Therapy,* 1971, **2**, 477–487.

Levitt, E. E. *The psychology of anxiety.* Indianapolis: Bobbs-Merrill, 1967.

Lewis, O. The culture of poverty. *Scientific American,* October 1966.

Lichtenstein, E., et al. Comparison of rapid smoking, warm, smoky air, and attention placebo in the modification of smoking behavior. *Journal of Consulting and Clinical Psychology,* 1973, **40**, 92–98.

Lieberman, M. A. Psychological correlates of impending death: Some preliminary observations. In B. L. Neugarten (Ed.), *Middle age and aging.* Chicago: University of Chicago Press, 1968.

Liebert, R. M., and Baron, R. A. Some immediate effects of televised violence on children's behavior. *Developmental Psychology,* 1972, **6**, 469–475.

Liebert, R. M., and Neale, J. M. TV violence and child aggression: Snow on the screen. *Psychology Today,* April 1972.

Lifton, R. J. *Thought reform and the psychology of totalism.* New York: Norton, 1961.

Limpus, L. The liberation of women: Sexual repression and the family. In H. Gadlin and B. E. Garskof (Eds.), *The uptight society: A book of readings.* Belmont, Calif.: Brooks/Cole, 1970.

Lindzey, G. Seer vs. sign. *Journal of Experimental Research on Personality,* 1965, **1**, 17–26.

Lindzey, G., and Rogolsky, S. Prejudice and identification of minority group membership. *Journal of Abnormal and Social Psychology,* 1950, **45**, 37–53.

Lipinski, E., and Lipinski, B. G. Motivational factors in psychedelic drug use by male college students. In R. E. Hormon and A. M. Fox (Eds.), *Drug awareness.* Discus Books/Published by Avon, 1970.

Looft, W. R. The psychology of more. *American Psychologist,* 1971, **26**, 561–565.

Lorenz, K. Z. The companion in the bird's world. *Auk,* 1937, **54**, 245–273.

Lorenz, K. Z. *King Solomon's ring.* New York: Crowell, 1952.

Lotter, V. Epidemiology of autistic conditions in young children: Some characteristics of the parents and children. *Social Psychiatry,* 1967, **1**, 163–173.

Louria, D. *Nightmare drugs.* New York: Pocket Books, 1966.

Lowe, C. M. Value orientations: An ethical dilemma. *American Psychologist,* 1959, **14**, 687–693.

Luce, G. G., and Peper, E. Mind over body, mind over mind. *New York Times Magazine,* September 12, 1971.

Luce, G. G., and Segal, J. What time is it? The body clock knows. *New York Times Magazine,* April 3, 1966.

Luckey, E., and Nass, G. D. A comparison of sexual attitudes and behavior in an international sample. *Journal of Marriage and the Family,* 1969, **31**, 364–379.

Ludwig, A. M. Altered states of consciousness. *Archives of General Psychiatry,* 1966, **15**, 225–233.

Ludwig, A. M. "Psychedelic" effects produced by sensory overload. *American Journal of Psychiatry,* 1972, **128**, 114–117.

Luria, A. *The role of speech in the regulation of normal and abnormal behavior.* New York: Liveright, 1961.

Luria, A. R. *The mind of a mnemonist.* New York: Basic Books, 1968.

Luria, A. R. The functional organization of the brain. *Scientific American,* March 1970.

Lykken, D. T. A study of anxiety in the sociopathic personality. *Journal of Abnormal and Social Psychology,* 1957, **55**, 6–10.

Lyman, S. M. Japanese-American generation gap. *Society,* January-February 1973.

Lynn, D. B., and Sawrey, W. L. The effects of father absence on Norwegian boys and girls. *Journal of Abnormal and Social Psychology,* 1959, **59**, 258–262.

MacDonald, A. P., Jr., and Majunder, R. K. Do the poor know how we see them? Preliminary study. *Perceptual and Motor Skills,* 1972, **34**, 47–49.

Mack, R. *Transforming America: Patterns of social change.* New York: Random, 1967.

Maier, W. J. Sensory deprivation therapy of an autistic boy. *American Journal of Psychotherapy,* 1970, **25**, 228–245.

Mann, L. Perceptual training: Misdirections and redirections. *American Journal of Orthopsychiatry,* 1970, **40**, 30–38.

Mannes, M. Ain't nobody here but us commercials. *Reporter,* 1957, **17**(6).

Marden, C. F., and Meyer, Gladys. *Minorities in American society.* (3rd ed.) New York: American Book Co., 1968.

Margolis, M. The mother-child relationship in bronchial asthma. *Journal of Abnormal and Social Psychology,* 1961, **63**, 360–387.

Maris, R. W. *Forces in urban suicide.* Homewood, Ill.: Dorsey, 1969.

Marks, H. H. Characteristics and trends of cerebral vascular disease. In P. H. Hoch and J. Zubin (Eds.), *Psychopathology of aging.* New York: Grune & Stratton, 1961.

Markson, E. A hiding place to die. *Trans-action,* November-December, 1971.

Marmor, J. "Normal" and "deviant" sexual behavior. *Journal of the American Medical Association,* 1971, **217**, 165–170.

Marquis, D. G. Scientific methodology in human relations. *Proceedings of the American Philosophical Society,* 1948, **92**, 411–416.

Marrow, A. J. Risks and uncertainties in action research. *Journal of Social Issues,* 1964, **20**, 5–20.

Marshall, D. S. Too much in Mangaia. *Psychology Today,* February 1971.

Marshall, J. The evidence: Do we see and hear what is? Or do our senses lie? *Psychology Today,* February 1969.

Maslow, A. H. A theory of human motivation. *Psychological Review,* 1943, **50**, 370–396.

Maslow, A. H. *Toward a psychology of being.* New York: Van Nostrand Reinhold, 1962.

Massaro, D. W. Forgetting: Interference or decay? *Journal of Experimental Psychology,* 1970, **83**, 238–243.

Maupin, E. W. Individual differences in response to a Zen meditation exercise. *Journal of Consulting Psychology,* 1965, **29**, 139–145.

May, R. Contribution to: The therapeutic process in cross-cultural perspective: A symposium. *American Journal of Psychiatry,* 1968, **124**, 1179–1183.

Mayer, J., and Harris, T. G. Affluence: The fifth horseman of the apocalypse. *Psychology Today,* January 1970.

McArthur, C. Personalities of first and second children. *Psychiatry,* 1956, **19**, 47–54.

McArthur, C. C. Clinical vs. actuarial prediction. In *Proceedings of the 1955 Invitational Conference on Testing Problems.* Princeton, N.J.: Educational Testing Service, 1956.

McCandless, B. *Adolescents: Behavior and development.* Hinsdale, Ill.: Dryden, 1970.

McClelland, D. C. The uses of measures of human motivation in the study of society. In J. W. Atkinson (Ed.), *Motives in fantasy, action, and society.* Princeton, N.J.: Van Nostrand, 1958.

McClelland, D. C. *The achieving society.* Princeton, N.J.: Van Nostrand, 1961.

McClelland, D. C. Toward a theory of motive acquisition. *American Psychologist,* 1965, **20**, 321–333.

McClelland, D. C. Testing for competence rather than for "intelligence." *American Psychologist,* 1973, **28**, 1–14.

McClelland, D. C., Atkinson, J. W., Clark, R. A., and Lowell, E. L. *The achievement motive.* New York: Appleton-Century-Crofts, 1953.

McConnell, J. V. Memory transfer through cannibalism in planarians. *Journal of Neuropsychiatry,* 1962, **3**(suppl. 1), 542–548.

McConnell, J. V. Criminals can be brainwashed—Now. *Psychology Today,* April 1970.

McDavid, R. I. Dialect differences and social differences in an urban society. In W. Bright (Ed.), *Sociolinguistics: Proceedings of the UCLA Sociolinguistics Conference 1964.* The Hague: Mouton, 1966.

McFall, R. M., and Hammen, C. L. Motivation, structure, and self-monitoring: Role of nonspecific factors in smoking reduction. *Journal of Consulting and Clinical Psychology,* 1971, **37**, 80–86.

McGaugh, J. L. Time-dependent processes in memory storage. In J. L. McGaugh and M. J. Herz (Eds.), *Controversial issues in consolidation of the memory trace.* New York: Atherton, 1970.

McGee, R. K. The suicide prevention center as a model for community mental health programs. *Community Mental Health Journal,* 1965, **1**, 162–172.

McGhee, P. E. Development of the humor response: A review of the literature. *Psychological Bulletin,* 1971, **76**, 328–348.

McGregor, D. *The human side of enterprise.* New York: McGraw-Hill, 1960.

McGuire, F. L. Smoking, driver education, and other correlates of accidents among young males. *Journal of Safety Research,* 1972, **4**, 5–11.

McGuire, W. J. Attitudes and opinions, In P. R. Farnsworth et al. (Eds.), *Annual review of psychology,* Vol. 17. Palo Alto, Calif.: Annual Reviews, 1966.

McGurk, H., and Lewis, M. Birth order: A phenomenon in search of an explanation. *Developmental Psychology,* 1972, **7**, 366.

McKinney, J. P., and Keele, T. Effects of increased mothering on the behavior of severely retarded boys. *American Journal of Mental Deficiency,* 1963, **67**, 556–562.

McManus, V. *Not for love.* New York: Putnam's, 1960.

McMurray, G. A. Experimental study of a case of insensitivity to pain. *Archives of Neurological Psychiatry,* 1950, **64**, 650–667.

McNeil, E. B. Waging experimental war: a review. *Journal of Conflict Resolution,* 1962, **6**, 77–81.

McNeil, E. B. *Human socialization.* Belmont, Calif.: Brooks/Cole, 1969.

McNeil, E. B. *Neuroses and personality disorders.* Englewood Cliffs, N.J.: Prentice-Hall, 1970.

McNeil, E. B., and Blum, G. S. Handwriting and psychosexual dimensions of personality. *Journal of Projective Techniques,* 1952, **16**, 476–484.

McRae, C. F., and Nelson, D. M. Youth to youth communication on smoking and health. *Journal of School Health,* 1971, **41**, 445–447.

Mead. M. *Culture and commitment: A study of the generation gap.* Garden City, N.Y.: Natural History Press/Doubleday, 1970.

Mead, M. Future Family. *Trans-action,* September 1971.

Mech, V. E. Factors influencing routine performance under noise: The influence of set. *Journal of Psychology,* 1953, **35**, 283–298.

Mednich, S. A. The associative basis of the creative process. *Psychological Review,* 1962, **69**, 220–232.

Meehl, P. E. *Clinical versus statistical prediction: A theoretical analysis and a review of the evidence.* Minneapolis: University of Minnesota Press, 1954.

Meehl, P. E. Seer over sign: The first good example. *Journal of Experimental Research in Personality,* 1965, **1**, 27–32.

Meissner, W. W. Family dynamics and psychosomatic process. *Family Process,* 1966, **5**, 142–161.

Meltzoff, J., and Komreish, M. *Research in psychotherapy.* New York: Atherton, 1970.

Melzack, R. Phantom limbs. *Psychology Today,* October 1970.

Melzack, R., and Scott, T. H. The effects of early experience on the response to pain. *Journal of Comparative and Physiological Psychology,* 1957, **50**, 155–161.

Mendel, W. M., and Rapport, S. Determinants of the decision for psychiatric hospitalization. Paper presented at the annual meetings of the American Psychiatric Association, Boston, May 1968.

Merbaum, A. D. Need for achievement in Negro children. Master's thesis, University of North Carolina, 1960.

Messenger, J. C. The luck of the Irish. *Psychology Today,* February 1971.

Metzner, R. *Maps of consciousness.* New York: Collier, 1971.

Meyerson, A. Theory and principles of the "total push" method in the treatment of chronic schizophrenics. *American Journal of Psychiatry,* 1939, **95**, 1197–1204.

Milgram, S. Behavioral study of obedience. *Journal of Abnormal and Social Psychology,* 1963, **67**, 371–378.

Milgram, S. Issues in the study of obedience: A reply to Baumrind. *American Psychologist,* 1964, **19**. 848–852.

Milgram, S. Reply to the critics. *International Journal of Psychiatry,* 1968, **6**, 294–295.

Miller, A. R. *The assault of privacy.* Ann Arbor: University of Michigan Press, 1971.

Miller, G. A. On turning psychology over to the unwashed. *Psychology Today,* December 1969.

Miller, N. E. Learning of visceral and glandular responses. *Science,* 1969, **163**, 434–445.

Miller, N. E., and Banuazizi, A. Instrumental learning by curarized rats of a specific visceral response, intestinal, or cardiac. *Journal of Comparative and Physiological Psychology,* 1968, **65**, 1–7.

Miller, N. E., and Bugelski, B. Minor studies in aggression: The influence of frustrations imposed by the in-group on attitudes expressed toward out-groups. *Journal of Psychology,* 1948, **25**, 437–442.

Miller, P. R. The Chicago demonstrators: A study in identity. *Bulletin of the Atomic Scientists,* 1969, **25**, 3–6.

Miller, W. B. Lower-class culture as a generating milieu of gang delinquency. *Journal of Social Issues,* 1958, **14**, 5–19.

Mitchell, D., and Wilson, W. Relationship of father absence to masculinity and popularity of delinquent boys. *Psychological Reports,* 1967, **20**, 1173–1174.

Montagu, A. *The humanization of man.* New York: Grove, 1962.

Montagu, A. (Ed.) *Man and aggression.* New York: Oxford University Press, 1968.

Montagu, A. *Touching. The human significance of the skin.* New York: Harper, 1971.

Mora, G. History of psychiatry. In A. M. Freedman and H. I. Kaplan (Eds.), *Psychiatry.* Baltimore: Williams & Wilkins, 1967.

Morgan, C. T., and King, R. N. *Introduction to psychology.* (4th ed.) New York: McGraw-Hill, 1971.

Moritz, A. P., and Zamchech, N. Sudden and unexpected deaths of young soldiers. *American Medical Association Archives of Pathology,* 1946, **42**, 459–494.

Morris, D. *The naked ape.* New York: McGraw-Hill, 1967.

Morse, W., and Skinner, B. A second type of "superstition" in the pigeon. *American Journal of Psychology,* 1957, **70**, 308–311.

Morse, W. C., and Weiss, R. S. The function and meaning of work and the job. In D. G. Zytowski (Ed.), *Vocational behavior.* New York: Holt, 1968.

Moscovici, S., Lage, E., and Naffrechoux, M. Influence of a consistent minority on the responses of a majority in a color perception task. *Sociometry,* 1969, **32**, 365–380.

Mosher, L. R., and Feinsilver, D. *Special report on schizophrenia.* Rockville, Md.: National Institute of Mental Health, April 1970.

Moss, T., Chang, A. F., and Levitt, M. Long-distance ESP: A controlled study. *Journal of Abnormal Psychology,* 1970, **76**, 288–294.

Mowrer, O. H. Hearing and speaking: An analysis of language learning. *Journal of Speech and Hearing Disorders,* 1958, **23**, 143–151.

Mungo, R. *Total loss farm.* New York: Dutton, 1971.

Murphy, G. *Challenge of psychical research.* New York: Harper, 1961.

Murtagh, J., and Harris, S. *Cast the first stone.* New York: McGraw-Hill, 1957.

Mussen, P. Differences between the TAT responses of Negro and white boys. *Journal of Consulting Psychology,* 1953, **17**, 373–376.

Myers, J. K., and Roberts, B. H. *Family and class dynamics in mental illness.* New York: Wiley, 1959.

Nabokov, P. The peyote road. *New York Times Magazine,* March 9, 1969.

Naranjo, C., and Ornstein, R. E. *On the psychology of meditation.* New York: Viking, 1971.

National Commission on the Causes and Prevention of Violence. *To establish justice, to insure domestic tranquility.* New York: Award Books, 1969.

Neill, A. S. *Summerhill: A radical approach to child rearing.* New York: Hart, 1960.

Nelson, H. Feelin' groovy? A third of the nation doesn't. *Los Angeles Times,* November 19, 1968.

Nelson, L. L., and Kagan, S. Competition: The star-spangled scramble. *Psychology Today,* September 1972.

Nemaih, J. C. Conversion reaction. In A. M. Freedman and H. I. Kaplan (Eds.), *Psychiatry.* Baltimore: Williams & Wilkins, 1967.

Neugarten, B. L. Personality and the aging process. *Gerontologist,* 1972, **12**, 15.

Neuhaus, R. *In defense of people: Ecology and the seduction of radicalism.* New York: Macmillan, 1971.

Newcomb, T. M. *The acquaintance process.* New York: Holt, 1961.

Newcomb, T. M., Turner, R., and Converse, P. *Social Psychology,* New York: Holt, 1965.

Newman, E. B. Forgetting of meaningful material during sleep and waking. *American Journal of Psychology,* 1939, **52**, 65–71.

Newton, N. Childbirth and culture. *Psychology Today,* November 1970.

Newton, N., Foshee, D., and Newton, M. Parturient mice: Effect of environment on labor. *Science,* 1966, **151**, 1560–1561.

Nietzke, A. The American obsession with fun. *Saturday Review,* August 26, 1972.

Nisbett, R. E. Determinants of food intake in human obesity. *Science,* 1968, **159**, 1254–1255.

Nisbett, R. E. Birth order and participation in dangerous sports. *Journal of Personality and Social Psychology,* 1968, **8**, 351–353.

Ober, D. C. Modification of smoking behavior. *Journal of Consulting and Clinical Psychology,* 1968, **32**, 543–549.

Oden, M. H. The fulfillment of promise: 40-year follow-up of the Terman gifted group. *Genetic Psychology Monographs,* 1968, **77**, 3–93.

Oettinger, A. G. (with S. Marks). *Run, computer, run: The mythology of educational innovation.* New York: Collier, 1969.

Olds, J. Self-stimulation of the brain. *Science,* 1958, **127**, 315–324.

O'Neill, C. C., and O'Neill, N. Patterns in group sexual activity. *Journal of Sex Research,* 1970, **6**, 101–112.

Orbach, J., Ehrlich, D., and Heath, H. A. Reversibility of the necker cube: An examination of the concept of satiation of orientation. *Perceptual Motor Skills,* 1963, **17**, 439–458.

Orlansky, H. Infant care and personality. *Psychological Bulletin,* 1949, **46**, 1–48.

Ornati, O. Poverty in America. In L. A. Ferman, J. L. Kornbluh, and A. Haber (Eds.), *Poverty in America.* Ann Arbor: University of Michigan Press, 1971.

Ornstein, R. E. Right and left thinking. *Psychology Today,* May 1973.

Oskamp, S., and Perlman, D. Effects of friendship and disliking on cooperation in a mixed motive game. *Journal of Conflict Resolution,* 1966, **10**, 221–226.

Packard, V. *The sexual wilderness.* New York: McKay, 1968.

Palmore, E. Predicting longevity: A follow-up controlling for age. *Gerontologist,* 1969, **9**, 247–250.

Palson, C., and Palson, R. Swinging in wedlock. *Society,* February 1972.

Parsons, T. Certain primary sources and patterns of aggression in the social structure of the Western world. *Psychiatry,* 1947, **10**, 167–181.

Pasamanick, B., and Knobloch, H. Epidemiologic studies on the complications of pregnancy and the birth process. In G. Caplan (Ed.), *Prevention of mental disorders in children.* New York: Basic Books, 1961.

Patterson, G. R., Littman, R. G., and Bricker, W. Assertive behavior in children: A step toward a theory of aggression. *Monographs of the Society for Research in Child Development,* 1967, No. 32.

Pattie, F. A. A brief history of hypnotism. In J. E. Gordon (Ed.), *Handbook of clinical and experimental hypnosis.* New York: Macmillan, 1967.

Pearson, P. H. Relationships between global and specified measures of novelty seeking. *Journal of Consulting and Clinical Psychology,* 1970, **34**, 199–204.

Peck, E. *The baby trap.* New York, Pinnacle, 1971.

Penfield, W. The interpretive cortex. *Science,* 1959, **129**, 1719–1725.

Piaget, J. *The moral judgment of the child.* Glencoe, Ill.: Free Press, 1948. (Originally published in 1932.)

Piaget, J. *The psychology of intelligence.* New York: Harcourt, 1950.

Piaget, J. *The origins of intelligence in children.* New York: International Universities Press, 1952.

Piaget, J., and Inhelder, B. *Le développement des quantités physiques chez l'enfant.* Neuchâtel, Switzerland: Delachaux and Niestlé, 1962.

Pierrel, R., and Sherman, J. G. Train your pet the Barnabus way. *Brown Alumni Monthly,* February 1963.

Pinkney, A. *Black Americans.* Englewood Cliffs, N.J.: Prentice-Hall, 1969.

Pintner, R., Dragositz, A., and Kushner, R. *Supplementary guide for the revised Stanford-Binet scale.* Stanford, Calif.: Stanford University Press, 1944.

Pitts, J. R. The structural-functional approach. In H. T. Christiansen (Ed.), *Handbook of marriage and family.* Chicago: Rand McNally, 1964.

Plumb, J. H. The great change in children. *Intellectual Digest,* April 1972.

Polednak, A. P., and Damon, A. College athletics, longevity, and cause of death. *Human Biology,* 1970, **42**, 28–46.

Polsky, N. *Hustlers, beats, and others.* Garden City, N.Y.: Doubleday, 1967.

Porterfield, E. Mixed marriage. *Psychology Today,* January 1973.

Postman, N., and Weingartner, C. *Teaching as a subversive activity.* New York: Delacorte, 1969.

Powell, D. H., and Driscoll, P. F. Middle-class professionals face unemployment. *Society,* January-February 1973.

Premack, A. J., and Premack, D. Teaching language to an ape. *Scientific American,* November 1972.

Pressey, S. L. A simple apparatus which gives tests and scores—and teaches. *School and Society,* 1926, **23**, 373–376.

Pressey, S. L. Concerning the nature and nurture of genius. *Scientific Monthly,* September 1955.

Preston, G. H. *Psychiatry for the curious.* New York: Rinehart, 1940.

Rabbie, J. M., and Horowitz, M. Arousal of ingroup-outgroup bias by a chance win or loss. *Journal of Personality and Social Psychology,* 1969, **13**, 269–277.

Rabkin, Y., and Rabkin, K. Children of the kibbutz. *Psychology Today,* March 1969.

Ramey, J. W. Communes, group marriage and the upper middle-class. *Journal of Marriage and the Family,* 1972, **34**, 647–655.

Ratner, S. C. Comparative aspects of hypnosis. In J. F. Gordon (Ed.), *Handbook of clinical and experimental hypnosis.* New York: Macmillan, 1967.

Raush, H. L., and Raush, C. L. *The halfway house movement: A search for sanity.* New York: Appleton-Century-Crofts, 1968.

Redlich, F. C., and Freedman, D. X. *The theory and practice of psychiatry.* New York: Basic Books, 1966.

Regestein, Q. R., and Howe, L. P. A psychotherapy group for skid-row alcoholics. *Massachusetts Journal of Mental Health,* 1972, **2**, 4–24.

Reimer, E. *School is dead: Alternatives in education: An indictment of the system and a strategy of revolution.* New York: Doubleday, 1971.

Reiss, I. L. How and why America's sex standards are changing. *Trans-action,* March 1968.

Resnick, J. H. Effects of stimulus satiation on the overlearned maladaptive response of cigarette smoking. *Journal of Consulting and Clinical Psychology,* 1968, **32**, 501–505.

Rheingold, H. L., Gewirtz, J. L., and Ross, H. W. Social conditioning of vocalizations on the infant. *Journal of Comparative and Physiological Psychology,* 1959, **52**, 68–73.

Rhine, J. B. Evidence of precognition in the covariation of salience ratios. *Journal of Parapsychology,* 1942, **6**, 111–143.

Ribble, M. A. Infantile experience in relation to personality development. In J. M. Hunt (Ed.), *Personality and the behavior disorders,* Vol. II. New York: Ronald Press, 1944.

Rice, H. K., and McDaniel, M. W. Operant behavior in vegetative patients. *Psychological Record,* 1966, **16**, 279–281.

Rice, H. K., McDaniel, M. W., Stallings, V. D., and Gatz, M. J. Operant behavior in vegetative patients, II. *Psychological Record,* 1967, **17**, 449–460.

Richter, C. P. The self-selection of diets. In *Essays in biology.* Berkeley and Los Angeles: University of California Press, 1943.

Richter, C. P. On the phenomenon of sudden death in animals and man. *Psychosomatic Medicine,* 1957, **19**, 191–198.

Rivers, C. Genetic engineering portends a grave new world. *Saturday Review,* April 8, 1972.

Rivers, W. L. Jim Crow journalism. *Stanford Today,* Autumn 1967.

Roberts, R. E. *The new communes coming together in America.* Englewood Cliffs, N.J.: Prentice-Hall, 1971.

Rock, I., and Kaufman, L. The moon illusion, II. *Science,* 1962, **136**, 1023–1031.

Roe, A. The psychology of the scientist. *Science,* 1961, **134**, 456–459.

Roethlisberger, F. J., and Dickson, W. J. *Management and the worker.* Cambridge: Harvard University Press, 1939.

Rogers, C. R., and Skinner, B. F. Some issues concerning the control of human behavior: A symposium. *Science,* 1956, **124**, 1057–1066. In M. Karlins and L. M. Andrews (Eds.), *Man controlled: Readings in the psychology of behavior control.* New York: Free Press, 1972.

Rogers, J. M. Drug abuse: Just what the doctor ordered. *Psychology Today,* September 1971.

Rokeach, M. *The three Christs of Ypsilanti.* New York: Knopf, 1964.

Rollin, B. Motherhood: Who needs it? *Look Magazine,* September 22, 1970.

Rorschach, H. *Psychodiagnostics: A diagnostic test based on perception.* New York: Grune & Stratton, 1942.

Rorvik, D. M. The wave of the future brain waves. *Look Magazine,* October 6, 1970.

Rosen, B. C., and D'Andrade, R. The psychosocial origins of achievement motivation. *Sociometry,* 1959, **22**, 188–218.

Rosenberg, B. G. Psychology through the looking glass. *Psychology Today,* June 1971.

Rosenberg, C. M. Complications of obsessional neurosis. *British Journal of Psychiatry,* 1968, **114**, 477–478.

Rosenberg, S. D. Hospital culture as collective defense. *Psychiatry,* 1970, **33**, 21–35.

Rosenfelt, R. H. The elderly mystique. *Journal of Social Issues,* 1965, **21**, 37–43.

Rosenhan, D. L. On being sane in insane places. *Science,* 1973, **179**, 250–258.

Rosenthal, D. Changes in some moral values following psychotherapy. *Journal of Consulting Psychology,* 1955, **19**, 431–436.

Rosenthal, R., and Jacobson, L. *Pygmalion in the classroom: Teacher expectation and pupils' intellectual development.* New York: Holt, 1968.

Rosnow, I. And then we were old. *Trans-action,* January-February 1965.

Rosnow, R. L. When he lends a helping hand, bite it. *Psychology Today,* April 1970.

Ross, M. Suicide among physicians. *Psychiatry in Medicine,* 1971, **2**, 189–197.

Rostow, E. G. Conflict and accommodation. In H. M. Ruitenbeek (Ed.), *Sexuality and identity.* New York: Delta, 1970.

Rowe, F. B., Brooks, S., and Watson, B. Communication through gestures. *American Annals of the Deaf,* 1960, **105**, 232–237.

Rudhyar, D. *The practice of astrology.* Baltimore: Penguin, 1968.

Ruff, G., Levy, E. Z., and Thaler, V. H. Factors influencing reactions to reduced sensory input. In P. Solomon et al. (Eds.), *Sensory deprivation.* Cambridge: Harvard University Press, 1961.

Ruitenbeek, H. M. *The male myth.* New York: Dell, 1967.

Ruitenbeek, H. M. *The new group therapies.* New York: Avon, 1970.

Russell, W., and Nathan, P. Traumatic amnesia. *Brain,* 1964, **69**, 280.

Sacerdote, P. Hypnosis in cancer patients. *American Journal of Clinical Hypnosis,* 1966, **9**, 100–108.

Safdie, M. Habitat '67. In W. R. Ewald (Ed.), *Environment for man.* Bloomington: Indiana University Press, 1967.

Sage, W. ESP and the psychology establishment. *Human Behavior,* September-October 1972.

Salisburg, W. W., and Salisburg, F. Youth and the search for intimacy. In L. A. Kirkendall and R. N. Whitehurst (Eds.), *The new sexual revolution.* New York: Donald W. Brown, 1971.

Sampson, E. E. *Social psychology and contemporary society.* New York: Wiley, 1971.

Sandler, S. A. Somnambulism in the armed forces. *Mental Hygiene,* 1945, **29**, 236–247.

Sanford, F. H. *Psychology.* (2nd ed.) Belmont, Calif.: Wadsworth, 1965.

Saranson, S., and Gladwin, T. Psychological and cultural problems in mental subnormality: A review of research. *Genetic Psychology Monograph,* 1958, **57**, 3–290.

Sarbin, T. R. Schizophrenia is a myth, born of metaphor, meaningless. *Psychology Today,* June 1972.

Sargant, W. The physical treatments of depression: Their indicators and proper use. *Journal of Neuropsychiatry,* 1961, **2**, 1–10.

Sarnoff, I., and Zimbardo, P. G. Anxiety, fear, and social affiliation. *Journal of Abnormal and Social Psychology,* 1961, **62**, 356–363.

Saturday Review. The skyjacker and how to stop him. *Saturday Review,* August 26, 1972.

Sava, S. G. When learning comes easy. *Saturday Review,* November 16, 1968.

Savitsky, J. C., Rogers, R. W., Izard, C. E., and Liebert, R. M. The role of frustration and anger in the imitation of filmed aggression against a human victim. *Psychological Reports,* 1971, **29**, 807–810.

Scarf, M. Brain researcher Jose Delgado asks: "What kind of humans would we like to construct?" *New York Times Magazine,* November 15, 1970.

Schachter, S. Deviation, rejection and communication. *Journal of Abnormal and Social Psychology,* 1951, **46**, 190–208.

Schachter, S. *The psychology of affiliation.* Stanford, Calif.: Stanford University Press, 1959.

Schachter, S. Birth order, eminence, and higher education. *American Sociological Review,* 1963, **28**, 757–767.

Schachter, S. Eat, eat. *Psychology Today,* April 1971.

Schachter, S., Goldman, R., and Gordon, A. Effects of fear, food deprivation, and obesity on eating. *Journal of Personality and Social Psychology,* 1968, **10**, 91–97.

Schachter, S., and Singer, J. Cognitive, social, and physiological determinants of emotional state. *Psychological Review,* 1962, **69**, 379–399.

Schein, E. H., Schneider, I., and Barker, C. H. *Coercive Persuasion.* New York: Norton, 1961.

Schein, E. H. *Organizational psychology.* Englewood Cliffs, N.J.: Prentice-Hall, 1965.

Schiller, H. I. Polls are prostitutes for the establishment. *Psychology Today,* July 1972.

Schmeidler, G. R. (Ed.) *Extra-sensory perception.* New York: Atherton, 1969.

Schmeidler, G. R., and McConnell, R. A. *ESP and personality patterns.* New Haven, Conn.: Yale University Press, 1958.

Schmidt, H., and Fonda, C. The reliability of psychiatric diagnosis: A new look. *Journal of Abnormal and Social Psychology,* 1956, **52**, 262–267.

Schofield, W. *Psychotherapy: The purchase of friendship.* Englewood Cliffs, N.J.: Prentice-Hall, 1964.

Schofield, W., and Balian, L. A comparative study of the personal histories of schizophrenic and nonpsychiatric patients. *Journal of Abnormal and Social Psychology,* 1959, **59**, 216–225.

Schorr, A. L. The family cycle and income development. In L. A. Ferman, J. L. Kornbluh, and A. Haber (Eds.), *Poverty in America.* Ann Arbor: University of Michigan Press, 1971.

Schultz, D. P. The human subject in psychological research. *Psychological Bulletin,* 1969, **72**, 214–228.

Schultz, J. H., and Luthe, W. *Autogenic training.* New York: Grune & Stratton, 1959.

Schwartz, D. A unitary formulation of the manic-depressive reactions. *Psychiatry,* 1961, **24**, 238–245.

Schwebel, M. *Who can be educated?* New York: Grove, 1968.

Schwitzgebel, R. L. Preliminary socialization for psychotherapy of behavior-disordered adolescents. *Journal of Consulting and Clinical Psychology,* 1969, **33**, 71–77.

Scott, J. P. A time to learn. *Psychology Today,* March 1969.

Sears, R. R. Ordinal position in the family as a psychological variable. *American Sociological Review,* 1950, **15**, 397–401.

Sears, R. R., Maccoby, E. E., and Levin, H. *Patterns of Child Rearing.* Evanston, Ill.: Row, Peterson, 1957.

Sears, R. R., Pintler, M., and Sears, P. S. Effect of father separation on preschool children's doll play aggression. *Child Development,* 1946, **17**, 219–243.

Seiden, R. H. Campus tragedy: A study of student suicide. *Journal of Abnormal Psychology,* 1966, **71**, 389–399.

Seiden, R. H. We're driving young blacks to suicide. *Psychology Today,* August 1970.

Seidenberg, R. Drug advertising and perception of mental illness. *Mental Hygiene,* 1971, **55,** 21–31.

Seligman, M. E. P. Fall into helplessness. *Psychology Today,* June 1973.

Selye, H. *The stress of life.* New York: McGraw-Hill, 1956.

Senden, M. V. (Trans. by P. Heath.) *Space and sight.* New York: Free Press, 1960.

Sexton, P. C. *The feminized male.* New York: Vintage, 1969.

Seymour, D. Z. Black English. *Intellectual Digest,* Fall 1972.

Shapiro, D. *Neurotic styles.* New York: Basic Books, 1965.

Sheehan, B. W. Indian-white relations in early America: A review essay. In H. M. Bahr, B. A. Chadwick, and R. C. Day (Eds.), *Native Americans today: Sociological perspectives.* New York: Harper, 1972.

Sheldon, W. H. *Varieties of human physique.* New York: Harper, 1940.

Sheldon, W. H., et al. *Atlas of man: A guide for somatotyping the adult male at all ages.* New York: Harper, 1954.

Shepard, M., and Lee, M. *Marathon 16.* New York: Putnam's, 1970.

Sherif, M. *The psychology of social norms.* New York: Harper, 1936.

Sherif, M., Harvey, O. J., White, B. J., Hood, W. E., and Sherif, C. W. *Intergroup conflict and cooperation: The Robber's Cave experiment.* Norman: University of Oklahoma Book Exchange, 1961.

Sherif, M., and Sherif, C. W. *Groups in harmony and tension.* New York: Harper, 1953.

Shirer, W. L. *The rise and fall of the Third Reich.* New York: Simon and Schuster, 1960.

Shirley, M. M. *The first two years: A study of twenty-five babies.* Vol. II. *Intellectual development.* Minneapolis: University of Minnesota Press, 1933.

Shneidman, E. S. You and death. *Psychology Today,* June 1971.

Shodell, M. J., and Reiter, H. H. Self-mutilative behavior in verbal and nonverbal schizophrenic children. *Archives of General Psychiatry,* 1968, **19,** 453–455.

Shopland, C., and Gregory, R. L. The effects of touch on a visually ambiguous three-dimensional figure. *Quarterly Journal of Experimental Psychology,* 1964, **16,** 66–70.

Shostrom, E. L. Group therapy: Let the buyer beware. *Psychology Today,* May 1969.

Sifneos, P. E. *Short-term psychotherapy and emotional crisis.* Cambridge: Harvard University Press, 1972.

Sigel, I. E., and Perry, C. Psycholinguistic diversity among "culturally deprived" children. *American Journal of Orthopsychiatry,* 1968, **38,** 122–126.

Sigelman, C. K. Social class and ethnic differences in language development. In L. S. Wrightsman, *Social psychology for the 1970's.* Monterey, Calif.: Brooks/Cole, 1972.

Siipola, E. M. A study of some effects of preparatory set. *Psychological Monographs,* 1935, **46**(210).

Silberman, C. E. *Crisis in black and white.* New York: Vintage, 1964.

Silberman, C. E. *Crisis in the classroom.* New York: Random, 1970.

Singer, J. E. The use of manipulative strategies: Machiavellianism and attractiveness. *Sociometry,* 1964, **27,** 128–150.

Singer, J. L. The importance of daydreaming. In *Readings in Psychology Today.* Del Mar, Calif.: CRM, 1969.

Singer, J. E., Brush, C. A., and Lublin, S. C. Some aspects of deindividuation: Identification and conformity. *Journal of Experimental Social Psychology,* 1965, **1,** 356–378.

Singh, J. A. L., and Zingg, N. R. *Wolf-children and feral man.* New York: Harper, 1942.

Skinner, B. F. *Walden two.* New York: Macmillan, 1948.

Skinner, B. F. *Science and human behavior.* New York: Macmillan, 1953.

Skinner, B. F. The science of learning and the art of teaching. *Harvard Educational Review,* 1954, **24,** 86–97.

Skinner, B. F. *Verbal behavior.* New York: Appleton-Century-Crofts, 1957.

Skinner, B. F. *Beyond freedom and dignity.* New York: Knopf, 1971.

Skodak, M., and Skeels, H. M. A final follow-up of one hundred adopted children. *Journal of Genetic Psychology,* 1949, **75,** 3–19.

Slater, P. *The pursuit of loneliness.* Boston: Beacon, 1970.

Slobin, D. I. They learn the same way all around the world. *Psychology Today,* May 1972.

Slovic, P. Risk-taking in children: Age and sex differences. *Child Development,* 1966, **37,** 169–176.

Smart, R. Subject selection bias in psychological research. *Canadian Psychologist,* 1966, **79,** 115–121.

Smart, R. G., and Fejer, D. Drug use among adolescents and their parents: Closing the generation gap in mood modification. *Journal of Abnormal Psychology,* 1972, **79,** 153–160.

Smigel, E. O., and Seiden, R. The decline and fall of the double standard. In E. Sagavin (Ed.), *Sex and the contemporary American scene. The Annals,* 1968, **376,** 6–17.

Smith, B. M. The polygraph. *Scientific American,* January 1967.

Smith, G. H., and Engel, R. Influence of a female model on perceived characteristics of an automobile. *Proceedings of the 76th Annual Convention of the American Psychological Association,* 1968, **3,** 681–682.

Smith, J. M. Eugenics and utopia. In F. E. Manuel (Ed.),

Utopias and utopian thought. New York: Houghton Mifflin, 1966.

Smith, J. R., and Smith, L. G. Co-marital sex and the sexual freedom movement. *Journal of Sex Research,* 1970, **6,** 131–142.

Smith, R. N. Characteristics of creativity research. *Perceptual and Motor Skills,* 1968, **26,** 698.

Snyder, S. H. The true speed trip: Schizophrenia. *Psychology Today,* January 1972.

Soal, S. G., and Bateman, F. *Modern experiments in telepathy.* New Haven, Conn.: Yale University Press, 1964.

Solomon, F., and Fishman, J. R. Youth and peace: A psychosocial study of student peace demonstrators in Washington, D.C. *Journal of Social Issues,* 1964, **20,** 54–73.

Spelt, D. K. The conditioning of the human fetus in utero. *Journal of Experimental Psychology,* 1948, **38,** 338–346.

Sperry, R. W. The great cerebral commissure. *Scientific American,* January 1964.

Sperry, R. W. The effects of hemisphere deconnection on conscious awareness. *American Psychologist,* 1968, **23,** 117–121.

Spielberger, C. D. (Ed.) *Anxiety and behavior.* New York: Academic Press, 1966.

Spitz, R. A. Hospitalism. *Psychoanalytic Study of the Child,* 1945, **1,** 53–74.

Spitz, R. A. Anaclitic depression. *Psychoanalytic Study of the Child,* 1946, **1,** 313–342.

Spradlin, J. E., and Girardeau, F. L. The behavior of moderately and severely retarded persons. In N. R. Ellis (Ed.), *International review of research in mental retardation,* Vol. 1. New York: Academic Press, 1966.

Srole, L., Langer, T. S., Michael, S. T., Opler, M. K., and Rennie, T. A. C. *Mental health in the metropolis: The midtown Manhattan study.* New York: McGraw-Hill, 1962.

Stacey, C. L., and De Martino, M. F. *Understanding human motivation.* Cleveland: Howard Allen, 1958.

Stagner, R. Personality dynamics and social conflict. *Journal of Social Issues,* 1961, **17,** 28–44.

Staples, F. R., and Walters, R. H. Anxiety, birth order, and susceptibility to social influence. *Journal of Abnormal and Social Psychology,* 1967, **62,** 716–719.

Steele, B. F., and Pollock, C. B. A psychiatric study of parents who abuse infants and small children. In R. E. Helfer and C. H. Kempe (Eds.), *The battered child.* Chicago: University of Chicago Press, 1968.

Stewart, W. A. Urban Negro speech: Sociolinguistic factors affecting English teaching. In R. W. Shuy (Ed.), *Social dialects and language learning.* Champaign, Ill.: National Council of Teachers of English, 1964.

Still, J. W. Why can't we live forever? *Better Homes and Gardens,* August 1958.

Stock, R. W. Will the baby be normal? *New York Times Magazine,* March 23, 1969.

Stolz, L. M., et al. *Father relations of war born children.* Stanford, Calif.: Stanford University Press, 1954.

Stone, C. P. Wildness and savageness in rats of different strains. In K. S. Lashley (Ed.), *Studies in the dynamics of behavior.* Chicago: University of Chicago Press, 1932.

Stone, S. Psychiatry through the ages. *Journal of Abnormal and Social Psychology,* 1937, **32,** 131–160.

Storms, M. D., and Nisbett, R. E. Insomnia and the attribution process. *Journal of Personality and Social Psychology,* 1970, **16,** 319–328.

Stotland, E., and Hillmer, M. L., Jr. Identification, authoritarian defensiveness, and self-esteem. *Journal of Abnormal and Social Psychology,* 1962, **64,** 334–342.

Strange, J. R. *Abnormal psychology: Understanding behavior disorders.* New York: McGraw-Hill, 1965.

Straughan, J. R., Potter, W. K., Jr., and Hamilton, S. H., Jr. The behavioral treatment of an elective mute. *Journal of Child Psychology and Psychiatry,* 1965, **6,** 125–130.

Strohmeyer, C. F., III. Eidetikers. *Psychology Today,* November 1970.

Stuart, R. B., and Davis, B. *Slim chance in a fat world.* Champaign, Ill.: Research Press, 1972.

Stunkard, A., and Koch, C. The interpretation of gastric motility: Apparent bias in the reports of hunger by obese persons. *Archives of General Psychiatry,* 1964, **11,** 74–82.

Sudnow, D. Dead on arrival. *Trans-action,* November 1967.

Sundberg, N. D., and Tyler, L. E. *Clinical psychology.* New York: Appleton-Century-Crofts, 1962.

Supa, M., Cotzin, M., and Dallenbach, K. M. Facial vision: The perception of obstacles by the blind. *American Journal of Psychology,* 1944, **57,** 133–183.

Suppes, P. C., and Morningstar, M. Computer-assisted instruction. *Science,* 1969, **166,** 343–350.

Surman, O. S., Gottlieb, S. K., and Hackett, T. P. Hypnotic treatment of a child with warts. *American Journal of Clinical Hypnosis,* 1972, **15,** 12–14.

Szasz, T. S. The ethics of addiction. *Harper's,* April 1972.

Taba, H. Cultural deprivation as a factor in school learning. *Merrill-Palmer Quarterly of Behavior and Development,* 1964, **10,** 147–159.

Taft, R. The ability to judge people. *Psychological Bulletin,* 1955, **52,** 1–23.

Talmon-Garber, Y. The family in Israel: The kibbutz. *Marriage and Family Living,* 1954, **16,** 346–349.

Tamerin, J. S. The psychodynamics of quitting smoking in a group. *American Journal of Psychiatry,* 1972, **129,** 589–595.

Taub, J. M., and Burger, R. J. Extended sleep and performance: The Rip Van Winkle effect. *Psychonomic Science,* 1969, **16,** 204–205.

Taub, J. M. Dream recall and content following various durations of sleep. *Psychonomic Science,* 1970, **16**, 204–205.

Taylor, D. W., Berry, P. C., and Bloch, C. H. Group participation, brainstorming and creative thinking. *Administrative Science Quarterly,* 1958, **3**, 23–47.

Taylor, W. S., and Martin, M. F. Multiple personality. *Journal of Abnormal and Social Psychology,* 1944, **39**, 281–300.

Terkel, S. *Hard times.* New York: Avon, 1970.

Thigpen, C. H., and Cleckley, H. M. A case of multiple personality. *Journal of Abnormal and Social Psychology,* 1954, **49**, 135–151.

Thigpen, C. H., and Cleckley, H. M. *The three faces of Eve.* New York: McGraw-Hill, 1957.

Thoms, H., and Bliven, B., Jr. Life before birth. *McCall's,* February 1958.

Thorndike, E. L. *Animal intelligence.* New York: Macmillan, 1911.

Thurstone, L. L. Primary mental abilities. *Psychometric Monographs,* No. 1. Chicago: University of Chicago Press, 1938.

Tilker, H. A. Socially responsible behavior as a function of observer responsibility and victim feedback. *Journal of Personality and Social Psychology,* 1970, **14**, 95–100.

Time. The new rebel cry: Jesus is coming. *Time,* June 2, 1971.

Time. The occult: A substitute faith. *Time,* June 19, 1972.

Tinbergen, N. On war and peace in animals and man. *Science,* 1968, **160**, 1411–1418.

Toman, W. Birth order rules all. *Psychology Today,* December 1970.

Torrey, E. F. What Western psychotherapists can learn from witchdoctors. *American Journal of Orthopsychiatry,* 1972, **42**, 69–76.

Tredgold, R. F., and Soddy, K. *A textbook of mental deficiency.* (9th ed.) Baltimore: Williams & Wilkins, 1956.

Trowill, J. A. Instrumental conditioning of the heart rate in the curarized rat. *Journal of Comparative and Physiological Psychology,* 1967, **63**, 7–11.

Tulkin, S. R. An analysis of the concept of cultural deprivation. *Developmental Psychology,* 1972, **6**, 326–339.

Turnbull, C. M. Some observations regarding the experiences and behavior of the Ba Mbuti pygmies. *American Journal of Psychology,* 1961, **74**, 304–308.

Turnbull, J. W. Asthma conceived as a learned response. *Journal of Psychosomatic Research,* 1962, **6**, 59–70.

Tyler, L. E. *The psychology of human differences.* (3rd ed.) New York: Appleton-Century-Crofts, 1965.

Ullman, L. P., and Krasner, L. *A psychological approach to abnormal behavior.* Englewood Cliffs, N.J.: Prentice-Hall, 1969.

Ulrich, R. E., Stachnik, T. J., and Stainton, N. R. Student acceptance of generalized personality interpretations. *Psychological Reports,* 1963, **13**, 831–834.

Underwood, B. J. Interference and forgetting. *Psychological Review,* 1957, **64**, 49–60.

Ungerleider, J. T., and Fisher, D. The problems of LSD-25 and emotional disorder. In R. E. Horman and A. M. Fox (Eds.), *Drug awareness.* Discus Books/Published by Avon, 1970.

U.S. Department of Health, Education, and Welfare. Mental health statistics: Current facility reports, 1967. Series MHB-H-11. U.S. Gov't. Printing Office.

Vernon, P. E. *Personality assessment: A critical survey.* London: Methuen, 1964.

Verville, E. *Behavior Problems of children.* Philadelphia: Saunders, 1967.

Vitols, M. M. Differing Negro-white mental illness patterns seen converging as equality grows between races. *Mental Health Scope,* 1967, **1**, 1–3.

Volar, E. *The manipulated man.* New York: Farrar, Straus & Giroux, 1973.

Wagar, J. A. Growth versus the quality of life. *Science,* 1970, **168**, 1179–1184.

Wahler, R. O. Infant social development: Some experimental analyses of an infant-mother interaction during the first year of life. *Journal of Experimental Child Psychology,* 1969, **7**, 101–113.

Walker, E. L., and Heyns, R. W. *An anatomy for conformity.* Belmont, Calif.: Brooks/Cole, 1967.

Wallace, R. K., and Benson, H. The physiology of meditation. *Scientific American,* May 1972.

Wallach, H. The role of head movements and vestibular and visual cues in sound localization. *Journal of Experimental Psychology,* 1940, **27**, 339–368.

Wallach, H. The perception of achromatic colors. *Scientific American,* October 1963.

Wallach, M. A., Kogan, N., and Bem. D. J. Diffusion of responsibility and level of risktaking in groups. *Journal of Abnormal and Social Psychology,* 1964, **68**, 263–274.

Wallach, M. A., and Kogan, N. Creativity and intelligence in children's thinking. *Trans-action,* January-February 1967.

Wallach, M. A., and Wing, C. W., Jr. *The talented student: A validation of the creativity-intelligence distinction.* New York: Holt, 1969.

Walsh, C. *God at large.* New York: Seaburg, 1971.

Walster, E. Passionate love. Paper presented at a conference on "Theories of interpersonal attraction in the dyad," New London, Conn., October 1970.

Walster, E., Aronson, E., and Abrahams, D. On increasing the persuasiveness of a low prestige communicator.

Journal of Experimental Social Psychology, 1966, **2**, 325–342.

Walster, E., and Berscheid, E. Adrenaline makes the heart grow fonder. *Psychology Today,* May 1971.

Ward, C. H., Beck, A. T., Mendelson, M., Mock, J. E., and Erbaugh, J. K. The psychiatric nomenclature. *Archives of General Psychiatry,* 1962, **7**, 198–205.

Ward, L. B. Problems in review: Putting executives to the test. *Harvard Business Review,* 1960, **38**, 6–7.

Warner, L. A second survey of psychological opinion on ESP. *Journal of Parapsychology,* 1952, **16**, 284–295.

Warren, J. R. Birth order and social behavior. *Psychological Bulletin,* 1966, **65**, 38–49.

Watkins, J. G. Psychotherapeutic methods. In B. B. Wolman (Ed.), *Handbook of clinical psychology.* New York: McGraw-Hill, 1965.

Watson, G. *Social psychology: Issues and insights.* Philadelphia: Lippincott, 1966.

Watson, J. B., and Rayner, R. Conditioned emotional reactions. *Journal of Experimental Psychology,* 1920, **3**, 1–14.

Watson, R. I. *Psychology of the child.* (2nd ed.) New York: Wiley, 1965.

Watts, W. A., Lynch, S., and Whittaker, D. Alienation and activism in today's college youth: Socialization patterns and current family relationships. *Journal of Counseling Psychology,* 1969, **16**, 1–7.

Weaver, T. R. The incidence of maladjustment among mental defectives in military environment. *American Journal of Mental Deficiency,* 1946, **51**, 238–246.

Wechsler, D. *Measurement of adult intelligence.* (3rd ed.) Baltimore: Williams & Wilkins, 1944.

Wecter, D. *The age of the Great Depression: 1929–1941.* New York: Macmillan, 1948.

Weinraub, B. Sweden discusses the impact of welfare system on freedom. *New York Times,* November 12, 1972.

Weinstein, E. A., Eck, R. A., and Lyerly, O. G. Conversion hysteria in Appalachia. *Psychiatry,* 1969, **32**, 334–341.

Weisman, A. Psychosocial death. *Psychology Today,* November 1972.

Weiss, J. M. Psychological factors in stress and disease. *Scientific American,* June 1972.

Weissman, M. M., and Paykel, E. S. Moving and depression in women. *Society,* July-August 1972.

Weisz, A. E., and Taylor, R. L. American presidential assassination. *Diseases of the Nervous System,* 1969, **30**, 659–668.

Welker, W. I. An analysis of exploratory and play behavior in animals. In D. W. Fiske and S. R. Maddi (Eds.), *Functions of varied experience.* Homewood, Ill.: Dorsey, 1961.

Werts, C. E., and Watley, D. J. Paternal influence on talent development. *Journal of Counseling Psychology,* 1972, **19**, 367–373.

West, L. J. Dissociative reaction. In A. M. Freedman and H. I. Kaplan (Eds.), *Psychiatry.* Baltimore: Williams & Wilkins, 1967.

Whalen, T. Wives of alcoholics. *Quarterly Journal of Studies on Alcohol,* 1953, **14**, 632–641.

White, R. W. Motivation reconsidered: The concept of competence. *Psychological Review,* 1959, **66**, 297–333.

White, R. W. *The abnormal personality.* (3rd ed.) New York: Ronald Press, 1964.

Whitney, L. R., and Barnard, K. E. Implications of operant learning theory for nursing care of the retarded child. *Mental Retardation,* 1966, **4**, 26–29.

Whittaker, D., and Watts, W. A. Personality characteristics associated with activism and disaffiliation in today's college-age youth. *Journal of Counseling Psychology,* 1971, **18**, 200–206.

Whitten, P., and Kagan, J. Jensen's dangerous half-truth. *Psychology Today,* August 1969.

Whyte, W. H., Jr. *The organization man.* New York: Simon and Schuster, 1956.

Wideman, J. Fear in the streets. *Intellectual Digest,* February 1972.

Willerman, L., and Churchill, J. A. Intelligence and birth weight in identical twins. *Child Development,* 1967, **38**, 623–629.

Williams, J. L. Personal space and its relation to extroversion-introversion. Master's thesis, University of Alberta, 1963.

Williamson, E. G. Value orientation in counseling. *Personnel and Guidance Journal,* 1958, **36**, 520–528.

Wilmer, H. A. Use of the television monologue with adolescent psychiatric patients. *American Journal of Psychiatry,* 1970, **126**, 1760–1766.

Winick, C. Clients' perceptions of prostitutes and of themselves. *International Journal of Social Psychiatry,* 1961–62, **8**, 289–297.

Winick, C., and Kinsie, P. M. *The lively commerce.* New York: New American Library, 1971.

Winterbottom, M. R. The relation of childhood training in independence to achievement motivation. Doctoral dissertation, University of Michigan, 1953.

Wittenborn, J. R., Plante, M., Burgess, F., and Livermore, N. The efficacy of electroconvulsive therapy, pronoizid and placebo in the treatment of young depressed women. *Journal of Nervous and Mental Disease,* 1961, **133**, 316–332.

Witthower, E. D., and White, K. L. Psychophysiologic aspects of respiratory disorders. In S. Arieti (Ed.), *American handbook of psychiatry.* New York: Basic Books, 1959.

Wohlford, P. Initiation of cigarette smoking: Is it related to parental smoking behavior? *Journal of Consulting and Clinical Psychology,* 1970, **34**, 148–151.

Wold, C. I. Characteristics of 26,000 suicide prevention center patients. *Bulletin of Suicidology,* 1970, **6**, 24–28.

Wolfe, J. B. Effectiveness of token rewards for chimpanzees. *Comparative Psychological Monographs,* 1936, **12**, 50.

Wolfenstein, M. *Children's humor.* Glencoe, Ill.: Free Press, 1954.

Wolff, P. H. The development of attention in young infants. *Annals of the New York Academy of Sciences,* 1965, **118**, 815–830.

Wolfgang, M. E. Who kills whom. *Psychology Today,* October 1969.

Wolpe, J., and Lazarus, A. A. *Behavior therapy techniques: A guide to the treatment of neurosis.* Elmsford, N.Y.: Pergamon, 1966.

Wolpe, J., and Rachman, S. Psychoanalytic "evidence": A critique based on Freud's case of little Hans. *Journal of Nervous and Mental Disease,* 1960, **131**, 135–148.

Wooldridge, D. E. *The machinery of the brain.* New York: McGraw-Hill, 1963.

Wrightsman, L. S., Jr. Effects of waiting with others on changes in level of felt anxiety. *Journal of Abnormal and Social Psychology,* 1960, **61**, 216–222.

Wrightsman, L. S. *Social psychology for the seventies.* Monterey, Calif.: Brooks/Cole, 1972.

Wrightsman, L. S., and Baker, N. J. Where have all the idealistic, imperturbable freshmen gone? *Proceedings of the 77th Annual Convention of the American Psychological Association,* 1969, **4**, 299–300.

Wyzanski, C. E. It is quite right that the young should talk about us as hypocrites. We are. *Saturday Review,* July 20, 1968.

Yang, C. K. *The Chinese family in the communist revolution.* Cambridge: Harvard University Press, 1959.

Yates, A. J. *Behavior therapy.* New York: Wiley, 1970.

Young, K. *Personality and problems of adjustment.* (2nd ed.) New York: Appleton-Century-Crofts, 1962.

Zajonc, R. B. Attitudinal effects of mere exposure. *Journal of Personality and Social Psychology Monograph Supplement,* 1968, **9**, 1–27.

Zajonc, R. B. Brainwash: Familiarity breeds comfort. *Psychology Today,* March 1970.

Zalba, S. R. Battered children. *Trans-action,* July-August 1971.

Zeigler, H. P., and Leibowitz, H. Apparent visual size as a function of distance for children and adults. *American Journal of Psychology,* 1957, **70**, 106–109.

Zigler, E. Familial mental retardation: A continuing dilemma. *Science,* 1967, **155**, 292–298.

Zigler, E., and Phillips, L. Psychiatric diagnosis and symptomatology. *Journal of Abnormal and Social Psychology,* 1961, **63**, 69–75.

Zimbardo, P. G. The human choice: Individuation, reason, and order versus deindividuation, impulse, and chaos. *Nebraska Symposium on Motivation,* 1969, **18**, 237–307.

Zimbardo, P. G. Symposium on social and developmental issues in moral research. Paper presented at the meeting of the Western Psychological Association, Los Angeles, April 1970.

Zimbardo, P., and Formica, R. Emotional comparisons and self-esteem as determinants of affiliation. *Journal of Personality,* 1963, **31**, 141–162.

Zimbardo, P. G., Weisenberg, M., Firestone, I., and Levy, B. Communicator effectiveness in producing public conformity and private attitude change. *Journal of Personality,* 1965, **33**, 233–256.

Zoellner, R. Confessions of a middle-aged moralist. *Commonweal,* June 7, 1968.

Zube. M. J. Changes concepts of morality: 1948–69. *Social Forces,* 1972, **50**, 385–393.

Zubeck, J. P., Puskar, D., Samson, W., and Gowing, J. Perceptual changes after prolonged isolation (darkness and silence). *Canadian Journal of Psychology,* 1961, **15**, 83–100.

Zuckerman, M. Theoretical formulations: I. In J. Zubek (Ed.), *Sensory deprivation: Fifteen years of research.* New York: Appleton-Century-Crofts, 1969.

Zuckerman, M. Dimensions of sensation seeking. *Journal of Consulting and Clinical Psychology,* 1971, **36**, 45–52.

Zuckerman, M., and Cohen, N. Sources of reports of visual and auditory sensations in perceptual isolation experiments. *Psychological Bulletin,* 1964, **62**, 11–20.

Zuckerman, M., Schultz, D. P., and Hopkins, T. R. Sensation seeking and volunteering for sensory deprivation and hypnosis experiments. *Journal of Consulting Psychology,* 1967, **31**, 358–363.

Zung, W. W., and Wilson, W. P. Time estimation during sleep. *Biological Psychiatry,* 1971, **3**, 159–164.

Photographic Acknowledgements

Page 202: Harry F. Harlow, University of Wisconsin Primate Laboratory
Page 209: Suzanne Arms, Jeroboam
Page 212: Suzanne Arms, Jeroboam
Page 214: Burk Uzzle, Magnum
Page 217: Claus Meyer, Black Star

CHAPTER NINE

Page 218: Nacio Jan Brown, BBM
Page 220: John Brook
Page 226: Jeffrey Blankfort, BBM
Page 227: U.S. Army
Page 229: Linda Montano, Jeroboam
Page 238: Nick Pavloff, Jeroboam

CHAPTER TEN

Page 244: Kay Y. James
Page 248: David Glaubinger, Jeroboam
Page 252: University of California, Santa Barbara
Page 254: Joanne Leonard
Page 259: Joanne Leonard
Page 265: Collection, The Museum of Modern Art, New York
Page 268: Charles Harbutt, Magnum

CHAPTER ELEVEN

Page 270: Nell Dorr
Page 276: The Psychological Corporation
Page 282: The Psychological Corporation
Page 289: Bob Smith, Rapho Guillumette
Page 291: Peter Goodman, BBM
Page 293: Joshua Popenoe, from *Inside Summerhill*, copyright 1970 Hart Publishing Company, Inc., New York

CHAPTER TWELVE

Page 300: Nacio Jan Brown, BBM
Page 303: Roger Lubin, Jeroboam
Page 310: Optic Nerve, Jeroboam

CHAPTER THIRTEEN

Page 320: Wallraf-Richartz Museum
Page 324: Collection, The Museum of Modern Art, New York, Larry Aldrich Foundation Fund
Page 325: The Art Institute of Chicago
Page 328: Optic Nerve, Jeroboam
Page 331: Len Sirman Press, Geneva

CHAPTER FOURTEEN

Page 340: John Brook
Page 342: Mitchell Payne, Jeroboam
Page 343: Eric Hass, Rapho Guillumette
Page 345: Frankfurter Goethe-Museum

Page 348:
Page 348: Steve Schapiro, Black Star
Page 351: Stern, Black Star
Page 352: Peter M. Witt, North Carolina Department of Mental Health
Page 356: Wells Fargo Bank History Room, San Francisco
Page 357: Suzanne Arms, Jeroboam
Page 362: Dr. Thelma Moss, University of California, Los Angeles
Page 363: The Bettman Archive

CHAPTER FIFTEEN

Page 368: John Brook
Page 370: Abigail Heyman, Magnum
Page 373: The Coca Cola Company
Page 374: David Powers, Jeroboam
Page 375: Hamilton Watch Company
Page 378: Robert Capa, Magnum
Page 383: Peeter Vilms, Jeroboam
Page 389: American Cancer Society, Inc.
Page 391: American Cancer Society, Inc.
Page 392: Mitchell Payne, Jeroboam
Page 393: American Cancer Society, Inc.

CHAPTER SIXTEEN

Page 394: John Pearson
Page 397: Joanne Leonard
Page 398: John Brook
Page 399: Roger Lubin, Jeroboam
Page 400: Wide World Photos
Page 406: Baron Wolman
Page 411: Dan Landi, Black Star
Page 413: Abigail Heyman, Magnum
Page 417: Hella Hammid, Rapho Guillumette
Page 418: Hella Hammid, Rapho Guillumette
Page 419: Bonnie Freer, Rapho Guillumette

CHAPTER SEVENTEEN

Page 426: John A. Knaggs, BBM
Page 429: Prado Museum
Page 430: Culver Pictures
Page 432: The Bettmann Archive
Page 433: N. Bouvier
Page 436: Roger Lubin, Jeroboam
Page 440: Michael Weisbrot, Black Star
Page 441: Nacio Jan Brown, BBM

CHAPTER EIGHTEEN

Page 442: John and Regina Hicks
Page 445: David Powers, Jeroboam
Page 448: Claus Meyer, Black Star
Page 450: David Glaubinger, Jeroboam
Page 453: David Margolin, Black Star
Page 457, top: John and Regina Hicks

Page 457, bottom: John Pearson
Page 458, bottom left: John Pearson
Pages 458–459: John & Regina Hicks
Page 461: Werner Wolff, Black Star
Page 463: Bemis Company, Inc.

CHAPTER NINETEEN

Page 466: Hide Shibata
Page 469: Prado Museum
Page 472: John Launois, Black Star
Page 473: Mitchell Payne, Jeroboam
Page 474: Mitchell Payne, Jeroboam
Page 475: Hide Shibata
Page 479: G. William Holland, Smith-Kline Corporation
Page 482: Roger Malloch, Magnum
Page 483: Lou de la Torre, BBM

CHAPTER TWENTY

Page 486: Baron Wolman
Page 490: Culver Pictures
Page 491: Baron Wolman
Page 494: Ed Turnbull, Delancey Street Foundation
Page 495: Ed Turnbull, Delancey Street Foundation
Page 496: Baron Wolman
Page 498: Len Sirman Press
Page 500: John and Regina Hicks
Page 501: G. William Holland, Smith-Kline Corporation
Page 502: David Glaubinger, Jeroboam
Page 504: Napa State Hospital, Imola, California
Page 505: Hide Shibata
Page 506: John Launois, Black Star

CHAPTER TWENTY-ONE

Page 512: Baron Wolman
Page 515: David Powers, Jeroboam
Page 517: Collection, The Museum of Modern Art, New York
Page 519: Prado Museum
Page 520: Nacio Jan Brown, BBM
Page 521: Juvenile Bureau, San Francisco Police Department
Page 524: Wells Fargo Bank History Room, San Francisco
Page 525: Federal Bureau of Investigation
Page 528: California Department of Highways
Page 529: Charles Gatewood, Magnum
Page 530: Ray Ellis, Rapho Guillumette

CHAPTER TWENTY-TWO

Page 534: John Brook
Page 536: State Historical Society of Wisconsin
Page 537: Philadelphia Museum of Art
Page 538: Michael Abramson, Black Star
Page 542, top: State Historical Society of Wisconsin
Page 542, bottom: Joanne Leonard

Page 544: Library of Congress
Page 546: NOW Legal Defense and Education Fund, Inc.
Page 548: Providence Public Library
Page 549, left: Providence Public Library
Page 549, right: Bob Adelman, Magnum
Page 552: Jan Lukas. Rapho Guillumette
Page 554: Louvre Museum

CHAPTER TWENTY-THREE

Page 556: W. Eugene Smith
Page 558: Wide World Photos
Page 561: Wide World Photos
Page 563: Nacio Jan Brown, BBM
Page 565: War Relocation Authority
Page 566: Wells Fargo Bank History Room, San Francisco
Page 569: Joseph Fay
Page 570: Philadelphia Museum of Art
Page 571: Michael Abramson, Black Star
Page 572: David Powers, Jeroboam
Page 573: John Pearson

CHAPTER TWENTY-FOUR

Page 578: David Glaubinger, Jeroboam
Page 580: Philadelphia Museum of Art
Page 581: Bob Combs, Rapho Guillumette
Page 583, top: Burk Uzzle, Magnum
Page 583, bottom: Whitney Museum of American Art
Page 584: David Glaubinger, Jeroboam
Page 586: Optic Nerve, Jeroboam
Page 589: The Fine Arts Museums of San Francisco, California Palace of the Legion of Honor
Page 597: Paul Sequeira, Rapho Guillumette
Page 599: Lynn McLaren, Rapho Guillumette

CHAPTER TWENTY-FIVE

Page 602: Stephen G. Williams, The Photography Place
Page 605: Wide World Photos
Page 607: Dennis Stock, Magnum
Page 608: Optic Nerve, Jeroboam
Page 610, top: Bill Stanton, Magnum
Page 610, bottom: Roger Lubin, Jeroboam
Page 613: Peeter Vilms, Jeroboam
Page 618: Joanne Leonard
Page 619: Bruce Davidson, Magnum

CHAPTER TWENTY-SIX

Page 622: W. Eugene Smith
Page 625: John Pearson
Page 627: Peter Goodman, BBM
Page 629: The Oakland Museum
Page 630: The Oakland Museum
Page 632: Bruce Davidson, Magnum
Page 635: David Powers, Jeroboam
Page 638: Nacio Jan Brown, BBM
Page 641: Ed Turnbull, Delancey Street Foundation

Glossary

Absolute threshold (limen)   The minimum amount of energy required for the nervous system to register a sensation.

Activity, in satisfying needs   (1) **Goal-directed**—acquiring the resources to satisfy the need. (2) **Preparatory**—ascertaining the availability of resources.

Activity level of measure of drive   A measurement of the strength of a drive according to the amount of activity required in its satisfaction.

Actualization   Maslow's term for the process by which innate needs, capacities, and talents become reality.

Acuity, visual   The ability to distinguish the details in the field of vision; keenness of sight.

Acupuncture   A medical therapeutic practice of inserting needles into parts of the body; developed in China.

Acute depression   The second stage of progressive depression, marked by increased alienation and self-accusation and by physical deterioration.

Acute mania   Considered the second stage of progressively manic behavior, characterized by intransigence and carelessness of personal appearance.

Adrenal glands   Situated above the kidneys, each consists of (1) **adrenal cortex,** which secretes corticosteroid and adrenal sex hormones and influences growth, metabolism, blood circulation, salt balance, healing, and the production of antibodies; and (2) **adrenal medulla,** which secretes the hormones epinephrine and norepinephrine and influences metabolism and the stimulation of the central nervous system under stress.

Adrenaline   A hormone secreted by the adrenal medulla, that affects the heartbeat, blood pressure, and blood sugar levels. Also called **epinephrine.**

Affective disorder   Mental disturbances causing changes of mood.

Agitated depression   An exaggerated form of anxiety.

Alarm reaction   The first stage of exposure to stress, in which the nervous system prepares a defense.

All-or-none principle   Of axon function: an impulse has to be of a certain strength before the axon will function, but when that strength is reached, the axon will fire completely.

Alpha wave   A rhythmic electric impulse of the brain, averaging ten cycles per second, occurring in wakefulness and relaxation.

Amnesia   Forgetfulness to the extreme of loss of personal identity; a defense mechanism against conflict too devastating to be handled.

Amniotic sac   The membrane containing the fluid that surrounds and protects the fetus.

Amphetamine psychosis   An effect, resembling the condition of psychotic disturbance, of amphetamine drugs, characterized by paranoid delusions, compulsions, and stereotyped behavior.

Amphetamines   A group of drugs that produce psychological stimulation by releasing epinephrine in the brain, but often cause extreme depression later. Popularly known as "speed," "uppers," and "pep pills."

Anal stage   In psychoanalytic theory, the stage in psychosexual development when bowel control is achieved and gratification centers on anal activities.

Androgens   Male sex hormones.

Andropause   See **Male climacteric.**

Anniversary reaction   The term used to describe the physical or psychological disturbance sometimes found in survivors on or about the anniversary of the death of someone close to them.

Anomia   The inability to put thoughts into words—a result of brain disease.

Anorexia nervosa   The nervous loss of appetite; symptomatic of emotional disorder.

Antidepressant   See **Energizer.**

Anxiety   Vague apprehension and feeling of disquiet, frequently the result of conflicting motives; a pervading symptom of neuroses. Freud distinguished three types: (1) **Moral**—the guilt that follows the contravention of whatever moral code one learned very early in life. (2) **Neurotic**—the fear that learned responses and defenses may break down and that behavior will become controlled by the instincts. (3) **Reality**—the fear of one's environment; disquiet about everyday living.

Aphasia   The loss of the ability to understand or use words—a result of brain disease. **Syntactical aphasia**   An incapacity to form coherent sentences.

Aphonia   The inability to speak.

Apparent-distance theory   Used to explain the moon illusion; holds that the further away an object, the smaller it appears.

Approach-approach conflict   The problem of choosing between two equally attractive goals.

Approach-avoidance conflict   The problem attached to making the choice between temptation and denial.

Archetype   According to Jung, an idea or way of thinking inherited from the experience of the race and remaining in the unconscious of the individual to influence his perception of the world. Also called **primordial image.**

Area sample   In surveying, the method of choosing suitable subjects by pinpointing the residents of a specific house, or houses, in a specific segment of a geographic region (area), the houses (or dwelling units) having been chosen at random.

Arithmetic mean (average)   In statistics, the quantity with a value intermediate between two or more quantities, derived by dividing the sum of the quantities in question by the number of those quantities.

Arteriosclerosis, cerebral   The thickening of the arteries of the brain, thereby reducing the supply of blood and impairing its functioning.

Associational cortex   The part of the human brain that shows no specific response when electrically stimulated.

Attention   The psychological process of selecting and responding to certain stimuli while suppressing reaction to others.

Attitude   The manner of acting, feeling, or thinking that shows one's disposition or opinion.

Autism   A form of schizophrenia characterized by morbid preoccupation with the self, the inability to relate to others or to the environment, and a tendency toward pathological fantasies. Found frequently in children and, when occurring in babies, also known as **infantile autism.**

Autokinetic effect   The effect on the perceiver of an object seen without any perceptual anchor, usually cited as the apparent movement of a small light in a dark room.

Autonomic nervous system   The part of the nervous system that controls muscles and glands, which are not usually subject to voluntary control. The **sympathetic** division is activated by stress. The **parasympathetic** division directs the body to relax after stress and also regulates ruminative and restorative functions.

Autonomic response   An unconscious physiological reaction to a stimulus.

Autonomous morality   Piaget's term for the developing child's ability, at about age 10, to modify rules to fit prevailing situations.

Average   See **Arithmetic mean.**

Aversive conditioning   An element of behavior therapy whereby unacceptable behavior becomes linked in the patient's mind with painful stimuli and therefore to be avoided.

Avoidance-avoidance conflict   The problem attached to the necessity of making a choice between two unacceptable goals.

Axon   A long fiber extending away from the neuron that transmits stimuli to other neurons, to muscles, or to glands.

Axon terminal   The knob on the end of each of the small fibers that begin to branch out toward the end of the axon.

Axonal transmission   The movement of stimuli within a nerve.

Barbiturates   Drugs with sedative or pain-deadening effects.

Basic trust   Erikson's term for the sense of security that the infant needs from early babyhood to enable him to develop as an independent person without feeling constantly threatened by the world.

Behavior modification   The process of changing behavior by small, successive steps of rewarding acceptable behavior without punishing the unacceptable, thus giving the patient evidence of some success even in the early stages of treatment.

Behavior prediction   (1) **Clinical**—by which personal judgments and opinions, as well as analyzed data, are used. (2) **Statistical**—by which data are analyzed statistically, generalizations made, and personal impressions eliminated.

Behavior therapy   A method of changing undesirable patterns of behavior by rewarding acceptable responses until the unacceptable responses have been extinguished; that is, a matter of altering habits to the point where the patient himself has acquired self-perpetuating, internal reinforcers for his new behavior. It is considered effective for mental disorder even though no attempt is made to ascertain the causes of the disorder.

Behavioral engineering   The process of regulating or instilling acceptable behavior, especially in child rearing, by manipulating the individual in much the same way that a dog is trained: compliance is rewarded, failure is ignored.

Behavioral theory   A theory of personality development holding that behavior is determined by the reinforcement received from the environment, and may be changed by extinguishing existing responses and substituting acceptable responses.

Benzedrine   A drug used medically to overcome fatigue or nervous exhaustion; by drug users as a consciousness stimulant. Popularly known as "bennies."

BFT   See **Biofeedback Training.**

Bi-modal distribution   In statistics, a frequency distribution with two modes.

Binet-Simon Test of Intelligence   The original test of intelligence, using the concept of mental age; developed in France in 1904.

Binocular parallax   See **Retinal disparity.**

Binocular vision   Visual perception by the simultaneous use of two eyes. Since the eyes are about 2½ inches apart and therefore see slightly different images, the quality of binocular vision governs the perception of depth.

Biofeedback   A technique for stimulating the brain by using electronic monitoring instruments that signal bodily fluctuations in certain involuntary functions such as heartbeat, blood pressure, and respiration, so that, it is hoped, a person can identify the changes and perhaps control them.

Biofeedback Training (BFT) A form of learning that enables an individual to control certain involuntary physiological functions.

Biological engineering The science of chemically or surgically altering biological characteristics.

Black English The language used by much of the black population of the United States; grammatically and syntactically different (and, depending on the theorist, incomparable with or inferior to) **standard English.**

Blind spot The area of the retina where the optic nerve enters the eye.

Body English Nonverbal communication imparted by stance and position of the body or parts of it. See also *Vibratese.*

Brain syndrome, acute Biochemical changes in brain function, provoking delirium, stupor, or coma.

Brain waves Rhythmic electric impulses given off by the neurons in the cerebral cortex. See also **Alpha wave.**

Brainstem The central core of the brain, issuing from the spinal cord.

Brainstorming An approach to problem solving which assumes that the more ideas that are put forward, the better are the group's chances of reaching the best possible solution.

Brainwashing The technique of clearing the mind of established ideas and loyalties by indoctrination under duress and persistent psychological pressure.

Cannon-Bard theory Of emotion: holds that the thalamus and hypothalamus of the brain perceive emotional stimuli and also control the reactions to them.

Case history A comprehensive study which, of an individual, might include personality and intelligence tests, biography, interviews, and observations.

Catatonia A form of schizophrenia characterized by total preoccupation with perceived danger and an apparently deliberate lack of cooperation, with sudden occasional violence punctuating the long spells of immobility.

Catharsis, aggressive A theory of human behavior holding that people are naturally violent and must alleviate their hostility by expressing it.

Central sulcus See **Fissures of the brain.**

Central traits Traits in others so vivid that we tend to base our entire estimate of their personality on them.

Cerebellum The part of the brain that controls movement and coordination.

Cerebral cortex The largest area of the brain and that which controls thought and consciousness.

Chaining In learning theory, the process of mastering a series of related activities to one end.

Choice measure of drive A measure of the relative strength of motivations made by noting which of two needs is satisfied first.

Chromosomes Large, chainlike molecules of DNA and proteins that contain the genes responsible for heredity. All human cells, except sex cells, contain 46 (23 from each parent).

Clairvoyance The power of discerning objects not apparent to the normal senses.

Client-centered therapy A form of treatment for anxiety that enables the patient to realize what his true self is and thereby resolve the contradictions that have been troubling him. Also called *Rogerian therapy.*

Clones Offspring produced by grafting, budding, or chemically induced division, from single cells; asexual (and therefore identical to the single parent) reproduction of sexually reproducing organisms.

Cochlea The spiral-shaped part of the inner ear containing the auditory nerve endings.

Coefficient of correlation In statistics, a measure of how two variables are related, the measure varying from -1 (perfect negative correlation) to $+1$ (perfect positive correlation), with 0 representing no correlation.

Cognitive consistency Agreement between one's beliefs and/or feelings and one's behavior. Attempts to achieve such agreement may often involve distorted perception.

Cognitive dissonance Awareness of a discrepancy between one's beliefs and/or feelings and one's behavior. The desire to eliminate the discrepancy is considered a major human motivation.

Cognitive rigidity Perseverance to the point of absurdity—a symptom of psychopathic obsession.

Cognitive theory of motivation An explanation of behavior based on the notion that man is rational and able to choose his responses.

Color blindness (1) **Achromatic**—the inability to see anything but black, white, and shades of gray; rare. (2) **Dichromatic**—the inability to distinguish one of the three primary colurs; a sex-linked deficiency, considerably more common in males than in females.

Common fate A principle of perceptual stimulus organization by which elements that are perceived to function, move, or change in the same way tend to be perceived as belonging together.

Common-ground analytic psychotherapy Treatment of mental disorder based on the assumption that, if the patient's anxiety can be diminished, he will be able to gain insight into what is disturbing him.

Concrete operations Piaget's term for the stage in child development (about ages 7 through 11) in which the child can think things out without having to enact them physically.

Conditioned stimulus A stimulus, hitherto neutral, that will evoke a response in a subject who has been taught to associate it with whatever stimulus will instinctively evoke the required response.

Conditioning   The process of teaching subjects to produce learned responses on cue. (1) **Respondent (Classical; Pavlovian)**—the cue is provided by two stimuli applied simultaneously: an unconditioned stimulus (one that will evoke an instinctive response) and a neutral stimulus (one that does not necessarily evoke any response and that certainly does not evoke the cued response). After a number of trials, the neutral stimulus will evoke the response even without the unconditioned stimulus (2) **Operant**—used in behavior therapy; the process by which existing behavior is reinforced or obliterated by the application or withholding (depending on the desired effect) of rewarding or punishing stimuli. Operant, unlike classical, conditioning is used on voluntary responses.

Conduction deafness   The inability to hear resulting from injury to the sound-conducting mechanisms of the ear; hearing aids will remedy it.

Cones   Nerve cells in the eyes, containing light-sensitive chemicals that change when struck by light and, in changing, signal the brain; the color receptors of the eye.

Consciousness expansion   See **Psychedelics.**

Consolidation theory   A theory holding that information becomes permanently part of the memory only after it has been held in the mind a certain length of time without disruption.

Consummatory behavior   The final activity in satisfying a need.

Contingency theory of leadership   A theory holding that leaders are made—by the situation and the group to be led—not born.

Conversion hysteria   A mental disorder characterized by sudden physical malfunction or failure with no discernible physical cause; the repressed impulse is converted into a physical symptom.

Copying   In child development, the child's deliberate duplicating of behavior in another; a method of learning.

Cornea   The transparent, outer skin of the eyeball.

Corpus callosum   The mass of nerve fibers connecting the two hemispheres of the brain; when severed, the result is a "split brain."

Correlation   In statistics, a measure of the relationship between two things: (1) **Positive**—$+1.00$. (2) **None**—$.00$. (3) **Negative**—-1.00.

Correlational studies   Investigations made to determine the extent of the relationship (correlation) between characteristics.

Counterconditioning   See **Extinction.**

Counterphobic behavior   A reaction toward extreme fear that causes the individual to seek out occasions on which to expose himself to the feared object to prove to himself and others that he is able to conquer his fears.

Craft neuroses (craft palsies)   Symptoms of conversion hysteria that manifest themselves as a paralysis or other debilitation preventing the victim from functioning in his role or career when that is a source of his anxiety.

Cretinism   A type of mental deficiency associated with a poorly functioning thyroid gland.

Critical-period effect   A major and lasting result engendered by a relatively small amount of learning at a particular time in early development. See also **Imprinting.**

Cryonics   The science of freezing.

Culturalism   See **Neo-Freudianism.**

Cumulative deficit   A hypothesis about the existence of Black English, which, it holds, stems from an early ignorance about the relationships among words and which will lead to cognitive deficiency, especially in complex and abstract reasoning.

Deafferentation   See **Sensory deprivation.**

Decompensation   A failure to adjust; in psychology, the disorganization and disorientation of behavior and personality resulting from a massive but ultimately doomed effort to cope with stress; often accompanied by physical impairment.

Defense mechanism   The denial, often unconscious, that frustration and conflict and the concomitant anxiety exist, thereby preserving self-esteem. Symptoms may include delusions, hallucinations, obsessions, compulsions, and morbid fears.

Defensive identification   In child development, the child's patterning himself on another in the hopes of achieving similar status.

Deficit motivators   Conditions of deprivation that provoke action in order that they might be removed.

Deindividuation   The effect, on the individual, of his anonymity when in a large group.

Delirious mania   See **Hyperacute mania.**

Delta sleep   The stage of deepest sleep.

Démence précoce   The name given to the mental disorder later classified as **dementia praecox** and now as **schizophrenia.**

Dementia   See **Simple schizophrenia.**

Dementia praecox   A former name for **schizophrenia.**

Demoralization   The state of mental deterioration that results from an individual's failure and perceived powerlessness to change.

Dendrites   Fibers projecting from the neurons that receive stimuli from adjacent neurons.

Deoxyribonucleic acid   See **DNA.**

Depersonalization   A mental disorder characterized by loss of a sense of personality, reality, and identity.

Depression As a mental disorder, gloom in extreme form, against which the patient has no defenses and must submit to whatever fate his delusions are providing for him.

Deprivation As a mental disorder, gloom in extreme form, against which the patient has no defenses and must submit to whatever fate his delusions are providing for him.

Deprivation A lack of some element of psychological, physical, or social balance that provokes activity toward obtaining it; a need.

Descriptive statistics Numbers that describe other numbers.

Desensitization A method of treatment for phobia that progressively confronts the patient with the object of his fears so that increasing familiarity will decrease the threat.

Development identification In child development, the affection between mother and infant before the latter realizes that he is a separate person.

Developmental lag A hypothesis of the existence of Black English that holds the language to be a retarded form of standard English developed in a culturally impoverished environment,

Dialect The form or variety of a spoken language peculiar to a region, a community, or a social or occupational group.

Difference hypothesis An explanation of the development of Black English that holds the language to be a dialect of what is considered standard English, with no implication that it is inferior or limited.

Difference threshold The point at which the nervous system detects a change in stimuli.

Discrimination The ability to distinguish between one stimulus and another.

Displacement The act of substituting a desired but unattainable goal with one less favored but more accessible.

Dissociative hysteria A mental disorder caused by inadequately repressed impulses that, in manifesting themselves, cause the personality to disintegrate.

Distractions In psychology, stimuli that at first cannot be ignored but, if continued long enough, stop being perceived.

DNA (deoxyribonucleic acid) The cellular molecules of the genes that carry the genetic code of hereditary factors.

Down's syndrome (Mongolism) A chromosomal deviation caused by the presence of extra chromosomal material, resulting in mental retardation and considered to be connected with the mother's age.

Downer Popular or slang term among drug users for drugs that have a calming or sedative effect.

Drive Usually biological (as opposed to social or psychological *motives*) direction of the organism toward a specific goal.

Drive theory of motivation An explanation of behavior that would have it rooted in the necessity to satisfy deprivation by means of learned responses.

Ecology In sociology, the relationship between human groups and material resources, and the social and cultural patterns of that relationship.

Ectomorph The slender physical type, characterized by an extensively developed nervous system.

EEG See **Electroencephalogram; Electroencephalograph.**

Effectors Muscles and glands that receive and act upon nerve stimuli.

Ego In psychoanalytic theory, that part of the personality governed by reason, experiencing the external world through the senses, censoring the id, and answerable to the superego. In general terms, the self-concept of the individual.

Eidetiker An individual endowed with an unusually vivid memory for images.

Electroencephalogram (EEG) The record of the brain waves made on an electroencephalograph.

Electroencephalograph (EEG) The instrument used to record the electrical activity of the brain.

Electroshock Electric current passed through the brain to produce unconsciousness and convulsions; used in treating mental illness.

Embryo In man, the prenatal organism from the second through the eleventh week after conception.

Emotion A broad term covering the complex feeling of experience, sensation, internal and external physical response, and motivation.

Encopresis The lack of bowel control and, in children, symptomatic of mental and emotional disorder.

Encounter A method of helping people to relate to one another by having them, in small groups, usually under the leadership of a psychotherapist, meet to promote personal contact in an open, intimate atmosphere.

Endomorph The abdominal physical type, characterized by a strong digestive system and tending to roundness, with relatively weak muscles and bones; flabby.

Energizer (antidepressant) A drug that stimulates the brain; used in psychotherapy to rouse depressed or anxious patients out of their gloom, even if briefly.

Enuresis The lack of bladder control; the result of ineffective toilet training and symptomatic, in children, of mental and emotional disorder.

Epilepsy A convulsive disorder produced by malfunction of the brain, accompanied by mental blackout and sometimes seizures.

Epinephrine See **Adrenaline.**

ESP See **Extrasensory perception.**

Estrogens Female sex hormones.

Eugenics The science of improving races and breeds, especially the human race, by controlling hereditary factors.

Euthanasia Mercy killing; painless death for victims of incurable illness, serious mental deficiency, or extreme accidents.

Existential therapy A treatment for anxiety that makes the patient aware of the choices he is making so that he realizes that it is he who is responsible for his life.

Existentialism In psychology, a theory of personality based on the belief that man is free (that is, not bound by instinct or inherited patterns of behavior) and responsible for his own existence and experience; thus, disorder results from his negatinng or being denied that responsibility.

Experiment An action or process undertaken to discover something not yet known or to demonstrate something known. A careful and controlled study of cause and effect made by manipulating an independent variable (or condition affecting the subject) and observing its effect on a dependent variable (or the subject's behavior in response to changes in the independent variable).

Experimental method The most highly formalized scientific practice, in which hypothesis are tested under precisely specified conditions.

Externalization of drive The term used for the practice of following established habits even in the absence of the original reason for their existence.

Extinction The process of changing a conditioned response by separating the conditioned stimulus from the unconditioned and applying the former with a new unconditioned stimulus that evokes a different response. Thus the original conditioned response is not obliterated; it is simply overridden by a new response, by a process also called **counterconditioning.**

Extrasensory perception (ESP) The perception of things, mental and physical, by means, usually unknown and/or undefined, outside those of the normal senses.

Fatigue theory An explanation of optical illusion holding that the nervous system, wearied of one set of perceptions, shifts to its alternative. The theory is also used to explain indecision: both perceptions cannot be right, but both are perceived.

Fetus In man, the prenatal organism after the eleventh week following conception.

Figure The foreground of the perceptual field; that part to which one directs most of his attention. See also **Ground.**

Fissure of Silvius See **Fissures in the brain.**

Fissures in the brain Two grooves, the **central sulcus** (*sulcus* being Latin for "furrow") and the **fissure of Silvius,** running across the cerebral cortex, dividing it into sections called lobes.

Formal operations Piaget's term for the final stage in child development (about ages 12 through 15) in which thought about abstractions is possible.

Fovea A depression in the retina containing only cones; the point of clearest color reception.

Free will The human will regarded as uninhibited by restraints, compulsions, or antecedent conditioning—giving the individual entire responsibility for decision or choice.

Frequency distribution In statistics, how often each score is obtained.

Frequency method A means of determining the limits of perceptible stimuli by testing only that range of stimuli that immediately precedes and follows the assumed point of perception.

Frequency polygon In statistics, a graph consisting of points joined by a line, indicating the frequency with which specific results occur.

Freudian theory Freud's theory of personality, which, he maintained, develops, in unconscious desires, in infancy and early childhood, is established by about age 7 and thereafter is only elaborated and refined. Also called **Psychoanalytic theory.**

Fright drug Succinycholine.

Functional autonomy An explanation of activity that is continued even though the original motivation is no longer applicable.

Functional fixedness The inability to see a new use for a familiar object; an indication of inflexibility and lack of imagination.

Galvanic skin reflex (GSR) A change in the electrical conductivity of the skin, caused by activity of the sweat glands.

Gate-control mechanisms Barriers in the nervous system that, depending on whether they are open or closed, permit or block the transmission of pain; the concept was put forward as an explanation of acupuncture.

General-adaptation syndrome Selye's term for the adjustment made in facing stress.

Generalization (1) The process by which similar stimuli produce identical responses; for example, dogs conditioned to salivate at the sound of a tuning fork will also salivate on hearing a whistle, buzzer, metronome, or bell. (2) the process by which a substitute response will be made if the subject is prevented from making the conditioned response.

Generativity According to Erikson, the ability in a mature personality to be concerned with others and being, thereby, productive and happy instead of self-centered.

Genes Molecules of DNA found in the chromosomes and determining the individual pattern of heredity. (1) **Dominant**—the genes for certain physical characteristics (for example, curly hair) will always prevail. (2) **Recessive**—the genes for the complementary characteristics (for example, straight hair) that have no visible effect unless paired with another recessive gene.

Genetics The biological study of heredity and variation.

Genotype The fundamental hereditary constitution of an organism. Compare **Phenotype.**

Gestalt   A German word meaning "form" or "organization." (1) **Gestalt psychology**—the study of mental activities in general and perception in particular, with the emphasis on the functioning of the whole of the human mind, not on its parts. (2) **Gestalt therapy**—treatment for anxiety that tries to put the patient back into contact with all the facets of his personality.

Glands   Organs that separate certain elements from the blood and convert them into substances for the body to use (such as adrenaline) or excrete (such as urine).

Glia   Cells in the brain that surround, cushion, and probably nourish the nerve cells.

Glove anaesthesia   Insensitivity from the wrist down, from psychic, not organic, causes.

Gray matter   Grayish nerve tissue of the brain and spinal cord, consisting mainly of nerve cells, with few nerve fibers. See also **White matter.**

Green-light stage   In brainstorming, the period of problem solving when the group is producing as many ideas as possible without stopping to criticize them.

Ground   The background of the perceptual field. See also **Figure.**

Group (mass) therapy   A method of treating mental disturbances in meetings or gatherings of groups of patients and a number of therapists.

GSR   See **Galvanic skin reflex.**

Habituation   A process whereby an organism ceases to respond both psychologically and physiologically to specific repeated stimuli which have carried no significant information.

Hallucination   A perception accepted without question, notwithstanding the complete absence of external sensory cues; a vision.

Hallucinogen   Usually, a drug that will produce hallucinations in the mind of the user.

Hawthorne effect   The term is used for the concept that attitudes and interpersonal relations are important motivators in work.

Hebephrenia   A form of schizophrenia that appears early in life, characterized by emotional disorganization and rapid personality disintegration.

Hedonistic theory of motivation   An early (eighteenth- and nineteenth-century) explanation of behavior that would have man making calculated choices in favor of the pleasurable over the painful.

Hemispheres of the brain   The two dome-shaped structures of the brain, joined by a network of nerves, and each controlling the opposite side of the body.

Heredity   The transmission from parent to offspring of certain biological factors.

Heroin   Derived from morphine, a very powerful, habit-forming narcotic that creates immensely pleasant feelings.

Heterozygous trait   A characteristic transmitted by the dominant of two parental genes, which will obscure the effectiveness of the other, recessive, gene.

High Mach   See **Machiavellianism, scale of.**

Histogram   In statistics, a diagram showing frequency distribution.

Holmgren wools test   A test of color blindness, in which the subject sorts threads of wool into color groups.

Homeostasis   The condition of physiological balance, the necessity for maintaining which constitutes a major motive for physiological functioning.

Homozygous trait   A characteristic found in identical form in the genes of both parents and resulting in an offspring running true to type.

Hormones   Secretions of the endocrine glands that control metabolism and behavior.

Humanistic theory of personality   A theory holding that each individual is unique and that his desires for dignity and self-esteem and the extent to which he attains or misses them will determine his behavior.

Hyperacute depression   The final stage of progressive depression wherein the patient is confused, totally absorbed with his delusions, and unresponsive.

Hyperacute (delirious) mania   The last stage of progressively manic behavior, characterized by frenzied excitement and culminating in his collapse into depression.

Hypertension   High blood pressure.

Hypnosis   A sleeplike condition, psychically induced, in which the subject loses consciousness but will still respond, to a limited extent, to suggestion.

Hypnotherapy   The treatment of disease by hypnotism.

Hypoglycemia   The deficiency of sugar in the blood.

Hypomania   The most mild stage of progressively manic behavior, characterized by excitability and apparently inexhaustible energy and drive.

Hypophonia   The inability to speak above a whisper.

Hypophysis   See **Pituitary gland.**

Hypothalamus   The part of the brain that controls the emotions and is active in almost every kind of physiological motivation.

Hypothyroidism   Inadequate functioning of the thyroid gland, resulting in a condition of mental deficiency and physical abnormality known as **cretinism** if it exists from birth and **myxedema** if it occurs later.

Hysteria   A psychoneurosis characterized by emotional excitability, excessive anxiety, sensory and motor disturbance, and the simulation of organic disorders (such as blindness or deafness).

Id   In Freud's theory, the unlearned basic drives of the personality, which are unbound by reality, morality, prudence, or social responsibility.

Identification In child development, the process by which the child patterns himself on another. **Identification with the aggressor** The child's patterning himself on the hostile, angry, punishing peer or parent; aggression begetting aggression.

Identity crisis The stage, in Erikson's theory of personality, reached between the ages of 12 and 18, in which the individual must determine who and what he is.

Idiocy The most severe degree of mental retardation, marked by an IQ of between 20 and 25 and a mental age of between 2 and 3 years.

Idiographic approach to personality An approach assuming that personality does not admit of generalization: each individual is unique and must be studied in isolation. Compare **Nomothetic approach to personality.**

Idiot Savant An otherwise mentally defective person who has one mental skill, usually some manifestation of an extraordinary memory.

Imbecile A mental defective with an IQ ranging from 20 to 25 and a mental age ranging from 3 to 7 years.

Imitation In child development, conscious or unconscious copying of adults.

Implosive therapy A form of treatment for anxiety in which the patient is helped to face the most terrifying experience he can imagine and thereby gain the courage of success to enable him to handle his other terrors.

Imprinting A form of learning in which certain stimuli very early in life evoke behavior patterns that are not generally reversible. Susceptibility to the imprinting of responses occurs only at critical periods during development.

Incidence In statistics, the frequency of the occurrence over a fixed period of time.

Incus One of the three small bones of the ear; somewhat anvil-shaped.

Individual psychology The term used to describe Adler's theory of psychology, since he held that each person organizes his personality differently.

Individuation In Jung's theory, the stage in personality development when the constituents of the personality are balanced.

Inductive thinking The process of starting with observed facts and constructing a theory that is consistent with them.

Infantile autism See **Autism.**

Infantile psychosis Mental disorder in children, the symptoms of which—abnormal language development, compulsions, and stereotyped mannerisms—manifest themselves in infancy.

Inhibition As a general term, the suppression or restraint of behavior. In learning, the confusion and forgetting of material learned at different times. (1) **Proactive**—the material learned first can confuse the learning of additional material. (2) **Retroactive**—the material learned later may cause the previously learned material to be forgotten.

Inkblot test See **Rorschach test.**

Insight The ability to see and understand clearly the inner nature of things.

Instinct Inborn, unlearned, biologically purposeful response produced whenever the appropriate stimulus is received; well developed in animals, vestigial in man. In psychoanalysis, the forces of energy that convert tension and drives into action.

Instinctual theory of behavior An explanation of behavior that considers it to be the result of physiological inheritance and learned responses.

Insulin A hormone secreted by the pancreas that regulates the blood sugar level.

Intellectualization The means by which threats to the emotions are analyzed in the abstract and are therefore no longer immediately threatening.

Intelligence Mental ability.

Intelligence Quotient (IQ) A measure of intelligence obtained by dividing the subject's mental age (gauged on his performance of a standardized test) by his chronological age and multiplying the answer by 100. The average Intelligence Quotient is 100.

Interference with reality contact See **Sensory deprivation.**

Interindividual communication A system of responses enabling one to talk to others.

Intraindividual communication A system of responses useful for organizing one's own thoughts and actions.

Investigatory responses The actions of making familiar an unfamiliar object.

Involutional melancholia A mental disorder occurring in middle age and characterized by abnormal anxiety, agitation, delusions, and depression.

IQ See **Intelligence Quotient.**

Isolation As a defense mechanism, the effect of separating thought from the appropriate emotion to the extent that it is meaningless and therefore no longer threatening.

James-Lange theory of emotion A theory holding that the specific physical reaction to a stimulus determines the emotional response to that stimulus.

Kinesics The nonverbal expression of emotion, conveyed by body position, posture, gesture, and other movement.

Kinesthesis The sensation of the body's position, movement, and tension.

Klinefelter's syndrome A chromosomal deviation caused by the presence of one extra chromosome (47 instead of 46) and resulting in the failure of the male genitals to develop normally.

Koan In Japanese Zen religion, a theme on which to meditate.

Land color phenomenon The ability to combine separate images in red and green tints mentally to form a completely colored picture.

Language The vocal expression or communication of thoughts and feelings.

Laws of probability In statistics, the laws of probability hold that each one of all possible results has an equal chance of occurring.

Learned helplessness A conditioned lack of response considered similar to the apathy and negativism of depressed patients.

Learning theory of personality A theory that personality, as manifest in behavior, is the result of responses learned by reinforcement.

Least-preferred co-worker score An index, devised by Fiedler, of leadership style, calculated on ratings given by subordinates and colleagues.

Lesion Injury or other alteration of any organ or tissue resulting in functional loss or impairment.

Levels of aspiration The ordering of goals according to the individual's success or failure in achievement. By and large, success tends to raise the level; failure tends to lower it.

Levels of significance In statistics, the frequency, beyond the likelihood of chance, that a result will occur. Most commonly used are .01 level (1% level): 1 time in 100, and .05 level (5% level): 5 times in 100.

Libido For Freud, the driving energy force for gratification, principally sexual, but also for food, comfort, and happiness. For Jung, psychic energy in general.

Lie detector See **Polygraph.**

Limen See **Absolute threshold.**

Lobectomy Surgical removal of the frontal lobes of the brain.

Lobotomy Surgical severance of the frontal lobes from the rest of the brain.

Low Mach See **Machiavellianism, scale of.**

LPC See **Least-preferred co-worker score.**

Lysergic acid diethylamide (LSD-25) A drug chemically derived from ergotic alkaloids and capable of inducing vivid imagery, hallucinations, and mental disorganization.

MA See **Mental age.**

Machiavellianism, scale of (Mach scale) A questionnaire used to measure motivation and scored according to closeness of the subject's answers to the sentiments of Machiavelli. **High Mach** scorers tend to manipulate people and to be careless of moral considerations. **Low Mach** scorers tend to be susceptible to social pressure, empathetic, and vulnerable.

Machismo A Spanish word denoting an attitude of exaggerated male pride, virility, and fearlessness, usually adopted by young men attempting to compensate for humiliation received as children.

Male climacteric (andropause) Neurological and endocrinological balance change occurring in middle age, but often imperceptibly, even to the subject, and rarely affecting his emotional balance.

Malleus The largest of the three small bones in the ear; somewhat hammer-shaped.

Manic-depression A psychosis characterized by swings from extreme elation to extreme melancholy, punctuated by periods of normalcy.

Mantra An invocation.

Marasmus A wasting of the flesh without fever or apparent disease; a progressive emaciation.

Marathon encounter Intensive group therapy conducted in meetings lasting twenty-four hours or more at a stretch.

Mass therapy See **Group therapy.**

Matched-dependent behavior A form of imitation in children that is an approximation rather than a copy of behavior in another.

Maturation The process of development and bodily change that is independent of learning, but may be hampered by the environment.

Median In statistics, the result that occurs halfway across the range of results, that is, the middle number in an uneven series of numbers; the number halfway between the two middle numbers in an even series.

Meditation The act and process of serious contemplation.

Medulla oblongata The part of the brain that controls autonomic physiological function.

Melancholia A mental disorder characterized by excessive gloom, mistrust, and depression.

Membrane potential The difference in electrical voltage between the internal and external chemical solutions of the axon.

Memory trace A physical change in the nervous system produced by learning, which, if used, would strengthen the change; if unused, would cause the change to fade and revert.

Menopause Cessation, in middle age, of menstruation; often accompanied by physiological and emotional imbalance.

Mental age (MA) A measurement of intellectual ability obtained from standardized tests which are scored by formulae based on the age at which average children obtain the given score. See also **Intelligence Quotient.**

Mescal buttons The buttonlike tops of the small, spineless mescal cactus, which contain a narcotic and may be chewed for a stimulating effect.

Mescaline A narcotic, hallucinogenic substance derived from the mescal cactus.

Mesomorph The muscular or athletic physical type.

Method of limits The means of determining the nervous system's sensitivity to stimuli by running the gamut from absence to most extreme form of the stimulus being tested and noting the subject's awareness.

Microsleep Momentary loss of awareness induced by long periods—100 hours or more—of wakefulness.

Midbrain A segment of the brainstem which helps to relay complex reflexes involving hearing and vision. Also involved in the reception of pain. Also called mesencephalon.

Mode (modal point) In statistics, the result in a number of results that occurs most often.

Mongolism See **Down's syndrome.**

Monologue therapy A form of treatment for adolescent drug users in which the patient records and then reviews his actions on videotape.

Moral realism Piaget's term for the child's accepting the immutability of given rules (between the ages of 3 and 8).

Moron A mental defective whose mental age is considered to be between 7 and 12 years of age and whose IQ is between 50 and 75. The highest classification of mental deficiency.

Morpheme In linguistics, any word or part of a word that conveys meaning, that cannot be broken down further without losing its meaning, and that retains its meaning even though it may be used in several contexts.

Müller-Lyon illusion An optical illusion that, of two straight lines of the same length, the one with arrow points at each end is the shorter.

Multiple personality Two or more diverse personalities in the same body.

Mutism The inability to speak; the term as used in psychology indicates that the cause is psychic rather than organic.

Myelin A white, fatty substance forming a sheath about certain nerve fibers.

Myxedema See **Hypothyroidism.**

Natural selection The process, first suggested by Darwin, by which the individuals of a species best fitted for their environment survive, propagate, and spread, while the less fitted individuals die out.

Necker cube An ambiguous graphic representation of a cube.

Need The condition of deprivation—physiological, social, or psychological—that stimulates activity toward satisfaction.

Neo-Freudianism (culturalism) Modern (*neo* meaning "new") psychoanalytic theory in which Freud's theories have been modified by, among other things, less emphasis being placed on early sexuality.

Neural efficiency analyzer An instrument invented by Ertl that measures brain-wave patterns and, ostensibly, the brain's ability to learn.

Neurons Nerve cells forming the basic units of the nervous system. (1) **Afferent (sensory) neurons** transmit stimuli from outside and inside the body to the spinal cord and the brain. (2) **Efferent (motor) neurons** transmit stimuli from the spinal cord or the brain to muscles and glands. (3) **Association neurons** make the connection between incoming and outgoing stimuli.

Neuropsychology The study of nervous and psychic disorders.

Neurosis Emotional or mental disorder characterized by apprehension, use of defense mechanisms, and impairment of function to the point where the victim cannot cope with reality. Also called **psychoneurosis.**

Neurotic breakdown The disintegration of personality that follows a forced increase in defense mechanisms, leaving no resources available to cope with everyday living.

Neurotic personality A personality in which symptoms of neurosis may be apparent but in mild form and with no certainty that they will develop into full-blown neurosis.

Nomothetic approach to personality An approach assuming that patterns of personality follow laws that may be generalized for all individuals and that the study of personality consists in discovering the laws.

Non-Rapid Eye Movement Sleep See **NREM sleep.**

Nonreversal shift The ability to change responses when the stimuli change. See also **Reversal shift.**

Noradrenaline A hormone secreted by the adrenal medulla and released in association with situations of anger or fighting. Also called **Norepinephrine.**

Normal (ideal) curve In statistics, the range of a normal probability distribution when expressed as a symmetrical curve.

"Normal neuroses" of childhood The persistent, irrational fears common to children.

NREM sleep Non-Rapid Eye Movement Sleep, which comprises about 75% of the time spent asleep.

Obsessive-compulsive disorder A mental disorder characterized by anxiety; persistent, unwanted thoughts; and repeated, ritualistic behavior.

Obstacle (obstruction) reaction measure of drive A calculation of the amount of opposition that an organism will overcome in order to satisfy a need.

Oedipus complex In psychoanalytic theory, the repressed desire for sex relations with the parent of the opposite sex and jealousy of the other parent; appears between the ages of 2½ and 6 years; specifically used of attitudes of a boy toward his mother.

Operational definition The statement determining and limiting an experiment in terms of the procedure to be used.

Opiate A medicine containing opium or any of its derivatives and acting as a sedative and narcotic.

Oral stage In psychoanalytic theory, the stage in psychosexual development in which the mouth is the primary source of pleasure.

Paradoxical heat The sensation of heat transmitted by the stimulation of hot and cold receptors simultaneously.

Paradoxical sleep The stage of sleep during which one dreams.

Paranoia A mental disturbance characterized by complex, systematized delusions and little serious impairment of other mental functions.

Parascience The study of supernatural phenomena, such as telepathy, clairvoyance, extrasensory perception, and the like.

Paresis A disease of the brain, caused by syphilis of the central nervous system and characterized by mental and emotional instability and attacks of paralysis.

Pathological togetherness A term used by Calhoun to describe the shortened life-spans, and high incidence of still-births or death in childbirth, characteristic of overcrowded rats.

Pentobarbitol A sedative, hypnotic, analgesic drug.

Percentile In statistics, the set of partitioned values that divide the total frequency [entire sample] into 100 equal parts.

Perceptual filtering The effect of one's cultural heritage on what he sees or how he interprets his perceptions.

Perceptual isolation See **Sensory deprivation.**

Perceptual set The combination of past experience and expectation that makes an individual interpret what he sees in ways peculiar to himself.

Performance measure of drive A means of gauging the strength of a drive according to the increasing action required to satisfy it.

Personal dispositions See **Trait theory.**

Personality The pattern of behavior and thinking characteristic of an individual.

Personality, psychological test of An instrument that evaluates a person by comparing him with others who have taken the same test.

Personality inventory A measure of traits by means of a number of statements to which the subject is asked to respond.

Peyote The Mexican name for the mescal cactus, which yields a narcotic substance.

Phallic stage In psychoanalytic theory, the stage in psychosexual development (between ages 3 and 5) when interest and gratification center on the genital organs.

Phenomenologism In psychology, especially Rogers's, the theory that personality is governed by the image each person has of himself and the extent to which that image is reinforced or fragmented by others.

Phenotype The visible, not necessarily hereditary, characteristics of an organism. Compare **Genotype.**

Phenylalanine A chemical in the blood that, in excess—as a result of impaired protein metabolism—destroys brain cells.

Phenylketonuria (PKU) A disease caused by impaired protein metabolism and resulting in severe retardation, hyperactivity, and seizures. PKU is transmitted by recessive genes and may be contained by diet if diagnosed in early infancy.

Phobia A morbid fear, which can take the form of an exaggeration of a common emotional experience—death, snakes, solitude, hostility—or of a fear peculiar to the individual, such as claustrophobia.

Phonemes In linguistics, a class of closely related sounds, all designated by a single symbol. The sequential patterns of phonemes show differences in various languages.

Pica The abnormal craving for certain unnatural foods.

Pituitary gland (hypophysis) The master gland, situated in the head and secreting hormones that influence growth, puberty, the function of other glands, and lactation.

PKU See **Phenylketonuria.**

Placebo A pill or liquid given a patient; any benefits it may have will be psychological, stemming from its having been taken, not physiological.

Placenta A vascular organ within the uterus that provides food for and eliminates the waste matter of the fetus by way of the umbilical cord.

PMA See **Thurstone Primary Mental Abilities Test.**

Polarization of nerves The condition of the nerve when the internal solution of sodium and potassium is electrically negative while the external solution is positive.

Polygraph (lie detector) An instrument that measures physical changes that accompany heightened emotion—heartbeat, breathing, galvanic skin reflexes, blood pressure. Used on the assumption that deliberate lying will produce guilt, anxiety, or fear, which in turn will trigger physical reactions.

Pons (pons Variolii) A band of nerve fibers joining the cerebral cortex, the cerebellum, and the medulla oblongata of the brain.

Preoperational stage In Piaget's scheme of child development, the stage in which the child between ages 2 and 7 does not distinguish between the symbol and what it symbolizes.

Presbyopia A form of farsightedness occurring after middle age and caused by a diminished elasticity of the lens.

Prevalence The number of incidents of an occurrence extant at any one time.

Primal scream An agonized, convulsive cry, ostensibly indicating the release of long-pent feelings and signaling the cure of neuroses—a form of psychotherapy devised by Janov.

Primordial image See **Archetype.**

Process schizophrenia A mental disorder of gradual, but progressively disturbed behavior and personality.

Projection A process of judging others by oneself; of attributing to others motives in oneself that cause anxiety.

Projective test A means of measuring personality traits using neutral stimuli that the subject is free to interpret as he will.

Prolactin A pituitary hormone released to stimulate lactation in nursing females.

Propaganda Systematic, deliberate, widespread indoctrination; the word now usually carries the connotation of deception or distortion.

Proxemics Nonverbal expression, communication through the relative distances between people and their orientation toward each other, as conveyed by touch and eye contact.

Psilocybin A hallucinogenic drug, derived from mushrooms.

Psychedelics Drugs causing extreme changes in the conscious mind, such as delusions, hallucinations, intensification of awareness and sensory perception—effects also termed "consciousness expanding."

Psychiatry A medical specialization in the diagnosis and treatment of mental illness.

Psychic secretions Pavlov's term for the salivation of dogs that had learned to associate food with the person who fed them. In investigating the mechanisms of these "secretions," Pavlov discovered the process of conditioning.

Psychoanalysis (1) A method, developed by Freud, for treating neuroses and other disorders of the mind. A basic assumption is that mental disorders are caused by the conscious mind's rejecting factors that lurk in the unconscious mind as "dynamic repressions." With therapy, these repressions are discovered and resolved. (2) A theory of behavior.

Psychoanalytic theory See **Freudian theory.**

Psychodynamic theory A theory of personality classification stressing that patterns of personalaty are not static and will be influenced by experience. The most prominent of the psychodynamic theories is **psychoanalytic,** or **Freudian, theory.**

Psychogenic disorder A disorder of mental (as opposed to physical—somatogenic) origin.

Psychokinesis The influencing of a physical object by exercise of will. Also defined as "violent cerebral action due to objective inhibition."

Psychological tests Instruments used to ascertain personality traits, aptitudes, vocational preferences, general intelligence, and other behavior, and are used also, to compare an individual with the rest of the population.

Psychologist A specialist in psychology.

Psychology The science of behavior, studied that it may be measured, explained, or changed.

Psychomimetic drug A drug with effects similar to manifestations of psychosis.

Psychoneurosis See **Neurosis.**

Psychopath A person afflicted with psychopathy.

Psychopathology (1) The science of abnormalities and diseases of the mind. (2) Loosely: disorders of the mind.

Psychopathy A mental disorder characterized by emotional instability, impaired judgment, perverse, impulsive (often criminal) behavior, inability to learn from experience, amoral and asocial feelings.

Psychosis A severe mental disorder manifest in a disintegration of the personality and loss of contact with reality.

Psychosocial death A psychological death occurring before physical death, when the will to live is gone.

Psychosomatic illness A physical illness originating in the psyche or emotions.

Psychostimulant A drug that will raise the activity level of the mind.

Psychosurgery Surgery on the brain in order to change behavior.

Psychotropic drugs A general term for medications intended for mental disorders.

Punishment In conditioning, punishment consists in either withholding a rewarding stimulus or applying a discouraging stimulus, the desired effect being to reduce or eliminate the response. Compare **Reinforcement.**

Quota sample In surveys, subjects are chosen as being representative of whatever proportion of the total population they reflect.

Rapid Eye Movement (REM) sleep The stage of sleep during which one dreams most.

Rationalization A means by which irrational, impulsive action, or even failure, is justified to others and oneself by substituting acceptable explanations for the real but unacceptable reasons.

Reaction formation A defense mechanism consisting in action directly contrary to the repressed wish.

Reactive courage The ability to expose oneself deliberately to a feared object.

Reactive schizophrenia A mental disorder occurring as a result of trauma with which the individual is unable to cope. If the cause of stress can be removed, the victim is likely to recover.

Reasoning (1) **Deductive**—the process of coming to a conclusion by adding up the implications of previous experience or available data. (2) **Inductive**—the process of coming to a conclusion by starting from available data and intuitively solving the problem, working out the rational justification, if there be one, afterward.

Receptors Cells in the sense organs that are sensitive to stimuli.

Reconditioning The process by which a conditioned response, having been extinguished, is evoked again—a faster learning process than the original conditioning.

Red-light stage In brainstorming, the stage when the suggestions put forward earlier about the problem are examined, criticized, and evaluated.

Reduced sensory input   See **Sensory deprivation.**

Reflex   An immediate, involuntary, instinctive response to a specific stimulus.

Refractory periods of nerves   (1) **Absolute**—the interval of time immediately after an axon has been fired, during which it is unexcitable and cannot be fired at all. (2) **Relative**—the interval of time during which the axon, returning to normal, can be fired, but only by an extra-strong stimulus.

Regression   The unconscious return to attitudes or behavior more appropriate to an earlier stage of psychosocial development—a defense mechanism.

Reinforcement   The process in conditioning by which a response is strengthened or weakened by repeated application of the rewarding or punishing stimulus. Also called **positive reinforcement** to distinguish the process from the elicitation of negatively reinforced responses, which are responses that are strengthened by the removal of stimuli.

Reinforcers   Stimuli that follow a response and increase the probability of its occurrence. **Secondary reinforcers** Objects that, through association with reinforcing stimuli, become reinforcers themselves.

REM   See **Rapid Eye Movement sleep.**

Replication of an experiment   The exact repetition of an experiment to determine the validity of the original result.

Repression   Freud's term for the unconscious tendency to exclude from conscious awareness unpleasant or painful ideas.

Response   The reaction to a stimulus; a complex pattern of responses is sometimes called a **reaction.**

Reticular activating system   The nerve fibers going from the reticular formation to the higher centers of the brain, the medulla oblongata and the pons, that act as a general arousal system, regulating action and alertness.

Reticular formation   A network of nerves in the brainstem and hypothalamus constituting the source of the reticular activating system and filtering out unimportant messages from the sensory organs.

Retinal disparity   The term used for the fact that, because of their relative positions, each eye gives us a slightly different image of what we are seeing. Also called **binocular parallax.**

Reversal shift   The ability to change responses when the rewards are changed, so that what was hitherto rewarded is rejected and the previously fruitless response favored. See also **Nonreversal shift.**

Reversible figure   The element in the perceptual field that is not easily distinguished from the background.

Ribonucleic acid (RNA)   An essential component of all living matter, found in all cells, active in protein synthesis, functioning as a carrier for genetic information and, it is thought, in learning and memory.

RNA   See **Ribonucleic acid.**

Rodopsin (visual purple)   A chemical in the nerve cells of the eye that changes when exposed to light, the change signaling the brain.

Rods   Nerve cells in the eyes containing light-sensitive chemicals, blind to color, but after adapting themselves, effective in twilight.

Rogerian therapy   See **Client-centered therapy.**

Rolfing   A form of physical therapy in which the skeleton of the patient is ostensibly lengthened by manipulation and massage to improve posture and respiration.

Rorschach test   A test of personality traits obtained by studying the responses to a series of inkblots. Also called **inkblot test.**

Savings   In learning theory, the fact that relearning requires less time and effort than the original learning did.

Schedules of reinforcement   A refinement of the conditioning process whereby subjects are taught to expect reinforcement at varying intervals of time.

Schizophrenia   A mental disorder characterized by apathy, withdrawal, hallucinations, and delusions of persecution and omnipotence, often with impaired intelligence.

Scholastic-performance intelligence   Mental ability when applied to reading, writing, and arithmetic.

School phobia   Found mostly in very young children, the feeling that school is a terrifying or at least acutely uncomfortable place; usually one among other symptoms of emotional disturbance.

Scientific method   The way in which scientific investigation is undertaken, involving the selection of a problem, the systematic observation of important variables, and the organization and interpretation of the facts that are revealed.

Script analysis   A form of psychotherapy based on the assumption that attitudes and behavior are formed for life between the ages of 3 and 7.

Self-actualizing theory of personality   An explanation of personality according to which man is constantly striving to realize his inherited potential. According to Rogers, the struggle is against low self-esteem, anxiety, or conflict. According to Maslow, it is against attitudes, social pressure, accidents, or habits.

Self-esteem   Belief in and respect for oneself.

Senile brain disease   The atrophy and/or degeneration of the central nervous system.

Sensation Seeking Scale (SSS)   Developed by Zuckerman to gauge levels of response to stimulation in individuals.

Sensitivity training   Training in interpersonal relationships.

Sensory adaptation   Changes in the thresholds at which the nervous system is aware of stimuli.

Sensory deprivation   The condition of lacking the normal psychological and physiological stimulation provided by the senses. Also called **isolation; perceptual isolation; reduced sensory input; interference with reality contact; deafferentation.**

Sensory gating The process by which the reticular formation permits urgent or important nerve impulses to go through to the higher brain centers while stopping others until the brain has time to deal with them.

Sensory-motor stage In Piaget's scheme of child development, the stage in which, until about the age of 2, the child concentrates on the structure of objects and develops an elementary form of reasoning without benefit of language.

Sensory overload Levels of stimulation beyond those normally felt that may cause distortions in perception.

Serial position effect In learning theory, the term used to indicate that the first and last items of a list will be remembered better than the other items because of their position.

Sexuality, infantile Interest in and concern with sex, in particular the genital area, manifest in tiny babies and considered by Freud to be central in personality development.

Simple depression The mildest form of progressive depression, similar to dejection, except that it is characterized by listlessness and helplessness.

Simple schizophrenia (dementia) A fairly mild form of mental disorder, characterized by apathy, withdrawal, and antisocial behavior.

Skew In statistics, a description of a frequency distribution when most of the results fall at one of the two extremes: **right skew** when the results are toward the lower end of the range; **left skew** when toward the upper end.

Social instincts Genetically transmitted, interrelated patterns of behavior. The existence of such patterns is currently doubted.

Socialization The process by which the values and customs of a culture are acquired by the young, usually by direct training.

Somatic nervous system That part of the nervous system that controls bodily movements.

Somatic therapy Treatment for mental disorder that is applied to the body by, for example, chemicals or electric shock.

Somatotype The classification of individuals according to physical characteristics.

Specificity theory of pain The theory, held by Western cultures, that pain receptors in particular parts of the body signal the brain when stimulated and thus pain is felt wherever the stimulus is. The theory is contradicted by the principles of acupuncture.

Spinal cord A cylindrical structure of nerve tissues enclosed in the spinal canal and the vertebrae and stretching from the medulla oblongata in the brain to the second lumbar vertebra.

Spontaneous recovery The reappearance of an apparently extinguished conditioned response, as a result of the repetition of the original conditioning or simply after a rest interval.

SSS See **Sensation Seeking Scale.**

Stage of exhaustion The final phase of exposure to stress that the organism can no longer withstand.

Stage of resistance The second stage of response to stress, in which the organism defends itself as well as it can.

Stanford-Binet Test of Intelligence An adaptation of the original Binet-Simon test, published in 1916; used to test mental ability in reading, writing, and arithmetic.

Stapes The small, stirrup-shaped bone in the ear.

Stimoceiver A transmitting and receiving instrument, invented by José Delgado, that stimulates the brain by radio waves and records the resulting electrical activity; it has been used to regulate behavior, particularly aggression.

Stimulus Any action that causes a change in the receptor.

Stocking anaesthesia Psychogenic numbness of the feet.

Stress Any human condition that mobilizes physiological resources and causes an increase in energy expenditure.

Stroke In transactional analysis, a unit of recognition that may be positive or negative.

Stuttering An impairment of the fluence of speech that is considered to be indicative of mental imbalance.

Sublimation A process by which a socially accepted activity is substituted for an unacceptable one.

Subliminal perception The unconscious awareness of stimuli.

Superego In psychoanalytic theory, the conscience, or that part of the personality that imposes moral standards and limits on the ego and the id; it functions in the unconscious.

Swinging The practice of group sex in America.

Symptom neurosis An emotional disorder displaying reactive symptoms: anxiety, phobia, obsession, compulsion.

Synapse The space between the axon terminals of one neuron and the next.

Synaptic transmission The movement of stimuli from one neuron to another.

Synaptic vesicles Oval sacs in some axon terminals that are burst by nerve impulses and release a chemical transmitter substance that travels across the synapse and fires the adjoining axons.

Syntactical aphasia See **Aphasia.**

Syphilis, cerebral Syphilis of the brain.

Tarantism A mental disorder held, in the seventeenth century, to be caused by the bite of the tarantula spider. Now considered to have been a condition of mania or hysterical excitement.

TAT See **Thematic Apperception Test.**

Telepathy The awareness of another's thoughts without benefit of the normal sensory channels; transference of thought.

Testosterone A sex hormone considered to influence the sexual urge.

T-group   A small group of people meeting for therapy or personal growth, designed to provide interpersonal experience in an atmosphere of honesty and sensitivity. Also called **Encounter group.**

Thalamus   The part of the brain controlling the relaying of messages as nerve impulses.

Thematic Apperception Test (TAT)   A test of attitudes, used by psychiatrists to apply appropriate therapy.

Thinking   The mental activity of formulating and using concepts.

Threshold of maximum intensity   The maximum amount of stimulation that can be perceived; for stimuli that, in excess, cause pain (for example, light, sound), the point at which a normal response becomes a pain response.

Thurstone Primary Mental Abilities Test (PMA)   A test of intelligence that gauges seven elements of mental acumen that were thought to be independent but are actually highly correlated.

Thyroid gland   Situated in the neck and secreting the hormones that influence growth, the development of the central nervous system and the reproductive organs, the conversion of food to energy, and immunity.

Token economy   A system of reward used mainly in mental hospitals: socially constructive behavior is reinforced by tokens that may be exchanged for privileges.

Trait theory   A theory of personality classification that uses numerous characteristics (traits) of personality to describe the pattern for the individual. (1) **Common traits** are found in all individuals. (2) **Individual traits** (which Allport called "personal dispositions") are peculiar to individuals and possibly unique.

Transactional analysis   A form of psychotherapy that probes the interactions (transactions) of people with one another.

Transcendent function   In Jung's theory, the ultimate stage of personality development in which the self is fully realized.

Transduction   The process by which physical energy is converted into electrical impulses in the nervous system.

Transsexual   An individual physically male, psychologically female.

Trauma   Specifically, a wound or injury. The term has been broadened to include mental shock, severe disappointment, and tragedy.

Trepanning   The operation of cutting a hole in the skull.

Twins   Two young born at the same birth. (1) **Fraternal twins** result from two ova, each with its own placenta and amniotic sac. (2) **Identical twins** result from one ovum that split so that both fetuses share the same placenta and amniotic sac. (3) **Siamese twins** are identical twins still joined together at some point of the body, the result of an incomplete splitting of the ovum. The term is derived from twin boys born in Siam in 1811.

Type theory   The earliest theory of personality classification. Unsophisticated in that personality is too complex to be described in terms merely of central characteristics, type theories are not much used.

Umbilical cord   A cordlike structure connecting the fetus with the placenta of the mother and conveying food to, and waste matter away from, the fetus.

Unconscious   In Jung's theory, the **collective unconscious** is the pool of archetypes or primordial images of universal human experience, uncolored by culture or the passage of time. The **personal unconscious** is repressed or forgotten material.

Undoing   A defense mechanism involving action, reaction, and action again in order to check and double-check on past action—a vicious circle that only stimulates the obsession.

Variables   (1) **Dependent**—the result of an experiment. In psychology, almost always a response. (2) **Independent**—an event, value (or, in psychology, almost always a stimulus) chosen arbitrarily and upon which the result (in psychology, response) will depend.

Verbal mediator   A label that, in categorizing an unknown, allows us to respond to it.

Vibratese   A term coined by Geldard to designate a system of signals used as a language comprehensible by the skin. See also **Body English.**

Visual purple   See **Rodopsin.**

Waxy flexibility   The description of the immobile, but not rigid, posture that victims of catatonic schizophrenia are apt to assume.

Wechsler Adult Intelligence Scale (WAIS)   A test to measure the intelligence of adults in which the items are arranged in order of difficulty, and thus the scores are weighted.

White matter   Whitish nerve tissue of the brain and spinal cord, consisting mainly of nerve fibers. See also **Gray matter.**

Yoga   A mystic and ascetic practice involving intense and complete concentration on something, especially the deity, in order to accomplish an identity of the consciousness with the object of contemplation.

Zygote   The fertilized egg resulting from the union of two cells, male and female, to form a single cell.

Index